Accounting for Managers

Interpreting Accounting Information for Decision Making

Fifth Edition

Paul M. Collier

Formerly Professor of Accounting at Monash University in Melbourne, Australia; and Senior Lecturer, Aston Business School, Birmingham, UK

D1279162

WILEY

Registered office

John Wiley & Sons Ltd, The Atrium, Southern Gate, Chichester, West Sussex, PO19 8SQ, United Kingdom

For details of our global editorial offices, for customer services and for information about how to apply for permission to reuse the copyright material in this book please see our website at www.wiley.com.

Library of Congress Cataloging-in-Publication Data

Collier, Paul M.
    Accounting for managers : interpreting accounting information for decision making / Paul M. Collier,
Formerly Professor of Accounting at Monash University in Melbourne, Australia; and Senior Lecturer,
Aston Business School, Birmingham, UK.—Fifth edition.
        pages cm
    Includes bibliographical references and index.
    ISBN 978-1-119-00294-9 (pbk.)—ISBN 978-1-119-09710-5 (ebk.)
        1. Managerial accounting.   I. Title.
HF5657.4.C647 2015
658.15'11—dc23   2015002800

ISBN: 978-1-119-00294-9 (pbk)
ISBN: 978-1-119-09710-5 (ebk)
ISBN: 978-1-119-13383-4 (ebk)

British Library Cataloguing in Publication Data

A catalogue record for this book is available from the British Library

Typeset in 9/13pt Trump Mediaeval by SPi Global

For Loredana and Alexis

Contents

Preface to the Fifth Edition   **xiii**

About the Author   **xvii**

Acknowledgements   **xix**

PART I Context of Accounting   1

1 Introduction to Accounting   3
    Accounting, accountability, and the account   3
    A short history of accounting   5
    Introducing the functions of accounting   7
    The role of financial accounting   7
    The role of management accounting   8
    Recent developments in accounting   10
    The relationship between financial accounting and management accounting   12
    A critical perspective   14
    Conclusion   16
    References   16
    Questions   17

2 Accounting and its Relationship to Shareholder Value and Corporate Governance   19
    Capital and product markets   19
    Shareholder value-based management   21
    Shareholder value, strategy, and accounting   23
    Company regulation and corporate governance   25
    Risk management, internal control, and accounting   28
    A critical perspective   29
    Conclusion   30

References   30
Questions   31

3 Recording Financial Transactions and the Principles of Accounting   33
Business events, transactions, and the accounting system   33
The double entry: recording transactions   35
Extracting financial information from the accounting system   38
Basic principles of accounting   42
Cost terms and concepts: the limitations of financial accounting   45
Conclusion   47
References   47
Questions   47

4 Management Control, Accounting, and its Rational-Economic Assumptions   51
Management control systems   51
Planning and control in organizations   54
Non-financial performance measurement   58
A theoretical framework for accounting   64
Conclusion   65
References   65
Websites   67
Questions   67

5 Interpretive and Critical Perspectives on Accounting and Decision Making   69
Research and theory in management control and accounting   70
Alternative paradigms   73
The interpretive paradigm and the social construction perspective   75
Culture, control, and accounting   77
The radical paradigm and critical accounting   78
Power and accounting   80
Creative accounting, ethics, and accounting   84
Conclusion   90
References   91
Questions   93

PART II The Use of Financial Statements for Decision Making   95

6 Constructing Financial Statements: IFRS and the Framework of Accounting   97
International Financial Reporting Standards (IFRS)   98
Framework for the Preparation and Presentation of Financial Statements   100

True and fair view   103
Reporting profitability: the Income Statement and Statement of Comprehensive Income   104
Reporting financial position: the Balance Sheet or Statement of Financial Position   107
The matching principle and accruals accounting   109
Depreciation   111
Specific IFRS accounting treatments   112
Reporting cash flow: the Statement of Cash Flows   116
Differences between the financial statements   118
A theoretical perspective on financial statements   120
A critical perspective on financial statements and accounting standards   121
Conclusion   122
Reference   122
Websites   122
Appendix to Chapter 6: List of IFRS and FRS   123
Questions   125

7 Interpreting Financial Statements   129
Annual Reports   129
The context of financial statements   131
Ratio analysis   132
Profitability   133
Liquidity   135
Gearing   135
Activity/efficiency   136
Working capital   137
Managing receivables   138
Managing inventory   138
Managing payables   139
Managing working capital   139
Shareholder return   140
The relationship between financial ratios   141
Interpreting financial statements using ratios   143
Using the Statement of Cash Flows   145
Limitations of ratio analysis   152
A wider view on corporate reporting   156
Intellectual capital   157
Institutional theory   158
Corporate social and environmental responsibility   158
Applying different perspectives to financial statements   161
Conclusion   162

References   163
Questions   163

8 Accounting for Inventory   171
Introduction to inventory   171
Methods of costing inventory in manufacturing   175
Management accounting statements   180
Conclusion   181
Questions   182

PART III Using Accounting Information for Decision Making, Planning, and Control   185

9 Accounting and Information Systems   187
Introduction to accounting and information systems   187
Methods of data collection   188
Big data   190
Types of information system   190
Business processes   192
Information systems design and controls   194
Conclusion   196
References   196
Questions   196

10 Marketing Decisions   197
Marketing strategy   197
Cost behaviour   199
Cost–volume–profit analysis   201
Alternative approaches to pricing   208
Segmental profitability   212
Customer profitability analysis   216
Conclusion   219
References   219
Questions   220

11 Operating Decisions   223
The operations function   223
Managing operations – manufacturing   225
Managing operations – services   227
Accounting for the cost of spare capacity   228

Capacity utilization and product mix   229
Theory of Constraints   231
Operating decisions: relevant costs   232
Supply chain management, total cost of ownership, and supplier cost analysis   237
The cost of quality   239
Environmental cost management   241
Conclusion   246
References   247
Questions   247

12 Human Resource Decisions   251
Human resources and accounting   251
The cost of labour   252
Relevant cost of labour   255
Conclusion   261
References   262
Questions   262

13 Overhead Allocation Decisions   267
Cost classification   267
The overhead allocation problem   271
Shifts in management accounting thinking   272
Alternative methods of overhead allocation   273
Differences between absorption and activity-based costing   282
Contingency theory   285
International comparisons   286
Behavioural implications of management accounting   287
Conclusion   290
References   291
Questions   292

14 Strategic Investment Decisions   297
Strategy   297
Capital expenditure evaluation   298
Accounting rate of return   301
Payback   304
Discounted cash flow   304
Comparison of techniques   307
Conclusion   311
References   311

Appendix to Chapter 14: Present value factors   311
Questions   313

15 Performance Evaluation of Business Units   317
Structure of business organizations   317
The decentralized organization and divisional performance measurement   320
Controllability   323
Comparison of methods   326
Transfer pricing   327
Transaction cost economics   329
Conclusion: a critical perspective   330
References   331
Questions   332

16 Budgeting   335
What is budgeting?   335
The budgeting process   336
The profit budget   339
Cash forecasting   345
A behavioural perspective on budgeting   349
A critical perspective: beyond budgeting?   350
Conclusion   354
References   354
Questions   354

17 Budgetary Control   359
What is budgetary control?   359
Variance analysis   361
Flexible budgets and sales variances   362
Flexible budgets and cost variances   363
Interpreting variances   365
Criticism of variance analysis   366
Applying different perspectives to management accounting   368
Conclusion   368
References   369
Questions   369

18 Strategic Management Accounting   371
Trends in management accounting   371
Strategic management accounting   372

Accounting techniques to support strategic management accounting   374
Lean production, lean accounting, and backflush costing   381
Conclusion   384
References   384
Further reading   385
Questions   386

PART IV Supporting Information   387

Readings   389
  Reading 1 Cooper and Kaplan (1988). How cost accounting distorts product costs   390
  Reading 2 Dent (1991). Accounting and organizational cultures: a field study of the
             emergence of a new organizational reality   403

Glossary of Accounting Terms   **435**

Solutions to Questions   **449**

Index   **509**

Preface to Fifth Edition

My own education as an accountant many years ago was aimed at achieving professional recognition and emphasized an uncritical acceptance of the tools and techniques that I was taught. Teaching accounting hasn't changed much since then. However, it was only after moving from financial to general management positions in industry that I began to see the limitations and questionable assumptions that underlay the accounting tools and techniques I had learned. When I returned to study later in my career, I was exposed for the first time to alternative perspectives on accounting that helped me to understand the assumptions and limitations of accounting that I had seen in practice. This book is therefore as much a result of my practical experience as a producer and user of accounting information as it is a result of my teaching and training experience.

The title of the book, *Accounting for Managers: Interpreting Accounting Information for Decision Making*, emphasizes the focus on accounting to meet the needs of managers. As accounting increasingly becomes decentred from the accounting department in organizations, line managers in all functional areas of business are expected to be able to prepare budgets, develop business cases for capital investment, calculate prices, and exercise cost control to ensure that profit targets are achieved. Managers are also expected to analyse and interpret accounting information so that marketing, operations, and human resource decisions are made in the light of an understanding of the financial consequences of those decisions.

The challenge that this book aims to address is for non-accounting managers to understand the numbers sufficiently well to be able to contribute to the formulation and implementation of business strategy and communicate with accountants. Those managers who do not understand, or who do not want to understand, the numbers are likely to be increasingly marginalized in their organizations.

The material contained in the book stresses the interpretation of accounting information as well as a critical (rather than unthinking) acceptance of the underlying assumptions behind accounting. This book has been continually motivated by my experience in teaching accounting at postgraduate level (MBA and MSc) at Aston Business School in Birmingham (UK) and subsequently in the MBA at Monash University in Melbourne (Australia). It has also been used to support customized training programmes for non-financial managers in the use of financial tools and techniques in their own organizations. Hence the emphasis in this book is on *using* accounting, not *doing* accounting. Most accounting texts are a 'cut down' version of a text used to train accountants, but this book takes a *user*, not a *preparer*, focus. It has been written specifically focused on the needs of non-financial managers who need a solid grounding in accounting.

There is a focus in most accounting texts on manufacturing organizations, perhaps because many of those books have been issued as revised editions for many years and have not adequately reflected the changing nature of the economies in the developed world. The growth of service businesses and the knowledge economy is not sufficiently explored in most accounting texts. This book uses examples, case studies, and questions that are more equally balanced between the needs of organizations in manufacturing, retail, and services. It also uses corporate examples, rather than small business examples that lack realism for practising managers. Most of the examples and illustrations in this book are simplified versions of real-life business problems, drawn from my experiences with various organizations.

In most accounting books there is insufficient attention to theory, particularly for postgraduate students who should have a *wider theoretical understanding* of the assumptions and limitations of accounting information. Theory should encourage the reader to enquire more deeply into the alternative theoretical positions underlying accounting as well as its social and behavioural consequences, both within their own organizations and in the wider society. This book introduces the reader to some of the journal literature that is either fundamental to the role of accounting or is 'ground breaking'. This book provides, through the references in each chapter, an accessible route for those who want to reach into the wider academic literature.

Accounting books are often inaccessible to those from non-English-speaking backgrounds, because of the complexity of the language used. Many of the examples and questions in accounting texts rely on a strong knowledge of the nuances of the English language to interpret what the question is asking, before students can make any attempt to answer them. This book adopts a more plain English style that addresses the needs of European and Asian students.

Finally, the examples in most accounting books focus on the calculations that accountants perform, rather than on the *interpretive needs* of managers who use those reports. While some calculation questions are needed to ensure that readers understand how information is produced, the emphasis for the non-financial manager should be on a *critical understanding and questioning* of the accounting numbers and of the underlying assumptions behind those numbers, and on the need to supplement accounting reports with non-financial performance measures and broader perspectives than satisfying shareholder wealth alone.

An important change to the last (4th) edition was to include illustrations, questions, and solutions using multiple currency symbols: the £, €, and $. This was aimed at being more relevant to users across national boundaries but also reflects the internationalization of accounting tools and techniques. This 5th edition has involved a thorough review: deleting older material, reflecting changes in corporate regulation and accounting standards, and updating case studies and examples. Some chapters have been extensively rewritten – especially Chapters 4, 7, 17, and 18.

Outline of the book

The book is arranged in four parts. The first part describes the context and role of accounting in business. The first two chapters are provided for those students who are coming to business studies for the first time, although even the experienced reader should find value in reading them. Chapter 3 provides a basic introduction to accounting, without the confusion that usually accompanies 'debits' and 'credits'.

Some theoretical frameworks are provided in Chapters 4 and 5. This should provide a foundation for readers' understanding that accounting is more than a technical subject but is grounded in competing theories and values. These theories and values are themselves rooted in historical, political, economic, and social causes. The theoretical framework should help to make the subject more meaningful to students and practitioners alike.

In Part II, Chapters 6 and 7 provide a comprehensive review of financial statements and ratio analysis from the perspective of a user of financial statements and reflect the latest practice under International Financial Reporting Standards (IFRS). Chapter 8, which looks at inventory valuation, provides an important link between Parts II and III of the book.

The third part of the book shows the reader how accounting information is used in decision making, planning, and control. In this third part the accounting tools and techniques are explained and illustrated. Beginning with an introduction to accounting and information systems in Chapter 9, subsequent chapters review how accounting is integral to decisions about marketing (Chapter 10), operations (Chapter 11), and human resources (Chapter 12). The problem of overhead allocation is covered in Chapter 13, followed by capital expenditure decisions (Chapter 14), the evaluation of business unit performance (Chapter 15), budgeting (Chapter 16), and budgetary control (Chapter 17). Chapter 18 introduces a range of the more recent, strategic management accounting approaches.

Theory is integrated with tools and techniques, and case studies, drawn mainly from real business examples, help draw out the concepts in each chapter. A critical approach to the assumptions underlying financial information is presented, building on the theoretical framework provided in Chapters 4 and 5. The questions at the end of each chapter rely on knowledge gained from reading that chapter and the preceding chapters. Consequently, there is a greater level of detail involved in questions in the later chapters. Attempting these questions will help the reader to understand how accountants produce information needed by non-accounting managers. The end-of-chapter case studies provide the reader with the opportunity to interpret and analyse financial information produced by an accountant for use by non-accounting managers in decision making.

Part IV provides a wealth of supporting material, including an extensive glossary of accounting terms. Two readings from the accounting literature cover a broad spectrum and support the most important theoretical concepts in the book. They present two different yet complementary perspectives on accounting in organizations. The fourth part of the book also contains solutions to the end-of-chapter questions.

About the Author

Dr Paul M. Collier PhD (Warwick), BBus (NSWIT), MComm (NSW), Grad Dip Ed (UTS), CPA (Aust) has, through his long career, been chief financial officer and general manager (operations) for a Stock Exchange-listed company, a senior public sector manager, and, after making a late-career transition to academia, a professor of accounting. His industry and academic experience is spread between the UK, where he worked for 13 years, and Australia, where he now lives.

Dr Collier's academic career commenced at Aston Business School in Birmingham, UK, where he was senior lecturer and Director of Executive Education. He became Professor and head of the management accounting and information systems discipline at Monash University in Melbourne before becoming Associate Dean for research training in the Faculty of Business and Economics. He was Head of the Business School at La Trobe University before retiring from a full-time academic position.

Paul has now returned to his roots by investing in a hospitality business, although he retains his academic interests as a member of the academic board for a private university and his involvement in writing course material for CPA Australia's professional examinations.

Paul has been a board member and chair of the audit committee of a not-for-profit social housing association in the UK with assets of £200 million; and a board member, chair of the finance and resources committee, and member of the audit committee of a health service in Australia with a budget of over $350 million. He has been an examiner in risk and control strategy for the Chartered Institute of Management Accountants (CIMA) in the UK and in strategic management accounting for CPA Australia, and has written study material for both professional bodies.

Paul was Secretary of the Management Control Association in the UK and in Australia, founding Chair of the Qualitative Research special interest group of AFAANZ – the association for accounting and finance academics in Australia/New Zealand.

This book uses material developed by the author based on his experience as a practitioner, in his teaching at Aston and Monash, and in delivering financial training to non-financial managers in diverse industries over many years. Paul's research interests are in the use of management accounting and non-financial performance information in decision making and the behavioural aspects of management accounting and management control systems. He has published many case studies of accounting in academic journals and as book chapters. He is also the author of *Fundamentals of Risk Management for Accountants and Managers*, published in 2009.

Acknowledgements

I acknowledge the contribution of colleagues at Aston Business School and Monash University with whom I have taught, especially Stan Brignall at Aston and Bob Cornick at Monash.

Many academics have provided valuable comments on each edition of the text, and wherever possible their feedback and suggestions have been built in. Thanks also to the many students who have invariably identified errors or ambiguities which have been corrected, despite careful proofreading.

I am also grateful to the staff at John Wiley, particularly Steve Hardman for his support from the beginning, and to Georgia King and Joshua Poole for this 5th edition. The John Wiley staff have always provided excellent support and helpful advice throughout the writing and updating of each edition of this book.

I would also like to thank those academics who have made an important contribution to my career, but more importantly to my understanding of the role of management control in organizations and society: Professors Brendan McSweeney, A J (Tony) Berry, Richard Laughlin, Jane Broadbent, the late Clive Emmanuel, Bob Scapens, David Otley and the late Tony Lowe (UK); Kim Langfield-Smith, Robert Chenhall, and Lee Parker (Australia). I would also like to thank Margaret Woods (Aston), Deryl Northcott (Auckland UT), John Burns (Exeter), Robyn Pilcher (Curtin), and members of the Management Control Association for the contribution, direct or indirect, they have made to me and my work.

I

Context of Accounting

Part I describes the context and role of accounting in business and provides some theoretical frameworks. It is hoped that this will offer a foundation for readers' understanding that accounting is more than a technical subject. Accounting presents a particular view of the world, but by no means the only view of the world. As such it has strengths, but also weaknesses. Accounting itself is grounded in competing theories, and these theories are derived from various historical, political, economic, and social roots. The theoretical framework presented in Part I should help to make the subject more meaningful to students and practitioners alike.

Chapter 1 provides an introduction to accounting, and an overview of accounting history as well as describing how the role of accounting has changed, including the influence that this changed role has had on non-financial managers. Chapter 2 describes the context in which management accounting operates: the capital market emphasis on shareholder value, as well as the business context of corporate governance and company regulation.

Chapter 3 describes how transactions are recorded by accounting systems and the principles that underlie the preparation and presentation of financial statements.

Chapter 4 covers the rational, economics-based theoretical approach to management control, which encompasses management accounting and performance measurement.

Chapter 5 offers alternative perspectives on the role of accounting, including the roles of culture and power. The theoretical framework in Chapters 4 and 5 is important to support the interpretive analysis and critical perspective taken by this book.

1

Introduction to Accounting

This chapter introduces accounting and its functions and provides a short history of accounting, highlighting the roles of both financial and management accounting, and the interaction between both. It also describes the recent developments that have changed the roles of accountants and non-financial managers in relation to the use of financial information. The chapter concludes with a brief critical perspective on accounting.

Accounting, accountability, and the account

Businesses exist to provide goods or services to customers in exchange for a financial reward (profit). Public-sector and not-for-profit organizations also provide services, although their funding may be a mix of income from service provision, government funding, and charitable donations. While this book is primarily concerned with profit-oriented businesses, most of the principles are equally applicable to the public and not-for-profit sectors. Business is not about accounting. It is about markets, products and services, people, and operations (the delivery of products or services to customers), although accounting is implicated in all of these decisions because it is the financial representation of business activity.

The definitions applied by professional bodies to the meaning of 'accounting' have changed over time because the expectations of stakeholders (the users of accounting information) have changed, as has the technology with which accounting is carried out.

The Institute of Chartered Accountants in England and Wales (ICAEW) defines accounting as the systematic recording, reporting, and analysis of financial transactions of an organization. Accounting allows an organization to analyse the financial performance of the business, looking at statistics such as net profit (Source: http://careers.icaew.com/university-students-graduates/about-the-aca/glossary-of-terms, downloaded April 2014).

The American Institute of Certified Public Accountants (AICPA) and the American Accounting Association (AAA) view the role of the accounting profession as being to produce, analyse, interpret, and prepare reports about financial and operational information, including assurance about that information. This role is an important one because stakeholders throughout the economy base critical decisions on information provided by the accounting profession (Source: http://www.aicpa.org/Press/PressReleases/2010/Pages/AAAandAICPACreatePathwaysCommission.aspx).

These are important definitions because they highlight two quite separate aspects of the accounting role:

- Accounting as the process of recording and reporting business transactions (its 'passive' role). That process is concerned with capturing business events, recording their financial effects, summarizing and reporting the result of those effects (we cover this in Chapter 3); and
- Accounting as the analysis of financial information for users (its 'active' role). This emphasizes the decision usefulness of accounting information and the broad spectrum of 'users' of that information.

The passive role of accounting, which is a development of the traditional bookkeeping role, is how non-accountants often view the practice of accounting. However technology has gradually replaced much of this role, while the global and highly competitive business environment of the twenty-first century demands a far more active role for accounting in contributing to business decisions through analysis and performance improvement.

While the primary concern of this book is the use of accounting information for decision making, the book takes a broad stakeholder perspective that users of accounting information include all those who may have an interest in the survival, profitability, and growth of a business: shareholders, employees, customers, suppliers, financiers, government, and society as a whole.

The notion of accounting for a narrow (shareholders and financiers) or a broad (societal) group of users is an important philosophical debate to which we will return throughout this book. This debate derives from questions of accountability: to whom is the business accountable? For what is the business accountable? And what is the role of accounting in that accountability?

In the context of this book, accountability relates to the responsibility of management of an organization to its diverse stakeholders, a responsibility to which we will return time and again throughout successive chapters. Much of this accountability is carried out through accounting. However accountability can also be seen in a broader way than its use in accounting. Boland and Schultze (1996) defined accountability as:

> The capacity and willingness to give explanations for conduct, stating how one has discharged one's responsibilities, an explaining of conduct with a credible story of what happened, and a calculation and balancing of competing obligations, including moral ones (p. 62).

ac - count (-kount) *n.*
- A narrative or record of events.
- A reason given for a particular action or event.
- A report relating to one's conduct.
- To furnish a reckoning (to someone) of money received and paid out.
- To make satisfactory amends.
- To give satisfactory reasons or an explanation for actions.

Exhibit 1.1   Definitions of 'account'

There are many definitions of accountability, but they all derive from the original meanings of the word *account*. Exhibit 1.1 provides a number of different definitions for the word 'account'.

Accounting is a collection of systems and processes used to record, report, and interpret business transactions. Accounting provides an account – *an explanation or report in financial terms* about the transactions of an organization.

An account enables managers to satisfy the *stakeholders* in the organization that they have acted in the best interests of stakeholders rather than themselves. This is the notion of accountability to others, a result of the *stewardship* function of managers by which accounting provides the ability for managers to show that they have been responsible in their use of resources provided by various stakeholders. Stewardship is an important concept because in all but very small businesses, the owners of businesses are not the same as the managers. This separation of ownership from control makes accounting particularly influential due to the emphasis given to increasing shareholder wealth (or shareholder value) as well as the broader stakeholder perspective that organizations need to contribute to the sustainability of natural resources and the environment (we cover corporate social responsibility in Chapter 7).

A short history of accounting

The history of accounting is intertwined with the development of trade between tribes and there are records of tokens used as an early form of currency and the recording of commercial transactions in clay tablets in Mesopotamia dating back to 3300 BC (Gleeson-White, 2011). In fact, historians believe that the origins of writing can be found in simple accounting records. Gleeson-White (p. 14) found that the Code of Hammurabi recorded laws about accounting in Babylon in 1790 BC: 'If the merchant has given to the agent corn, wool, oil, or any sort of goods to traffic with, the agent shall write down the price and hand over to the merchant; the agent shall take a sealed memorandum of the price which he shall give to the merchant.'

However, accounting as we know it today began in the fourteenth century in the Italian city-states of Florence, Genoa, and Venice as a result of the growth of maritime trade and banking institutions. Ship-owners used some form of accounting to hold the ships' captains accountable for the profits derived from trading the products they exported and imported. The importance of maritime trade led to the first bank with customer facilities opening in Venice in 1149. Trade enabled the movement of ideas between countries and the Lombards, Italian merchants, established themselves as moneylenders in England at the end of the twelfth century.

The 'double entry' (debits and credits) of cash receipts and payments had spread through Italian firms by about 1300, providing balance sheet data and the separate accounting of capital and revenue, including concepts such as accruals and depreciation (Murray, 2010). Surviving accounting records of the Florence-based Medici (1397–1494) show the rich and systematic nature of the accounting of the time (Kuran, 2010).

The first treatise on accounting (although it was contained within a book on mathematics) was the work of a monk, Luca Pacioli, in 1494. The first professional accounting body was formed in Venice in 1581. Gleeson-White (2011) has written a fascinating history of the origins of accounting and particularly its development in the Italian city states in her book *Double Entry*.

Much of the language of accounting is derived from Latin roots. 'Debtor' comes from the Latin *debitum*, something that is owed; 'assets' from the Latin *ad+satis*, to enough, i.e. to pay obligations; 'liability' from *ligare*, to bind; 'capital' from *caput*, a head (of wealth). Even 'account' derives initially from the Latin *computare*, to count, while 'profit' comes from *profectus*, advance or progress. 'Sterling' and 'shilling' came from the Italian *sterlino* and *scellino*, while the pre-decimal currency abbreviation 'LSD' (pounds, shillings, and pence) stood for *lire, soldi, denarii*.

Little changed in terms of accounting until the Industrial Revolution. Chandler (1990) traced the development of the modern industrial enterprise from its agricultural and commercial roots in the last half of the nineteenth century. By 1870, the leading industrial nations – the USA, Great Britain, and Germany – accounted for two-thirds of the world's industrial output. One of the consequences of growth was the shift from home-based work to factory-based work and the separation of ownership from management. Although the corporation, as distinct from its owners, had been in existence in Britain since 1650, the separation of ownership and control was enabled by the first British Companies Act, which formalized the law in relation to 'joint stock companies' and introduced the limited liability of shareholders during the 1850s. The London Stock Exchange had been formed earlier in 1773. These changes increased the importance of accounting and accountability.

The era of mass production began in the early twentieth century with Henry Ford's assembly line. Organizations grew larger and this led to the creation of new organizational forms. Based on an extensive historical analysis, Chandler (1962) found that in large firms strategic growth and diversification led to the creation of decentralized, multidivisional corporations. Chandler's work thus emphasized organizational structure following organizational strategy. Chandler studied examples like General Motors, where remotely located managers made decisions on behalf of absent owners and central head office functions.

In the 1930s large firms such as General Motors shifted their strategy from production to a market focus, and budgets were developed to coordinate diverse activities. In the first decades of the twentieth century, the DuPont chemicals company developed a model to measure the return on investment (ROI). ROI (see Chapters 7, 14, and 15) was used to make capital investment decisions and to evaluate the performance of business units, including the accountability of managers to use capital efficiently.

Introducing the functions of accounting

Accounting is traditionally seen as fulfilling three functions:

- *Scorekeeping:* capturing, recording, summarizing, and reporting financial performance.
- *Attention directing:* drawing attention to, and assisting in the interpretation of, business performance, particularly in terms of the trend over time, and the comparison between actual and planned, or a benchmark measure of performance.
- *Problem solving:* identifying the best choice from a range of alternative actions.

In this book, we acknowledge the role of the scorekeeping function in Chapters 6 through 8. We are not concerned with how investors make decisions about their investments in companies, so we emphasize attention directing and problem solving as taking place through three inter-related functions, all part of the role of non-financial (marketing, operations, human resources, etc.) as well as financial managers:

- *Planning:* establishing goals and strategies to achieve those goals.
- *Decision making:* using financial (and non-financial performance) information to make decisions consistent with those goals and strategies.
- *Control:* using financial (and non-financial) information to improve performance over time, relative to what was planned, or using the information to modify the plan itself.

Planning, decision making and control are particularly relevant as increasingly businesses have been decentralized into many business units, where much of the planning, decision making, and control is focused.

Accountability results in the production of financial statements, primarily for those interested parties who are external to the business. This function is called financial accounting. Managers need financial and non-financial information to develop and implement strategy by planning for the future (budgeting); making decisions about products, services, prices and what costs to incur (decision making using cost information); and ensuring that plans are put into action and are achieved (control). This function is called management accounting. A third function, *corporate finance*, is concerned with how business organizations raise funds and make capital investment decisions, as well as with transactions such as foreign exchange. Corporate finance is largely beyond the scope of this book, although we touch on shareholder value in Chapter 2 and capital investment decisions in Chapter 14.

The role of financial accounting

Financial accounting is the recording of financial transactions, aimed principally at reporting performance to those outside the organization, with a primary focus on shareholders. In countries like the UK, USA, Canada, and Australia, corporations legislation usually dictates that directors of companies are required to report the financial performance of the companies to shareholders. They do so through an Annual Report which comprises four financial statements: the Statement of Comprehensive Income (or Income Statement, but commonly referred to as the Profit and Loss Account, or P&L); the Statement of Financial Position (more commonly called the Balance Sheet); the Statement of Changes in Equity; and the Statement of Cash Flows (these four statements are the topics of Chapters 6 and 7).

Financial statements are regulated by legislation and by accounting standards, and are subject to independent audit in order to provide comparisons between different companies (we explain this in more detail in Chapter 2). However, the information provided by financial statements is of limited decision usefulness for managers because the financial information is produced only once per year, is highly aggregated and provides no comparison to target (although the financial statements do provide a prior year comparison).

While financial accounting is extremely important for investors, it is also important for managers for two reasons. First, many managerial decisions, whether they relate to planning, decision making, or control, involve decisions that will ultimately be reported in financial statements and affect shareholder reaction in stock markets. Hence the decisions of managers are influenced by how those decisions will be presented to (and interpreted by) users of financial statements. Second, the accounting system that produces financial reports is the same system that managers use for planning, decision making, and control. This financial accounting information is supplemented by non-financial performance measures and by more detail and analysis derived from outside the financial accounting system. However, financial accounting still provides the foundation on which managers plan, make decisions, and exercise managerial control. As a result of these two reasons, managers need to understand financial accounting in order to take full advantage of the range of management accounting techniques that are available.

The role of management accounting

The advent of automated production following the Industrial Revolution increased the size and complexity of production processes, which employed more people and required larger sums of capital to finance machinery. Accounting historians suggest that the increase in the number of limited companies that led to the separation of ownership from control caused an increase in attention to what was called 'cost accounting' (the forerunner of 'management accounting') in order to determine the cost of products and enable the exercise of control by absent owners over their managers. Reflecting this emergence, the earlier title of management accountants was cost or works accountants.

Typically situated in factories, cost or works accountants tended to understand the business at a technical level and were able to advise non-financial managers in relation to operational decisions. Cost accounting was concerned with determining the cost of an object, whether a product, an activity, a division of the organization, or a market segment. The first book on cost accounting is believed to be Garcke and Fell's *Factory Accounts*, which was published in 1897.

Historians, such as Chandler (1990), have argued that the new corporate structures that were developed in the twentieth century – multidivisional organizations, conglomerates, and multinationals – placed increased demands on accounting. These demands included divisional performance evaluation and budgeting. It has also been suggested that developments in cost accounting were driven by government demands for cost information during both world wars. It appears that 'management accounting' became a term used only after World War II.

In their acclaimed book *Relevance Lost*, Johnson and Kaplan (1991) traced the development of management accounting from its origins in the Industrial Revolution supporting process-type industries such as textile and steel conversion, transportation, and distribution. These systems were concerned with evaluating the efficiency of internal processes, rather than measuring organizational profitability. Financial reports were produced using a separate transactions-based system that reported financial performance. Johnson and Kaplan (1991) argued that 'virtually all management accounting practices used today had been developed by 1925' (p. 12).

Calculating the cost of different products was unnecessary because the product range was homogeneous, but Johnson and Kaplan (1991) described how the early manufacturing firms attempted to improve performance through *economies of scale* by increasing the volume of output in order to lower unit costs. This led to a concern with measuring the efficiency of the production process. Over time, the product range of businesses expanded to meet the demands of the market and so businesses sought *economies of scope* through producing two or more products in a single facility. This led to the need for better information about how the mix of products could improve total profits.

Johnson and Kaplan (1991) described how

> a management accounting system must provide timely and accurate information to facilitate efforts to control costs, to measure and improve productivity, and to devise improved production processes. The management accounting system must also report accurate product costs so that pricing decisions, introduction of new products, abandonment of obsolete products, and response to rival products can be made (p. 4).

They argued that the developments in accounting theory in the first decades of the twentieth century came about by academics who

> emphasized simple decision-making models in highly simplified firms – those producing one or only a few products, usually in a one stage production process. The academics developed their ideas by logic and deductive reasoning. They did not attempt to study the problems actually faced by managers of organizations producing hundreds or thousands of products in complex production processes (p. 175).

They concluded:

> Not surprisingly, in this situation actual management accounting systems provided few benefits to organizations. In some instances, the information reported by existing management accounting systems not only inhibited good decision-making by managers, it might actually have encouraged bad decisions (p. 177).

Johnson and Kaplan (1991) described how the global competition that has taken place has left management accounting behind in terms of its decision usefulness. Developments such as total quality management, just-in-time inventory, computer-integrated manufacturing, shorter product life cycles (see Chapters 11 and 18), and the decline of manufacturing and rise of service industries have led to the need for 'accurate knowledge of product costs, excellent cost control, and coherent performance measurement' (p. 220). And 'the challenge for today's competitive environment is to develop new and more flexible approaches to the design of effective cost accounting, management control, and performance measurement systems' (p. 224).

A joint consultation document by UK and US accounting bodies (CIMA and AICPA, 2014) argues that management accountants use relevant and accurate information to improve the organization's performance through better decision taking. This helps to ensure that long-run value is created for stakeholders: 'Management accounting creates value and ensures sustainable success by contributing to sound decision making through the comprehensive analysis and provision of information that enables and supports organisations to plan, implement and control the execution of their strategy' (p. 5). The three 'global management accounting principles' are:

1. Preparing relevant information (along three dimensions: past, present and future; internal and external; and financial and non-financial information);
2. Modelling value creation (to understand the cause-effect relationships between inputs and outcomes);
3. Communicating with impact to drive better decisions about strategy execution.

There have been many changes since *Relevance Lost* was published in 1991. However, most of those changes have been in financial accounting. The next section describes relatively recent developments in accounting practice.

Recent developments in accounting

Compared to 20 or so years ago, financial accounting has gained in importance relative to management accounting. This is due to two reasons. First, the globalization of financial markets and the ability of investors to invest in stock markets around the world increased the need for financial statements that were comparable across different countries, rather than being based on local legislation and standards. The development of the UK-led International Financial Reporting Standards (IFRS) has resulted in almost all significant economies adopting a single set of reporting standards that enables investors to compare company performance across national boundaries. The only significant economy not to have yet adopted IFRS is the USA, which still relies on Generally Accepted Accounting Principles (GAAP), although it is moving towards IFRS. The topic of financial reporting standards is discussed in detail in Chapter 6.

The second reason has been the large corporate failures that raised questions about why financial statements have not provided early warning signals about the risk of failure. The size of some of these failures, with Enron and WorldCom as notable examples, and the increasing complexity of business transactions (some of which have been designed to improve the perception of reported performance, rather than the underlying reality) have led to a continual change in accounting standards in trying to improve their usefulness to investors.

The need for change was exemplified by the Global Financial Crisis that reached its height in 2007–8 and the global recession that followed from 2008–12. A housing bubble in the US (the 'sub-prime mortgage crisis') that burst and the failure of many high risk and overly complex debt instruments linked to those mortgages were the immediate causes of the crisis. However, there were other contributing factors: the failure of regulatory bodies, failures by boards of directors to exercise sound governance and risk management practices, and the failure by credit rating agencies adequately to recognize risk. Failures of banks and financial institutions were overtaken by financial crises in whole nations, particularly in Europe.

The advent of IFRS, corporate failures, and transactional complexity has led to an emphasis (and this author would argue an undue overemphasis) on reporting past and typically short-term performance designed to satisfy stock market investors, rather than improving the value-added capability of organizations to be successful in the longer term. While there have been significant management accounting developments in the last 20 years, these have tended to be overshadowed by financial reporting. We will return to these issues throughout this book. Of particular importance is recognizing that financial accounting is essential in *reporting* historic business performance and demonstrating accountability to investors, but management accounting comprises the set of tools and techniques that will help to *improve and sustain* business performance.

Value-based management is more fully described in Chapter 2, but it is in brief a concern with improving the value of the business to its shareholders. A fundamental role of non-financial managers is to make marketing, operational, human resource, and investment decisions that contribute to increasing the value of the business. Accounting provides the information base to assist in planning, decision making, and control.

The limitations of accounting information, particularly as a lagging indicator of performance, have led to an increasing emphasis on non-financial performance measures, which are described more fully in Chapter 4. Non-financial measures are a major concern of both accountants and non-financial managers, as they tend to be leading indicators of the financial performance that will be reported at some future time.

Activity-based management is an approach that emphasizes the underlying business processes that cut across the traditional organizational structure but are essential to produce goods and services. This approach reflects the need to identify the drivers or causes of those activities in order to be able to plan and control costs more effectively. Activity-based approaches are introduced throughout Part III.

Improving the quality of products and services is also a major concern, since advances in production technology and the need to improve performance by reducing waste have led to management tools such as total quality management (TQM), and continuous improvement processes such as Six Sigma and the Business Excellence model. Greater attention to environmental issues as a result of climate change has also led companies to better understand the short-term and long-term consequences of inefficient energy usage and environmental pollution. Managers can no longer ignore these issues and accounting has a role to play in measuring and reporting quality and environmental costs (see Chapter 11).

Strategic management accounting, which is described more fully in Chapter 18, is an attempt to shift the perceptions of accountants and non-financial managers from inward-looking to outward-looking, recognizing the need to look beyond the business to the whole supply chain with suppliers and customers, and beyond the current accounting period to product life cycles, and to seek ways of achieving and maintaining competitive advantage.

Lean accounting is a consequence of lean manufacturing, itself a development of the just-in-time philosophy which focuses on the elimination of inventory. Lean approaches emphasize reducing all waste, and their application to accounting is to identify and eliminate wasteful accounting practices which contribute little to management decision making. We discuss these developments more in Chapters 17 and 18.

In addition to these changes has been the rapid improvement in information and communications technologies. Computerization has eliminated many routine accounting processes (which were more correctly book keeping processes) and has expanded information systems beyond accounting to enterprise resource planning systems (ERPS, see Chapter 9) which integrate marketing, purchasing, production, distribution, and human resources information with accounting. The ready availability of information systems has also enabled detailed financial reports to be available for non-financial managers soon after the end of each accounting period.

These changes have had two impacts: (i) to change the role of accountants and (ii) to change the role of non-financial managers. Computerization has taken (especially management) accountants away from their 'bean counter' image to a role where they are more active participants in formulating and implementing business strategy, and act more as internal business consultants and advisers to management, providing information and advice that support improving business performance. These changes have also increased the responsibility of non-financial managers from their technical areas of expertise. Most non-financial managers now have responsibilities for setting budgets and meeting financial targets. This means that non-financial managers need an increased understanding of accounting to fulfil their accountability to higher levels of management.

The relationship between financial accounting and management accounting

Financial accounting is focused on the needs of external users and demonstrates accountability to shareholders under the stewardship principle. Financial statements have to comply with accounting standards (see Chapter 6) and are subject to audit. They are produced annually, are highly aggregated using historical figures, and provide only a comparison to the prior year. There is a common form of presentation of the Income Statement, Statement of Financial Position, and Statement of Cash Flows that applies to all companies.

Management accounting meets the needs of internal users (directors and managers) for planning, decision making, and control purposes. Reports are not subject to audit or accounting standards so organizations can present the information that is relevant to the needs of their business. Management accounting reports typically are produced more frequently (e.g. monthly) and are disaggregated to business unit level with more detail, often supplemented by non-financial information (see Chapter 4) with comparison to budget targets.

Table 1.1 shows the principal differences between financial and management accounting.

Table 1.1   Principal differences between financial and management accounting.

	Financial accounting	Management accounting
Focus	Production of financial statements, primarily for those interested parties who are external to the business	Production of financial and non-financial information, primarily for internal use within the business (boards of directors and management)
Time horizon	Past financial year	Future (planning/budgeting) and current (decision making and control)
Level of analysis	Summarizing data for a financial year. Highly aggregated (e.g. total expenses), for the organization as a whole	At least monthly with a greater level of detail (e.g. individual expenses), and at the level of each business unit
Decision-making use	Investment decisions	Decisions about products/services, pricing, etc.
Comparative information	Prior year	Budget and prior periods

Both financial and management accounting are important and useful for managers. Importantly, both are derived from the accounting records of the business, although management accounting supplements this with other, often non-financial sources of information. The needs of shareholders drive many business decisions and influence how those business decisions are likely to be reflected in the financial statements reported to those outside the business. Therefore the decisions that are made by managers in organizations need to integrate the day-to-day operational choices (management accounting) with the result of those choices as they impact on financial statements (financial accounting).

Finally, financial accounting is largely the domain of qualified accountants, as it is a specialist activity requiring a great deal of knowledge and skill. The term 'management accountant' is less common in practice because it has become incorporated into a variety of financial and increasingly non-financial positions. The title 'management accountant' is more prevalent in the UK where it has been institutionalized by the Chartered Institute of Management Accountants (CIMA). In Continental Europe the specific terminology of management accountant has never existed and 'controller' is a more common title (Hopwood, 2008).

Many non-financial roles now incorporate many of the roles carried out by management accountants. This is particularly so for managers with engineering or technical backgrounds who as line managers have considerable financial autonomy, including responsibility for budgets, cost control, pricing, and proposing new capital expenditure.

A critical perspective

Although the concepts and assumptions underlying accounting are yet to be introduced, having begun this book with an introduction to accounting history, it is worthwhile introducing here a contrasting viewpoint. While this viewpoint is one that may not be accepted by many practising managers, it is worth being aware of the role that accounting plays in the capitalist economic system in which we live and work.

The Marxist historian Hobsbawm (1962) argued that the cotton industry once dominated the UK economy, and this resulted in a shift from domestic production to factory production. Sales increased but profits shrank, so labour (which was three times the cost of materials) was replaced by mechanization during the Industrial Revolution.

Entrepreneurs purchased small items of machinery and growth was largely financed by borrowings. The Industrial Revolution produced 'such vast quantities and at such rapidly diminishing cost, as to be no longer dependent on existing demand, but to create its own market' (Hobsbawm, 1962, p. 32).

Advances in mass production followed the development of the assembly line, and were supported by the ease of transportation by rail and sea, and communications through the electric telegraph. At the same time, agriculture diminished in importance. Due to the appetite of the railways for iron and steel, coal, heavy machinery, labour, and capital investment, 'the comfortable and rich classes accumulated income so fast and in such vast quantities as to exceed all available possibilities of spending and investment' (Hobsbawm, 1962, p. 45).

While the rich accumulated profits, labour was exploited with wages kept at subsistence levels. Labour had to learn how to work, unlike agriculture or craft industries, in a manner suited to industry, and the result was a draconian master–servant relationship. In the 1840s a depression led to unemployment and high food prices, and 1848 saw the rise of the labouring poor in European cities, who threatened both the weak and obsolete regimes and the rich.

This resulted in a clash between the political (French) and industrial (British) revolutions, the 'triumph of bourgeois-liberal capitalism' and the domination of the globe by a few Western regimes, especially the British in the mid-nineteenth century, which became a 'world hegemony' (Hobsbawm, 1962). These concepts of industrial production and exploitation of labour were exported to developing countries in the centuries before the twentieth, through the process of British colonialism, and hence the 'British' capitalist system was exported throughout the world, not least with the support of a colonial expansionist Empire that lent large sums of money in return for countries' adoption of the British system. Similar approaches were taken by other European countries as they colonized countries in the African continent and in South-East Asia.

This 'global triumph' of capitalism in the 1850s (Hobsbawm, 1975) was a consequence of the combination of cheap capital and rising prices. Stability and prosperity overtook political questions about the legitimacy of existing dynasties and technology cheapened manufactured products. There was high demand but the cost of living did not fall, so labour became dominated by the interests of the new owners of the means of production. 'Economic liberalism' became the recipe for economic growth as the market ruled labour and helped national (and especially British) economic expansion. Industrialization made wealth and industrial capacity decisive in international power, especially in the USA, Japan, and Germany. National colonialism, it can be argued, has been superseded by a system of colonialism by multinational corporations, largely based in the USA, and to a lesser extent by British and European companies.

Armstrong (1987) traced the historical factors behind the comparative pre-eminence of accountants in British (and probably in most English-language economy) management hierarchies (in relation to other professions) and the emphasis on financial control. He concluded that accounting controls were installed by accountants as a result of their power base in global capital markets, which was achieved through their role in the allocation of the profit surplus to shareholders. Armstrong argued that mergers led to control problems that were tackled by

> American management consultants who tended to recommend the multidivisional form of organization . . . [which] entirely divorce[s] headquarters management from operations. Functional departments and their managers are subjected to a battery of financial indicators and budgetary controls . . . [and] a subordination of operational to financial decision-making and a major influx of accountants into senior management positions (p. 433).

A different reading of history is designed to do more than raise readers' awareness that accounting is not a neutral tool, objectively reporting performance. Accounting is intimately bound up with reinforcing a capitalist system, and privileging shareholders over other stakeholders. This raises a significant question: whether accounting should only be concerned with maximizing short-term profits for current shareholders, or whether it should be more concerned with longer-term performance to satisfy a broader range of stakeholders. This implies notions of corporate social responsibility, sustainability for future generations, and a consideration of ethics. Roberts (1996) suggested that organizational accounting embodies the separation of instrumental and moral consequences, which is questionable. He argued:

> The mystification of accounting information helps to fix, elevate and then impose upon others its own particular instrumental interests, without regard to the wider social and environmental consequences of the pursuit of such interests. Accounting thus serves as a vehicle whereby others are called to account, while the interests it embodies escape such accountability (p. 59).

This is a more critical perspective than that associated with the traditional notion of accounting as a report to shareholders and managers. We will revisit the critical perspective throughout this book.

Conclusion

This chapter introduces the notion of accountability and the function of accounting. It identifies the different roles played by financial accounting and management accounting, and the interaction between those roles. A short history of accounting and a summary of recent developments in accounting are supplemented by a critical perspective on the historically derived position of accounting in Western economies. This chapter provides a broad introduction to many concepts that will be developed further throughout this book.

While this book is designed to help non-financial managers understand the tools and techniques of accounting, it is also intended to make readers think critically about the role and limitations of accounting. One intention is to reinforce to readers that

> accounting information provides a window through which the real activities of the organization may be monitored, but it should be noted also that other windows are used that do not rely upon accounting information (Otley and Berry, 1994, p. 46).

References

Armstrong, P. (1987). The rise of accounting controls in British capitalist enterprises. *Accounting, Organizations and Society*, 12(5), 415–36.

Boland, R. J. and Schultze, U. (1996). Narrating accountability: cognition and the production of the accountable self. In R. Munro and J. Mouritsen (Eds), *Accountability: Power, Ethos and the Technologies of Managing*, London: International Thomson Business Press.

Chandler, A. D. J. (1962). *Strategy and Structure: Chapters in the History of the American Industrial Enterprise.* Cambridge, MA: Harvard University Press.

Chandler, A. D. J. (1990). *Scale and Scope: The Dynamics of Industrial Capitalism.* Cambridge, MA: Harvard University Press.

Chartered Institute of Management Accountants & American Institute of Certified Public Accountants (CIMA & AICPA, 2014). *Consultation Draft: Global Management Accounting Principles: Driving better business through improved performance.* Source: http://www.cgma.org/Resources/Reports/DownloadableDocuments/global-management-accounting-principles.pdf.

Gleeson-White, J. (2011). *Double Entry: How the merchants of Venice shaped the modern world – and how their invention could make or break the planet.* Sydney: Allen & Unwin.

Hobsbawm, E. (1962). *The Age of Revolution: Europe 1789–1848.* London: Phoenix Press.

Hobsbawm, E. (1975). *The Age of Capital: 1848–1875.* London: Phoenix Press.

Hopwood, A. G. (2008). Management accounting research in a changing world. *Journal of Management Accounting Research*, 20, 313.

Johnson, H. T. and Kaplan, R. S. (1991). *Relevance Lost: The Rise and Fall of Management Accounting.* Boston, MA: Harvard Business Press Books.

Kuran, T. (2010). The Scale of Entrepreneurship in Middle Eastern History. In Landes, D. S., Mokyr, J. and Baumol, W. J. (eds). *The Invention of Enterprise: Entrepreneurship from Ancient Mesopotamia to Modern Times.* Princeton: Princeton University Press.

Murray, J. M. (2010) Entrepreneurs and Entrepreneurship in Medieval Europe. In Landes, D. S., Mokyr, J. and Baumol, W. J. (eds). *The Invention of Enterprise: Entrepreneurship from Ancient Mesopotamia to Modern Times*. Princeton: Princeton University Press.

Otley, D. T. and Berry, A. J. (1994). Case study research in management accounting and control. *Management Accounting Research*, 5, 45–65.

Roberts, J. (1996). From discipline to dialogue: individualizing and socializing forms of accountability. In R.Munro and J. Mouritsen (Eds), *Accountability: Power, Ethos and the Technologies of Managing*. London: International Thomson Business Press.

Questions

1.1   Explain the difference between accounting, an account, and accountability.

1.2   Summarize the main activities of (i) financial accountants and (ii) management accountants.

1.3   Briefly explain the critical view of the role of accounting and accountants.

2

Accounting and its Relationship to Shareholder Value and Corporate Governance

This chapter relates the role of accounting in terms of shareholder value and strategy. The reader is introduced to the difference between capital and product markets and the importance of shareholder value. This is then developed through the relationship between shareholder value, strategy, and accounting. The regulation of companies and corporate governance is explained as the context in which accounting operates, including the role of directors, audit, and Stock Exchange listing rules. A brief coverage of risk, internal control, and accounting is followed by a critical perspective, introducing a concern with stakeholder compared to shareholder value.

Capital and product markets

Since the seventeenth century, companies have been formed by shareholders in order to consolidate resources and invest in opportunities. Shareholders have *limited liability* through which their personal liability in the event of business failure is limited to their investment in the company's share capital. Shareholders appoint directors to direct and control the business, and the directors in turn employ managers. Shareholders have few direct rights in relation to the conduct of the business. Their main powers are to elect the directors, approve the directors' recommendation of a dividend, and appoint the auditors in an annual general meeting of shareholders. They are also entitled to an Annual Report containing details of the company's financial performance (see Chapter 7).

The market in which investors buy and sell the shares of companies (the term commonly used in North America is 'stock', but we retain the Anglo term 'shares' throughout this book) is called the capital market, which is normally associated with a Stock Exchange. Companies obtain funds raised from shareholders (capital, or equity) and borrowings from financiers (debt). Both of these constitute the capital employed in the business.

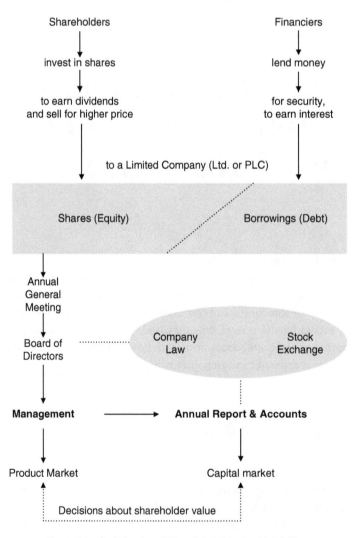

Figure 2.1   Capital and product market structure and interaction.

The cost of capital represents the cost incurred by the organization to fund all its investments, comprising the cost of equity and the cost of debt weighted by the mix of debt and equity. The cost of debt is interest, which is the price charged by the lender. The cost of equity is partly dividend and partly capital growth, because most shareholders expect both regular income from profits (the dividend) and an increase in the value of their shares over time in the capital market. Thus the different costs of each form of capital, weighted by the proportions of different forms of debt and equity, constitute the weighted average cost of capital (WACC). The management of the business relationship with capital markets is called financial management or corporate finance. The calculation of the WACC is beyond the scope of this book and is covered by texts on corporate finance. It will be assumed as given when required in this book.

Companies use their capital to invest in technologies, people, and materials in order to make, buy, and sell products or services to customers. This is called the product market. The focus of shareholder wealth, according to Rappaport (1998), is to obtain funds at competitive rates from capital markets and invest those funds to exploit imperfections in product markets. Where this takes place, shareholder wealth is increased through dividends and increases in the share price. The relationship between capital markets and product markets is shown in Figure 2.1.

Shareholder value-based management

Since the mid-1980s, there has been more and more emphasis on increasing the value of the business to its shareholders. Traditionally, business performance has been measured through accounting ratios such as return on capital employed (ROCE), return on investment (ROI), earnings per share, and so on (which are described in Chapter 7). However, it has been argued that these are historical rather than current measures, and they vary between companies as a result of different accounting treatments.

Rappaport (1998) described how companies with strong cash flows diversified in the mid-twentieth century, often into uneconomic businesses, which led to the 'value gap' – the difference between the market value of the shares and the value of the business if it had been managed to maximize shareholder value. The consequence was the takeover movement and subsequent asset stripping of the 1980s, which provided a powerful incentive for managers to focus on creating value for shareholders. The takeover movement itself led to problems as high acquisition premiums (the excess paid over and above the calculated value of the business, i.e. the goodwill – see Chapter 6) were paid to the owners and financed by high levels of debt. During the 1990s institutional investors (pension/ superannuation funds, insurance companies, investment trusts, etc.), through their dominance of share ownership, increased their pressure on management to improve the financial performance of companies.

The global financial crisis (GFC) which commenced in 2007 and reached its peak in 2008 has had wide-ranging impacts on individual countries, global financial markets and institutions, and national economies. A recession affecting most global markets lasted until 2012 and its repercussions are still being felt in Europe and North America.

Two particular causes of the GFC have been given by commentators. The first was the practice of securitization, where loans were packaged and resold by banks to other financial institutions (including insurance companies) to raise funds for further lending. The second and related cause of the GFC was said to be the rewards offered to directors and senior managers, especially in the financial services industry, for continuously improving performance that was unsustainable and did not take into account the risks that were being faced.

The GFC and its aftermath were at least in part a consequence of the relentless pursuit of short-term financial performance, without any real concern for risk or the sustainability of performance over the longer term.

Nevertheless, value-based management (VBM) emphasizes shareholder value, on the assumption that this is the primary goal of every business. Research into the use of value-based management approaches by UK companies was described by Cooper *et al.* (2001). VBM approaches include:

- total shareholder return;
- market value added;
- shareholder value added; and
- economic value added.

Total shareholder return (TSR) compares the dividends received by shareholders and the increase in the share price with the original shareholder investment, expressing the TSR as a percentage of the initial investment.

Market value added (MVA) is the difference between total market capitalization (number of shares issued times share price plus the market value of debt) and the total capital invested in the business by debt and equity providers. This is a measure of the value generated by managers for shareholders.

Rappaport (1998) coined the term *shareholder value added (SVA)* to refer to the increase in shareholder value over time. He defined shareholder value as the economic value of an investment, which can be calculated by using the cost of capital to discount estimated future cash flows (which he called *free cash flows*) into present values (free cash flow is discussed in more detail in Chapter 6; discounted cash flow techniques are described in detail in Chapter 14). The business must generate profits in product markets that exceed the cost of capital in the capital market for value to be created (if not, shareholder value is eroded).

Rappaport developed a shareholder value network model which identifies seven drivers of shareholder value: sales growth rate; operating profit margin; income tax rate; working capital investment; fixed capital investment; cost of capital; and forecast duration. Managers make three types of decisions that influence these value drivers and lead to shareholder value:

- Operating decisions – product mix, pricing, promotion, customer service, etc., which are then reflected in the sales growth rate, operating profit margin, and income tax rate.
- Investment decisions – in both inventory and capacity, which are then reflected in both working capital and fixed capital investment.
- Financing decisions – the mix of debt and equity and the choice of financial instrument determine the cost of capital, which is assessed by capital markets in terms of business risk.

The forecast duration is the estimated number of years over which the return from investments is expected to exceed the cost of capital.

The seven value drivers determine the cash flow from operations, the level of debt, and the cost of capital, all of which determine shareholder value. However, a detrimental consequence of the emphasis on shareholder value is that it has led to a focus on short-term financial performance, sometimes at the expense of longer-term investment and sustainable performance.

Economic Value Added™ (EVA) is a financial performance measure developed by consultants Stern Stewart & Co. It claims to capture the economic profit of a business that leads to shareholder value creation. In simple terms, EVA is net operating profit after deducting a charge to cover the opportunity cost of the capital invested in the business (when by taking one course of action you lose the opportunity to undertake an alternative course). EVA or 'economic profit' is the amount by which earnings exceed (or fall short of) the minimum rate of return that shareholders and financiers could get by investing in other securities with a comparable risk.

EVA accepts the assumption that the primary financial objective of any business is to maximize the wealth of its shareholders. The value of the business depends on the extent to which investors expect future profits to be greater or less than the weighted average cost of capital. Returns over and above the cost of capital increase shareholder wealth, while returns below the cost of capital erode shareholder wealth. Stern Stewart argues that managers understand this measure because it is based on operating profits. By introducing a notional charge based on assets held by the business, managers (whether at a corporate or divisional level) manage those assets as well as the profit generated.

EVA has its critics. For example, the calculation of EVA allows a large number of adjustments to reported accounting profits in order to remove distortions caused by arbitrary accounting rules, although Stern Stewart argues that most organizations need only a few of these. EVA also estimates the risk-adjusted cost of capital, which can be argued as being subjective. The increase in shareholder value is reflected in compensation strategies for managers whose goals, argues Stern Stewart, are aligned to increasing shareholder wealth through bonus and share option schemes that are paid over a period of time to ensure consistent future performance.

Irrespective of the VBM approach adopted, the pursuit of shareholder value (or economic value added) can be achieved through new or redesigned products and services, expansion to new markets, introduction of new technologies, the management of costs, the development of performance measurement systems, and improved decision making. Value-based management aims to improve shareholder wealth, however it may be measured. Improving shareholder value is inextricably linked with both strategy and accounting.

Shareholder value, strategy, and accounting

This book treats accounting as integral to the formulation and implementation of strategy, through decisions about the functional areas of marketing, operations, and human resources. The purpose of strategy 'is to pursue profit over the long term' (Grant, 1998, p. 34). Strategy is concerned with long-term direction, achieving and maintaining competitive advantage, identifying the scope and boundaries of the organization, and matching the activities of the organization to its environment. Strategy is also about building on resources and competences to create new opportunities and take advantage of those opportunities by managing change within the organization.

There is also a link between strategy and operational decisions in order to turn strategy formulation into strategy implementation. Implementation is about converting strategy into action by setting performance targets (both financial and non-financial) for the business as a whole and for individual business units and then measuring and controlling performance against those targets (this is the subject of Chapter 4).

The strategic focus of accounting in business organizations is reporting and improving the value of the business to its shareholders through dividends from profits and/or through capital growth. Strategy both influences, and is influenced by, shareholder value. Strategy therefore also influences accounting: what performance is measured, how it is measured, and how it is reported. The organization's accounting system (which we introduce in Chapter 3) is about providing useful information to two distinct groups: external parties and managers.

Financial accounting relates to the stewardship function (Chapter 1), which holds that managers are accountable to those with a financial interest in the business. Accounting produces financial statements to satisfy that accountability (Chapters 6 and 7) and measures, to some extent, the creation of shareholder value. Management accounting provides the information for managers to assist in planning, decision making, and control (Chapters 9 through 18). Management accounting is more concerned with strategy and supplements the accounting system data with additional non-financial information and analysis and provides more detail, as managers have quite different requirements to those outside the business. The principal focus of this book is on how accounting provides information to assist non-financial managers.

The importance of strategy for accounting and the information it provides is that strategy involves taking a longer-term view about the sustainable performance of the business. Financial accounting reports are essential in reporting and enabling decisions by investors and lenders; however, they focus on short-term, highly aggregated financial performance. Management accounting comprises a set of tools and techniques to support planning, decision making, and control by managers in business organizations. So management accounting is about creating shareholder value through strategic planning, while financial accounting is more concerned with reporting the results of strategic decisions to investors.

However, as we saw in Chapter 1, these two are inter-related and that inter-relationship goes further when we introduce strategy. Strategy, as we have seen, is focused on achieving shareholder value, and whether or not shareholder value is achieved is commonly gauged through financial statements. Hence, decisions made using management accounting information are made in the context not only of whether those decisions are likely to lead to delivery of the desired strategy and shareholder value in the longer term, but also as to how those decisions will appear in the short term when they are reported in the financial statements for the current year. Equally, the pursuit of short-term profits to be reported in the current financial year (despite the lessons of the global financial crisis) can lead to a failure to take decisions that are beneficial strategically but which may have a negative impact on the financial statements in the short term.

Beyond its role in strategy and shareholder value, accounting is a requirement of legislation, and reporting to shareholders is a fundamental role of boards of directors. The next section provides the context of accounting in terms of the regulation of companies and corporate governance.

Company regulation and corporate governance

The regulation of companies

The Companies Act of 2006 is the primary UK legislation governing companies. Similar legislation operates throughout most Commonwealth countries. The Act sets out the need for companies to have a constitution, formally known as the *Memorandum of Association* and *Articles of Association*. Each company has a share capital, enabling ownership to be divided over many 'shareholders' or 'members' of the company (the term 'stock holders' is used in the United States). The Act sets out the effects of incorporation, i.e. the 'limited liability' of shareholders for any unpaid portion of the shares they own. In most cases, issued shares are fully paid and therefore shareholders have no liability beyond their initial investment in the event of a company's failure.

Shareholders appoint directors to manage the company on their behalf. Those directors have various duties. Directors may authorize the company to borrow money. The directors must keep accounting records and produce financial statements in a specified format. If the company makes a profit, the directors may recommend that a dividend be paid out of profits. An auditor must be appointed to report annually to shareholders. Shareholders have no management rights. However, shareholders receive an Annual Report (see Chapter 7) containing the financial statements and an annual general meeting of shareholders must be held which elects directors, ratifies the dividend, and appoints auditors, etc.

Corporate governance

Corporate governance is the system by which companies are directed and controlled. Boards of directors are responsible for the governance of their companies. The responsibilities of the board include setting the company's strategic goals, providing leadership to senior management, monitoring business performance, and reporting to shareholders.

Corporate governance in the UK dates back to a report by Sir Adrian Cadbury in 1992 and followed several major corporate collapses. The high-profile failures of companies, and the press coverage given to the major failures of Enron and WorldCom in the United States, brought corporate governance to worldwide attention. Large-scale failures have become a feature of business history throughout the world, with the most recent spate of collapses attributed to the global financial crisis. The increased attention to corporate governance has also been global, with many Commonwealth countries following the Cadbury principles which have evolved into codes of corporate governance.

The UK Corporate Governance Code (Financial Reporting Council, 2014: https://www.frc.org.uk/Our-Work/Publications/Corporate-Governance/UK-Corporate-Governance-Code-2014.pdf) is the most recent code of practice. The Code adopts a principles-based approach that provides best practice guidelines for corporate governance in companies. The Code is aimed at Stock Exchange-listed companies (whether incorporated in the UK or elsewhere) which are required to either comply with the Code or explain reasons for any departure from it (the 'comply or explain' approach). The Code is also regarded as best practice for unlisted companies.

Even before the advent of corporate governance codes, a growing number of institutional investors were encouraging greater disclosure of governance processes, emphasizing the quality and sustainability of earnings, rather than short-term profits alone. Research has shown that an overwhelming majority of institutional investors are prepared to pay a significant premium for companies exhibiting high standards of corporate governance.

The introduction of the *Sarbanes–Oxley Act* in 2002 (often referred to as SOX) was the legislative response in the USA to the financial and accounting scandals of Enron and WorldCom and the misconduct at the accounting firm Arthur Andersen. Although not a corporate governance code as such, Sarbanes–Oxley focused on financial reporting and introduced the requirement to disclose all material off-balance-sheet transactions (transactions that avoided, through technical loopholes, being disclosed in financial statements). The Act requires the certification of annual and quarterly financial statements by the chief executive and chief financial officer of all companies with US securities registrations, with criminal penalties for knowingly making false certifications.

In other countries, there are similar requirements to Sarbanes–Oxley and the UK Corporate Governance Code, including:

- Canadian equivalent of Sarbanes–Oxley Act known as C-SOX;
- German Corporate Governance Code of 2002;
- King Report on Corporate Governance (2002) (and the King II and King III Reports) in South Africa;
- Financial Security Law in France of 2003;
- Corporate Law Economic Reform Program Act (CLERP9) in Australia in 2004.

It is important to note that while practices may differ in each country, the underlying principles of corporate governance are quite similar.

Principles of corporate governance

The role of a company's board of directors is to provide entrepreneurial leadership of the company within a framework of prudent and effective controls which enables risk to be assessed and managed. The board should set the company's strategic aims, and ensure that the necessary financial and human resources are in place for the company to meet its objectives and review management performance. The board should set the company's values and standards and ensure that its obligations to its shareholders and others are understood and met.

The five main principles of corporate governance found in the *UK Corporate Governance Code* are in relation to: leadership by the board; the effectiveness of the board; accountability; remuneration of board directors; and relations with shareholders.

Responsibility of directors

Under Companies legislation, the financial statements of a company are the responsibility of directors, not managers. Directors are responsible for keeping proper accounting records which disclose with reasonable accuracy the financial position of the company and for ensuring that financial statements comply with the Companies Act. They are also responsible for safeguarding the company's assets and for taking reasonable steps to prevent and detect fraud.

The financial statements must show a 'true and fair view' (see Chapter 6) of the state of affairs of the company and of the profit or loss for that year. The US equivalent of the true and fair view is to *present fairly*' in conformity with generally accepted accounting principles. In preparing the financial statements, directors must select suitable accounting policies and apply those policies consistently, make judgements and estimates that are reasonable and prudent, and prepare financial statements on a going concern basis unless it is inappropriate to presume that the company will continue in business (see Chapter 3 for a discussion of these principles).

Although in practice these functions will be delegated to a company's managers, the accountability for financial records and financial statements cannot be delegated by the board of directors. Both are, however, subject to audit.

Audit

Audit is a periodic examination of the accounting records of a company carried out by an independent accountant to ensure that those records have been properly maintained and that the financial statements which are drawn up from those records present a true and fair view. An audit includes examination, on a test basis, of evidence relevant to the amounts and disclosures in financial statements. It also includes an assessment of significant estimates and judgements made by directors in the preparation of financial statements, and whether the company's accounting policies are appropriate, consistent, and adequately disclosed. Auditors carry out their audit in accordance with UK Auditing Standards, issued by the Financial Reporting Council.

Each year the auditors present a report to shareholders, giving their opinion as to whether the financial statements present a true and fair view and are properly prepared in accordance with the Companies Act and applicable accounting standards (see Chapters 6 and 7).

Stock Exchange Listing Rules

The primary aim of a Stock Exchange is to provide issuers, intermediaries, and investors with attractive, efficient, and well-regulated markets in which to raise capital and fulfil investment and trading requirements. Stock exchanges in the UK are subject to oversight by the UK Listing Authority, part of the Financial Conduct Authority. All companies are subject to the Companies Act, but publicly listed companies (i.e. those listed on a Stock Exchange) have to abide by additional regulations called the 'Listing Rules' (http://media.fshandbook.info/content/full/LR.pdf). These rules are set by the UK Listing Authority.

The Listing Rules set out mandatory standards for any company wishing to list its shares or securities for sale to the public, and are aimed at protecting investors and maintaining standards of transparency, conduct, shareholder rights, and due diligence. The Listing Rules dictate such matters as the contents of the prospectus on an initial public offering (IPO) of shares, and ongoing obligations such as the disclosure of price-sensitive information, and communications on new share offers, rights issues, and potential or actual takeover bids for the company.

The Listing Rules require listed companies to disclose how they have applied the principles in the *UK Corporate Governance Code*; and to confirm either that the company complies with the Code's provisions or, if it does not comply, to provide an explanation (the 'comply or explain' approach referred to above).

Risk management, internal control, and accounting

The benefits of applying good corporate governance are to reduce risk, stimulate performance, improve access to capital markets, enhance the marketability of products/services by creating confidence among stakeholders, and demonstrate transparency and accountability.

The *UK Corporate Governance Code* takes a strong position in relation to risk. Risk is defined as 'uncertain future events which could influence the achievement of the organization's strategic, operational and financial objectives' (International Federation of Accountants, 1999). Risk may be business or operational, arising from the normal course of business (loss of customers, failure of computer systems, poor quality products, etc.); financial (arising from changes in interest rates, foreign currency exposure, poor credit control, etc.); environmental (arising from changes in political, economic, social, or technological factors); or reputational. Risk may be considered in relation to downside factors ('bad things may happen') or upside factors ('good things may not happen'). This recognizes that taking risks is a necessary part of conducting business, with returns being the compensation for taking risks. The *UK Corporate Governance Code* requires that boards of directors institute a system of internal control based on the organization's risk appetite and the identification and assessment of risks facing the organization. A comprehensive approach to risk management ensures appropriate risk responses, monitoring and reporting processes, and the development of appropriate internal controls to help manage risk.

Internal control is the whole system of internal controls, financial and otherwise, established in order to provide reasonable assurance of effective and efficient operation, internal financial control, and compliance with laws and regulations. The *UK Corporate Governance Code* provides that the board should maintain a sound system of internal control to safeguard shareholders' investment and the company's assets. The board should, at least annually, conduct a review of the effectiveness of the system of internal controls and should report to shareholders that they have done so. The review should cover all material controls, including financial, operational, and compliance controls and risk management systems.

Although there are forms of control other than financial ones (see Chapter 4), internal financial controls are established to provide reasonable assurance of the safeguarding of assets against unauthorized use or disposition, the maintenance of proper accounting records, and the reliability of financial information used within the business or for publication.

Accounting controls are important in all organizations. They include control over cash, receivables, inventory, payables, and the business infrastructure (non-current assets, see Chapter 7), as well as borrowings, income, and expenses. Financial controls also exist over the costing of products and services (Chapters 10–13), capital investment decisions (Chapter 14), divisional performance evaluation (Chapter 15), and budgets and budgetary control (Chapters 16 and 17). Accounting is fundamental to a system of internal control, and is the subject of Part III of this book, although the theoretical foundations are laid in Chapters 4 and 5.

A critical perspective

Shareholders' interests dominate business and accountants occupy a privileged position as those who establish the rules and report business performance. This can be seen as a historical development (see Chapter 1). However, the dominant concern with shareholder value has subsumed much consideration of the wider accountability of business to other stakeholders.

In a 2013 paper, Harvard Business School's George Serafeim argued that increasing concentration of economic activity and power in the world's largest corporations, the Global 1000, has opened the way for managers to consider the interests of a broader set of stakeholders rather than only shareholders (Serafeim, 2013).

Stakeholder theory looks beyond shareholders to those groups who influence, or are influenced by, the organization. The theory argues that shareholders are not representative of society and stakes are held in the organization by employees, customers, suppliers, government, and the wider community. Stakeholder theory is concerned with how the power of stakeholders, with their competing interests, is managed by the organization in terms of its broader accountabilities. Although this chapter has been concerned with shareholder value and corporate governance, a critical approach questions this emphasis on the privilege accorded to shareholder value.

The stakeholder model takes a broader view, for example that found in South Africa, where the King Committee on Corporate Governance provides an integrated approach to corporate governance in the interest of all stakeholders, embracing the social, environmental, and economic aspects of organizational activities. While not legislation, it is a requirement for companies listed on the Johannesburg Stock Exchange. In the King III Report of 2009, governance, strategy, and sustainability were integrated. The report recommended that organizations produce an integrated report in place of an annual financial report and a separate sustainability report (see Chapter 7 for a discussion of sustainability reporting).

The shareholder and stakeholder models represent different means by which the functioning of boards of directors and top management can be understood. However, in company law, there is no doubt that shareholders are in a privileged position compared with other stakeholders. A critical perspective merely asks why this is so, and whether such a position ought to be taken for granted.

The idea of strategy oriented towards achieving goals is also open to criticism. Mintzberg (1994) was critical of the theory of strategic planning, particularly focused on financial projections, branding it a 'calculating style of management' which results in strategies that are extrapolated from the past or copied from others. Mintzberg saw some strategy as deliberate, but other strategy as an emergent process, which should lead to continual learning. He argued:

> Strategic planning often spoils strategic thinking, causing managers to confuse real vision with the manipulation of numbers (p. 107).

The pursuit of shareholder value implies a particular goal-oriented, economic, and rational theory of management behaviour and organizational action. We will consider the theoretical assumptions behind this perspective in Chapters 4 and 5.

Conclusion

While Chapter 1 provided an introduction to accounting, its history, and the changing role of the accountant, this chapter has provided the context for accounting. First, we considered the importance of capital markets and how they dictate the drive for shareholder value-based management through strategic planning. We then introduced the notions of company regulation and corporate governance that underlie the functioning of business organizations. The roles of boards of directors, auditors, stock exchanges, and their regulators are intimately bound up with the practice of accounting, risk management, and internal control. Finally, we concluded with a critical perspective that challenges the dominant (and narrow) view of shareholder value and contrasts it with a broader stakeholder view.

References

Cooper, S., Crowther, D., Davies, M., and Davis, E. W. (2001). *Shareholder or Stakeholder Value: The Development of Indicators for the Control and Measurement of Performance*. London: Chartered Institute of Management Accountants.

Financial Reporting Council (2014). *The UK Corporate Governance Code*. https://www.frc.org.uk/Our-Work/Publications/Corporate-Governance/UK-Corporate-Governance-Code-2014.pdf.

Grant, R. M. (1998). *Contemporary Strategy Analysis: Concepts, Techniques, Applications*. Oxford: Blackwell.

International Federation of Accountants (1999). *Enhancing Shareholder Wealth by Better Managing Business Risk*.

King Committee on Corporate Governance (2002). *King Report on Corporate Governance for South Africa 2002 (King II Report)*. Institute of Directors, South Africa. http://www.mervynking.co.za/downloads/CD_King2.pdf.

Mintzberg, H. (1994). The fall and rise of strategic planning. *Harvard Business Review*, Jan–Feb, 107–14.

Rappaport, A. (1998). *Creating Shareholder Value: A Guide for Managers and Investors*. New York: Free Press.

Serafeim, G. (2013). *The Role of the Corporation in Society: An Alternative View and Opportunities for Future Research*. Harvard Business School. SSRN-id2270579.pdf at http://papers.ssrn.com/sol3/papers.cfm?abstract_id=2270579.

Questions

2.1 Explain the idea of value-based management and how shareholder value relates to the interaction between product and capital markets.

2.2 Explain the key issues in corporate governance as they relate to accounting.

2.3 Explain the key differences between a shareholder value and a stakeholder approach to the accountability of organizations.

3

Recording Financial Transactions and the Principles of Accounting

In order to understand the accounting process, we need to understand how accounting captures information that is subsequently used for producing financial statements and for managerial planning, decision-making, and control purposes. This chapter describes how business events are recorded as transactions into an accounting system using the double-entry method that is the foundation of accounting. The elements of the accounting system are introduced: assets; liabilities; income; expenses, and equity. We introduce a simple form of the Income Statement and Statement of Financial Position (Balance Sheet) and explain the basic principles of accounting that underlie how financial statements are produced. Finally, the chapter introduces one of the first limitations of accounting systems – the calculation of 'cost' for decision making, and how cost may be interpreted in multiple ways.

Business events, transactions, and the accounting system

Businesses exist to make a profit. They do this by producing goods and services and selling those goods and services at a price that covers their cost. Conducting business involves a number of *business events* such as buying equipment, purchasing goods and services, paying expenses, making sales, distributing goods and services, etc. In accounting terms, each of these business events is a transaction. A transaction is the financial description of each business event.

It is important to recognize that transactions are a financial representation of the business event, measured in monetary terms. This is only one perspective on business events, albeit the one considered most important for accounting purposes. A broader view is that business events can also be recorded in non-financial terms, such as measures of product/service quality, speed of delivery, customer satisfaction, etc. These non-financial performance measures (which are described in detail in Chapter 4) are important aspects of business events that are not captured by financial transactions. This is a limitation of accounting as a tool of business decision making that the reader must always bear in mind.

Each transaction is recorded on a source document that forms the basis of recording in a business's accounting system. Examples of source documents are invoices and cheques, although increasingly source documents are records of electronic transactions, such as electronic funds transfer. The accounting system, typically computer based (except for very small businesses), comprises a set of accounts that summarize the transactions that have been recorded on source documents and entered into the accounting system. Accounts can be considered as 'buckets' within the accounting system containing similar transactions (e.g. sales income, salary payments, inventory).

There are five types of accounts:

- **Assets**: things the business *owns*.
- **Liabilities**: debts the business *owes*.
- **Income**: the *revenue* generated from the *sale* of goods or services.
- **Expenses**: the *costs* incurred in *producing* the goods and services
- **Equity (or capital)**: the investment made by shareholders into the business.

The main difference between these categories is that business profit is calculated as:

$$\textbf{profit = income – expenses}$$

while the equity or capital of the business (the owner's investment) is calculated as

$$\textbf{equity = assets – liabilities}$$

Financial statements comprise the Income Statement (which used to be called the Profit and Loss account and which now forms part of the Statement of Comprehensive Income) and the Statement of Financial Position (previously termed Balance Sheet, although this term is still commonly used). Both are produced from the information in the accounting system (see Chapter 6).

Figure 3.1 shows in diagrammatic form the relationship between business events, the recording of transactions in the accounting system, and how the five types of accounts are presented in the Income Statement and Statement of Financial Position (or Balance Sheet).

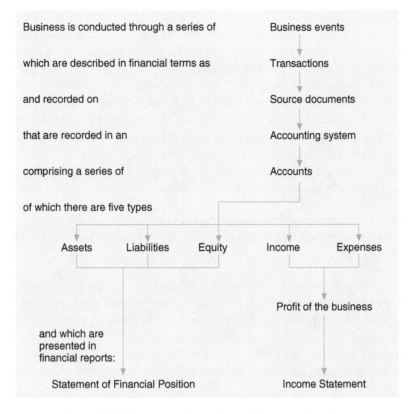

Figure 3.1   Business events, transactions, and the accounting system.

The double entry: recording transactions

Businesses use a system of accounting called double entry, which derives from the late fifteenth-century Italian city-states (see Chapter 1). The double entry means that every business transaction affects two accounts. Those accounts may *increase* or *decrease*. Accountants record the increases or decreases as debits or credits, but it is not necessary for non-accountants to understand this distinction. It is sufficient for our purposes to:

1. identify what type of account is affected (assets, liability, income, expense, or equity); and
2. determine whether the transaction increases or decreases that account.

Transactions may take place in one of two forms:

Cash: If the business sells goods/services for cash, the double entry is an increase in income and an increase in the bank account (an asset). If the business buys goods/services for cash, either an asset or an expense will increase (depending on what is bought) and the bank account will decrease.

Credit: If the business sells goods/services on credit, the double entry is an increase in debts owed *to* the business (called Receivables in financial statements but commonly referred to as Debtors, an asset) and an increase in income. If the business buys goods/services on credit, either an asset or an expense will increase (depending on what is bought) and the debts owed *by* the business will increase (called Payables in financial statements, but commonly referred to as Creditors, a liability).

Note that the double entry does not necessarily involve an increase in one account and a decrease in another account. Two accounts may increase, or two accounts may decrease, or one may increase and one decrease. This is because the accounting treatment of assets, liabilities, income, expenses, and equity is different, as we will see later.

When goods are bought for resale, they become an asset called Inventory (commonly referred to as Stock). When the same goods are sold, there are two transactions:

1. the sale, either by cash or credit, as described above; and
2. the transfer of the cost of those goods, now sold, from inventory to an expense, called either cost of sales, or cost of goods sold.

In this way, the profit is the difference between the *price* at which the goods were sold (1 above) and the purchase *cost* of the same goods (2 above). Note the distinction between price (what the business charges customers for its products or services; and the cost, which the business pays for its goods or services).

Increases or decreases in inventory only reflect a change in the asset *Inventory*. Importantly, the purchase of goods into inventory does not affect profit until the goods are sold, when they become the *cost of sales*.

Some examples of business transactions and how the double entry affects the accounting system are shown in Table 3.1.

Table 3.1   Business transactions and the double entry.

Business event	Transaction	Source document	Accounts affected	Type of account	Increase or decrease
Install new equipment for production	Buy equipment for cash £25,000	Cheque	Equipment	Asset	Increase £25,000
			Bank	Asset	Decrease £25,000
Receive stock of goods for resale	Purchase stock on credit £15,000	Invoice from supplier	Inventory	Asset	Increase £15,000
			Payables	Liability	Increase £15,000
Pay weekly wages	Pay wages £3,000	Cheque	Wages	Expense	Increase £3,000
			Bank	Asset	Decrease £3,000
Sell goods to customer from stock	Sell stock on credit £9,000	Invoice to customer	Receivables	Asset	Increase £9,000
			Sales	Income	Increase £9,000
Deliver goods from stock	The goods that were sold for £9,000 cost £4,000 to buy	Goods delivery note	Cost of sales	Expense	Increase £4,000
			Inventory	Asset	Decrease £4,000

Business event	Transaction	Source document	Accounts affected	Type of account	Increase or decrease
Advertising	Pay £1,000 for advertising	Cheque	Advertising	Expense	Increase £1,000
			Bank	Asset	Decrease £1,000
Receive payment from customer for earlier sale on credit	Receive £4,000 from customer	Bank deposit	Bank	Asset	Increase £4,000
			Receivables	Asset	Decrease £4,000
Pay supplier for goods previously bought on credit	Pay £9,000 to supplier	Cheque	Bank	Asset	Decrease £9,000
			Payables	Liability	Decrease £9,000

The accounts are all contained within a ledger, which is simply a collection of all the different accounts for the business. The ledger summarizes the transactions for each account, as shown in Table 3.2.

Table 3.2   Summarizing business transactions in a ledger.

Account transaction	Asset Equipment	Asset Inventory	Asset Receivables	Asset Bank	Liability: Payables	Income: Sales	Expenses
Buy equipment for cash £25,000	+25,000			−25,000			
Purchase stock on credit £15,000		+15,000			+15,000		
Pay wages £3,000				−3,000			+3,000
Sell stock on credit £9,000			+9,000			+9,000	
The goods that were sold for £9,000 cost £4,000 to buy		−4,000					+4,000
Pay advertising £1,000				−1,000			+1,000
Receive £4,000 from customer			−4,000	+4,000			
Pay £9,000 to supplier				−9,000	−9,000		
Total of transactions for this period	+25,000	+11,000	+5,000	−34,000	+6,000	+9,000	+8,000

In the example in Table 3.2 there would be a separate account for each type of expense (wages, cost of sales, advertising), but for ease of presentation in this text these accounts have been placed in a single column. The ledger is the source of the financial statements that report the performance of the business. However, the ledger also contains the balance of each account brought forward from the previous period. In our simple example, assume that the business commenced with £50,000 in the bank account that had been contributed by the owner (the owner's *equity*). Table 3.3 shows the effect of the opening balances.

Table 3.3   Summarizing business transactions with opening balances in a ledger.

Account	Equity	Asset Equipment	Asset Inventory	Asset Receivables	Asset Bank	Liability: Payables	Income: Sales	Expenses
Investment by owner	+50,000				+50,000			
Total of transactions for this period		+25,000	+11,000	+5,000	−34,000	+6,000	+9,000	+8,000
Totals of each account at end of period	+50,000	+25,000	+11,000	+5,000	+16,000	+6,000	+9,000	+8,000

Extracting financial information from the accounting system

To produce financial statements we need to separate the accounts for income and expenses from those for assets and liabilities. In this example, we would produce an Income Statement (see Table 3.4) based on the income and expenses.

The Statement of Financial Position lists the assets and liabilities of the business, as shown in Table 3.5. The double-entry system records the profit earned by the business as an addition to the owner's investment in the business. This is because owners have the rights to the profit of the business. This is termed retained profits.

Table 3.4   Income Statement.

Income		9,000
Less expenses:		
Cost of sales	4,000	
Wages	3,000	
Advertising	1,000	8,000
Profit		1,000

Table 3.5   Statement of financial position (simple version).

Assets		Liabilities	
Equipment	25,000	Payables	6,000
Inventory	11,000	**Equity**	
Receivables	5,000	Owner's original investment	50,000
Bank	16,000	Plus profit for period	1,000
		Total equity	51,000
Total assets	57,000	Total liabilities plus equity	57,000

The Balance Sheet must *balance*, i.e. assets are equal to liabilities plus equity.

$$\text{assets}(£57,000) = \text{liabilities}(£6,000) + \text{equity}(£51,000)$$

This is called the accounting equation and reflects that all the assets of the business must be financed either by liabilities or by equity (as we saw in Chapter 1). Although shown separately, equity is a kind of liability as it is owed by the business to its owners, although for a company there must be special circumstances for it ever to be repaid.

The accounting equation can also be restated as:

$$\text{equity}(£51,000) = \text{assets}(£57,000) - \text{liabilities}(£6,000)$$

Table 3.5 is a format no longer used for the Statement of Financial Position, but it is shown here as an example because it more clearly shows the accounting equation. The Statement of Financial Position has for many years been shown in a vertical format as shown in Table 3.6. Note that net assets refers to the difference between total assets and total liabilities. Net assets must be equal to total equity (i.e. the Statement of Financial Position 'balances').

Table 3.6   Statement of Financial Position.

Assets:	
Equipment	25,000
Inventory	11,000
Receivables	5,000
Bank	16,000
Total assets	57,000
Liabilities:	
Payables	6,000
Net assets	51,000
Equity:	
Owner's original investment	50,000
Plus profit for period	1,000
Owner's equity	51,000

There are some important points to note about the transactions shown in Table 3.6:

1. The purchase of equipment of £25,000 has not affected profit (although we will consider depreciation in Chapter 6).
2. Although there has been a profit of £1,000, the bank balance has reduced by £34,000 (from £50,000 to £16,000).
3. Most of the cash has gone into the new equipment (£25,000), but some has gone into working capital.

Cash flow (which we cover in more detail in Chapter 6) is, for the purposes of this chapter, equivalent to the movement in the Bank account (although as we will see in Chapter 6 it is more involved than this). It is important to recognize at this point that profit and cash flow are quite different, as cash flow (unlike profit) is affected by changes in Payables, Receivables, and Inventory, i.e. by 'working capital'.

Working capital (see Chapter 7) is the investment in assets (less liabilities) that continually revolve in and out of the bank, comprising receivables, inventory, payables, and the bank balance itself (in this case £32,000 less £6,000 = £26,000). Note that Equipment (£25,000) is not part of working capital as it forms part of the business infrastructure. The purchase of infrastructure is commonly called capital investment or capital expenditure (often abbreviated as **cap ex**), and is also referred to as capitalizing an amount of money paid out, which does not affect profit. Whether a payment is treated as an expense (which affects profit) or as an asset (which appears in the Statement of Financial Position) is important, as it can have a significant impact on profit, which is one of the main measures of business performance. We will consider this issue in more detail in Chapters 6 and 7.

You should attempt the following worked example without looking at the solution. Then check your answer against the solution in Tables 3.7–3.9.

Worked Example: Scott Stores

Jim and Jane Scott have started a retail hardware business by investing $10,000 of their cash. They also borrowed $5,000 from their bank.

They paid the first month's rent on their store for $2,000, and paid for store fittings (shelving, cash register, etc.) totalling $10,000. They purchased inventory on credit from several suppliers with a total cost of $8,000.

In their first month Scott Stores banked cash sales for goods sold totalling $10,000. Based on the product bar codes scanned into their electronic cash register, the cost of sales for those goods was $5,000.

The business paid wages of $1,000 and other expenses of $1,000.

The business paid those of its suppliers who expected to be paid before month end, totalling $4,000.

Complete a spreadsheet showing the business transactions for the month by account. Use this spreadsheet to produce an Income Statement and Statement of Financial Position for the business.

Table 3.7   Business transactions for Scott Stores for May.

	Asset Bank	Asset Store Fittings	Asset: Inventory	Liability: Bank Debt	Liability: Payables	Income from Sales	Cost of Sales	Expenses	Equity
Cash invested by Jim and Jane	+10,000								+10,000
Bank borrowing	+5,000			+5,000					
Paid rent	−2,000							+2,000	
Paid for store fittings	−10,000	+10,000							
Purchased inventory on credit			+8,000		+8,000				
Cash sales	+10,000					+10,000			
Cost of sales			−5,000				+5000		
Paid wages	−1,000							+1,000	
Paid other expenses	−1,000							+1,000	
Paid suppliers	−4,000				−4,000				
Totals	+7,000	+10,000	+3,000	+5,000	+4,000	+10,000	+5,000	+4,000	+10,000
Profit (Income − Expenses) transferred to Equity							Profit $1,000		+1,000

Table 3.7 shows the spreadsheet for all the transactions of Scott Stores. You should note that where a transaction refers to 'paid' it should be treated as a transaction affecting the Bank account. Transactions 'on credit' do not affect Bank.

Note also that purchasing inventory is not an expense until the goods are sold. Inventory is an asset. When the goods are sold, there is a transfer of the *cost* of those goods to the 'Cost of Sales' account, which is matched (see the 'Matching principle' below) with the 'Income from Sales account', which is at the business's *selling price*. Payments to suppliers for goods previously bought on credit do not affect Inventory (as the goods had been recorded as cost of sales when they were received) and do not create an expense, but reduce the liability 'Payables' (the debt owed to the suppliers). Finally, the profit of the business for the month increases the owners' equity in the business.

Table 3.8 shows the Income Statement and Table 3.9 the Statement of Financial Position.

Both the Income Statement and the Statement of Financial Position are described in detail in Chapter 6. In financial reporting, as this chapter and Chapters 6 and 7 will show, there are strict requirements for

Table 3.8   Income Statement for Scott Stores for May.

Sales		10,000
Cost of sales	5,000	
Rent	2,000	
Wages	1,000	
Other expenses	1,000	9,000
Profit		1,000

Table 3.9   Statement of Financial Position for Scott Stores at end of May.

Assets:	
Store fittings	10,000
Inventory	3,000
Bank	7,000
	20,000
Liabilities:	
Bank debt	5,000
Payables	4,000
	9,000
Net assets	11,000
Equity	
Investment by owners	10,000
Profit for the month	1,000
	11,000

the content and presentation of financial statements. One of these requirements is that the reports (produced from the ledger accounts) are based on line items. Line items are the generic types of assets, liabilities, income, expenses, and equity that are common to all businesses. This is an important requirement as all businesses are required to report their expenses using much the same line items, to ensure comparability between companies. Each of the items with amounts in the Income Statement and the Statement of Financial Position in the preceding examples are 'line items'.

Basic principles of accounting

Basic principles or conventions have been developed over many years and form the basis upon which financial information is reported. These principles include:

1. accounting entity;
2. accounting period;
3. matching principle;

4. monetary measurement;
5. historical cost;
6. going concern;
7. conservatism;
8. consistency.

Each is dealt with in turn below.

Accounting entity

Financial statements are produced for the business, independent of the owners – the business and its owners are separate entities. This is particularly important for owner-managed businesses where the personal finances of the owner must be separated from the business finances. The problem caused by the entity principle is that complex organizational structures are not always clearly identifiable as an 'entity' (see the Enron case study in Chapter 5).

Accounting period

Financial information is produced for a financial year. The accounting period is arbitrary and has no relationship with business cycles. Businesses typically end their financial year at the end of a calendar or national fiscal year. The business cycle is more important than the financial year, which after all is nothing more than the time taken for the Earth to revolve around the Sun. If we consider the early history of accounting, merchant ships did not produce monthly accounting reports. They reported to the ships' owners at the end of the business cycle, when the goods they had traded were all sold and profits could be calculated meaningfully. However, companies are required to report to shareholders on an annual basis (companies listed on Stock Exchanges have to report some financial information to shareholders semi-annually, or in the USA quarterly).

Matching principle

Closely related to the accounting period is the matching (or accruals) principle, in which income is recognized when it is *earned* and expenses when they are *incurred*, rather than on a cash basis. Income is earned when property in the goods passes from seller to buyer, or when services are provided. This is usually evidenced by the payment of money (for cash sales) or the generation of an invoice (credit sales). The accruals method of accounting provides a more meaningful picture of the financial performance of a business from year to year. However, the preparation of accounting reports requires certain assumptions to be made about the recognition of income and expenses. One of the criticisms made of many companies is that they attempt to 'smooth' their reported performance to satisfy the expectations of stock market analysts in order to maintain shareholder value. This practice has become known as 'earnings management'. A significant cause of the difficulties faced by WorldCom was that expenditure had been treated as an asset in order to improve reported profits (see the case study in Chapter 5).

Monetary measurement

Despite the importance of market, product/service quality, human, technological, and environmental factors, accounting records transactions and reports information in purely financial terms. This provides an important but limited perspective on business performance. The criticism of accounting numbers is that they are *lagging* indicators of performance. Chapter 4 considers non-financial measures of performance that are more likely to present *leading* indicators of performance. An emphasis on financial numbers tends to overlook important issues of customer satisfaction, quality, innovation, and employee morale, which have a major impact on *sustainable* business performance. The financial emphasis also means that these essential ingredients to a successful business may not be given the same weighting as that given to financial information.

Historical cost

Accounting reports record transactions at their original cost less depreciation (see Chapter 6), not at market (realizable) value or at current (replacement) cost. The historical cost may be unrelated to market or replacement value. Under this principle, the Statement of Financial Position does *not* attempt to represent the value of the business. The owner's equity is merely a calculated figure based on the historical cost of assets and liabilities rather than a valuation of the business. The Statement of Financial Position excludes assets that have not been purchased by a business but have been built up over time, such as customer goodwill, brand names, etc. (Goodwill is covered in Chapter 6.)

It is the stock market that values a business, usually based on the judgements made by investors about the expected *future* earnings of the business. Consequently, there will often be a significant difference between the Statement of Financial Position and the market value or *market capitalization* of the business (the number of shares issued by the company times the current share price). The *market-to-book ratio (MBR)* is the market value of the business divided by the original capital invested. Major service-based and high technology companies such as Apple and Microsoft, which have enormous goodwill and intellectual property but a low asset base, have high MBRs because the stock market values shares by taking account of future earnings expectations and information that is not reflected in accounting reports, including recent information about technological and market advancements.

Going concern

The financial statements are prepared on the basis that the business will continue in operation. Many businesses have failed soon after their financial statements have been prepared on a going concern basis, making the asset values in the Statement of Financial Position impossible to realize. As asset values after the liquidation of a business are unlikely to equal historical cost, the continued operation of a business is an important assumption. Were financial statements to be prepared on a 'fire sale' basis, asset values would be virtually worthless. The going concern principle can be a significant limitation of financial statements as the case study on Carrington Printers in Chapter 7 reveals.

Conservatism

Accounting is a prudent practice, in which the sometimes over-optimistic opinions of non-financial managers are discounted. A conservative approach tends to recognize the downside of events rather than the upside. Hence, likely future prospects are ignored, while likely future negative events may be reflected in the financial statements (we cover provisions for such events in Chapter 6). However, as mentioned above, the pressure on listed companies from analysts to meet stock market expectations of profitability has resulted from time to time in earnings management practices, such as those that led to problems at Enron and WorldCom.

Consistency

The application of accounting principles should be consistent from one year to the next. Where those principles vary, the effect on profits must be separately disclosed. However, some businesses have tended to change their rules, even with disclosure, in order to improve their reported performance, explaining the change as a once-only event.

These eight basic principles have been elaborated by International Financial Reporting Standards (IFRS) and the *Framework for the Preparation and Presentation of Financial Statements*, both of which are described in Chapter 6.

Cost terms and concepts: the limitations of financial accounting

One of the most important pieces of financial information for managers concerns cost, which forms the basis for most of the chapters in Part III. The calculation of cost is influenced in large part by accounting principles and the requirements of financial reporting. However, the cost that is calculated for financial reporting purposes may have limited decision usefulness for managers. The problematic nature of calculating costs may have been the source of the comment – still very relevant – by American economist John Clark (1923) that there were 'different costs for different purposes'.

Cost can be defined as 'a resource sacrificed or foregone to achieve a specific objective' (Horngren *et al.*, 1999, p. 31). The official terminology of the Chartered Institute of Management Accountants (CIMA) states that the word 'cost' can rarely stand alone and should be qualified as to its nature and limitations.

For planning, decision-making, and control purposes, cost is typically defined in relation to a cost object, which is anything for which a measurement of costs is required. While the cost object is often an *output* – a product or service – it may also be a resource (an *input* to the production process), a *process* of converting resources into outputs, or an *area of responsibility* (a department or cost centre) within the organization. Examples of *inputs* are materials, labour, rent, advertising, etc. These are line items in accounting (see above). Examples of *processes* are purchasing, customer order processing, order fulfilment, dispatch, etc. *Departments or cost centres* may include Purchasing, Production, Marketing,

Accounting, etc. Other cost objects are possible when we want to consider profitability, e.g. the cost of dealing with specific customers is important for customer profitability analysis, or the costs of a distribution channel when we compare the profitability of different methods of distribution.

Businesses typically report in relation to line items (the resource inputs) and responsibility centres (departments or cost centres). This means that decisions requiring cost information about business processes and product/service outputs may be difficult to obtain, because most accounting systems (except activity-based systems, as will be described in Chapter 13) do not provide adequate information about these other cost objects. Reports on the profitability of each product, each customer, or each distribution channel are rarely able to be produced from the traditional financial accounting system and must be determined through management accounting processes that use, but are not incorporated within, traditional accounting systems (however, the more sophisticated enterprise resource planning systems, see Chapter 9, can provide much of this more comprehensive information).

Businesses may adopt a system of management accounting to provide this kind of information for management purposes, but rarely will this second system reconcile with the external financial statements because the management information system may not follow the same accounting principles described in this chapter and in Chapter 6. Therefore, the requirement to produce financial statements based on line items and responsibility centres, rather than more meaningful cost objects (customers, processes, etc.), is a limitation of accounting as a tool of decision making.

Accountants define costs in monetary terms, and while this book focuses on monetary costs, readers should recognize that there are not only financial costs but non-financial (or at the very least difficult to measure) human, social, and environmental costs, and these latter costs are not reported in the financial statements of companies. For example, making employees redundant causes family problems (a human cost) and transfers to society the obligation to pay social security benefits (a social cost). Pollution causes long-term environmental costs that are also transferred to society. These are as important as (and perhaps more important than) financial costs, but they are not recorded by accounting systems (but see Chapter 7 for a discussion of corporate social responsibility). The exclusion of human, social, and environmental costs is a second and significant limitation of accounting.

The notion of cost is also problematic because we need to decide how cost is to be defined. If, as Horngren *et al.* defined it, cost is a resource sacrificed or forgone, then one of the questions we must ask is whether that definition implies a cash cost or an opportunity cost. A cash cost is the amount of cash expended (a valuable resource), whereas an opportunity cost is the lost opportunity of not doing something, which may be the loss of time or the loss of a customer, or the diminution in the value of an asset (e.g. machinery), all equally valuable resources. If it is the cash cost, is it the *historical* (past) cost or the *future* cost with which we should be concerned?

For example, is the cost of an employee:

- the historical cash cost of salaries and benefits, training, recruitment, etc. paid?
- the future cash cost of salaries and benefits to be paid?
- the lost opportunity cost of what we could have done with the money had we not employed that person, e.g. the benefits that could have resulted from expenditure of the same amount of money on advertising, computer equipment, external consulting services, etc?

Past or historical costs are irrelevant to current or future decisions because we can't do anything about them. We call these past costs sunk costs.

This, then, is our third limitation of accounting: what do we mean by cost and how do we calculate it? We return to many of these issues throughout Part III of this book. The point to remember here is that, while financial statements are important and do report many costs, they are not necessarily the costs that should be used by managers for decision making.

Conclusion

This chapter has described how an accounting system captures, records, summarizes, and reports financial information using the double-entry system of recording financial transactions in accounts. It has introduced the Income Statement and Statement of Financial Position. The simple examples of financial statements introduced in this chapter (which are dealt with in more detail in Chapters 6 and 7) rely on the separation between assets, liabilities, income, expenses, and equity. This chapter has also identified the basic principles underlying the accounting process. One of the limitations of financial accounting for managerial decision making is highlighted through a brief introduction to 'cost'.

References

Clark, J. M. (1923). *Studies in the Economics of Overhead Costs*. Chicago: University of Chicago Press.
Horngren, C. T., Bhimani, A., Foster, G., and Datar, S. M. (1999). *Management and Cost Accounting*. London: Prentice Hall.

Questions

3.1   An accounting system comprises accounts that can be grouped into:

a.   income, expenses, assets, liabilities, and profit
b.   financial position, profit, and cash flow
c.   assets, liabilities, income, expenses, and equity
d.   profit, capital, financial position, and cash flow

3.2   A transaction to record the sale of goods on credit would involve a double entry for the sales value to the following accounts:

a.   increase sales and reduce inventory
b.   increase sales and increase inventory
c.   increase payables and increase sales
d.   increase receivables and increase sales

3.3   A retail business has cash sales of £100,000, the cost of sales for which was £35,000. Salaries of £15,000, rental of £4,000 and advertising of £8,000 have been paid in cash. The owners have contributed equity of £25,000. In addition, the business paid cash of £40,000 for stock and purchased equipment on credit for £20,000. The financial statements of the business would show:

a.   Profit of £38,000, cash of £13,000, and equity of £25,000
b.   Profit of £38,000, cash of £58,000, and equity of £63,000
c.   Profit of £65,000, cash of £33,000, and equity of £38,000
d.   Profit of £63,000, cash of £33,000, and equity of £25,000

3.4   A Statement of Financial Position (Balance Sheet) shows liabilities of £125,000 and assets of £240,000. The Income Statement shows income of £80,000 and expenses of £35,000. Equity is:

a.   £45,000
b.   £115,000
c.   £160,000
d.   £365,000

3.5   A transaction to record the purchase of asset equipment on credit would involve:

a.   increasing asset equipment and reducing payables
b.   reducing asset equipment and reducing payables
c.   increasing payables and increasing asset equipment
d.   increasing payables and reducing asset equipment

3.6 For each of the following transactions, identify whether there is an increase or decrease in profit, cash flow, assets, liabilities or equity:

Transaction	Profit (Income minus Expenses)	Cash flow	Assets (excl. cash)	Liabilities	Equity
Issues shares to public					
Borrows money over 5 years					
Pays cash for equipment					
Buys inventory on credit					
Sells goods on credit					
Pays cash for salaries, rent, etc.					
Pays cash to suppliers					
Receives cash from customers					

3.7 The following balances are shown in alphabetical order in a professional service firm's accounting system at the end of a financial year:

	£
Advertising	15,000
Bank	5,000
Equity	71,000
Income	135,000
Equipment	100,000
Payables	11,000
Receivables	12,000
Rent	10,000
Salaries	75,000

Calculate:

a. the profit for the year
b. the equity at the end of the year

4

Management Control, Accounting, and its Rational-Economic Assumptions

Accounting needs to be understood in its broader context as part of a management control system. In this chapter, we describe management control systems and their relationship with accounting; and planning and control systems including the role of feedback and feedforward, with particular reference to cybernetic forms of control. This chapter also explains the importance of non-financial performance measurement and introduces the Balanced Scorecard and strategy mapping processes. We conclude with a brief introduction to a theoretical framework for accounting.

Management control systems

In his seminal work on the subject, Anthony (1965) defined management control as:

> The process by which managers assure that resources are obtained and used effectively and efficiently in the accomplishment of the organization's objectives.

Management control encompasses both financial and non-financial performance measurement. Anthony developed a model that differentiated three planning and control functions:

- Strategy formulation was concerned with goals, strategies and policies. This fed into
- Management control, which was concerned with the implementation of strategies and in turn led to
- Task control, which comprised the efficient and effective performance of individual tasks.

Anthony was primarily concerned with the second of these functions. However, Otley (1994) argued that such a separation was unrealistic and that management control was 'intimately bound up with both strategic decisions about positioning and operating decisions that ensure the effective implementation of such strategies' (p. 298). Building on Anthony's earlier definition, Anthony and Govindarajan (2000) defined management control as a 'process by which managers at all levels ensure that the people they supervise implement their intended strategies' (p. 4).

Berry *et al.* (1995) defined management control as:

> the process of guiding organizations into viable patterns of activity in a changing environment . . . managers are concerned to influence the behaviour of other organizational participants so that some overall organizational goals are achieved (p. 4).

These organizational goals, as we have seen in previous chapters, are generally financial goals. Companies need to produce profits and generate increases in their share price in order to achieve wealth for their shareholders. Managers must plan, make decisions, and exercise control to ensure that these goals are achieved. We introduced the distinction between financial and management accounting in Chapter 1. Management control is concerned with both generating shareholder wealth (which involves the use of management accounting) and reporting shareholder wealth (the predominant concern of financial accounting).

The accounting system is often at the centre of the information system used by top management and boards of directors to ensure that the organization is on track to meet its objectives. However, management control is a broader function that incorporates a wide range of controls: accounting systems; non-financial performance information (described in detail later in this chapter); strategic plans; organizational policies and procedures; and human resource recruitment, training, and socialization processes (Chapter 5 describes this kind of control in more detail).

Management controls have been described through different forms of categorization over the last few decades:

- Through the market in which prices convey the information necessary for decisions; through bureaucracy, characterized by rules and supervision; and as an informal social mechanism – a clan – which operates through socialization processes that are part of an organizational culture (Ouchi, 1979).
- Strategic plans; long-range plans; annual operating budgets; periodic statistical reports; performance appraisal; and policies and procedures (Daft and Macintosh, 1984).

- Formal, informal, and crisis modes of control where '[i]ndividual measures are used to direct short-term attention, cultural norms are the basis for guiding long-term behaviour, and a crisis mode of operation is adopted whenever performance of a unit falls outside of acceptable parameters' (Euske *et al.*, 1993, p. 294).
- Personnel, action, and results controls (Merchant, 1998).
- Objectives, strategies and plans, target-setting, incentive and reward structures, and information feedback loops (Otley, 1999).

In this chapter we are concerned with management control as a *system* (a collection of inter-related mechanisms) of rules which include, but are not limited to, accounting. However, controls may not be inter-related if they are developed organically over time rather than systematically (Machin, 1983). The problem for many organizations is that elements of the control system such as strategic plans, budgets, non-financial performance measures, and human resource policies may give different signals to employees as to what is expected of them. Hence the idea of a management control *system* may be inappropriate where controls are piecemeal and not integrated – the result of their having emerged over time rather than being the subject of a deliberate design.

The term 'control package' may better reflect the idea of a set of controls that operate towards common goals, but not necessarily as an integrated management control 'system'. One recent typology of the management control package includes planning, cybernetic, reward and compensation, administrative, and cultural elements (Malmi and Brown, 2008). Cybernetic controls include the more formal budgets, financial, and non-financial measurement systems. Administrative controls include the governance and organization structure, policies, and procedures. Culture includes clans, values, and symbols. The concept of a package 'points to the fact that different systems are often introduced by different interest groups at different times, so the controls in their entirety should not be defined holistically as a single system' (Malmi and Brown, 2008, p. 291).

While in many organizations, one type of control may be dominant (often accounting-based controls), Alvesson and Karreman (2004) have argued for understanding various forms of control as simultaneously active. As controls may be linked to and supporting of each other, they argue that it might be counterproductive to assume the existence of a dominating form of control. Building on Otley's (1999) argument that performance management provides a better integrating framework for management control systems, Ferreira and Otley (2009) developed a framework for performance management systems (PMS) which contains eight core elements: vision and mission; key success factors; organization structure; strategies and plans; key performance measures; target setting; performance evaluation; and reward systems. These are influenced by four other factors: PMS change; PMS use; strength and coherence of the core elements; and information flows, systems, and networks. The PMS exists within a set of broader contextual and cultural influences.

Simons (1994; 1995) identified how top managers can simultaneously operate with four types of control systems: boundary; belief; diagnostic; and interactive. Boundary systems establish explicit limits and rules. Belief systems are concerned with values, purpose, and direction. Diagnostic control systems provide formal feedback to enable corrections from preset standards. Interactive control systems are used by managers to regularly and personally involve themselves in the decisions of subordinates. Simons described the actions taken by newly appointed top managers attempting strategic change, all of whom used control systems to: overcome inertia; communicate the substance of their agenda; structure implementation timetables; ensure continuing attention through incentives; and focus organizational learning on strategic uncertainties.

Macintosh and Quattrone (2010) argue that there needs to be a 'wise balance between an excess of control, which would lead to resistance and organizational turmoil, and a lack of it, which would cause organizational chaos and disintegration' (p. 5).

Irrespective of which approach is taken to management control, it is clear that the definition of management control systems has evolved from formal, financially quantifiable information to include external information relating to markets, customers, and competitors; non-financial information about production processes; predictive information; and a broad array of decision support mechanisms and informal personal and social controls (Chenhall, 2003).

Planning and control in organizations

We can distinguish systems for planning from systems for control. *Planning systems* interpret environmental demands and constraints and use a set of numbers to provide a 'common language which can be used to compare and contrast the results obtained by each activity' (Otley, 1987, p. 64). These numbers may be financial or non-financial performance expectations, represented in accounting and in non-financial performance measurement reports. Otley *et al.* (1995) noted that:

> accounting is still seen as a pre-eminent technology by which to integrate diverse activities from strategy to operations and with which to render accountability (p. S39).

Control systems are concerned with *feedback* control, in which 'the observed error is fed back into the process to instigate action to cause its reduction' (Otley, 1987, p. 21). By contrast, planning systems are also concerned with *feedforward* control, 'because it is only an expected error that is used to stimulate the control process' (p. 21).

Both feedback and feedforward are used as methods of management control to improve performance. While a simple financial example of feedback is comparing actual with budget results in an Income Statement, a non-financial example is the customer satisfaction survey after a telephone sales or service call (for example from a bank or telecoms provider). Customers are asked various questions which are aggregated, analysed, and reported back to management for comparison with targets. Where customer satisfaction is lower than expected, corrective action (e.g. staff training) is taken with the intention of improving performance.

Feedforward in a financial example is setting a budget, then looking at the impact of that budget on cash flows and the likely impact on the expectations of the stock market (taking into account the views of investment advisers such as stock brokers and investment analysts). Where the budget is unlikely to meet those expectations (and may lead to a fall in share price), budget revisions will follow to improve the likely performance. A non-financial example of feedforward is developing alternative scenarios of the future, and using the insights gained to develop strategies to move the organization away from high risk scenarios towards more acceptable ones. A famous example of scenario planning was developed by Shell in the 1980s, which helped it avoid the worst effects of an international oil crisis (de Geus, 1988).

We can consider the management planning and control system as a single system in which both feedback and feedforward are concerned with reducing the performance gap (Downs, 1966). Downs defined this as 'the difference in utility [an individual] perceives between the actual and the satisfactory level of performance' (p. 169). According to Downs, the larger the gap, the greater is the motivation to undertake a more intensive search for ways of bridging that gap.

Both feedback and feedforward need to be integrated in the management control system in order to reduce the performance gap as they share common targets, the need for corrective action to be reflected either in goal adjustment or in changed behaviour, and the allocation or utilization of resources (i.e. budgeting and budgetary control, which are covered in Chapters 16 and 17).

There are five major standards against which performance can be compared (Emmanuel et al., 1990):

1. Previous time periods;
2. Similar organizations;
3. Estimates of future organizational performance ex ante;
4. Estimates of what might have been achieved ex post;
5. The performance necessary to achieve defined goals.

The process of comparison is at the centre of the control system. According to Anthony and Govindarajan (2000), every control system has at least four elements:

1. A detector or sensor that measures what is happening;
2. An assessor that determines the significance of what is happening by comparing it with a standard or expectation;
3. An effector (feedback) that alters behaviour if the assessor indicates the need to do so;
4. A communication network that transmits information between the other elements.

This can be represented in the diagram in Figure 4.1.

Hofstede (1981) provided a typology for management control: routine, expert, trial-and-error, intuitive, judgemental, or political. The first three are cybernetic and are described in this chapter. Non-cybernetic controls are described in Chapter 5. A *cybernetic control* process involves four conditions (Berry et al., 1995, originally published in Otley and Berry, 1980):

1. The existence of an objective that is desired;
2. A means of measuring process outputs in terms of this objective;
3. The ability to predict the effect of potential control actions;
4. The ability to take actions to reduce deviations from the objective.

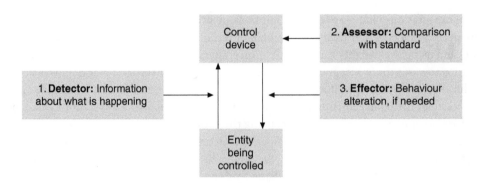

Figure 4.1   Elements of a control system.
Source: Reprinted from Anthony, R. N. and Govindarajan, V. (2000). *Management Control Systems* (10th edn), McGraw-Hill Irwin.

The simplest example of a cybernetic control system is a thermostat. A desired room temperature is set (1); a thermometer measures the room temperature (2); knowledge is available to enable heating and cooling in response to deviations from the desired room temperature (3); and the heating/cooling system is automatically engaged in response to the measured deviation (4).

However, Otley and Berry (1980) recognized that in organizations, cybernetic control was more difficult than in the simple thermostat example, because:

> organizational objectives are often vague, ambiguous and change with time . . . measures of achievement are possible only in correspondingly vague and often subjective terms . . . predictive models of organizational behaviour are partial and unreliable, and . . . different models may be held by different participants . . . the ability to act is highly constrained for most groups of participants, including the so-called 'controllers' (p. 241).

Based on work by Berry *et al.* (1995), Emmanuel *et al.* (1990) presented a simplified diagram of the control process as a regulator. This is shown in Figure 4.2.

Figure 4.2 emphasizes the importance for control of a *predictive model*, which is necessary for both feedback (reactive) and feedforward (anticipatory) modes of control. The predictive model is essential in organizational control because it defines the explicit or implicit cause–effect or action–outcome relationships, i.e. the expectation that if something is done, there will be a likely result, e.g. that advertising will lead to increased sales orders; or that increasing price may cause the volume of sales to fall. The predictive model has to be defined by each organization to suit its particular strategy and its competitive environment. For example, mainstream airlines charge higher prices, provide flights at times that suit business travellers, depart from/arrive at major airports, and provide ancillary services like meals free of charge. Low-cost airlines charge lower prices to passengers, and may appeal more to holiday makers who have more flexibility in when and from where their flights depart and arrive, and who may be willing to pay extra for reserved seats, luggage, meals, and drinks. This predictive model is central to both the strategy and the control system adopted by organizations.

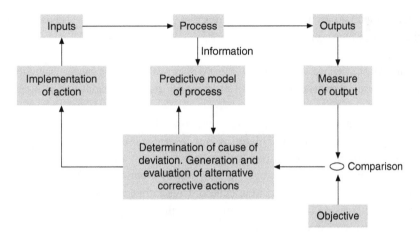

Figure 4.2   Necessary conditions for control.

Source: Reprinted from Emmanuel, C., Otley, D. and Merchant, K. (1990). *Accounting for Management Control* (2nd edn). London: Chapman & Hall.

The difficulty with any form of control is the reliability of the predictive model. It is also critical that the organization's management control system reflects the predictive model adopted by the business. A management control or accounting system that fails to reflect the nature of the business and its strategy is likely to impede, rather than assist, the organization in achieving its goals: 'Attempting to design control systems without having a detailed knowledge of how the business works is likely to prove a recipe for disaster' (Otley, 1999, p. 381).

Understanding the predictive model means that managers can try to influence behaviour and measure results. Ouchi (1977) argued that there were 'only two phenomena which can be observed, monitored, and counted: behavior and the outputs which result from behavior' (p. 97). To apply behaviour control, organizations need agreement or knowledge about means–ends relationships. To apply output control, a valid and reliable measure of the desired outputs must be available. Ouchi argued that as organizations grow larger and hierarchy increases, there is a shift from behaviour to output control.

Otley and Berry (1980) defined four types of control in response to deviations from desired performance:

1. First-order control adjusts system inputs (e.g. resources) and causes behaviour to alter.
2. Second-order control alters system objectives (e.g. goals) or the standards to be attained.
3. Internal learning amends the predictive model on the basis of past experience and the measurement and communication processes associated with it.
4. Systemic learning or adaptation changes the nature of the system itself: inputs, outputs, and predictive models.

Accounting should be understood in this broader context of management control. Emmanuel *et al.* (1990) believed that accounting was important because it represents 'one of the few integrative mechanisms capable of summarizing the effect of an organization's actions in quantitative terms' (p. 4). Because management information can be expressed in monetary terms, it can be aggregated across time and across diverse organizational units and provides a means of integrating activities. Otley and Berry (1994) described how in management control:

> accounting information provides a window through which the real activities of the organization may be monitored, but it should be noted also that other windows are used that do not rely upon accounting information (p. 46).

Otley (1994) called for a wider view of management control, with less emphasis on accounting-based controls. Criticizing Anthony's model of planning and control (see earlier in this chapter), Otley argued that '[t]he split between strategic planning, management control and operational control, which was always tendentious, now becomes untenable' (p. 292). Otley claimed that there was widespread agreement that undue emphasis was given to financial controls rather than to a more 'balanced scorecard' approach, hence the increasing importance given to non-financial (or multidimensional) performance management in the study of management control systems. Otley *et al.* (1995) argued for expanding management control beyond accounting, distinguishing financial control from management control, the latter as:

> a general management function concerned with the achievement of overall organizational aims and objectives . . . management control is concerned with looking after the overall business with money being used as a convenient measure of a variety of other more complex dimensions, not as an end in itself (p. S33).

The next section introduces the importance of non-financial performance measures to supplement financial ones.

Non-financial performance measurement

The limitations of financial measures were identified most clearly by Johnson and Kaplan (1987), who argued that there was an excessive focus on short-term financial performance. They commented:

> Managers discovered that profits could be 'earned' not just by selling more or producing for less, but also by engaging in a variety of non-productive activities: exploiting accounting conventions, engaging in financial entrepreneurship, and reducing discretionary expenditures (p. 197).

Examples of exploiting accounting conventions have been seen in corporate collapses such as Enron and WorldCom, while financial entrepreneurship can be seen as one of the causes of the Global Financial Crisis. The discretionary costs that could be 'eliminated' in pursuit of short-term profit include:

> R&D, promotion, distribution, quality improvement, applications engineering, human resources, and customer relations all of which, of course, are vital to a company's long-term performance. The immediate effect of such reductions is to boost reported profitability, but at the expense of sacrificing the company's long-term competitive position (p. 201).

Johnson and Kaplan (1987) emphasized the importance of non-financial indicators, arguing:

> Short-term financial measures will have to be replaced by a variety of non-financial indicators that provide better targets and predictors for the firm's long-term profitability goals (p. 259).

There have been many attempts at non-financial performance measurement, as early as the *tableaux de bord* that had been developed by 'sub-departments' in French factories (Innes, 1996). These comprise non-financial measures that managers identified as critical to success and that were developed and monitored locally, rather than being part of the formal reporting process.

Many types of performance measures exist, including:

- input measures (human, physical, or financial resources used by the organization);
- activity or process measures (e.g. number of hours worked, number of material issues, number of deliveries);
- output measures (e.g. quantity of goods and services produced, sales revenue);
- efficiency measures (e.g. ratios of outputs to inputs, such as productivity per hour);
- effectiveness measures (measures of output conforming to specified characteristics such as quality pass rate or on-time delivery);
- impact measures (how outcomes contribute to achieving organizational strategy, such as customer satisfaction, or reduced wastage or energy consumption); and
- investment measures (e.g. capital expenditure, distribution channel expansion, research and development expenditure).

These measures may be financial (expressed in a currency), non-financial quantitative (e.g. % of satisfied customers), or a combination of both (e.g. sales dollars per square foot of retail floor space).

The development of the Balanced Scorecard (Kaplan and Norton, 1992; 1993; 1996; 2001) has received extensive coverage in the business press and is perhaps the best-known example of a more balanced approach to performance measurement than was available from financial performance alone. The Balanced Scorecard took as a starting point the goal to generate long-term economic value, which required other than financial measures as drivers of long-term performance and growth. Kaplan and Norton (1996) argued that the Scorecard provided the ability to link a company's long-term strategy with its short-term actions, emphasizing that:

> meeting short-term financial targets should not constitute satisfactory performance when other measures indicate that the long-term strategy is either not working or not being implemented well (p. 80).

The Balanced Scorecard (BSC) presents four different perspectives and complements traditional financial indicators with measures of performance for customers, internal processes, and learning and growth, and 'translates a company's strategic objectives into a coherent set of performance measures' (Kaplan and Norton, 1993, p. 134) with the customer, business process, and learning and growth perspectives being leading indicators of performance (measures of what is happening now) while financial indicators are the lagging indicators of performance which measure what has happened in the past as a consequence of performance in the other three perspectives. The Balanced Scorecard is shown in Figure 4.3.

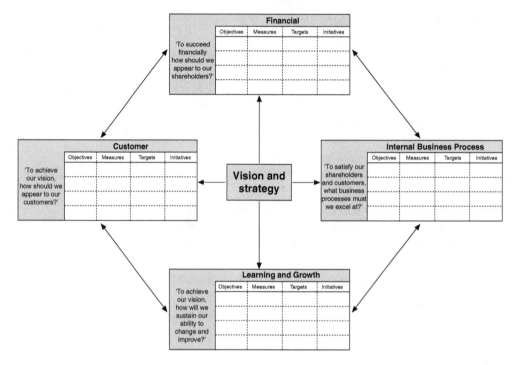

Figure 4.3 Translating vision and strategy: four perspectives.

Source: Reprinted by permission of *Harvard Business Review*. From 'Using the Balanced Scorecard as a strategic management system' by R. S. Kaplan and D. P. Norton, JanFeb 1996. Copyright 1996, Harvard Business School Publishing Corporation; all rights reserved.

Kaplan and Norton did not prescribe the specific performance measures that should be used for each perspective, but suggested that organizations developed performance measures linked to their strategy and competitive position.

Examples of performance measures in the customer perspective may include market share, customer satisfaction, net promoter score, and brand reputation. Performance measures in the business process perspective may include quality pass rate, on-time delivery, cycle time (from order to delivery), and productivity. In the learning and growth perspective, performance measures may include employee retention and motivation, investment in training, research and development expenditure, and new patent registrations.

Kaplan and Norton argued that at top management level, three or four performance measures for each perspective should be sufficient (12 to 16 in total) as any more than that becomes difficult to monitor and issues can subsequently arise about the relative importance of some performance measures over others. Kaplan and Norton also showed that the organizational-level performance measurement approach needed to cascade down through each layer of the organization to business units and ultimately to each employee, so that everyone's goals were linked hierarchically to achieving the organizational goals. Therefore, in a complex organization, there may be dozens or even hundreds of different performance measures which vary by manager based on differences in business unit strategy, or individual job function.

The relative importance of performance measures is addressed to some extent in the BSC by the assumption of a hierarchical relationship between the four perspectives, and hence between the four sets of performance measures. Improving learning and growth will, according to Kaplan and Norton, transform business processes, which will in turn lead to more satisfied customers and finally to financial performance. However, Norreklit *et al.* (2008) have questioned whether such causal relationships actually exist. For example, assuming that increased advertising will lead to more sales revenue, or that high customer satisfaction levels will lead to higher profits.

It is risky to assume that a change in one measure will have a cause–effect change on another measure. One of the difficulties in setting objectives and performance measures is the accuracy of the predictive model used by the organization. BSCs are a simplification of the complexity of any business organization, its predictive model, and the competitive environment. The cause and effect assumptions must be simplistic in order to overcome real-life complexity and it is problematic whether, in fact, improved non-financial performance does lead to improved financial performance. For example, quality and customer satisfaction may improve beyond the capacity of the business to reflect the costs of improved quality and customer care in its prices (we discuss the value chain in Chapter 11) and hence profit may fall.

One of the distinguishing features of the BSC is the notion of 'balance', that organizations cannot maximize performance on all four perspectives simultaneously. Rather, optimum overall performance is the likely result of finding the right balance between performance as measured by all four perspectives.

Strategy mapping (Kaplan and Norton, 2001) is a development of the Balanced Scorecard approach, and reflects the assumptions of the organization's predictive model. A strategy map identifies the assumed cause–effect relationships. An example of a strategy map for a professional services firm is shown in Figure 4.4. It shows the assumed cause–effect relationships (i.e. the predictive model of the firm) between seeking to maintain knowledge (learning and growth), winning new business (customer), carrying out work and managing productivity (business process), and achieving financial returns (financial).

Performance targets are developed for each of the elements in the strategy map, and financial resources are allocated (through the budget process) to support the achievement of those targets. Regular monitoring and review of performance takes place by comparing actual performance against targets. Where performance needs to be improved, the strategy mapping process involves making resource reallocations through changing budgets. This approach is challenging to the traditional accounting view of fixed resource allocations for the year. In few organizations are budgets reallocated mid-year due to performance shortfalls. However, this is a logical extension of managing performance more flexibly and lies at the heart of the strategy mapping process. Strategy mapping is a continual process through which performance measures are used as a method of learning what works and what doesn't work. Learning results in changes to the assumed cause–effect relationships, and to performance measures and targets.

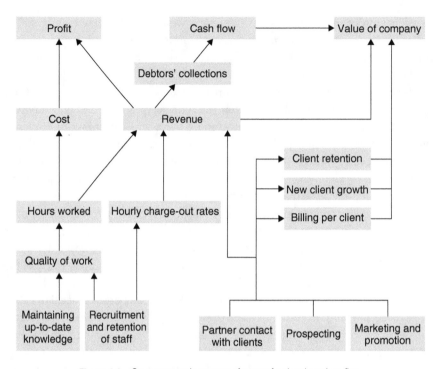

Figure 4.4   Strategy mapping process for a professional services firm.

The difficulty with performance measurement systems is that there are multiple stakeholders inside and outside the organization, and their expectations may need to be reconciled. The *Performance Prism* was developed at Cranfield University by Neely, Adams, and Kennerley (2002). It differs from other non-financial performance measurement systems in that it takes a stakeholder approach (see Chapter 2) to the organization, defined broadly to include investors, customers, employees, regulators, communities, and suppliers (Neely, Kennerley, and Adams 2007). The framework has five facets:

1. stakeholder satisfaction (what stakeholders *want*);
2. stakeholder contribution (what the organization *needs* from its stakeholders);
3. the strategies;
4. processes; and
5. capabilities that an organization needs to satisfy the wants and needs.

Each of the five facets has its own measures but the overall focus of the performance prism is on stakeholder satisfaction.

Importantly, linking performance measurement with strategy is critical to long-term sustainable performance (compared with a focus on short-term financial results). But measuring strategic and operational performance requires a different set of performance measures. Operational measures help to measure the short-term performance of an organization, often measured in terms of profitability, while strategic measures focus on the implementation of the organization's long-term strategy. What these strategic performance measures are will be determined by the organization's strategy. Chenhall (2005) has argued that a key element of strategic measures is that they provide integrated information to help managers deliver positive strategic outcomes.

Market research carried out by Oracle (2011) found that 71% of respondents described the links between strategic goals, operational plans, and budgets in their organizations as 'fragmented'. An important implication of Oracle's research is their finding that, on average, 1.7 months will pass before the finance department becomes aware that operational plans and/or market circumstances for the company have changed. In terms of performance data, for the 89% of managers with departmental performance measures who responded to the survey, it takes, on average, just under two months for information about departmental performance against targets to filter up to the senior management team or the board of directors.

The lack of reliable, accurate, and timely data is compounded by a lack of stability in the organization's environment with strategic plans needing to be continually updated to stay relevant to the latest business conditions. Turbulence in the business environment is caused by:

- economic uncertainty;
- changing technology;
- the rapid introduction of new products;
- changing customer demand; and
- increased regulation and competition.

Researchers at the UK's Cranfield University are critical of traditional approaches to performance measurement which rely on stability and predictability and have developed a Performance Management for Turbulent Environments (PM⁴TE) model (Barrows and Neely, 2012). They argue that:

> many traditional performance management practices do not work well in turbulent environments. In turbulent environments the need for timely information grows significantly. Managers must detect and interpret information much more rapidly. They have to make faster decisions. They have to execute more quickly with a narrower margin for error. And they must embrace new ways of operating versus exclusively focusing on exploiting core businesses (Barrows and Neely, 2012, p. 17).

The PM⁴TE model comprises:

- a performance management cycle;
- an execution management cycle that explicitly links *projects* to performance (as it is through projects that most organizations drive change and improvement); and
- enablers such as leadership and strategic intelligence. A key enabler is the recognition that performance measurement should be used for learning rather than control (as learning is central to success in turbulent environments).

We have focused on the importance of a more holistic management control system that is focused on achieving strategy through the organization's predictive model. We have also seen the need for a broader view of performance, moving from an accounting-dominated perspective to a more balanced approach that incorporates both financial and non-financial information. We have also seen the importance of balancing short-term operational with longer-term strategic performance. Finally, we have introduced the need to recognize stakeholders beyond shareholders in control and performance, and how a turbulent environment can impact on management control and performance measurement.

A key point is the need for accountants and non-financial managers to have a better understanding of the operational activities and predictive model of the business and to build this understanding into control systems design, connecting control systems with business strategy and developing an appropriate and balanced set of performance measures.

A theoretical framework for accounting

We can now move on to a concern with understanding the assumptions inherent in the model of management control and performance measurement that we have just described. We have identified accounting as part of a broader management control system that is driven by goals and strategy. We have also expanded the notion of management control to incorporate non-financial performance measurement. This description of management control systems implies a cybernetic system of control, with feedforward and feedback processes that influence behaviour and resource allocation decisions.

There are certain assumptions underlying the cybernetic model that are based on what is called a rational, functional, or economic *paradigm*, or view of the world. *Rational* means following reasoning as opposed to experience or observation (which is called *empiricism*). The traditional approach to decision making for management control and accounting has been from an *economically rational* perspective. Under this perspective, alternatives can be evaluated and decisions computed as a result of economic preferences.

March and Simon (1958) laid the basis for economic theories of the firm in distinguishing the neoclassical assumption that economic decisions were made by perfectly rational actors possessing relatively complete information aimed at *maximizing* rather than *satisficing* behaviour. Satisficing is based on *bounded rationality*: actors with general goals searching for whatever solution more or less attained those goals. March and Simon used the example of searching a haystack for the sharpest needle (maximizing) versus searching for a needle sharp enough to sew with (satisficing). March and Simon's notion of bounded rationality recognized that decision makers have limited information and limited ability to process that information in an uncertain and complex environment.

Scott (1998) described three perspectives on organizations: as rational systems, natural systems, and open systems. We consider natural and open systems in Chapter 5. The *rational perspective* sees organizations as 'purposeful collectivities', i.e. in which the actions of participants are coordinated to achieve defined goals. Organizations are highly formalized with rules governing behaviour and roles which are determined independent of the attributes of the people occupying those roles. For students of management theory, Taylor's scientific management, Fayol's administrative theory, Weber's bureaucracy, and Simon's theory of administrative behaviour are all examples of rational systems. Rational systems are predicated on the division of labour and specialization of tasks, reducing transaction costs, efficiently processing information, and monitoring the work of agents.

Within the rational perspective, accounting has been dominated by the notion of contract, which is reflected in two theories: agency and transaction cost economics. *Agency theory* (see Chapter 6) focuses on the contractual relationship between owners and managers and on the cost of the information needed by owners to monitor contractual performance. The cost of information is also an important aspect of *transaction cost economics* (see Chapter 15), which considers whether transactions should take place in the marketplace (outsourcing) or within the organizational hierarchy (in-house).

The rational perspective and the notion of contract determine how the accounting and control systems used by organizations are viewed. However, different perspectives to the rational one will suggest different interpretations of events, grounded in the different ways in which the preparers and users of accounting information may see the world. We return to the theoretical framework of accounting, its assumptions and limitations, throughout this book. We begin with a contrast to the economically rational approach in Chapter 5.

Conclusion

This chapter has shown that in delivering shareholder value, accounting cannot be seen as separate from the organizational control system. Accounting is integral to management control, but many elements of management control do not rely on accounting information. The importance of non-financial performance measurement has been emphasized, particularly the important role played by Kaplan and Norton in developing the Balanced Scorecard and subsequently the strategy mapping approach. Both reflect accounting numbers as lagging measures, with strategy implementation more a question of getting the balance right with performance on customer, business process, and learning and growth perspectives.

Accounting and the Balanced Scorecard are, however, rooted in the rational, economics-based paradigm, which emphasizes a goal orientation and a cybernetic control system based on feedback and feedforward. The next chapter provides alternative perspectives on the inter-relationship between accounting and organizations.

References

Alvesson, M. and Karreman, D. (2004). Interfaces of control. Technocratic and socio-ideological control in a global management consultancy firm. *Accounting, Organizations and Society*, 29, 423–44.

Anthony, R. N. (1965). *Planning and Control Systems: A Framework for Analysis*. Boston, MA: Harvard Business School Press.

Anthony, R. N. and Govindarajan, V. (2000). *Management Control Systems* 10th edn. New York: McGraw-Hill Irwin.

Barrows, E. and Neely, A. (2012). *Managing Performance in Turbulent Times: Analytics and Insight*. New Jersey: John Wiley & Sons.

Berry, A. J., Broadbent, J., and Otley, D. (1995). The domain of organizational control. In A. J. Berry, J. Broadbent, and D. Otley (Eds), *Management Control: Theories, Issues and Practices*. London: Macmillan.

Chenhall, R. H. (2003). Management control systems design within its organizational context: findings from contingency-based research and directions for the future. *Accounting, Organizations and Society*, 28(23), 127–68.

Chenhall, R.H. (2005). Integrative strategic performance measurement systems, strategic alignment of manufacturing, learning and strategic outcomes: an exploratory study. *Accounting, Organizations and Society*, 30(5), 395–422.

Daft, R. L. and Macintosh, N. B. (1984). The nature and use of formal control systems for management control and strategy implementation. *Journal of Management*, 10(1), 43–66.

de Geus, A. P. (1988). Planning as Learning. *Harvard Business Review*. March/April. P70–74.

Downs, A. (1966). *Inside Bureaucracy*. Boston, MA: Little, Brown.

Emmanuel, C., Otley, D., and Merchant, K. (1990). *Accounting for Management Control* (2nd edn). London: Chapman & Hall.

Euske, K. J., Lebas, M. J., *et al.* (1993). Performance management in an international setting. *Management Accounting Research*, 4, 275–99.

Ferreira, A. and Otley, D. (2009). The design and use of performance management systems: an extended framework for analysis. *Management Accounting Research*, 20(4), 263–82.

Hofstede, G. (1981). Management control of public and not-for-profit activities. *Accounting, Organizations and Society*, 6(3), 193–211.

Innes, J. (1996). Activity performance measures and tableaux de bord. In I. Lapsley and F. Mitchell (Eds), *Accounting and Performance Measurement: Issues in the Private and Public Sectors*. London: Paul Chapman.

Johnson, H. T. and Kaplan, R. S. (1987). *Relevance Lost: The Rise and Fall of Management Accounting*. Boston, MA: Harvard Business School Press.

Kaplan, R. S. and Norton, D. P. (1992). The Balanced Scorecard Measures that drive performance. *Harvard Business Review, Jan–Feb*, 71–9.

Kaplan, R. S. and Norton, D. P. (1993). Putting the Balanced Scorecard to work. *Harvard Business Review, Sept–Oct*, 134–47.

Kaplan, R. S. and Norton, D. P. (1996). Using the Balanced Scorecard as a strategic management system. *Harvard Business Review, Jan–Feb*, 75–85.

Kaplan, R. S. and Norton, D. P. (2001). *The Strategy-Focused Organization: How Balanced Scorecard Companies Thrive in the New Business Environment*. Boston, MA: Harvard Business School Press.

Machin, J. L. J. (1983). Management control systems: whence and whither? In E. A. Lowe and J. L. J. Machin (Eds), *New Perspectives in Management Control*. London: Macmillan, pp. 22–42.

Macintosh, N. & Quattrone, P. (2010). *Management Accounting and Control Systems: An Organizational and Sociological Approach* 2nd edn. Chichester: John Wiley & Sons.

Malmi, T. and Brown, D. A. (2008). Management control systems as a package opportunities, challenges and research directions. *Management Accounting Research*, 19, 287–300.

March, J. G. and Simon, H. A. (1958). *Organizations*. Chichester: John Wiley & Sons.

Merchant, K. A. (1998). *Modern Management Control Systems: Text and Cases*. Upper Saddle River, NJ: Prentice Hall.

Neely, A., Adams, C., and Kennerley, M. (2002). *The Performance Prism: The Scorecard for Measuring and Managing Business Success*. London: Prentice Hall.

Neely, A., Kennerley, M., and Adams, C. (2007). Performance measurement frameworks. In Neely, A. (Ed.) *Business Performance Measurement: Unifying Theories and Integrating Practice*. Cambridge: Cambridge University Press. pp. 143–62.

Norreklit, H., Jacobsen, M., and Mitchell, F. (2008) Pitfalls in using the balanced scorecard. *Journal of Corporate Accounting & Finance*, October, 65–8.

Oracle (2011). Performance management: An incomplete picture. *The Oracle Report*. http://www.oracle.com/webapps/dialogue/ns/dlgwelcome.jsp? p_ext=Y&p_dlg_id=10077790&src=7038701&Act=29, (sign up to Oracle is required which is free of charge).

Otley, D. (1987). *Accounting Control and Organizational Behaviour*. London: Heinemann.

Otley, D. (1994). Management control in contemporary organizations: towards a wider framework. *Management Accounting Research*, 5, 289–99.

Otley, D. (1999). Performance management: a framework for management control systems research. *Management Accounting Research*, 10, 363–82.

Otley, D. T. and Berry, A. J. (1980). Control, organization and accounting. *Accounting, Organizations and Society*, 5(2), 231–44.

Otley, D. T. and Berry, A. J. (1994). Case study research in management accounting and control. *Management Accounting Research*, 5, 45–65.

Otley, D. T., Berry, A. J., and Broadbent, J. (1995). Research in management control: an overview of its development. *British Journal of Management*, 6, Special Issue, S31–S44.

Ouchi, W. G. (1977). The relationship between organizational structure and organizational control. *Administrative Science Quarterly*, 22, 95–113.

Ouchi, W. G. (1979). A conceptual framework for the design of organizational control mechanisms. *Management Science*, 25(9), 833–48.

Scott, W. R. (1998). *Organizations: Rational, Natural, and Open Systems* 4th edn. Upper Saddle River, NJ: Prentice Hall.

Simons, R. (1994). How new top managers use control systems as levers of strategic renewal. *Strategic Management Journal*, 15, 169–89.

Simons, R. (1995). *Levers of Control: How Managers Use Innovative Control Systems to Drive Strategic Renewal*. Boston, MA: Harvard Business School Press.

Websites

A useful website on performance measurement and management is provided by the Performance Measurement Association at www.performanceportal.org.

The Management Control Association promotes the study of management control and management accounting. Its website is www.managementcontrolassociation.ac.uk.

Questions

4.1   Explain the key ingredients of a cybernetic management control system.

4.2   Outline the benefits of a Balanced Scorecard (BSC) approach to performance measurement and how the four perspectives in the BSC are inter-related.

4.3   Describe what is meant by an economic/rational perspective as it applies to management control and accounting.

CHAPTER 5

Interpretive and Critical Perspectives on Accounting and Decision Making

In Chapter 4 we described the rational-economic paradigm that underpins management control systems in general and accounting reports in particular. There are, however, alternative paradigms. For example, Otley and Berry (1980) questioned the usefulness of cybernetic controls (goal-oriented, with targets and using feedback to take corrective action) given the limitations of accounting systems as a result of organizational complexity and rapid environmental change. Accounting systems provide an important, but limited, perspective on organizations which is enhanced by non-financial performance measurement (as we saw in Chapter 4). However, organizations are typified by more informal, and often more subtle, forms of control than formal systems like accounting and the Balanced Scorecard.

While Chapter 4 assumed a rational paradigm (a paradigm is a way of viewing the world), this chapter explores alternative ways to understand the role played by accounting and management control in organizations. We look at the role of research and review the interpretive paradigm and the social constructionist perspective and how organizational culture is implicated in accounting. We then consider the radical paradigm and how power has become of interest in critical accounting theory. These alternative paradigms to the rational-economic one described in Chapter 4 are an important focus of this book to which we return in subsequent chapters, because alternative paradigms bring our attention to the underlying assumptions and the limitations of accounting information. Chapter 5 concludes with an introduction to ethics as it affects the accountant and manager, but we commence with a review of the role of research and theory in management control and accounting.

Research and theory in management control and accounting

Theory is an explanation of what is observed in practice. This is not the 'ivory tower' idealism for which academics are often criticized, but the use of 'real-world' evidence to inform and explain practice. The development of theory from practice is the result of a process of research. Practice informs theory, which in turn, via various forms of dissemination and education, can influence the spread of practice between organizations and countries.

An understanding of management control and accounting tools and techniques without an understanding of theory has the same problems as theories divorced from business practice. An understanding of the underlying assumptions, and the limitations, of the tools and techniques of management control and accounting is essential. If we ignore those assumptions and limitations, we are likely to make decisions on the basis of numbers alone that do not adequately reflect the complexity of the competitive business environment and the predictive model which underlies the way organizations carry on business (the predictive model was discussed in Chapter 4).

Theory typically takes one of two forms:

* Quantitative studies of a large number of business organizations through surveys or analysis of publicly available (e.g. stock exchange) data that can be analysed statistically in order to produce generalizations about accounting practice.
* Qualitative studies of a single organization or a small number of organizations through case studies comprising interviews, observation, and documentary research that aims to explain accounting practice in the context in which it is situated.

Both methods are valuable in helping to understand management control and accounting practice. The reader is encouraged to look at some of the academic research literature referred to in the chapters throughout this book in order to understand the context of management control and accounting in organizations. The Readings in Part IV of this book are intended to provide readers with an exposure to some key academic accounting literature.

Hopper *et al.* (2001) traced the development of accounting research through four approaches:

* conventional teaching emphasizing the needs of the professional accounting bodies;
* the application of economics and management science;
* history and public-sector accounting;
* behavioural and organizational approaches.

The first approach is that traditionally taken by students of accounting. The second approach relies heavily on econometric and mathematical models, which are outside the scope of this book. As we have taken the view that managers and accountants should take a more interpretive and critical perspective, we present a conventional approach (as managers need to know how to read financial information) but also one situated in its historical context, within a behavioural and organizational approach, rooted in the unique circumstances of each organization. This enables managers to go beyond reading, to interpreting and using financial information.

Research in accounting tends to fall into two distinct categories:

- The normative view – *what ought to happen* – that there is one best way of doing accounting, that accounting information is economically rational and serves an instrumental purpose in making decisions in the pursuit of shareholder value. The normative view was reflected in Chapter 4 and is evident through the presentation of accounting tools and techniques in each chapter in Part III.
- The interpretive and critical view – *what does happen* – the explanation of how accounting systems develop and are used in particular organizational settings. This is the subject of this chapter. This view recognizes that people do not necessarily make decisions based on economically rational reasons but have limited information and limited cognitive ability and are influenced not only by formal organizational structures and systems (including, but not limited to, accounting systems) but also by the norms and values of their social groups and by organizational power and influence. We contrast the normative view with interpretive and critical perspectives in each chapter.

While the normative view is most commonly associated with quantitative studies which examine, for example, the variables that are most likely to be related to improving organizational performance, the interpretive and critical view tends to be more descriptive or qualitative rather than statistical. This is a necessary approach to explain the practice of accounting in both its organizational setting and the wider social, political, and historical context in which it exists.

The study of organizations is important because what happens may be contrary to what management control theory suggests. Kaplan (1986) argued for empirical studies of accounting systems in their organizational contexts, by 'observing skilled practitioners in actual organizations' (p. 441). Kaplan described empirical research methods, especially case or field studies that communicate the 'deep, rich slices of organizational life' (p. 445) and are 'the only mechanism by which management accounting can become a scientific field of inquiry' (p. 448).

The interpretive or critical view has tended to be developed through case study research. The quantitative approach is important in making broad generalizations based on statistical analysis, while the qualitative approach is more situation-specific, and while both research approaches contribute to the development of theory, quantitative studies lead to statistical generalizations while qualitative studies lead to analytic or theoretical generalizations. Case study research is more appropriate when 'why?' or 'how?' questions are asked about contemporary events.

Birnberg (2009) described three periods of accounting research in the USA. In the pre-World War II period, the dominant market for accounting research was practitioner. The post-war period was a transitional period and can be characterized as one reflecting the professionalization of management education. The modern period has been predominantly interested in using tools to contribute to the theoretical literature, i.e. research for research's own sake, and to a far lesser degree with the concerns of practice. Much of the cause of research for its own sake may be due to the way government research grants are allocated and the ranking of academic journals, which are more interested in developing theory than contributing to practice. Birnberg argued that researchers not only needed to concern themselves with the academic rigour of research, but to make it relevant to practice as well.

Otley (2001) argued that management accounting research 'has, in a number of respects, lost touch with management accounting practices' (p. 255), having concentrated too much on accounting and not enough on management. Otley reinforced his earlier arguments that management accounting had become 'irrelevant to contemporary organizations, but worse that it was often actually counter-productive to good management decision making' (p. 243) and that we need to 'put the management back into management accounting' (p. 259). Hopper et al. (2001) argued that there have been few British scholars who have achieved innovation in practice, either because of 'the anti-intellectualism of British managers and accountants . . . or the marginal role of academics in British policy making' (p. 285), a criticism that could equally be applied to most other English-speaking countries.

Hopper et al. (2001) emphasized the rise of behavioural and organizational accounting research since 1975. In the UK, a paradigm shift occurred that did not happen in the USA (where shareholder value using agency theory – see Chapter 6 – remains the dominant research approach), as more sociological and political approaches drew from European social theory and were influenced by Scandinavian case-based research. Under the 'new public management' reforms of the Thatcher and Reagan governments, private-sector approaches were adopted in the public sector, where:

> accounting data and the consulting arms of accounting firms had been central to economic and policy debates, involving privatization, industrial restructuring, reform of the public sector, and worries about de-industrialization . . . it appeared apparent that accounting had to be studied in its broader social, political and institutional context (Hopper et al., 2001, p. 276).

The adoption of efficiency-based practices, often termed 'managerialism' in the public-sector context, is important in the private sector in terms of delivering profitability, but is more questionable in the public sector where there is a far greater focus by professionals on the quality of service delivery, whether that be improved education, health, or justice outcomes, etc.

Hence the need to closely study how management control and accounting are actually used in organizations, and affect organizational decision making. Humphrey and Scapens (1996) argued for the capacity of explanatory case studies 'to move away from managerialist notions of accounting and to provide more challenging reflections on the nature of accounting knowledge and practice' (p. 87) and its 'intricacies, complexities and inconsistencies' (p. 90).

Theory is integrated with practical examples in this book to reflect the importance not only of taking the rational or economics-based paradigm which is most commonly associated with management control and accounting in particular, but supplementing this with an interpretive and critical perspective on management control and financial statements to provide a more holistic, and perhaps more useful, understanding.

Alternative paradigms

One non-rational (as opposed to irrational) approach to decision making is the 'garbage can', which March and Olsen (1976) used as an analogy to describe management decision making as a 'fortuitous confluence' whereby problems, solutions, participants, and choice opportunities somehow come together. Cooper *et al.* (1981) detailed the rational model of financial and management accounting systems as planning and control devices that measure, report, and evaluate individuals and business units. By contrast, the garbage-can view recognizes that systems provide an appearance of rationality and create an organizational history, but that 'the sequence whereby actions precede goals may well be a more accurate portrayal of organizational functioning than the more traditional goal–action paradigm' (p. 181).

Scott (1998) conceptualized organizations as rational, natural, and open systems. Figure 5.1 shows the different perspectives in diagrammatic form.

As we have already seen, the *rational perspective* is of the organization as a goal-oriented collective that acts purposefully to achieve those goals through a formal structure governing behaviour and the roles of organizational members (see Chapter 4). The *natural perspective* is based on the human relations school of thought, arguing that rules and roles do not significantly influence the actions of people in organizations. In the natural perspective, people are motivated by self-interest and the informal relations between them are more important in understanding organizational behaviour than the formal organizational structure. These informal relations emphasize the social aspect of organizations, which may operate in *consensus* where common goals are shared or in *conflict*. Conflictual approaches stress organizational structures as systems of power where weaker groups are dominated by more powerful ones.

Both rational and natural perspectives view the organization as a *closed system*, separate from its environment. By contrast, the *open systems perspective* emphasizes the impact of the environment on organizations. In the open perspective, organizations are seen as shifting coalitions of participants affecting a collection of interdependent activities that may be tightly or loosely coupled. Thompson (1967) contrasted the technical core of the organization with its goal achievement and control-oriented rationality, implying a closed system and the elimination of uncertainty, with the organization's dependency and lack of control at an institutional level where the greatest uncertainty existed, implying an open system. Thompson argued that at a managerial level there was mediation between the two, provided by a range of manoeuvring devices and organizational structures (which include management control and accounting systems).

Research studies result in competing theories being developed to explain practice. Rational theories are often based on the one 'best way' of doing things, which was developed through the work study methods of Frederick Taylor (1911) and termed 'scientific management'. It is also founded on the work of philosophers like Max Weber (1922/1947) on bureaucracy. Shareholder value (see Chapter 2) lies at the heart of rational theories.

Agency theory (see Chapter 6) is the foundation of the practice of accounting, with boards of directors and managers acting as the agents of their principals, the shareholders. The natural perspective is based on *behavioural theory* and what is often called the 'Human Relations School' which developed

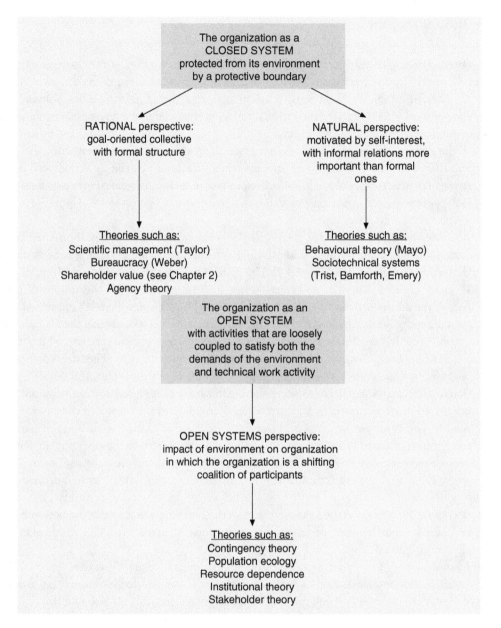

Figure 5.1   Organizations as closed or open systems: Rational, natural, and open systems perspectives.
Source: Based on Scott (1998).

from the work of management researchers such as Elton Mayo (1945) and his experiments at the Hawthorne plant of General Electric, and with the socio-technical systems theory of Trist and Bamforth (1951).

Within the open systems perspective, *contingency theory* (see Chapter 13) suggests that there is no one best way of exercising management control or of accounting. Rather, appropriate systems emerge from the influence of the environment (which may be turbulent or static), technology, organizational size, and the need to fit controls and accounting to the organizational strategy, structure, and culture. *Population ecology theory* is based on the biological analogy of natural selection and holds that environments select organizations for survival on the basis of the fit between the organizational form and the characteristics of the environment. *Resource dependence theory* emphasizes adaptation as organizations act to improve their opportunity to survive, particularly through the relationships of power that impact the organization. *Institutional theory* (see Chapter 7) stresses the rules that are imposed by external parties, especially by government; the values and norms that are internalized in roles as part of socialization processes; and the cultural controls that underpin the belief systems that are supported by the professions. *Stakeholder theory* (see Chapter 2) recognizes that organizations should be accountable to a variety of stakeholders (and not just shareholders as in agency theory). These theories help to explain practice, but they do so in different ways, from different standpoints, and often with different conclusions.

One problem that has arisen in academic research is the variety of theories used to explain practice, which Humphrey and Scapens (1996) believe excessively dominate the analysis of case study evidence. Similarly, Hopper *et al.* (2001) argued the need 'to integrate and consolidate the variety of theories and methodologies which have emerged in recent years, rather than seeking to add yet more' (p. 283).

In his classification of the types of management control, Hofstede (1981) separated cybernetic (rational) models from non-cybernetic ones, which were dependent on values and rituals. The cybernetic model of control systems is located in the rational paradigm (which we described in Chapter 4). Non-cybernetic systems are located in interpretive or critical paradigms. We turn first to the interpretive paradigm and then to the critical paradigm. Each paradigm is a different way of seeing the world – think of it as taking off one pair of glasses and replacing it with another pair which sees the same things, but in a different way or from a different perspective.

The interpretive paradigm and the social construction perspective

While the rational paradigm assumes an objectively knowable world, the interpretive view reflects a subjectively created, emergent social reality. Objectivity is fact-based, measurable, and observable. Subjectivity is based on interpretations and points of view, involving experience, emotion, and judgement. We may think that objectivity is superior but few facts are truly objective. Witness, for example, the different interpretations and judgement about topics such as politics, religion, education, health, military action, immigration, crime, climate change, the social responsibility of business, etc. Different interpretations, opinions, and judgements are applied to the same set of 'facts' with very different conclusions. The same applies to the interpretation of accounting numbers. Are they objective representations of some fact, or interpretations and judgements?

Hopwood (1983) coined the term *accounting in action* to describe the 'ways in which accounting reflects, reinforces or even constrains the strategic postures adopted by particular organizations' (p. 302). Hopwood (1987) contrasted the constitutive as well as reflective roles of accounting. By separating these, Hopwood recognized that accounting does not merely report (the reflective role) but actually creates the organizational reality (the constitutive role). This distinction has been at the centre of much behavioural and organizational research, i.e. that accounting is involved in *constructing* a particular view of reality (of an organization's performance and its relationship with the world around it) rather than merely reporting some objective facts.

The aim of the interpretive perspective is:

> to produce rich and deep understandings of how managers and employees in organizations understand, think about, interact with, and use management accounting and control systems (Macintosh, 1994, p. 4).

Individuals perceive things differently, as a result of their education, past experiences, values, etc. Individuals act towards things on the basis of the *meaning* that things have for them. But meaning is not inherent; it is brought to the situation by the individual, who then acts in accordance with that meaning. But how individuals construct meaning is affected significantly by the social groups to which individuals belong (family groups, national cultures, professions, sporting or work groups, etc.). So reality, which in the interpretive paradigm is subjective rather than objective, is not just the result of individual perceptions, but is influenced by social groups who both construct and share meanings. We call this '*socially constructed*' reality such that members of particular social groups construct meanings, which are then internalized and shared between individuals in that group.

It is through that socially constructed process that members of the social group make sense of reality in a similar way. For example, in an organizational setting, it is common for marketing and sales people to see 'reality' quite differently from people in the operations/ production/ distribution function, and differently again from those in finance and administration roles.

Preston (1995) added that the social constructionist perspective does not preclude the existence of organizational structures and processes, but suggests that these are symbolic representations of a particular view of organizational reality. These meanings are also expressed symbolically through language. In this context accounting information is a symbolic representation of reality. Individual behaviour is guided by the meanings, values, and beliefs that are constructed and shared by organizational members. These symbols are then subject to interpretation by individuals, who act towards them on the basis of the meaning they have for them. However, Preston recognized that these structures and processes may influence the development of an organizational culture – the shared values, beliefs, and meanings that are collectively held by organizational participants.

Whilst what Alvesson and Karreman (2004) call 'technocratic control' emphasizes plans, arrangements, and systems which focus on behaviour and measurable outputs, 'socio-ideological control' comprises efforts to persuade people to adapt to certain values, norms, and ideas about what is good, important, and praiseworthy in terms of work and organizational life. It comprises methods of controlling worker mindsets through social relations, identity formation, and ideology – through organizational culture. This distinction between formal and informal elements of control is important because of the role that culture plays in management control and accounting.

Culture, control, and accounting

Allaire and Firsirotu (1984) contrasted a *sociostructural* system based on formal structures, strategies, policies, and management processes with a *cultural* system based on myths, ideology, values, and artefacts and shaped by society, the history of the organization, and the contingent factors affecting it. They argued that sociostructural and cultural systems were in a complex relationship, with potential for stress when an organization is subject to sudden pressures for change.

The review of research on organizational culture undertaken by Smircich (1983) reflected a convergence of views around culture as 'shared key values and beliefs' (p. 345). These values and beliefs convey a sense of identity, generate commitment, enhance social system stability, and serve as a sense-making device to guide and shape behaviour. Smircich also identified the existence of multiple organization subcultures – a multiplicity of cultures within an organization, rather than one pervading culture.

Schein (1988/1968) described the process that brings about change in the values and attitudes of different groups of people throughout their career as 'organizational socialization' – a key element in sustaining an organization's culture. It occurs whenever an individual enters an organization, changes departments, or is promoted. Socialization determines employee loyalty, commitment, productivity, and turnover. It is the process whereby a new member of a group learns the values, norms, and behaviour patterns – the 'price of membership' (p. 54). These norms, values, and behaviours are learned from organizational publications, from training, line managers, peers and role models, and from the rewards and punishments that exist. Where the values of the immediate group that the individual joins are out of line with the value system of the organization as a whole, the individual learns the values of the immediate group more quickly than those of the organization. The essence of management, according to Schein, is that managers must understand organizations as social systems that socialize their members, and then gain control over those forces.

Some of the control system frameworks we introduced in Chapter 4 included culture. Ouchi (1979) identified three mechanisms for control: market (based on prices); bureaucracy (based on rules); and clan (based on tradition). Clan mechanisms are represented in professions, where different organizations have the same values. Ouchi used the example of a hospital, where a highly formalized and lengthy period of socialization leads to both skill and value training. Simons (1994; 1995) referred to belief systems, and Ferreira and Otley (2009) and Malmi and Brown (2008) both recognized cultural elements in management control.

Scott (1998) described accounting systems as 'one of the most important conventions connecting institutionally defined belief systems with technical activities' (p. 137). Scott argued that some organizations rely less on formal controls and more on developing a set of beliefs and norms to guide behaviour.

Hofstede (1981) argued that control systems must be sensitive to organizational cultures and that those controls running counter to culture are unlikely to be successfully imposed. Markus and Pfeffer (1983) suggested that resistance to and failure of accounting control systems was common, arguing that control systems will be implemented when they are consistent with the dominant organizational culture in their implications for values and beliefs. The idea of resistance to control brings us to the radical paradigm and a consideration of the role of power in management control and accounting.

The radical paradigm and critical accounting

Radical approaches emphasize broader structural issues such as the role of the State, distribution of the surplus of production, and class difference (Hopper *et al.*, 1987). Those writers who sought a more radical interpretation than the interpretive one drew on the work of Karl Marx. In Chapter 1, we saw through the perspective of the Marxist historian Eric Hobsbawm that much of what we take for granted in capitalist society and the role of accounting is a result of the history of industrial revolution and British colonialism, and subsequently American industrial power.

There are three approaches within the radical perspective: political economy, labour process, and critical theory (Roslender, 1995). All are concerned with promoting change in the status quo. The *political economy* approach recognizes power and conflict in society and the effect that accounting has on the distribution of income, power, and wealth. *Labour process theory* focuses on the corruption of human creativity in the pursuit of wealth, especially deskilling in which management control is a reproducer of capitalism, a point taken up effectively by Braverman (1974) who wrote of the degradation of work as a result of industrialization. Labour process theorists emphasize:

> the structural instabilities that characterize capitalism's unequal and antagonistic social relations (Neimark and Tinker, 1986, p. 378).

Neimark and Tinker emphasized the 'on-going conflict among and between social classes over the disposition and division of the social surplus' (p. 379) and how '[s]ocial and organizational control systems are not neutral mechanisms in these struggles but are attached to and legitimate concrete power interests' (p. 380). Having undertaken the examples in Chapter 3, readers will know that in accounting, the profit at the end of a period is transferred to become an addition to the owners' equity.

A radical approach would argue that through this simple transfer, accounting supports the unequal relations of capitalism.

The third radical perspective, *critical theory*, emphasizes a critique of the status quo and emancipation towards a better life. Hopper and Powell (1985) argued that critical studies show how 'accounting measures alienate through subordinating behaviour to perceived imperatives which are in fact socially created' (p. 454). The role of accounting, according to critical theorists, is to challenge the status quo.

An example of the application of critical theory is provided by Perrow (1991), who argued:

> If one raised profits by externalizing many costs to the community, exploiting the workforce, evading government controls by corrupting officials, manipulating stock values, and controlling the market by forming quasi-cartels or other predatory practices – all common practices in the nineteenth and twentieth century – then profits will not reflect the efficient use of labor, capital, and natural resources (p. 746).

Of course, writing in 1991, Perrow did not realize that these same practices would still exist in the twenty-first century, and hence critique remains important if society is to improve.

Critical theory does not necessarily imply a Marxist view of the world and a desire to overthrow capitalism, but it does imply a questioning and critical approach to the role of accounting in organizations and society. Laughlin (1999) defined *critical accounting* as providing:

> a critical understanding of the role of accounting processes and practices and the accounting profession in the functioning of society and organizations with an intention to use that understanding to engage (where appropriate) in changing these processes, practices and the profession (p. 73).

Much of critical theory is concerned with opening up the discourse from a narrow economic-rational application of accounting to question its underlying assumptions and its (often dysfunctional) consequences. *Discourse* is a conversation, albeit an informed one, through which arguments and counter-arguments are considered. Accounting is implicated in discourse because in its written form, it presents ostensibly objective 'facts' that contain implicit rather than explicit assumptions. An accounting discourse of profit is dominated by an economic-rational logic. Thus, accounting 'serves to construct a particular field of visibility' (Miller and O'Leary, 1987, p. 239). While this makes some things (i.e. financial numbers) more visible, it makes other things (e.g. the quality of the product/service, the treatment of workers, the organization's impact on the environment, etc.) invisible, or at least less visible.

In promoting critical theory, Broadbent and Laughlin (1997) emphasized 'recognition of the choice between seeking to develop change through meaningful debate [rather than] through the application of power or coercion' (p. 645). However, power is evident in how organizations actually work, and we must consider the role of power in relation to accounting.

Power and accounting

We have seen how control systems and accounting are aimed at influencing behaviour to achieve goals. This is inextricably bound up with a consideration of power. Pfeffer (1992) defined power as:

> the potential ability to influence behavior, to change the course of events, to overcome resistance, and to get people to do things that they would not otherwise do (p. 30).

Morgan (1986) identified power as either a resource or a social relation, defining it as 'the medium through which conflicts of interest are ultimately resolved' (p. 158). As a resource, power is concerned with the dependency of one party on particular resources, and the control over the distribution of that resource by another party. As a social relation, power is concerned with domination of one person (or group) over another. By contrast, Giddens (1976) argued that power does not of itself imply conflict. Because power is linked to the pursuit of interest, it is only when interests do not coincide that power and conflict are related. Hence, power may also be used in a consensual way, to achieve agreed goals.

Various writers have commented on how power is implicit in what is seen to be important in organizational functioning. Child (1972) concluded:

> . . . one is recognizing the operation of an essentially political process in which constraints and opportunities are functions of the power exercised by decision-makers in the light of ideological values (p. 16).

Markus and Pfeffer (1983) argued that accounting and control systems are related to power:

> because they collect and manipulate information used in decision making . . . [and] because they are used to change the performance of individuals and the outcomes of organizational processes (pp. 206–7).

One only has to observe the budget-setting process in organizations, when accountants exert considerable power over resource allocations to particular business units or functions, and approval over bids for capital expenditure (we explore these issues more in Chapters 14 and 16). In Chapter 4 we described the strategy mapping process whereby strategy should drive performance targets and in turn budget allocations. However, in most organizations, different power structures are often in place to establish strategic plans, control the budget, and set non-financial targets. Different power bases can result in a lack of systematic management control, with each dominant coalition wishing to retain its own power base (i.e. the strategic plan, the budget, or the Balanced Scorecard).

Figure 5.2 shows a representation of the main differences between the rational (economic), interpretive, and radical (or critical) paradigms.

In this chapter, we have introduced the interpretive and radical paradigms, suggesting the interaction between accounting and control systems, culture, and power relations, in contrast with the economically rational paradigm introduced in Chapter 4. Readers should not see any one of these perspectives as better or worse than any other. However, using the analogy of wearing different pairs of glasses to gain different perspectives, alternately looking through each set of glasses is more likely to give a more holistic picture than relying on a single pair of glasses alone.

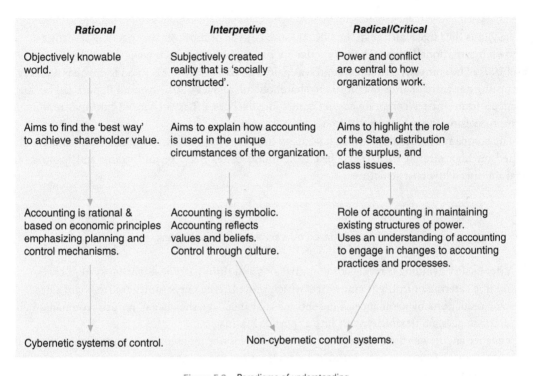

Figure 5.2   Paradigms of understanding.

Case study 5.1: easyJet

easyJet provides an interesting and well-known example to illustrate many of the aspects of management control described in Chapter 4 and this chapter as it illustrates rational-economic, interpretive, and critical perspectives.

Background

easyJet, the low-cost airline, was founded by Sir Stelios Haji-Ioannou in 1995 and floated on the London Stock Exchange in late 2000, which then valued the company at £777 million. Through his family company, Sir Stelios retains ownership of over one third of the business and retains important rights over the 'easy' brand name. At the time of writing this edition (January 2015) the company's market capitalization was £6,685 million and it was part of the FTSE 100 index. In its 2013 Annual Report, easyJet reported that it had over 200 aircraft flying over 600 routes in 32 countries and employed 8,300 staff. In financial year 2013, the company carried over 60 million passengers, earning revenue of £4.2 billion and a net profit before tax of £478 million.

easyJet is the largest airline in the UK measured by the number of passengers. The airline is well known internationally through the popular TV series 'Airline', which was televised between 1999 and 2007. The company's first dividend was paid for financial year 2011 and it now has a policy of returning one third of after-tax profits to shareholders. easyJet's 2013 Annual Report can be downloaded from http://corporate.easyjet.com/~/media/Files/E/Easyjet-Plc-V2/pdf/investors/result-center-investor/annual-report-2013.pdf.

The company borrowed its low cost strategy from Southwest Airlines in the USA. This strategy relied on high aircraft utilization, fast turnaround times between unloading and loading, and maintaining a low cost structure.

Cost advantages

The company's low cost strategy is based on various cost advantages:

- direct sales, avoiding travel agent commissions and third-party reservation system costs;
- no free catering or in-flight amenities, which provides the opportunity for on-board sales;
- cost reductions by avoidance of exceptions that incur overheads e.g. no unaccompanied children, no pets, no flexibility with late airport check-ins;
- cheaper and newer high seating density aircraft (easyJet pitched Boeing against Airbus in the aircraft manufacturers' battle to win orders from easyJet in 2002);
- lower crew costs through fast airport turnaround, hence higher productivity;
- lower airport costs through use of secondary airports (although the company now has a large base at Gatwick);
- higher seat density – more seats per aircraft;
- use of marginal pricing formula and yield management to maximize capacity utilization and revenue – the average load factor on their aircraft in the 2013 financial year was 89%;
- hedging the cost of aircraft fuel; and
- maintaining a strong Balance Sheet with low borrowings.

Performance measurement

As well as cost control and revenue maximization, the key performance measures reported in the company's 2013 Annual Report were:

- million seats flown;
- number of passengers;
- revenue, cost, and profit per seat;
- load factor (i.e. % of seat capacity utilized);
- available seat kilometres (ASK) – the total number of seats available for passengers multiplied by the number of kilometres flown;

- revenue passenger kilometres (RPK) – the total number of paying passengers carried multiplied by the number of kilometres flown;
- number of sectors (point-to-point destinations);
- average sector length (kilometres);
- aircraft utilization hours per day;
- customer satisfaction (and whether customers are likely to recommend easyJet);
- on-time performance;
- staff turnover; and
- safety.

It is likely that the company reports internally other performance measures that it does not make public.

Importantly, many of these performance measures are common across the airline industry, including load factor, ASK, and RPK. Costs and revenues are monitored for each route, to support the company's stated strategy of targeting capacity which has the highest return.

A rational-economic perspective

easyJet is clearly focused on shareholder value through its focus on revenue growth and profitability. The company's approach to shareholder value was that it preferred to retain its funds for use in the business and did not pay a dividend until its first dividend for the year ended September 2011. However, the company's substantial growth has benefited shareholders through increases in the share price. If a shareholder purchased 100 shares in late 2001 at the then market price of £4.00 each, those shares (at the market price in January 2015 of £16.83 each) would now be worth £1,683 – a fourfold increase.

An interpretive perspective

The interpretive perspective reveals aspects of socially constructed reality and different aspects of interpreting easyJet's performance. easyJet promotes its culture as informal with a very flat management structure and informal dress code in an open plan office environment. However, there have been criticisms of its industrial relations practices, with the CEO admitting in 2011 to a continued deterioration in relationships between the company and its pilots and the pilots union over several years. It is only recently that easyJet has recognized trade unions, preferring to deal directly with employees. From the passenger perspective, the low-cost focus of easyJet means that it can be criticized for some of its decisions. The 'Airline' TV documentary series often revealed passenger complaints about easyJet's inflexibility, especially over late airport check-ins. In 2004, easyJet was criticized for failing to observe European Union rules on compensation to passengers who had been denied boarding, or who experienced delays or cancellations. In 2008, the Advertising Standards Authority criticized easyJet's misleading environmental claim in its corporate publicity that its aircraft had lower carbon emissions than its competitors. Nevertheless, negative publicity has not affected easyJet's performance, and there is evidence that even negative publicity in the 'Airline' TV series was more beneficial than harmful to the airline.

A critical perspective

Power is also an important element in understanding easyJet. The company was founded by Stelios Haji-Ioannou who was forced to stand down as chairman of the board when easyJet listed on the Stock Exchange in 2000. However, Stelios remained a director of the company until he resigned in 2010 following pressure from the corporate governance lobby. The Haji-Ioannou family holds over one third of easyJet's shares, and in addition held (through a separate company) a restrictive agreement that controlled the 'easy' brand name. These rights were reduced following litigation and agreement between the company and its founder. A new 50-year brand licence signed in 2010 awarded the founder a £300,000 annual fee together with 0.25% of revenues. These impacts demonstrate the power of an important and influential shareholder set against the expectations of the Stock Exchange for good governance by the board of directors.

Source: http://corporate.easyjet.com/ and http://corporate.easyjet.com/investors/reports-and-accounts.aspx?sc_lang=en).

Finally in this chapter, we turn to the issue of ethics and how ethical issues affect accounting information and the roles of financial and non-financial managers.

Creative accounting, ethics, and accounting

Accounting choices are moral choices:

> Accounting is important precisely to the extent the accountant can transform the world, can influence the lived experience of others in ways which cause that experience to differ from what it would be in the absence of accounting, or in the presence of an alternative kind of accounting (Francis, quoted in Gowthorpe and Blake, 1998, p. 3).

However, some accountants and non-financial managers have not adopted particularly ethical – or even legal – approaches to the preparation, reporting and use of financial information. 'Creative accounting' is a process of artificially manipulating accounting figures by taking advantage of loopholes in accounting rules or making estimates or judgements that are unrealistic, the purpose of which is to present financial statements in a way that shareholders or other stakeholders may prefer. Creative accounting practices have been justified by managers for reasons of income smoothing, to bring profits closer to forecasts or stock market expectations; changing accounting policies to distract attention from poor performance; or maintaining or boosting share prices (Gowthorpe and Blake, 1998).

Despite the role of accounting standards (see Chapter 6) and other regulations, creative accounting has always played a part in the efforts made by a few companies to present their performance in a better light. However, although accounting standards continually improve, there are always loopholes that accountants seem to find as quickly as standards are produced.

This desire for an income smoothing effect can be achieved by practices such as accruals, stock valuation, creating or reducing provisions, capitalizing or expensing costs (WorldCom fraudulently capitalized expenses as assets), and off-Balance Sheet financing (creating special-purpose entities that hid liabilities from shareholders, which was the main factor in Enron's downfall in the USA). While there is nothing wrong *per se* in these standard practices which involve subjective judgements based on estimation, they are inappropriate when they are done solely for the purpose of income smoothing to manipulate reported performance. The term 'creative accounting' has tended to be replaced with 'earnings management', perhaps to disguise the negative connotations of the former term. Earnings management is aimed at avoiding the criticism of being creative with financial information; however, whatever the practice is called, boards of directors still like to satisfy stock market expectations influenced by stock analysts.

De la Torre (2009) uses a series of case studies to describe more recent efforts by companies including Lucent Technologies, L'Oréal, Deutsche Bank, American International Group, and Vodafone to 'bend rather than break' the rules of revenue and expense recognition, accounting for stock options, and off-Balance Sheet financing.

We now consider (in Case studies 5.2 to 5.5) some high-profile examples of corporate failure in order to understand the differences between practices which may be illegal, unethical, or simply due to poor decision making.

Case study 5.2: Enron

In December 2001, US energy trader Enron collapsed. Enron was the largest bankruptcy in US history. Even though the USA was believed by many to be the most regulated financial market in the world, it was evident from Enron's collapse that investors were not properly informed about the significance of off-Balance Sheet transactions. Enron had taken out large loans that were created through special-purpose entities such that they were not treated as liabilities in Enron's financial reports. US accounting rules may have contributed to this, in that they are concerned with the strict legal ownership of investment vehicles rather than with their effective control. There were some indications that Enron may have actively lobbied against changing the treatment in US financial reporting of special-purpose entities used in off-Balance Sheet financing.

Former chief executive Kenneth Lay died in 2006 before he could stand trial. Enron's former chief financial officer Andrew Fastow was sentenced to prison in 2006 for stealing from Enron and devising schemes to deceive investors about the energy company's true financial condition. Lawyers have to date won settlements totalling US$7.3 billion from banks including JPMorgan Chase, Bank of America, and Citigroup.

Case study 5.3: WorldCom

WorldCom filed for bankruptcy protection in June 2002. The company had used accounting tricks to conceal a deteriorating financial condition and to inflate profits. It was at the time the biggest corporate fraud in history, largely a result of treating operating expenses as capital expenditure. WorldCom (now renamed MCI) admitted in March 2004 that the total amount by which it had misled investors over the previous 10 years was almost US$75 billion (£42 billion) and reduced its stated pre-tax profits for 2001 and 2002 by that amount. The Securities and Exchange Commission (SEC) said WorldCom had committed 'accounting improprieties of unprecedented magnitude' – proof, it said, of the need for reform in the regulation of corporate accounting.

Former WorldCom chief executive Bernie Ebbers resigned in April 2002 amid questions about US$366 million in personal loans from the company and a federal probe of its accounting practices. Ebbers was subsequently charged with conspiracy to commit securities fraud and filing misleading data with the SEC and is currently serving a 25-year prison term. Scott Sullivan, former chief financial officer, pleaded guilty to three criminal charges and was sentenced to five years in prison as part of a plea agreement in which he testified against Ebbers.

As a consequence of the failures of Enron and WorldCom, the USA introduced Sarbanes–Oxley legislation (see Chapter 2) to address many of the criticisms of reporting and auditing practice.

Case study 5.4: Arthur Andersen

Before the 'Big Four' accounting firms, there was a 'Big Five', one of which was Arthur Andersen. The firm was found guilty of criminal charges in relation to the audit of Enron and its actions in relation to disguising Enron's off-Balance Sheet transactions, with the firm having instructed its employees to destroy documents pursuant to its document retention policy. As a result, the firm surrendered its licence to practise as accountants in the US. While the criminal verdict was subsequently overturned by the US Supreme Court on the basis that the jury was misdirected as to the law, the damage to Arthur Andersen's reputation was substantial and the firm ceased to exist, with other accounting firms taking over its client business.

The failure of Enron highlighted the over-dependence of an auditor (Arthur Andersen) on one particular client, the employment of staff by Enron who had previously worked for their auditors, the process of audit appointments and reappointments, the rotation of audit partners, and how auditors are monitored and regulated. The practice of auditing financial statements was permanently affected by the cases of Enron, WorldCom, and Arthur Andersen. In particular, audit firms are now required to demonstrate independence and clearly separate their audit and non-audit (e.g. consulting) services.

Case study 5.5: The failure of the Royal Bank of Scotland

In October 2008, the Royal Bank of Scotland (RBS) in effect failed and was part nationalized, relying on Bank of England Emergency Liquidity Assistance to fund itself. RBS's failure imposed large costs on UK citizens. To prevent collapse the government injected £45.5 billion of equity capital, a stake reduced to about £20 billion when the Financial Services Authority's (FSA) report was written.

The report concluded that some of the causes of RBS's failure were systemic – common to many banks – or the consequence of unstable features of the entire financial system. This was exacerbated by a deficient global framework for bank capital regulation, together with an FSA supervisory approach which assigned a relatively low priority to liquidity, and created conditions in which some form of systemic crisis was more likely to occur.

The FSA report argued that key prudential regulations being applied by itself, and by other regulatory authorities across the world, were dangerously inadequate. There was an erroneous belief that financial markets were inherently stable, and that the Basel II capital adequacy regime would ensure a sound banking system. The FSA's supervisory approach entailed inadequate focus on the core prudential issues of capital, liquidity, and asset quality, and insufficient willingness to challenge management judgements and risk assessments. The FSA report highlighted that it operated within the context of frequent political demands to avoid imposing burdens which could undermine the competitiveness of UK financial organizations.

However, the FSA report held that ultimate responsibility for poor decisions must lie with the bank. The multiple poor decisions that RBS made suggested that there were likely to have been underlying deficiencies in RBS management, governance, and culture which made it prone to make poor decisions. The FSA report found that the RBS failure was caused by errors of judgement and execution made by RBS management, which resulted in RBS being one of the banks that failed during the 2007–8 global financial crisis: in particular, the decision by RBS to go ahead with the ABN AMRO acquisition on the basis of a due diligence study which was clearly inadequate relative to the risks involved.

However, the FSA report found that there was not sufficient evidence of dishonesty or incompetence to bring enforcement actions which had a reasonable chance of success in court proceedings.

Source: Financial Services Authority. (2011). *The failure of the Royal Bank of Scotland*. FSA Board Report. Financial Services Authority Board Report. http://www.fsa.gov.uk/pubs/other/rbs.pdf.

Subsequent to the global financial crisis, global prudential regulations have been changed radically, with Basel III introducing capital adequacy standards far above previous levels, and for the first time introducing quantitative global liquidity rules. The Financial Services Authority no longer exists. The Financial Conduct Authority now regulates the financial services industry in the UK, while the

Prudential Regulation Authority is a part of the Bank of England and is now responsible for the prudential regulation and supervision of banks, building societies, credit unions, insurers, and major investment firms.

The issue of whether an accounting treatment is proper or otherwise is often a subjective judgement, although the case studies of Enron and WorldCom reveal clear illegality, while the Royal Bank of Scotland case reveals errors of judgement and poor decision-making processes rather than any evidence of dishonesty or incompetence.

WorldCom's and Enron's focus on performance was almost exclusively financial, oriented on short-term profits and share prices. This focus was supported by bonuses and share options to reward executives for short-term profits that resulted in a culture in which ethical principles were largely ignored. The actions of Arthur Andersen in destroying records, despite no illegality being proven, are clearly unethical. This brings us to a discussion of ethics.

Ethics is important for accountants and non-accountants alike. The members of any of the professional accounting bodies are governed by their ethical rules. These rules also provide useful guidance for non-accountants, not only in their dealings with professional accountants, but also in terms of their own behaviour.

A *Code of Ethics for Professional Accountants* was introduced in 2006 by the International Federation of Accountants (IFAC) and has been subsequently updated (IFAC, 2010). The Code is in three parts. Part A establishes the fundamental principles of professional ethics for professional accountants and provides a conceptual framework which gives guidance on fundamental ethical principles. Part B applies to professional accountants in public practice. Part C applies to professional accountants in business. The Code states that a distinguishing mark of the accountancy profession is its responsibility to act in the public interest, and not exclusively to satisfy the needs of an individual client or employer. This is an important point and one often overlooked by accountants who seek to serve their clients or employers without regard to the wider effects of their actions.

The conceptual framework states that a professional accountant is required to comply with the following fundamental principles:

- *Integrity*: A professional accountant should be straightforward and honest in all professional and business relationships.
- *Objectivity*: A professional accountant should not allow bias, conflict of interest, or undue influence of others to override professional or business judgements.
- *Professional competence and due care*: A professional accountant has a continuing duty to maintain professional knowledge and skill at the level required to ensure that a client or employer receives competent professional service based on current developments in practice, legislation, and techniques. A professional accountant should act diligently and in accordance with applicable technical and professional standards when providing professional services.
- *Confidentiality*: A professional accountant should respect the confidentiality of information acquired as a result of professional and business relationships and should not disclose any such information to third parties without proper and specific authority unless there is a legal or professional right or duty to disclose.

- *Professional behaviour*: A professional accountant should comply with relevant laws and regulations and should avoid any action that discredits the profession.

The conceptual framework underlying the fundamental principles requires a professional accountant to identify, evaluate, and address threats to compliance with the fundamental principles, rather than merely comply with a set of specific rules. Compliance with the fundamental principles may potentially be threatened by a broad range of circumstances. Threats may fall into the following categories:

- Self-interest threats, which may occur as a result of the financial or other interests of a professional accountant or of an immediate or close family member.
- Self-review threats, which may occur when a previous judgement needs to be re-evaluated by the professional accountant responsible for that judgement.
- Advocacy threats, which may occur when a professional accountant promotes a position or opinion to the point that the accountant's objectivity may be compromised.
- Familiarity threats, which may occur when, because of a close personal relationship, a professional accountant becomes too sympathetic to the interests of others.
- Intimidation threats, which may occur when a professional accountant may be deterred from acting objectively by threats, whether actual or perceived.

In attempting to resolve potential ethical problems, a professional accountant should determine the appropriate course of action that is consistent with the fundamental principles. The professional accountant should also weigh the consequences of each possible course of action. It may be in the best interests of the professional accountant to document the substance of the issue and details of any discussions held or decisions taken, concerning that issue.

Where a matter involves a conflict with, or within, an organization, a professional accountant should also consider consulting with those charged with governance of the organization, such as the board of directors or the audit committee. If a significant conflict cannot be resolved, a professional accountant may wish to obtain professional advice from the relevant professional body or legal advisers, and thereby obtain guidance on ethical issues without breaching confidentiality. The professional accountant should consider obtaining legal advice to determine whether there is a legal requirement to report. If, after exhausting all relevant possibilities, the ethical conflict remains unresolved, a professional accountant should, where possible, refuse to remain associated with the matter creating the conflict. The professional accountant may determine that, in the circumstances, it is appropriate to withdraw from the specific assignment, or to resign altogether from the engagement, the firm, or the employing organization.

While non-financial managers are not bound by any accounting Code of Ethics, different professions may have their own codes that do apply. Nevertheless, the basic principles of integrity, objectivity, competence and due care, confidentiality, and standards of behaviour are societal expectations of most people and are difficult to ignore. Therefore, all managers, when faced with ethical issues, need to consider and weigh the consequences of alternative courses of action. For example, if you had been employed by Enron, WorldCom, or Arthur Andersen, and had become aware of their practices and been concerned about illegal or unethical conduct, would you have said anything? One simple test is whether you would be happy to see your name and your actions reported on the front page of a daily newspaper. If you would find such a report embarrassing and necessitating your accountability for those actions, this may be an indication that the actions might be unethical. Such a standard was clearly not applied by the staff of Enron, WorldCom, and Arthur Andersen.

Conclusion

This chapter has contrasted the rational, economics-based paradigm of management control in Chapter 4 with a more interpretive and critical approach. We began with an overview of how research has developed different insights into accounting and broader management control practices and briefly mentioned a number of theories that are aimed at explaining how organizations actually work. We then considered alternative paradigms through open/closed systems, and rational/natural approaches. We looked at the interpretive paradigm and how reality can be socially constructed, and the relationship between culture, control, and accounting. We then examined the radical or critical paradigm and the relationship between power and accounting. While much of accounting relies on the rational-economic paradigm, we will return to make comparisons with interpretive and critical perspectives throughout this book. So for example, Chapter 7 applies these different perspectives to financial statements, Chapter 13 applies them to costs, and Chapter 17 addresses budgets. However, a practical difficulty in adopting a perspective other than the rational-economic one is that organizational discourse suggests that the rational-economic perspective of shareholder value is the only valid one, although individuals often act in line with particular values or norms, and sometimes in the pursuit of power and self-interest.

We concluded the chapter with a discussion of creative accounting (or earnings management) and ethics and how they have been implicated in some major corporate collapses.

An advantage in understanding interpretive and critical alternatives to the rational-economic one is what Covaleski et al. (1996) called 'paradigmatic pluralism . . . alternative ways of understanding the multiple roles played by management accounting in organizations and society' (p. 24). Otley et al. (1995) suggested that while the definition of management control was 'managerialist in focus . . . this should not preclude a critical stance and thus a broader choice of theoretical approaches' (p. S42). Hence, whether or not you see the world predominantly through a rational, interpretive, or critical pair of glasses, this should not prevent you from occasionally exchanging those glasses in order to see a broader perspective, and perhaps understand the perspectives of other people a little better.

Now and again, it is worthwhile removing our rational-economic glasses and looking at the world through the lens of interpretive and critical theory. Having read Chapters 4 and 5, you should now read and think about Reading B in Part IV of this book. Reading B describes the development of approaches to management control and the role of accounting in terms of open/closed and rational/natural system perspectives.

References

Allaire, Y. and Firsirotu, M. E. (1984). Theories of organizational culture. *Organization Studies*, 5(3), 193–226.

Alvesson, M. and Karreman, D. (2004). Interfaces of control. Technocratic and socio-ideological control in a global management consultancy firm. Accounting, *Organizations and Society*, 29, 423–44.

Birnberg, J. G. (2009). The case for post-modern management accounting: thinking outside the box. *Journal of Management Accounting Research*, 21, 318.

Braverman, H. (1974). *Labor and Monopoly Capital: The Degradation of Work in the Twentieth Century*. New York: Monthly Review Press.

Broadbent, J. and Laughlin, R. (1997). Developing empirical research: an example informed by a Habermasian approach. *Accounting, Auditing and Accountability Journal*, 10(5), 622–48.

Child, J. (1972). Organizational structure, environment and performance: the role of strategic choice. *Sociology*, 6, 122.

Cooper, D. J., Hayes, D., and Wolf, F. (1981). Accounting in organized anarchies: understanding and designing accounting systems in ambiguous situations. *Accounting, Organizations and Society*, 6(3), 175–91.

Covaleski, M. A., Dirsmith, M. W., and Samuel, S. (1996). Managerial accounting research: the contributions of organizational and sociological theories. *Journal of Management Accounting Research*, 8, 135.

De la Torre, I. (2009). *Creative Accounting Exposed*. Basingstoke: Palgrave Macmillan.

Ferreira, A. and Otley, D. (2009). The design and use of performance management systems: an extended framework for analysis. *Management Accounting Research*, 20(4), 263–82.

Financial Services Authority. (2011). *The failure of the Royal Bank of Scotland*. FSA Board Report. Financial Services Authority Board Report. http://www.fsa.gov.uk/pubs/other/rbs.pdf.

Giddens, A. (1976). *New Rules of Sociological Method: A Positive Critique of Interpretative Sociologies*. London: Hutchinson.

Gowthorpe, C. and Blake, J. (Eds) (1998). *Ethical Issues in Accounting*. London: Routledge.

Hofstede, G. (1981). Management control of public and not-for-profit activities. *Accounting, Organizations and Society*, 6(3), 193–211.

Hopper, T. and Powell, A. (1985). Making sense of research into the organizational and social aspects of management accounting: a review of its underlying assumptions. *Journal of Management Studies*, 22(5), 429–65.

Hopper, T., Otley, D., and Scapens, B. (2001). British management accounting research: whence and whither: opinions and recollections. *British Accounting Review*, 33, 263–91.

Hopper, T., Storey, J. and Willmott, H. (1987). Accounting for accounting: towards the development of a dialectical view. *Accounting, Organizations and Society*, 12(5), 437–56.

Hopwood, A. G. (1983). On trying to study accounting in the contexts in which it operates. *Accounting, Organizations and Society*, 8(2/3), 287–305.

Hopwood, A. G. (1987). The archaeology of accounting systems. *Accounting, Organizations and Society*, 12(3), 207–34.

Humphrey, C. and Scapens, R. W. (1996). Theories and case studies of organizational and accounting practices: limitation or liberation? *Accounting, Auditing and Accountability Journal*, 9(4), 86–106.

International Federation of Accountants (IFAC, 2010). *Handbook of the Code of Ethics for Professional Accountants*.

Kaplan, R. S. (1986). The role for empirical research in management accounting. *Accounting, Organizations and Society*, 11(4/5), 429–52.

Laughlin, R. (1999). Critical accounting: nature, progress and prognosis. *Accounting, Auditing and Accountability Journal*, 12(1), 73–8.

Macintosh, N. B. (1994). *Management Accounting and Control Systems: An Organizational and Behavioral Approach*. Chichester: John Wiley & Sons.

Malmi, T. and Brown, D. A. (2008). Management control systems as a package opportunities, challenges and research directions. *Management Accounting Research*, 19, 287–300.

March, J. G. and Olsen, J. P. (1976). *Ambiguity and Choice in Organizations*. Bergen: Universitetsforiagen.

Markus, M. L. and Pfeffer, J. (1983). Power and the design and implementation of accounting and control systems. *Accounting, Organizations and Society*, 8(2/3), 205–18.

Mayo, E. (1945). *The Social Problems of an Industrial Civilization*. Boston, MA: Harvard Business School Press.

Miller, P. and O'Leary, T. (1987).Accounting and the construction of the governable person. *Accounting, Organizations and Society*, 12(3), 235–65.

Morgan, G. (1986). *Images of Organization*. Newbury Park, CA: Sage.

Neimark, M. and Tinker, T. (1986). The social construction of management control systems. *Accounting, Organizations and Society*, 11(4/5), 369–95.

Otley, D. (2001). Extending the boundaries of management accounting research: developing systems for performance management. *British Accounting Review*, 33, 243–61.

Otley, D. T. and Berry, A. J. (1980). Control, organization and accounting. *Accounting, Organizations and Society*, 5(2), 231–44.

Otley, D. T., Berry, A. J., and Broadbent, J. (1995). Research in management control: an overview of its development. *British Journal of Management*, 6, Special Issue, S31–S44.

Ouchi, W. G. (1979). A conceptual framework for the design of organizational control mechanisms. *Management Science*, 25(9), 83348.

Perrow, C. (1991). A society of organizations. *Theory and Society*, 20(6), 725–62.

Pfeffer, J. (1992). *Managing with Power: Politics and Influence in Organizations*. Boston, MA: Harvard Business School Press.

Preston, A. (1995). *Budgeting, creativity and culture*. In D. Ashton, T. Hopper, and R. W. Scapens (Eds), *Issues in Management Accounting* 2nd edn. London: Prentice Hall.

Roslender, R. (1995). *Critical management accounting*. In D. Ashton, T. Hopper, and R. W. Scapens (Eds), *Issues in Management Accounting* 2nd edn. London: Prentice Hall.

Schein, E. H. (1988/1968). Organizational socialization and the profession of management. *Sloan Management Review*, Fall, 53–65.

Scott, W. R. (1998). *Organizations: Rational, Natural, and Open Systems* 4th edn. Upper Saddle River, NJ: Prentice Hall.

Simons, R. (1994). How new top managers use control systems as levers of strategic renewal. *Strategic Management Journal*, 15, 169–89.

Simons, R. (1995). *Levers of Control: How Managers Use Innovative Control Systems to Drive Strategic Renewal*. Boston, MA: Harvard Business School Press.

Smircich, L. (1983). Concepts of culture and organizational analysis. *Administrative Science Quarterly*, 28, 339–58.

Taylor, F. W. (1911). *Scientific Management: Comprising Shop Management; the Principles of Scientific Management; Testimony before the Special House Committee*. New York: Harper & Brothers.

Thompson, J. (1967). *Organizations in Action: Social Science Bases of Administrative Theory*. New York: McGraw-Hill.

Trist, E. L. and Bamforth, K. W. (1951). Social and psychological consequences of the Longwall method of coal-getting. *Human Relations*, 4, 32–8.

Weber, M. (1922/1947). *The Theory of Social and Economic Organization*. Oxford: Oxford University Press.

Questions

5.1   Compare the normative approach with interpretive or critical approaches to research in management control and accounting.

5.2   Explain what is meant by 'socially constructed reality'.

5.3   Describe the role that *discourse* plays in critical theory.

The Use of Financial Statements for Decision Making

The major concern of this book is with accounting information for decision making, so financial statements provide a crucial ingredient to decision making due to the importance of shareholder value (as we saw in Chapter 2). Therefore, the concept of 'decision usefulness', i.e. the value of information for making decisions, while largely based on notions of cost (the recurrent theme in Part III), is also intertwined with the value of the business as perceived by shareholders and capital markets. Thus the focus of Part II is on understanding and interpreting financial statements. Our focus here is not so much on how investors use financial information to make investment decisions, but on how managers can interpret and use the expectations of shareholders and the financial information they have at hand to make decisions that contribute to improving shareholder value.

Chapter 6 describes the main financial statements (Income Statement, Balance Sheet, and Statement of Cash Flows) and the accruals basis of accounting and International Financial Reporting Standards (IFRS) that underpin them. Chapter 7 helps the reader to interpret the main financial statements using the tools of ratio analysis. Chapter 8 is concerned with accounting for inventory, which is a crucial link between financial accounting and management accounting. The introduction to financial accounting in these chapters is an important building block for an understanding of management accounting in Part III.

CHAPTER 6

Constructing Financial Statements: IFRS and the Framework of Accounting

The chapter begins with International Financial Reporting Standards (IFRS) and the *Framework for the Preparation and Presentation of Financial Statements* which sets out the concepts underlying the preparation and presentation of financial statements for external users. The chapter then introduces each of the principal financial statements: Statement of Comprehensive Income; Statement of Financial Position; and Statement of Cash Flows. It describes examples of the accruals or matching principle, which emphasizes prepayments, accruals, and provisions such as depreciation. The chapter then describes four important accounting treatments: sales taxes; goodwill; research and development; and leases. The chapter concludes with an introduction to agency theory and a critical perspective on financial statements and accounting standards.

As we saw in Chapter 1, accounting provides an account – an explanation or report in financial terms about the transactions of an organization. Accounting enables managers to satisfy the *stakeholders* in the organization (owners, government, financiers, suppliers, customers, employees, etc.) that they have acted in the best interests of stakeholders rather than themselves. We referred to this in Chapter 1 as *accountability*.

These explanations are provided to stakeholders through financial statements, often referred to as the company's 'accounts'. The main financial statements are: the Income Statement (previously called the Profit and Loss account); the Statement of Comprehensive Income (which is an extended Income

Statement); the Statement of Financial Position (previously, and still more commonly, called the Balance Sheet); and Statement of Cash Flows. The first two of these were introduced briefly in Chapter 3.

International Financial Reporting Standards (IFRS)

Accounting standards reflect the basic accounting principles that are generally accepted by the accounting profession (see Chapter 3) and which are an essential requirement under the Companies Act for reporting financial information. Historically, each country had its own set of accounting standards. The move towards the harmonization of accounting standards between countries through the work of the International Accounting Standards Board (IASB) has been a consequence of the globalization of capital markets, with the consequent need for accounting rules that can be understood by international investors. The dominance of multinational corporations and the desire of companies to be listed on multiple stock exchanges have led to the need to rationalize different reporting practices in different countries to enable comparisons between the financial statements of companies irrespective of national jurisdiction.

International Financial Reporting Standards (IFRS) are published by the IASB (2011), which has sole responsibility for setting accounting standards and comprises 14 individuals drawn from the accounting profession, industry, and academia. The predecessor of the IASB was the Board of the International Accounting Standards Committee (IASC) which published International Accounting Standards (IAS), some of which still exist. The term International Financial Reporting Standards (IFRS) includes both the newer IFRS and the older IAS, together with Interpretations issued under these standards.

IFRS set out recognition, measurement, presentation, and disclosure requirements dealing with transactions and events that are important in general-purpose financial statements, although some standards refer to specific industries. General-purpose financial statements are directed towards the common information needs of a wide range of users. A full list of IFRS is contained in the Appendix to this chapter.

In the UK, the Financial Reporting Council (FRC) is the independent regulator responsible for promoting high-quality corporate governance and reporting to foster investment. The FRC promotes high standards of corporate governance through the UK Corporate Governance Code (see Chapter 2), sets standards for corporate reporting, and monitors and enforces accounting and auditing standards. The Conduct Committee and the Monitoring Committee of the FRC carry out the functions of reviewing company accounts for compliance with the law and accounting standards, and monitoring audit firms.

The Financial Reporting Council assumed responsibility for UK accounting standards in 2012. A Codes and Standards Committee was established to advise the FRC Board on maintaining an effective framework of UK codes and standards. At the same time, the Accounting Council replaced the Accounting Standards Board (ASB), assuming an advisory role to the Codes & Standards Committee and the FRC Board.

Accounting standards developed by the FRC or, previously, by the ASB are contained in UK 'Financial Reporting Standards' (FRSs). The ASB adopted the standards issued by the Accounting Standards Committee (ASC) when the ASB took over the work of the ASC in 1990, so all standards fall within the legal definition of accounting standards. These earlier standards are designated 'Statements of Standard Accounting Practice' (SSAPs). Whilst some of the SSAPs have been superseded by FRSs, some remain in force. A full list of the current (at the time of writing) FRSs is included in the Appendix to this chapter.

Since 2005, the European Union has mandated that all companies are required to prepare their consolidated financial statements ('consolidated' financial statements apply to a group of companies with common ownership) in accordance with IFRS. Almost all other groups and companies have a choice between following IFRSs or UK Generally Accepted Accounting Principles (GAAP). Small companies (as defined by legislation) have an additional option of following the Financial Reporting Standard for Smaller Entities (FRSSE).

From 1 January 2015 a new financial reporting framework will be put in place for the UK. The FRC has published new accounting standards which together form the basis of the new UK approach. The revisions fundamentally reform financial reporting with three new Financial Reporting Standards (a fourth standard applies to insurance contracts). These are:

- FRS 100 – Application of Financial Reporting Requirements. This sets out the overall reporting framework;
- FRS 101 – Reduced Disclosure Framework. This permits disclosure exemptions from the requirements of EU-adopted IFRSs for certain qualifying entities;
- FRS 102 – The Financial Reporting Standard applicable in the UK and Republic of Ireland. This will ultimately replace all existing FRSs and SSAPs.

FRS 102 was released in March 2013 and replaces almost 3,000 pages of current UK GAAP with just over 300 pages. The main purpose of FRS 102 is to make reporting requirements proportionate to the size of the organization. The majority of large and medium-sized UK entities will in future apply FRS 102 when preparing their annual financial statements. More specifically, the new standard will apply to all entities that are neither required nor elect to apply EU-adopted IFRSs.

In the UK, accounting standards are said to be 'principles-based' rather than the 'rules-based' approach in the USA. The rules-based approach has been criticized following the failures of Enron and WorldCom. In the USA, the equivalent of IFRS is Generally Accepted Accounting Principles (GAAP). The IASB and the US Financial Accounting Standards Board (FASB) have been involved in a long-term convergence project which is continuing. PricewaterhouseCoopers (PwC) has produced a summary of similarities and differences between IFRS and GAAP which is beyond the scope of this text, but the summary is available online at http://www.pwc.com/en_US/us/issues/ifrs-reporting/publications/assets/ifrs-and-us-gaap-similarities-and-differences-2014.pdf. PwC emphasize 'the importance of being financially bilingual in the US capital markets' (p. 2) and that IFRS is increasingly relevant to many US businesses as they engage in cross-border mergers and acquisitions, report to their non-US stakeholders, and manage their overseas operations. The current status of the convergence project between IFRS and GAAP can be accessed from the IFRS website at http://www.ifrs.org/Use-around-the-world/Global-convergence/Convergence-with-US-GAAP/Pages/Convergence-with-US-GAAP.aspx.

Because IFRS remain the current (at the time of writing) international accounting standards, we will focus on these standards, although the differences between the new US GAAP and IFRS are not likely to be sufficiently different to concern readers of this book in their roles as non-financial managers interpreting and using financial information for decision making.

Framework for the Preparation and Presentation of Financial Statements

The IASB has produced a *Framework for the Preparation and Presentation of Financial Statements*. All IFRS are based on the *Framework* (IASB, 2011). A complete set of financial statements includes a:

- Statement of Financial Position (commonly called the Balance Sheet);
- Income Statement and/or Statement of Comprehensive Income;
- Statement of Changes in Equity (i.e. showing changes in shareholders' funds);
- Statement of Cash Flows;
- Explanatory Notes to the Financial Statements.

Information about financial position is primarily provided in the Statement of Financial Position. Information about performance is primarily provided in the Statement of Comprehensive Income. Information about changes in financial position is largely in the Statement of Cash Flows.

Users of financial statements are defined as:

- investors;
- employees;
- lenders;
- suppliers and trade creditors;
- customers;
- government and their agencies;
- the public.

Importantly, management is not defined as a user in terms of financial statements. This is because management has the ability to determine the form and content of additional information to meet its needs. The reporting of information to meet such needs is beyond the scope of the *Framework*. Part III of this book is concerned with the information needs of managers, although, as we will see in Chapter 7, the analysis and interpretation of financial performance trends and benchmarks through ratio analysis is important for managers in improving shareholder value.

The *Framework* sets out the concepts underlying the preparation and presentation of financial statements for external users. Where there is conflict between the requirements of a Standard and the *Framework*, the Standard prevails. The *Framework* is concerned with:

1. the objectives of financial statements;
2. the qualitative characteristics that determine decision usefulness;

3. the definition, recognition, and measurement of the elements from which financial statements are constructed;
4. concepts of capital maintenance.

Each of these is considered in turn.

Objectives of financial statements

The *Framework* states that the objective of financial statements is to provide information about the financial position, performance, and changes in financial position (i.e. cash flow) of an entity (the term 'entity' is used in accounting standards to refer to any form of business organization) that is useful to a wide range of users in making economic decisions (i.e. 'decision usefulness'). The financial statements show the results of the stewardship or accountability of management for the resources entrusted to them by shareholders.

FRS 102 in the UK has a similar view of the objective of financial statements: to provide information about the financial position, performance, and cash flows of an entity that is useful for economic decision making by a broad range of users who are not in a position to demand reports tailored to meet their particular information needs.

Qualitative characteristics of financial statements

The underlying assumptions of financial statements are that they are prepared on an accruals basis and as a going concern (see Chapter 3, but note that accruals accounting is covered later in this chapter). The following qualitative characteristics make the information useful to users. These are:

1. *Understandability:* users are assumed to have a reasonable knowledge of business and economic activities and accounting.
2. *Relevance:* information must be relevant to the decision-making needs of users. The relevance of information is affected by its nature and *materiality*. Information is material if its omission or misstatement could influence the economic decisions of users taken on the basis of financial statements.
3. *Reliability:* information is reliable when it is free from material error and bias and can be depended upon by users to *represent faithfully* that which it purports to represent. To be represented faithfully, it is necessary that transactions are accounted for and presented in accordance with their substance and economic reality and not merely their legal form, which may be contrived (this is called *'substance over form'* – see the case studies of Enron and WorldCom in Chapter 5). Information may lose its relevance and reliability if there is undue delay in reporting.
4. *Comparability:* users must be able to compare the financial statements of an entity through time and compare the financial statements of different entities in order to evaluate their relative financial position, performance, and changes in financial position. Measurement and presentation must therefore be consistent throughout an entity and over time (see 'Elements of financial statements' below). Importantly, users must be informed of the accounting policies employed in the preparation of financial statements, any

changes in those policies, and the effects of those changes (the principle of consistency, introduced in Chapter 3). However, it is not appropriate for an entity to leave its accounting policies unchanged when more relevant and reliable alternatives exist. The corresponding information for the preceding period is essential for comparability.

To this list, FRS 102 adds further qualitative characteristics: prudence, completeness, timeliness, and the balance between benefit and cost.

Elements of financial statements

Financial reports portray the financial effects of transactions by grouping them into broad classes according to their economic characteristics. These broad classes are the *elements* of financial statements. The elements related to the measurement of financial position in the Statement of Financial Position are assets, liabilities, and equity. The elements related to the measurement of performance in the Statement of Comprehensive Income are income and expenses.

Recognition is the process of incorporating in the Statement of Financial Position or Statement of Comprehensive Income an item that meets the definition of an element. Recognition depicts an item in words and a monetary amount and the inclusion of that figure in the Statement of Financial Position or Statement of Comprehensive Income totals. An item that meets the definition of an element should be recognized if:

- it is probable that any future economic benefit associated with the item will flow to or from the entity; and
- the item has a cost or value that can be measured with reliability.

An item that has the characteristics of an element but does not meet these criteria for recognition may warrant disclosure in a Note to the financial statements (see Chapter 7).

An asset is not recognized in the Statement of Financial Position when expenditure has been incurred for which it is considered improbable that economic benefits will flow to the entity beyond the current accounting period. This should be treated as an expense (see the WorldCom case study in Chapter 5).

A liability is recognized in the Statement of Financial Position when it is probable that an outflow of resources which have economic benefit will result from the settlement of a present obligation.

Measurement is the process of determining the monetary amounts at which the elements of the financial statements are to be recognized and carried in the Statement of Financial Position and Statement of Comprehensive Income. There are four bases of measurement:

- *Historical cost:* assets are recorded at the cash or fair value ('fair value' is defined below) consideration given at the time of their acquisition.
- *Current cost:* assets are carried at the cash amount that would have to be paid if the same or equivalent asset was acquired currently.

- *Realizable value:* assets are carried at the cash amount that could currently be obtained by selling the asset.
- *Present value:* assets are carried at the present discounted value of the future net cash inflows that the item is expected to generate (see Chapter 14 for a full explanation of present discounted value).

The most common measurement basis is historical cost. However:

- inventories are usually carried at the lower of cost or net realizable value (see Chapter 8);
- marketable investments are carried at market value;
- pension liabilities are carried at present value.

Concepts of capital maintenance

The *financial* concept of capital comprises invested money, being equal to net assets or the equity of a company. The *physical* concept of capital refers to the productive capacity of the business. The concept chosen indicates the goal to be attained in determining profit.

Capital maintenance provides the linkage between concepts of capital and profit because it provides the point of reference as to how profit is measured. Under *financial capital maintenance*, a profit is earned only if the financial amount of net assets at the end of a period exceeds the financial amount of net assets at the beginning of a period, excluding distributions to (i.e. dividends) and contributions from (i.e. share issues) shareholders. Under *physical capital maintenance*, a profit is earned only if the physical productive capacity of the business at the end of a period exceeds the physical productive capacity at the beginning of a period, after excluding distributions to and contributions from shareholders.

The physical capital maintenance concept requires the adoption of the current cost basis of measurement, which is not a requirement of financial capital maintenance. The principal difference between the two concepts is the treatment of changes in the prices of assets and liabilities. For the purposes of this book, we will assume that the concept of financial capital maintenance applies.

True and fair view

In addition to the need to comply with IFRS, the presentation of financial statements must comply with Chapter 4 of the Companies Act 2006, which requires the financial statements to represent a '*true and fair view*' of the state of affairs of the company and its profits. In the USA, the equivalent requirement is to '*present fairly*'. The Companies Act requires directors to state whether the accounts have been prepared in accordance with accounting standards and to explain any significant departures from those standards. For companies listed on the Stock Exchange, there are 'Listing Rules' that require the disclosure of additional information (see Chapter 2). Although the *Framework* does not deal directly with the need for a 'true and fair view', the application of the qualitative characteristics and the appropriate accounting standards normally results in financial statements that convey what is generally understood as a true and fair view.

The requirement for a true and fair view has never been tested at law, but it takes precedence over accounting standards. The notion of 'true and fair' is somewhat subjective and it can be argued that it encourages flexibility and can provide the potential to ignore accounting standards because of the 'true and fair view' override. The Financial Reporting Council has the power to seek revision of a company's financial statements where they do not comply with accounting standards and if necessary to seek a court order to ensure compliance.

We now turn to the first financial statement: the Statement of Comprehensive Income.

Reporting profitability: the Income Statement and Statement of Comprehensive Income

Businesses exist to make a profit. Thus, as we saw in Chapter 3, the basic accounting concept is that:

$$\textbf{profit} = \textbf{income} - \textbf{expenses}$$

If expenses exceed income, the result is a loss.

Profits are determined by the matching principle – *matching income earned with the expenses incurred in earning that income.* Income is the value of sales of goods or services produced by the business. The IFRS definition is that income is increases in economic benefits during the accounting period. Expenses are all the costs incurred in buying, making, or providing those goods or services and all the marketing and selling, production, logistics, human resource, information technology, financing, administration, and management costs involved in operating the business. Expenses are decreases in economic benefits during the accounting period.

The definition of income includes both revenue and gains. Revenue arises in the ordinary course of business (e.g. sales, fees, interest, dividends, royalties, and rent). This is often called turnover. Gains represent other items such as income from the disposal of assets or revaluations of investments. Gains are usually disclosed separately from revenue in the financial statements.

The definition of expenses includes those *expenses* that arise in the ordinary course of business (e.g. salaries, advertising, etc.) as well as losses. Losses represent other items such as those resulting from disasters such as fire and flood and following the disposal of assets or losses following changes in foreign exchange rates. Losses are usually disclosed separately from expenses in the financial statements.

In the past, some items were shown in financial statements as 'extraordinary' but this is no longer possible under IFRS. However, the results (revenue, expenses, profit or loss, and income tax) of any discontinued operations (e.g. where a part of the business is disposed of) are shown separately in the Income Statement.

In both financial accounting and management accounting, we distinguish gross profit and operating (or net) profit.

Gross profit is the difference between the selling *price* and the purchase (or production) *cost* of the goods or services sold. Using a simple example, a retailer selling baked beans may buy each tin for 5p and sell it for 9p. The gross profit is 4p per tin.

$$\textbf{gross profit = sales – cost of sales}$$

Gross margin is gross profit expressed as a percentage of sales. So in our baked beans example the gross margin is 44.4% (4p/9p).

The cost of sales is either:

- the cost of providing a service; or
- the cost of buying goods sold by a retailer; or
- the cost of raw materials and production costs for a product manufacturer.

However, not all the goods bought by a retailer or used in production will have been sold in the same period as the sales are made. The matching principle requires that the business adjusts for increases or decreases in *inventory* – the stock of goods bought or produced for resale but not yet sold (this is described in detail in Chapter 8). Therefore, the cost of sales in the financial statements is more properly described as the cost of goods *sold*, not the cost of goods *produced*. Because the production and sale of services are simultaneous, the cost of services produced always equals the cost of services sold (there is no such thing as an inventory of services).

Expenses deducted from gross profit will include all the other (selling, administration, finance, etc.) costs of the business (in the USA, the term commonly used is General and Administrative expenses, or G&A), that is those expenses not directly concerned with buying, making or providing goods or services, but supporting that activity:

$$\textbf{operating profit = gross profit – expenses}$$

The operating profit is one of the most significant figures because it represents the profit generated from the ordinary operations of the business. It is also called net profit, profit before interest and taxes (PBIT), or earnings before interest and taxes (EBIT).

As for gross margin, operating margin is operating (or net) profit expressed as a percentage of sales.

After interest and taxes are deducted, the amount remaining for shareholders is the *net profit after tax (NPAT)*. This is transferred to the Statement of Changes in Equity where other adjustments (including the payment of dividends) are made, before the final figure is transferred to shareholders' funds (or equity) in the Statement of Financial Position.

The distinction between cost of sales and expenses can vary between industries and organizations. A single retail store may treat only the product cost as the cost of sales, and salaries and rent as expenses. A large retail chain may include the salaries of staff and the store rental as cost of sales with expenses limited to purchasing, central warehousing, and head office costs. Many service businesses do not disclose cost of sales or gross profit figures as they are not required to do so. It is only in manufacturing where accounting standards dictate what costs should be included in the cost of production (see Chapter 11). For any particular business, it is important to determine the demarcation between cost of sales and expenses in order to be able to understand the gross profit calculation.

From operating profit, a company must pay *interest* to its lenders, and *income tax* to the government. The profit (or loss) of a business for a financial period (after income tax is deducted) is reported in a Statement of Comprehensive Income or Income Statement (known previously as a Profit and Loss Account, although this term – or P&L – is still in common usage).

Companies have two options in reporting comprehensive income:

- a single Statement of Comprehensive Income; or
- two statements, one an Income Statement, and the second a statement beginning with profit or loss and also showing the components of other comprehensive income.

The Income Statement (with which we are predominantly concerned) will typically appear as in Table 6.1.

Table 6.1   Income Statement.

Revenue	2,000,000
Less: cost of sales	1,500,000
Gross profit	500,000
Less: selling and administration expenses	400,000
Operating profit	100,000
Less: interest costs	16,000
Profit before income tax	84,000
Less: income tax	14,000
Net profit after tax	70,000

'Other comprehensive income' can best be explained by way of examples. It includes: foreign currency translation adjustments on investments in overseas subsidiaries; actuarial gains and losses arising from a defined benefit pension plan for employees; revaluations of property, plant, and equipment; and changes in the fair value of financial assets. (IFRS defines *fair value* as the amount for which an asset or liability could be exchanged between knowledgeable, willing parties in an arm's length transaction.) Many of the examples of other comprehensive income refer to movements in the price or valuation of something resulting in a change in measurement (measurement is one of the *Framework* elements) although some changes in price or valuation are included in the main Income Statement. This is quite a difficult concept, and is outside the scope of this book as it is not necessary for non-financial managers to understand this level of detail.

Chapter 3 explained that profit is transferred to equity – in a company this is called shareholders' funds – in the Statement of Financial Position (or Balance Sheet). From the company's after-tax profits, a *dividend* is usually paid to shareholders (for their share of the profits as they, unlike lenders, do not receive an interest rate for their investment). The *Statement of Changes in Equity* shows the profit from the Income Statement, other comprehensive income, and the payment of dividends out of profits. It also shows various other movements in shareholders' funds, including the issue of new shares, the purchase of a company's own shares and so on. In other words, it shows the change between the shareholders' funds from one year to the next. The Statement of Changes in Equity is shown in Table 6.2.

Table 6.2   Statement of Changes in Equity.

At beginning of year	**960,000**
Profit for the year	70,000
Other comprehensive income	0
Total comprehensive income	70,000
Less: dividend	30,000
At end of year	**1,000,000**

Reporting financial position: the Balance Sheet or Statement of Financial Position

Not all business transactions appear in the Statement of Comprehensive Income. The Statement of Financial Position (previously and still more commonly referred to as the Balance Sheet) shows the financial position of the business – its assets, liabilities and equity at the *end* of a financial period.

Some business payments are to acquire assets. The IFRS definition of an asset is a resource controlled by an entity as a result of past events and from which future economic benefits are expected to flow to the entity. An entity acquires assets to produce goods or services capable of satisfying customer needs. Physical form is not essential. Non-current assets (which used to be called fixed assets) are things that the business *owns* and uses as part of its infrastructure. There are two types of non-current assets: tangible and intangible. Tangible assets comprise those physical assets that can be seen and touched, such as buildings, machinery, vehicles, computers, etc. Intangible assets comprise non-physical assets such as the goodwill of a business (described later in this chapter) or its intellectual property, e.g. its ownership of patents and trademarks.

Current assets include money in the bank, Receivables (also called Debtors: the sales to customers on credit, but not yet received) and Inventory (the stock of goods bought or manufactured, but unsold). The word *current* in accounting means 12 months, so current assets are those that will change their form during the next year. They are part of *working capital* (see below). By contrast, non-current assets (see above) do not normally change their form in the ordinary course of business; as part of the business infrastructure they have a longer term role.

Sometimes assets are acquired or expenses incurred without paying for them immediately. In doing so, the business incurs liabilities. Liabilities are debts that the business *owes*. The IFRS definition of a liability is a present obligation of the entity arising from past events, the settlement of which is expected to result in an outflow from the entity of resources embodying economic benefits. Current liabilities include Payables (also called Creditors: purchases from suppliers on credit, but unpaid), loans due to be repaid, amounts due for taxes, etc. As for assets, the word current means that the liabilities will be repaid within 12 months. Current liabilities also form part of working capital.

Working capital (discussed in more detail in Chapter 7) comprises those current assets and current liabilities (Receivables, Payables, Inventory, Bank, etc.) that continually revolve in the business, i.e. Inventory purchases on credit increase Payables, which when due are paid out of the Bank account. The Bank account increases when customers pay what they owe (reducing Receivables) for the Inventory they purchased on credit.

Non-current liabilities include loans to finance the business that are repayable after 12 months, other amounts owing that are not current, and certain kinds of provisions (see later in this chapter). Equity (or shareholders' funds, both of which are commonly referred to as 'capital') is a particular kind of liability, as it is the money invested by the owners in the business. As we saw in Chapter 3, equity is increased by the retained profits of the business (the profit after paying interest and income tax) and reduced by payment of dividends, as was described above for the Statement of Changes in Equity. Equity is defined by IFRS as the residual interest (of owners/shareholders) in the assets of the entity after deducting all its liabilities.

The Statement of Financial Position will typically appear as in Table 6.3. In the Statement of Financial Position, Net assets is the difference between total assets and total liabilities, which must 'balance' with the total of equity. This is called the accounting equation, which can be shown in a number of different ways:

$$\textbf{net assets} = \textbf{total assets} - \textbf{total liabilities} \ (\textit{as shown in a Statement of Financial Position,}$$
$$\textit{equal to equity})$$

$$\textbf{total assets} = \textbf{liabilities} + \textbf{equity} \ \left(\textit{reflecting the total capital employed in a business, see Chapter 7}\right)$$

or

$$\textbf{assets} - \textbf{liabilities} = \textbf{equity} \ (\textit{reflecting the shareholders' investment in the business})$$

Importantly, the equity of the business does *not* represent the value of the business. It represents the funds initially invested by owners (or the shareholders in a company) plus the retained profits (after payment of taxes and dividends). In Table 6.3, equity represents the initial investment and retained earnings, which is calculated in the Statement of Changes in Equity in Table 6.2.

IAS1 is the standard concerned with the Presentation of Financial Statements. However, IAS1 does not prescribe either the order or format in which items are presented in the Statement of Financial Position. The size, nature, or function of an item or the degree to which items are aggregated and the actual terminology used in the Statement of Financial Position therefore varies somewhat between companies. The key requirement under IFRS is that the presentation must be relevant to understanding a company's financial position.

Table 6.3   Statement of Financial Position.

Assets	
Non-current assets	
Property, plant & equipment	<u>1,150,000</u>
Current assets	
Receivables	300,000
Inventory	<u>200,000</u>
	500,000
Total assets	<u>1,650,000</u>
Liabilities	
Non-current liabilities	
Long-term loans	<u>300,000</u>
Current liabilities	
Payables	300,000
Bank overdraft	<u>50,000</u>
	350,000
Total liabilities	650,000
Net assets	<u>1,000,000</u>
Equity	
Share capital	900,000
Retained earnings	<u>100,000</u>
Total equity	<u>1,000,000</u>

We can now consider some of the specific accounting treatments which lead to how amounts are shown in the Income Statement and Statement of Financial Position.

The matching principle and accruals accounting

An important principle that is particularly relevant to the interpretation of accounting reports is the matching principle. The matching (or accruals) principle recognizes income when it is *earned* and recognizes expenses when they are *incurred*.

Income is earned when a sale of goods or services takes place, typically evidenced by an invoice (where the sale is on credit) or payment by a customer (for a cash sale). Expenses are incurred when a good or service is received and a debt is due to the supplier of the goods or services, again evidenced by the supplier's invoice (for a purchase on credit) or by a payment of cash.

While cash accounting (recognizing only what is received into and paid out of a business bank account) may be used by very small businesses, *accrual accounting* is the method of accounting used by businesses which make sales and/or purchases using credit, where the timing of the receipt or payment of cash is earlier or later than when the business *earns* income or *incurs* expenses (as described above). The accruals method provides a more meaningful picture of the financial performance of a business from year to year.

Accruals accounting recognizes Receivables (a current asset, being sales on credit not yet paid for by customers), Inventory (a current asset, stock purchased or made but not yet sold), and Payables (a current liability, payments due to suppliers for goods and services purchased on credit) and also makes adjustments for other timing differences:

* prepayments;
* accruals; and
* provisions.

The matching principle requires that certain cash payments made in advance are treated as prepayments, i.e. made in advance of when they are treated as an expense for profit purposes. Other expenses are treated as expenses for profit purposes even though no cash payment has yet been made. This is called an accrual.

A good example of a prepayment is insurance, which is paid 12 months in advance. Assume that a business which has a financial year ending 31 March pays its 12-month insurance premium of €12,000 in advance on 1 January. At its year end, the business will only treat €3,000 (3/12 of €12,000) as an expense and will treat the remaining €9,000 as a prepayment (a current asset in the Statement of Financial Position).

A good example of an accrual is electricity, which like most utilities is paid (often quarterly) in arrears. If the same business usually receives its electricity bill in May (covering the period March to May) it will need to accrue an expense for the month of March, even if the bill has not yet been received. If the prior year's bill was €2,400 for the same quarter (allowing for seasonal fluctuations in usage) then the business will accrue €800 (1/3 of €2,400).

The effect of prepayments and accruals on profit, the Statement of Financial Position and cash flow is shown in Table 6.4.

A further example of the matching principle is in the creation of provisions. Provisions are estimates of possible liabilities that may arise, but where there is uncertainty as to the timing or the amount of money. Some provisions are shown as a liability in the Statement of Financial Position. An example of a possible future liability is a provision for warranty claims that may be payable in relation to the sales of products. The estimate will be based on the likely costs to be incurred in the future, based on past experience.

Table 6.4   Prepayments and accruals.

	Effect on profit in Income Statement	Effect on Statement of Financial Position	Effect on Cash flow
Prepayment	Expense of €3,000	Prepayment (current asset) of €9,000	Cash outflow of €12,000
Accrual	Expense of €800	Accrual (current liability) of €800	No cash flow until quarterly bill received and paid

Other types of provisions are reductions in asset values such that only the net asset value is shown on the face of the Statement of Financial Position, with the gross asset value and the provision being shown in the Notes to Financial Statements. The main examples of provisions are:

- *Doubtful debts:* customers may experience difficulty in paying their accounts and a provision may be made based on past experience that a proportion of those customers will never pay. This provision is deducted from the current asset Receivables and treated as an expense called Doubtful Debts in the Income Statement.
- *Inventory:* some stock may be obsolete but still held in the store. A provision reduces the value of the obsolete stock to its sale or scrap value (if any). This provision is deducted from the current asset Inventory and is treated as an expense Obsolete Stock in the Income Statement.
- *Depreciation:* this is a charge against profits, intended to write off the value of each non-current asset over its useful life. This provision is deducted from each type of non-current asset and treated as a Depreciation expense in the Income Statement.

The most important provision, because it typically involves a large cost, is for depreciation.

Depreciation

Non-current assets are capitalized in the Statement of Financial Position so that the purchase of non-current assets does not affect profit. Depreciation is an expense that spreads the cost of the asset over its useful life. The following example illustrates the matching principle in relation to depreciation.

A non-current asset costs €100,000. It is expected to have a life of four years and have a resale (e.g. trade-in) value of €20,000 at the end of that time. The depreciation charge is:

$$\frac{asset\ cost - resale\ value}{expected\ life} = \frac{100,000 - 20,000}{4} = 20,000 \text{p.a.}$$

It is important to recognize that the cash outflow of €100,000 occurs when the asset is bought. The depreciation charge of €20,000 per annum is a *non-cash expense* each year (there is no payment out of the bank account for depreciation). However, the value of the asset in the Statement of Financial Position reduces each year as a result of the depreciation charge, as Table 6.5 shows. The asset can be depreciated to a nil value in the Statement of Financial Position even though it is still in use. If the asset is sold, any profit or loss on sale is treated as a separate item in the Income Statement. While buildings may be depreciated, land is never depreciated.

Non-current assets may be measured at their historical cost or revalued. Historical cost, while commonly used, results in a potentially misleading picture as to the value of non-current assets. Revaluation provides more relevant information to users of the financial statements than the asset's historical cost. Under accounting standards, revaluing tangible non-current assets remains optional. However, the

Table 6.5   Effect of depreciation charges on Statement of Financial Position.

	Original asset cost €	Provision for Depreciation €	Net value in Statement of Financial Position €
End of year 1	100,000	20,000	80,000
End of year 2	100,000	40,000	60,000
End of year 3	100,000	60,000	40,000
End of year 4	100,000	80,000	20,000
End of year 5	100,000	100,000	Nil

standards require that where a policy of revaluation is adopted, it must be applied to a whole class of assets (not individual assets) and the valuations must be kept up to date through regular independent valuations. This ensures consistency in the treatment of similar assets from year to year.

A type of depreciation used for intangible assets, such as goodwill (see later in this chapter) or lease-hold property improvements, is called amortization, which has the same meaning and is calculated in the same way as depreciation. However, intangible assets and securities may also be valued at fair value. *Fair value* is a measure of market value, defined as the value which would be agreed between knowledgeable and willing buyers and sellers in arm's-length transactions. This is a subjective judgement as no transaction has actually taken place. The dramatic falls in the value of many financial assets following the global financial crisis has called the fair value method into question.

In reporting profits, some companies show the profit before depreciation (or amortization) is deducted, because it can be a substantial cost, but one that does not result in any cash flow. A variation of EBIT (see earlier in this chapter) is EBITDA: earnings before interest, taxes, depreciation, and amortization. This is often an important figure used in assessing business units or managers, who have little or no control over interest, tax, or depreciation expenses.

Specific IFRS accounting treatments

The full list of IFRS and their predecessor IAS is contained in the Appendix to this chapter, along with a list of UK FRSs. Many relate to specific accounting treatments or specific industries that are beyond the scope of this book. However, some important standards are as follows:

- IAS1 *Presentation of Financial Statements* requires that an entity whose financial statements comply with IFRS must make an explicit and unreserved statement of compliance in the Notes to the financial statements. The impact of changed accounting policies must also be shown in the financial statements.
- IFRS2 *Share Based Payment*: companies have increasingly used grants of shares through share options, and share ownership plans to employees. Previously, these were not reflected in financial

statements until such time as the option was exercised. There has been much criticism of this accounting treatment by shareholders. The Standard now requires an entity to reflect in its Statement of Comprehensive Income the effects of share-based payment transactions based on the fair value of the equity instruments granted, measured at the date of the grant. Some companies changed their employee share schemes as a result of this standard.

- IAS2 *Inventory*: stock is valued at the lower of cost and net realizable (i.e. sales proceeds less costs of sale). The cost of inventory includes all costs of purchase, costs of conversion, and other costs incurred in bringing the inventory to its present location and condition. Costs of purchase include import duties and transport, less any discounts or rebates. Accounting for Inventory is covered in detail in Chapter 8. Costs of conversion include direct labour and a systematic allocation of fixed and variable production overheads (this is covered in detail in Chapters 11 through 13).
- IAS11 *Construction Contracts*: how profits generated over long-term constructions are brought into the financial statements is covered briefly in Chapter 8.
- IAS16 *Property, Plant & Equipment*: assets are valued at either cost less accumulated depreciation or are regularly revalued independently (explained above).
- IAS17 *Leases*: requires accounting for most non-rental leases as though they were owned and depreciated by the lessee. Lease accounting is described later in this chapter.
- IAS19 *Employee Benefits*: from time to time, stock market losses have resulted in defined pension fund liabilities (to pay pensions for retired employees) exceeding their assets. Where this occurs, companies must recognize the liability for any deficit in their pension funds in their financial statements. A result of this Standard has been to close many defined benefit pension schemes and replace them with accumulation schemes.
- IAS36 *Impairment of Assets*: impairment refers to the reduction in value of an intangible asset such as goodwill (see later in this chapter for an example of goodwill and impairment).
- IAS37 *Provisions, Contingent Liabilities and Contingent Assets*: a provision is a liability of uncertain timing or amount. Examples include warranty obligations (explained above). The amount recognized as a provision is the best estimate of the expenditure required to settle the obligation.
- IAS38 *Intangible Assets*: internally generated goodwill, brands, customer lists, etc. are not recognized as assets. Intangible assets can only arise when they are purchased (see later in this chapter for examples of goodwill and research and development).

There are also standards relating to accounting for hedging and changes in foreign exchange (IAS21) and financial instruments (IAS39) but these are outside the scope of this book.

Four accounting treatments are important for managers to understand and each is treated in turn:

- accounting for sales taxes;
- accounting for goodwill and impairment testing;
- accounting for research and development expenditure;
- accounting for leases.

Accounting for sales taxes

Sales taxes are taxes added to the sale price of goods and services. These taxes are remitted to taxation authorities, after deducting sales taxes on purchased goods and services. In the UK Value Added Tax (or VAT) is not shown in most financial statements (although an exception is in some retail businesses). VAT is added to sales by businesses selling goods and services. When businesses purchase goods and services, they have to pay VAT. The business must remit the difference between the VAT it recovers from customers and the VAT it pays its suppliers to the tax authorities. As a transaction, the receipts (from sales) equal the payments (to suppliers and to the tax authorities) and hence these are not shown in the Income Statement although the unremitted liability to the taxation authorities appears in the Statement of Financial Position as a current liability. In retail businesses, where VAT is more complex (as some retail transactions are exempt from VAT), the VAT-inclusive and VAT-exclusive turnover may both be shown in the Income Statement.

Accounting for goodwill and impairment testing

Goodwill is an intangible asset. It arises where a company buys a business and pays more than the fair value of the tangible assets. Goodwill represents the value of brands, customer lists, location, reputation, etc. and is reflected in an expectation of future profits and cash flows. Goodwill cannot be created on a Statement of Financial Position from internally generated sources, but only arises on the acquisition of another business. Goodwill is amortized (amortization is the same principle as depreciation, but the term is used in relation to intangible assets) over a maximum of 20 years.

IAS36 requires intangibles like goodwill to be subject to an impairment test. Impairment involves the annual assessment of the recoverable amount of an asset. The *recoverable amount* is the higher of its fair value less costs to sell, and the value in use, i.e. the present value of future cash flows (see Chapter 14 for the calculation of present value of future cash flows). An increase in the amortization provision would need to be made (reducing the net goodwill carried in the Statement of Financial Position) if future cash flows were unable to justify the existing carrying value.

Example of goodwill

Negotiations are completed for the acquisition of a business for €1 million. The fair value of tangible assets purchased is €700,000. The goodwill is therefore €300,000 and the acquiring business decides to amortize the goodwill over 10 years. The annual amortization cost is therefore €30,000. At year end, the Statement of Financial Position will show:

Intangible asset goodwill	€300,000
Less provision for amortization	30,000
	€270,000

The €30,000 annual charge will need to be reassessed annually to determine if the goodwill has been impaired. This is called an annual impairment test. As most businesses are bought on a price/earnings multiple (or P/E ratio, covered in Chapter 7) based on discounted future cash flows, the annual impairment test essentially repeats the exercise each year to determine whether the goodwill carried is excessive.

Although the detailed method of calculating impairment is beyond the scope of this book, a simple example would be a case where, at year end, the impairment test results in a maximum goodwill figure of €250,000, in which case the company would need to increase its provision for amortization to €50,000, and the net goodwill in its Statement of Financial Position would reduce to €250,000.

In Chapter 5, we described the case study of Royal Bank of Scotland. That bank would have placed a significant value on goodwill following its acquisition of ABN Amro, but following the bank's failure, that goodwill value would have been significantly impaired and written down in the Statement of Financial Position.

Accounting for research and development expenditure

In companies that invest heavily in research and development (e.g. pharmaceuticals), expenditure on research is recognized as an expense although expenditure on development may be recognized as an asset provided specific criteria can be satisfied. Examples of *research* include activities aimed at gaining new knowledge and the search for, evaluation, and selection of alternative materials, products, processes, services, and so on. Examples of *development* include design, construction, and testing of prototypes; design of tooling, moulds, and dies; design, construction, and operation of a pilot plant; and the design, construction, and testing of a selected alternative for improved materials, products, processes, and services. Whilst research is expensed as it is incurred because any future cash flows are less certain, development may be capitalized and amortized over a number of years in line with expectations of future cash flows. However, as for goodwill, an annual impairment test needs to be carried out.

Accounting for leases

Leasing arose as a method of finance for equipment used by business organizations, in which a business needing equipment (the lessee) 'rented' that equipment from a financial institution (the lessor) which in turn paid the supplier for the equipment. The lessee pays a fixed monthly sum over a number of years to the lessor in payment of the debt. Many businesses finance at least some of their tangible non-current assets through leasing facilities.

There are two types of leases: operating and finance. Under an operating lease, all the risks and rewards are with the lessor, so lease payments are no more than rental payments. In the case of finance leases, the substance and economic reality are that the lessee acquires the economic benefits of the use of the leased asset for the major part of its useful life in return for entering into an obligation to pay an amount, usually in instalments, approximating the fair value of the asset and the interest cost.

Accounting standards require lessees to capitalize material finance leases because the transaction is considered to be the economic equivalent of borrowing to acquire an asset; accordingly, the lessee records the asset and the liability to pay lease rentals in its Statement of Financial Position.

The lessee capitalizes the fair value of the asset, or the present value of the minimum lease payments (described in Chapter 14), as the cost of the non-current asset and this same amount (the total of the future lease payments) is recorded as the liability (some of which will be current and some non-current). The leased asset has to be depreciated over the shorter of the period of the lease or the useful life of the asset, as though it were owned. Depreciation expense appears in the Income Statement and reduces the Statement of Financial Position asset value through a provision for depreciation as though the leased asset were owned. As for other assets, there needs to be an annual impairment test.

Lease payments owing are shown as a (current and/or non-current) liability in the Statement of Financial Position. The periodic (usual monthly) lease payment is not simply a revenue expense but represents both the repayment of the capital element of the loan and also the interest charge on the loan. The interest on the lease is treated as an expense to give a constant periodic return on the balance of the outstanding loan.

Operating lease payments, where risk and rewards are maintained by the lessor (the most common example is the company motor vehicle) are treated as an expense and are not capitalized in the Statement of Financial Position, although a disclosure of the lease liability must be made in the Notes to the financial statements.

Apart from the Income Statement and Statement of Financial Position, the third very important financial statement is the Statement of Cash Flows.

Reporting cash flow: the Statement of Cash Flows

The Statement of Cash Flows shows the movement in cash for the business during a financial period. It includes:

- cash flows from operations (profit adjusted by non-cash expenses and movements in working capital);
- cash flows from investing (purchase and sale of non-current assets);
- cash flow from financing (borrowings and repayment of debt; new share issues and purchase of a company's own shares);

The cash flow from operations differs from the operating profit because of:

- depreciation, and
- increases (or decreases) in working capital.

Depreciation is a non-cash expense (there is no payment after the initial asset is purchased) and because it has already been included as an expense in the Income Statement (and so has already reduced profit), it must be added back to profit to show the cash flow from operations.

Changes in working capital (e.g. changes in Receivables, Inventory, Prepayments, Payables, and Accruals) increase or decrease cash flow from operations. If Receivables or Inventory increase, some of the income *earned* has not yet turned into cash, so the cash flow from operations must be reduced. Likewise, if Payables increase, the costs of buying Inventory or expenses which have been incurred but not yet paid out increase the cash flow from operations.

IFRS allow two different presentation formats for showing cash flow from operations in the Statement of Cash Flows:

- the direct method, disclosing major classes of gross cash receipts and payments; and
- the indirect method, whereby profit or loss is adjusted for the effect of non-cash transactions.

In this book, we will only show the indirect method as it is more commonly used in practice and more clearly shows the link between the profit or loss in the Statement of Comprehensive Income and the Statement of Cash Flows.

An example of a Statement of Cash Flows using the indirect method is shown in Table 6.6.

Table 6.6   Statement of Cash Flows.

Cash flows from operating activities	
Profit before tax	100,000
Plus Depreciation	20,000
	120,000
Movement in inventories	−10,000
Movement in receivables	−15,000
Movement in payables	20,000
Cash generated from operations	**115,000**
Income tax paid	−12,000
Net cash flows from operating activities	**103,000**
Cash flows from investing activities	
Purchase of plant & equipment	−100,000
Cash flows from financing activities	
Additional borrowing	50,000
Interest paid	−16,000
Dividends paid	−25,000
Net cash flows from financing activities	9,000
Net increase in cash and cash equivalents	12,000
Opening cash and cash equivalents	−62,000
Closing cash and cash equivalents	−50,000

In the Statement of Cash Flows, *cash equivalents* are short-term, highly liquid investments that are readily convertible to known amounts of cash and which are subject to an insignificant risk of changes in value. Cash equivalents are held for the purpose of meeting short-term cash commitments rather than for investment or other purposes and include cash at bank and bank overdrafts (monies owing to a bank in a bank account where payments exceed receipts) that are an integral part of an entity's cash management.

IFRS does not specify where cash flows from interest or dividends received or paid should be shown in the Statement of Cash Flows, and so each company must decide whether to classify interest and dividends paid as either operating or financing activities; and interest and dividends received as either operating or investing activities. In reading the Statement of Cash Flows, it is important to note that the amounts shown for taxation, interest, and dividend payments are not the same as the amounts shown in the Income Statement because of timing differences between when those items are treated as expenses and when the cash payment is made, which is normally after the end of the financial year.

Differences between the financial statements

The Income Statement shows the profit (or loss) of a business for a financial year, using the accruals method by which income earned is matched with expenses incurred in earning that income, irrespective of the timing of receipts from sales and payment of expenses.

The Statement of Cash Flows shows the movements in and out of the company's bank account (or cash equivalents) during a financial year. This is split into three sections: cash flows from operations; cash flows from investing activities; and cash flows from financing activities.

Cash flows from operations in the Statement of Cash Flows are not the same as profit. First, non-cash items such as depreciation are added back to profit. Second, working capital changes increase or decrease the cash flows from operations (increases in Receivables or Inventory reduce cash flows, while increases in Payables increase cash flows).

Other items in the Statement of Cash Flows do not appear in the Income Statement at all. The major items are: capital expenditure or the disposal of non-current assets (cash flows from investing); borrowings and repayments of debt; and changes in shareholders' equity (cash flows from financing) – all of which affect cash flow, but not profit.

The Statement of Financial Position shows the assets, liabilities, and equity on the last day of the financial year. The Statement of Cash Flows reflects the movements between the Statement of Financial Position at the beginning and end of the financial year, while the Income Statement and the Statement of Comprehensive Income and the Statement of Changes in Equity show the movement in equity between the beginning and end of the financial year.

Illustration

The following illustration shows how several typical transactions influence the three main financial statements.

ABC Ltd buys a new computer system for $150,000 on the first day of the financial year and on the same day borrows $100,000 to do so. XYZ depreciates its computers at the rate of 20% per annum. During the year $10,000 of the loan was repaid together with $1,000 interest.

Prepare a simple Income Statement, Statement of Financial Position, and Statement of Cash Flows to show how each of these transactions would appear.

The double entry (see Chapter 3) is carried out using Table 6.7, which is then used to construct the financial statements which are shown in Table 6.8.

Table 6.7   Double entry for transactions.

	Non-current asset	Non-current liability	Bank account	Expense
Purchase of computer system	+150,000		−150,000	
Borrowing		+100,000	+100,000	
Depreciation 20% of $150,000	−30,000			+30,000
Repayment of loan		−10,000	−10,000	
Interest on loan			−1,000	+1,000
Total	120,000	90,000	61,000	31,000

Table 6.8   Effect of transactions on financial statements.

Income Statement:	
Depreciation expense	$30,000
Interest cost	$1,000
Loss (total expense)	$31,000
Statement of Financial Position:	
Non-current asset $150,000 less depreciation $30,000 Net	$120,000
Liability $100,000 less repayment $10,000 balance	−$90,000
Bank overdraft balance (see below)	−$61,000
Net assets	−$31,000
Equity (loss, see above)	−$31,000
Statement of Cash Flows:	
Loss	−$31,000
Add back depreciation	$30,000
Cash flow from operations	−$1,000
Cash flow from investing activities	
Cash paid for purchase of asset	−$150,000
Cash flow from financing activities	
Borrowing	+$100,000
Repayment	−$10,000
Reduction in bank balance	−$61,000

It is very important to understand the differences between these three financial statements as they each tell the user something different. However, a fuller understanding can only be gained by looking at the three statements together, which provides a more holistic understanding. Interpreting these financial statements is the subject of Chapter 7.

A theoretical perspective on financial statements

A necessary ingredient for shareholder value (see Chapter 2), given the separation of ownership from control in most large business organizations, is the control of what managers actually do. Control is considered in the rational-economic paradigm (see Chapter 4) through the notion of *contract*, in which the role of control is to measure and reward performance such that there will be greater *goal congruence*, i.e. that individuals pursuing their own self-interest will also pursue the collective organizational interest.

There are two main versions of contractual theory: agency theory and transaction cost economics. Agency theory sees the economy as a network of interlocking contracts. The transaction cost approach sees the economy as a mixture of markets, hierarchies, and networks (transaction cost economics is discussed further in Chapter 15).

Agency theory

Agency theory is concerned with contractual relationships within the firm, between a *principal* (shareholders) and an *agent* (directors and managers), whose rights and duties are specified by a real or notional contract of employment. This theory recognizes the behaviour of an agent, whose actions the management control and accounting system seeks to influence and control. Both principals and agents are assumed to be rational-economic persons motivated solely by self-interest, although they may differ with respect to their preferences, beliefs, and the information that is available to them.

The principal wishes to influence what the agent does, but delegates tasks to the agent in an uncertain environment. The agent expends effort in the performance of these tasks. The outcome of the agent's efforts depends on both environmental factors and the effort expended by the agent. Under the *sharing rule*, the agent usually receives a reward, being a share of the outcome (typically a bonus, share options, and so on). The reward will depend on the information system used to measure the outcome. Consequently, financial statements play an important role in regulating the actions of agents, who may be tempted to report profits so as to maximize their own remuneration. The assumption of agency theory is that the agent obtains utility (a benefit) from the reward but disutility from expending effort.

The agency model involves seeking an employment contract that specifies the sharing rule and the information system. An accounting system can provide output measures from which an agent's efforts can be inferred, but the measures may not accurately reflect the effort expended. This leads to uncertainty about the relationship between the accounting measure and the agent's effort. If the principal cannot observe the agent's effort, or infer it from measured output, the agent may have an incentive to act in a manner different from the employment contract and this is called *moral hazard*. A principal who can observe the agent's effort but does not have access to all the information held by the agent does not know whether the effort expended has been based on the agent's information or whether the agent has 'shirked'. This is called *adverse selection*.

Moral hazard and adverse selection are both a consequence of *information asymmetry*. This happens because principal and agent have different amounts of information. Although both principals and agents will have access to financial statements, only managers will have access to the vastly more comprehensive management accounting information available within the organization. A function of accounting under agency theory is to improve efficiency by minimizing the losses caused through moral hazard and adverse selection.

We see simple examples of agency transactions, for example in buying or renting real estate, in booking travel through a travel agent, or using an insurance broker. When we apply the same principle to organizations, agency theory becomes more complex because there are multiple principals (rather than a single shareholder) and multiple agents (the board may be unified but is composed of individuals, including the chief executive officer). Agency theory ignores the effect of capital markets by assuming a single owner rather than a group of owners. The model also focuses on single-period behaviour rather than the longer term. Many individuals violate the assumptions of rational self-interested behaviour because of their norms and values, and in the agency perspective there is no regard given to power, trust, ethical issues, or equity (see Chapter 5), all of which may affect behaviour. We consider some alternative theories to agency in the next chapter.

A critical perspective on financial statements and accounting standards

There have been various criticisms of accounting standards including:

- The almost continual introduction of new and amended standards, making comparisons over longer time periods difficult.
- Standards that fail to consider practical implementation issues, e.g. the impact of pension fund accounting (IAS19) and accounting for stock options (IFRS2).
- 'International' standards that do not yet incorporate the USA.
- Divergence between IFRS and the UK's implementation of UK GAAP from 2015.
- Lobbying which may influence the development of standards (there is evidence from the USA of lobbyists attempting to influence standard setters – see the case study of Enron in Chapter 5).
- The absence of any explicit statement in IFRS about the relationship between the legal requirement for a 'true and fair view' and compliance with accounting standards.
- The potential for standards to lead to more creative accounting or earnings management (see Chapter 5) through a focus on presentation rather than the underlying business reality (i.e. form over substance).
- Standards having a narrow accounting focus rather than being inclusive of non-financial performance and broader accountability issues such as social and environmental reporting (see Chapter 7 for a discussion of these issues).

Perhaps the biggest criticism of financial statements is that the ever-increasing complexity of accounting standards has made financial statements so much more difficult to understand, even for accountants themselves, who increasingly rely on the expertise of auditors to advise them in terms of detailed presentational aspects of accounting standards compliance. Stock market analysts often discount financial statements and use supplementary sources of data to make judgements about company performance and prospects. The absence of comparisons to plan (even though financial statements make comparison to prior years) also limits the usability of financial statements, which are rarely available publicly earlier than two months after the end of each financial year. Perhaps most importantly, financial statements reinforce the dominant stock market focus on short-term profits rather than the longer term sustainability of performance.

Conclusion

This chapter has covered the three main financial statements: Income Statement, Statement of Financial Position, and Statement of Cash Flows. It has introduced International Financial Reporting Standards (IFRS) and the *Framework for the Preparation and Presentation of Financial Statements*, and the UKs introduction of a new GAAP from 2015. The principles of accrual accounting (including prepayments, accruals, and depreciation) as well as accounting for sales tax, goodwill, research and development, and leases have all been covered. The chapter concluded with an introduction to what has been historically one of the main theories underlying the construction of financial statements, agency theory, and has provided a brief critique of financial statements and accounting standards. In the next chapter, we introduce the tools and techniques that are used to interpret financial statements and consider some alternative theoretical perspectives.

Reference

International Accounting Standards Board (2011). *International Financial Reporting Standards IFRSs 2011 version*. Bound Volume. London: IASB.

Websites

The website of the International Accounting Standards Board is http://www.ifrs.org/Home.htm.
The website of the Financial Reporting Council in the UK is http://www.frc.org.uk/.

Appendix to Chapter 6: List of International Financial Reporting Standards (IFRS) as at January 2015

Source: http://www.iasplus.com/en/standards

IFRS

IFRS 1: First-time Adoption of International Financial Reporting Standards
IFRS 2: Share-based Payment
IFRS 3: Business Combinations
IFRS 4: Insurance Contracts
IFRS 5: Non-current Assets Held for Sale and Discontinued Operations
IFRS 6: Exploration for and Evaluation of Mineral Assets
IFRS 7: Financial Instruments: Disclosures
IFRS 8: Operating Segments
IFRS 9: Financial Instruments
IFRS 10: Consolidated Financial Statements
IFRS 11: Joint Arrangements
IFRS 12: Disclosure of Interests in Other Entities
IFRS 13: Fair Value Measurement
IFRS 14: Regulatory Deferral Accounts
IFRS 15: Revenue from Contracts with Customers

IAS

IAS 1: Presentation of Financial Statements
IAS 2: Inventories
IAS 7: Statement of Cash Flows
IAS 8: Accounting Policies, Changes in Accounting Estimates and Errors
IAS 10: Events After the Reporting Period
IAS 11: Construction Contracts
IAS 12: Income Taxes
IAS 16: Property, Plant and Equipment
IAS 17: Leases
IAS 18: Revenue
IAS 19: Employee Benefits
IAS 20: Accounting for Government Grants and Disclosure of Government Assistance
IAS 21: The Effects of Changes in Foreign Exchange Rates
IAA 23: Borrowing Costs
IAS 24: Related Party Disclosures
IAS 26: Accounting and Reporting by Retirement Benefit Plans
IAS 27: Consolidated and Separate Financial Statements
IAS 28: Investments in Associates

IAS 29: Financial Reporting in Hyperinflationary Economies
IAS 31: Interests In Joint Ventures
IAS 32: Financial Instruments: Presentation
IAS 33: Earnings Per Share
IAS 34: Interim Financial Reporting
IAS 36: Impairment of Assets
IAS 37: Provisions, Contingent Liabilities and Contingent Assets
IAS 38: Intangible Assets
IAS 39: Financial Instruments: Recognition and Measurement
IAS 40: Investment Property
IAS 41: Agriculture

UK Financial Reporting Standards as at January 2015

Source: https://www.frc.org.uk/Our-Work/Codes-Standards/Accounting-and-Reporting-Policy/Standards-in-Issue.aspx

FRS 100 – Application of Financial Reporting Requirements
FRS 101 – Reduced Disclosure Framework
FRS 102 – The Financial Reporting Standard applicable in the UK and Republic of Ireland
FRS 103 – Insurance Contracts

FRS 1 – Cash Flow Statements (Revised 1996)
FRS 2 – Accounting for Subsidiary Undertakings
FRS 3 – Reporting Financial Performance
FRS 4 – Capital Instruments
FRS 5 – Reporting the Substance of Transactions
FRS 6 – Acquisitions and Mergers
FRS 7 – Fair Values in Acquisition Accounting
FRS 8 – Related Party Disclosures
FRS 9 – Associates and Joint Ventures
FRS 10 – Goodwill and Intangible Assets
FRS 11 – Impairment of Fixed Assets and Goodwill
FRS 12 – Provisions, Contingent Liabilities and Contingent Assets
FRS 13 – Derivatives and other Financial Instruments: Disclosures
FRS 14 – Earnings per Share
FRS 15 – Tangible Fixed Assets
FRS 16 – Current Tax
FRS 17 – Retirement Benefits
FRS 18 – Accounting Policies

FRS 19 – Deferred Tax

FRS 20 (IFRS2) – Share-based Payment

FRS 21 (IAS 10) – Events after the Balance Sheet Date

FRS 22 (IAS 33) – Earnings per share

FRS 23 (IAS 21) – The Effects of Changes in Foreign Exchange Rates

FRS 25 (IAS 32) – Financial Instruments: Presentation

FRS 26 (IAS 39) – Financial Instruments: Recognition and Measurement

FRS 27 – Life Assurance

FRS 28 – Corresponding Amounts

FRS 29 (IFRS 7) – Financial Instruments: Disclosures

FRS 30 – Heritage Assets

SSAP 4 – Accounting for government grants

SSAP 5 – Accounting for value added tax

SSAP 9 – Stocks and long-term contracts

SSAP 13 – Accounting for research and development

SSAP 15 – Status of SSAP 15

SSAP 17 – Accounting for post balance sheet events

SSAP 19 – Accounting for investment properties

SSAP 20 – Foreign currency translation

SSAP 21 – Accounting for leases and hire purchase contracts

SSAP 24 – Accounting for pension costs

SSAP 25 – Segmental reporting

Questions

6.1 Kazam Services begins the month with capital of £200,000 and the following assets and liabilities:

Assets	**Liabilities**
Non-current assets £500,000	Bank overdraft £35,000
Receivables £125,000	Payables £90,000
	Long-term loan £300,000

The following transactions took place in the accounting records of the business during the last month:

Take out long-term loan for new building £150,000.

Receivables reduce by £45,000 as customers pay their accounts.

Payables reduce by £30,000 as suppliers are paid.

Invoice customers for £70,000 for services carried out.

Pay salaries £15,000.
Pay various office expenses £5,000.
In addition, depreciation of £20,000 is to be provided for the period.

- Produce a schedule of transactions under appropriate headings for each account.
- Total each account and produce an Income Statement and Statement of Financial Position.

6.2 Vibro plc has non-current assets of £250,000, current assets of £125,000, long-term debt of £125,000, and payables of £75,000.

- What is the working capital?
- What is the capital employed in the company?
- What is the shareholders' capital?

6.3 XYZ Ltd's Income Statement shows the following:

	2015	2014
	€	€
Sales	1,250,000	1,175,000
Cost of sales	787,000	715,000
Selling and admin expenses	324,000	323,000

Based on these figures, which of the following statements is true?
a. Sales, cost of sales, and expenses have all increased, therefore profit, gross margin, and operating margin have all increased.
b. The operating profit has increased due to sales growth, higher gross margins, and similar expenses.
c. Although the operating profit has decreased, the operating margin has increased as a result of sales growth and an increase in gross profit.
d. The operating profit has decreased due to lower gross margins and higher expenses, despite sales growth.
e. Although the operating profit has increased, the operating margin has decreased as a result of a reduction in the gross margin and higher expenses, despite sales growth.

6.4 What is the impact of the following prepayment, accrual, and provision transactions on profit, the Statement of Financial Position, and cash flow?
a. A business has 24 motor vehicles that it leases in return for a monthly payment, excluding insurance. The company's financial year is 1 April/31 March, but the annual insurance premium of $400 per vehicle for the calendar year January–December is due for payment on 31 December.

b. A business budgets for energy costs of $6,000 per annum over its financial year 1 January/31 December. Bills for usage are sent each quarter on the last days of each of February, May, August, and November. Historically, 70% of the annual energy cost is spent during the autumn and winter (September–February).

c. A business with a financial year of 1 April/31 March purchases a new computer network server for $12,000 on 30 June. The business depreciates computer hardware at the rate of 20% of cost per annum, beginning the month following purchase.

6.5 NOP plc has recently acquired a business, for which it paid £12 million. The assets and liabilities of the acquired business comprise:

Plant & Equipment	£7,000,000
Receivables	£1,500,000
Inventory	£2,300,000
Payables	£ 500,000

The directors decide to amortize any goodwill over a period of 10 years. Calculate the goodwill in the Statement of Financial Position (ignoring any impairment) at the end of the first year after the business was purchased.

6.6 PUH Ltd leases all of its assets. In its Statement of Financial Position, PUH shows a current liability of £750,000 and a long-term debt of £1,640,000 for lease commitments. What type of expenses will a user of PUH's financial statements expect to see in the Income Statement?

6.7 A business sells a non-current asset for less than its Statement of Financial Position value. Under IFRS, how will the difference between the asset value in the Statement of Financial Position and the amount received on the sale of the asset be disclosed in the Income Statement?

6.8 A business sells a non-current asset for more than its Statement of Financial Position value. Under IFRS, how will the difference between the asset value in the Statement of Financial Position and the amount received on the sale of the asset be disclosed in the Income Statement?

6.9 A manufacturing business has invoiced customers $5,875,000 including sales taxes of 17.5%. What sales value will be shown in the Income Statement?

6.10 MNJ Ltd borrows €200,000 from a finance company. The next day, the company uses those funds to purchase new plant and equipment for €150,000. MNJ depreciates its plant and equipment at the rate of 20% per annum. During the year MNJ also incurs advertising expenditure of €5,000. Present an extract from each of the Income Statement, Statement of Financial Position, and Statement of Cash Flows to show how these transactions would be presented.

Interpreting Financial Statements

This chapter begins with an overview of a company's Annual Report and shows how ratio analysis can be used to interpret financial statements. This interpretation covers profitability, liquidity (cash flow), gearing (borrowings), activity/efficiency, and shareholder return. We also look at working capital management in detail. Two case studies demonstrate how ratios can be used to look 'behind the numbers' contained in financial statements. The chapter concludes with alternative theoretical perspectives on financial reporting including corporate social and environmental reporting together with new developments in integrated reporting.

Annual Reports

For all companies, the Companies Act requires the preparation of financial statements. Financial statements are an important part of a company's Annual Report, which must be available to all shareholders for all companies listed on the Stock Exchange.

The Annual Report for a listed company typically contains:

- A financial summary – the key financial information.
- A list of the main advisers to the company: legal advisers, bankers, auditors, and so on.
- The chairman's, directors', and/or chief financial officer's report(s). These reports provide a useful summary of the key factors affecting the company's performance over the past year and its prospects for the future. It is important to read this information as it provides background and context to the

financial statements, and the company's products/services and major market segments. The user must 'read between the lines' in this report, since an intention of the Annual Report is to paint a realistic yet often 'glossy' picture of the business. However, as competitors will also read the Annual Report, the company takes care not to disclose more than is necessary.

- The statutory reports (i.e. those required by the Companies Act) by the directors. These will contain a summary of financial performance, major policies, strategies and activities, details about the board of directors and the remuneration of board members and senior managers, and statements about corporate governance, risk management, and internal control.
- The audit report which will define the auditors' responsibilities, an opinion as to whether the financial statements give a true and fair view and are compliant with the Companies Act and IFRS (see Chapter 6), and the basis upon which that opinion has been formed.
- The financial statements: Income Statement and/or Statement of Comprehensive Income; Statement of Changes in Equity; Balance Sheet (or Statement of Financial Position); and Statement of Cash Flows (see Chapter 6). Where consolidated figures are provided, these should be used, as they are the total figures for the group of companies that comprise the whole business. Prior year figures must be shown for comparative purposes.
- Notes to the financial statements, which provide detailed explanations to the figures in the financial statements, and usually run to many pages. As well as a breakdown of many of the figures contained in the Income Statement, Balance Sheet (or Statement of Financial Position), and Statement of Cash Flows, the Notes will include details such as: the major accounting policies adopted; staff numbers and staff costs; directors' remuneration; depreciation of assets; investments; taxation; share capital; capital expenditure contracted for; pension liabilities; lease liabilities; subsidiaries; and events occurring after the end of the financial year.

Operating and Financial Review (OFR)

The Accounting Standards Board (ASB) published a *Reporting Statement: Operating and Financial Review* (OFR) in 2006 (available at https://www.frc.org.uk/Our-Work/Publications/ASB/Reporting-Statement-Operating-and-Financial-Review-File.pdf). The ASB believes that the Reporting Statement on Operating and Financial Review provides best practice guidance for all UK companies that are required to prepare a business review.

The Standard has to some extent been reinforced by section 417 of the Companies Act 2006 (see http://www.legislation.gov.uk/ukpga/2006/46/section/417) which requires UK quoted companies to undertake an enhanced business review. The purpose of the business review is to inform members of the company (i.e. shareholders) and help them assess how the directors have performed their duty under section 172 of the Companies Act (i.e. their duty to promote the success of the company). Under section 417, the business review must contain a fair review of the company's business, and a description of the principal risks and uncertainties facing the company. It must provide a balanced and comprehensive analysis of the development and performance of the company's business during the financial year, and the position of the company's business at the end of that year, consistent with the size and complexity of the business.

Listed companies must also include the main trends and factors likely to affect the future development, performance, and position of the company's business; and information about the impact of the company's business on the environment, the company's employees, and social and community issues, using financial and other key performance indicators (KPIs: see the Balanced Scorecard in Chapter 4).

The context of financial statements

Before we begin analysing the financial statements themselves, it is particularly important to understand the context in which the business operates. While much information can be obtained from the Annual Report and the company's website, it must be remembered that these are at least in part produced for public relations purposes, hence it is important to seek out broader information about the company which will then provide a broader context in which the financial statements can be interpreted and understood.

Access to past newspaper articles using library databases (Factiva is one example) can provide a more rounded picture of a company, including criticisms of its operations. However, it is important to remember that press reports themselves can be inaccurate and biased. Nevertheless, making enquiries into a company through newspaper articles can help to understand the 'bigger picture'.

In the UK, the Office for National Statistics provides aggregated statistical data of interest to many industries. This bigger picture can also be obtained from industry publications, trade associations, and exhibitions, where information extends not just to individual companies but to a whole industry. Market research and consulting firms also produce detailed analyses of industries but these can be expensive to purchase, while credit rating agencies provide independent information about a company's financial position including any litigation and credit reputation. Stock market analysts undertake their own analysis and use that to support the buy or sell recommendations they give to their investment clients.

Personal experience is also important. If you are looking at the financial statements of a large supermarket chain such as Sainsbury's or Tesco in the UK, personal experience of shopping can help to understand the business operations. So for example, if you notice that food prices are lower, it may be that supermarkets are carrying out a price war to win market share, and this may affect their profits in the short term.

The key issue in interpreting financial statements is to understand the context: what is happening in the company's market? Is customer demand changing? What technological and regulatory changes are affecting it? Who are the major competitors? Only with this contextual awareness can we begin to understand financial statements.

Ratio analysis

Ratio analysis is perhaps the most important tool used to analyse financial statements: the Income Statement, Balance Sheet (or Statement of Financial Position), and Statement of Cash Flows. *Ratios* are typically two numbers, with one being expressed as a percentage of the other. Ratio analysis can be used to help interpret *trends* in performance year on year by *benchmarking* to industry averages or to the performance of individual competitors, or by comparison against a predetermined *target*. As companies are required to show a comparison with their prior year financial statements, ratios should be applied, at the very least, to current and past years. However, trends can really only be interpreted properly over a longer period, ideally five years. Trade association, market research, and consultancy reports often benchmark companies in an industry and some government statistical data is published (e.g. on retail sales and automobile registrations). Annual Reports do not provide comparisons against target, so this kind of ratio analysis is only possible for managers within the company. Most financial statements provide consolidated (or group) data and data for the parent (or holding) company. We are usually only concerned with the consolidated or group figures. However, companies are required to show some detailed segmental analysis of major parts of their business, which is often very important in understanding business performance.

Ratio analysis can be used to interpret performance against five criteria:

- the rate of profitability;
- liquidity, i.e. cash flow;
- gearing, i.e. the proportion of borrowings to shareholders' equity;
- how efficiently assets are utilized; and
- returns to shareholders.

There are different definitions that can be used for each ratio. Different text books, credit rating agencies, and stock market analysts use varying definitions. However, it is important that whatever ratios are used, they are meaningful to the business and applied consistently. The most common ratios follow. The calculations refer to the example Income Statement and Statement of Financial Position in Chapter 6 which are repeated below in Tables 7.1, 7.2, and 7.3. Ratios may be calculated on the end-of-year Balance Sheet (Statement of Financial Position) figures (as has been done in the examples that follow) or on the basis of the average of Balance Sheet figures over two years.

Table 7.1   Income Statement.

Revenue	2,000,000
Less: cost of sales	1,500,000
Gross profit	500,000
Less: selling and administration expenses	400,000
Operating profit	100,000
Less: interest costs	16,000
Profit before income tax	84,000
Less: income tax	14,000
Net profit after tax	70,000

Table 7.2   Statement of Changes in Equity.

At beginning of year	**960,000**
Profit for the year	70,000
Other comprehensive income	0
Total comprehensive income	**70,000**
Less: dividend	30,000
At end of year	**1,000,000**

Table 7.3   Statement of Financial Position.

Assets	
Non-current assets	
Property, plant & equipment	1,150,000
Current assets	
Receivables	300,000
Inventory	200,000
	500,000
Total assets	1,650,000
Liabilities	
Non-current liabilities	
Long-term loans	300,000
Current liabilities	
Payables	300,000
Bank overdraft	50,000
	350,000
Total liabilities	650,000
Net assets	1,000,000
Equity	
Share capital	900,000
Retained earnings	100,000
Total equity	1,000,000

Ratios are nearly always expressed as a percentage (by multiplying the answer by 100). In the following examples, only £'000 (thousands of pounds) are shown.

Profitability

Return on (shareholders') investment (ROI)

$$\frac{\text{net profit after tax}}{\text{shareholders' funds}} = \frac{70}{1,000} = 7\%$$

Return on capital employed (ROCE)

$$\frac{\text{operating profit before interest and tax}}{\text{shareholders' funds} + \text{long-term debt}} = \frac{100}{1,000 + 300} = 7.7\%$$

Operating margin (or operating profit/sales)

$$\frac{\text{operating profit before interest and tax}}{\text{sales}} = \frac{100}{2,000} = 5\%$$

Gross margin (or gross profit/sales)

$$\frac{\text{gross profit}}{\text{sales}} = \frac{500}{2,000} = 25\%$$

Overheads/sales

$$\frac{\text{overheads}}{\text{sales}} = \frac{400}{2,000} = 20\%$$

Each of the profitability ratios provides a different method of interpreting profitability. Satisfactory business performance requires an adequate return on shareholders' funds and total capital employed in the business (the total of the investment by shareholders and lenders). ROI will often be higher when shareholders' funds are low, but this involves higher risk (see Gearing, below). Profit must also be achieved as a percentage of sales. The operating profit and gross profit margins emphasize different elements of business performance. It is important to maximize gross margin (the difference between selling price and the cost of sales for the volume of goods or services sold) and to control the proportion of overhead in relation to sales, but it is also essential to grow sales volume and value.

Sales growth

A further method of interpreting performance is sales growth, which is simply

$$\frac{\text{sales in year 2} - \text{sales in year 1}}{\text{sales in year 1}}$$

Hence, had the sales in the previous year been £1,800,000 (not shown in the example in Table 7.1), the sales growth would be

$$\frac{2,000 - 1,800}{1,800} = \frac{200}{1,800} = 11.1\%$$

Businesses and the stock market not only like to see increasing profitability but also increasing sales, which is an important measure of the long-term sustainability of profits.

Liquidity

Working capital

$$\frac{\text{current assets}}{\text{current liabilities}} = \frac{500}{350} = 143\%$$

Acid test (or quick ratio)

$$\frac{\text{current assets} - \text{inventory}}{\text{current liabilities}} = \frac{500 - 200}{350} = 86\%$$

Working capital is explained in more detail later in this chapter, but is essentially the liquid funds that circulate in and out of the bank account, comprising, in the main, receivables, inventory, payables, and bank account (or overdraft). Many businesses will aim for a working capital ratio of around 150% and an acid test of around 100%. A business that has an acid test of less than 100% may experience difficulty in paying its debts as they fall due. On the other hand, a company with too high a working capital ratio may not be utilizing its assets effectively. However, there are substantial variations between industries. In retail for example, a lot of inventory is held and this is reflected in payables to suppliers, but there are no receivables from customers. Customers pay cash as they buy goods and hence the working capital and acid test ratios will often be less than 100. This demonstrates the importance of understanding the business context and method of operation, rather than applying ratio analysis unthinkingly.

Gearing

Gearing ratio

$$\frac{\textit{long-term debt}}{\textit{shareholders' funds} + \textit{long-term debt}} = \frac{300}{1,000 + 300} = 23.1\%$$

Interest cover

$$\frac{\text{profit before interest and tax}}{\text{interest payable}} = \frac{100}{16} = 6.25 \text{ times}$$

Gearing is the amount of borrowings relative to shareholders' equity. The higher the gearing, the higher the risk of repaying debt and interest. In the short term, repaying interest is more important, so the lower the interest cover, the more pressure there is on profits to fund interest charges. However, because borrowings are being used, the *rate of profit* earned by shareholders is higher where there are higher borrowings. The relationship between risk and return is an important feature of interpreting business performance. Consider the example in Table 7.4 of risk and return for a business under different assumptions of the mix between debt and equity (which was covered in Chapter 2) in financing the total assets of the company.

Table 7.4   Risk and return – effect of different debt/equity mix.

	100% equity	50% equity 50% debt	10% equity 90% debt
Capital employed	100,000	100,000	100,000
Equity	100,000	50,000	10,000
Debt	0	50,000	90,000
Operating profit before interest and tax	20,000	20,000	20,000
Interest at 10% on debt	0	5,000	9,000
Profit after interest	20,000	15,000	11,000
Tax at 30%	6,000	4,500	3,300
Profit after tax	14,000	10,500	7,700
Return on investment	14%	21%	77%
Interest cover	N/A	4	2.2

While in the example in Table 7.4 the return on capital employed is a constant 20% (an operating profit of £20,000 on capital employed of £100,000), the return on shareholders' funds increases as debt replaces equity. This improvement to the return to shareholders shows the value of leveraging other people's money, but it carries a risk, which increases as the proportion of profits taken by the interest charge increases (reflected in the lower interest cover ratio). If profits turn down, there are substantially more risks carried by the highly geared business in repaying both interest and the loan principal.

Many businesses aim for a gearing in the range of 40–60%, but there are wide variations between industries and in the risk attitude of companies within industries.

Activity/efficiency

Asset turnover

$$\frac{\text{sales}}{\text{total assets}} = \frac{2{,}000}{1{,}150 + 500} = 121\%$$

Investment in assets has as its principal purpose the generation of sales. Asset turnover is a measure of how efficiently assets are utilized to generate sales, with the goal being to work the assets as hard as possible to generate sales.

We now consider three aspects of asset efficiency, the components of working capital.

Working capital

The management of working capital is a crucial element of cash flow management. Working capital is the difference between current assets and current liabilities. In practical terms, we are primarily concerned with inventory and receivables (debtors), although prepayments are a further element of current assets. Current liabilities comprise trade payables (creditors) and accruals. The other element of working capital is bank, representing either surplus cash (a current asset) or short-term borrowing through a bank overdraft facility (a current liability).

The working capital cycle is shown in Figure 7.1. If not properly managed, money tied up in receivables and inventory puts pressure on the business, which can lead to late payments to suppliers (and potentially a higher cost of sales). Managing working capital is essential for success, as the ability to avoid a cash crisis and pay debts as they fall due depends on:

- managing receivables through effective credit approval, invoicing, and collection activity;
- managing inventory through effective ordering, storage, and identification of stock;
- managing payables by negotiation of trade terms and taking advantage of settlement discounts; and
- managing cash by effective forecasting, short-term borrowing, and/or investment of surplus cash where possible.

Ratios to determine the efficiency of the management of working capital and methods for managing and monitoring receivables, inventory, and payables are described below.

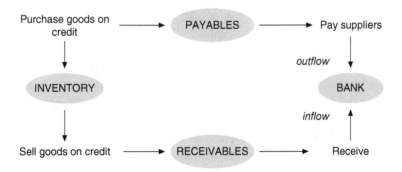

Figure 7.1   The working capital cycle.

Managing receivables

The main measure of how effectively receivables (debtors) are managed is the number of days' sales outstanding. Days' sales outstanding (DSO) is:

$$\frac{\text{receivables}}{\text{average daily sales}}$$

The business has sales of £2,000,000 and receivables of £300,000. Average daily sales are £5,479 (£2,000,000/365). There are therefore 54.75 average days' sales outstanding (£300,000/£5,479). Management of receivables will aim to reduce days' sales outstanding over time and minimize bad debts. The target number of days' sales outstanding will be a function of the industry, the credit terms offered by the firm, and its efficiency in both credit approval and collection activity. In practice, a firm with 30-day trading terms will typically aim to have its days' sales outstanding at no more than 45–50.

Acceptance policies will aim to determine the creditworthiness of new customers before sales are made. This can be achieved by checking trade and bank references, searching company accounts, and consulting a credit bureau for any adverse reports. Credit limits can be set for each customer. Collection policies should ensure that invoices are issued quickly and accurately, that any queries (e.g. delivery quantity, price, etc.) are investigated as soon as they are identified, and that continual follow-up of late-paying customers is carried out. Discounts may be offered for settlement within credit terms.

Bad debts may occur because a customer's business fails. For this reason, firms establish a provision (see Chapter 6) to cover the likelihood of customers not being able to pay their debts.

Managing inventory

The main measure of how effectively inventory (stock) is managed is the inventory turnover (or stock turn). Inventory turnover is:

$$\frac{\text{cost of sales}}{\text{stock}}$$

In the example, cost of sales is £1,500,000 and inventory is £200,000. The inventory turnover is therefore 7.5 (£1,500,000/£200,000). This means that inventory turns over (is bought or manufactured and sold) 7.5 times per year, or on average every 49 days (365/7.5). Sound management of inventory requires an accurate and up-to-date inventory control system.

Often in inventory control the *Pareto principle* (also called the 80/20 rule) applies. This recognizes that a small proportion (often about 20%) of the number of inventory items accounts for a relatively large proportion (say 80%) of the total value. In inventory control, ABC analysis takes the approach that, rather than attempt to manage all stock items equally, efforts should be made to prioritize the

'A' items that account for most value, then 'B' items and only if time permits the many smaller value 'C' items. Increasingly manufacturing businesses adopt *just-in-time* (*JIT*) methods to minimize investment in inventory, treating any inventory investment as a wasted resource. JIT requires sophisticated production planning, inventory control, and supply chain management so that inventory is only received as it is required for production or sale. Stock may be written off because of stock losses, obsolescence, or damage. For this reason, firms establish a provision to cover the likelihood of writing off part of the value of stock. Accounting for Inventory is the subject of Chapter 8.

Managing payables

Just as it is important to collect debts from customers, it is also essential to ensure that suppliers are paid within their credit terms. As for receivables, the main measure of how effectively payables (creditors) are managed is the number of days' purchases outstanding. Days' purchases outstanding (DPO) are:

$$\frac{\text{payables}}{\text{average daily purchases}}$$

The business has cost of sales (usually its main credit purchases, as most other expenses, e.g. salaries, rent, are not on credit) of £1,500,000 and creditors of £300,000. Average daily purchases are £4,110 (£1,500,000/365). There are therefore 73 average days' purchases outstanding (£300,000/£4,110).

The number of days' purchases outstanding will reflect credit terms offered by the supplier, any discounts that may be obtained for prompt payment, and the collection action taken by the supplier. Failure to pay trade payables will likely lead to a higher cost of sales, and may result in the loss or stoppage of supply, which can then affect the ability of a business to satisfy its customers' orders. The average payment time for trade payables has to be disclosed in a company's Annual Report to shareholders.

Managing working capital

Importantly, improving days' sales outstanding or inventory turnover will not improve the working capital ratio as there is only a shift from one type of current asset to another. Table 7.5 shows the effect of changes in working capital.

In the first column the working capital ratio is 150% and acid test 100%. In the second column, faster collection of receivables and faster inventory turnover converts those current assets into money in the bank. While this will show improved days' sales outstanding and inventory turnover, there is no change in the working capital ratio, although there is an improvement in the acid test (as inventory has fallen). In the third column, the cash funds are used to reduce payables. This improves our days' purchases outstanding ratio and increases our working capital ratio as there are now more current assets relative to current liabilities. In the final column, some of the cash funds are used to repay long-term debt (a non-current

Table 7.5   Effects of changes in working capital.

	1. Original working capital	2. Improved DSO and Inventory turnover	3. Improved DPO	4. Repayment of long-term loan
Bank	10,000	15,000	9,000	6,000
Receivables	10,000	7,000	7,000	7,000
Inventory	10,000	8,000	8,000	8,000
Total current assets	30,000	30,000	24,000	21,000
Payables	20,000	20,000	14,000	14,000
Total current liabilities	20,000	20,000	14,000	14,000
Working capital ratio	150%	150%	171%	150%
Acid test ratio	100%	110%	114%	93%

liability). This will improve the gearing ratio but results in a fall (still to an acceptable level) in the working capital and acid test ratios, as there are now fewer current assets available to meet current liabilities.

One of the issues in calculating the receivables, inventory, and payables ratios is the number of days to be used in calculating average daily sales, inventory, or purchases. Provided you are consistent, it doesn't matter too much, but in practice it is best to try to approximate the number of days a business is open. So a retail business operating 365 days per year could use that number while a professional service firm operating five days per week for 52 weeks may use only 260 days.

The final group of ratios comprises measures used by shareholders as measures of investment performance.

Shareholder return

For these ratios we need some additional information:

$$\text{number of shares issued} \quad 100,000$$
$$\text{market value of shares} \quad £2.50$$

Dividend per share

$$\frac{\text{dividends paid}}{\text{number of shares}} = \frac{30,000}{100,000} = £0.30 \text{ per share}$$

Dividend payout ratio

$$\frac{\text{dividends paid}}{\text{profit after tax}} = \frac{30,000}{70,000} = 43\%$$

Dividend yield

$$\frac{\text{dividends paid per share}}{\text{market value per share}} = \frac{0.30}{2.50} = 12\%$$

Earnings per share (EPS)

$$\frac{\text{profit after tax}}{\text{number of shares}} = \frac{70,000}{100,000} = £0.70 \text{ per share}$$

Price/earnings (P/E) ratio

$$\frac{\text{market value per share}}{\text{earnings per share}} = \frac{2.50}{0.70} = 3.57 \text{ times}$$

The shareholder ratios are measures of returns to shareholders on their investment in the business. The dividend and earnings ratios reflect the annual return to shareholders. Stock market investors have an expectation of stable or increasing dividends per share, hence the dividend payout ratio may have to increase to maintain a stable dividend. It is quite common for companies to pay out around half their after-tax profits as dividend, retaining the balance for reinvestment in the business. However, there are substantial variations between companies. The P/E ratio measures the number of years over which the investment in shares will be recovered through earnings. The long-term average P/E ratio for Stock Exchange listed companies in the UK, USA, and Australia is around 15. Earnings per share represent the 'return' to shareholders through profits (even though part of the profits is paid as dividend and part reinvested in the company as retained earnings). Because share issues can take place during the year, the number of shares needs to be weighted. Companies are required to calculate this weighting in a particular way and show their earnings per share with the Income Statement.

The relationship between financial ratios

As can be seen from the ratios, some are drawn from only the Income Statement, some from only the Balance Sheet (Statement of Financial Position), and some are drawn from both. While ratios can provide useful information individually, it is important to understand the relationships between the ratios. Figure 7.2 shows the relationships between the 'elements' (see the *Framework* in Chapter 6 for an explanation of elements) in the Income Statement and Balance Sheet and the financial ratios. In Figure 7.2, the light blue elongated box contains the elements in the Income Statement while the darker blue box includes the Balance Sheet elements. Outside the boxes are the ratios, with arrows showing the sources of financial data used in calculating those ratios.

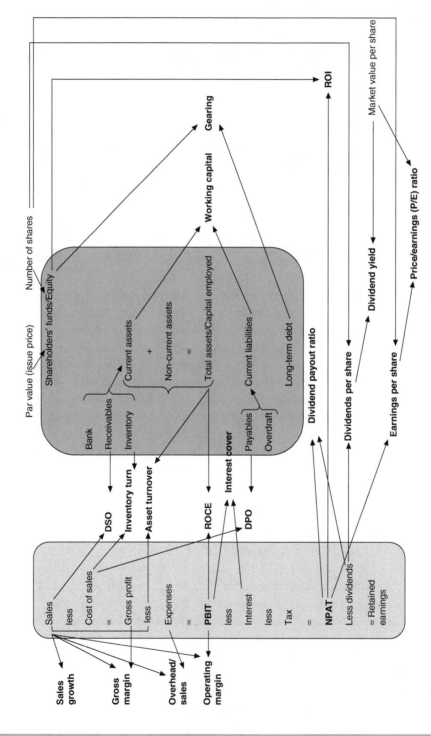

Figure 7.2   Structure of financial statement elements (Income Statement and Statement of Financial Position) and financial ratios.

Although this is rather a complex diagram, it can help to see how different ratios affect each other. So, for example, total assets (capital employed) in the Balance Sheet affect both ROCE, a profitability measure (because capital employed is the denominator in that ratio), and asset turnover, an efficiency measure (where capital employed is also the denominator). These relationships between ratios will help you to interpret financial information.

Interpreting financial statements using ratios

The interpretation of any ratio depends on the industry. In particular, the ratio needs to be interpreted as a trend over time, or by comparison to industry averages or to competitor ratios (benchmarking) or to predetermined targets. These comparisons help determine whether performance is improving and where further improvement may be necessary. Based on an understanding of the business context and competitive conditions, and the information provided by ratio analysis, users of financial statements can make judgements about the pattern of past performance, financial strength, and future prospects. Our focus is not on how investors use financial ratios to make investment decisions (a topic that falls more easily into corporate finance) but on how ratios are used by boards of directors and managers in their own organization. There will be two particular emphases: how to improve performance as measured by ratios over time; and how the company appears to its investors when they look at the company's financial ratios. In addition, managers will also be concerned with the financial statements of competitors, customers, and suppliers.

Broadly speaking, businesses seek:

- increasing rates of profit on shareholders' funds, capital employed, and sales, as well as sales growth;
- adequate liquidity (a ratio of current assets to liabilities of not less than 100%) to ensure that debts can be paid as they fall due, but not an excessive rate to suggest that funds are inefficiently used;
- a level of debt commensurate with the business risk taken;
- high efficiency as a result of maximizing sales from the business's investments in assets; and
- a satisfactory and sustainable return on the investment made by shareholders.

When considering the movement in a ratio over two or more years, it is important to look at possible causes for the movement. The cause can be that either the numerator (top number in the ratio) or denominator (bottom number in the ratio) – or both – can influence the change. Some of the possible explanations behind changes in ratios are described below.

Profitability

Improvements in operating profitability as a proportion of sales (PBIT or EBIT) are the result of profitability growing at a faster rate than sales growth, a result either of a higher gross margin or lower overheads. Note that sales growth may result in a higher profit but not necessarily in a higher rate of profit as a percentage of sales.

Improvement in the rate of gross profit may be the result of higher selling prices, lower cost of sales, or changes in the mix of product/services sold or different market segments in which they are sold, which may reflect differential profitability. Naturally, the opposite explanations hold true for deterioration in gross profits.

Improvements in the returns on shareholders' funds (ROI) and capital employed (ROCE) may be because profits have increased and/or because the capital used to generate those profits has altered (new shares may be issued or the company may buy back shares as a method of returning cash to shareholders). When businesses are taken over by others, one way of improving ROI or ROCE is to increase profits by reducing costs (often as a result of economies of scale), but another is to maintain profits while reducing assets and repaying debt. By shifting from debt to equity for example, the ROCE may not alter (because capital employed is a combination of debt and equity) but the ROI will decrease (assuming constant profits) as there is more equity.

Liquidity

Improvements in the working capital and acid test ratios are the result of changing the balance between current assets and current liabilities. As the working capital cycle in Figure 7.1 showed, and as illustrated in Table 7.5, money changes form between receivables, inventory, bank, and payables and results in changes to liquidity ratios. Borrowing over the long term in order to fund current assets will improve working capital ratios, as will profits that generate cash flow. By contrast, using liquid funds to repay long-term loans or incurring losses will reduce the working capital available.

Gearing

The gearing ratio reflects the balance between long-term debt and shareholders' equity. It changes as a result of changes in either shareholders' funds (more shares may be issued, or there may be a buyback of shares), raising new borrowings, or repayments of debt. As debt increases in proportion to shareholders' funds, the gearing ratio will increase.

Interest cover may increase as a result of higher profits or lower borrowings (and reduce as a result of lower profits or higher borrowings), but even with constant borrowings, changes in the interest rate paid will also influence this ratio.

Activity/efficiency

Asset turnover improves either because sales increase or the total assets used reduce, but the goal is to make the business assets work harder to generate sales, and to sell off assets that are no longer productive. As discussed above, improvement also comes from minimizing investments in receivables and inventory.

Shareholder return

Decisions made by directors about the dividend to be paid influence the dividend payout ratio. Dividends are a recommendation by directors to an annual general meeting of shareholders on the basis of the proportion of profits the directors want to distribute and the capital needed to be retained in the business to fund growth. Often, shareholder value considerations will dictate the level of dividends. On a per share basis, stock markets prefer to see stable or increasing dividends over time, rather than fluctuating in line with rising or falling profits. This is sometimes at the cost of retaining fewer profits and then having to borrow additional funds to support growth strategies. However, the number of shares issued also affects this ratio, as share issues will result in a lower dividend *per share* unless the total dividend is increased.

As companies have little influence over their share price, which is a result of market expectations of future performance as much as past performance, dividend yield, while influenced by the dividend paid per share, is more readily influenced by changes in the market price of the shares.

Earnings per share are influenced, as for profitability, by the profit but also (like dividends) by the number of shares issued. As for the dividend yield, the price/earnings (P/E) ratio is often more a result of changes in the share price based on future expectations of stock market investors than in the profits reflected in the earnings per share.

One way of improving shareholder value is through a share buyback. A buyback occurs when a company purchases its own shares and then either cancels them or holds them as treasury shares for reissue in the future. A company can buy its shares in the open market as for any other investor, or it may make a proportional offer to all shareholders (in much the same way that a rights issue offers new shares to shareholders in proportion to their existing shareholding). Companies normally buy back their shares from their retained earnings. Large-scale share buybacks are a way in which companies can distribute surplus cash by carrying out a return of equity to shareholders. One advantage of a buyback is that by reducing the number of issued shares, the share price increases (as the market value of the business is spread over fewer shares), resulting in a capital gain to shareholders. An alternative to increasing dividends is to carry out a small buyback of shares each year. This results in a capital gain to shareholders rather than income, and does not commit the company to any future dividend payment, given the desire to maintain constant dividends per share.

Using the Statement of Cash Flows

While financial ratios do not use information from the Statement of Cash Flows, cash flow information does provide valuable information that helps in interpreting ratios. You will recall that the Statement of Cash Flows separates cash flows into their operating, investing, and financing components. Changes in profitability, affected by changes in working capital, are revealed in the operating cash flows, so increasing or decreasing profits and/or improved or worsening working capital management will be reflected here. Where capital employed has increased, you would expect to see the purchase of new non-current assets or business acquisitions (including goodwill) under investing activities, where you would also see proceeds of sale of any surplus non-current assets. This kind of investment is also likely to influence the asset turnover ratio.

Financing decisions will appear under the cash flow from financing section. Here you would expect to see proceeds from borrowings or repayments of debt, equity raised from shareholders, or payments for share buybacks, as well as the payment of dividends. These affect gearing ratios. In interpreting the financial ratios, check your interpretation with the Statement of Cash Flows as this will reinforce (or challenge) your interpretation.

Case study 7.1 provides an example of how to interpret financial ratios.

Case study 7.1: W H Smith PLC – interpreting financial statements

W H Smith is one of the UK's biggest retailers, selling a range of stationery, books, newspapers, magazines, and 'impulse' products such as confectionery. The company is part of the FTSE 250 index. The Annual Report (the latest available at the time of writing is for the year ended 31 August 2013, at http://www.whsmithplc.co.uk/investors/company_reports/annual_reports/) states that the business goal is to 'improve the Company's profitability and cash flow generation, delivering sustainable returns to shareholders' (p. 6).

The company prepares its financial statements in accordance with the Companies Act 2006 and the IFRSs as adopted by the European Union (see Chapter 6 for a discussion).

As mentioned above, the context in which the business operates is important, and before undertaking any ratio analysis and interpretation, it is important to read the Annual Report and undertake some research through websites and press reports to better understand the retail context in which W H Smith operates as well as its business model.

The business employs almost 15,000 staff and comprises two segments: High Street shops and shops in travel centres (e.g. railway stations, motorway services, airports, etc. including over 100 outside the UK).

A reading of W H Smith's Annual Report for 2013 reveals some key facts about the business, in particular the quite different performance in each of the two segments of 'High Street' and 'Travel'. The High Street segment has a wider selection of products, with 615 outlets producing sales of £726 million and profits of £56 million (7.7%) while the Travel segment has a more tailored selection of products, with 673 outlets producing sales of £460 million and profits of £66 million (14.3%). The Directors' Report and Business Review disclose that the average store size in the High Street segment is about five times that in the Travel segment, with Travel producing a Return on Capital Employed of 110% while the High Street segment earns a ROCE of 47%. The differential profits in each segment are an important part of understanding the business context, and would not likely be apparent to a customer of W H Smith who shops in both High Street and Travel outlets.

The financial statements of W H Smith are shown below in Tables 7.6 to 7.10.

The number of shares issued in financial year 2013 was 123 million, a reduction from 130 million in 2012. W H Smith's share price was £6 in August 2012, £8.47 in August 2013, and £11 at the time of writing in July 2014, valuing the company at £1.3 billion.

Current prices of UK-listed shares are available from the London Stock Exchange at http://www.londonstockexchange.com/prices-and-markets/stocks/stocks-and-prices.htm and similar data is available from US, Australian, and other stock markets.

Table 7.6   Income Statement for W H Smith PLC.

£m	2013	2012
Group income statement		
Revenue	1186	1243
Operating profit	107	102
Net interest revenue	1	0
Profit before tax	108	102
Income tax expense	21	22
Profit for the year	87	80

Table 7.7   Statement of Comprehensive Income for W H Smith PLC.

£m	2013	2012
Profit for the year	87	80
Actuarial losses on defined benefit pension schemes	–5	–3
Tax on defined benefit schemes	–1	–1
Mark to market valuation of derivative financial assets	1	0
Total comprehensive income	82	76

Although ratios can be calculated without reference to the Notes, more meaningful ratios can often be calculated using the additional information in the Notes. The Notes provide more detailed information about figures in the financial statements.

Ratios for W H Smith for 2013 and 2012 are shown in Table 7.12. The interpretation of these ratios follows, based on contextual information and other information contained in the Annual Report, although it should be understood that these are subjective interpretations (see Chapters 4 and 5) which are made without the information that would only be available to management and directors within the W H Smith business.

One of the first things to note about the financial statements is that the ratios tell a story which must be interpreted in light of the figures themselves. Looking at the ratios in isolation from the figures can lead to a misleading interpretation, as the following discussion illustrates.

The profitability ratios should be looked at together even though they are calculated individually. They show that sales actually fell by 4.5% between 2012 and 2013. However profits increased, and each ratio fills out part of the picture.

First, the gross profit which fell by £9 million. This is not shown in the Income Statement but in Note 3 to the financial statements (we have shown this in Table 7.11 – always use the Notes to look for the detail behind the numbers on the face of the financial statements). Gross profit fell because sales fell, but the gross margin – the rate of gross profit on sales – increased from

Table 7.8   Balance Sheet for W H Smith PLC.

£m	2013	2012
Non-current assets		
Goodwill	33	32
Other intangible assets	22	22
Property, plant & equipment	149	155
Deferred tax assets	23	24
Trade & other receivables	3	4
	230	237
Current assets		
Inventories	148	151
Trade & other receivables	51	54
Current tax asset	3	5
Cash & cash equivalents	31	36
	233	246
Total assets	463	483
Current liabilities		
Trade & other payables	232	246
Retirement benefit obligations	11	10
Current tax liabilities	42	45
Short-term provisions	3	4
	288	305
Non-current liabilities		
Retirement benefit obligations	51	61
Deferred tax liabilities	2	4
Long-term provisions	4	3
Other non-current liabilities	16	15
	73	83
Total liabilities	361	388
Total net assets	102	95
Shareholders' equity		
Share capital, retained earnings & reserves	102	95

Table 7.9   Statement of Changes in Equity for W H Smith PLC.

£m	2013	2012
Balance brought forward from prior year	95	94
Total comprehensive income	82	76
Share-based payments & employee shares	9	6
Dividends paid	−34	−31
Purchase of own shares for cancellation	−50	−50
Balance at end of year	102	95

Table 7.10   Statement of Cash Flows for W H Smith PLC.

£m	2013	2012
Net cash flow from operating activities	119	115
Investing activities		
Purchase of property, plant & equipment	–32	–38
Purchase of intangible assets	–6	–5
Proceeds of disposal of property, plant & equipment		6
Acquisition of business	–1	
Net cash outflow from investing activities	–39	–37
Financing activities		
Dividend paid	–34	–31
Purchase of own shares	–51	–52
Net cash used in financing activities	–85	–83
Net decrease in cash and cash equivalents	–5	–5
Opening net cash & cash equivalents	36	41
Closing net cash & cash equivalents	31	36

Reconciliation of operating profit to net cash inflow from operations (Note 22)		
£m	2013	2012
Operating profit	107	102
Depreciation & amortisation	37	39
Share-based payments	7	7
Decrease in inventories	3	3
Decrease in receivables	4	3
Decrease in payables	–6	–6
Pension funding	–12	–13
Income taxes paid	–19	–17
Change in provisions	–2	–3
Net cash inflow from operating activities	119	115

53.4% to 55.2%. As gross margin is the difference between what a business buys its goods for (the cost), and what it sells them for (the price), we know that the difference between the cost and price is greater. We do not know if this is because prices increased, or because costs were lower as a result of better purchasing (or perhaps both), or if the increase is a result of a sales mix whereby there were more sales of the more profitable products. Remember that the profitability of the Travel segment is greater than that of the High Street segment so that may also help to explain the increase. We would need access to detailed management data in order to know precisely how the increase was obtained, but increasing gross margin at a time of falling sales is certainly a good achievement.

Second, overheads have increased from 45.2% to 46.2% of sales, although the Income Statement reveals that overheads actually fell by £16 million. While overheads represent a higher proportion of sales, they have fallen more than gross profit. This demonstrates management control of

Table 7.11   Additional information for W H Smith PLC.

£m	2013	2012
Group operating profit (Note 3)		
Turnover	1,186	1,243
Cost of sales	−531	−579
Gross profit	655	664
Distribution costs	−475	−486
Administrative expenses	−73	−76
Group operating profit	107	102
Trade debtors (Note 16)	23	20
Trade creditors (Note 17)	99	101
Number of shares issued (Note 24)	123	130
Share price at 31 August	847	600

Table 7.12   Ratios for W H Smith PLC.

	2013	2012
Profitability:		
ROI	85.3%	84.2%
ROCE (debt free, as no interest cost)	104.9%	107.4%
Operating margin	9.0%	8.2%
Gross margin	55.2%	53.4%
Overheads/sales	46.2%	45.2%
Sales growth	−4.6%	
Liquidity:		
Working capital	80.9%	80.7%
Acid test	29.5%	31.1%
Gearing:		
Gearing	NA	NA
Interest cover	NA	NA
Activity/efficiency:		
Asset turnover	2.6	2.6
Days' sales outstanding	7.1	5.9
Inventory turnover	3.6	3.8
Inventory days	101.7	95.2
Days' payables outstanding	68.1	63.7
Shareholder return:		
Dividend per share (Note 11)	£0.28	£0.24
Dividend payout ratio	39.1%	38.8%
Dividend yield	3.3%	4.0%
Earnings per share (Note 12)	£0.71	£0.62
P/E ratio	12.0	9.8

expenses in line with falling sales. The result is a profit increase of £6 million (from 8.2% to 9% of sales – many retail businesses achieve only a profit of 3–5% of sales).

The ROI and ROCE ratios tell a similar story, although they are affected not just by profit increase, but also by the change in shareholders' equity (for ROI) and capital employed (for ROCE). In both cases the ratios are very healthy and any shareholder would be more than happy to achieve this kind of return (85%) on their investment. As the shareholder return ratios show (see below), this figure is a bit misleading because it is based on the historical cost principle (see Chapter 3) and not on the current market value of the business. While ROI has increased, ROCE has fallen but this is largely because the change in profits and shareholders' funds between the two years is quite small. W H Smith is an unusual case in that it has no long-term debt, hence the denominator for ROCE (shareholders' funds plus long-term debt) is the same as that for ROI.

The liquidity ratios must be interpreted with caution, highlighting the importance of understanding the predictive model of the business. Working capital is steady at just over 80% while the acid test (adjusting for inventory) has fallen to around 30%. While (as previously discussed) these ratios should normally be more than 100% to ensure that the business can pay its debts as they fall due, the nature of retail businesses is that all their sales are cash sales (hence there are no receivables) so that general rule does not apply as cash coming in to the business each day does not form part of the ratio calculation. We can see from the Balance Sheet and Statement of Cash Flows that the business has cash of around £30 million, little changed from the previous year. The working capital ratios (days' sales outstanding, inventory turn, and days' payables outstanding) reinforce this. Here again, it is important not to take the figures from the face of the Balance Sheet but to look more carefully at the Notes (the information from Notes 16 and 17 is in Table 7.11). Days' sales outstanding (as discussed above) is meaningless as the business does not make sales on credit (there must be some but the nature of these is not known from the Annual Report). Days' purchases outstanding have increased from 63.7 to 68.1. On the surface, this is not a good sign but the reader must remember that the ratio we are able to calculate is based on annual purchases and the payables on the last day of the financial year. A far more accurate figure will be held by the company. In fact, its internal information is reported in Note 17 as an average credit period taken of 59 days, compared with 60 days in the previous year.

Stock turn for W H Smith is quite low at 3.6, a slight reduction in the previous year, increasing stock levels from just over 3 months (95 days in 2012) to 3 ⅓ months. This is quite a lot of inventory for a retail store which must guard against the risk of obsolescence.

In terms of overall efficiency/activity, asset turnover has remained constant at 2.6, meaning that every £1 of investment in assets generates £2.60 in sales revenue.

The gearing ratios are meaningless when a company has no debt, and consequently no net interest cost. The financial review section in the Directors' report provides the useful explanation that W H Smith's stores are mainly held under operating leases that are not capitalized and are therefore not included as debt for accounting purposes (see Chapter 6 for a discussion of the difference between finance leases and operating leases).

Shareholder returns are affected by the increased share price, a function of stock market expectations for future earnings. The dividend per share has increased (remember that the number of shares has fallen due to the share buyback – explained earlier in this chapter) as has the dividend payout ratio (the proportion of after-tax profits distributed to shareholders) but the dividend yield has decreased, due to the increase in the share price. Earnings per share (calculated in Note 12 to the financial statements) has increased but the increase in share price has led to an increase in the price/earnings ratio to 12. In other words, the current market price of shares will be recovered, at the level of current earnings, in 12 years – remember that the average long-term P/E ratio for the stock market as a whole is around 15.

The Statement of Changes in Equity (Table 7.9) shows that the total comprehensive income has been returned to shareholders through a combination of dividends and share buyback. The Statement of Cash Flows (Table 7.10) reveals capital expenditure of £32 million, down from £38 million in the preceding year. The business has some £30 million in the bank.

Overall, we can say that not much has changed for W H Smith between 2012 and 2013. Sales did fall but margin increased and overheads were reduced so that profits increased – a sign of good management. The business has a sound cash flow from operations and has a programme of capital expenditure. Being debt free means that the company has less risk – but note the effect of risk and return in relation to gearing we discussed earlier in this chapter and illustrated in Table 7.4.

W H Smith makes regular and increasing returns to shareholders through dividends, the proceeds of share buy backs, and the increased market price of the shares – a capital gain for investors. Investors would no doubt be happy with the returns the company has achieved.

Importantly however, our analysis is restricted to two years. This is far too short a period of time from which to make significant judgements and at least a five-year trend would lead to a fuller picture. A perusal of press reports since the publication of the 2013 Annual Report suggests a repeating cycle of falling sales due to lower High Street spending and less travel, affecting the Travel segment stores. However, this is continuing to be offset by tightly controlled gross margins and overhead costs. Nevertheless, the share price continues to increase over time. By the time this book is published, readers will be able to access the 2014 Annual Report which is unlikely to show any significant change from that of 2013.

Limitations of ratio analysis

The limitations of financial statements were discussed in Chapter 6. In particular for ratio analysis purposes, financial statements are historical records and backwards-looking. Inflation can impact on the values shown in financial statements, particularly where assets are held at historical cost in the Balance Sheet (Statement of Financial Position). The Balance Sheet, it should also be recognized, is merely a 'snapshot' of assets and liabilities on the last day of the financial year.

The calculation of profit in financial statements is arrived at after estimates which involve significant subjective judgement, as we saw in relation to estimates such as accruals, prepayments, depreciation, goodwill amortization, and provisions (see Chapter 6). There is also some flexibility in how accounting standards are applied which involves issues of earnings management, i.e. reporting financial performance that the stock market expects (see Chapters 3 and 5). These judgements all influence the financial numbers that are the basis of ratio analysis.

Ratios are of little value unless calculated over several years when a trend can be identified, or in comparison with similar organizations for benchmarking purposes. Ratios need to be interpreted in the context of economic, industry, and competitive factors, and the organization's unique strategy. Ratios are only able to be calculated once per year on the basis of published financial statements but, of course, accountants within organizations will have access to much more detailed figures and will typically have those figures on a monthly basis, so the ratios calculated internally will be even more reliable in terms of identifying trends and opportunities for improvement. More detailed information is contained in the Notes to financial statements than in the financial statements themselves and judgements need to be made about whether to use data on the face of financial statements, or contained within the Notes (some of the examples in the W H Smith case study illustrated this).

Finally, there are different definitions of ratios used in different textbooks and by different financial statement analysts. However, the consistent use of a ratio definition is more important than the particular definition selected.

Consequently, care needs to be exercised in calculating and interpreting ratios and time needs to be spent understanding the economic and competitive context in which ratios are being interpreted (for example, thinking about the nature of the retail industry is necessary to properly interpret some of the ratios for W H Smith in this chapter). This broader contextual understanding can be gained for example by reading the company's Annual Report, financial and trade press, internet reports, market research, consultant and analyst reports – all of which provide broader information about economic change, the industry, competitive conditions, supply chain issues, customer behaviour, regulatory change, and so on.

Case study 7.2 highlights some of these limitations.

Case study 7.2: Carrington Printers – an accounting critique

Carrington Printers was a privately owned, 100-year-old printing company employing about 100 people and operating out of its own premises in a medium-sized town. Although the company was heavily indebted and had been operating with a small loss for the past three years, it had a fairly strong Balance Sheet and a good customer base spread over a wide geographical area. Carrington's simplified Balance Sheet is shown in Table 7.13. Although the case study is several years old (the organization was real, but the name has been changed), the data has been presented in the format of current accounting standards.

Table 7.13   Carrington Printers' Balance Sheet.

	$
Non-current assets	
Land and buildings at cost less depreciation	1,000,000
Plant and equipment at cost less depreciation	450,000
	1,450,000
Current assets	
Receivables	500,000
Inventory	450,000
	950,000
Total assets	2,400,000
Non-current liabilities	
Borrowings	750,000
Current liabilities	
Payables	850,000
Bank overdraft	250,000
	1,100,000
Total liabilities	1,850,000
Net assets	550,000
Equity	
Issued capital	100,000
Retained earnings	450,000
Shareholders' funds	550,000

The nature of the printing industry at the time the financial statements were prepared was one of excess production capacity and over the previous year a price war had been fought between competitors in order to retain existing customers and win new business. The effect of this had been that selling prices (and consequently profit margins) had fallen throughout the industry. Carrington's plant and equipment were, in the main, quite old and not suited to some of the work that it was winning. Consequently, some work was being produced inefficiently, with a detrimental impact on profit margins. Before the end of the year the sales director had left the company and had influenced many of Carrington's customers, with whom he had established a good relationship, to move to his new employer. Over several months, Carrington's sales began to drop significantly.

Lost sales and deteriorating margins affected cash flow. Printing companies at that time typically carried a large stock of paper in a range of weights, sizes, and colours, while customers often took more than 60 days to pay their accounts. Because payment of taxes and employees takes priority, suppliers are often the last group to be paid. The major suppliers of printers are paper merchants, who stop supply when their customers do not pay on time. The consequence of Carrington's cash flow difficulties was that suppliers limited the supply of paper that Carrington needed to satisfy customer orders.

None of these events was reflected in the financial statements and the auditors, largely unaware of changing market conditions and the *increased level of competition*, had little understanding of the gradual detrimental impact on Carrington that had taken place at the time of the audit.

Although aware of the cash flow tightening experienced by the company, the auditors signed the accounts, being satisfied that the business could be treated as a going concern.

As a result of the problems identified above, Carrington approached its bankers for additional loans. However, the bankers declined, believing that existing loans had reached the maximum percentage of the asset values against which they were prepared to lend. The company attempted a sale and leaseback of its land and buildings (through which a purchaser pays a market price for the property, with Carrington becoming a tenant on a long-term lease). However, investors interested in the property were not satisfied that Carrington was a viable tenant and the property was unable to be sold on that basis.

Cash flow pressures continued and the shareholders were approached to contribute additional capital. They were unable to do so and six months after the Balance Sheet was produced the company collapsed, and was placed into receivership and subsequently liquidation by its bankers.

The liquidators found, as is common in failed companies, that the values in the Balance Sheet were substantially higher than what the assets could be sold for. In particular:

- Land and buildings were sold for far less than an independent valuation had suggested, as the property would now be vacant.
- Plant and machinery were almost worthless given their age and condition and the excess capacity in the industry.
- Receivables were collected with substantial amounts being written off as bad debts. Customers often refuse to pay accounts giving spurious reasons and it is often not cost-effective for the liquidator to pursue a collection action through the courts.
- Inventory was discovered to be largely worthless. Substantial stocks of paper were found to have been held for long periods with little likelihood of ever being used and other printers were unwilling to pay more than a fraction of its cost.

As the bankers had security over most of Carrington's assets, there were virtually no funds remaining after repaying bank loans to pay the unsecured creditors.

This case raises some important issues about the value of audited financial statements:

1. The importance of understanding the context of the business, that is how its market conditions and its mix of products or services are changing over time, the impact of key members of staff on business viability, and how well (or in this case badly) the business is able to adapt to these changes.
2. The preparation of financial statements assumes a going concern, but the circumstances facing a business can change quickly and the Balance Sheet can become a meaningless document.
3. The auditors rely on information from the directors about significant risks affecting the company. The directors did not intentionally deceive the auditors, but genuinely believed that the business could be turned around and become profitable by winning back customers. They also believed that the large inventory would satisfy future customer orders. The directors also genuinely believed that

the property could be sold in order to eliminate debt. This was unquestioned by the auditors. These different perspectives are an illustration of the socially constructed reality (see Chapter 5) of the directors and senior managers who were not able to stand back and make an objective judgement about Carrington's business viability, although the auditors should have been in a better position to have done so.

The company's failure was repeated over the next few years as Carrington's competitors also faced liquidation as technological change eroded much of the market that these companies sold into.

This case highlights the limitations of both financial statements (see Chapter 6) and the use of ratios based on those financial statements, without a thorough knowledge of the broader environment facing the business.

The Carrington case illustrates not only the limitations of financial statements but the additional information held by management that is not available to those outside the organization. Chapters 8 onwards are concerned with information that is used for managerial planning, decision making, and control. But as earlier chapters have already suggested, we must not overlook the inter-relationship between financial and management accounting. The content of current and projected financial statements and how users perceive the information they contain influences managerial plans and decisions. Equally, the actions of managers are reflected in the performance reported in future financial statements.

However, before we move on, we need to consider how a focus on responsibilities to a wider group of stakeholders has increased the prominence of reporting beyond the domain of accounting.

A wider view on corporate reporting

Chapter 6 described the traditional theoretical perspective that has informed financial statements: agency theory. The role of financial statements in agency theory is to hold directors and managers accountable to shareholders. One of the key roles of top management is to communicate with shareholders through 'signalling' the performance and financial position of the business. The Annual Report provides information that is much more than financial, and acts as the primary focus for signalling between the company and its shareholders. Financial statements, for example, are signals prepared by directors for shareholders, about their performance in carrying out the operations of the organization (reported in the Income Statement), and in building the assets of the organization (reported in the Balance Sheet or Statement of Financial Position). Financial statements are therefore important signals to current and potential shareholders about the company.

However, signalling does not just occur between the organization and outside stakeholders. Management in large organizations often devotes much time to competing for resources for their business unit, project, or team. Performance measures can be used internally in organizations to support claims by managers for additional resources for their business units. Managers who can demonstrate success in achieving their performance goals are more likely to be given increased access to resources in the future.

In the remainder of this chapter, we consider some alternative perspectives to agency theory: intellectual capital and institutional theory. We also introduce corporate social and environmental reporting including the Global Reporting Initiative and new developments in integrated reporting.

Intellectual capital

Edvinsson and Malone (1997) defined intellectual capital as 'the hidden dynamic factors that underlie the visible company' (p. 11). Stewart (1997) defined intellectual capital as 'formalized, captured and leveraged knowledge' (p. 68). Intellectual capital is of particular interest to accountants in increasingly knowledge-based economies in which the limitations of traditional financial statements erode their value as a tool supporting meaningful decision making (Guthrie, 2001). Three dimensions of intellectual capital have been identified in the literature: human (developing and leveraging individual knowledge and skills); organizational (internal structures, systems, and procedures); and customer (loyalty, brand, image, and so on).

The disclosure of information about intellectual capital as an extension to financial reporting has been proposed by various accounting academics through an *intellectual capital statement*. The most publicized example is the *Skandia Navigator* (see Edvinsson and Malone, 1997). Intellectual capital statements report on the activities that management initiates and supports. Bukh *et al.* (2001) argued that there are three dimensions of intellectual capital: (i) an identity story, a grand narrative of innovation, flexibility, or knowledge; (ii) a management model specifying the management activities that give substance to the grand story in areas such as technology, structure, or employee development; and (iii) a presentation model that identifies the objects that are committed to numbers in the intellectual capital statements. The intellectual capital statement 'is more than just a set of metrics . . . Together these metrics, sketches/visualisations and stories/narratives form a network, which constitutes the report . . . The sketches/visualisations construct a certain "wholeness" in the organization of metrics or measurements, while the story/narrative suggests how the legitimacy of the intellectual capital statement is created' (Bukh *et al.*, 2001, p. 99).

Intellectual capital statements reveal the limitations of financial statements and how additional contextual knowledge is important, especially as Western companies move increasingly away from manufacturing into service and knowledge-based businesses.

While most businesses espouse a commitment to employees and the value of their knowledge, as well as to some form of social or environmental responsibility, this is often merely rhetoric, a facade to appease the interest groups of stakeholders. The *institutional* setting of organizations provides another perspective from which to view financial statements.

Institutional theory

Institutional theory is valuable because it locates the organization within its historical and contextual setting. It is predicated on the need for legitimation and on isomorphic processes. Scott (1995) describes *legitimation* as the result of organizations being dependent, to a greater or lesser extent, on support from the environment for their survival and continued operation. Organizations need the support of governmental institutions where their operations are regulated (and few organizations are not regulated in some form or other). Organizations are also dependent on the acquisition of resources (labour, finance, technology, and so on) for their purposes. If an organization is not legitimated, it may incur sanctions of a legal, economic, or social nature.

The second significant aspect of institutional power is the operation of *isomorphism*, the tendency for different organizations to adopt similar characteristics. DiMaggio and Powell (1983) identified three forms of isomorphism: coercive, as a result of political influence and the need to gain legitimacy; mimetic, following from standard responses to uncertainty; and normative, associated with profession-alization. They held that isomorphic tendencies between organizations were a result of wider belief systems and cultural frames of reference. Processes of education, inter-organizational movement of personnel, and professionalization emphasize these belief systems and cultural values at an institu-tional level, and facilitate the mimetic processes that result in organizations imitating each other. We can see the results of isomorphism in, for example, the similarity of banks to each other, retailers to each other, and professional firms like accountants and lawyers to each other. Legitimacy can come from, for example, the use of international firms of management consultants or software packages such as Oracle or SAP – again leading to isomorphism.

These legitimating and isomorphic processes become taken for granted by organizations as they strive to satisfy the demands of external regulators, resource suppliers, and professional groups. These taken-for-granted processes themselves become institutionalized in the systems and processes – including accounting and reporting – adopted by organizations.

One significant institutional influence on organizations has been the emergence of investor concern with corporate social and environmental responsibility.

Corporate social and environmental responsibility

The concern with stakeholders rather than shareholders (introduced in Chapter 2) began in the 1970s and is generally associated with the publication in 1975 of *The Corporate Report*. From that time, accounting academics began to question profit as the sole measure of business performance and sug-gested a wider social responsibility for business.

Stakeholder theory argues that managers should serve the interests of anyone with a 'stake' in (that is, anyone who is affected by) the organization. Stakeholders include shareholders, but also encompass employees, suppliers, customers, government, and the communities in which the business operates.

Managers need to strike an appropriate balance between these interests when directing activities so that no one stakeholder group is satisfied to the detriment of others. Much of the argument behind stakeholder theory is that economic pressures to satisfy only shareholders is short-term thinking and organizations need to ensure their survival and success in the long term by satisfying other stakeholders as well – this is called *sustainability* (see below). A concern with a broader group of stakeholders has led to a wider view about what should be included in Annual Reports.

Concepts of *corporate social responsibility*, or corporate social and environmental reporting (CSR), attempt to highlight the impact of organizations on society, and to incorporate such information into company Annual Reports to supplement the economic focus of financial statements. During the 1980s and 1990s, environmental accounting (see for example Gray, Owen, and Adams, 1996) focused on responsibility for the natural environment and in particular on sustainability as a result of concerns about ozone depletion, the greenhouse effect, and climate change. Part of the appeal of environmental accounting was that issues of energy efficiency, recycling, and reductions in packaging had cost-saving potential for companies and therefore profits and social responsibility came to be seen as not necessarily mutually exclusive.

The best-known definition of sustainability comes from *Our Common Future* (the so-called 'Brundtland Report') prepared under the auspices of the World Commission on Environment and Development in 1987, which defines sustainable development as that which 'meets the needs of the present without compromising the ability of future generations to meet their own needs'. In other words, sustainability is a condition where the demands placed upon the environment by people and business organizations can be met without reducing the capacity of the environment to provide for future generations. Some of the major sustainability issues are population, climate change, and energy use.

A broader understanding of sustainability is that economic sustainability and social and environmental sustainability are not mutually exclusive. Sustainability should not be seen as being just about 'green' issues but about the sustainability of economic performance to enable improvements in the environment and society. Equally, unless organizations pay attention to environmental and societal issues, they may not survive to generate sustainable profits for investors in the future. This is the 'triple bottom line': a concern with profits, with the environment, and with improving society.

In its broadest sense, the triple bottom line captures the spectrum of values that organizations must embrace – economic, environmental, and social. In practical terms, triple bottom line reporting means expanding the traditional company reporting framework to take into account not just financial outcomes but also environmental and social performance. Such a framework is provided by the Global Reporting Initiative.

Global Reporting Initiative

The Global Reporting Initiative (GRI) (www.globalreporting.org) argues that sustainability reporting helps organizations to set goals, measure performance, and manage change in order to make their operations more sustainable. The GRI G4 Sustainability Reporting Guidelines provide Reporting Principles, Standard Disclosures, and an Implementation Manual for the preparation of sustainability reports by organizations, regardless of their size, sector, or location.

G4 Sustainability Reports include the disclosure of the governance approach and of the environmental, social, and economic performance and impacts of organizations. Importantly, the economic dimension of sustainability concerns the organization's impacts on the economic conditions of all its stakeholders and on economic systems at local, national, and global levels rather than on the financial condition of the organization.

In addition to the general standard disclosures in G4 that concern strategy, stakeholder engagement, governance, and ethics there are specific standard disclosures on the management approach and performance indicators under the following headings:

1. economic;
2. environmental; and
3. social:
   a. labour practices;
   b. human rights;
   c. society; and
   d. product responsibility.

A full set of the GRI G4 disclosures can be viewed at https://www.globalreporting.org/resourcelibrary/GRIG4-Part1-Reporting-Principles-and-Standard-Disclosures.pdf.

The Global Reporting Initiative co-founded the International Integrated Reporting Council (IIRC) because it believed the future of corporate reporting is the integration of financial and sustainability strategy and reporting.

Integrated reporting

Through the integrated report, an organization provides a concise communication about how its strategy, governance, performance, and prospects lead to the creation of value over time. The integrated report is not intended to be an extract of the traditional Annual Report nor a combination of the annual financial statements and sustainability reports. An integrated report is a concise communication about how an organization's strategy, governance, performance, and prospects lead to the creation of value over the short, medium, and long term.

The International IR (Integrated Reporting) Framework document ('the Framework') was issued by the International Integrated Reporting Council in 2013 (see http://www.theiirc.org/wp-content/uploads/2013/12/13-12-08-THE-INTERNATIONAL-IR-FRAMEWORK-2-1.pdf).

An integrated report is defined in the *Framework* as:

> a concise communication about how an organization's strategy, governance, performance and prospects, in the context of its external environment, lead to the creation of value over the short, medium and long term (IIRC 2013, para 1.1).

The *Framework* takes a principles-based approach. It does not prescribe specific key performance indicators, measurement methods, or the disclosure of individual matters, but does include a small number of requirements that are to be applied before an integrated report can be said to be in accordance with the Framework. The Framework refers to a collection of 'capitals' (building on the notion of intellectual capital discussed earlier in this chapter):

- financial capital (funds for use in the business);
- manufactured capital (machines);
- natural capital (air, water, and land);
- human capital (skill, experience, and motivation);
- intellectual capital (the intangibles); and
- social and relationship capital (community stakeholders).

Integrated reporting is a broader view of business, reflecting the ability of an organization to create financial returns to shareholders and the value the organization creates for stakeholders and society at large through the resources and relationships that are used by, and affected by, an organization.

Integrated reporting takes advantage of new and emerging technologies such as eXtensible Business Reporting Language (XBRL) to link information within the primary report and to facilitate access to further detail online where that is appropriate.

XBRL is a language for the electronic communication of business and financial data and is becoming a standard means of communicating information between businesses and on the internet. Instead of treating financial information as a block of text (as in a standard internet page or a printed document) it provides a unique computer-readable identifying tag for each individual item of data (e.g. net profit after tax). Computers can treat XBRL data intelligently. They can recognize the information in an XBRL document, select it, analyse it, store it, exchange it with other computers, and present it automatically in a variety of ways for users.

Applying different perspectives to financial statements

In Chapters 4 and 5 we considered rational-economic, interpretive, and critical perspectives that help to provide multiple views about the world in which we live. Chapters 6 and 7 have introduced many aspects of the construction and interpretation of financial statements.

Implicit in most of what is contained in Chapters 6 and 7 is an acceptance of the rational-economic perspective described in Chapter 4. Financial statements support the agency model (see Chapter 6) by holding managers-as-agents accountable to shareholders-as-principals. The actions of managers, whose performance is represented in financial statements, are oriented to increasing shareholder value and financial statements are the most important device by which directors and managers provide signals to shareholders about the business.

How then can other perspectives inform the views we take about financial statements? The interpretive perspective (Chapter 5) relies on the notion of a reality that is socially constructed, as we saw in the

Carrington Printers case. This perspective accepts that shareholder value is a valid way of seeing the world, but it is not the only way of seeing the world. For example, a common phrase in many organizations is that 'people are our greatest asset' yet they do not appear in financial statements except in relation to salary expenses. Human resource managers may be critical of the focus on financial performance rather than issues of employee selection, retention, training, and motivation which are equally important for long-term business success. Similarly, marketing managers will value customer retention and satisfaction as necessary for achieving financial performance. Non-financial performance measures like the Balanced Scorecard (see Chapter 4) take a broader perspective, yet non-financial measures of performance on customer, process, and learning and growth perspectives are not reflected in financial statements. The brief discussion of intellectual capital in this chapter reflected a broader approach to reporting on these kinds of issues which has been developed through an increased attention by organizations to corporate social and environmental responsibility and sustainability. The Global Reporting Initiative and the work on integrated reporting has provided a framework for a more stakeholder-oriented view.

The critical perspective (Chapter 5) questions the taken-for-granted assumptions behind financial statements and profit determination. At its extreme, this perspective questions why shareholders are in a privileged position and receive all the profits from business (because the profit for a period is always transferred to shareholders' funds in the Balance Sheet). For example, Marxists ask why capital is more important than labour. A less extreme example is in relation to moral and ethical considerations. The discussion of creative accounting and ethics and the examples of WorldCom, Enron, and Arthur Andersen (see Chapter 5) reflect the unintended but often dysfunctional consequences of the shareholder value model. Power is a central issue in the critical perspective and institutional theory shows how power reinforces the status quo, through the way capital markets work and in the regulation of financial statements. This power is reinforced by top managers who use financial statements and rewards to reinforce their position. While this is to be expected under the rational-economic model, reinforcing the existing managerial hierarchy is not taken for granted in the critical perspective, which aims at questioning existing structures.

A good example of the interpretive and critical perspective is in relation to corporate social and environmental responsibility. This is a reflection of wider perspectives on a business (interpretive) and of power being exerted to require businesses to report in different ways, which by choice they are not likely to have done (critical).

Conclusion

This chapter has introduced the Annual Report and the importance of understanding the context of a business in order to interpret its financial performance. We have explained and illustrated the ratios for analysing financial statements in terms of profitability, liquidity, gearing, efficiency, and shareholder return. We have looked in detail at interpreting these ratios using the case study of W H Smith and the chapter has identified some of the limitations of financial statement analysis, including a case study of the privately owned Carrington Printers. It has also set financial statements in the context of alternative theoretical perspectives which can provide a different way of reading and using financial statements and accounting information. These alternative perspectives continue throughout the third part of this book.

References

Accounting Standards Board (2006). *Reporting Statement: Operating and Financial Review*. London: ASB.

Bukh, P. N., Larsen, H. T. *et al.* (2001). Constructing intellectual capital statements. *Scandinavian Journal of Management*, 17, 87–108.

DiMaggio, P. J. and Powell, W. W. (1983). The iron cage revisited: institutional isomorphism and collective rationality in organizational fields. *American Sociological Review*, 48, 147–60.

Edvinsson, L. and Malone, M. S. (1997). *Intellectual Capital*. London: Piatkus.

Gray, R. H., Owen, D. L. and Adams, C. (1996). *Accounting and Accountability: Changes and Challenges in Corporate Social and Environmental Reporting*. London: Prentice Hall.

Guthrie, J. (2001). The management, measurement and the reporting of intellectual capital. *Journal of Intellectual Capital*, 2(1), 27–41.

International Integrated Reporting Council (IIRC, 2013). *The International IR (Integrated Reporting) Framework document*. http://www.theiirc.org/wp-content/uploads/2013/12/13-12-08-THE-INTERNATIONAL-IR-FRAMEWORK-2-1.pdf.

Scott, W. R. (1995). *Institutions and Organizations*. Thousand Oaks, CA: Sage.

Stewart, T. A. (1997). Intellectual Capital: The New Wealth of Organizations. London: Nicholas Brealey.

World Commission on Environment and Development (1987). *Our Common Future* (Brundtland Report). Annex to General Assembly document A/42/427. http://www.un-documents.net/our-common-future.pdf.

Questions

7.1 Following are the accounts for Drayton Ltd (Tables 7.14 and 7.15). Calculate the following ratios for Drayton for both 2014 and 2013:

- return on shareholders' investment (ROI);
- return on capital employed (ROCE);
- operating profit/sales;
- sales and expense growth;
- gearing;
- asset turnover.

Draw some conclusions from the change in the ratios over the two years.

Table 7.14   Drayton Ltd Income Statement for the year ended 31 December.

In £m	2014	2013
Turnover	141.1	138.4
Net operating costs	−113.9	−108.9
Operating profit	27.2	29.5
Non-operating income	1.4	1.3
Interest payable	−7.5	−8.8
Profit before tax	21.1	22.0
Income tax	−7.3	−5.7
Profit after tax	13.8	16.3
Dividends	−8.0	−8.0
Retained profit	5.8	8.3

Table 7.15   Balance Sheet as at 31 December.

In £m	2014	2013
Assets		
Non-current assets		
Tangible assets	266.7	265.3
Current assets		
Inventory	5.3	5.8
Trade receivables	15.7	20.9
Other receivables and prepayments	2.4	2.0
Bank	4.9	6.3
	28.3	35.0
Total assets	295.0	300.3
Liabilities		
Non-current liabilities		
Long-term loan	96.7	146.1
Current liabilities		
Trade payables	66.8	27.6
Total liabilities	163.5	173.7
Net assets	131.5	126.6
Equity		
Share capital	81.9	82.8
Retained earnings	49.6	43.8
Shareholders' funds	131.5	126.6

7.2 Jupiter Services has produced some financial ratios for the past two years (see Table 7.16). Use the ratios that have already been calculated to draw some conclusions about Jupiter's:

- profitability;
- liquidity;
- gearing;
- efficiency.

Table 7.16   Jupiter Services financial ratios.

	Current year	Previous year
Return on (shareholders') investment (ROI)		
$\dfrac{\text{net profit after tax}}{\text{shareholders' funds}}$	$\dfrac{193.4}{2,610.1} = 7.4\%$	$\dfrac{251.9}{2,547.0} = 9.9\%$
Return on capital employed (ROCE)		
$\dfrac{\text{net profit before interest and tax}}{\text{shareholders' funds} + \text{long-term debt}}$	$\dfrac{367.3}{2,610.1 + 1,770} = 8.4\%$	$\dfrac{394.7}{2,547 + 1,537.7} = 9.7\%$
Net profit/sales		
$\dfrac{\text{net profit before interest and tax}}{\text{sales}}$	$\dfrac{367.3}{1,681.6} = 21.8\%$	$\dfrac{394.7}{1,566.6} = 25.2\%$
Working capital		
$\dfrac{\text{current assets}}{\text{current liabilities}}$	$\dfrac{613.3}{1,444} = 42.5\%$	$\dfrac{475.3}{1,089.2} = 43.6\%$
Gearing ratio		
$\dfrac{\text{long-term debt}}{\text{shareholders' funds} + \text{long-term debt}}$	$\dfrac{1,770}{2,610.1 + 1,770} = 40.4\%$	$\dfrac{1,537.7}{2,547 + 1,537.7} = 37.6\%$
Interest cover		
$\dfrac{\text{profit before interest and tax}}{\text{interest payable}}$	$\dfrac{367.3}{161.1} = 2.28$	$\dfrac{394.7}{120.7} = 3.27$
Days' sales outstanding		
$\dfrac{\text{Receivables}}{\text{average daily sales}}$	$\dfrac{414.7}{1,681.6 / 365 = 4.607} = 90$	$\dfrac{353.8}{1,566.6 / 365 = 4.292} = 82.4$
Asset turnover		
$\dfrac{\text{Sales}}{\text{total assets}}$	$\dfrac{1,681.6}{5,304.5 + 613.3} = 28.4\%$	$\dfrac{1,566.6}{4,794.6 + 475.3} = 29.7\%$

7.3 Jones and Brown Retail Stationery sells its products to other businesses. It has provided the following information:

Sales	€1,200,000
Cost of sales	€450,000
Inventory at end of year	€200,000
Receivables at end of year	€200,000
Payables at end of year	€100,000

Using 250 days as the number of days the business is open, calculate:

- the days' sales outstanding;
- the inventory turnover; and
- the days' purchases outstanding.

7.4 The five-year financial statements of RST plc show the following sales figures:

	2014	2013	2012	2011	2010
Sales (in €m)	155	144	132	130	120

Calculate the sales growth figures for each year.

7.5 RST's Income Statement for 2014 shows:

	€m
Sales	155
Cost of sales	45
Gross profit	110
Selling, administration expenses	65
Operating profit before interest and taxes	45
Interest	10
Profit before tax	35
Income tax	7
Profit after tax	28

Calculate the overhead to sales ratio.

Case study question 7.1: Paramount Services plc

Paramount Services provides a range of business consultancy services. Its financial statements for the last year with prior year comparison are reproduced in Table 7.17.

Table 7.17   Paramount Services plc.

Income Statement

In $'000	2014	2013
Income	34,000	29,000
Less expenses	16,500	13,000
Operating profit before interest	17,500	16,000
Less interest expense	4,000	2,700
Profit before tax	13,500	13,300
Income tax expense	5,400	5,320
Net profit after tax	8,100	7,980

The Statement of Changes in Equity shows the following:		
Dividends paid	4,000	3,750
Number of shares issued	10,000,000	10,000,000
Earnings per share	£0.81	£0.80
Dividend per share	£0.40	£0.38
Market price of shares	£8.55	£10.20

Statement of Financial Position

In $'000	2014	2013
Assets		
Non-current assets	21,933	17,990
Current assets		
Receivables	7,080	4,750
Bank	377	1,250
	7,457	6,000
Total assets	29,390	23,990
Liabilities		
Non-current liabilities		
Long-term loans	2,750	2,000
Current liabilities		
Payables	4,300	3,750
Total liabilities	7,050	5,750
Net assets	22,340	18,240
Equity		
Capital and reserves		
Shareholders' funds	10,000	10,000
Retained profits	12,340	8,240
	22,340	18,240

An analyst has produced the following ratio analysis (Table 7.18) and has asked you to comment on any aspects that you think are important.

Table 7.18   Paramount Services plc.

Ratio analysis

	2014	2013
Sales growth	17.2%	
Expense growth	26.9%	
Profit growth	9.4%	
Interest cover	4.4	5.9
PBIT/Sales	39.7%	45.9%
ROCE (PBIT/SHF+L/TD)	69.7%	79.1%
ROI (NPAT/SHF)	36.3%	43.8%
Dividend payout	49.4%	47.0%
Dividend yield	4.7%	3.7%
P/E ratio	10.56	12.78
Asset efficiency (Sales/TA)	1.2	1.2
Days' sales outstanding	76.0	59.8
Working capital (CA/CL)	1.7	1.6
Gearing (LTD)/(SHF+LTD)	11.0%	9.9%

Case study question 7.2: General Machinery Ltd

General Machinery manufactures computer numerical control (CNC) equipment for its customers who use the equipment in the manufacture of electronic circuit boards. Ratios have been calculated from annual reports for the last five years and are shown in Table 7.19. The Statement of Cash Flows is shown in Table 7.20.

Table 7.19   Ratios.

	2014	2013	2012	2011	2010
ROI	5.0%	3.2%	3.6%	6.2%	5.8%
ROCE	9.2%	7.1%	6.2%	7.6%	6.4%
Operating margin	16.8%	13.9%	12.6%	15.7%	14.1%
Gross margin	70.0%	71.0%	72.0%	74.0%	75.0%
Overhead to sales	53.2%	57.1%	59.4%	58.3%	60.9%
Sales growth	11.4%	9.4%	6.7%	9.1%	
Working capital	198%	360%	340%	368%	326%
Acid test	135%	287%	270%	275%	243%
Gearing	42.0%	40.5%	38.6%	36.5%	37.4%
Interest cover	182%	162%	202%	376%	517%
Asset turnover	48%	46%	44%	44%	41%
Days' sales outstanding	60	63	68	70	73
Inventory turn	3.3	3.1	2.8	2.2	2.3
Days' purchases outstanding	78	88	102	105	111

Table 7.19   Continued

	2014	2013	2012	2011	2010
Dividend per share	$0.036	$0.027	$0.025	$0.036	$0.036
Dividend payout ratio	48.4%	57.9%	49.0%	41.4%	45.7%
Dividend yield	3.0%	2.5%	2.5%	4.5%	5.6%
EPS	$0.075	$0.047	$0.052	$0.088	$0.080
P/E ratio	16.0	23.4	19.3	9.1	8.2

General Machinery's Statement of Cash Flows is also shown for the last few years (Table 7.20).

Table 7.20   Statement of Cash Flows.

	2014	2013	2012	2011
Cash flow from operating activities				
Cash receipts	772,000	700,000	635,000	595,000
Cash payments	−628,000	−601,000	−537,200	−503,000
Interest paid	−72,000	−60,000	−40,000	−25,000
Income tax paid	−17,700	−11,100	−12,240	−20,700
Net cash from operating activities	54,300	27,900	45,560	46,300
Cash flow from investing activities				
Payments for property, plant & equipment	−200,000	−50,000	−50,000	–
Net cash used in investing activities	−200,000	−50,000	−50,000	–
Cash flow from financing activities				
Proceeds from borrowings	50,000	50,000	50,000	–
Dividends paid	−20,000	−15,000	−14,000	−20,000
Net cash from/used in financing activities	30,000	35,000	36,000	−20,000
Net increase/(decrease) in cash	−115,700	12,900	31,560	26,300
Cash at beginning of year	135,700	122,800	91,240	64,940
Cash at end of year	20,000	135,700	122,800	91,240

1. Discuss the major issues facing the company.
2. Recommend what actions the company should take to improve its overall performance, addressing each of profitability, liquidity, gearing, activity, and shareholder return measures.
3. In what way does the Statement of Cash Flows help you to interpret the ratios and financial performance of the company?

CHAPTER 8

Accounting for Inventory

Inventory is a crucial link between the Income Statement (as it affects the calculation of profit) and the asset value in the Balance Sheet (or Statement of Financial Position). However, it is also an important component of cost with which we are concerned throughout Part III of this book. Therefore, it is a useful bridging chapter on which to end our treatment of financial statements and lead into the use of accounting information for decision making, planning, and control.

This chapter begins with an explanation of inventory as it relates to financial statements. It then looks at the alternative methods of inventory valuation (average cost and first in–first out) and then explains the two main costing systems used for inventory: job costing and process costing. The chapter also looks briefly at contract costing for long-term projects such as construction and concludes by looking at the management accounting statements for manufacturing businesses that are used by managers for internal decision making.

Introduction to inventory

Inventory (or stock) is the term used for goods bought or manufactured for resale but which are as yet unsold. Inventory enables the matching of sales income with cost of goods sold, adjusting for the timing difference between purchasing or producing products and the sale of those products to customers. The value of inventory according to IAS2 *Inventories* is the lower of cost and net realizable value.

The cost of inventory includes all costs of purchase, conversion (i.e. manufacture), and other costs incurred in bringing the inventory to its present location and condition. Costs of purchase therefore include import duties and transportation, less any rebates or discounts. Costs of conversion include production labour and an allocation of production overheads (overheads are covered in Chapter 13). Special methods of calculating inventory value apply to construction contracts, agriculture, and commodities trading.

The matching principle (see Chapter 3) requires that business adjusts for changes in inventory in its Income Statement (the 'cost of sales', or 'cost of goods sold') and in its Balance Sheet (where inventory is a current asset).

The cost of sales is calculated as shown in Table 8.1.

Table 8.1   Cost of sales.

	£
Opening inventory (at beginning of period)	12,000
Plus purchases (or cost of manufacture)	32,000
= Stock available for sale	44,000
Less closing inventory (at end of period)	10,000
= Cost of sales	34,000

For a retailer or wholesaler, inventory is the cost of goods bought for resale. For a manufacturer, there are three different types of inventory:

• raw materials;
• work-in-progress;
• finished goods.

Manufacturing firms purchase raw materials (unprocessed goods) and undertake the *conversion process* through the application of labour, machinery, and know-how to manufacture finished goods. The finished goods are then available to be sold to customers. Work-in-progress (or WIP) consists of goods that have begun but have not yet completed the conversion process.

Flow of costs

Figures 8.1 and 8.2 show in diagrammatic form the flow of costs from purchasing to sales for a retail or wholesale business (Figure 8.1) and for a manufacturer (Figure 8.2).

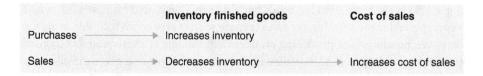

Figure 8.1   The flow of costs in purchasing.

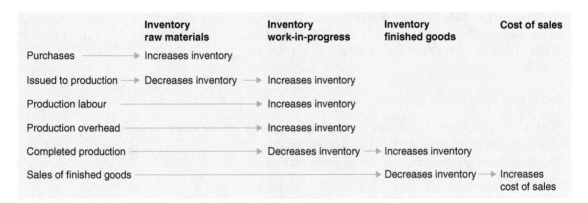

	Inventory raw materials	Inventory work-in-progress	Inventory finished goods	Cost of sales
Purchases	→ Increases inventory			
Issued to production	→ Decreases inventory	→ Increases inventory		
Production labour		→ Increases inventory		
Production overhead		→ Increases inventory		
Completed production		→ Decreases inventory	→ Increases inventory	
Sales of finished goods			→ Decreases inventory	→ Increases cost of sales

Figure 8.2   The flow of costs in manufacturing.

Cost formulae for inventory

Inventory valuation is important as the determination of the cost of inventory affects both:

- cost of sales in the Income Statement; and
- the inventory valuation in the Balance Sheet.

As inventory cost is an important element in management decision making, the valuation of inventory is also an important link between financial accounting and management accounting.

The costs of inventory items that are distinct are assigned their individual costs. So, for example, a component purchased for a specific customer order with a cost of £600 but unused, would be valued at £600. A motor vehicle held for resale by a dealer would be valued at its purchase (or trade-in) cost. In each case, the inventory items would need to be readily identifiable from other similar items.

However, if inventory items are similar and cannot be differentiated (which would be the case for most goods bought in bulk for resale), costs are assigned by using either the weighted average cost or first in–first out (FIFO) methods. The last in–first out (LIFO) method, common in the USA, is not used in the UK or Australia.

Inventory valuation under the weighted average method

Under the weighted average method, the cost of each item is determined from the weighted average of the cost of similar items at the beginning of a period and the cost of similar items purchased or produced during the period.

For example, a product is purchased on three separate occasions:

Units	Unit price	Total cost
5,000	£1.20	£6,000
2,000	£1.25	£2,500
3,000	£1.27	£3,810
10,000		£12,310

We need to calculate the cost of 6,000 units sold and the value of inventory using the weighted average method. The weighted average cost is £12,310/10,000 or £1.231 per unit. The cost of sales is 6,000 @ £1.231 = £7,386. The value of inventory is 4,000 @ £1.231 = £4,924.

Inventory valuation under FIFO

FIFO assumes that items of inventory purchased or produced first are sold first, so that those remaining in inventory are those most recently purchased or produced.

Using the same information as in the previous example:

Units	Unit price	Total cost
5,000	£1.20	£6,000
2,000	£1.25	£2,500
3,000	£1.27	£3,810
10,000		£12,310

We now need to calculate the cost of 6,000 units sold and the value of inventory using the FIFO method.

Under FIFO, the 6,000 units sold come first from the original 5,000 purchased, and the balance of 1,000 from the second purchase of 2,000 units. The cost of sales is therefore:

$$
\begin{array}{ll}
 & 5,000 @ £1.20 = £6,000 \\
\text{and} & 1,000 @ £1.25 = \underline{£1,250} \\
\text{Total} & £7,250
\end{array}
$$

The remaining inventory is the last purchased, i.e. 1,000 from the second purchase of 2,000 and 3,000 from the third purchase. The value of inventory is therefore:

$$
\begin{array}{ll}
 & 1,000 @ £1.25 = £1,250 \\
\text{and} & 3,000 @ £1.27 = \underline{£3,810} \\
\text{Total} & £5,060
\end{array}
$$

Note that depending on the method used, the cost of sales (and therefore profit) differs. If the 6,000 units were sold at a price of £2.00:

- under weighted average the gross profit would be £4,614 (£12,000 – £7,386);
- under FIFO the gross profit would be £4,750 (£12,000 – £7,250).

Over time, these differences level out, but differences in gross profit when calculated under the two methods are most common where the value of inventory is increasing or decreasing.

Retail method

The retail method is used for the measurement of inventory cost for retail organizations where there are large numbers of rapidly changing items with similar margins. The retail method of inventory valuation determines the cost of inventory by deducting an appropriate percentage profit margin from the sales value of inventory. That margin would be based on past experience of margins for each group of products.

Net realizable value

Where the net realizable value is less than cost, this value should be used for inventory valuation. The net realizable value is the proceeds of sale, less any costs of disposal (e.g. transport, cleaning). The realizable value could be a discounted sales value, trade-in value, or scrap value where that value is lower than the cost of purchase (or cost of production).

Methods of costing inventory in manufacturing

There are different types of manufacturing and it is important to differentiate alternative production methods to which different methods apply for the calculation of cost of sales and the valuation of inventory:

- *Custom*: where unique, custom products are produced singly, e.g. a building.
- *Batch*: where a quantity of the same goods are produced at the same time (often called a production run), e.g. textbooks.
- *Continuous*: where products are produced in a continuous production process, e.g. oil and chemicals, soft drinks.

For custom and batch manufacture, costs are collected through a job costing system that accumulates the cost of raw materials as they are issued to each *job* (either a custom product or a batch of products) and the cost of time spent by different categories of labour. To each of these costs, overhead is allocated to cover the manufacturing costs that are a necessary part of production but that are not included in materials or labour (overhead will be explained in Chapter 13). When a custom product is completed, the accumulated cost of materials, labour, and overhead is the cost of that custom product. For each batch, the total job cost is divided by the number of units produced (e.g. the number of copies of the textbook) to give a cost per unit (i.e. cost per textbook).

For continuous manufacture a process costing system is used, under which costs are collected over a period of time, together with a measure of the volume of production. At the end of the accounting period, the total costs are divided by the volume produced to give a cost per unit of volume. Under a process costing system, materials are issued to production, but as labour hours cannot be allocated to continuously produced products, conversion costs comprise the production labour and production overhead. In process costing, equivalent units combine the number of completed units of production with the proportion of partially completed units expressed as completed units (e.g. 1,000 units 50% complete are calculated as the equivalent of 500 completed units).

We now present examples of job and process costing. In both cases, two important documents record the costs being incurred:

- Material issues: record the quantity of each type of raw material issued to production.
- Timesheets: record the number of hours worked by production labour to convert the raw material to finished goods.

Job costing illustration

Helo Europe manufactures components for helicopters. It does so in batches of 100 components. Each batch requires 500 kg of rolled and formed steel, which takes 15 hours of labour. During the course of a month, the following transactions take place:

- Purchase of steel 1,000 kg @ €12/kg;
- Issue of steel to production 500 kg;
- Labour to roll and form 500 kg steel 15 hours @ €125/hour;
- Overhead allocated at completion of production of 100 components €2,000;
- 60 of the components manufactured in the batch were sold for €130 each.

At month end, 500 kg of steel has been issued to production and 7 hours have been worked. The job is incomplete. We need to calculate the value of work-in-progress at month end.

Using this information, work-in-progress will comprise:

Materials: steel 500 kg @ €12/kg	€6,000
Labour: 7 hours @ €125	875
Work-in-progress	€6,875

After completion of the job, it is necessary to calculate the:

- unit cost of production;
- gross profit;
- value of inventory.

The job cost for the production of a batch of 100 components is as follows:

Materials: steel 500 kg @ €12/kg	€6,000
Labour: 15 hours @ €125	1,875
Overhead	2,000
Total job cost	€9,875
Cost per component	€98.75 (€9,875/100)

The cost of sales of the 60 components sold is €5,925 (60 @ €98.75). The sales income is €7,800 (60 @ €130) and the gross profit is €1,875.

The stock of finished goods is €3,950 (40 @ €98.75). The stock of raw materials is the cost of 500 kg of steel that has been purchased but remains unused at its purchase cost of €12/kg, a value of €6,000.

Job costing and work-in-progress for services

Whilst inventory may be thought of as only relating to manufacturers and retailers, it also relates to professional service firms. Accountants and lawyers are examples of firms with large work-in-progress inventories covering work carried out on behalf of clients but not yet invoiced. While these firms have no raw materials or finished goods in inventory, timesheets record the time spent by professionals on behalf of their clients.

PLC Accountants have been conducting ABC's audit. At month end 15 partner hours and 60 audit hours have been allocated to ABC's work, which has not been invoiced. The hourly cost rates used by PLC are $200/hour for partners and $80/hour for auditors.

The calculation of the work-in-progress for PLC at month end is:

15 partner hours @ $200	$3,000
60 audit hours @ $80	4,800
Total	$7,800

Process costing illustration

Voxic Co. manufactures lubricants. It does so in a continuous production process 24 hours per day, 7 days per week. During the course of a month, raw materials costing £140,000 were purchased and 100,000 litres of lubricant were produced. Materials issued to production cost £75,000 and conversion costs incurred were £55,000. 80,000 litres of lubricant were sold for £1.50/litre.

At the end of the month, calculations are necessary for the:

* unit cost of production;
* gross profit;
* value of inventory.

The cost of production for the month was £130,000 (materials £75,000 + conversion £55,000). As 100,000 litres were produced, the cost per litre is £1.30 (£130,000/100,000 litres).

The cost of sales for the 80,000 litres sold was £104,000 (80,000 @ £1.30). Sales proceeds were £120,000 (80,000 @ £1.50) and gross profit was £16,000.

Finished goods inventory is £26,000 (20,000 litres unsold @ £1.30). Raw materials inventory is valued at £65,000 (£140,000 purchased less £75,000 issued).

Process costing with partially completed units – weighted average method

Kazoo produced oils on a process basis during a month.

The opening work-in-progress was 7,000 units, consisting of materials €12,000 and conversion costs €30,000.

12,000 units commenced production during the month.

The closing work-in-progress was 4,000 units, 75% complete.

The cost of materials issued to production during the month was €140,000.

The conversion costs for production during the month were €80,000.

It is necessary to calculate:

- the number of units completed;
- the equivalent units in work-in-progress;
- the cost per unit, using the weighted average method;
- the cost of work-in-progress and finished goods at month end.

Note: in process costing examples, materials are usually assumed to be added at the beginning of the process (but in practice you would need to determine the stage at which they are added), and conversion costs are added uniformly throughout the process. Table 8.2 shows the calculations.

Table 8.2   Process costing example with partially completed units – Kazoo.

	Units
Opening WIP	7,000
Units commenced	12,000
	19,000
Closing WIP	4,000
Completed	15,000

Cost per unit:

	Opening WIP €	Cost for month €	Total €	Completed units	WIP equivalent units	Total equivalent units	Cost per equivalent unit* €
Material	12,000	140,000	152,000	15,000	4,000	19,000	€8.00
Conversion	30,000	80,000	110,000	15,000	3,000[†]	18,000	€6.11
Total	€42,000		€262,000				€14.11

Work-in-progress:

Materials 4,000 @ €8	€32,000
Conversion 3,000 @ €6.111	€18,333
	€50,333

Finished goods:

15,000 units @ €14.111	€211,666
Total costs	€262,000

*Total cost divided by total equivalent units.

[†]4,000 units, 75% complete at end of month = 3,000 equivalent units.

Note: if a FIFO method of costing and inventory valuation was used in this process costing example, a variation to this calculation would be necessary. However, for most purposes the weighted average method is sufficient for process costing with partially completed units.

Long-term contract costing

Long-term contract costing is a method of job costing that applies to large units that are produced over a long period of time, e.g. construction or software development projects. Because of the length of time the contract takes to complete, it is necessary to apportion the profit over several accounting periods. Although the goods that are the subject of the contract have not been delivered, IAS11 *Construction Contracts* requires that revenue and costs be allocated over the period in which the contract takes place (e.g. the construction period). The *stage of completion method* is the most common method to be applied to long-term contracts. Under this method, profit recognized is based on the proportion of work carried out, taking into account any known inequalities at the various stages of the contract. The costs incurred in reaching the relevant stage of completion are then matched with income. However, where the outcome of a contract is not known with reasonable certainty, no profit should be recognized, although losses should be recognized as soon as they are foreseen.

Long-term contracts will frequently allow for progress payments to be made by a customer at various stages of completion. For construction contracts, there will typically be an architect's certificate to support the stage of completion. Contracts may also include a retention value, a proportion of the total contract price that is retained by the customer and not paid until a specified period after the end of the contract.

Long-term contract costing illustration

Macro Builders has entered into a two-year contract to construct a building. The contract price is $1.2 million, with an expected cost of construction of $1 million. After one year, the following costs have been incurred:

Material delivered to site	$500,000
Salaries and wages paid	130,000
Overhead costs	170,000

The architect certifies the value of work completed to the contractual stage for a progress payment as $600,000. Macro estimates that it will cost $250,000 to complete the contract over and above the costs already incurred.

Table 8.3 shows the calculations for the:

* anticipated profit on the contract;
* amount of profit that can be considered to have been earned to date.

Table 8.3   Long-term contract costing example.

Costs of construction:	
Material delivered to site	$500,000
Salaries and wages paid	130,000
Overhead costs	170,000
	$800,000
Less work not certified	200,000
Cost of work certified	$600,000
Anticipated profit:	
Cost of work certified	$600,000
Work not certified	200,000
Estimated cost to complete	250,000
	1,050,000
Contract price	1,200,000
Anticipated profit	$150,000

Expected cost of construction $1,000,000 (or $1,050,000)
Percentage complete 60% ($600,000/$1,000,000)
Take up profit of 60% of $150,000 = $90,000

The calculation of the value of inventory is necessary before we can calculate gross profits and produce an Income Statement. In Chapter 6 we saw the format of an Income Statement for financial accounting purposes. However, directors and managers in organizations need far more detailed information than that prepared for external reporting. The next section presents a typical set of financial statements produced for management accounting purposes.

Management accounting statements

The collection and analysis of financial data on manufacturing activities, adjusted by the valuations of inventory for raw materials, work-in-progress, and finished goods, results in a manufacturing statement and cost of sales statement produced for management accounting purposes. These statements are shown in Table 8.4. Note that in a retail or services organization that buys in goods or services but does not manufacture, there would be no manufacturing statement but there would still be a cost of sales statement and an income statement.

With the exception of the Income Statement, the information contained in Table 8.4 is presented only for management purposes. It is not published as part of the Annual Report and is not disclosed to shareholders or others outside the organization.

Table 8.4   Management accounting statements.

Manufacturing statement

Material:

Raw material inventory at beginning of period	50,000	
Purchases of raw materials	150,000	
Raw material available for use	200,000	
Less raw material inventory at end of period	40,000	
Raw material usage in production		160,000
Production labour		330,000
Manufacturing overhead:		
Factory rental	50,000	
Depreciation of plant & equipment	30,000	
Light & power	10,000	
Salaries & wages of non-production labour	60,000	150,000
Total manufacturing costs		640,000
Add work-in-progress inventory at beginning of period		100,000
		740,000
Less work-in-progress inventory at end of period		60,000
Cost of goods manufactured		680,000

Cost of sales statement

Finished goods inventory at beginning of period	160,000
Cost of goods manufactured	680,000
Goods available for sale	840,000
Less finished goods inventory at end of period	120,000
Cost of sales	720,000

Income statement

Sales	1,000,000
Less cost of sales	720,000
Gross profit	280,000
Less selling and administrative expenses	150,000
Net profit	130,000

Included in the Notes to the Accounts in the financial statements would be a breakdown of the valuation of inventory in the current assets section of the Balance Sheet. This would show:

Inventory raw materials	40,000
Inventory work-in-progress	60,000
Inventory finished goods	120,000
Total	220,000

Conclusion

In this chapter we have looked at several methods of calculating the value of inventory and cost of sales, the main ones being weighted average and first in–first out (FIFO). We have also looked at the two main methods of costing for the production of goods and services: job costing and process costing, and a method of long-term contract costing. We then presented the management accounting statements prepared for internal use and which support the published Income Statement. This is a useful point at which to make the transition from Part II of this book and its concern with financial statements for external parties to the concern of Part III with the use of accounting information for decision making, planning, and control.

Importantly for Part III, while it is essential to value inventory for financial statement purposes, inventory costs may not be suitable for decision-making purposes, as Chapters 10, 11, and 12 will show. In these chapters we demonstrate that the assumptions and limitations of costs based on accounting standards have to be understood and questioned in terms of their relevance for day-to-day decision making by managers.

Questions

8.1   Opening inventory for a month is €25,000 and closing inventory for the same month is €30,000. Cost of sales for that month is €35,000. Purchases for the month are:

a.   €20,000
b.   €30,000
c.   €40,000
d.   €50,000

8.2   Goods that complete production in a manufacturing business:

a.   Increase work-in-progress inventory and decrease finished goods inventory
b.   Decrease work-in-progress inventory and increase finished goods inventory
c.   Decrease work-in-progress inventory and decrease finished goods inventory
d.   Decrease finished goods inventory and increase cost of sales

8.3   An item of stock is purchased for £1,500. The sales price was £2,000 but as the item has now been superseded it can only be sold for a discounted price of £1,350. The scrap value of the item is £1,100. To sell or scrap the stock will involve transport costs of £100. The value of the stock for Statement of Financial Position purposes is:

a.   £1,500
b.   £1,350
c.   £1,250
d.   £1,000

8.4   The following purchases are made during a month:

Feb 10	6,000 @ $2
Feb 20	3,000 @ $2.20
Feb 28	2,000 @ $2.30

Calculate the cost of 8,000 units sold in the month and the value of inventory at month end, using the:

a.   weighted average method;
b.   FIFO method.

8.5   Bluesky Ltd's Assembly Department had 20,000 units in WIP on 1 March 2014. Materials are added at the beginning of the assembly process. An additional 60,000 units were started during March, and 15,000 units were in WIP on 31 March 2014. The units in WIP on 31 March were 30% complete with respect to conversion. Costs incurred in the Assembly Department for March 2014 were as follows:

	WIP 1 March	Costs incurred in March
	£	£
Material	62,000	192,000
Conversion	25,000	85,150

Using the weighted average method of process costing, calculate the cost of goods completed and transferred to finished goods inventory during March AND the cost of WIP at 31 March 2014.

8.6   Fisher Ltd manufactures custom furniture and uses a job costing system. On 1 January 2015, there were no balances in work-in-process or finished goods inventories. The following events occurred in January 2015:

- The company began two jobs A101 (comprising 40 tables) and B202 (comprising 60 chairs).
- 400 square metres of timber were purchased at a total cost of £5,800.
- 80 litres of glue were purchased at a cost of £6 per litre.
- The following raw materials were issued during the month:
  Issue #1: Job A101 200 square metres of timber
  Issue #2: Job B202 150 square metres of timber
  Issue #3: 20 litres of glue were used on each job.
- The following amount of labour hours were spent on the two jobs:
  A101: 200 labour hours
  B202: 100 labour hours.
  Actual labour cost per hour was £30.
- Overhead should be charged to each job on the basis of £25 per labour hour.
- Job A101 was completed, and 30 tables from the job were sold for a total price of £15,000. Job B202 was unfinished at month end.

Calculate the inventory value at month end of:

- raw materials;
- work-in-progress; and
- finished goods.

Calculate the cost of sales and gross profit for the month.

8.7 Jerry's Engineering has a three-year contract to construct a large piece of capital equipment for its client. The contract price is €4 million. At the end of the first financial year of the project, material, labour, and overheads charged to the job totalled €850,000. Jerry estimates a further €2.65 million is still to be spent to complete the job. An independent valuer has certified the value of the work completed as €850,000 which the client has paid under the contract as a progress payment. Calculate the amount of profit that Jerry can recognize as having been earned in the current year.

8.8 The following transactions relate to Mammoth Product Company for the year ended 31 December 2014.

	$
Sales revenue	900,000
Purchases of raw materials	250,000
Factory labour	450,000
Factory rental	75,000
Depreciation of plant and equipment	50,000
Factory light and power	25,000
Salaries and wages of factory labour	100,000
Selling and administrative expenses	75,000
Opening inventory 1 January 2014:	
Finished goods	150,000
Work-in-progress	300,000
Raw materials	100,000
Closing inventory 31 December 2014:	
Finished goods	250,000
Work-in-progress	400,000
Raw materials	150,000

Prepare a:

- Manufacturing Statement;
- Cost of Sales Statement; and
- Income Statement.

Calculate the value of inventory to be shown in the Balance Sheet (Statement of Financial Position).

PART III

Using Accounting Information for Decision Making, Planning, and Control

Part II was concerned with the use of financial information, primarily for external reporting purposes. Part III shows the reader how accounting information is used by managers. While an analysis of financial statements is useful, particularly for external interested parties (e.g. shareholders, bankers and financiers, the government), the information is of limited use to the internal management of the business because:

- it is aggregated to the corporate level, whereas managers require information at the business unit level;
- it is aggregated to annual figures, whereas managers require timely information, usually at not less than monthly intervals (and for sales information, weekly or even daily);
- it is aggregated to headline figures (e.g. total sales), whereas managers require information in much greater detail (e.g. by customer, product/service, geographical area, business unit);
- it does not provide a comparison of plan to actual figures to provide a gauge on progress towards achieving business goals.

Consequently, the chapters in Part III are concerned with management accounting: the production of accounting information for use by managers. This information is disaggregated (to business unit level), more regular (typically monthly), and is more detailed for management decision making, planning, and control. Management accounting is not regulated by accounting standards and is not subject to audit. This means that an organization's method of management accounting can be developed to meet its particular needs, which may be different from other companies, even in the same industry (this is called a 'contingent' explanation). However, the information used in management accounting comes from the same accounting system as that which produces financial statements (although it is supplemented by other data) and the accounting system must still satisfy the requirement to produce financial statements for external parties. Management accounting cannot be divorced from the practices of financial accounting – it is intertwined, not just because of the need to produce financial statements for external parties, but because the results of decisions made using management accounting today are reflected in tomorrow's financial statements; and because the demands of users of financial statements influence the decisions made by managers.

In Part III, the accounting tools and techniques are explained and illustrated by straightforward examples. Case studies, drawn mainly from real business examples, help draw out the concepts. Theory is integrated with the tools and techniques, and the use of quotations from the original sources is intended to encourage readers to access the accounting academic literature they may find of interest.

These chapters in Part III do not take an approach to accounting that is common to other accounting textbooks. The chapters in this Part are aimed particularly at non-financial managers in functional roles, for example operations, marketing, purchasing, distribution, human resources, and information technology. These managers are not accountants but their role often encompasses responsibility for budgets, pricing, cost control, and capital investment proposals that require an understanding of how accounting is used in planning, decision making, and control. The chapters in Part III therefore take a user-focused rather than a preparer-focused approach, demonstrating techniques that do not require any prior management accounting knowledge.

Chapter 9 provides a framework of accounting and information systems through which to understand the nature of business processes and how information systems are used in planning, decision making, and control. Chapters 10, 11, and 12 consider the accounting techniques that are of value in marketing, operations, and human resource decisions, respectively. The more traditional accounting focus is left to Chapter 13, by which time the reader should have little difficulty in understanding issues of overhead allocation. Chapter 14 focuses on strategic decisions such as capital investment and Chapter 15 on divisional performance measurement. Chapter 16 covers the subject of budgeting and Chapter 17 discusses budgetary control. Chapter 18 introduces the reader to the topic of strategic management accounting.

CHAPTER 9

Accounting and Information Systems

This chapter considers the use of accounting information systems. We look at different methods of data collection and different types of information systems, with a particular focus on enterprise resource planning systems. The chapter also reviews the importance of a horizontal business process perspective on organizational functioning, rather than a vertical, hierarchical, or functional business unit perspective. The chapter concludes with an overview of the importance of systems design and internal controls for information systems.

Introduction to accounting and information systems

An information system is a system that collects information and presents it, usually in summarized form, for management. Data is a set of raw facts. Information is different from data because it has been made usable by some form of summarization and/or analysis. For example, daily sales data can be summarized and analysed as trends by customer and/or product/service in a monthly sales analysis report and thereby become meaningful management information which can be used for decision making.

Organizations will typically have an information systems (IS) strategy which follows the organizational business strategy and determines the long-term information requirements of the business. The IS strategy provides an 'umbrella' for different information technologies to help ensure that appropriate information is acquired, retained, shared, and available for use in strategy implementation. The IS strategy can be distinguished from the information technology (IT) strategy which defines the specific systems that are required to satisfy the information needs of the organization, including the hardware, software, and operating systems. The third element is the information management (IM) strategy which is concerned with ensuring that the necessary information is being provided to users. This includes the type of database that is used, data warehousing, and reporting systems.

Information is an essential tool of management, but it needs to be relevant, timely, accurate, complete, concise, and understandable. The benefits of quality information that meets these criteria may include improved decision making, better customer service, improved product/service quality, enhanced productivity, and reduced staffing and waste. However, the collection, processing, analysis, and reporting of information is an expensive process (e.g. the cost of hardware, software development, staff time), and organizations need to ensure that the value of the information obtained is greater than the cost of providing that information.

An accounting information system is one that uses technology to capture, store, process, and report accounting information. However, in this chapter we consider accounting to be only one component, albeit an important one, of management information systems.

Methods of data collection

Most data collection in organizations takes place as a by-product of transaction recording through computer systems, which have automated tasks that were carried out before computers by manual processing of documents and entries into journals and ledgers (Chapter 3 described the recording of financial transactions).

Computer systems have substantially automated routine tasks with multiple aspects of a transaction being carried out simultaneously. For example, credit sales typically incorporate the whole process of delivering goods (or services) by producing a delivery docket that accompanies goods, reducing inventory, producing an invoice, updating the receivables (debtor) records to show the amount owed by customers, producing a sales analysis by customer/product, and calculating the gross profit margin on the sale by deducting the cost of sales. This information is transferred into the general ledger, where along with all other similar transactions it is summarized and reported as sales and gross profit.

Retailers make extensive use of electronic point of sale (EPOS) technology which uses bar code scanning to reduce inventory, price goods and calculate margins, and print a cash register listing for the customer. Over a time period (day, week, or month) the outputs from such a system include a detailed analysis of business volume (e.g. number of customers, number of items sold, scanning time at the checkout), sales analysis by product, product profitability, and inventory reorder requirements. Additional benefits of EPOS include information about peak sales times during each day, products that may need to be discounted, and sales locations that may need to be expanded. More recently, supermarkets have introduced self-scan units where customers scan, pack, and pay for their own purchases without the need for a checkout operator. In many stores, a single member of staff can supervise up to a dozen self-scan terminals, a significant labour cost saving for supermarkets. Even small businesses like restaurants can take advantage of modern point of sale terminals that are relatively inexpensive and can enable business owners to monitor customer seating, generate orders for the kitchen, price goods and calculate bills, and provide detailed management reporting on inventory, sales trends, etc.

The use of electronic funds transfer at point of sale (EFTPOS – whether debit or credit cards) means that customers do not have to pay cash (which is expensive for retailers to deal with due to security requirements) but can automatically transfer funds from their bank account (or credit card) to the retailer's bank account, thereby eliminating further transactions. 'Pay pass' or 'pay wave' technology allows customers to merely pass their card over a terminal to pay for smaller value purchases without the need to enter account and PIN details, saving time for staff taking customer money. Some banks now provide their merchant customers with demographic data on customer spending using debit/credit cards, including number of transactions and average spend by customer age, gender, place of residence, etc.

The increase in e-commerce for business-to-consumer (B2C) sales means that for many products and services, purchasing over the internet enables customers to carry out the data processing previously carried out by a retailer's own employees. Companies such as Amazon and iTunes save costs by not needing expensive retail premises or staff taking customer orders. Customers order and pay online. All the retailer has to do is ship the goods (and for iTunes, Apple doesn't even have to do that as the customer downloads the purchased product). For business-to-business (B2B), electronic data interchange (EDI) enables supplier and customer systems to be linked by a common data format so that purchase orders raised by the customer are automatically converted into sales orders on the supplier. For example, in the automotive industry, orders from the major vehicle assemblers are placed on suppliers using EDI. EDI transactions enable the supplier to confirm their ability to meet the order by online means. The use of EDI enables automatic generation of invoicing by the supplier, tracing of deliveries by the logistics supplier, and receipt of goods by the vehicle assembler, ultimately leading to payment to the supplier (for a case study, see Berry and Collier, 2007).

An important part of data collection is collecting the financial details of a transaction. Also important is capturing as much information as possible about the transaction from a non-financial perspective. An example of this is the information collected from customers through retail credit cards, store loyalty cards, frequent flyer, and similar programmes. These enable retailers to maintain a detailed knowledge of their customers' purchasing habits to enable targeted promotional campaigns aimed at specific customers.

Another source of data is that which is available from and about suppliers. For example, in the automotive industry, the large vehicle assemblers collect vast quantities of information about their suppliers' costs: their cost of labour; the cost of manufacturing equipment and its capacity; the cost of raw materials such as steel. Much of this information is publically available but retaining it in an organization's information system supports subsequent negotiations between the automotive assembler's purchasing department and its suppliers. By using this information, buyers can check the reasonableness of supplier prices for component parts, as buyers can perform their own checks on what it should cost to produce the same components. This more strategic use of accounting information is described further in Chapter 18.

Of course, the more that is expected of an information system, the more data has to be collected, stored, and reported. Accounting is one type rather than the only type of information that is collected. In Chapter 4, we saw that Balanced Scorecard-type performance measurement systems collate and report information about customers, business processes, and innovation to supplement financial performance measures. Therefore, organizations need to capture information from their marketing, purchasing, production, distribution, and human resource activities. Information about key factors such as customer satisfaction, cycle times (from order to delivery), quality, waste, and on-time delivery need to be part of an information system and integrated with and reported together with financial information for management purposes.

Big data

Large volumes of information are now available from public sources. The term 'big data' refers to very large and complex data sets, which can be seen in the massive data resources of the internet and the results provided by search engines such as Google, or data held on Facebook. Organizations are able to access this information (for a fee) to enable targeted marketing. According to IBM (2012), 90% of the data in the world today has been created in the last two years. This data comes from, for example, sensors used to gather climate information, posts to social media sites, digital pictures and videos, purchase transaction records, and mobile phone signals.

Strategic intelligence and learning are more feasible with the advent of technologies to access 'big data'. It is now possible to collect extensive data about potential customers through their interaction with a business's website and through interaction with social media such as Facebook and Twitter. This data can be mined to learn about customers, competitors, and products/services. Parise, Iyer, and Vesset (2012) distinguish social analytics (non-transactional, social data) from performance management (business intelligence using transactional data). In non-transactional data, Parise, Iyer, and Vesset describe the use of social metrics to help inform managers about the success of their external and internal social marketing campaigns and the ability to calculate a 'digital footprint'.

However, big data faces the problem of how to analyse multiple pictures to devise the optimum strategy. Buytendijk (2010) has emphasized the limitations of analytics in performance measurement because, as he explains, strategy is concerned with satisfying the often differing expectations of different stakeholders. Developing strategy is full of dilemmas and analytical thinking is only partly helpful in dealing with these dilemmas. Rather than analysis, Buytendijk emphasizes the importance of synthesis, the process of taking multiple, sometimes contradictory, ideas and bringing them together to create a single picture.

From an accounting perspective, while these sources of data can provide valuable information, it can come at a significant cost to the business. A cost-benefit analysis needs to be conducted to ensure that the value to the business of this information exceeds its cost of acquisition, storage, and analysis.

Types of information system

There are various types of information system.

Transaction processing systems collect source data about each business transaction, for example customer orders, sales, purchases, inventory movements, payments, and receipts. Transaction processing reports are important for control and audit purposes but provide little usable management information. Data from transaction processing systems is predominantly financial in nature. The most common form of delivering management information to users has been the 'hard copy' report, a computer-generated report that may list transactions (a transaction report or audit trail), exceptions (an exception report, such as product sales below a predetermined price level), or a summarized report (e.g. a sales analysis) for a period.

Management information systems (MIS) may extend from financial to non-financial information and typically are more oriented to support management decisions. For example, displays of key performance data with graphical representation are becoming increasingly common. Traffic lights (red/amber/green) draw attention to those aspects of performance that are meeting target (green), those that are in need of urgent attention (red), and those that need to be considered as they are borderline (amber). However, these systems do not integrate accounting, manufacturing, and distribution systems. Market research carried out by Oracle (2011) identified criticisms by respondents including an over-reliance on spreadsheets, working with out-of-date data from multiple 'silos' of information, and a lack of data sharing between departments.

An *enterprise resource planning* (ERP) system helps to integrate data flow and access to information over the whole range of a company's activities. ERP systems typically capture transaction data for accounting purposes, together with operational, customer, and supplier data which are then made available through data warehouses against which custom-designed reports can be produced. ERP systems take a whole-of-business approach. ERP system data can be used to update performance measures in a Balanced Scorecard system (Chapter 4) and can be used for activity-based costing (Chapter 13), shareholder value analysis (Chapter 2), strategic planning, customer relationship management, and supply chain management (Chapter 18). ERP systems are a development of earlier material requirements planning (MRP), distribution requirements planning (DRP), and manufacturing resource planning (MRP2) systems.

Strategic enterprise management systems (SEM) are a type of ERP system that provide support for the strategic management process. They are based on data stored in a data warehouse which is then used by a range of analytical tools. An SEM can be an important driver of organizational performance as it enables faster and better decision making at all organizational levels.

Decision support systems (DSS) go a step further and contain data analysis models that provide the ability for managers to simulate scenarios or ask 'What if?' questions so that different options can be considered to aid in decision making. DSS may be contained in a spreadsheet or in a complex software package.

Executive information systems (EIS) are systems used for decision support which incorporate access to summarized data, often in graphical form, to enable senior managers to evaluate information about the organization and its environment. An EIS utilizes a 'drill-down' facility to move from aggregated data down to a more specific and detailed level (e.g. customer, product, business unit). Information is typically also available from external sources, for example public databases. Ease of use is an important feature so that enquiries can be made without a detailed knowledge of the underlying data structures.

Expert systems store data relevant to a specialist area and are populated with knowledge gained from experts which is retained in a structured format or knowledge base. Expert systems provide solutions to problems that require discretionary judgement. Users access data through a graphical user interface (GUI) to ask questions of the system, which prompts the user for more information. Various rules are then applied by the expert system to make decisions. The best example of an expert system is that used for credit approval. Information is entered to the system in response to prompts, such as postcode, telephone number, age, employment history, which is compared with confidential data held by credit reference agencies on a large number of similar applicants to make an automated judgement about an applicant's creditworthiness and the allocation of a credit limit.

In this chapter, we will use the term 'enterprise resource planning' (ERP) systems to refer to information systems that are not limited to accounting but integrate different functional areas of the business and take a business process perspective. The best-known examples of these systems include SAP and Oracle. These systems can be extended with tools such as Business Intelligence (or BI) or tools that enable SEM, DSS, EIS, or expert applications. ERP systems avoid 'information silos' that provide limited and specialist information to narrow groups of managers. Often these silos (typical of older transaction processing or MIS systems) are based on different software packages, use different databases, and do not always report timely, accurate, or consistent data to users. Although different modules exist in an ERP (e.g. customer order entry, inventory, invoicing, accounts receivable, management reporting), these are all integrated so that each module provides consistent information to users.

While an ERP system makes reporting easy in terms of the hierarchical or vertical structure of organizations, as reflected in the traditional organization chart, increasingly businesses are looking at the horizontal business processes that cut across departmental structures.

Business processes

We typically think of an organization in terms of its hierarchical structure: a head office with departments responsible for marketing, production, and administration; or a business unit structure with autonomous units responsible for particular products/services or geographic territories. Financial information about the hierarchical structure is important for internal financial reporting, comparing actual with budget performance and holding managers accountable for the performance of their departments or business units.

However, an organization can also be thought of as a collection of processes or activities that when combined form part of the value chain (see Chapter 11) delivering value to customers. The hierarchical perspective is based on functions carried out such as selling or accounting, with different specialists responsible for each. The business process perspective is a horizontal rather than a vertical perspective on the organization, where the focus is on *how things are done* to satisfy customer demand, with more emphasis on generalists rather than specialists. One example of a business process starts with accepting a customer's order and ends with delivering it to the customer, including the accounting transaction of invoicing the customer. Another business process is that of placing an order with a supplier through to receiving the goods or services and making payment to the supplier.

Flowcharting and process mapping are commonly used methods for representing business processes. Process maps are graphical representations of business processes showing the activities and flows of data between activities and the areas responsible for carrying out those activities. These can be simple or complex.

Figure 9.1 shows a simplified example of a process map for processing a customer order and its computer entry through the physical picking of goods from a warehouse to dispatch and invoicing. To

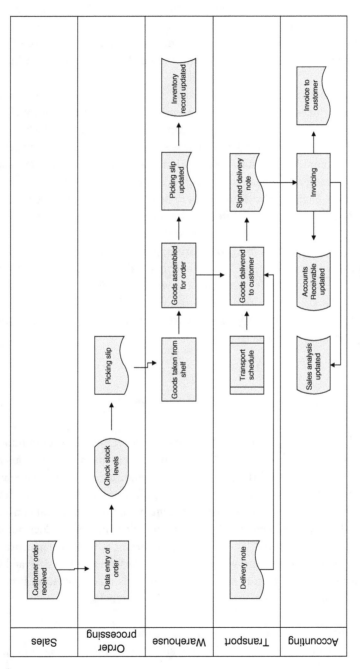

Figure 9.1   Customer order processing.

satisfy the customer, this needs to be an effective, seamless, and error-free process. However, in this example five separate departments are involved (Sales, Order Processing, Warehouse, Transport, and Accounting). As we will see in Chapter 13, accounting systems generally capture costs for departments (i.e. at the vertical or hierarchical level), but what is more important in terms of cost, efficiency, and quality is the cost of the business process itself, and the need to streamline that business process as much as possible.

Business process re-engineering (or BPR) is defined as 'the fundamental rethinking and radical design of business processes to achieve dramatic improvements in critical contemporary measures of performance, such as cost, quality, service, and speed' (Hammer and Champy, 1993). This approach can lead to improvements that eliminate duplication and waste and identify gaps where failures in quality, delivery, or service can occur. A continual re-evaluation of business processes can lead to continuous improvement, increased competitiveness, and profitability. ERP systems take a business process perspective and can help to re-engineer those processes to be more efficient and effective.

A business process perspective enables a different view of cost than the traditional approach to departments or product/services. Activity-based costing systems (see Chapter 13) provide a means by which costs can be accumulated both for hierarchical reporting purposes and on a horizontal or business process basis in relation to business activities. This means that, using Figure 9.1 as an example, in addition to accumulating costs for each of the five departments, we could produce total costs for customer order processing, and in an ERP system, link this to non-financial data such as the number of customer orders, number of picking slips, number of inventory items, and number of deliveries to produce useful analytical data about the cost of these activities.

Information systems design and controls

The sheer volume of data now available to organizations and the variety of types of information systems that can be utilized make the design of information systems to meet the needs of the business particularly important. This is particularly so when the complexity of accounting for both the hierarchical organizational structure and the business processes is required. Organizations will frequently need to improve or change their ERP systems to meet changing customer demand or environmental constraints. However, there is a significant risk in the development of these systems that the system does not meet user needs, is late, or costs more than was estimated. Therefore, it is important to have strong controls over information systems design. This is necessary even where proven ERP systems such as SAP and Oracle are introduced as these systems will usually require customization to meet an organization's specific needs.

The key elements of project management for information systems are:

- specification of requirements and obtaining top management support;
- project organization: defining the roles and responsibilities of the steering committee and project manager;
- resource planning – both staff and money;

- quality control and progress monitoring;
- user participation and involvement.

A steering committee should monitor the system implementation and have overall responsibility to ensure that the system meets requirements in terms of quality, time, and cost. Systems development projects should comprise four distinct stages:

- Feasibility study stage: there should be a clear understanding about the objectives of the new system, the deliverables, its cost, and time to completion.
- System design stage: data security and levels of authorization need to be built into the system design. During this stage, the internal auditor should review system documentation, interfaces with other systems, and acceptance of design by all in the project team, especially users.
- Testing stage: comprehensive testing by systems development staff, programmers, users, and internal auditors.
- Implementation stage: a review of training and documentation, file conversion, and operational issues, e.g. staffing and supervision.

An implementation plan will cover parallel running, where the new system is operated in conjunction with the existing system until such time as the new system is proven to work by reconciling outputs from both systems; and ensuring that users are satisfied with the new system and are confident about discontinuing the existing system. If there is a changeover without parallel running, then testing prior to implementation becomes more important and additional monitoring may be needed during the early stages of implementation. A post-implementation review of the new system should also be carried out to establish whether the system is operating as intended and to confirm that user needs are being satisfied.

As organizations increasingly rely on their ERP systems, information system controls are essential to ensure the security of data and the reliability of information once an information system is operational. There are four main types of controls in relation to information systems:

1. Security controls: the prevention of unauthorized access, modification, or destruction of stored data. Recruitment, training, and supervision need to be in place to ensure the competency of those responsible for programming and data entry. Access controls, e.g. through passwords, provide security over unauthorized access to data.
2. Application controls are designed for each individual application, such as payroll, accounting, and inventory control. The aim of application controls is to prevent, detect, and correct transaction processing errors.
3. Network controls have arisen in response to the growth of distributed processing and e-commerce and the need for protection against hacking and viruses. A firewall comprises a combination of hardware and software located between the company's private network (intranet) and the public network.
4. Contingency controls are relied upon if other controls fail; there must be a back-up facility and a contingency plan to restore business operations as quickly as possible (e.g. a business continuity or disaster recovery plan).

Conclusion

This chapter has shown the important role that information systems play in planning, decision making, and control. We have not limited ourselves to purely accounting systems here but have focused on the role of enterprise resource planning systems (ERP, such as Oracle and SAP) which increasingly play a key role in providing financial and non-financial information for managers. In using ERP systems, organizations are able to refocus on business processes rather than the hierarchical organizational structures that are more allied with externally oriented financial reporting. We have also looked at the importance of the design of information systems to ensure they can meet organizational needs.

References

Berry, A. J. and Collier, P. M. (2007). Risk management in supply chains: processes, organisation for uncertainty and culture. *International Journal of Risk Assessment and Management*, 7(8), 1005–26.

Buytendijk, F. (2010). *Dealing with Dilemmas: Where Business Analytics Fall Short*. New Jersey: John Wiley & Sons.

Hammer, M. and Champy, J. (1993). *Reengineering the Corporation: A Manifesto for Business Revolution*. London: Nicholas Brealey.

IBM (2012). *What is big data?* http://www-01.ibm.com/software/data/bigdata/what-is-big-data.html (accessed August 2014).

Oracle (2011). Performance management: An incomplete picture. *The Oracle Report*. http://www.oracle.com/webapps/dialogue/ns/dlgwelcome.jsp?p_ext=Y&p_dlg_id=10077790&src=7038701&Act=29 (accessed August 2014, sign up to Oracle is required which is free of charge).

Parise, S., Iyer, B., and Vesset, D. (2012). Four strategies to capture and create value from big data. *Ivey Business Journal*, July/August http://www.iveybusinessjournal.com/topics/strategy/four-strategies-to-capture-and-create-value-from-big-data (accessed August 2014).

Questions

9.1   Explain the differences between transaction processing systems, management information systems, and enterprise resource planning systems.

9.2   Compare and contrast the value of financial information under the hierarchical or vertical perspective and the horizontal or business process perspective.

9.3   Explain the importance and role of information systems design and information systems controls.

CHAPTER 10

Marketing Decisions

This chapter considers the use of accounting information in making marketing decisions. It begins with an overview of some of the key elements of marketing theory and introduces cost behaviour: the distinction between fixed and variable costs, average and marginal costs. Decisions involving the relationship between price and volume are covered through the technique of cost–volume–profit (CVP) analysis and a consideration of how a different product/sales mix and operating leverage affects profitability. Different approaches to pricing are covered: cost-plus pricing; target rate of return; the optimum selling price; and special pricing decisions. The chapter concludes with an introduction to segmental profitability and customer profitability analysis.

Marketing strategy

Marketing is the business function that aims to understand customer needs and satisfy those needs more effectively than competitors. Marketing can be achieved through a focus on selling products and services or through building lasting relationships with customers (customer relationship management). Marketing texts emphasize the importance of adding value through marketing activity. Adding value differentiates product/services from competitors, and enables a price to be charged that equates to the benefits obtained by the customer. However, for any business to achieve profitability, customers must be prepared to pay more for the product/service benefit than the benefit costs to provide.

Porter (1980) identified five forces that affect an industry: the threat of new entrants; the bargaining power of customers; the bargaining power of suppliers; the threat of substitute product/services; and the threat from competitors, each of which develops strategies for success. In a later book, Porter (1985) identified three generic strategies that businesses can adopt in order to achieve a sustainable competitive advantage. The alternative strategies were to be a low-cost producer, to be a higher-cost producer that can differentiate its product/services, or to focus on a market niche.

Understanding business costs, especially product/service cost, is important in marketing decisions, but it will be more important for a low-cost strategy than for a differentiation or focus strategy, where the focus will be more on brand reputation, after-sales service, and various non-financial performance measures (see the Balanced Scorecard in Chapter 4) rather than cost alone.

Pricing of product/services is setting a price that customers are willing to pay for a product/service in a competitive market. Setting the right price is crucial to business success, in terms of increasing the perceived value so as to maximize the margin between price and cost and to increase volume and market share without eroding profits. Pricing strategies may be aimed at *penetration* – achieving long-term market share – or *skimming* – maximizing short-term profits from a limited market size. Accounting can assist in understanding the profitability impact of high-volume/low-margin versus low-volume/high-margin strategies. A further element of marketing is the distribution channel to be used. This may range from the company's own sales force to retail outlets, direct marketing, and the number of intermediaries between the product/service provider and the ultimate customer. The cost of distribution can significantly affect profits and so distribution channel profitability, like customer profitability, is an important focus for accounting.

The price customers are willing to pay depends on what has been termed the factors which drive up utility. Utility can derive from product, service, personnel, and image drivers. Product drivers include performance, features, reliability, operating costs, and serviceability. Services drivers include ease of credit availability, ordering, delivery, installation, training, after-sales service, and guarantees. Personnel drivers include the professionalism, courtesy, reliability, and responsiveness of staff. Image drivers reflect the confidence of customers in the company or brand name, which is built through the other three drivers and by advertising and promotional activity. However each of these value drivers has cost drivers. Consequently, accounting needs to pay attention to the drivers of customer utility so that the costs of those drivers can be compared with the price which can be charged to customers.

The product mix or sales mix is the mix of product/services offered by the business, each of which may be aimed at satisfying different customer needs. Businesses develop marketing strategies to meet the needs of their customers in different *market segments*, each of which can be defined by its unique characteristics (e.g. different geographic areas or distribution channels). These segments may yield different prices and incur different costs as customers demand more or less of different product/services. Product/service mix can significantly affect profitability as businesses aim to increase sales of the more profitable product/services relative to others.

A focus on customer relationship management entails taking a longer-term view than product/service profitability and emphasizes the profits that can be derived from a satisfied customer base. The cost of winning new customers is high (advertising, sales representation, negotiation, etc.), and loyal customers tend to buy more regularly, spend more, and are often willing to pay premium prices. This is an element of the business goodwill that is shown in financial statements where a business is acquired (Chapter 6) and part of the 'intellectual capital' that lies behind financial statements (see Chapter 7).

Marketing texts typically introduce marketing strategy as a combination of the 4 Ps of product, price, place, and promotion. The marketing strategy for a business will encompass decisions about product/service mix, customer mix, market segmentation, value and cost drivers, pricing, and distribution channel. Each element of marketing strategy requires an understanding of accounting, which can help to answer questions such as:

- How can accounting information support the marketing strategy?
- What is the volume of product/services that we need to sell to maintain profitability?
- What alternative approaches to pricing can we adopt?
- What is our customer, product/service, and distribution channel profitability in each of our market segments?

This chapter is concerned with answering these questions. Although information on competitors, customers, and suppliers is likely to be limited, strategic management accounting approaches (see Chapter 18) can apply the same tools and techniques in the pursuit of competitive advantage.

Cost behaviour

Marketing decisions cannot be made in isolation from knowledge of the costs of the business and the impact that marketing strategy has on operations and on business profitability. Profitability for marketing decisions is the difference between *revenue* – the income earned from the sale of product/services – and cost. As we saw in Chapter 3, it is the notion of cost that is problematic.

For many business decisions, it is helpful to distinguish between how costs behave, i.e. whether they are fixed or variable. Fixed costs are those that do not change with increases in business activity (such as rent). This is not to say that fixed costs never change (obviously rents do increase in accordance with the terms of a lease) but there is no connection (except sometimes in large retail shopping centres) between cost and the volume of activity. By contrast, variable costs do increase/decrease in proportion to an increase/decrease in business volume, so that as a business produces more units of a good or service, the business incurs proportionately more costs.

For example, advertising is a fixed cost because there is no relationship between spending on advertising and generating revenue (although we may wish there was). However, sales commission is a variable cost because the more a business sells, the more commission it pays out.

A simple example shows the impact of fixed and variable cost behaviour on total and average cost. XYZ Limited has the capacity to produce between 10,000 and 30,000 units of a product each period. Its fixed costs are £200,000. Variable costs are £10 per unit. The example is shown in Table 10.1.

In this example, even if the business produces no units, costs are still £200,000 because fixed costs are independent of volume. Total costs increase as the business incurs variable costs of £10 for each unit produced. However, the average cost declines with the increase in volume because the fixed cost is spread over more units.

Table 10.1   Cost behaviour – fixed and variable costs.

Activity (number of units sold)	Fixed costs (£200,000)	Variable costs (£10 per unit)	Total cost (£)	Average cost (per unit)
10,000	200,000	100,000	300,000	£30.00
15,000	200,000	150,000	350,000	£23.33
20,000	200,000	200,000	400,000	£20.00
25,000	200,000	250,000	450,000	£18.00
30,000	200,000	300,000	500,000	£16.67

Not all costs are quite so easy to separate between fixed and variable. Some costs are semi-fixed, while others are semi-variable. Semi-fixed costs (also called step fixed costs) are constant within a particular level of activity, but can increase when activity reaches a critical level. This can happen, for example, with changes from a single-shift to a two-shift operation, which requires not only additional variable costs but also additional fixed costs (e.g. extra supervision). Semi-variable costs have both fixed and variable components. A simple example is a telephone bill, which will have a fixed component (rental) and a variable component (calls). Maintenance of motor vehicles can be both time based (the fixed component) and mileage based (the variable component).

This example introduces the notion of marginal cost. The marginal cost is the cost of producing one extra unit. In the above example, to increase volume from 10,000 to 15,000 units incurs a marginal cost of £50,000 (which in this case is 5,000 additional units at a variable cost of £10 each). However, in some circumstances marginal costs may include a fixed-cost element (in the case of semi-fixed costs).

The contribution margin is important in marketing decisions. Contribution margin is the difference between sales revenue and variable costs of sale. It differs from gross profit (which we introduced in Chapter 6) which includes both fixed and variable costs in the cost of sales. The value of the contribution margin approach is that we can understand the marginal contribution of a sale towards profits because fixed costs, while they may be included in the cost of a product or service, do not change whether or not the sale takes place. Hence, a more meaningful presentation of information is:

Sales revenue	€400,000
Less variable cost of sales	180,000
Contribution margin	220,000
Less fixed cost of sales	130,000
Gross profit	€90,000

The notion of cost is therefore quite difficult. Is the cost in Table 10.1 the average cost or the marginal cost? If it is the average cost, what level of activity is chosen to determine that average, given fluctuating volumes of sales from period to period? There are several possible answers: if our activity level last year was 10,000 units, we may say the cost is £30 per unit, but if we expect to have an activity level of 15,000 units this year, perhaps the cost is £23.33. Then again, if our marginal cost to produce one extra unit is only £10, isn't that our cost? One of the earliest writers on management accounting described 'different costs for different purposes' (Clark, 1923) so we need to understand the purpose for which we want to use the cost before deciding what the appropriate measure of cost is.

Cost–volume–profit analysis

A method for understanding the relationship between profit, cost, and sales revenue is cost–volume–profit analysis, or CVP. CVP is concerned with understanding the relationship between changes in activity (the number of units sold) and changes in selling prices and costs (both fixed and variable). Typical questions that CVP may help with are:

- What is the likely effect on profits of changes in selling price or the volume of activity?
- If we incur additional costs, what changes should we make to our selling price or to the volume that we need to sell?

CVP is used by accountants in a relatively simplistic manner. While most businesses will sell a wide range of product/services at many different prices (e.g. quantity discounts), accountants assume a constant sales mix and average selling prices per unit. The assumption is that these relationships are linear, rather than the curvilinear models preferred by economists that reflect economies and diseconomies of scale. The accountant limits this problem by recognizing the relevant range. The relevant range is the volume of activity within which the business expects to be operating over the short-term planning horizon, typically the current or next accounting period, and the business will usually have experience of operating at this level of output. Within the relevant range, the accountant's model and the economist's model are similar.

Profit can be shown as the difference between revenue and costs (both fixed and variable). This relationship can be shown in the following formula:

net profit = revenue – (fixed costs + variable costs)
net profit = (units sold × selling price) – [fixed costs + (units sold × unit variable cost)]

In mathematical terms, this is:

$$N = Pu - (F + Bu)$$

where:

N = net profit
u = number of units sold
P = selling price per unit
F = total fixed costs
B = variable cost per unit

Using the example of XYZ Limited, a selling price of £25 for 20,000 units would yield a net profit of:

$N = (£25 \times 20,000) - [£200,000 + (£10 \times 20,000)]$
$N = £500,000 - £400,000$
$N = £100,000$

CVP permits sensitivity analysis. Sensitivity analysis is an approach to understanding how changes in one variable (e.g. price) affect other variables (e.g. volume). This is important, because revenues and costs cannot be predicted with certainty and there is always a range of possible outcomes, i.e. different mixes of price, volume, and cost.

Using sensitivity analysis, a business may ask questions such as: What is the selling price (P) required for a profit (N) of £150,000 on sales of 25,000 units? To calculate this, we enter the data we know in the formula and solve for the missing figure (in this case price):

$$£150,000 = £P \times 25,000 - \left[£200,000 + (£10 \times 25,000)\right]$$

$$£150,000 = £25,000P - £450,000$$

$$P = \frac{£600,000}{25,000}$$

$$P = £24 \ per \ unit$$

The breakeven point is the point at which total costs equal total revenue; that is, where there is neither a profit nor a loss. How many units have to be sold for the business to break even? This question can be answered by using simple algebra to solve the above equation for u (the number of units), where N (net profit) is 0, as follows:

$$0 = Pu - (F + Bu)$$

$$0 = 20u - (200,000 + 10u)$$

$$u = \frac{200,000}{10}$$

$$u = 20,000$$

However, a simpler formula for breakeven is:

$$breakeven \ sales \ (in \ units) = \frac{fixed \ costs}{selling \ price \ per \ unit - variable \ cost \ per \ unit} = \frac{£200,000}{20 - 10} = 20,000 \ units$$

Note that £10 is the *unit contribution*, i.e. the contribution to profit – the difference between the selling price and the variable cost per unit. The unit contribution can also be expressed as a percentage of sales of 0.5 or 50% (£10/£20), which applies to any level of sales as the ratio of contribution (£10) to selling price (£20) remains constant within the relevant range.

$$breakeven \ sales \ (in £s) = \frac{fixed \ costs}{unit \ contribution \ as \ a \ \% \ of \ sales} = \frac{£200,000}{0.5} = £400,000$$

This is equivalent to the breakeven units of 20,000 at £20 selling price per unit.

Businesses establish profit targets, and a variation on the above formulae is to calculate the number of units that need to be sold to generate a target net profit.

$$sales\,(in\ units)\,for\ profit\ of\ \pounds150,000 = \frac{fixed\ costs + target\ profit}{selling\ price\ per\ unit - variable\ cost\ per\ unit}$$

$$= \frac{\pounds200,000 + \pounds150,000}{20 - 10}$$

$$= 35,000\ units$$

$$sales\,(in\ \pounds s)\,for\ profit\ of\ \pounds150,000 = \frac{fixed\ costs + target\ profit}{unit\ contribution\ as\ a\ \%\ of\ sales}$$

$$= \frac{\pounds200,000 + \pounds150,000}{0.5}$$

$$= \pounds700,000$$

This is equivalent to the sales in units of 35,000 at £20 selling price per unit. However, if the business has a maximum capacity of 25,000 units, the limit of its relevant range, this profitability may not be achievable and the cost structure of the business reflected in the CVP relationship would have to be revised.

CVP can be understood through a graphical representation. Using the same data, the CVP graph is shown in Figure 10.1. In this CVP diagram, the vertical axis represents money (both revenue and cost) and the horizontal axis represents volume (the number of units sold). Fixed costs are seen to be constant, as increases in volume do not influence total fixed cost within the relevant range. Variable costs are nil at zero level of activity and increase in proportion to that activity. Total costs are the sum of variable and fixed costs. They begin above zero because, even with zero level of activity, fixed costs are still incurred. Total revenue starts at nil and increases with the volume sold.

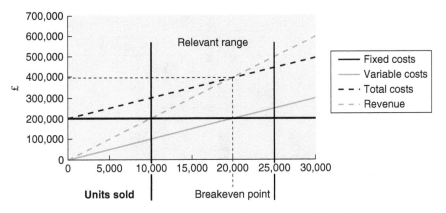

Figure 10.1   Breakeven chart for XYZ Ltd.

As fixed costs remain constant, profit per unit will vary at different levels of activity. The point at which the total cost line intersects the total revenue line is the breakeven point.

The breakeven point is shown by the dotted line and can be read as the revenue required (£400,000) to sell a given volume (20,000 units) at a selling price of £20 per unit. The area of profit is found to the right of the breakeven point, between total revenue and total cost. The area of loss is found to the left of the breakeven point, between total cost and total revenue. Note, however, that outside the relevant range (shown in the diagram as between 10,000 and 25,000 units) cost behaviour may be different and so the CVP diagram may have to be redrawn. The breakeven chart shows the margin of safety, which becomes larger as volume moves to the right of the breakeven point. The margin of safety is a measure of the difference between the anticipated and breakeven levels of activity. It is expressed as a percentage:

$$margin\ of\ safety\,(\%) = \frac{expected\ sales - breakeven\ sales}{expected\ sales} \times 100$$

Using the same example, the margin of safety assuming anticipated sales of 25,000 units is:

$$\frac{25,000 - 20,000}{25,000} \times 100 = 20\%$$

The lower the margin of safety, the higher the risk, as sales do not have to fall much before reaching the breakeven point. Conversely, there is less risk where businesses operate with higher margins of safety.

Whereas the breakeven graph shows the breakeven point, the *profit–volume graph* shows the profit or loss at different levels of activity. For the same example, the profit–volume graph is shown in Figure 10.2.

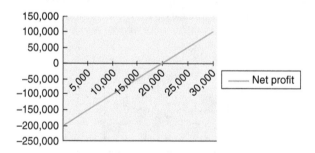

Figure 10.2   Profit–volume graph for XYZ Ltd.

At any level of output the net profit (or loss) can be seen in Figure 10.2. This example shows the breakeven point of 20,000 units and the small margin of safety to the anticipated sales level of 25,000 units, compared with the risk of substantial loss following from any level of activity below 20,000 units.

Sales mix and breakeven with multiple products

Sales mix is a particularly important factor in understanding profitability. A business that achieves its sales target may not achieve its profit target if the sales mix varies and profitability varies between products, as Tables 10.2 and 10.3 illustrate.

Table 10.2   Sales mix and profitability with multiple products – sales mix 1.

Sales mix 1	Sales mix			
	M	N	O	Total
Sales volume (units)	200	150	100	450
Selling price per unit	$10	$11	$15	
Sales revenue	$2,000	$1,650	$1,500	$5,150
Variable costs %	55%	45%	35%	
Variable costs	$1,100	$742	$525	$2,367
Contribution margin	$900	$908	$975	$2,783 54.0%
Less fixed costs				$1,400
Profit				$1,383

In sales mix 1 (Table 10.2), the business sells 450 units in total, but the sales volume, selling prices, and variable costs are quite different for each of products M, N, and O. The contribution margin is 54% of sales revenue.

Table 10.3   Sales mix and profitability with multiple products – sales mix 2.

Sales mix 2	Sales mix			
	M	N	O	Total
Sales volume (units)	300	150	30	480
Selling price per unit	$10	$11	$15	
Sales revenue	$3,000	$1,650	$450	$5,100
Variable costs %	55%	45%	35%	
Variable costs	$1,650	$742	$158	$2,550
Contribution margin	$1,350	$908	$292	$2,550 50.0%
Less fixed costs				$1,400
Profit				$1,150

In sales mix 2 (Table 10.3), more units have been sold in total and sales revenue in total is almost the same as in sales mix 1, but the mix of sales of products M, N, and O has changed significantly. The contribution per unit for M is $4.50, for N $6.05, and for O $9.75. In sales mix 2, more of the less profitable M products have been sold while less of the more profitable product O has been sold. The result is a decrease in total contribution margin (and hence profit) by $233 or 4% of sales revenue between sales mix 1 and sales mix 2. This highlights the value of monitoring sales mix using management accounting information.

Although businesses typically sell more than one product, CVP can still be used, but the sales mix does need to be fairly constant when using breakeven calculations, although CVP can still be applied by weighting the sales and margins of each product.

In the example in Table 10.4, a company has fixed costs of €200,000 for a period. During the same period, Product A constitutes 60% of a company's sales and each unit is sold for €30 each, with variable costs of €12 each. Product B represents the other 40% of sales, with each unit selling for €15 and variable costs of €7.

The contribution per unit is calculated and weighted by the sales mix to give a breakeven number of units. Table 10.4 shows the calculation of the breakeven point.

Table 10.4   Breakeven with multiple products.

	Product A (60% sales mix)	Product B (40% sales mix)
Selling price	€30	€15
Variable costs	€12	€7
Contribution per unit	€18	€8
Weighting of contribution by sales mix	60% × €18 = €10.80	40% × €8 = €3.20
Breakeven	$\frac{€200,000}{€10.80 + €3.20} = \frac{€200,000}{€14} =$ 14,286 units (both products A & B)	
Units by product to breakeven	14,286 × 60% = 8,572	14,286 × 40% = 5,714
Sales	8,572 @ €30 = €257,160	5,714 @ €15 = €85,710
Variable costs	8,572 @ €12 = €102,864	5,714 @ €7 = €39,998
Contribution	€154,296	€45,712
Total Contribution (Products A & B)	€200,008	

In this example, the breakeven is 14,286 units but this number represents combined sales of both products A and B. The sales mix (60/40) is applied again to derive the number of units for each of Products A and B. The accuracy of the result can be seen by calculating the contribution for the break-even level of sales for each unit which is equal to fixed costs.

Importantly, if 14,286 units are sold but (compared to the calculation in Table 10.4) there are more units of Product A sold and less of Product B, the business will earn a higher total contribution because the contribution per unit from Product A is higher than that for Product B. The opposite is also true, that if the mix changes and more are sold of Product B than Product A, even though 14,286 units may be sold in total, breakeven will not be reached. Hence, whilst this method is useful, it does rely on a close monitoring of the sales mix itself.

Operating leverage

Operating leverage refers to the mix of fixed and variable costs in a business and its ability to use its fixed costs to generate a contribution. A high operating leverage means that there are high fixed costs, low variable costs, and a high contribution margin per unit sold. Assume that two companies sell the same number of products at the same price and make the same profit. However, the mix of fixed and variable costs is different between the two companies. Table 10.5 shows an example.

Table 10.5   Operating leverage: fixed and variable costs.

	Company A		Company B	
Sales	200,000 @ $1.50	$300,000	200,000 @ $1.50	$300,000
Variable costs	90 cents per unit	180,000	30 cents per unit	60,000
Contribution	60 cents per unit	120,000	$1.20 per unit	240,000
Fixed costs		100,000		220,000
Profit		$20,000		$20,000
Breakeven point	$100,000/$0.60	166,667 units @$1.50 $250,000	$220,000/$1.20	183,333 units @ $1.50 $275,000 Higher risk
Contribution from 50,000 units sold (after breakeven)	50,000 @ $0.60	$30,000	50,000 @ $1.20	$60,000 Higher return

Table 10.5 shows that Company B has a higher operating leverage. This leads to a higher breakeven point as more units must be sold to achieve breakeven. However, Company B also has a higher contribution margin per unit, which means that once it has passed the breakeven point and recovered its fixed costs, it will generate profits faster for each additional unit sold because its contribution margin per unit sold is higher than that for Company A. Company B can make a higher return but because of its higher fixed costs, also faces a higher risk if the breakeven point is not reached.

Limitations of CVP analysis

Despite the advantages presented by CVP analysis, there are some significant limitations arising from the assumptions made. The assumptions are:

- Volume is the only factor that causes prices and variable costs to alter (in practice, production efficiencies, product/service mix, price levels, etc. all influence costs and revenues).
- There is a single product/service or a product/service mix that remains constant (in practice, product/service mix can vary significantly and different product/services may have different cost structures, prices, and contributions).
- Costs can be accurately divided into fixed and variable elements (although in practice many costs are semi-variable and semi-fixed – we develop this idea further in Chapter 13).
- Fixed costs do not change (although in practice they vary with the range of items produced and with product complexity, as we will see in Chapter 13).
- Total costs and revenues are linear (while this is reasonably likely within the relevant range, increases in volume may still lead to lower unit prices or economies of scale and curvilinear costs and revenues may be more accurate).
- The CVP analysis applies only to the relevant range (although decisions may be made in the current period to move outside this range).
- The analysis applies only to the short term and cannot reliably be used in the longer term.

Despite its limitations, CVP analysis is a useful tool in making decisions about pricing and volume, based on an understanding of the cost structure of the business. The next section describes how businesses make decisions about what price to charge.

Alternative approaches to pricing

Accounting information can be used for pricing by a variety of approaches:

- cost-plus pricing;
- target rate of return pricing;
- optimum selling price; and
- special pricing decisions.

However, it is important to remember that in most cases (unless a business has a monopoly or is a *price-maker*/price leader in the marketplace), selling prices will be dictated by what customers are prepared to pay and the prices set by competitors. The company will then be a *price-taker*. Hence, accounting-based costs may not be a reliable guide to setting prices. In these cases, cost information will be used, not in price setting, but in calculating product/service profitability, and in decisions about product or market discontinuance, which we look at later in this chapter.

An understanding of the firm's marketing strategy is essential in using cost information for pricing decisions.

As well as being price-makers or price-takers, businesses also adopt *market-skimming* or *market-penetration* strategies at different phases of the product/service life cycle (see Chapter 18). A common marketing strategy is *differential pricing*, where prices vary between each market segment. Where products/services are sold in different market segments at different prices, the price can be considered in different ways:

- A minimum short-term price taking into account only marginal, i.e. usually variable, costs.
- A minimum long-term price that covers the full product/service cost.
- A target long-term price that takes into account the return on investment necessary to increase shareholder value.

In each case, cost will be an important, but by no means the only, factor taken into account in pricing decisions.

Cost-plus pricing

Accounting information may be used in pricing decisions, particularly where the firm is a market leader or *price-maker*. In these cases, firms may adopt cost-plus pricing, in which a margin is added to the total product/service cost in order to determine the selling price. In CVP analysis, we differentiated variable costs from fixed costs and argued that in certain circumstances, a product/service could be sold where the contribution was positive, even though fixed costs were not covered. However, in the long term, the prices at which a business sells its goods/services must cover all of its costs. If it is unable to do so, it will make losses and may not survive. For every product/service the full cost must be calculated, to which the desired profit margin is added. Full cost includes an allocation to each product/service of all the costs of the business, including producing and delivering a good or service, and all its marketing, selling, finance, and administration costs. The calculation of full cost is covered in Chapter 13, but it is taken as given for the purposes of this chapter.

Using the CVP example provided earlier, the average cost was £20 assuming a level of activity of 20,000 units. The cost-plus pricing formula may be applied as a *mark-up* on any element of cost. For example, a mark-up of 25% would result in a selling price of £25:

$$\textbf{cost} + \textbf{mark-up on cost} = \textbf{selling price}$$
$$£20 + (25\% \ of \ £20) \quad = £25$$

The profit margin is the profit as a percentage of the selling price. Using the same example, the profit *margin* of £5 is 20% of the selling price of £25. A mark-up is the percentage added to cost for profit, whereas the margin is the percentage of the selling price that is represented by profit.

Often the mark-up will be an arbitrary figure, based on past experience, but it may be based on a ratio (see Chapter 7) such as return on sales (as in the above example). When considering the gross and operating margin ratios in Chapter 7, it is important to remember that achieving a ratio for the business as a whole means that individual products/services must all contribute towards that ratio, even though in practice some products/services will achieve higher returns, and others lower.

Another way of looking at the price is in terms of a return on the investment.

Target rate of return pricing

Target rate of return pricing estimates the (fixed and working) capital investment required for the business and the need to generate an adequate return on that investment to satisfy shareholders.

For example, if the investment required to produce a product/service is €1,000,000 and the company wants a 12% return on investment, the desired profit is €120,000 (€1,000,000 @ 12%). Assuming a volume of 20,000 units, each unit would need to generate a profit of €6 (€120,000/20,000 units). If the total cost was €20, the selling price would be €26. This represents a 30% mark-up on cost and a 23.1% margin on selling price. Target rate of return pricing is likely to lead to pricing decisions that are more closely linked to shareholder value than adding an arbitrary margin to total cost.

Optimum selling price

While cost-plus and target rate of return pricing is useful, it ignores the relationship between price and demand in a competitive business environment. The sensitivity of demand to changes in price is reflected in the *price elasticity of demand*. *Elastic demand* exists when a price increase leads to a fall in demand as customers place little value on the product/service or switch to substitutes. *Inelastic demand* exists where small price increases/decreases cause only a small change in demand because customers value the product or because no substitute is available.

The optimum selling price is the point at which profit is maximized. To ascertain the optimum selling price, a business must understand cost behaviour in terms of variable or fixed costs and have some ability, via market research, to predict likely changes in volume as prices increase or decrease.

MNO Limited has used market research to estimate the likely increase in demand as the selling price falls. For each level of activity we can calculate the revenue, variable costs, and total contribution. The figures are shown in Table 10.6.

Table 10.6   MNO Ltd – contribution at different activity levels.

Selling price per unit ($)	Volume expected at given selling price (units)	Revenue (selling price × volume) ($)	Variable costs (@ $10 per unit) ($)	Contribution (revenue – variable costs) ($)
40	10,000	400,000	100,000	300,000
35	15,000	525,000	150,000	375,000
30	20,000	600,000	200,000	400,000
25	25,000	625,000	250,000	375,000
20	30,000	600,000	300,000	300,000

An approach that seeks to maximize sales revenue will result in a strategy that seeks to sell 25,000 units at $25 each, with total revenue being $625,000. However, taking account of the price/volume relationship and costs (which were estimated at $10 variable cost per unit) shows that the business will *maximize its contribution* towards fixed costs and profit at $400,000 with an optimum selling price of $30. This is so even though the number of units sold will be less at 20,000 with total revenue of $600,000.

The highest contribution will always be the highest profit as the fixed costs will be unchanged at each level of activity within the relevant range. Although businesses seek to *increase* sales revenue, they wish to *maximize* contribution and therefore profitability. This issue is often the cause of conflict between marketing and finance staff in business organizations, especially where sales revenue is rewarded by commission payments to sales representatives.

Special pricing decisions

Special pricing decisions are usually one-time orders at a price below that usually sold in the market. In the long term, all the costs of the business must be covered by the selling price if the business is to be profitable. However, in the short term, spare capacity may lead to decisions to accept orders from customers at less than the full cost. As fixed costs remain the same irrespective of volume, provided that the selling price covers the variable costs, a selling price at less than full cost can make a positive contribution to recovering some of the fixed costs of the business and therefore to a greater profit (or lower loss).

A business may have adopted a marketing strategy to sell at a price of £30, but only 17,000 units have been sold. The business profitability will be:

		£'000
Revenue	17,000 @ £30	510
Variable costs	17,000 @ £10	170
Contribution		340
Fixed costs		200
Net profit		140

Accepting an order of 3,000 units at £12 will increase profits by £6,000 (3,000 at a selling price of £12 less variable costs of £10) because fixed costs will remain unchanged. The business profitability will then be:

		£'000
Revenue	17,000 @ £30	510
	3,000 @ £12	36
		546
Variable costs	20,000 @ £10	200
Contribution		346
Fixed costs		200
Net profit		146

Consequently, provided that the business can sell at a price that at least covers variable costs, in the short term the business will be better off. This argument does not follow through into the long term, over which the business must cover all its costs in order to be profitable. A business will also minimize its losses by selling at a price that covers variable costs but not full costs. If volume falls below the breakeven point:

		£'000
Revenue	8,000 @ £30	240
Variable costs	8,000 @ £10	80
Contribution		160
Fixed costs		200
Net loss		40

If an order of 3,000 units at £12 is accepted, the loss will be reduced by £6,000:

		£'000
Revenue	8,000 @ £30	240
	3,000 @ £12	36
		276
Variable costs	11,000 @ £10	110
Contribution		166
Fixed costs		200
Net loss		34

However, consideration needs to be given to the long-term marketing implications of accepting orders at less than normal selling price:

1. The future selling price may be affected by accepting a special order, if competitors adopt similar pricing tactics.
2. Customers who receive or become aware of a special selling price may expect a similar low price in the future.
3. Accepting this order may prevent the firm from accepting a more profitable order at a higher price if one subsequently comes along.
4. It is assumed that the business has spare capacity that has no alternative use.
5. It is assumed that fixed costs are unavoidable in the short term.

Segmental profitability

Companies typically decentralize their operations to multiple business units, all of which are expected to be profitable. These business units (we discuss the evaluation of business unit profitability in more detail in Chapter 15) may be based on the function they carry out, or on the basis of some form of market segmentation. *Market segments* may be defined geographically, by customer or by customer groups, by product/service or by product/service groups, or by different distribution channels. In any of these cases, decisions may be made about expanding or contracting in different segments based on the relative profitability of those segments. These are important decisions, but the methods by which costs are allocated over each segment must be understood before informed decisions about the profitability, or even discontinuance, of a market segment can be made.

As we will see in Chapter 13, major assumptions are involved in how costs are allocated within a business. However, for the purposes of the present chapter, we need to separate fixed costs into unavoidable business-wide costs and avoidable segment-specific costs. Unavoidable costs typically include the top management, finance and treasury, human resource specialists, and the company's IT system. Companies often charge these costs out to different business units or market segments using an arbitrary method (for example in proportion to sales revenue). These costs are only able to be influenced at the corporate level and hence at the level of the individual business unit or market segment the costs cannot be avoided. Avoidable costs are identifiable with and are able to be influenced by decisions made at the business unit level. Hence, if a decision is made to close a market segment, these costs would be avoidable. So for example in a retail chain, a poorly performing shop could be closed down and this would avoid the fixed costs of shop rental and salaries of local staff. However, the head office costs of the retail chain would be unaffected and so are unavoidable.

The idea of contribution (sales revenue less variable costs) introduced earlier in this chapter can be extended to the case of different market segments. This requires the separation of avoidable from unavoidable fixed costs.

An example is an accounting practice that prepares tax returns on behalf of clients. The clients are grouped into three market segments: business accounting (where the practice also carries out accounting services); business tax (where the practice only completes the tax return); and personal returns. The practice thinks that personal returns may be unprofitable and a partner has produced the data in Table 10.7.

Table 10.7 Profitability of business segments for an accounting practice.

	Business (accounting services)	Business (tax only)	Personal	Total
Revenue	120,000	50,000	30,000	200,000
Variable costs	50,000	22,000	18,000	90,000
Contribution	70,000	28,000	12,000	110,000
Avoidable fixed costs for administrative support	20,000	10,000	5,000	35,000
Contribution to overhead	50,000	18,000	7,000	75,000
Unavoidable fixed business expenses (rent, partner salaries etc.) – allocated as a percentage of revenue	30,000	12,500	7,500	50,000
Profit	20,000	5,500	(500)	25,000
Note: unavoidable fixed costs have been allocated across the three market segments in proportion to sales	60%	25%	15%	

As the example in Table 10.7 shows, despite the loss made by the personal tax returns market segment, these clients contribute £7,000 in the period towards the unavoidable overhead. If this segment were discontinued, the profit of the practice would fall by £7,000 to £18,000. The same example, without the personal tax market segment, can be seen in Table 10.8.

This result in Table 10.8 arises because, even though the fixed costs for administrative support of personal tax would be saved if the segment were discontinued, the whole of the unavoidable costs of £50,000 would continue. Table 10.8 shows that the reported profits of the two remaining segments would appear to fall as they now carry a higher proportion of the unavoidable fixed costs.

Case study 10.1 illustrates segmental profitability.

Table 10.8   Profitability of business segments for an accounting practice – discontinuance of personal tax.

	Business (accounting services)	Business (tax only)	Personal	Total
Revenue	120,000	50,000		170,000
Variable costs	50,000	22,000		72,000
Contribution	70,000	28,000		98,000
Avoidable fixed costs for administrative support	20,000	10,000		30,000
Contribution to overhead	50,000	18,000		68,000
Unavoidable fixed business expenses (rent, partner salaries etc. – allocated as a percentage of revenue	35,300	14,700		50,000
Profit	14,700	3,300		18,000
Note: unavoidable fixed costs have been allocated across the three market segments in proportion to sales	70%	30%		

Case study 10.1: Retail Stores plc – the loss-making division

Retail Stores has three segments, producing the results in Table 10.9. The contribution as a percentage of sales, assuming a constant sales mix, is 70.6% (€600,000/€850,000).

Table 10.9   Retail Stores – analysis of trading results.

€	Clothing	Electrical	Toys	Total
Sales	400,000	300,000	150,000	850,000
Variable costs %	25%	30%	40%	
Variable costs	100,000	90,000	60,000	250,000
Contribution	300,000	210,000	90,000	600,000
Segment-specific fixed costs	120,000	100,000	60,000	280,000
Allocated business-wide costs (as a % of sales revenue)	120,000	90,000	45,000	255,000
Profit/(loss)	60,000	20,000	(15,000)	65,000

The company's breakeven point in sales is calculated as:

$$\frac{fixed\ costs}{unit\ contribution\ as\ a\ \%\ of\ sales} \quad \frac{280,000 + 255,000}{0.706} = \frac{535,000}{0.706}$$

or €758,000.

Current sales of €850,000 represent a margin of safety of:

$$\frac{expected\ sales - breakeven\ sales}{expected\ sales} \times 100 = \frac{£850,000 - £758,000}{£850,000}$$

or 10.8%.

Management is considering dropping the Toys segment due to its reported loss after deducting avoidable segment-specific fixed costs and unavoidable business-wide costs, which are allocated as a percentage of sales revenue.

However, an understanding of cost behaviour helps to identify that each segment is making a positive contribution to business-wide costs after deducting the segment-specific fixed costs, as the modification to the reported profits in Table 10.10 demonstrates.

Table 10.10   Retail Stores – contribution by business segment.

€	Clothing	Electrical	Toys	Total
Sales	400,000	300,000	150,000	850,000
Variable costs %	25%	30%	40%	
Variable costs	100,000	90,000	60,000	250,000
Contribution	300,000	210,000	90,000	600,000
Segment-specific fixed costs	120,000	100,000	60,000	280,000
Segment contribution to business-wide costs and profit	180,000	110,000	30,000	320,000
Allocated business-wide costs (as a % of sales revenue)	120,000	90,000	45,000	255,000
Profit/(loss)	60,000	20,000	(15,000)	65,000

Based on the figures in Table 10.10, despite the Toys segment making a loss, it makes a positive contribution of €30,000 to allocated business-wide costs. If the Toys segment was discontinued, total profit would fall by €30,000, as Table 10.11 shows.

Table 10.11   Retail Stores – effect of closure of Toys business segment.

€	Clothing	Electrical	Toys	Total
Sales	400,000	300,000		700,000
Variable costs %	25%	30%		
Variable costs	100,000	90,000		190,000
Contribution	300,000	210,000		510,000
Segment-specific fixed costs	120,000	100,000		220,000
Segment contribution to business-wide costs and profit	180,000	110,000		290,000
Allocated business-wide costs (as a % of sales revenue)	146,000	109,000		255,000
Profit/(loss)	34,000	1,000		35,000

This is because the loss of the contribution by the Toys segment to business-wide costs and profits amounts to €30,000 (after deducting avoidable segment-specific fixed costs). The business-wide costs of €255,000 are reallocated over the two remaining business segments in proportion to sales revenue, which in turn makes the Electrical segment appear only marginally profitable.

If the Toys division were discontinued, the impact would be to reduce costs by €60,000 and a new, higher contribution as a percentage of sales results (€510,000/€700,000=72.9%, up from 70.6%). Consequently, Retail Stores' breakeven point in sales can be revised to:

$$\frac{fixed\ costs}{unit\ contribution\ as\ a\ \%\ of\ sales} = \frac{220,000 + 255,000}{0.729} = \frac{475,000}{0.729}$$

or €652,000.

Current sales of €700,000 represent a margin of safety of 6.8%, a fall of 4% from the three-division breakeven calculation. This is calculated by:

$$\frac{expected\ sales - breakeven\ sales}{expected\ sales} \times 100 = \frac{£700,000 - £652,000}{£700,000}$$

Segmental profitability is the result of distinguishing avoidable variable costs and fixed costs that are segment-specific from an allocation of unavoidable business-wide fixed costs. It is important to differentiate these costs in decision making. We will return to the overhead cost allocation problem in Chapter 13.

Another example of segmental profitability is concerned with customer profitability analysis.

Customer profitability analysis

Just as some products/services are more profitable than others, so are particular customers, industry groups, or geographic territories. Understanding customer profitability is essential to customer relationship management as the organization faces three alternatives:

- reducing the costs of servicing unprofitable customers;
- increasing prices to unprofitable customers to cover those costs;
- no longer doing business with unprofitable customers.

For example, some customers may make heavy demands on costs so as to make them unprofitable. An example is banking where corporate banking, mortgage lending, credit cards, and so on are far more profitable for banks than 'mum and dad' banking. This is because many people have many bank accounts, often with small amounts of money, but banks provide a very expensive network of branches to support that particular customer type. Banks would most likely be more profitable if they eliminated this type of business, although there would be political and reputational consequences in doing so. However, technology has reduced the cost of processing large volumes of small-value customer transactions, e.g. automatic teller machines (ATMs) for cash withdrawals, and EFTPOS (electronic funds transfer at point of sale) and BACS (Bank Automated Clearing System) for making payments instead of using cheques which are costly for banks to process.

In the following example (see Table 10.12), Marquet Company is an engineering company which has four major customers located in different parts of the country: North, South, East, and West. The customers in North and West are fairly well established but lower prices are charged in South and East where there is more price competition. While variable production costs are the same, selling and distribution costs are higher for South and West than for North and East. Each customer is supported by a local office with its own fixed costs.

Table 10.12 shows that South and East are unprofitable customers. In the short term it would be

Table 10.12   Marquet Company.

	North	South	East	West	Total
Sales units	4,000	2,000	1,000	7,000	14,000
Average price per unit	£10	£7	£7	£11	
Sales revenue £	£40,000	£14,000	£7,000	£77,000	£138,000
Variable production costs (£3 per unit)	12,000	6,000	3,000	21,000	42,000
Variable selling and distribution costs (£2 per unit for North & East; £3 per unit for South & West)	8,000	6,000	2,000	21,000	37,000
Contribution	20,000	2,000	2,000	35,000	59,000
Fixed costs specific to customer	10,000	3,000	3,000	15,000	31,000
Contribution to corporate overhead	10,000	(1,000)	(1,000)	20,000	28,000
Corporate overhead					15,000
Net profit £					£13,000

better to discontinue business with them, but the business needs to consider whether it can either increase the selling price, increase the volume (which will contribute to the recovery of more of the fixed costs incurred to support the customer), or reduce its variable selling and distribution costs to the loss-making customers. Using customer profitability analysis, like business segment contribution analysis, allows organizations to take a strategic view of multiple dimensions of profitability (products/services, customers, business units, etc.) and make strategic decisions about which should be retained, which need further investment, which need price or cost adjustments, and which should be abandoned.

Case study 10.2 shows how an understanding of financial information can assist more directly in carrying out the marketing function.

Case study 10.2: SuperTech – using accounting information to win sales

One of Global Enterprises' target customers is SuperTech, a high-technology company involved in making semiconductors for advanced manufacturing capabilities. SuperTech has grown rapidly and its sales are $35 million per annum. Variable costs consume about 60% of sales and fixed selling, distribution, and administrative expenses are about $10 million, leaving a profit of $4 million. The challenge facing SuperTech is to continue to grow while maintaining profitability. It plans to achieve this by continuing to re-engineer its production processes to reduce the lead time between order and delivery and improve the yield from its production by improving quality.

Global sees SuperTech as a major customer for its services. However, it operates in a highly price-competitive industry. Global is unwilling to reduce its pricing because it has a premium brand image and believes that it should be able to use its customer knowledge, including published financial information, to increase sales and justify the prices being charged. Global believes that its services can contribute to SuperTech's strategy of reducing lead time and improving yield.

Global has been able to ascertain the following information from the financial statements of SuperTech:

- Its cost of sales last year was $21.6 million and its inventory was $17.5 million. This is because the equipment made by SuperTech is highly technical and requires long production lead times.
- Employment-related costs for the 250 employees were $8 million, 25% of the total business costs of $31 million.
- The company has borrowings of $14.5 million, its gearing being 90%, and interest costs last year were $787,000.

We need to make a number of assumptions about the business, but these are acceptable in order to estimate the kind of savings that Global's services might obtain for SuperTech.

We can calculate the company's cost of production, assuming 240 working days per year, as $90,000 per day ($21.6 million/240). Given the low number of employees and the knowledge that many of these are employed in non-production roles, the vast majority (over 80%) of production cost is believed to be material costs. Using the inventory days ratio (see Chapter 7), we can calculate that the year-end inventory holding is 194 days ($17.5 million/$90,000), equivalent to 81% of working days (194/240).

Global's services will increase the production costs because of its premium pricing, and it expects the price differential to be $250,000 per annum. However, Global's services will generate savings for SuperTech. First, the service will reduce the lead time in manufacture by 10 days. The company's interest cost of $787,000 is 5.4% of its borrowings of $14.5 million. This is a very rough estimate as borrowings increased during the year and the company most likely had different interest rates in operation. However, it is useful as a guide. If Global's services can reduce SuperTech's lead time by 10 days, that will reduce the level of inventory by $900,000 ($90,000 per day × 10), which can be used to reduce debt, resulting in an interest saving of $48,600 ($900,000 @ 5.4%).

Second, Global also believes that its services will increase the yield from existing production because of the higher quality achieved. Global estimates that this yield improvement will lower the cost of sales from 60% to 59%. This 1% saving on sales of $35 million is equivalent to $350,000 per annum.

Global's business proposal (which of course needs to demonstrate how these gains can be achieved from a technical perspective) can contain the following financial justification:

	per annum
Savings:	
Interest savings on reduced lead time	$48,600
Yield improvements	$350,000
Total savings	$398,600
Additional cost of Global's services	$250,000
Net saving per annum	$148,600

This is equivalent to an increase of 3.7% in the net profit (after interest) to SuperTech.

Conclusion

This chapter has shown how accounting information can contribute to marketing decisions. We have introduced the separation of costs into their fixed and variable components and the importance of understanding contribution. The use of CVP analysis has been shown to provide information about breakeven points and the sales required to achieve target profits given a different sales mix and the different operating leverage of companies. Various approaches to pricing have also been introduced. We have also separated fixed costs into their avoidable and unavoidable components to consider the profitability of different market segments and the analysis of customer profitability.

While marketing is critical to business success, so too is the fulfilment of the promises made by marketing, therefore the operations function is the subject of the next chapter.

References

Clark, J. M. (1923). *Studies in the Economics of Overhead Costs*. Chicago: University of Chicago Press.

Porter, M. E. (1980). *Competitive Strategy: Techniques for Analyzing Industries and Competitors*. New York: Free Press.

Porter, M. E. (1985). *Competitive Advantage: Creating and Sustaining Superior Performance*. New York: Free Press.

Questions

10.1   National Retail Stores has identified the following data from its accounting system for the year ended 31 December: sales £1,100,000; purchases £650,000; overhead expenses £275,000. It had an opening inventory of £150,000 and a closing inventory of £200,000.
Calculate the:
- gross profit; and
- operating profit.

10.2   Plastic Emoluments has a relevant range between 100,000 and 200,000 units, fixed costs are €645,000, and variable costs are €7 per unit. Calculate the average costs at a production volume of each of 100,000, 150,000, and 200,000 units.

10.3   Hilltop Solutions has a planned level of activity of 150,000 units, fixed costs are $300,000, and variable costs are $7 per unit. The actual production volume is 140,000 units.
Identify the:
- actual cost per unit; and
- marginal cost per unit.

10.4   Corporate Document Service incurs variable costs of £7 every time a document is processed. The business providing the service has fixed costs of £100,000 per month. The selling price for each service is £25.
- By how much does the average cost change between processing 10,000 and 20,000 documents?
- Does the marginal cost change in the same way?
- Explain why the average cost changes.

10.5   The Cook Co. has two divisions, Eastern and Western. The divisions have the following revenue and expenses:

	Eastern €	Western €
Sales	550,000	500,000
Variable costs	275,000	200,000
Divisional fixed costs	180,000	150,000
Allocated corporate costs	170,000	135,000

The management of Cook is considering the closure of the Eastern division sales office. If the Eastern division were closed, the fixed costs associated with this division could be avoided but allocated corporate costs would continue.

Given this data:
- Calculate the effect on Cook Co.'s operating profit before and after the closure.
- Should the Eastern division be closed?

10.6   Jacobean Creek plc has provided the following data for last year:

Sales	5,000 units
Sales price	£80 per unit
Variable cost	£55 per unit
Fixed cost	£25,000

For the current year, Jacobean Creek believes that although sales volume will remain constant, the contribution margin per unit can be increased by 20% and total fixed cost can be reduced by 10%.
- Calculate the operating profit for last year and the current year.
- What is the increase in profit between the two years?

10.7   Relay Co. makes batons. It can make 300,000 batons a year at a variable cost of $750,000 and a fixed cost of $450,000. Relay predicts that next year it will sell 240,000 batons at the normal price of $5 per baton. In addition, a special order has been placed for 60,000 batons to be sold at a 40% discount. What will be Relay Co.'s total operating profit if the special order were accepted in addition to the planned sales at full price?

10.8   Yorkstar plans for a profit of £40,000 and expects to sell 20,000 units. Variable cost is £8 per unit and total fixed costs are £100,000. Calculate the selling price per unit if the target profit is to be achieved.

10.9   Jasper's IT consultancy has fixed costs of €450,000 per annum. There are 10,000 hours billed on average per annum. If variable costs are €35 per hour, calculate the breakeven charge rate per hour.

10.10   Hong Long Ltd has a product that is sold for $75, variable costs are $30, and fixed costs are $1,000 per month. Calculate how many products need to be sold to obtain a profit of $10,000 per annum.

10.11   John Richards plc has a cost per unit of £10 and an annual volume of sales of 18,000 units. If a £200,000 investment is required and the target rate of return is 12%, calculate the target mark-up per unit.

10.12   Victory Sales Co. predicts its selling price to be €20 per unit. Estimated variable costs are €13 per unit and fixed overhead €7,000. Calculate the number of units to be sold to generate a profit of €5,000.

10.13   Luffer Enterprises estimates the following demand for its services at different selling prices. All demand is within Luffer's relevant range. Variable costs are £15 per unit and fixed costs are £10,000.

Price (£)	Quantity
26	1,075
27	1,000
28	925
29	850
30	775

Calculate the level of sales that will generate the highest profit.

10.14   Godfrey Consultancy adopts a cost-plus pricing system for its services and applies a target rate of return of 25% on an investment of $750,000. Its labour costs are $25 per hour and other variable costs are $4 per hour. The consultancy anticipates charging 20,000 hours per year to clients and has fixed overheads of $250,000. Calculate Godfrey's target selling price per hour.

10.15   The marketing department of Giggo Hotels has estimated the number of hotel rooms (it has 120) that could be sold at different price levels. This information is shown below:

Number of rooms sold	Price per room per night (d)
120	90
100	105
80	135
60	155
50	175

Giggo Hotels has estimated its variable costs at £25 per room per night. Calculate the occupancy rate that Giggo will need in order to maximize its profits.

CHAPTER **11**

Operating Decisions

This chapter introduces the operations function: the fulfilment of a customer order following the marketing function. We consider operations through the value chain and contrast the different operating decisions faced by manufacturing and service businesses. Several operational decisions are considered, in particular capacity utilization, the cost of spare capacity, and the product/service mix under capacity constraints. Relevant costs are considered in relation to the make versus buy decision, equipment replacement, and the relevant cost of materials. We also look at supply chain management, the total cost of ownership, and supplier cost analysis, as well as the cost of quality and environmental costs.

The operations function

Operations is the function that produces the goods or services to satisfy demand from customers. This function, interpreted broadly, includes all aspects of purchasing, manufacturing, distribution, and logistics, whatever those activities may be called in particular industries. While purchasing and logistics may be common to all industries, manufacturing will only be relevant to a manufacturing business. There will also be different emphases such as distribution for a retail business and the separation of 'front office' (or customer-facing) functions from 'back office' (or support) functions for a service business or financial institution.

Irrespective of whether the business is in manufacturing, retailing, or services, we can consider *operations* as the all-encompassing processes that *produce* the goods or services that satisfy customer demand. In simple terms, operations is concerned with the conversion process between resources (materials, facilities and equipment, people) and the products/services that are sold to customers. There are five aspects of the operations function: quality, speed, dependability, flexibility, and cost (Slack, Brandon-Jones, and Johnston, 2014). For our present purposes, we focus on cost as each of the first four aspects of operations has cost implications and the lower the cost of producing goods and services, the lower can be the price to the customer, or the more profit may be retained by the business.

A useful analytical tool for understanding the conversion process is the *value chain* developed by Porter (1985). According to Porter every business is:

> a collection of activities that are performed to design, produce, market, deliver, and support its product . . . A firm's value chain and the way it performs individual activities are a reflection of its history, its strategy, its approach to implementing its strategy, and the underlying economics of the activities themselves (Porter, 1985, p. 36).

Porter separated the value chain into primary and support activities. Primary activities commence with the *upstream activities* of research and development, product design, and sourcing (which Porter calls 'inbound logistics'); the production and distribution functions ('operations' and 'outbound logistics'); and the *downstream activities* of marketing and after-sales customer service. Support activities included firm infrastructure, human resource management, technology development, and procurement.

The value chain, comprising both primary and support activities, contributes to the margin. We have discussed margin in previous chapters, but our concern here is to ensure that the costs incurred by a business in its value-adding activities can be reflected in the price charged to the customer with a sufficient margin remaining. It is all too easy to invest in primary and support activities that either do not add value or add value that customers are not willing to pay for. In those cases the margin will be smaller (or even negative, i.e. the business makes a loss).

Accounting systems categorize costs through the hierarchical organization structure and line items (see Chapter 3) such as salaries and wages, rental, and electricity. Porter argued that costs should be assigned to the value chain but that traditional accounting systems 'may obscure the underlying activities a firm performs' (Porter, 1985). For many management decisions, far better information would be available from the categorization of costs in terms of value activities that are technologically and strategically distinct. This idea is part of the business process approach introduced in Chapter 9 and to which we will return in Chapter 13.

Porter developed the notion of cost drivers, which he defined as the structural factors that influence the cost of an activity and are 'more or less' under the control of the business. He proposed that the cost drivers of each value activity be analysed to enable comparisons with competitor value chains (we consider this further in Chapter 18). This would result in the relative cost position of the business being improved by better control of the cost drivers or by reconfiguring the value chain, while maintaining a differentiated product.

The value chain as a collection of inter-related business processes is a useful concept to understand businesses that produce either goods or services. Each element of the value chain contributes to the price a customer is willing to pay, but also attracts costs. As we saw with Porter's views on competitive strategy in Chapter 10, accounting systems should provide cost and profitability information that supports both the operations strategy and the marketing strategy of the business. This strategy will vary considerably depending on the type and size of business, its competitive position, and its technology.

We first consider the role of operations in manufacturing and service industries. In describing operations throughout this book, we will use the term *production* to refer to either goods or services and use *manufacturing* where we specifically refer to the conversion of raw materials into finished goods.

Managing operations – manufacturing

A distinguishing feature between the sale of goods and services is the need for inventory or stock in the sale of goods. This topic was covered in detail in Chapter 8. Inventory enables the timing difference between production capacity and customer demand to be smoothed. This is of course not possible in the supply of services.

Manufacturing firms purchase raw materials (unprocessed goods) and undertake the *conversion process* through the application of labour, machinery, and know-how to manufacture finished goods The finished goods are then available to be sold to customers. There are actually three types of inventory in this example: raw materials, finished goods, and work-in-progress. Work-in-progress consists of goods that have begun but have not yet completed the conversion process.

As we saw in Chapter 8, there are different types of manufacturing and it is important to differentiate these production techniques as they lead to different costing methods:

- *Custom:* unique, custom products produced singly, e.g. a building.
- *Batch:* a quantity of the same goods produced at the same time (often called a production run), e.g. textbooks.
- *Continuous:* products produced in a continuous production process, e.g. oil and chemicals.

For continuous production processes, a process costing system is used. For custom and batch manufacture, costs are collected through a job costing system. In a manufacturing business the materials are identified by a bill of materials, a list of all the components that go to make up the completed project, and a routing, a list of the labour or machine-processing steps and times for the conversion process. To each of these costs, overhead is allocated to cover the manufacturing costs that are not included in either the bill of materials or the routing (overhead will be covered in Chapter 13). This chapter will assume a job costing system is used, but readers interested in process costing are encouraged to read Chapter 8.

The bill of materials and routing contain standard quantities of raw material and labour time for a unit (or batch) of product. Standard quantities are the expected raw material quantities, based on past and current experience and planned improvements in product design, purchasing, and methods of production. Standard costs are the standard quantities of raw materials or labour times multiplied by the current and anticipated purchase prices for materials and the labour rates of pay. The standard cost is therefore a budget cost for a unit or batch of a product. As actual costs are not known for some time after the end of the accounting period, standard costs are generally used for decision making. Standard costs are usually expressed *per unit*.

The manufacturing process and its relationship to accounting can be seen in Figure 11.1. When a custom product is completed, the accumulated cost of materials, labour, and overhead is the cost of that custom product. For a batch the total job cost is divided by the number of units produced. In process costing, at the end of the accounting period the total costs are divided by the volume produced to give a cost per unit of volume. The actual cost per unit can be compared to the budget or standard cost per unit. Any variation needs to be investigated and corrective action taken (we explain this in Chapter 17).

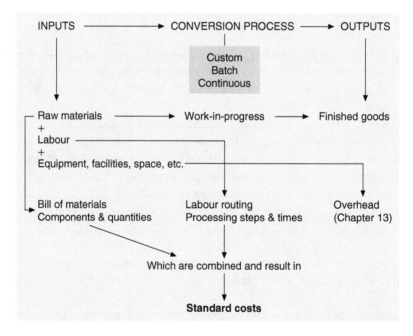

Figure 11.1   The manufacturing process and its relationship to standard costs.

The distinction between custom and batch is not always clear. Some products are produced on an assembly line as a batch of similar units but with some customization, because technology allows each unit to be unique. For example, motor vehicles are assembled as 'batches of one', since technology facilitates the sequencing of different specifications for each vehicle along a common production line. Within the same vehicle model, different colours, transmissions (manual or automatic), steering (right-hand or left-hand drive), and so on can all be accommodated.

Any manufacturing operation involves a number of sequential activities that need to be scheduled so that materials arrive at the appropriate time at the correct stage of production and labour is available to carry out the required process. Organizations that aim to have material arrive in production without holding buffer stocks are said to operate a just-in-time (JIT) manufacturing system. A case study of an automotive JIT can be found in Berry and Collier (2007).

Most manufacturing processes require an element of set-up or *make-ready* time, during which equipment settings are made to meet the specifications of the next production run (a custom product or batch). These settings may be made by manual labour or by computer through CNC (computer numerical control) technology. These investments involve substantial costs that need to be justified by an increased volume of production or by efficiencies that reduce production costs (we discuss investment decisions in Chapter 14). Set-up costs are built into the cost of production and are spread over the number of units in a batch.

The accumulated cost of materials, labour, and overhead is the cost of a custom product or a batch of the same products. We can illustrate this with the example of a production run or batch of textbooks. The standard cost for the printing of 5,000 copies of a textbook is as follows:

Raw materials (paper, ink, etc.) from bill of materials	12,000
Machine set-up time (paper size, ink colours, etc.)	2,000
Labour time for printing (from labour routing)	18,000
Overhead allocated	10,000
Total job cost	€42,000

For a batch the total job cost is divided by the number of units produced (e.g. the number of copies of the textbook) to give a cost per unit (cost per textbook). In this illustration, the standard cost per textbook is €8.40 (€42,000/5,000 copies).

The most important difference between manufacturing goods and providing services is the absence of raw materials from the conversion process. Services are more concerned with the application of human knowledge, skill, and experience, although often services can involve substantial investments in capital equipment, as the next section illustrates.

Managing operations – services

Service or knowledge-based industries have increasingly become the focus of Western economies. Fitzgerald *et al.* (1991) identified four key differences between products and services: intangibility, heterogeneity, simultaneity, and perishability. Services are *intangible* rather than physical and are often delivered in a 'bundle' such that customers may value different aspects of the service. Services involving high labour content are *heterogeneous*, i.e. the consistency of the service may vary significantly. The production and consumption of services are *simultaneous* so that services cannot be inspected before they are delivered. Services are also *perishable*, so that unlike physical goods, there can be no inventory of services that have been provided but remain unsold.

Fitzgerald *et al.* also identified three different service types. *Professional services* are 'front office', people based, involving discretion and the customization of services to meet customer needs in which the process is more important than the service itself. Examples include professional firms such as solicitors, auditors, and management consultants. *Mass services* involve limited contact time by staff and little customization, with services being equipment based and product oriented with an emphasis on the 'back office' and little autonomy. Examples here are rail transport, airports, and mass retailing. The third type of service is the *service shop*, a mixture of the other two extremes with emphasis on front and back office, people and equipment, and product and process. Examples of service shops are banking and hotels.

Fitzgerald *et al.* emphasized how cost traceability differed between each of these service types. Their research found that many service companies did not try to cost individual services accurately either for price-setting or profitability analysis, except for the time-recording practices of professional service firms.

In mass services and service shops, costs were controlled not by collecting the costs of each service but through responsibility centres (this topic is covered in more detail in Chapter 15). Following this argument, we can see that when you travel by rail, there is no calculation of the cost of your rail journey, or the cost of your hotel room. Nevertheless, these organizations must still understand their cost structures and ensure that the prices they charge, in the aggregate, cover all their costs and generate a profit.

Note that while there are no materials involved in the production of services in the same way that there are for manufacturing, retail business does have inventory (but only of finished goods) and professional service firms do have a work-in-progress inventory (time charged to customers but not yet invoiced) while other service firms do use items of inventory often classed as 'consumables' (e.g. hotels keep a stock of bed linen).

Accounting information has an important part to play in operational decisions. Typical questions that may arise include:

- What is the cost of spare capacity?
- What product/service mix should be produced where there are capacity constraints?
- What are the costs that are relevant for particular operational decisions?

This chapter considers each of these in turn.

Accounting for the cost of spare capacity

Production resources (material, facilities/equipment, and people) allocated to the process of supplying goods and services provide a capacity. The utilization of that capacity is a crucial performance driver for businesses, as the investment in capacity often involves substantial outlays of funds that need to be recovered by utilizing that capacity fully in the production of products/services. Capacity may also be a limitation for the production and distribution of goods and services where market demand exceeds capacity. So, for example, an airline will want to fully utilize all its seats on every flight. A factory will want to work its assets harder and maximize production volume. A professional services firm will want its professionals working all the time on behalf of clients.

A weakness of traditional accounting is that it equates the cost of *using* resources with the cost of *supplying* resources because financial statements reveal only the cost of resources supplied, not whether any of those resources were wasted through under-utilization. Activity-based costing (which is described further in Chapter 13) has as a central focus the identification and elimination of unused capacity. According to Kaplan and Cooper (1998), there are two ways in which unused capacity can be eliminated:

1. Reducing the supply of resources that perform an activity, i.e. spending reductions that reduce capacity.
2. Increasing the quantity of activities for the resources, i.e. revenue increases through greater utilization of existing capacity.

Identifying the difference between the cost of resources supplied and the cost of resources used as the cost of the unused capacity enables management to take appropriate corrective action.

$$\textbf{cost of resources supplied} - \textbf{cost of resources used} = \textbf{cost of unused capacity}$$

An example illustrates this.

Ten staff, each costing $30,000 per year, deliver banking services where the cost driver (the cause of the activity) is the number of banking transactions.

Assuming that each member of staff can process 2,000 transactions per annum, the cost of resources supplied is $300,000 (10 × $30,000) and the capacity number of transactions is 20,000 (10 × 2,000). The standard cost per transaction would be $15 ($300,000/20,000 transactions).

If in fact 18,000 transactions were carried out in the year, the cost of resources used would be $270,000 (18,000 @ $15) and the cost of unused capacity would be $30,000 (2,000 @ $15, or $300,000 resources supplied minus $270,000 resources used). If the cost of resources used is equated with the cost of resources supplied, the actual transaction cost becomes $16.67 ($300,000/18,000 transactions) and the cost of unused capacity is not identified separately. This is a weakness of traditional accounting systems.

Although there can be no carry forward of an 'inventory' of unused capacity in a service delivery function, management information is more meaningful if the standard cost is maintained at $15 and the cost of spare capacity is identified separately. Management action can then be taken to reduce the cost of spare capacity to zero, either by increasing the volume of business or reducing the capacity (i.e. the number of staff).

A different situation arises where there is insufficient capacity and management needs to make choices between alternative products/services.

Capacity utilization and product mix

Where demand exceeds the capacity of the business to produce goods or deliver services as a result of scarce resources (whether that is space, equipment, materials, or staff), the scarce resource is the limiting factor. Capacity utilization is concerned with maximizing profitability by selecting the optimum product/service mix. It is therefore necessary, where demand exceeds capacity, to rank the products/services with the highest contributions, per unit of the limiting factor (i.e. the scarce resource). This enables the business to utilize capacity in the most effective way to achieve the maximum profit from that capacity – subject of course to market demand.

For example, Beaufort Accessories makes three parts (F, G, and H) for a motor vehicle, each with different selling prices and variable costs and requiring a different number of machining hours. These are shown in Table 11.1. However, Beaufort has an overall capacity limitation of 10,000 machine hours.

Table 11.1   Beaufort Accessories cost information.

	Part F	Part G	Part H
Selling price per unit	£150	£200	£225
Variable material cost per unit	£50	£80	£40
Variable labour cost per unit	£50	£60	£125
Contribution per unit	£50	£60	£60
Machine hours per unit	2	4	5
Estimated sales demand (units)	2,000	2,000	2,000
Required machine hours based on estimated demand	4,000	8,000	10,000

The first step is to identify the ranking of the products by calculating the contribution per unit of the limiting factor (machine hours in this case) for each product. This is shown in Table 11.2.

Table 11.2   Beaufort Accessories product ranking based on contribution.

	Part F	Part G	Part H
Contribution per unit	£50	£60	£60
Machine hours per unit	2	4	5
Contribution per machine hour	£25	£15	£12
Ranking (preference)	1	2	3

Although both Part G and Part H have higher contributions per unit, the contribution per machine hour (the unit of limited capacity) is higher for Part F. Profitability will be maximized by using the limited capacity to produce as many Part Fs as can be sold, followed by Part Gs. Based on this ranking, the available production capacity can be allocated as shown in Table 11.3:

Table 11.3   Beaufort Accessories production mix and contribution.

Production	Contribution
2,000 of Part F @ 2 hours = 4,000 hours.	2,000 @ £50 per unit = £100,000
Based on the capacity limitation of 10,000 hours, there are 6,000 hours remaining, so Beaufort can produce 3/4 of the demand for Part G (6,000 hours available/8,000 hours to meet demand) equivalent to 1,500 units of part G (3/4 of 2,000 units).	
1,500 of Part G @ 4 hours = 6,000 hours	1,500 @ £60 per unit = £90,000
Maximum contribution	£190,000
There is no available capacity for Part H	

This example shows that managers should not be swayed by simple measures of sales revenue (the highest price) or even the highest contribution per unit of product/service (as we saw in Chapter 10) but should focus on optimizing the use of limited production capacity by comparing the contribution earned from the use of the available production capacity. However, there is an alternative to this approach to capacity utilization.

Theory of Constraints

A different approach to limited capacity was developed by Goldratt and Cox (1986), who focused on the existence of bottlenecks in production and the need to maximize volume through the bottleneck (throughput) rather than through production capacity as a whole. This is because a bottleneck resource can limit the overall production volume of a business. Goldratt and Cox developed the Theory of Constraints (ToC), under which only three aspects of performance are important: throughput contribution, operating expense, and inventory. Throughput contribution is defined as sales revenue less the cost of materials:

$$\textbf{throughput contribution = sales – cost of materials}$$

Goldratt and Cox considered all costs other than materials as fixed and independent of customers and products, so operating expenses included all costs except materials. Labour to them, at least in the short term, was a fixed cost. They emphasized the importance of maximizing throughput while holding constant or reducing operating expenses and inventory. Goldratt and Cox also recognized that there was little point in maximizing non-bottleneck resources if this leads to an inability to produce at the bottlenecks.

We can apply the Theory of Constraints to the Beaufort Accessories example by assuming that while machine hours provide the overall production constraint, specialized labour hours are a bottleneck resource. Table 11.4 shows the throughput ranking using the Theory of Constraints. The ranking is quite different to that in Table 11.2, which was based on overall production (i.e. machine capacity). Under the Theory of Constraints, which is concerned (i) with throughput contribution rather than total contribution and (ii) with bottlenecks (i.e. specialized labour hours rather than overall production

Table 11.4   Beaufort Accessories product ranking based on Theory of Constraints.

	Part F	Part G	Part H
Selling price per unit	£150	£200	£225
Variable material cost per unit	£50	£80	£40
Throughput contribution per unit	£100	£120	£185
Labour hours per unit	4	2	5
Return per labour hour	£25	£60	£37
Ranking (preference)	3	1	2

Note: The cost per labour hour for each Part is different due to the specialized labour associated with each Part.

capacity), Part G has the highest ranking, followed by Part H and Part F last. The difference is due to the treatment of variable costs other than materials, and the relative importance to the business of a bottleneck resource like specialized labour compared with overall production capacity.

Which is the preferred method? Both have value. As in many situations using management accounting information to make decisions, different assumptions can lead to different decisions. It is important to be explicit about your assumptions but to make assumptions that are most realistic in terms of the unique conditions that apply to each business. In the Beaufort example, it would depend on the extent to which variable labour costs were avoidable in the short term (we cover this aspect of labour in Chapter 12), and on the extent to which the specialized labour bottleneck really constrains overall production capacity – and how this might be overcome by management action. In many businesses, a bottleneck can have a serious impact on production volumes, with non-bottleneck resources standing idle because of the bottleneck.

This leads us to think about the issue of when costs are relevant to a particular decision at a particular point in time.

Operating decisions: relevant costs

Operating decisions imply an understanding of costs, but not necessarily those costs that are defined by accountants and are recorded in the company's accounting system. We have already seen in Chapter 10 the distinction between avoidable and unavoidable costs. This brings us to the notion of relevant costs. Relevant costs are those costs that are relevant to a particular decision. Relevant costs are the *future, incremental cash flows* that result from a decision. Relevant costs specifically do not include sunk costs, i.e. costs that have been incurred in the past, as nothing we can do can change those earlier decisions. Relevant costs are avoidable costs because, by taking a particular decision, we can avoid the cost. Unavoidable costs are not relevant because, irrespective of what our decision is, we will still incur those costs. Relevant costs may, however, be opportunity costs. An opportunity cost is not a cost that is paid out in cash. It is the loss of a future cash flow that takes place as a result of making a particular decision.

Three examples illustrate how relevant costs can be applied:

- make versus buy decisions;
- equipment replacement decisions;
- pricing decisions using the cost of materials.

Make versus buy?

A concern with subcontracting or outsourcing has dominated Western business in recent years as the cost of producing goods and services in-house has been increasingly compared with the cost of purchasing goods on the open market. This has often entailed a shift to outsourcing, especially to off-shore locations. The make versus buy decision should be based on which alternative is less costly on a *relevant cost* basis; that is, taking into account only future, incremental cash flows.

For example, the costs of in-house production of a computer processing service that averages 10,000 transactions per month are calculated as €25,000 per month. This comprises €0.50 per transaction for stationery and €2 per transaction for labour. In addition, there is a €10,000 charge from head office as the share of the depreciation charge for computer equipment. An independent computer bureau has tendered a fixed price of €20,000 per month.

Based on this information, we judge that stationery and labour costs are variable costs that are both avoidable if processing is outsourced. The depreciation charge will remain a cost to the business irrespective of the outsourcing decision. It is therefore unavoidable. The fixed outsourcing cost will only be incurred if outsourcing takes place.

The *total* costs for each alternative are compared in Table 11.5. The *relevant* costs for the alternatives are shown in Table 11.6. In Table 11.6 the €10,000 share of depreciation costs is not shown as it is not relevant to the decision because it is unavoidable.

Table 11.5   Total costs – make versus buy.

	Cost to make	Cost to buy
Stationery 10,000 @ €0.50	5,000	
Labour 10,000 @ €2	20,000	
Share of depreciation costs	10,000	10,000
Outsourcing cost	0	20,000
Total relevant cost	€35,000	€30,000

Table 11.6   Relevant costs – make versus buy.

	Relevant cost to make	Relevant cost to buy
Stationery 10,000 @ €0.50	5,000	
Labour 10,000 @ €2	20,000	
Outsourcing cost	0	20,000
Total relevant cost	€25,000	€20,000

Both Tables 11.5 and 11.6 show the same information, but the presentation is different. In either case there would be a €5,000 per month saving by outsourcing the computer processing service (total costs of €30,000 compared to €35,000; or relevant costs of €20,000 compared to €25,000).

Equipment replacement

A further example of the use of relevant costs is the decision to replace plant and equipment. Once again, the concern is with future incremental cash flows, not with historical or sunk costs or with non-cash expenses such as depreciation.

Mammoth Hotel Company wishes to expand the dining facility and needs a larger kitchen with additional capacity. A new kitchen will cost $150,000, and the kitchen equipment supplier is prepared to offer $25,000 as a trade-in for the old kitchen. The new kitchen will ensure that the dining facility earns additional income of $25,000 for each of the next five years.

The existing kitchen incurs operating costs of $40,000 per year. Due to labour-saving technology, the operating costs are expected to fall to $30,000 per year if the new kitchen is bought. These figures are shown in Table 11.7.

Table 11.7   Relevant costs – equipment replacement.

	Retain old kitchen	Buy new kitchen
Purchase price of new kitchen		−$150,000
Trade-in value of old kitchen		+$25,000
Additional income from dining of $25,000 p.a. for 5 years		+$125,000
Operating cost savings of $10,000 p.a. for 5 years		+50,000
Total relevant cost (saving)	0	$50,000

There are no relevant costs to retain the old kitchen as the capital cost is sunk, and a decision to retain the old kitchen will not affect the income from dining or the operating costs. If the new kitchen is purchased, the additional income and cost savings ($175,000) are offset by the net (after trade-in) purchase price of the new kitchen ($125,000). The purchase of a new kitchen therefore generates a relevant cost *saving* of $50,000 in future, incremental, cash flow terms.

However, we need to exercise caution here as what seems to be a sensible decision on a relevant cost basis has important implications in how the information is presented in financial statements. As we have seen in Chapters 6 and 7, the purchase price of the new kitchen would be capitalized and depreciated in Mammoth Hotel's Balance Sheet. The Income Statement would show additional income of $25,000 per year, cost savings of $10,000 per year, and a (non-cash) depreciation expense of $30,000 per year ($150,000/5), resulting in an incremental profit of $5,000 per year, which may not be sufficient to justify the investment (we consider investment evaluation in Chapter 14). A further aspect to consider is any loss on sale of the existing kitchen. While not affecting cash flow (and hence not a relevant cost), the Income Statement would disclose any loss on the kitchen (its value after depreciation as shown in the Balance Sheet, less the trade-in value). Any such loss may not be viewed well by financial statement users.

There is a tension between decisions based on future incremental cash flows and how those decisions (although positive for future profitability) may be seen by financial statement users. A result of this tension could be that managers do not take advantage of opportunities and so do not generate additional shareholder wealth because of the negative perceptions such a decision may leave in the minds of others. The political aspects of decisions were discussed in Chapter 5.

Relevant cost of materials

As the definition of relevant cost is the future incremental cash flow, it follows that the relevant cost of materials is not the historical (or sunk) cost but the replacement cost of the materials. This is particularly important in pricing decisions for special orders (see Chapter 10). It is irrelevant whether or not those materials are held in inventory, and they may well be used to fulfil a special order, but the relevant cost remains the future, incremental cash flow. In most cases this will be the replacement cost for the materials, but in some circumstances it may be the opportunity cost where the materials have only scrap value or an alternative use. The relevant cost of materials can be summarized as follows:

- If the material is purchased specifically for the special order, the relevant cost is the replacement price.
- If the material is already in stock and is used regularly in the business, the relevant cost is the replacement price.
- If the material is already in stock but is surplus to business requirements (other than for this special order), the relevant cost is the opportunity cost, which may be its scrap value or its value in any alternative use.

Stanford Potteries Ltd has been approached by a customer who wants to place a special order and is willing to pay £13,000. The order requires the materials shown in Table 11.8.

Table 11.8   Material requirements.

Material	Total kg required	Kg in stock	Original purchase price per kg	Scrap value per kg	Replacement purchase price per kg
A	750	0			6.00
B	1,000	600	3.50	2.50	5.00
C	500	400	3.00	2.50	4.00

In Table 11.8, the 'original purchase price' column is the cost of materials as would be shown in the company's accounting system when the stock was purchased. The 'replacement purchase price' column is the amount that is charged by suppliers for any stock to be purchased currently.

For this special order, Material A would have to be purchased specifically for this order. Material B is used regularly and any inventory used for this order would have to be replaced. Material C is surplus to requirements and has no alternative use. The calculation of relevant material costs is shown in Table 11.9.

As a result of the above, Stanford Potteries would accept the special order because the additional income exceeds the relevant cost of materials. In the case of A, the material is purchased at the replacement purchase price. For Material B, even though some inventory is held at a lower cost price, it is used

Table 11.9   Relevant cost of materials.

Material		Relevant cost £
A	750 kg @ £6 (replacement price)	4,500
B	1,000 kg @ £5 (replacement price)	5,000
C	400 kg @ £2.50 (opportunity cost of scrap value)	1,000
	100 kg @ £4 (replacement price)	400
Total relevant cost of materials		10,900
Revenue from special order		13,000
Future, incremental cash flow gain		2,100

regularly and has to be replaced at the current purchase price. It is important to note that the 600 kg of Material B in stock may physically be used, but will need to be replaced. Remember it is the future incremental cash flow of £5 and not the sunk cost of £3.50 that is relevant to this decision.

For Material C, the 400 kg in inventory has no other value than scrap, so the relevant cost is the opportunity cost (i.e. the loss of generating scrap value of 400 kg @ £2.50) by using Material C for this order. The 100 kg of Material C not in inventory has to be purchased at the replacement purchase price.

Remember that the relevant cost of materials in Table 11.9 is not the same as the cost that would be recorded in Stanford's accounting system. Table 11.10 shows how the accounting system would record the cost of materials. It would (as explained in Chapter 8) cost anything used from inventory using the original purchase price, and any inventory purchased would be at the replacement price. Table 11.10 shows the materials cost as £10,200 compared to the relevant cost of materials of £10,900 shown in Table 11.9.

Table 11.10   Comparison – accounting cost of materials.

Material		Accounting cost £
A	750 kg @ £6	4,500
B	600 kg in stock @ £3.50	2,100
	400 kg to be purchased @ £5	2,000
C	400 kg in stock @ £3	1,200
	100 kg to be purchased @ £4	400
Total		£10,200

So as in the equipment replacement example, the financial result reported in financial statements may be different from the financial result generated by a relevant cost calculation. In the cost of materials example, the relevant cost calculation shows that in future, incremental cash flow terms the special order achieves a gain of £2,100, but in the accounting records a profit of £2,800 (£13,000 – £10,200) will be recorded.

Which is correct? They both are. The accounting records report income and costs according to accounting principles relevant to financial reporting. Relevant costs are a future-oriented tool of management accounting to assist in decision making, based not on financial reporting principles but on future, incremental cash flows. Both provide useful, but different, information on which to make judgements. A relevant cost approach helps to understand the impact, in cash flow terms, of future decisions. Accounting costs are important signals of past performance, but can distort management decisions, which should be made in terms of whether a particular decision will improve shareholder value in the future.

As we saw in Chapter 10 in relation to marketing, management accounting provides the tools to look at the operations function more broadly. We can do so by considering supply chain management, supplier cost analysis, and the total cost of ownership.

Supply chain management, total cost of ownership, and supplier cost analysis

Supply chain management is concerned with activities beyond the organization's direct control, i.e. the quality, speed, dependability, flexibility, and cost of its suppliers, and of its distribution channel. Increasingly, organizations wish to reduce their holdings of inventory and receive that inventory on a just-in-time basis to meet their production plans. There are various costs associated with suppliers, over and above the cost of the purchased product. These costs include:

- *Purchasing costs* – the costs of finding and negotiating with suppliers, placing and receiving orders of goods and services, and paying suppliers;
- *Delivery failure costs* – costs of late deliveries from suppliers, including additional transport costs, lost production time due to late deliveries, and the opportunity cost of lost profits due to late deliveries impacting on the organization's own customers;
- *Quality failure costs* – costs of poor supplier quality, cost of returns/rework/scrap, lost production time due to poor quality materials, and the opportunity cost of lost profits due to poor quality impacting on the organization's own customers;
- *Inventory holding costs* – storage, insurance and handling costs for inventory, the risk of obsolete or damaged stock, and the financial cost due to the investment in inventory;
- *Compliance costs* – auditing supplier arrangements, inspections, and relationship management.

These costs can be even higher when the supply chain is a global one, an increasing trend as businesses aim to source products and services from the most economical source, wherever it is located. However, a global supply chain, despite lower purchase costs, carries with it higher transport costs and may have a higher risk of delivery or quality failure as well as a longer lead time between order placement and delivery. In addition there are foreign currency risks, customs duties and taxes, and risks from dealing with businesses subject to different language and culture, and different legal and political systems. There are also reputational consequences for businesses dealing with low labour cost countries where there are different laws and ethical standards in relation to minimum pay rates, child labour, health and safety, and environmental damage, etc.

Many of these costs associated with suppliers are hidden as overhead costs within the accounting system (overhead costs are not directly concerned with production – we cover these in detail in Chapter 13) and they are typically not identified by accountants as supply chain-related costs. A focus only on the invoiced price from suppliers can disguise substantial differences between the total costs of dealing with different suppliers.

The total cost of ownership is the total cost of the supply arrangement with a supplier, including purchasing costs, delivery failure, quality failure, inventory holding, and compliance costs. Table 11.11 illustrates a comparison between two suppliers, 'T' and 'W', based on an analysis of costs associated with purchasing the same product from each.

As the example in Table 11.11 illustrates, a comparison of the invoiced prices from 'T' and 'W' is overly simplistic as it would lead to purchasing from 'W' as the purchase cost is £2 per unit lower than from 'T'. However, an analysis of the total cost of ownership reveals that there are many hidden costs of purchasing: delivery failure, quality failure, inventory holding, and compliance. Many factors would drive these additional costs, which would be ascertained from a detailed analysis of the historical records of the purchasing company. This would involve comparing time spent on purchasing administration, and compliance; costs incurred in rectifying delivery, and quality failure; and the costs of holding inventory. This kind of analysis is referred to as activity-based costing (which is described in detail

Table 11.11   Comparison of total cost of ownership for two suppliers.

Cost	'T'	'W'
	£	£
Cost of product	15.50	13.50
Transport cost to store	1.50	2.15
Administration:		
Cost of placing an order	3.00	2.50
Cost of receiving an order	3.00	5.00
Cost of paying invoice	1.00	1.00
Delivery failure:		
Additional transport	0.75	0.50
Lost production time	1.25	1.00
Quality failure:		
Return/rework/scrap	1.20	1.50
Lost production time	1.25	1.75
Inventory holding:		
Storage & insurance	1.20	1.50
Compliance:		
Audit & inspection	1.00	1.50
Total cost of ownership	**£30.65**	**£31.90**

in Chapter 13) but for present purposes we can assume that the operations function has received the detailed cost analysis from accounting.

The analysis would reveal the differences in the business activities as a result of purchasing from 'T' and from 'W'. For example, 'W' may deliver in smaller packaging sizes leading to higher costs of unloading and placing stock into the store. Additional transport costs and lost production time are worse for 'T' while 'W' has experienced poorer quality leading to more costs in returns, rework, and scrap, and more lost production time. There have also been higher inspection costs associated with 'W'. As a result of this supplier cost analysis, the total cost of ownership is shown to be higher for 'W' than for 'T', even though the cost of the goods as invoiced by the supplier is lower for 'W'. Unless 'W' can improve its supplier performance in relation to these factors, it is better to purchase from 'T' and avoid many of the costs associated with purchasing, delivery failure, quality failure, inventory holding, and compliance.

One way of evaluating supplier performance using this information is through a supplier performance index, which is the ratio of the total overhead costs to the supplier's invoiced price. In Table 11.11, for 'T', overhead costs are £15.15 or 97.7% of the invoice cost. For 'W', the overhead cost is £18.40 or 136.3% of invoiced cost. Another way of looking at the supplier performance index is to see that the total cost of ownership for 'T' is 1.98 times the invoiced cost while for 'W' the ratio is 2.36.

Understanding the total cost of ownership and being able accurately to compare supplier performance is essential in minimizing the cost to the purchasing business, not just in financial terms but in the 'hidden' overheads associated with this wider view of supplier performance.

There are other important costs that rarely appear in financial statements, and if they do so, are rarely identifiable. Two particular costs worth considering are:

- costs of quality;
- environmental costs.

The cost of quality

One aspect of operational management that deserves particular attention is total quality management and the cost of quality. *Total quality management* (*TQM*) encompasses design, purchasing, operations, distribution, marketing, and administration. A TQM approach emphasizes continuous improvement through a systematic approach to quality management that focuses on customer expectations, re-engineers business processes, ensures the quality of goods and services from suppliers, and ensures that all employees are committed to quality improvement. Standardization of processes ensures consistency, which may be documented in a quality management system such as the ISO 9000 family of standards (see http://www.iso.org/iso/iso_9000).

TQM involves comprehensive measurement systems, often developed from statistical process control (SPC) approaches.

The *Six Sigma* approach, developed by Motorola, is a measure of standard deviation, i.e. how tightly clustered observations are around a mean (the average). Six Sigma aims to improve quality by removing

defects and the causes of defects. It is well developed as a management tool in high-technology manufacturing organizations and is part of a performance measurement model called DMAIC, an acronym
for Define, Measure, Analyse, Improve, and Control. Quality will likely be a measure included in the
business process perspective in a Balanced Scorecard (see Chapter 4).

Not only is non-financial performance measurement crucial in TQM, but accounting has a significant role to play because of its ability to record and report the cost of quality and how cost influences,
and is influenced by, continuous improvement in production processes.

Recognizing the cost of quality is important in terms of continuous improvement processes. The
Chartered Institute of Management Accountants defines the cost of quality as the difference between
the actual costs of production, selling, and after-sales service and the costs that would be incurred if
there were no failures during production or usage of products/services. There are two broad categories
of the cost of quality: conformance costs and non-conformance costs.

Conformance costs are those costs incurred to achieve the specified standard of quality and include
prevention costs such as quality measurement and review, supplier review, and quality training (i.e. the
procedures required by the ISO 9000 quality management standards). Costs of conformance also
include the costs of appraisal, such as inspection or testing to ensure that products or services actually
meet the quality standard.

The costs of *non-conformance* include the cost of internal and external failure. Internal failure is
where a fault is identified by the business before the product/service reaches the customer, typically
evidenced by the cost of waste or rework. The cost of external failure is identified after the product/
service is in the hands of the customer. Typical costs are warranty claims, discounts, and replacement costs.

The example in Table 11.12 illustrates how a cost statement might look for quality management
purposes.

Table 11.12   Costs of quality.

Conformance costs:	€
Prevention costs –	
Quality measurement	10,000
Quality training	5,000
Appraisal costs –	
Inspection & testing	7,000
	22,000
Cost of non-conformance:	
Internal failure –	
Waste & rework	12,000
External failure –	
Discounts	5,000
Warranty repairs	25,000
	42,000
Total costs of quality	64,000

Identifying the cost of quality is important to the continuous improvement process, as substantial
improvements to business performance can often be achieved by investing in conformance and so

avoiding the much larger costs usually associated with non-conformance, as in the example illustrated in Table 11.12. This is important not only for the production process, but, as we saw in the last section, in relation to goods delivered by suppliers and used in production.

Although SPC or Six Sigma-based systems will measure quality performance, accounting systems rarely reflect the costs of prevention, inspection, and internal and external failure costs, so the costs of quality tend to be buried in production costs as rework, waste, and so on. This leads to the problem that the true cost of quality to a business is not known and therefore action to address the cause of quality problems may not be undertaken.

A similar situation arises in respect to environmental costs.

Environmental cost management

Of increasing importance to organizations are costs relating to environmental protection (including land, water, and air pollution, and waste treatment) and the costs of remedying problems caused during the production process. Environmental costs involve recognition of the importance of corporate social responsibility (see Chapter 7). ISO 14000 (http://www.iso.org/iso/iso14000) is a family of international standards on environmental management. Like the ISO 9000 quality family, ISO 14000 provides a framework for the development of both the system and the supporting audit program and specifies a framework of control for an environmental management system against which an organization can be certified by a third party. ISO19011 (http://www.iso.org/iso/catalogue_detail?csnumber= 50675) provides a standard for auditing both quality and environmental management systems.

Environmental management accounting recognizes environmental costs for decision making, with the principles of measuring environmental costs being similar to those for measuring quality costs. Environmental management accounting is concerned with collecting, measuring, and reporting costs about the environmental impact of an organization's activities. As for quality management, these costs can be broken down into four types: prevention costs, to avoid environmental damage (e.g. the cost of equipment to reduce pollution and the training of employees); measurement costs, to determine the extent of the organization's environmental impact (including testing, monitoring, and external certification); internal failure costs, where remedial action has to be taken (e.g. cleaning up spillages or leakages, or employee health and safety-related damages); and external failure costs (e.g. penalties incurred for environmental damage).

As countries introduce carbon taxes or emissions trading schemes to reduce greenhouse gas emissions, environmental accounting is likely to increase in importance, not only in relation to external reporting and audit requirements, but also in how organizations take environment-related costs into consideration in their decision making. Environmental reporting is already part of GRI G4 Sustainability Reporting Guidelines (see Chapter 7).

For most organizations, as is the case for continuous quality improvement, continuous environmental improvement is likely to result from an investment in preventive measures and measurement to enable corrective action, rather than in remedying the cost of failure after the event. Failure can involve substantial costs, both financial and reputational (e.g. the 2010 *Deepwater Horizons* explosion and oil spill in the Gulf of Mexico, which severely damaged the reputation of BP).

As for the cost of quality, environmental cost management is only likely to result from management accounting systems that provide information that is not readily available in Annual Reports (other than to a limited extent in supplementary reports such as under the GRI).

Case studies 11.1, 11.2, and 11.3 illustrate the main concepts identified in this chapter.

Case Study 11.1: Quality Printing Company – pricing for capacity utilization

Quality Printing Company (QPC) is a listed company, a manufacturer of high-quality, multi-colour printed brochures and stationery. Historically, orders were for long-run, high-volume printing, but over recent years the sales mix has changed to shorter runs of greater variety. This market change has been reflected in a larger number of orders but a lower average order size. Expenses have increased throughout the business in order to process the larger number of orders. The result was an increase in sales value but a decline in profitability. By the latest year, QPC had virtually no spare production capacity to increase its sales but needed to improve profitability. The trend in business performance is shown in Table 11.13.

Table 11.13   Quality Printing Company – business performance trends.

	Last year £	One year ago £	Two years ago £
Sales	2,255,000	2,125,000	2,000,000
Production costs:			
Materials	1,260,000	1,105,000	980,000
Labour	250,000	225,000	205,000
Other production costs	328,000	312,000	295,000
	1,838,000	1,642,000	1,480,000
Contribution	417,000	483,000	520,000
Fixed selling and administration expenses	325,000	285,000	250,000
Net profit	92,000	198,000	270,000
Production capacity utilization (hours)	12,100	11,200	10,500

An analysis of these figures in Table 11.14 shows that while sales have increased steadily, profit has declined as a result of a lower gross margin (materials and other costs have increased as a percentage of sales). QPC noticed that the change in sales mix had led not only to a higher material content, and therefore to more working capital, but also to higher costs in manufacturing, selling, and administration, since employment had increased to support the larger number of smaller order sizes.

Table 11.14   Quality Printing Company – analysis of business performance.

	Last year	One year ago	Two years ago
Sales growth (%)	6.1	6.3	
Net profit as a % of sales	4.1	9.3	13.5
Gross margin as a % of sales	18.5	22.7	26.0
Materials as a % of sales	55.9	52.0	49.0
Labour and other costs as a % of sales	25.6	25.3	25.0
Fixed selling and administration expenses as a % of sales	14.4	13.4	12.5

A throughput contribution approach that calculates the sales less cost of materials and relates this to the production capacity utilization shows how the contribution per hour of capacity has declined. This is shown in Table 11.15.

Table 11.15   Quality Printing Comapny – throughput contribution.

	Last year	One year ago	Two years ago
Throughput contribution	995,000	1,020,000	1,020,000
No. production hours	12,100	11,200	10,500
Throughput contribution per hour	£82	£91	£97

As a result of the above analysis, QPC initiated a pricing strategy that emphasized the throughput contribution per hour in pricing decisions. Target contributions were set in order to force price increases and alter the sales mix to restore profitability. However, the salesforce, whose remuneration package included a commission on sales value, resisted these changes. The future of the company was doomed as share prices fell in line with continually disappointing profitability. This led to the company being taken over by a larger competitor.

Case Study 11.2: Vehicle Parts Company – the effect of equipment replacement on costs and prices

Vehicle Parts Company (VPC) is a privately owned manufacturer of components and a Tier 1 supplier to several major motor vehicle assemblers. The design of the machinery used by VPC meant that long set-up times were needed to make the machines ready for small production runs. The old equipment kept breaking down and quality was poor. As a result of these problems, about 35% of

VPC's production was delivered late. Consequently, there was a gradual loss of production volume as customers sought more reliable suppliers. Demand was unlikely to increase in the short term because of delivery performance. However, as the current machinery had been fully written off in the company's accounting system, the company incurred no depreciation expense. As a result, its reported profits were quite high.

The market for VPC's components now demands greater flexibility with more short runs of parts to meet the assemblers' just-in-time (JIT) requirements. New computer numerically controlled (CNC) equipment was bought in order to satisfy customer demand and provide the ability to grow sales volume. While the new CNC equipment substantially reduced set-up times, the significant depreciation charge increased the product cost and made the manufactured parts less profitable. The marketing manager believed that the depreciation cost should be discounted as otherwise the business would lose sales by retaining the existing mark-up on cost. VPC's accountant argued that depreciation is a cost that must be included in the cost of the product and prepared the summary in Table 11.16.

If the capital investment had not been made, volume would have declined as a result of quality and delivery performance. However, with the new CNC equipment and if existing prices were maintained, reported profitability would decline by €200,000 p.a. (the depreciation cost). If prices were increased to cover the depreciation cost, sales volume and therefore profitability might fall further.

Table 11.16:   Vehicle Parts Company.

	Existing machine	New CNC machine
Original cost	€250,000	€1,000,000
Depreciation at 20% p.a.	fully written off	200,000
Available hours (2 shifts)	1,920	1,920
Set-up time	35%	5%
Running time	65%	95%
Available running hours	1,248	1,824
Hours per part	0.5	0.35
Production capacity (number of parts)	2,496	5,211
Market capacity		2,500
	€	€
Depreciation cost per part	0	80
Material cost per part	75	75
Labour and other costs per part	30	20
Total cost per part	105	175
Mark-up 50%	53	88
Selling price	158	263
Maximum selling price		158
Effective markdown on cost (Price 158 – Cost 175 = 17)		10%

There had been little choice but to make the capital investment if the business was to survive. However, on a relevant cost basis, once the capital investment decision had been made, depreciation could be ignored as it did not incur any future, incremental cash flow. Hence, the 'effective mark down on cost' of 10% was illusory from a management decision-making point of view as the capital investment decision had already been made, although the financial statements of the company would show a worse position given that in accounting terms the depreciation would be shown as a very real business expense.

This case is a good example of the different information presented in financial statements and that used by managers for decision-making. It shows how accounting makes visible certain aspects of organizational performance and changes the way managers view events, i.e. that some events are 'socially constructed' by accounting, a concept that was introduced in Chapter 5.

Case Study 11.3:   Quality and waste at Planet Engineering

Planet Engineering is a manufacturing company that was acquired through a leveraged buy-out by investors whose objective is to float the company on the Stock Exchange within five years of its acquisition. As part of this goal, Planet Engineering is expected to maximize profits and cash flow and minimize any capital expenditure on new plant and equipment.

Planet's sales growth has been relatively stagnant despite gross profit margins falling from 35% to 30% over the last three years. Margins have been impacted by considerable rework of Planet's products due to plant and equipment that is ageing. Planet's production manager has brought the board of directors' attention to the fact that the inefficient equipment in the factory and the drive to reduce costs are resulting in waste and complaints from customers about product quality. However, the board does not accept these arguments and has blamed poor management practices for the falling gross profit margins.

The production manager has asked the company's accountant to identify the specific costs that are associated with poor quality and waste. The accountant has no financial information but does have some non-financial data. She undertakes an analysis of a sample of factory employee timesheets, which identifies about 5% of employee time being spent on rework rather than on productive work. She also reviews the cost of waste removal which is primarily from the factory. Information provided by the waste removal contractor identifies an estimated cost of $40,000 per annum that could be avoided if the results of poor quality production were not sent to land-fill sites.

Before submitting her figures to the production manager, the accountant speaks to Planet's human resources manager about the issues and is advised that as a result of the ageing plant and equipment, there have been a series of notifiable injuries to workers under health and safety legis-lation. The cost of lost time due to injuries, legal costs, and fines from the regulatory authority have averaged $50,000 over the last three years.

While the accountant is discussing the problem over coffee with Planet's sales manager, he tells her that several customers are lost each year due to complaints about poor quality. After a brief investigation, the sales manager reports back that lost customers over the last three years who have cited quality problems have cost Planet an average of $400,000 in lost sales each year. This does not include the inability to win new customers who are aware of Planet's reputation for poor quality.

Planet's accountant summarizes the estimated annual cost of quality and wastage as follows:

Production labour $1.2 million – estimated 5% rework	$60,000
Waste removal costs associated with poor quality production	40,000
Lost time due to injuries, legal costs, and fines	50,000
Lost sales $400,000 at gross margin of 30%	$120,000
Total	$270,000

Plus an indeterminate lost margin from reputational damage which affects the likelihood of attracting new customers and skilled employees.

The production manager undertakes his own review into the plant and equipment needs of Planet and determines that an investment of $500,000 would bring the plant and equipment to a standard that would effectively eliminate the rework, waste, and health and safety costs caused by the older plant. Over a five-year period, the depreciation cost to the company would be $100,000 per annum. Even ignoring the ability to win new customers once Planet's reputation improves, the figures prepared by the accountant suggest that the investment will be more than compensated by cost savings.

The production manager, in presenting this information to the board, is better able to argue that an investment in modern plant and equipment will reduce costs, improve the gross margin, and support efforts to achieve sales growth.

Conclusion

Operations decisions are critical in satisfying customer demand. Understanding the cost of each element in the value chain is an important ingredient in making operational decisions and this includes an under-standing of the difference between manufacturing and services costing, what constitutes the standard cost of a product or service, and the cost of spare capacity. It is also important that businesses maximize their existing production capacity through seeking out the mix of products/services that deliver the high-est contribution per unit of the limiting production capacity. It is also important to distinguish historical costs derived from an accounting system from relevant costs for decision making (defined as future incremental cash flows). The identification of the total cost of ownership and the ability to compare supplier performance accurately is essential, as is understanding the cost of quality and environmental costs. All of this information is available through various management accounting tools and techniques introduced in this chapter, all of which contribute to better planning, decision making, and control.

References

Berry, A. J. and Collier, P. M. (2007). Risk management in supply chains: processes, organisation for uncertainty and culture. *International Journal of Risk Assessment and Management*, 7(8), 100–526.

Fitzgerald, L., Johnston, R., Brignall, S. *et al.* (1991). *Performance Measurement in Service Businesses*. London: Chartered Institute of Management Accountants.

Goldratt, E. M. and Cox, J. (1986). *The Goal: A Process of Ongoing Improvement* (Revd. edn). Croton-on-Hudson, NY: North River Press.

Kaplan, R. S. and Cooper, R. (1998). *Cost and Effect: Using Integrated Cost Systems to Drive Profitability and Performance*. Boston, MA: Harvard Business School Press.

Porter, M. E. (1985). *Competitive Advantage: Creating and Sustaining Superior Performance*. New York: Free Press.

Slack, N., Brandon-Jones, A., and Johnston, R. (2014) *Operations Management*. 7th edition. London: Pearson Education.

Questions

11.1   The following data relate to activity and costs for two recent months:

	November	December
Activity level in units	5,000	10,000
	£	£
Variable costs	10,000	?
Fixed costs	30,000	?
Semi-variable costs	20,000	?
Total costs	60,000	75,000

Assuming that both activity levels are within the relevant range, calculate for December the:

- variable costs;
- fixed costs;
- semi-variable costs.

11.2   Maxitank makes two products. The prices and costs of each product are:

	Product R	Product S
	€	€
Selling price	12	20
Raw materials	4	11
Production labour hours	2	4
Machine hours	4	3

Maxitank's sales are limited by the machine capacity of the factory, which is the company's bottleneck. Which of the two products should be produced first in order to maximize the throughput generated from the limited capacity?

11.3   Goldfish Enterprises' costs for selling 15,000 hours of consultancy services are $345,000 and costs for 7,000 hours are $185,000. The company wishes to estimate its fixed and variable costs.

- What are the fixed and variable costs for Goldfish?
- What is the principal assumption behind your calculation?

11.4   Midlands Refrigeration estimates the costs per unit of a product as:

Materials	40 kg @ £2.50 per kg
Production labour	7 hours machining @ £12 per hour
	4 hours finishing @ £7 per hour

Variable production overhead @ £5 per labour hour. Fixed production overhead of £1,000,000 is based on a production volume of 12,500 units.
Calculate the:

- variable production cost;
- total production cost.

11.5   Harrison Products' capacity is 20,000 units a year. A summary of operating results for last year is:

Sales (12,000 units @ €100)	€1,200,000
Variable costs	588,000
Contribution margin	612,000
Fixed costs	245,000
Net operating income	€367,000

A foreign distributor has offered to buy a guaranteed 8,000 units at €95 per unit next year. Harrison expects its regular sales next year to be 15,000 units.

If Harrison accepts this offer and forgoes some of its expected sales to ensure that it does not exceed capacity, what would be the total operating profit next year assuming that total fixed costs increase by €100,000?

11.6   Global Conglomerates has a new product that requires 150 kg of material Y876, which is in constant use within the firm. There are 100 kg in stock that cost $11.00/kg. The replacement value is $12.50/kg and the scrap value is $2.00/kg. Calculate the relevant cost of the material to be used in the new product.

11.7   Magnificent Products makes three products, each requiring two machine hours per unit to produce. The following information has been provided by the sales department in relation to each product:

	Macro	Mezzo	Micro
Budgeted sales units	10,000	7,500	5,000
Selling price per unit	£12	£16	£18
Variable costs per unit	£6	£7	£4

If the company has a limited production capacity, preventing the sale of all the units budgeted by the sales department, how should Magnificent rank its products for manufacture in order to maximize profitability?

11.8   Europa manufactures its own Widgets. The company's costs to produce an annual requirement of 4,000 Widgets are: raw materials €15,000, production labour €10,000, and fixed manufacturing overheads €7,000. An overseas supplier has offered to produce the same volume of Widgets for Europa for €27,000. Europa determines that if it outsourced production, it could avoid €4,000 of its fixed manufacturing overhead. Calculate the cost per Widget under each alternative and recommend whether Europa should manufacture in-house or subcontract.

11.9   Buena Manufacturing has sales of $850,000. It used raw materials of $450,000, production labour of $175,000, and incurred other variable manufacturing expenses of $30,000. The business also incurred fixed non-manufacturing expenses of $65,000 and selling and administrative expenses of $40,000. Its opening stock of finished goods was $120,000 and its closing stock had reduced by $25,000. Calculate each of the:

- cost of production;
- cost of sales;
- contribution margin; and
- operating profit.

CHAPTER 12

Human Resource Decisions

Building on accounting for operations, this chapter explains the components of labour costs and how those costs are applied to decisions affecting the production of goods or services. The relevant cost of labour for decision-making purposes is also explained.

Human resources and accounting

According to Armstrong and Taylor (2014), human resource management is concerned with the management of people in a way that improves organizational performance and effectiveness. The management of human resources is concerned with job design; recruitment, training, and motivation; performance appraisal; industrial relations, employee participation, and team work; remuneration; redundancy; health and safety; and employment policies and practices including development of a workplace culture.

Historically, as Chapter 1 suggested, employment costs were a large element of the cost of manufacture. However, with improvements in manufacturing, information, and communications technologies and the shift to service and knowledge-based industries in most Western economies, people costs have tended to decline in proportion to total costs. In addition, many large-scale labour-intensive operations, such as in banking and call centres, have been outsourced to off-shore locations, which, while reducing business costs, has tended to exacerbate some problems of overall management, quality control, and customer satisfaction. Where those jobs have remained within the organization, the human resource management function has often been devolved to divisionalized business units and under line management control. Irrespective of structure, it is through human resources – people – that the marketing and production of goods and services takes place. Therefore, effective management of labour costs is an essential ingredient of business success and an important focus for accounting.

Many non-accounting readers ask why the Balance Sheet (or Statement of Financial Position) of a business does not show the value of its human assets (what has been called *human resource accounting*). The knowledge, skills, and abilities of people are a key resource in satisfying markets through the provision of goods and services. But people are not *owned* by a business. They are recruited, trained and developed, then motivated to accomplish tasks for which they are appraised and rewarded. People may leave the business for personal reasons or be made redundant when there is a business downturn. The value of people to the business is in the application of their knowledge, skills, and abilities towards the provision of goods and services. Intellectual capital, which was described in Chapter 7, goes some way towards trying to report to shareholders and others the value of human, as well as organizational and customer, capital.

In accounting terms, people are treated as *labour*, a resource that is consumed and therefore an expense rather than an asset. Labour may be consumed either *directly* in producing goods or services or *indirectly* as a business overhead. This distinction between *direct* and *indirect labour* is an important concept that is considered in more detail in Chapter 13.

The cost of labour

The cost of labour can be considered either over the short term or the long term. In the short term, the cost of labour is the total expense incurred in relation to that resource, which may be calculated as the cost per unit of production, for either goods or services. The cost of labour is the salary or wage cost paid through the payroll, plus the oncost. The labour oncost consists of the non-salary or wage costs that follow from the payment of salaries or wages. The most obvious of these in the UK are National Insurance contributions and pension (or superannuation) contributions made by the business. In other countries oncosts may include health insurance costs, payroll taxes, or workers' compensation insurance premiums. Virtually all oncosts are expressed as a percentage of salary. The *total employment cost* may include other forms of remuneration such as bonuses, profit shares, and non-cash remuneration, for example share options, expense allowances, business-provided motor vehicles, and so on.

Other than the payment of salaries, wages and oncosts, there are two other important elements of the cost of labour. A less visible but important element of the cost of labour is the period during which employees are paid but are not *at work*. This covers for example public holidays, annual leave, and sick leave. A second element of the cost of labour which is also hidden is the time when people are at work but are unproductive, such as when they are on refreshment or toilet breaks, socializing, or engaged in training or meetings, or during equipment downtimes. These unproductive times (which may benefit the business indirectly) all increase the cost of labour in relation to the volume of production of goods or services. The actual at-work and productive time is an important calculation in determining the production capacity of the business (see Chapter 11).

The following example shows how the total employment cost may be calculated for an individual (the oncosts are indicative only as they can vary widely depending on the location of the business and the industry in which it operates – they are not reflective of actual current costs):

	£	£
Salary		50,000
Oncosts:		
National insurance 12%	6,000	
Pension contribution 6%	3,000	9,000
		59,000
Bonus paid as share options		5,000
Total salary cost		64,000
Non-salary benefits:		
Cost of motor vehicle	10,000	
Expense allowance	2,000	12,000
Total employment cost		76,000

Assuming a five-day week and 20 days' annual leave, five days' sick leave, and eight public holidays per annum (the actual calculation will vary by location and industry), the actual days at work (the available production capacity) can be calculated as:

Working days 52 × 5		260
Less:		
Annual leave	20	
Sick leave	5	
Public holidays	8	33
Actual days at work		227

The total employment cost per working day for this employee is therefore £334.80 (£76,000/227 days). Assuming that the employee works eight hours per day and the employee is productive for 80% of the time at work, then the cost per hour worked is £52.31 (£334.80/(8 × 80%)).

The employee, taking home £50,000 for a 40-hour week, may consider their cost of employment as about £24 per hour (£50,000/52/40), even though they will not receive this amount as income tax has to be deducted. From the employer's perspective, however, this example shows the total employment cost and the effect of the paid but unproductive time, which more than doubles the cost to the employer – what is £24 per hour to the employee is over £52 per hour to the employer. Many business advisers recommend that an employee needs to generate at least three times their salary in earnings before his or her salary can be justified.

The cost per unit of production can be expressed either as the (total employment) cost per (productive) hour worked, in this case a *labour cost per hour* of £52.31, or as a cost per unit of production. If an employee during their productive hours completes four units of a product, the *labour cost per unit of production* is £13.08 (£52.31/4). If a service employee processes five transactions per hour, the *labour cost per unit of production* (a transaction is still a unit of production) is £10.46 (£52.31/5).

The calculation of the cost of labour per productive hour is shown in Table 12.1.

Table 12.1   The cost of productive labour.

Cost	Time
Salaries and wages + oncosts (pensions, national insurance, etc.) + non-salary benefits (motor vehicles, expenses, etc.) = total employment cost	Working days – annual leave, sick leave, public holidays, etc. = actual days at work × at work hours × productivity = productive hours worked

$$\frac{\text{total employment cost}}{\text{productive hours worked}} = \text{labour cost per hour}$$

In professional services firms such as accountants and lawyers, architects and consultants, labour is the largest cost. Each classification of employee from the most junior to partners record their time, often in 6-minute increments (tenths of an hour) on timesheets that ensure that all time spent on client work is billed to clients. Each classification of employee will have a different cost and a different *charge-out rate* to clients (this is the price at which the professional labour hours are charged). Labour hours will be captured in a job costing system (see Chapters 8 and 11), where each job is work undertaken for a client, rather than the production of a custom product or batch of products.

The charge-out rates differentiate between 'front office' workers whose times are charged to clients and 'back office' workers who provide support services to the front office workers. The costs of the back office need to be covered by the charge-out rates along with other business overhead costs such as office rental and the cost of computer systems, etc. (we discuss overheads in detail in Chapter 13).

In the longer term, a business may want to take a broader view of the total cost of employment. Many costs are incurred over and above the salary and wages paid to employees, who must be recruited and trained before they can be productive. A longer-term approach to the total cost of employment may include recruitment and training costs as additional costs of employment. In relation to short term and long term, an important issue arises as to whether the cost of labour is a fixed or variable cost, following the distinction made in Chapter 10.

It is clear that materials used in production are a variable cost, as no materials are consumed if there is no production, but the situation for labour is more complex. Accountants have historically considered labour that is consumed in producing goods or services as a variable cost. This is because it is usually expressed as a cost per unit of production, which, in total, increases or decreases in line with business activity (although it often ignores the cost of spare capacity, which was explained in Chapter 11). Changing legislation, the influence of trade unions, and business policies have meant that in the very short term, all labour takes on the appearance of a fixed cost. The consultation process for redundancy takes time, and legislation such as Transfer of Undertakings Protection of Employment (TUPE) in the UK or the European Union Transfers of Undertakings Directive secures the employment rights of labour even when it is transferred between organizations, a fairly common occurrence as a consequence of outsourcing arrangements or business mergers and acquisitions. Consequently, reflecting the underlying practicality, many businesses now account for production labour as a fixed cost, at least in the short term.

Relevant cost of labour

The distinction between fixed and variable costs is not sufficient for the purpose of making decisions about labour in the very short term as, in that short term, labour will still be paid irrespective of whether employees are fully utilized or have spare capacity. Therefore, in the short term, a business bidding for a special order should only take into account the *relevant* costs associated with that decision. As we saw in Chapter 11, the relevant cost is the *future, incremental cash flow*, i.e. the cost that will be affected by a particular decision to do (or not to do) something. As decision making is not concerned with the past, historical (or *sunk*) costs are irrelevant. The relevant cost may be an additional cash payment or an *opportunity cost*, i.e. the loss from an opportunity forgone. For example, in the case of full capacity, the relevant cost could be the additional labour costs (e.g. overtime or casual labour) that may have to be incurred, or the opportunity cost following from the inability to sell products/services (e.g. both the loss of income from a particular order and the wider potential loss of customer goodwill).

As we saw in Chapter 11, costs that are the same irrespective of the alternative chosen are irrelevant for the purposes of a particular decision, as there is no financial benefit or loss as a result of either choice. The costs that are relevant may change over time and with changing circumstances. This is particularly so with the cost of labour, where full capacity in one week or month may be followed by surplus capacity in the following week or month.

Where there is spare capacity, with surplus labour that will be paid irrespective of whether a particular decision is taken or not, the labour cost is irrelevant to the decision, because there is no future *incremental* cash flow. Where there is casual labour or use of overtime and the decision causes that cost to increase (or decrease), the labour cost is relevant. Where labour is scarce and there is full capacity, so that labour has to be diverted from alternative work involving an opportunity cost, the relevant cost is the cost of that lost opportunity.

For example, Brown & Co. is a small management consulting firm that has been offered a market research project for a client. The estimated workloads and labour costs (i.e. the costs, not the charge-out rates) for the project are:

	Hours	Hourly labour cost
Partners	120	€60
Managers	350	€45
Support staff	150	€20

For Brown & Co., there is at present a shortage of work for partners, but this is a temporary situation. Managers are fully utilized and if they are used on this project, other clients will have to be turned away, which will involve the loss of revenue of €100 per hour. Support staff are paid on a casual basis and are only hired when needed. Fixed costs are €100,000 per annum.

The relevant cost of labour to be used when considering this project can be calculated by considering the future, incremental cash flows:

Partners	120 hours – irrelevant as unavoidable surplus labour	Nil
Managers	350 hours @ €100 – the opportunity cost of the lost revenue from clients who are turned away	€35,000
Support staff	150 hours @ €20 cost – hired as needed	3,000
Relevant cost of labour		€38,000

However, the accounting system would have recorded the cost of labour (based on timesheets and hourly labour costs) as:

	Hours	Hourly labour cost	Total labour cost
Partners	120	€60	€7,200
Managers	350	€45	€15,750
Support staff	150	€20	€3,000
Total cost of labour			€25,950

While the accounting system records the historical cost, in this instance it does not take into account the opportunity cost of the lost revenue, or recognize that partners are paid irrespective of the firm's busyness. Accounting costs are therefore a limited way in which to make future-oriented management decisions.

The relevant cost approach identifies the future, incremental cash flows associated with acceptance of the order. The relevant cost ignores the cost of partners as there is no future, incremental cash flow. The cost of managers is the opportunity cost of the lost revenue from the work to be turned away. The support staff cost is due to the need to employ more temporary staff. Fixed costs are irrelevant as they are unaffected by this project. In this case, Brown & Co. would be worse off by taking the market research project at a price less than €38,000. If it is unable to achieve a higher price, the existing clients should be retained at the €100 charge-out rate for managers.

Chapter 11 introduced outsourcing as a business strategy that has been in favour with many businesses to reduce the cost of labour. The following example illustrates the relevant costs of labour in an outsourcing decision.

Newgo Industries operates a telephone call centre as part of a larger company. The call centre employs 10 telephone operators at a total employment cost of $40,000 per annum each. Each operator is on a short-term employment contract which is cancellable with a month's notice. Management salaries cost $50,000 per annum and the call centre is charged a rental and utilities cost by head office of $20,000 per annum. An offshore company has offered to undertake the call centre function for $325,000 per annum. If the call centre is outsourced, management salaries will continue unchanged and the head office charge cannot be avoided. Table 12.2 shows the total cost under each alternative. Table 12.3 shows the relevant costs for each alternative, by eliminating those costs which are unavoidable under both alternatives. Both Tables 12.2 and 12.3 show that the cost differential is $75,000 per annum and therefore, from a financial perspective, the outsourcing should proceed.

Table 12.2   Total costs of call centre and outsourcing.

	Retain call centre	Outsourcing
Telephone operators, 10 @ $40,000	400,000	
Management	50,000	50,000
Office rental and utilities	20,000	20,000
Outsourcing cost	0	325,000
Total relevant cost	$470,000	$395,000

Table 12.3   Relevant costs of call centre and outsourcing.

	Retain call centre	Outsourcing
Telephone operators, 10 @ $40,000	400,000	
Outsourcing cost		325,000
Total relevant cost	$400,000	$325,000

Note in this example that the salaries of telephone operators are a relevant cost as these costs can be avoided by giving a month's notice to the affected staff. Management salaries are not a relevant cost as they are incurred irrespective of the decision to outsource. This example shows how it is important in any calculation of relevant costs to be sure about which costs involve future incremental cash flows, i.e. which costs are avoidable and which costs are unavoidable. However, it is also important to remember that financial information is only one element of a business decision such as outsourcing. Other factors that must be considered (but which are often difficult to quantify) include quality, customer service, and reputation.

Case studies 12.1 and 12.2 illustrate how an understanding of labour costs and unused capacity can influence management decisions.

Case study 12.1: The Database Management Company – labour costs and unused capacity

The Database Management Company (DMC) is a call centre within a multinational company that has built a sophisticated database to hold consumer buying preferences. DMC contracts with large retail organizations to provide information on request and charges a fixed monthly fee plus a fee for each transaction (request for information). DMC estimates transaction volume based on past experience and recruits employees accordingly, to ensure that it is able to satisfy its customers' demands without delay.

Employees are on a mix of permanent and temporary contracts. Labour costs are separated into variable (transaction-processing costs, which can be directly attributable to specific contracts) and fixed elements (administration and supervision). DMC also incurs fixed costs, the main items being for building occupancy (a charge made by the parent company based on floor area occupied) and the leasing of computer equipment. As these costs follow staffing levels that relate to specific contracts, they can be allocated with a reasonable degree of accuracy.

DMC's budget (based on anticipated activity levels and standard costs) is shown in Table 12.4. As a result of declining retail sales the demand for transactions has fallen, but because of uncertainty in DMC about how long this downturn will last, it has only been able to reduce its variable labour cost by ending the contracts of a small number of temporary staff. DMC's actual results for the same period are shown in Table 12.5.

Table 12.4   DMC budget.

(In £'000)	Contract 1	Contract 2	Contract 3	Total
Budgeted no. of transactions	10,000	15,000	25,000	50,000
Fee per transaction	£1.00	£0.85	£0.70	
Budgeted transaction income	£10,000	£12,750	£17,500	£40,250
Fixed monthly fee	5,000	7,500	12,000	24,500
Total budgeted income	£15,000	£20,250	£29,500	£64,750
Variable labour costs	4,000	6,000	9,000	19,000
Contribution	£11,000	£14,250	£20,500	£45,750
Fixed labour costs	3,000	2,000	2,000	7,000
Occupancy costs	5,000	6,000	12,000	23,000
Computer costs	2,500	3,500	5,000	11,000
Budgeted net profit	£500	£2,750	£1,500	£4,750

Table 12.5   DMC actual results.

(In £'000)	Contract 1	Contract 2	Contract 3	Total
Actual number of transactions	9,000	10,500	22,000	41,500
Fee per transaction	£1.00	£0.85	£0.70	
Actual transaction income	£9,000	£8,925	£15,400	£33,325
Fixed monthly fee	5,000	7,500	12,000	24,500
Actual income	£14,000	£16,425	£27,400	£57,825
Variable labour costs	3,750	5,000	8,000	16,750
Contribution	£10,250	£11,425	£19,400	£41,075
Fixed labour costs	3,000	2,000	2,000	7,000
Occupancy costs	5,000	6,000	12,000	23,000
Computer costs	2,500	3,500	5,000	11,000
Actual net profit/(-loss)	−£250	−£75	£400	£75

How can the poor performance compared with budget be interpreted?

DMC's income has fallen across the board because of the reduced number of transactions on all its contracts. Because it has been unable to alter its variable labour cost significantly in the short term, the contribution towards fixed costs and profits has fallen. Therefore, although the business treats these costs as variable, in practice they are fixed costs, especially in the short term. The fixed salary and non-salary costs are constant despite the fall in transaction volume and so profit-ability has been eroded. DMC cannot alter its floor space allocation from the parent company or its computer lease costs despite having spare capacity.

What information can be provided to help in making a decision about cost reductions?

Calculating the variance (or difference) between the budget and actual income and variable costs shows how the difference between budget and actual profit of £4,675 (£4,750 – £75) is represented by a fall in income of £6,925 offset by a reduction in variable labour costs of £2,250 (all figures are in £'000). This is shown in Table 12.6.

Table 12.6   DMC loss of contribution.

(In £'000)	Contract 1	Contract 2	Contract 3	Total
Income reduction from budget	1,000	3,825	2,100	6,925
Variable labour costs reduction	250	1,000	1,000	2,250
Contribution reduction	£750	£2,825	£1,100	£4,675

Calculating the cost of unused capacity identifies the profit decline more clearly, as can be seen in Table 12.7.

Table 12.7   DMC cost of unused capacity.

(In £'000)	Contract 1	Contract 2	Contract 3	Total
Budgeted variable labour costs	£4,000	£6,000	£9,000	£19,000
Budgeted number of transactions	10,000	15,000	25,000	50,000
Budgeted cost per transaction	£0.40	£0.40	£0.36	
Actual number of transactions	9,000	10,500	22,000	41,500
Budgeted cost per transaction	£0.40	£0.40	£0.36	
Standard variable labour cost[1]	£3,600	£4,200	£7,920	£15,720
Cost of unused capacity (budget variable labour cost less standard variable labour cost)	£400	£1,800	£1,080	£3,280

Note: 1. The actual number of transactions multiplied by the budgeted variable labour cost per transaction.

Of the gap between budget and actual profit, £3,280 is accounted for by the cost of unused capacity in variable labour. This gap has been offset to some extent by the reduction in variable labour costs of £2,250. There remains the capability to reduce variable costs to meet the actual transaction volume, as Table 12.8 shows.

Table 12.8   DMC variable costs.

(In £'000)	Contract 1	Contract 2	Contract 3	Total
Actual variable labour costs	3,750	5,000	8,000	16,750
Standard variable labour costs	3,600	4,200	7,920	15,720
Difference	£150	£800	£80	£1,030

What conclusions can be drawn from this information?

It is clear that DMC either has to increase its income or reduce its costs in order to reach its profitability targets. The company has a significant cost of unused capacity. However, it can only reduce this unused capacity based on sound market evidence or else it may be constraining its ability to provide services to its customers in future, which may in turn result in a greater loss of income. DMC needs to renegotiate its prices and volumes with its customers.

Case study 12.2: Trojan Sales – the cost of losing a customer

Trojan Sales is a business employing a number of sales representatives, each costing the business €40,000 per annum, a figure that includes salary, oncosts, and motor vehicle running costs. Sales representatives also earn a commission of 1% on the orders placed by their customers. On average, each sales representative looks after 100 customers (one driver of activity) and each year, customers place an average of five orders, with an average order size of €2,500. Therefore, each representative generates sales of:

$$100 \times 5 \times €2,500 = €1,250,000$$

and earns commission of 1%, amounting to €12,500.

However, Trojan suffers from a loss to competitors of about 10% of its customer base each year. Consequently, only about 70% of each sales representative's time is spent with existing customers, while the remaining 30% is spent on winning replacement customers, with each representative needing to find 10 new customers each year (a second driver of activity). The business wants to undertake a campaign to prevent the loss of customers and has asked for a calculation of the cost of each lost customer.

A first step is to calculate the cost of the different functions carried out by each sales representative:

$$\frac{\text{employment cost of } €40{,}000 \times 70\% \text{ of time}}{100 \text{ existing customers}} = €280 \text{ per customer (account maintenance)}$$

$$\frac{\text{employment cost of } €40{,}000 \times 30\% \text{ of time}}{10 \text{ new customers}} = €1{,}200 \text{ per new customer}$$

The cash cost of winning a new customer is €1,200. However, the opportunity cost provides a more meaningful cost. If there were no lost business and sales representatives could spend all of their time with existing customers, each representative could look after 142 customers (100 × 100/70) in the same time.

If each of the 142 customers placed the average five orders with an average order size of €2,500, each representative could generate income of €1,775,000 and earn commission of €17,750. The opportunity cost is the loss of the opportunity by the company to generate the extra income of €525,000 (€1,775,000 − €1,250,000) and the opportunity cost to the representative personally of €5,250 (commission of €17,750 − €12,500).

Each customer lost costs Trojan €1,200 in time taken by sales representatives to find a replacement customer. However, on an opportunity cost basis, each lost customer potentially costs the company €52,500 in lost sales and the sales representative €525 in lost commission.

For this kind of reason, businesses sometimes adopt a strategy of splitting their salesforce into those representatives who are good at new account prospecting and those who are better at account maintenance.

Conclusion

This chapter has calculated the cost of labour and contrasted earnings from an employee's perspective with the total cost of employment to an employer. We have also developed the idea of relevant costs (introduced in Chapter 11) with examples of the relevant cost of labour.

Unfortunately, one of the first business responses to a downturn in profits is frequently to make staff redundant. Although the redundancy payments will be recognized as a cost in the Income Statement, there is a substantial social cost, not reflected in the financial reports of a business. These social effects will be borne by the redundant employee, while the financial burden of unemployment benefits may be borne by the taxpayer (see Chapter 5 for a discussion). This short-term concern with reducing labour costs often ignores the potential for cost improvement that can arise from a better understanding of business processes. It also ignores the investment in human capital: the knowledge, skills, and experience of employees made redundant and the long-term costs associated with recruitment and training that will have to be incurred again if business activity returns to higher levels.

References

Armstrong, M. and Taylor, S. (2014) *Armstrong's Handbook of Human Resource Management Practice* (13th edition). London: Kogan Page.

Questions

12.1   Grant & McKenzie is a firm of financial advisers that needs to calculate an hourly rate to charge customers for its services.

The average salary cost for its advisers is £40,000. National Insurance is 11% and the firm pays a pension contribution of 6%. Each adviser has four weeks' annual holiday and there are 10 days per annum when the firm closes for bank holidays and Christmas. Each adviser is expected to do chargeable work for clients of 25 hours per week, the remainder of the time being administrative work. Calculate an hourly rate (to the nearest whole £) to cover the cost of each financial adviser.

12.2   Local Bank does not know how much of its cheque-processing costs is fixed and how much is variable. However, total costs have been estimated at €750,000 for processing 1,000,000 transactions and €850,000 for processing 1,200,000 transactions.

What are the variable costs per transaction?
What are the fixed costs?

12.3   Cardinal Co. needs 20,000 units of a certain part to use in one of its products. The following information is available in relation to the cost to Cardinal to make each part:

Raw materials	$4
Production labour	16
Variable manufacturing overhead	8
Fixed manufacturing overhead	10
Total	$38

The cost to buy the part from the Oriole Co. is $36. If Cardinal bought the part from Oriole instead of making it, Cardinal would have no use for the spare capacity. Additionally, 60% of the fixed manufacturing overheads would continue regardless of what decision is made. Cardinal decides that production labour is an avoidable cost for the purposes of this decision.

Decide whether to make or buy the 20,000 parts, by comparing the relevant costs.

12.4   Cirrus Company has calculated that the cost to make a component is made up of raw materials £120, production labour £60, variable overhead £30, and fixed overhead of £25. Another company has offered to make the component for £140. If the company has spare capacity and wishes to retain its skilled labour force, should it make or buy the component?

12.5   Bromide Partners provides three services: accounting, audit, and tax. The total business overheads of €650,000 have been divided into two groups:

Partners	€200,000
Juniors	€450,000

Partner hours are a measure of complexity and junior hours define the duration of the work. The hours spent by each type of staff are:

	Accounting	Audit	Tax	Total
Partner hours	150	250	400	800
Junior hours	1,200	2,800	1,000	5,000

Calculate the total cost of providing audit services.

12.6   Bendix Ltd is considering the alternatives of either purchasing component VX-1 from an outside supplier or producing the component itself. Production costs to Bendix are estimated at:

Production labour	$200
Raw materials	600
Variable overheads	100
Fixed overheads	300
Total	$1,200

An outside supplier, Cosmo Ltd, has quoted a price of $1,000 for each VX-1 for an order of 100 of these components. However, if Bendix accepts the quote from Cosmo, the company will need to give three months' notice of redundancy to staff.

- Calculate the relevant costs of the alternative choices (show your workings) and make a recommendation to management as to which choice to accept.
- How would your recommendation differ if Bendix employees were on temporary contracts with no notice period?

• Explain the significance of a stock valuation of $1,300 for the VX-1 at the end of the last accounting period.

12.7   Victory Products Ltd manufactures high-technology products for the computer industry. Victory's accountant has produced a profit report showing the profitability of each of its three main customers for last year (Table 12.9).

Table 12.9   Victory Products profit report.

	Franklin Industries	Engineering Partners	Zeta PLC	Other customers	Total
Sales	1,000,000	1,500,000	2,000,000	1,500,000	6,000,000
Cost of materials	250,000	600,000	750,000	750,000	2,350,000
Cost of labour	300,000	200,000	300,000	75,000	875,000
Gross profit	450,000	700,000	950,000	675,000	2,775,000
Corporate overheads:					
Rental					250,000
Depreciation					350,000
Non- production salaries					600,000
Selling expenses					350,000
Administration					250,000
Corporate overheads allocated as 30% of sales	300,000	450,000	600,000	450,000	
Operating profit	150,000	250,000	350,000	225,000	975,000

Victory is operating at almost full capacity, but wishes to improve its profitability further. The accountant has reported that, based on the above figures, Franklin Industries is the least profitable customer and has recommended that prices be increased. If this is not possible, the accountant has suggested that Victory discontinues selling to Franklin and seeks more profitable business from Engineering Partners and Zeta.

Labour is the most significant limitation on capacity. It is highly specialized and is difficult to replace. Consequently, Victory does all it can to keep its workforce even where there are seasonal downturns in business. The company charges £100 per hour for all labour, which is readily trans-ferable between each of the customer products.

You have been asked to comment on the accountant's recommendations.

12.8   Seaford Group produces chocolate products including an exclusive range of chocolate Easter eggs, producing and selling a total of 100,000 eggs each year. The materials cost is $1.25 per egg and the labour cost is $0.70. Additional variable overhead costs are estimated at $0.20 per egg. Fixed overhead costs for Seaford Group total $150,000.

An international company has offered to produce the 100,000 Easter eggs to the same quality on behalf of Seaford for $2.50 per egg. If Seaford accepts this offer it can use its labour to produce other products and its fixed costs can be reduced by $50,000. However, there will be transportation costs that Seaford has to bear to bring the Easter eggs to its premises, amounting to $0.25 per egg.

Apply relevant cost principles to determine whether Seaford should continue to make the Easter eggs in-house or should subcontract to the international company.

Case study question 12.1: Call Centre Services plc

Call Centre Services (CCS) operates two divisions: a call centre that answers incoming customer service calls on behalf of its clients; and a telemarketing operation that makes outgoing sales calls to seek new business for its clients. In the call centre, each operator can handle on average about 6,000 calls per annum.

Although staff are allocated to one division or the other, when there is a high volume of incoming calls sales staff from the telemarketing division assist customer service staff in the call centre division. This is the result of a recruitment 'freeze' being in place.

The finance department has produced the information shown in Table 12.10.

Table 12.10   Call Centre Services.

	Call centre	Telemarketing	Total
Number of calls	70,000	25,000	
Fee per call	€5	€10	
Revenue	350,000	250,000	600,000
Less expenses:			
Staff costs 10 @ €15,000 p.a. 5 @ €22,000 p.a.	150,000	110,000	260,000
Lease costs on telecoms and IT equipment (shared 50/50)	20,000	20,000	40,000
Rent (shared in proportion to staffing: 2/3, 1/3)	80,000	40,000	120,000
Telephone call charges		20,000	20,000
Total expenses	250,000	190,000	440,000
Operating profit	€100,000	€60,000	€160,000

What conclusions can you draw about the performance of the two divisions?

CHAPTER 13

Overhead Allocation Decisions

This chapter explains how accountants determine the costs of products/services through differentiating product and period costs, and direct and indirect costs. The chapter emphasizes the overhead allocation problem: how indirect costs are allocated to determine product/service profitability and assist in pricing decisions. In doing so, it contrasts variable costing, absorption costing, and activity-based costing. The chapter includes an overview of contingency theory, a comparison between Western and international approaches to management accounting, and a consideration of the behavioural consequences of accounting choices.

Cost classification

In this chapter we are concerned with developing what we have simply referred to in earlier chapters as 'overhead' (or what in North American companies is commonly referred to as 'burden'). Overhead is defined in the CIMA official terminology as 'Expenditure on labour, materials or services that cannot be economically identified with a specific saleable cost unit' (CIMA, 2005, p. 15). Overheads are also called indirect costs. We first consider the classification of product and period costs, and then direct and indirect costs.

Product and period costs

The first categorization of costs made by accountants is between period and product. Period costs relate to the accounting period (year, month). Product costs relate to the cost of goods (or services) produced. This distinction is particularly important to the link between management accounting and financial accounting, because the calculation of profit is based on the separation of product and period costs. However, the value given to inventory is based only on product costs, a requirement of accounting standards. The IFRS accounting standard on Inventories (see Chapter 6), IAS2, requires that the cost of stock should:

> comprise that expenditure which has been incurred in the normal course of business in bringing the product or service to its present location and condition. Such costs will include all related production overheads.

Although Chapters 10, 11, and 12 introduced the concept of the contribution (sales less variable costs), as we saw in Chapter 6 there are two types of profit: gross profit and net profit:

$$\text{gross profit} = \text{sales} - \text{cost of sales}$$

The cost of sales is the product (or service) cost. It is either:

- the cost of providing a service; or
- the cost of buying goods sold by a retailer; or
- the cost of raw materials and production costs for a product manufacturer.

$$\text{net (or operating) profit} = \text{gross profit} - \text{expenses}$$

Expenses are the period costs, as they relate more to a period of time than to the production of products/services. These will include all the other (marketing, selling, administration, IT, human resources, finance, etc.) costs of the business, i.e. those not directly concerned with buying, making, or providing goods or services, but supporting that activity.

To calculate the cost of sales, we need to take into account the change in inventory, to ensure that we match the income from the sale of goods with the cost of the goods sold. As we saw in Chapter 6, *inventory (or stock)* is the value of goods purchased or manufactured that have not yet been sold.

$$\text{cost of sales} = \text{opening stock} + \text{purchases} - \text{closing stock}$$

for a retailer, or:

$$\text{cost of sales} = \text{opening stock} + \text{cost of production} - \text{closing stock}$$

for a manufacturer. For a service provider, there can be no inventory of services provided but not sold, as the production and consumption of services take place simultaneously, so:

$$\text{cost of sales} = \text{cost of providing the services that are sold}$$

As we know, sales, cost of sales, gross profit, expenses, and operating profit are all shown in the Income Statement.

Product costs are those that appear under cost of sales, while period costs are those that are deducted from gross profit to arrive at net or operating profit. While the valuation of inventory is prescribed by accounting standards, there are no such rules as to how gross profit is calculated and the distinction between product and period costs varies across different businesses. For example, in most large retail chains, the cost of sales reported in Income Statements includes not only the cost of the goods sold but also all the costs of the supermarkets (store rental, staff costs, etc.) in which we shop. Period costs include the distribution centres that hold the bulk of inventory and the head office functions. One reason for this is to avoid competitors knowing what the mark-up or margin (see Chapter 10) is on the company's sales. In service businesses, there is no requirement to show gross profit and there is considerable variation in how service businesses report.

Therefore, when we speak of 'overheads' we are not always sure what costs are included for any particular company. Perhaps a more meaningful distinction is that between direct and indirect costs.

Direct and indirect costs

Accounting systems typically record costs in terms of line items. As we saw in Chapter 3, line items reflect the structure of an accounting system around accounts for each type of expense, such as raw materials, salaries, rent, and advertising. Production costs (the cost of producing goods or services) may be classed as direct or indirect. Direct costs are readily traceable to particular products/services. Indirect costs are necessary to produce a product/service, but are not able to be readily traced to particular products/services. Any cost may be either direct or indirect, depending on its traceability to particular products/services. Because of their traceability, direct costs are nearly always variable costs because these costs increase or decrease with the volume of production. However, as we saw in Chapter 12, direct labour is sometimes treated as a fixed cost. Indirect costs may be variable (e.g. electricity) or fixed (e.g. rent). Indirect costs are often referred to as overheads.

Direct materials are traceable to particular products through *material issue* documents. For a manufacturer, direct material costs will include the materials bought and used in the manufacture of each unit of product. They will clearly be identifiable from a *bill of materials*: a detailed list of all the components used in production (see Chapter 11). There may be other materials of little value that are used in production, such as screws, adhesives, and cleaning materials, which do not appear on the bill of materials because they have little value and the cost of recording their use would be higher than the value achieved. These are still costs of production, but because they are not traced to particular products they are *indirect material* costs.

While the cost of materials will usually only apply to a retail or manufacturing business, the cost of labour will apply across all business sectors. *Direct labour* is traceable to particular products or services via a *time-recording* system. It is the labour directly involved in the conversion process of raw materials to finished goods or the cost of providing a service (the cost of labour was introduced in Chapter 12). Direct labour will be clearly identifiable from an instruction list or *routing*, a detailed list of all the steps required to produce a good or service. In a service business, direct labour will comprise those employees providing the service that is sold, such as the recording of chargeable hours in professional service firms like accountants, lawyers, architects, and consultants. In a call centre, for example, the cost of those employees making and receiving calls is a direct cost. Other labour costs will be incurred that do not appear on the routing, such as supervision, quality control, health and safety, cleaning, and maintenance. These are still costs of production, but because they are not traced to particular products, they are *indirect labour* costs.

Other costs are incurred that may be direct or indirect. For example, in a manufacturing business, the depreciation of machines (a fixed cost) used to make products may be a direct cost if each machine is used for a single product (because the cost will be traceable) or an indirect cost if the machine is used to make many products (because it may be more difficult to trace the depreciation cost applicable to different products). The electricity used in production (a variable cost) may be a direct cost if it is metered to particular products or indirect if it applies to a range of products. A royalty paid per unit of a product/ service produced or sold will be a direct cost. The cost of rental of premises, typically relating to the whole business, will be an indirect cost.

Prime cost is an umbrella term used to refer to the total of all direct costs. Overhead is divided into those overheads that are involved in production (i.e. indirect product costs) and those that are associated more with marketing and sales, finance, and administration (which are period rather than product costs). Production overhead is the total of all indirect material and labour costs and other indirect costs, i.e. all production costs other than direct costs. This distinction applies equally to the production of goods and services.

Non-production overheads (such as marketing, sales, distribution, finance, IT, administration) are period costs and are not included in production overhead. They are typically deducted from gross profit in the calculation of net profit. A simple way to think about the distinction is to imagine a factory and office complex. These are generally separated by a large wall. The office on one side has nicely dressed people working at desks. On the other side of the wall, people work with machines and wear overalls. This is a bit simplistic, but it does help to understand the distinction. Production overheads relate to the factory side of the wall, and non-production overheads to the office side. Hence, a factory manager and his production clerks who sit in the factory will be classed as production overhead. This distinction is not so straightforward where there is no factory, in which case each business will make its own distinction between product (or service) and period costs.

Distinguishing between production and non-production costs and between materials, labour, and overhead costs as direct or indirect is *contingent* on the type of product/service and the particular production process used in the organization. Contingency theory is described later in this chapter. There are no strict rules, as the classification of costs depends on the circumstances of each business and the decisions made by the accountants in that business. Consequently, unlike financial accounting, there is far greater variety between businesses – even in the same industry – in how costs are treated for management accounting purposes.

We do need to be careful when using the term 'overhead' to ensure that people we are talking to use the term in the same way, as its use may change from business to business and even from situation to situation. When we use the term, it may be limited to production overheads, or may comprise all the overheads of a business, both production and non-production. In this chapter, we will define overheads as comprising *indirect* product costs, i.e. those costs of production not readily traceable to products/services.

Figure 13.1 shows the relationship between the different classifications of costs.

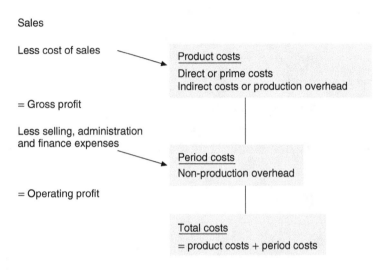

Cost classification.

The overhead allocation problem

We saw in Chapter 10 that there is an important distinction between fixed and variable costs, and the calculation of contribution (sales less variable costs) is important for short-term decision making. However, we also saw that in the longer term, all the costs of a business must be recovered if it is to be profitable. To assist with pricing, understanding profitability, and other decisions, accountants calculate the *full* or *absorbed* cost of products/services.

As direct costs by definition are traceable, this element of product/service cost is usually quite accurate. However, indirect costs, which by their nature cannot be traced to products/services, must in some way be *allocated* over products/services in order to calculate the full cost. Overhead allocation is the process of spreading production overhead (i.e. those overheads that cannot be traced directly to products/services) equitably over the volume of production. The overhead allocation problem can be seen in Figure 13.2.

The *overhead allocation problem* is a significant issue, as most businesses produce a range of products/services using multiple production processes. The most common form of overhead allocation employed by accountants historically has been to allocate overhead costs to products/services in proportion to direct labour, i.e. the more direct labour involved in producing a product/service, the more overhead is attributed to it. While this is probably a realistic assumption in professional services, it rarely accurately reflects the resources consumed in the production of most goods and services. For example, some processes may be resource intensive in terms of space, automation, people, or working

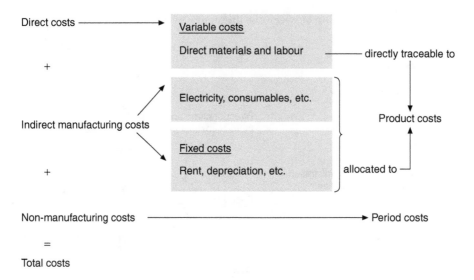

Figure 13.2   The overhead allocation problem.

capital. Some processes may be labour intensive while others use differing degrees of technology. The cost of labour, due to specialization and market forces, may also vary between different processes. Further, the extent to which these processes consume the (production and non-production) overheads of the business can be quite different. The allocation problem can lead to overheads being arbitrarily allocated across different products/services, which can lead to inappropriate pricing and misleading information about product/service profitability. As production overheads are a component of the valuation of inventory (because they are part of the cost of sales), an increase or decrease in inventory valuation will move profits between different accounting periods, so different methods of overhead allocation to products can influence reported profitability.

Shifts in management accounting thinking

In their book *Relevance Lost: The Rise and Fall of Management Accounting*, Johnson and Kaplan (1987) emphasized the limitations of traditional management accounting systems that have failed to provide accurate product costs:

> Costs are distributed to products by simplistic and arbitrary measures, usually direct-labor based, that do not represent the demands made by each product on the firm's resources . . . the methods systematically bias and distort costs of individual products . . . [and] usually lead to enormous cross subsidies across products (p. 2).

Management accounting, according to Johnson and Kaplan (1987), failed to keep pace with new technology and became subservient to the needs of external financial reporting, as costs were allocated by accountants between the valuation of inventory and the cost of goods sold. Johnson and Kaplan claimed that '[m]any accountants and managers have come to believe that inventory cost figures give an accurate guide to product costs, which they do not' (p. 145). They argued that:

> as product life cycles shorten and as more costs must be incurred before production begins . . . directly traceable product costs become a much lower fraction of total costs, traditional financial measures such as periodic earnings and accounting ROI become less useful measures of corporate performance (p. 16).

Inappropriate overhead allocation to products/services often leads to cross-subsidization. If a business sells a number of products and overheads are inappropriately allocated, then some products will bear unrealistically high costs and others unrealistically low costs. This is particularly so when indirect costs are a high proportion of total costs. The market will tend to recognize a bargain and so the business will sell many products/services where the cost (and therefore often the price) is understated. Sales volume will increase but profits will fall, as the revenue will be insufficient to cover the true costs of production. The market will also tend to recognize something that is too expensive and sales volume will fall, so the over costed (and often over priced) products/services will not earn enough revenue to compensate for the under costed, under priced products/services.

There are two methods of overhead allocation: absorption costing (the traditional method) and activity-based costing. These are compared in the next section, together with variable costing, a method that does not allocate overheads at all.

Alternative methods of overhead allocation

Variable costing

We have already seen (in Chapters 10, 11, and 12) the separation of fixed from variable costs. A method of costing that does not allocate fixed production overheads to products/services is variable (or marginal) costing. Under variable costing, the product cost only includes variable production costs. The business focus is on the contribution margin rather than gross profit. Fixed production costs are treated as period costs and charged to the Income Statement. This method avoids much of the overhead allocation problem, as most production overheads tend to be fixed rather than variable in nature. However, variable costing does not comply with accounting standard IAS2 which requires 'all related production overheads' to be included in the value of inventory. Variable costing cannot therefore be used in financial reporting. Although it can be, and is, used for internal management decision making, the effect of IAS2 is to require companies to account, for financial reporting purposes, on an absorption costing or activity-based basis, as 'all related production overheads' include both fixed and variable production costs. Nevertheless, it is a valuable tool for internal management decision making, as we saw in Chapter 10.

Absorption costing

Absorption costing is a system in which all (fixed and variable) production overhead costs are charged to products/services using an allocation base (a measure of activity or volume such as labour hours, machine hours, or the number of units produced). The allocation base used in absorption costing is often regarded as arbitrary because there is usually no logical connection between the allocation base and overhead costs. Businesses using absorption costing will select an appropriate allocation base for their business. The allocation base tends to be selected because it is already measured (e.g. direct labour hours). Under absorption costing, a *budgeted overhead rate* can be calculated as either:

- a business-wide rate; or
- a cost centre overhead rate.

A *business-wide budgeted overhead rate* is calculated by dividing the production overheads for the total business by the selected measure of activity. Overhead rates can also be calculated for each cost centre separately. A *cost centre* is a location within the organization to which costs are assigned (it may be a department or a group of activities within a department). A *cost centre budgeted overhead rate* is a result of determining the overheads that are charged to each cost centre separately and an allocation base that measures the activity of that cost centre. Different cost centres may use different allocation bases in the same company, as the costs and activity levels for each cost centre may be quite different. Remember that these are budgeted rates, based on expected costs and levels of activity. Businesses cannot wait until after the end of an accounting period when financial statements are produced to calculate actual costs and prices (we discuss differences between budget and actual overhead expenses and activity levels later in this chapter).

The overhead charged to each cost centre must be recovered as a rate based on the principal unit of activity within that cost centre, typically direct labour hours, machine hours, or the number of units produced. We therefore calculate a *direct labour hour rate* or a *machine hour rate* or a *rate per unit produced* for each production cost centre, or for the business as a whole, which allocates overheads.

Under both methods, the budgeted overhead rate is:

$$\frac{\text{estimated overhead expenditure for the period}}{\text{estimated activity for the period}}$$

For example, a business with budgeted overhead expenditure of £100,000 and an activity level of 4,000 direct labour hours would have a business-wide budgeted overhead rate of £25 per hour (£100,000/4,000). Most businesses are able to identify their overhead costs and activity to individual cost centre levels and determine cost centre overhead rates. This can be achieved using a three-stage process:

1. Identify indirect costs with particular cost centres. In many cases, although costs cannot be traced to products/services, they can be traced to particular cost centres. Accounting systems will separately record costs

incurred by each cost centre in order to hold the cost centre manager accountable (we discuss this further in Chapter15). For example, supervision costs may be traceable to each cost centre. Certain consumables may only be used in particular cost centres. Each cost centre may order goods and services and be charged for those goods and services separately.

2. Analyse each line item of expenditure that cannot be traced to particular cost centres and determine a suitable method of allocating each cost across the cost centres. There are no rules for the methods of allocation, which are contingent on the circumstances of the business and the choices made by accountants. However, common methods of allocating indirect costs include:

Expense	Allocation basis
Management salaries	Number of employees in each cost centre
Premises cost	Floor area occupied by each cost centre
Electricity	Machine hours used in each cost centre
Depreciation on equipment	Asset value in each cost centre

3. Identify those cost centres that are part of the production process and those service cost centres that provide support to production cost centres. Allocate the total costs incurred by service cost centres to the production cost centres using a reasonable method of allocation. Common methods of allocating service cost centres include:

Service cost centre	Allocation basis
Maintenance	Timesheet allocation of hours spent in each production cost centre
Canteen	Number of employees in each cost centre
Scheduling	Number of production orders

An example of cost allocation between departments is shown in Table 13.1. Using the previous example and the same overhead costs of £100,000, suitable methods of allocation have been identified for the five departments (stages 1 and 2) as follows:

Expense item	Method of allocation
Indirect wages	Allocated by payroll system
Factory rental	Floor area
Depreciation on equipment	Asset value
Electricity	Machine hours

Of the five departments, two are service departments. Their costs can be allocated as follows (stage 3):

Service cost centre	Method of allocation
Canteen	Number of employees
Scheduling	Number of production orders

Table 13.1 shows the figures produced to support the allocation process.

Table 13.1   Overhead allocations.

Expense	Total cost	Allocation calculation	Dept 1	Dept 2	Dept 3	Canteen	Scheduling
Indirect wages	£36,000	from payroll	£18,000	£9,000	£2,000	£2,000	£5,000
Factory rental	£23,000						
Area (sqm)	10,000	£2.30/sqm	5,000	2,500	1,500	500	500
Allocation £			£11,500	£5,750	£3,450	£1,150	£1,150
Depreciation	£14,000						
Asset value	£140,000	10% of asset value	40,000	60,000	30,000	7,000	3,000
Allocation £			£4,000	£6,000	£3,000	£700	£300
Electricity	£27,000						
Machine hours	9,000	£3/machine hour	3,000	2,000	4,000		
Allocation £			£9,000	£6,000	£12,000		
Total	£100,000		£42,500	£26,750	£20,450	£3,850	£6,450
Reallocate service cost centres							
Canteen	£3,850						
Employees	60	£64.16/employee	20	25	15		
Allocation £			£1,283	£1,604	£963	–£3,850	
Scheduling	£6,450						
Prod. orders	250	£25.80/order	100	70	80		
Allocation £			£2,580	£1,806	£2,064		–£6,450
Total cost	£100,000		£46,363	£30,160	£23,477	£0	£0

Once the costs have been allocated, a reasonable measure of activity is determined for each cost centre. While this is often direct labour hours (the most common measure of capacity), the unit of activity can be different for each cost centre (e.g. machine hours, material volume, number of units produced). For non-manufacturing businesses the unit of activity may be hotel rooms, airline seats, or consultancy hours. Using the above example and given the number of labour hours in each cost centre, we can now calculate a cost centre overhead rate, i.e. a budgeted overhead rate for each cost centre, as shown in Table 13.2.

Table 13.2   Cost centre budget overhead rate.

	Total cost	Dept 1	Dept 2	Dept 3
Total cost	£100,000	£46,363	£30,160	£23,477
Direct labour hours	4,000	2,000	750	1,250
Hourly rate	£25.00	£23.18	£40.21	£18.78

The most simplistic form of overhead allocation uses a single overhead rate for the whole business. As we previously calculated, the *business-wide budgeted overhead* rate is £25.00 *per direct labour hour* (£100,000/4,000). This rate would apply irrespective of whether the hours were worked in stages of production that had high or low machine utilization, different levels of skill, different pay rates, or required different degrees of support.

Under the *cost centre budgeted overhead rate*, the rate per direct labour hour varies from a low of £18.78 for Dept 3 to a high of £40.21 for Dept 2. This reflects the different cost structure and activity level of each cost centre.

Consider an example of two products, each requiring 10 machine hours. The extent to which each product requires different labour hours in each of the three departments will lead to quite different overhead allocations.

Assume that product A requires 2 hours in Dept 1, 5 hours in Dept 2, and 3 hours in Dept 3. The overhead allocation would be £303.77. If product B requires 5, 1, and 4 hours respectively in each department, the overhead allocation would be £231.25, as Table 13.3 shows.

Table 13.3   Overhead allocation to products based on cost centre budget overhead rate.

	Total cost	Dept 1	Dept 2	Dept 3
Hourly rate	£25.00	£23.18	£40.21	£18.78
Product A: direct labour hours		2	5	3
Overhead allocation	£303.77	£46.36	£201.07	£56.34
Product B: direct labour hours		5	1	4
Overhead allocation	£231.25	£115.91	£40.21	£75.13

The total cost of a product comprises the prime cost (the total of direct costs) and the overhead allocation. Whether a business-wide or cost centre overhead allocation rate is used, the prime cost is unchanged. Assuming that the direct costs per unit for our two example products are:

	Product A	Product B
Direct materials	110	150
Direct labour	75	90
Prime cost	185	240

The allocation of overhead based on cost centre rates (rounded to the nearest £) would be:

Prime cost (from above)	185	240
Overhead allocation	304	231
Full (or absorbed) cost	489	471

By contrast, the overhead allocation to both products (each of which requires 10 hours of production time) using a business-wide rate would be £250 (10 @ £25). The allocation of overhead based on the business-wide rate would be:

	Product A	*Product B*
Prime cost (from above)	185	240
Overhead allocation	250	250
Full (or absorbed) cost	435	490

As can be seen in the above example, the overhead allocation as a percentage of total cost can be very high relative to direct costs. This is not unusual in business, particularly in those organizations that have invested heavily in technology or in service businesses, where direct costs are a small proportion of total business costs. What is important here is that, just by varying the assumptions in the method of overhead allocation between using a cost centre rate or a business-wide rate, the result can be quite different product costs (£435 compared to £489 for product A; and £490 compared to £471 for product B).

The cost centre rate is more accurate than the business-wide rate because it does attempt to differentiate between the different cost structures of cost centres. However, the absorption method of allocating overhead costs to products/services has received substantial criticism because of the arbitrary way in which overheads are allocated. Most businesses use allocation bases such as direct labour hours, machine hours, or production units, because that data is readily available. The implicit assumption of absorption costing is that the allocation base chosen is a reflection of why business overheads are incurred. For example, if the allocation base is direct labour or machine hours, the assumption of absorption costing is that overhead costs are incurred in proportion to direct labour or machine hours. This is unlikely to be the case in most businesses as many overheads are caused by the scope and complexity of products/services.

As a result of the criticism of absorption costing, Kaplan and Cooper (1997) developed an alternative approach to overhead allocation: activity-based costing.

Activity-based costing

Activity-based costing (or ABC) is an attempt to identify a more accurate method of allocating overheads to products/services. In a later book by the authors of *Relevance Lost*, Kaplan and Cooper (1997) described how activity-based cost (ABC) systems:

> emerged in the mid-1980s to meet the need for accurate information about the cost of resource demands by individual products, services, customers and channels. ABC systems enabled indirect and support expenses to be driven, first to activities and processes, and then to products, services, and customers. The systems gave managers a clearer picture of the economics of their operations (p. 3).

ABC uses *cost pools* to accumulate the cost of significant business activities and then assigns the costs from the cost pools to products based on *cost drivers*, which measure each product's demand for activities.

Cost pools accumulate the cost of business processes, irrespective of the organizational structure of the business. The costs that correspond to the formal organization structure may still be accumulated for financial reporting purposes through a number of cost centres, but this will not be the method used for product costing. For example, the purchasing process can take place in many different departments, as we saw illustrated in Figure 9.1 in Chapter 9. A stores-person or computer operator may identify the need to restock a product. This will often lead to a purchase requisition, which must be approved by a manager before being passed to the purchasing department. Purchasing staff will have negotiated with suppliers in relation to quality, price, and delivery and will generally have approved suppliers and terms. A purchase order will be raised. The supplier will deliver the goods against the purchase order and the goods will be received into the store. The paperwork (a delivery note from the supplier and a goods received note) will be passed to the accounting department to be matched to the supplier invoice and payment will be made to the supplier. This business process cuts across several departments.

ABC collects the costs for the purchasing *process* in a cost pool, irrespective of the cost centre or department which incurred the cost. The next step is to identify a cost driver.

The cost driver is the most significant cause of the activity for each cost pool. In the purchasing example, the causes of costs are often recognized as the number of suppliers and/or the number of purchase orders. Cost drivers enable the cost of activities to be assigned from cost pools to cost objects (products/services). Rates are calculated for each cost driver and overhead costs are applied to products/services on the basis of the cost driver rates. There are no rules about what cost pools and cost drivers should be used, as this will be contingent on the circumstances of each business and the choices made by its accountants. Examples of cost pools and drivers are:

Cost pool	Cost driver
Purchasing	No. of purchase orders
Sales order entry	No. of sales orders
Material handling	No. of set-ups (i.e. batches)
Scheduling	No. of production orders
Machining	Machine hours (i.e. not labour hours)

For example, a rate will be calculated for each cost driver (e.g. purchase order, set-up) and assigned to each product based on how many purchase orders and set-ups the product has consumed. The more purchase orders and set-ups a product requires, the higher the overhead cost applied to it will be. ABC does not mean that direct labour hours or machine hours or the number of units produced are ignored. Where these are the significant cause of activities for particular cost pools, they are used as the cost drivers for those cost pools.

Using the same example as for absorption costing, assume for our two products that there are two cost pools: purchasing and scheduling. The driver for purchasing is the number of purchase orders and the driver for scheduling is the number of production orders. Costs are collected by an activity-based accounting system (which uses a coding structure to identify the cost pool as well as the cost centre) into cost pools and the measurement of cost drivers takes place, identifying how many activities are required for each product. The cost per unit of activity is the cost pool divided by the cost drivers, as shown in Table 13.4.

We can then calculate the overhead cost per product/service by dividing the total cost pool by the quantity of products/services produced. This is different from the absorption method which calculates

Table 13.4   Overhead accumulated in cost pools and allocated by cost drivers.

Cost pool and driver	Total cost	Product A	Product B
Purchasing	£40,000		
No. of purchase orders	4,000	3,000	1,000
	(£10 each)	£30,000	£10,000
Scheduling	£60,000		
No. of production orders	100	75	25
	(£600 each)	£45,000	£15,000
Total overhead	£100,000	£75,000	£25,000

the overhead costs per unit of product/service directly. Under the ABC method, overheads are identified with the total volume of a product/service produced and need to be divided by the volume of production to give the overhead per unit of product/service. This is shown in Table 13.5.

Table 13.5   Overhead per product based on ABC.

	Product A	Product B
Total overhead	£75,000	£25,000
Quantity produced	150	250
Per product (total overhead/quantity)	£500	£100

The prime cost (the total of direct costs) is not affected by the method of overhead allocation. The total cost of each product using ABC for overhead allocation is shown in Table 13.6. Table 13.7 compares the cost of each product calculated using both methods of absorption costing with that using ABC.

Table 13.6   Product costing under ABC.

	Direct materials	Direct labour	Production overhead	Total cost per table
Product A	£110	£75	£500	£685
Product B	£150	£90	£100	£340

Table 13.7   Comparison of product costs under absorption costing and activity-based costing.

	Product A	Product B
Cost using absorption costing–business-wide rate	£435	£490
Total cost using absorption costing–cost centre rate	£489	£471
Total cost using activity-based costing	£685	£340

Although this is an extreme example, significant differences can result in practice from the adoption of an activity-based approach to overhead allocation. In this example, overheads allocated using direct labour hours under absorption costing do not reflect the actual causes for overheads being incurred. Product A not only uses more purchasing and production order activity (the drivers of overheads in ABC), but also has a lower volume of production. Reflecting the *cause* (i.e. drivers) of overheads in overhead allocations more fairly represents the cost of each product. Under absorption costing, Product B was subsidizing Product A when compared with ABC. Cross-subsidization can be hidden where a business sells a mixture of high-volume and low-volume products/services, where there is a wide product/service variety, and where product/service complexity varies resulting in different demands on resources.

However, although conceptually attractive, surveys of practice show that ABC has not been considered by the majority of organizations, and that it has been abandoned by many organizations which adopted it in the 1990s (Gosselin, 2007), largely due to its complexity and the cost of implementation.

Time-driven activity-based costing (TDABC)

Time-driven activity-based costing (TDABC) was developed by Kaplan and Anderson (2007) and simplifies ABC through a two-step process:

1. Identifying all resources (e.g. order fulfilment, production scheduling) and the cost and capacity of each of those resources. The total cost of the resource (the same as the cost pool in ABC) is divided by the capacity measured in time (e.g. minutes) to give a cost per minute for each resource. While ABC divides each cost pool by a measure of activity appropriate to that cost pool, TDABC uses productive time, adjusted for idle and non-productive time.

2. For each activity carried out by resources, there is an estimate of the time taken to perform the activity. This time estimate is costed using the cost per minute for the resource and is used to reflect different time demands for different customers, products, distribution channels, etc.

For example, fulfilling a customer order may be a simple or more complex process, depending on customer-specific factors. Table 13.8 shows how two different customers may impact on the time required to fulfil an order:

Table 13.8   Illustration of TDABC for two customers.

Process	Customer 'Simple'	Customer 'Complex'
Receipt of order	Electronic: 1 minute (largely automated)	Fax machine requiring order entry: 10 minutes
Credit checking	Good payment history: 1 minute (automated)	Poor credit history – requires manual intervention: 10 minutes
Picking from stock	Standard quantity: 5 minutes	Requirement to break carton: 10 minutes
Packing & delivery	Standard packing & delivery: 5 minutes	Extra packing & faster delivery as customer frequently out-of-stock: 10 minutes
Total time for order fulfilment	**12 minutes**	**40 minutes**

Assuming customer order fulfilment in Table 13.8 – a resource of the business – costs €100,000 per month and this resource produces a capacity of 66,666 minutes, the cost per minute is €1.50. On that basis, TDABC would allocate a cost of €18 per order (12 @ €1.50) to the 'Simple' customer and a cost of €60 per order (40 @ €1.50) to the 'Complex' customer.

TDABC represents a variation on ABC that is easier to implement, although it does assume that the time basis is a valid measure of activity, especially given the criticism of labour hours in absorption costing.

Over- or under-recovery of overhead

The overhead rate per hour (or per unit of cost pool driver activity) is based on budgeted costs and the budgeted level of activity. However, both actual costs and actual activity levels are likely to differ from budget. The result is an under- or over-recovery of overhead.

For example, assume we budgeted for costs of £100,000 and 4,000 direct labour hours, resulting in an overhead rate of £25 per hour. Some alternative outcomes are:

- If actual costs are £105,000 but we still work 4,000 hours, we will charge £100,000 to production (4,000 × £25) and under-recover £5,000 (spending £105,000 less recovered £100,000).
- If actual costs are £102,000 and we work only 3,850 hours, we will charge £96,250 to production (3,850 × £25) and under-recover £5,750 (spending £102,000 less recovered £96,250).
- If actual costs are £98,000 and we work 4,100 hours, we will charge £102,500 to production (4,100 × £25) and over-recover £4,500 (spending £98,000 but recovering £102,500).

The same principle applies under ABC where there will be a variance between the total of planned cost driver activity and the actual cost driver activity level for each cost pool.

The under- or over-recovered overhead amount is most commonly charged to cost of sales but it may be allocated between cost of goods sold and any unsold inventory.

If budget costs and activity levels are not achieved, decisions about pricing or product profitability may be incorrect and the information used for business decisions may not be sound. Therefore it is important for spending to be controlled in line with budget (we discuss this further in Chapter 17) and for unused capacity to be reduced (we discussed the cost of spare capacity in Chapter 11).

Differences between absorption and activity-based costing

First, it is important to remember that under both methods, direct labour and material costs (i.e. prime costs) are the same. Also under both methods, the *total* overhead incurred by the company is the same. The difference between the two methods is because of different assumptions underlying the method of allocation of overhead costs over multiple products/services.

Under absorption costing, overheads are allocated in proportion to an arbitrary allocation base, typically direct labour hours. This means that the more labour hours allocated to a product/service, the more overhead will be allocated to it. While in some businesses this may be realistic (e.g. professional services), this is not necessarily the case. Under activity-based costing, overheads are traced through their drivers (the causes of activity) to the products/services that consume those activities, i.e. the more overheads a product/service causes to be incurred, the more overheads will be allocated to it. Under TDABC, while the cost pool is the same as under ABC, the driver is time.

Table 13.9 shows a comparison between the different methods.

Table 13.9   Alternative methods of overhead allocation.

Variable costing	Absorption costing	Activity-based costing	Time-driven activity-based costing
Allocates only variable costs as product costs	Allocates all fixed and variable production costs as product costs	Allocates all costs to products/services that can be allocated by cost drivers	
All fixed costs are treated as period costs	All non-production costs are treated as period costs	The distinction between production and non-production costs is less important	
	Accumulates costs in cost centres and measures activity in each cost centre (typically labour hours, machine hours or units produced)	Accumulates costs in cost pools based on business processes and measures the drivers of activities for each cost pool	Accumulates costs in cost pools based on business processes and measures the time-based drivers of activities for each cost pool
	Budgeted overhead rate = cost centre costs/unit of activity	Cost driver rate = activity cost pool/activity volume (e.g. purchase orders)	Cost driver rate = activity cost pool/time
	Calculates product/service cost for each cost centre as the unit of activity (e.g. labour hours) × budgeted overhead rate and adds this for all cost centres to give total product/service cost	Calculates product/service cost for each cost pool as activity volume × cost driver rate and adds this for all pools to give total product/service cost	Calculates product/service cost for each cost pool as time taken × cost per minute and adds this for all pools to give total product/service cost

One significant difference that the example in this chapter has not shown is in the distinction between production overhead and non-production overhead. While we have been concerned with allocating production overheads to products/services, to calculate the total cost of a product where a cost-plus approach to pricing is used (see Chapter 10) there is a need to allocate non-production overheads to products/services. This is more difficult as, by definition, these overheads are applicable more to the accounting period than to products.

Under ABC and TDABC, the distinction between fixed and variable costs and between production overhead and non-production overhead that applies to absorption costing is less important and can help with the allocation of a wider definition of overhead (both production and non-production) to products/services. Rather than focus on the simplistic fixed/variable distinction we introduced in Chapter 10, under an ABC approach costs are identified as follows:

- *Unit-level activities*: these are performed each time a unit is produced, e.g. direct labour, direct materials, and variable manufacturing costs such as electricity. These activities consume resources in proportion to the number of units produced. If we are printing books, then the cost of paper, ink and binding, and the labour of printers, are unit-level activities. If we produce twice as many books, unit-level activities will be doubled.
- *Batch-related activities*: these are performed each time a batch of goods is produced, e.g. a machine set-up. The cost of these activities varies with the number of batches, but is fixed irrespective of the number of units produced within the batch. Using our book example, the cost of set-up, or making the printing machines ready for printing, e.g. washing up, changing the ink, changing the paper, is fixed irrespective of how many books are printed in that batch, but variable on the number of batches that are printed.
- *Product-sustaining activities*: these enable the production and sale of multiple products/services, e.g. maintaining product specifications, after-sales support, product design, and development. The cost of these activities increases with the number of products, irrespective of the number of batches or the number of units produced. For each differently titled book published, there is a cost incurred in dealing with the author, obtaining copyright approval, typesetting the text, and so on. However many batches of the book are printed, these costs are fixed. Nevertheless, the cost is variable depending on the number of books that are published. Similarly, *customer-sustaining activities* support individual customers or groups of customers, e.g. different costs may apply to supporting retail, that is end-user customers, compared with resellers. In the book example, particular costs are associated with promoting a textbook to academics in universities in the hope that it will be set as required reading. Fiction books will be promoted through advertising and in-store retail bookstore displays.
- *Facility-sustaining activities*: these support the whole business and are common to all products/services. Examples of these costs include senior management and administrative staff, and premises costs. Under ABC these costs are fixed and unavoidable and irrelevant for most business decisions, being unrelated to the number of products, customers, batches, or units produced.

While unit-level activities are purely variable and facility-sustaining activities purely fixed, the ability to differentiate batch and product-sustaining activities provides more flexibility in understanding the drivers (i.e. causes) of overheads and enables a more accurate allocation of overheads to be carried out.

Because costs are assigned under ABC to cost pools rather than cost centres, and as business processes cross through many cost centres, the distinction between production and non-production overheads also breaks down under ABC. While the distinction is still important for stock valuation (as IAS2 requires the inclusion of production overheads), this distinction is not necessary for management decision making. The more (production and non-production) overheads that are able to be allocated accurately to products/services, the more accurate will be the information for decision making about contribution margins, relevant costs, pricing, and product/service profitability.

The ABC method is generally preferred because the allocation of costs is based on *cause-and-effect* relationships, while the absorption costing system is based on an *arbitrary* allocation of overhead costs. In their 2009 report *Management accounting tools for today and tomorrow*, the Chartered Institute of Management Accountants (CIMA, 2009) found that ABC is used by only 22% of small organizations in the survey, compared with 46% of very large organizations. This is likely to be due to ABC being costly to implement because of the need to analyse business processes in detail; requiring an accounting system that collects costs for both cost centres and cost pools; and the need to identify cost drivers and measure the extent to which individual products/services consume resources.

Why, then, do different organizations adopt different methods of management accounting? One explanation is provided by contingency theory.

Contingency theory

The central argument of contingency theory is that there is no control system (which, as described in Chapter 4, includes accounting systems) that is appropriate to all organizations. Fisher (1995) contrasts contingency with situation-specific and universalist models. The situation-specific approach argues that each control system is developed as a result of the unique characteristics of each organization. The universalist approach is that there is an optimal control system design that applies at least to some extent across different circumstances and organizations. The contingency approach is situated between these two extremes, in which the appropriateness of the control system depends on the particular circumstances faced by the business. However, generalizations in control systems design can be made for different classes of business circumstances.

Fisher (1995) reviewed various contingency studies and found that the following variables have been considered in research studies as affecting control systems design:

- *External environment*: whether uncertain or certain, static or dynamic, simple or complex.
- *Competitive strategy*: whether low cost or differentiated (e.g. Porter, see Chapter 10) and the stage of the product life cycle (see Chapter 18).
- *Technology*: the type of production technology (see Chapter 11).
- *Industry and business variables*: size, diversification, and structure (see Chapter 15).
- *Knowledge and observability of outcomes and behaviour*: the transformation process between inputs and outputs (see Chapter 4).

Otley (1980) argued that a simple linear explanation which assumed that contingent variables affected organizational design, which in turn determined the type of accounting/control system in use and in turn led to organizational effectiveness, was an inadequate explanation. Otley emphasized the importance of other controls outside accounting, the number of factors other than control system design influencing organizational performance, and that organizational effectiveness is itself difficult to measure. He argued that the contingent variables were outside the control of the organization, and those that could be influenced were part of a package of organizational controls including personnel selection, promotion, and reward systems. Otley also argued that there were other factors that, together with the contingent variables, influenced organizational effectiveness. He believed that an organization 'adapts to the contingencies it faces by arranging the factors it can control into an appropriate configuration that it hopes will lead to effective performance' (p. 421).

The choice of an absorption or activity-based approach to the overhead allocation problem is one example of how a control system will be influenced by contingent factors: the environment, competition, technology, business, and observability factors. The comment by Clark (1923), mentioned previously in this book, that there were 'different costs for different purposes' can be seen as an early understanding of the application of the contingency approach. Clark further commented that 'there is no one correct usage, usage being governed by the varying needs of varying business situations and problems'. Most important is the need to use cost information in different ways depending on the business circumstances, which has been the focus of Chapters 10 to 12.

However, we should not assume that the techniques in Chapters 10–13 are universally applicable. In many cases they are Western constructions, linked to the particular Anglo-centric capitalist system that is most evident in the UK, USA, Canada, and Australia. It is therefore worthwhile highlighting some key international differences.

International comparisons

Nobes and Parker (2008) described various approaches to categorizing international differences in accounting, including:

* different legal systems;
* whether accounting was commercially driven, government-driven, or governed by professional regulation;
* the relative strength of equity markets.

Nobes and Parker argued that legal systems, tax systems, and the strength of the accountancy profession all influence the development of accounting, but the main explanation for the most important international differences in financial reporting is the financing system (such as the size and spread of corporate shareholding). For example, the growth of institutional investors (such as pension/superannuation funds, insurance companies) has reduced the size of individual shareholdings in companies. In Germany, it is common for banks to own shares in the companies they lend to, but this is unheard of in the UK.

Financial reporting is largely harmonized within the European Union and elsewhere, using IFRS as the global accounting standards (see Chapter 6). This is likely to be a continuing trend given the globalization of capital markets which is likely to encompass the USA over the next few years. Whether there will be any effect of harmonization on management accounting practices is as yet unknown. In understanding management accounting, practising managers and students of accounting receive little exposure to management accounting practices outside the Anglo-centric economies.

In Germany, for example, the term 'controlling' is far more evident than is 'management accounting', implying a greater strategic emphasis. German teachers of accounting, and German textbooks, reveal that the Anglo-centric division between financial and management accounting is less relevant in Germany where there is a greater concern with the inter-relationship between both. In Anglo countries there is a greater operational emphasis, revealed in the focus on cost.

In Japan, there is a strong history of *keiretsu*, the interlocking shareholdings of industrial conglomerates and banks, with overlapping board memberships. This has, at least in part, influenced long-term strategy because of the absence of strong stock market pressures for short-term performance, as is the case in Anglo-centric countries. Japanese companies exhibit a more strategic planning style of management control rather than an emphasis on financial control and there is less attention to accounting and management control in Japan than to smooth production and quality products. Performance targets are set in the context of strategy but results are expected in the longer term. Pressures to meet short-term financial targets are not allowed to detract from long-term progress. The main emphasis in Japan is on market-driven product costing, i.e. target costing and continuous improvement (see Chapter 18), aimed at increasing market share over time by accepting lower short-term profits.

Research has shown that Japanese managers are uninterested in new management accounting techniques such as activity-based costing, since knowledge that some products are more expensive to produce than others is not important to product strategy decisions. On the contrary, expensive products are likely to have strategic value to the company.

Research by the University of Bath & CIMA (Van der Stede and Malone, 2010) identified the different business models and customs of the fast-growing economies of China and India, especially where State-owned enterprises carry out business and where executives place significant weight on personal relationships rather than on the contractual relationships that are most evident in the West.

It is important to contrast the approach taken in this text, as in all Anglo-centric accounting texts, with the practices in other countries. These practices are different because they are predicated on different assumptions, particularly the different emphases on long-term strategies for growth versus short-term strategies for profit. There are contingent factors – historical, cultural, political, legal, and economic influences – underlying the development of different management accounting techniques in countries such as Japan, Germany, and China.

The final section of this chapter addresses some behavioural issues associated with management accounting.

Behavioural implications of management accounting

Hopper, Otley, and Scapens (2001) traced the rise of behavioural and organizational accounting research in management accounting. In the UK, a paradigm shift occurred that did not happen in the USA (where agency theory – see Chapter 6 – has been the dominant research approach). In the UK, contingency theory and neo-human relations approaches were abandoned for more sociological and political approaches that drew from European social theory and were influenced by Scandinavian case-based research. Burchell *et al.* (1980) argued:

> What is accounted for can shape organizational participants' views of what is important, with the categories of dominant economic discourse and organizational functioning that are implicit within the accounting framework helping to create a particular conception of organizational reality (p. 5).

Reality in the economics and agency-based discourse is about shareholder value, while more sociological and political perspectives (see Chapter 5) see reality as socially constructed or the result of domination by one group over another. Along the same lines, Miller (1994) argued that accounting was not a neutral device that merely reports 'facts' but a set of practices that affects the type of world in which we live, the way in which we understand the choices able to be made by individuals and organizations, and the way in which we manage activities. Miller argued that 'to calculate and record the costs of an activity is to alter the way in which it can be thought about and acted upon' (p. 2).

Cooper, Hayes, and Wolf (1981) reflected that accounting systems are a significant component of power in organizations:

> Internal accounting systems by what they measure, how they measure and who they report to can effectively delimit the kind of issues addressed and the ways in which they are addressed (p. 182).

We have seen through the examples in Chapters 10–13 how accounting can change the way we see things. Choices about contribution margin or gross profit, avoidable or unavoidable costs, historical cost or relevant cost, cash costs or opportunity costs, and the choice of absorption or activity-based costing approaches all change our understanding of the cost and profitability of a product/service, a business unit, a market segment, and therefore the decisions we take with that understanding.

Information such as that provided by financial and management accounting, and by non-financial performance information affects human behaviour. People may feel they have insufficient information, that the information is inaccurate or misleading, or feel overwhelmed by the huge volume of information available from computer systems, especially (as we saw in Chapter 9) where different information systems provide different clues about performance.

Individual goals are not necessarily congruent with those of the business, and accounting information may motivate – or demotivate – people, especially where rewards (financial or otherwise, or sanctions) are linked to achieving performance targets.

Change management typically is met by resistance. Some people do not like change, while others see change as affecting their power base. Implementing a new system like activity-based costing can be threatening when it challenges individual preconceived notions of what products or customers are profitable. Resistance can come from sales people whose behaviour may be channelled towards selling different products to different customers.

We will consider the behavioural implications of budgeting and budgetary control in Chapters 16–17 but suffice to say here that the extent to which employees participate in setting budgets and targets is likely to be significantly motivational to those managers compared with budgets and targets being imposed by the organization. This is equally true in the degree of difficulty in meeting budget targets, especially where there are rewards or sanctions for doing so.

Various published research studies have adopted an interpretive or critical perspective in understanding the link between accounting systems, organizational change, and the behaviour of people in organizations as a result of culture and power (see Chapter 5 for the theoretical framework of these subjects). The interpretive perspective has provided a number of interesting studies. For example, Dent (1991) carried out a longitudinal field study of accounting change in EuroRail (which is one of the readings in this book), in which organizations were portrayed as cultures, i.e. systems of knowledge, belief, and values. Prior to Dent's study the dominant culture in EuroRail was engineering and production, in which accounting was incidental. This was displaced by economic and accounting concerns that constructed the railway as a profit-seeking enterprise. Dent described how accounting played a role 'in constructing specific knowledges' (p. 727) by tracing the introduction of a revised corporate planning system, the amendment of capital expenditure approval procedures, and the revision of budgeting systems, each of which shifted power from railway to business managers.

It is important in making choices about accounting methods to understand that these choices have behavioural consequences, some intended, some unintended, particularly where existing power structures are threatened, or where changes made are inconsistent with the norms and values, or culture, within the organization. In each case, management may face considerable resistance.

In Chapters 4 and 5, we considered rational-economic, interpretive, and critical perspectives that help to provide multiple views about the world in which we live. Chapters 10 through 13 have introduced many aspects of costs and how management accounting techniques are used in planning, decision making, and control in relation to marketing, operations, human resources, and accounting.

Implicit in most of what is contained in these four chapters is an acceptance of the rational-economic paradigm described in Chapter 4. The notion of shareholder value and the importance of profit have dictated acceptable approaches to calculating costs, at least for financial reporting purposes to shareholders. In financial reporting, regulation and audit generally prevents (except in creative accounting or earnings management) any but a single interpretation, the rational-economic one. However, as we have seen through the examples in these chapters, different interpretations of cost are possible, and all are defensible depending on the assumptions used.

The interpretive perspective applied to management accounting accepts that different understandings do exist. So there are alternative approaches to pricing (Chapter 10) in which different solutions are possible, yet all are correct if based on specific assumptions. Different methods of judging the best use of capacity are also possible (Chapter 11). Relevant costs are an entirely different approach to traditional historical costing (Chapters 11 and 12) while variable, absorption, and activity-based costing are very different interpretations of the treatment of overhead costs (this chapter). The critical paradigm privileges one or other treatment in each of these examples as a result not necessarily of rational choice, but of the power of the dominant management group (including the role of accountants in that group) which can influence the particular techniques adopted.

We conclude this chapter on overhead allocation with Case study 13.1, illustrating the overhead allocation problem in Tektronix.

Case study 13.1: Tektronix Portables division

Using a case study of the Portables division of Tektronix (a real company) that was facing considerable Japanese competition, Turney and Anderson (1989) argued that 'the accounting function has failed to adapt to a new competitive environment that requires continuous improvement in the design, manufacturing, and marketing of a product' (p. 37).

In their research, Turney and Anderson found that many of the accounting systems in use in Tektronix were obsolete, reporting information that was no longer used. The traditional focus for cost collection was labour, material, and overhead for a work order. Overhead was 'bloated' due to 'the enormous complexity of the production process' and 'long production runs tended to produce large inventories of the wrong product' (p. 44). The 'additional cost of unique components was not fully reflected in the standard cost of the product' (p. 44) and 'the low-volume and tailored products consumed significantly more support services per unit than did the high-volume, mainline products' (p. 45).

Tektronix introduced new measures of continuous improvement and the role of accounting changed 'from being a watchdog to being a change facilitator' (p. 41). The focus on costs changed to the output of a production line based on standard costs. This shifted attention from improving individual worker performance to improving overall process effectiveness. Production was stopped when a defect was found, something that in Western companies had been unimaginable given the focus on maximizing production volume. A new method of overhead allocation which 'shifts product cost from products with high-volume common parts to those with low-volume unique parts' (p. 46) was introduced.

Source: Turney, P. B. B. and Anderson B. (1989). Accounting for continuous improvement. *Sloan Management Review*, Winter, 37–47.

Conclusion

In Chapters 10, 11, and 12, various accounting techniques were identified that can be used by non-financial managers as part of the decision-making process. With the shift in most Western economies to service and knowledge-based industries and high-technology manufacture, overheads have increased as a proportion of total business costs. This chapter has shown the importance to decision making of the assumptions and methods used by accountants to allocate overheads to products/services. Understanding the methods used, and their limitations, is essential if informed decisions are to be made by accountants and non-financial managers.

This chapter has also shown that we need to consider the underlying assumptions behind the management accounting techniques that are in use. Other countries adopt different approaches and we have something to learn from different approaches and the need to consider the behavioural consequences of the choices made in relation to accounting systems.

The reader is encouraged to read and think about Reading A (Cooper and Kaplan: *How cost accounting distorts product costs*) which ultimately led its authors to develop activity-based costing. This is an early but still relevant critique of traditional cost allocation processes. In particular, the example of two identical plants producing the same overall volume but with a different product mix is a powerful illustration of the advantages of activity-based costing. Reading B is Dent's classic case study of EuroRail (*Accounting and organizational cultures; a field study of the emergence of a new organizational reality*) (discussed briefly in the section on behavioural implications above), which reflects the interpretive approach and shows the importance of culture and power in changing accounting systems. As such, it is a useful illustration of the behavioural implications of accounting. Both Readings are in Part IV of this book.

References

Burchell, S., Clubb, C., Hopwood, A., and Hughes, J. (1980). The roles of accounting in organizations and society. *Accounting, Organizations and Society*, 5(1), 5–27.

Chartered Institute of Management Accountants (CIMA 2005). *CIMA Official Terminology: 2005 Edition*. London: CIMA/Elsevier.

Chartered Institute of Management Accountants (CIMA, 2009). Management accounting tools for today and tomorrow. http://www.cimaglobal.com/Documents/Thought_leadership_docs/CIMA%20Tools%20and%20Techniques%2030-11-09%20PDF.pdf.

Clark, J. M. (1923). *Studies in the Economics of Overhead Costs*. Chicago: University of Chicago Press.

Cooper, D. J., Hayes, D., and Wolf, F. (1981). Accounting in organized anarchies: understanding and designing accounting systems in ambiguous situations. *Accounting, Organizations and Society*, 6(3), 175–91.

Dent, J. F. (1991). Accounting and organizational cultures: a field study of the emergence of a new organizational reality. *Accounting, Organizations and Society*, 16(8), 705–32.

Fisher, J. (1995). Contingency-based research on management control systems: categorization by level of complexity. *Journal of Accounting Literature*, 14, 24–53.

Gosselin, M. (2007). A review of activity-based costing: technique, implementation, and consequences. In C. S. Chapman, A. G. Hopwood, and M. D. Shields (Eds), *Handbook of Management Accounting Research* (Vol. 2, pp. 641–71). Oxford: Elsevier.

Hopper, T., Otley, D., and Scapens, B. (2001). British management accounting research: whence and whither: opinions and recollections. *British Accounting Review*, 33, 263–91.

Johnson, H. T. and Kaplan, R. S. (1987). *Relevance Lost: The Rise and Fall of Management Accounting*. Boston, MA: Harvard Business School Press.

Kaplan, R. S. and Anderson, S. R. (2007). The innovation of time-driven activity-based costing. *Cost Management*, 21(2), 5–15

Kaplan, R. S. and Cooper, R. (1997). *Cost and Effect: Using Integrated Cost Systems to Drive Profitability and Performance*. Boston, MA: Harvard Business Press Books.

Miller, P. (1994). Accounting as social and institutional practice: an introduction. In A. G. Hopwood and P. Miller (Eds), *Accounting as Social and Institutional Practice*. Cambridge: Cambridge University Press.

Nobes, C. and Parker, R. H. (Eds.). (2008). *Comparative International Accounting*. London: Pearson Education.

Otley, D. (1980). The contingency theory of management accounting: achievement and prognosis. *Accounting, Organizations and Society*, 5(4), 413–28.

Turney, P. B. B. and Anderson B. (1989). Accounting for continuous improvement. *Sloan Management Review*, Winter, 37–47.

Van der Stede, W. A. and Malone, R. (2010). *Accounting Trends in a Borderless World*. CIMA. http://www.cimaglobal.com/Documents/Thought_leadership_docs/AccountingTrends.pdf.

Questions

13.1 Intelco, a professional services firm, has overheads of $500,000. It operates three divisions and an accountant's estimate of the overhead allocation per division is 50% for Division 1, 30% for Division 2, and 20% for Division 3. The divisions respectively bill 4,000, 2,000, and 3,000 hours. Calculate the:

- blanket (organization-wide) overhead recovery rate; and
- cost centre overhead recovery rate for each division.

13.2 BCF Ltd manufactures a product known as a Grunge. Direct material and labour costs for each Grunge are €300 and €150 respectively. To produce a Grunge requires 20 hours, comprising 10 hours in machining, 7 hours in assembly, and 3 hours in finishing. Information for each department is:

	Machining	*Assembly*	*Finishing*
Overhead costs (€)	120,000	80,000	30,000
Labour hours	20,000	10,000	10,000

Calculate the cost of producing a Grunge using a departmental overhead recovery rate.

13.3 Engineering Products plc produces Product GH1, which incurs costs of £150 for direct materials and £75 for direct labour. The company has estimated its production overhead and direct labour hours for a period as:

	Dept A	*Dept B*	*Dept C*
Overheads £	150,000	200,000	125,000
Direct labour hours	5,000	10,000	5,000

Product GH1 is produced using 10 hours in Dept A, 12 hours in Dept B, and 5 hours in Dept C. Calculate the total cost of each GH1 using:

- a plant-wide overhead recovery rate; and
- cost centre overhead recovery rates.

13.4 Haridan Co. uses activity-based costing. The company has two products, A and B. The annual production and sales of Product A are 8,000 units and of product B 6,000 units. There are three activity cost pools, with estimated total cost and expected activity as follows:

Activity cost pool	Estimated cost	Product A	Expected activity Product B	Total
Activity 1	$20,000	100	400	500
Activity 2	$37,000	800	200	1,000
Activity 3	$91,200	800	3,000	3,800

Calculate the cost per unit of Product A and Product B under activity-based costing.

13.5 Cooper's Components uses an activity-based costing system for its product costing. For the last quarter, the data in Table 13.10 relates to costs, output volume, and cost drivers:

Table 13.10   Cooper's Components ABC data.

Overhead costs			€
Machinery			172,000
Set-ups			66,000
Materials handling			45,000
Total			€283,000

Product	A	B	C
Production and sales	4,000 units	3,000 units	2,000 units
Number of production runs	12	5	8
Number of stores orders	12	6	4
	per unit	per unit	per unit
Direct costs	€25	€35	€15
Machine hours	5	2	3
Direct labour hours	4	2	4

a. If set-up costs are driven by the number of production runs, what is the set-up cost per unit traced to product A?

b. If materials handling costs are driven by the number of stores orders, what is the materials handling cost per unit traced to product B?

13.6 Elandem PLC produces 20,000 units of Product L and 20,000 units of Product M. Under activity-based costing, £120,000 of costs are purchasing-related. If 240 purchase orders are produced each period, and the number of orders used by each product is:

	Product L	Product M
No. of orders	80	160

• Calculate the per-unit activity-based cost of purchasing for Products L and M.
• Calculate the overhead recovery for purchasing costs if those costs were recovered over the number of units of the product produced.

13.7   Heated Tools Ltd uses activity-based costing. It has identified three cost pools and their drivers as follows:

	Purchasing	*Quality control*	*Despatch*
Cost pool	$60,000	$40,000	$30,000
Driver	12,000	4,000	2,000
	Purchase orders	Stores issues	Deliveries

Product Hekla uses $100 of direct materials and $75 of direct labour. In addition, each Hekla has been identified as using five purchase orders, eight stores issues, and two deliveries. Calculate the total cost of each Hekla.

13.8   Samuelson uses activity-based costing. The company manufactures two products, X and Y. The annual production and sales of Product X are 3,000 units and of Product Y 2,000 units. There are three activity cost pools, with estimated total cost and expected activity as shown in Table 13.11.

Table 13.11   ABC data for Samuelson.

		Expected activity		
Cost pool	**Estimated cost**	**X**	**Y**	**Total**
Activity 1	€12,000	300	500	800
Activity 2	€15,000	100	400	500
Activity 3	€32,000	400	1200	1600
Total costs	€59,000			

a.   Calculate the overhead cost per unit of Products X and Y under activity-based costing.
b.   Samuelson wishes to contrast its overhead allocation with that under the traditional costing method it previously used. Samuelson charged its overheads of €59,000 to products in proportion to machine hours. Each unit of X and Y consumed five machine hours in production. Calculate the overhead cost per unit of Products X and Y under the traditional method of overhead allocation.

13.9   Brixton Industries plc makes three products: Widgets, Gadgets, and Helios. The following budget information relates to Brixton for next year (Table 13.12).

Table 13.12   Brixton Industries budget information.

	Widgets	**Gadgets**	**Helios**
Sales and production (units)	50,000	40,000	30,000
Selling price (£ per unit)	£45	£95	£73
Direct labour and materials (£ per unit)	£32	£84	£65
Machine hours per unit in machining dept	2	5	4
Direct labour hours per unit in assembly dept	7	3	2

Overheads allocated and apportioned to production departments (including service cost centres) were to be recovered in product costs as follows:

Machining department at £1.20 per machine hour.
Assembly department at £0.825 per direct labour hour.

However, you have determined that the overheads could be re-analysed into cost pools as in Table 13.13.

Table 13.13   Brixton Industries activity cost pools and drivers.

Cost pool	£ Cost	Cost driver	Quantity
Machining services	£357,000	Machine hours	420,000
Assembly services	£318,000	Direct labour hours	530,000
Set-up costs	£26,000	Set-ups	520
Order processing	£156,000	Customer orders	32,000
Purchasing	£84,000	Supplier orders	11,200

You have also been provided with the following estimates for the period as shown in Table 13.14.

Table 13.14   Brixton Industries estimates.

	Widgets	Gadgets	Helios
Number of set-ups	120	200	200
Customer orders	8,000	8,000	16,000
Supplier orders	3,000	4,000	4,200

- Prepare and present a profit calculation showing the profitability of each product using traditional absorption costing.
- Prepare and present a profit calculation showing the profitability of each product using activity-based costing.
- Explain the differences between the product profitability using absorption and activity-based costing.

13.10   Klingon Holdings has prepared a marketing study that shows the following demand and average price for each of its services for the following period:

	A	B	C
Volume	150,000	200,000	350,000
Estimated selling price per unit	$50	$35	$25
The variable costs for each are	$20	$17	$14

Fixed expenses have been budgeted as $6,900,000.

Using the above information:

- Calculate the contribution per unit of volume (and in total) for each service. Which is the preferred service? Why? What should the business strategy be?
- Determine the absorption (full) cost per unit for the three services using three different methods of allocating overheads.
- How do the results of these different methods compare?
- Assuming a constant mix of the services sold, calculate the breakeven point for the business.

Strategic Investment Decisions

We introduced strategy in Chapter 2 to explain its link with achieving shareholder value. One of the most important elements of strategy implementation is capital investment decision making, because investment decisions provide the physical infrastructure through which businesses produce and sell goods and services. This is the topic of this chapter. In evaluating capital expenditure decisions, we compare three techniques: accounting rate of return; payback; and discounted cash flow techniques to see how investment decisions are evaluated.

Strategy

Strategy has often been viewed as a road map to achieve an organization's objectives. It has been described by Michael Porter (whose work has been introduced in earlier chapters) as 'offensive or defensive actions to create a defensible position in an industry . . . [to] yield a superior return on investment for the organization' (Porter, 1980, p. 34).

The traditional approach to strategy formation was described by Ansoff (1988). This approach reflected the cybernetic approach to management control introduced in Chapter 4. For Ansoff, strategy formulation involved setting objectives and goals; and carrying out an internal appraisal of strengths and weaknesses and an external appraisal of opportunities and threats (called SWOT analysis). This led to strategic decisions such as investment, diversification, and the development of competitive strategy. External opportunities and threats are assessed by considering political, economic, social, and technological issues in the environment (called PEST analysis, sometimes extended to PESTLE to include legal and environmental factors).

A contrasting approach was developed by Quinn (1980), which he called *logical incrementalism*. Quinn argued against formal planning systems, which he believed had become 'costly paper-shuffling exercises', observing that 'most major strategic decisions seemed to be made outside the formal planning structure' (p. 2). Reflecting the critique of planning we introduced in Chapter 4, Quinn further argued that:

> the real strategy tends to evolve as internal decisions and external events flow together to create a new, widely shared consensus for action among key members of the top management team (p. 15).

To some extent the work by Mintzberg and Waters (1985) bridges these two extremes. Mintzberg and Waters defined strategy as a pattern in a stream of decisions and contrasted *intended* and *realized* strategy, arguing that *deliberate* strategies provided only a partial explanation, as some intended strategies were unable to be realized while other strategies *emerged* over time.

Strategy is crucial in enabling a business to be proactive in increasingly competitive and turbulent business conditions. The absence of strategy can lead to reactivity and a steady erosion of market share. Strategy *implementation* needs to be flexible because businesses in the twenty-first century must continually adapt to technological and market change, which may not have been foreseen during the strategy formulation cycle.

Strategy implementation involves ensuring that resource allocations follow strategy. Maritan (2001) used a case study to illustrate how a manufacturing firm invests in production equipment. Maritan found that the financial evaluation of capital investment decisions took place in the context of a complex organizational decision process in which multiple processes were used simultaneously to make capital investments that were associated with capabilities. This might be investing in new capacity or the capability to achieve lower costs, becoming more flexible, or producing a new product.

Kim and Mauborgne (2005) argued that most strategy is based on competing in established industries with limited growth opportunities, what they called 'red oceans'. They contrasted this with 'blue ocean' strategy which involved the creation of new industries or changing the basis of competition in old industries, in both cases making competition irrelevant. Amazon is a good example of a company developing a blue ocean strategy in book retailing, as is Apple in its development of iTunes.

Management accounting and control systems are used to manage risks and ensure that goals are achieved (see Chapter 4). In this chapter we are primarily concerned with how to evaluate capital investment decisions as a critical element in strategy formulation and implementation.

Capital expenditure evaluation

Capital investment or capital expenditure (often abbreviated as 'cap ex') means spending money now in the hope of getting it back later through future cash flows. The process of evaluating or appraising potential investments is to:

- generate ideas based on opportunities or identifying solutions to problems;
- research all relevant information;
- consider possible alternatives;
- evaluate the financial consequences of each alternative;
- assess non-financial aspects of each alternative;
- decide to proceed;
- determine an implementation plan and implement the proposal;
- control implementation by monitoring actual results compared to plan.

There are three main types of investment: new facilities for new product/services; expanding capacity to meet demand; or replacing assets in order to reduce production costs or improve quality or service. Most capital expenditure evaluations consider decisions such as: whether or not to invest; whether to invest in one project or one piece of equipment rather than another; and whether to invest now or at a later time. Capital expenditure evaluations are also used for business mergers and acquisitions.

There are three main methods of evaluating investments:

1. accounting rate of return;
2. payback;
3. discounted cash flow.

While the first method is concerned with accounting profits, the second and third are concerned with cash flows from a project. For any project, capital expenditure evaluation requires an estimation of future incremental cash flows, i.e. the additional cash flow (income less expenses and income taxes, and adjusting for increases in working capital) that will result from the investment, compared with the cash outflow for the initial investment. Depreciation is, of course, an expense in arriving at profit that does not involve any cash flow (see Chapter 6). Cash flow is usually considered to be more important than accounting profit in capital expenditure evaluation because it is cash flow that drives shareholder value (see Chapter 2).

In capital expenditure decision making, we usually refer to *free cash flow*. Free cash flow is a measure of financial performance defined as operating cash flow after deducting capital expenditure. As we have seen in Chapter 6, cash flow from operations comprises operating profit before tax, plus depreciation and amortization, adjusted by the increase or decrease in working capital.

> Free cash flow = operating profit before tax + depreciation & amortization +/− change in working capital − capital expenditure

Free cash flow represents the cash that a company is able to generate after investing in maintaining or expanding its asset base which enables the business to take advantage of opportunities to improve shareholder value.

In evaluating capital expenditure decisions, it is important to note the following:

- The financing decision is treated separately from the investment decision. Hence, even though there may be no initial cash outflow for the investment (because it may be wholly financed), all capital expenditure evaluation techniques assume an initial cash outflow. If a decision is made to proceed, then the organization is faced with a separate decision about how best to finance the investment. This is more a matter for corporate finance decisions about the mix of debt and equity.

- For the above reason, interest is never an expense shown in a forecast for capital expenditure evaluation purposes.
- The outflows are not just additional operating costs, as any new investment that generates sales growth is also likely to have an impact on working capital, since inventory, receivables, and payables are likely to increase along with sales growth (see Chapter 7).
- Income tax is treated as a cash outflow as it is a consequence of the cash inflows from the new investment.

The detailed work in arriving at these profit and cash flow forecasts is not shown here, but will be the result of estimating an increase in sales volume, pricing, cost of sales, additional expenses and working capital, income taxes, and so on using the same process as applies for budgeting (see Chapter 16). This estimation process will typically be developed using a spreadsheet that non-financial managers may have to develop, often with assistance from accountants in the business. Many assumptions will be made in developing these forecasts, which need to be made explicit in order that the forecasts can be understood. Most cap ex proposals need to be approved at board level and hence must be presented in terms that can be interpreted and evaluated. A summary of a typical profit and cash flow forecast produced for capital expenditure evaluation purposes is shown in Table 14.1 below.

Table 14.1   Illustration of forecast for capital expenditure purposes.

Forecast for cap ex proposal	Year 1	Year 2	Year 3	Year 4	Year 5	Total
Additional product sales (units)	15,000	20,000	25,000	14,000	12,000	86,000
Additional revenue @ $30 per unit	$450,000	$600,000	$750,000	$420,000	$360,000	$2,580,000
Additional variable & fixed costs	−$300,000	−$400,000	−$500,000	−$280,000	−$240,000	−$1,720,000
Profit before interest and taxes	$150,000	$200,000	$250,000	$140,000	$120,000	$860,000
Depreciation expense added back	$100,000	$100,000	$100,000	$100,000	$100,000	$500,000
Profit before depreciation	$250,000	$300,000	$350,000	$240,000	$220,000	$1,360,000
Working capital change	−$60,000	−$80,000	−$60,000	$30,000	$20,000	−$150,000
Income tax paid		−$65,000	−$90,000	−$85,000	−$60,000	−$300,000
Cash flow	$190,000	$155,000	$200,000	$185,000	$180,000	$910,000

In this simple example, the cap ex proposal assumes additional product sales at a price of $30 per unit, with additional variable and fixed costs being incurred (note: the original investment is a non-current asset in the Balance Sheet; the fixed costs are recurring costs each year such as additional rent, salaries, depreciation, etc. in the Income Statement). Depreciation is added back as a non-cash expense and for cash flow purposes, adjustments are made for changes in working capital (receivables, inventory, and payables), and estimated additional income tax payments are included. The resulting forecast is the *increased* profit and cash flow if the cap ex proposal is approved and implemented.

In the following example, we will assume three alternative investments as we consider each of the three methods of capital expenditure evaluation. Table 14.2 shows the estimated cash flows for each of the three alternatives, which are assumed to follow from the more comprehensive spreadsheet process explained and illustrated above (although there is no connection between Tables 14.1 and 14.2).

Table 14.2   Cash flows for three alternative investments.

Year	£ Project 1	£ Project 2	£ Project 3
0 initial investment	−100,000	−125,000	−200,000
1 inflows	25,000	35,000	60,000
2 inflows	25,000	35,000	60,000
3 inflows	25,000	35,000	80,000
4 inflows	25,000	35,000	30,000
5 inflows	25,000	35,000	30,000

In this example five years is used as the planning horizon, but this is only an example. The *planning horizon* used by each company will be different, contingent on the industry, the rate of technological change, anticipated competition, and so on. In practice it is how far ahead a company is reasonably comfortable in predicting. The planning horizon will commonly be equal to the period over which the investment is depreciated, but this does not have to be the case. A mining company like BHP Billiton making a major investment may plan 20–50 years in advance. A rapidly changing technology company like Apple may have a time horizon of only a year or two. Capital expenditure evaluations are also used for business acquisitions. As one component of the purchase price of another business is goodwill then the planning horizon will usually be the period over which goodwill is amortized (accounting for goodwill is covered in Chapter 6).

For simplicity, in capital expenditure evaluation we assume that each of the cash flows occurs at the end of each year. Year 0 represents the beginning of the project when the initial funds are paid out. If we add up the cash flows in the above example, Project 1 returns £125,000 (5 @ £25,000), Project 2 returns £175,000 (5 @ £35,000), and Project 3 returns £260,000 (2 @ £60,000 + £80,000 + 2 @ £30,000), although the initial investment in each is different.

Accounting rate of return

The accounting rate of return (ARR) is the profit after tax generated as a percentage of the initial investment. This is equivalent to the return on investment (ROI) that was introduced in Chapter 7. ARR is used here rather than ROI because ROI is based on the ratio of net profit after tax to shareholders' funds, but capital expenditure evaluation does not differentiate the source of funds to finance the investment, i.e. whether the investment is financed through debt or equity. The investment value for ARR is the depreciated value each year. The depreciated value each year, assuming a life of five years with no residual value at the end of that time, is shown in Table 14.3.

Table 14.3   Depreciated value of alternative investments.

End of year	£ Project 1	£ Project 2	£ Project 3
1	80,000	100,000	160,000
2	60,000	75,000	120,000
3	40,000	50,000	80,000
4	20,000	25,000	40,000
5	0	0	0

The accounting rate of return varies annually, as Table 14.4 shows for Project 1.

Table 14.4   ARR for Project 1.

Year	Cash flow £	Depreciation £	Profit £	Investment £	ARR
1	25,000	20,000	5,000	80,000	6.25%
2	25,000	20,000	5,000	60,000	8.3%
3	25,000	20,000	5,000	40,000	12.5%
4	25,000	20,000	5,000	20,000	25%
5	25,000	20,000	5,000	0	

It is quite common that ARR in earlier years is lower than in later years, as the asset has a higher depreciated value than in later years and cash flows often grow and then decline over the life cycle of an investment. In the final year, when the asset is fully depreciated, the return is infinite, because the ARR is based on an investment of zero. Different businesses use different ways of calculating the annual ARR – based on opening written-down value (the difference between historical cost and the accumulated depreciation), based on closing written-down value (as in the example in this chapter), or based on the average of opening and closing written-down values each year.

For the whole investment period, the accounting rate of return is the average annual return divided by the average investment. The average annual return is the total profit for the forecast period divided by the number of years. As we assume that depreciation is spread equally throughout the life of the asset, the average investment is half the value of the initial investment.

$$\frac{\text{total profits/no.of years}}{\text{initial investment/2}}$$

The average ARR for Project 1 is:

$$\frac{25,000/5}{100,000/2} = \frac{5,000}{50,000} = 10\%$$

The accounting rate of return for Project 2 is shown in Table 14.5.

Table 14.5   ARR for Project 2.

Year	Cash flow £	Depreciation £	Profit £	Investment £	ARR
1	35,000	25,000	10,000	100,000	10%
2	35,000	25,000	10,000	75,000	13.3%
3	35,000	25,000	10,000	50,000	20%
4	35,000	25,000	10,000	25,000	40%
5	35,000	25,000	10,000	0	

The average ARR for Project 2 is:

$$\frac{50,000/5}{125,000/2} = \frac{10,000}{62,500} = 16\%$$

The accounting rate of return for Project 3 is shown in Table 14.6.

Table 14.6   ARR for Project 3.

Year	Cash flow £	Depreciation £	Profit £	Investment £	ARR
1	60,000	40,000	20,000	160,000	13%
2	60,000	40,000	20,000	120,000	17%
3	80,000	40,000	40,000	80,000	50%
4	30,000	40,000	–10,000	40,000	–25%
5	30,000	40,000	–10,000	0	

The average ARR for Project 3 is:

$$\frac{60,000/5}{200,000/2} = \frac{12,000}{100,000} = 12\%$$

Project 3 in particular has substantial fluctuations in ARR from year to year. Using this method, Project 2 shows the highest return. However, it does not take into account either the scale of the investment required or the timing of the cash flows. Given that throughout this book we have emphasized that cash flow is more important than profit, it makes sense for capital expenditure evaluation to look not only at profits but also at cash flow. However, we must not forget that if a company has a target ROI (or ROCE, see Chapter 7), then every individual investment must contribute to achieving that ratio. Hence companies will typically have an ARR hurdle rate that reflects the overall company ROI and ROCE ratios it is aiming for.

Payback

This second method of capital investment evaluation calculates how many years it will take in cash terms to recover the initial investment, on the assumption that the shorter the payback period, the better the investment because the risk of technological or market change is less in the short term. Based on the cash flows for each project:

- Project 1 takes four years to recover its £100,000 investment (4 @ £25,000).
- Project 2 has recovered £105,000 by the end of the third year (3 @ £35,000) and will take less than seven months (20/35 = .57 of 12 months) to recover its £125,000 investment. The payback is therefore 3.57 years.
- Project 3 recovers its investment of £200,000 by the end of the third year (£60,000 + £60,000 + £80,000).

Based on the payback method, Project 3 is preferred (followed by Projects 2 and 1) as it has the fastest payback. However, the payback method ignores the size of the investment and any cash flows that take place after the investment has been recovered. This is a particular weakness of the payback method.

Discounted cash flow

Neither the accounting rate of return nor the payback method considers the *time value of money*, i.e. that £100 is worth more now than in a year's time, because it can be invested now at a rate of interest that will increase its value. For example, £100 invested today at 10% interest is equivalent to £110 in a year's time. Conversely, receiving £100 in a year's time is not worth £100 today. Assuming the same rate of interest it is worth only £91, because the £91, invested at 10%, will be equivalent to £100 in a year's time.

The time value of money needs to be recognized in capital investment evaluations in order to compare investment alternatives with different initial cash outflows, and different cash inflows over different time periods. The third method of capital expenditure evaluation therefore involves discounted cash flow (DCF) techniques. DCF discounts future cash flows to their present values using a discount rate (or interest rate) that is usually the firm's weighted average cost of capital (the risk-adjusted cost of borrowing for the investment, see Chapter 2). The cost of capital may be risk adjusted, i.e. a higher hurdle may be set where an investment is perceived as being more risky.

There are two discounted cash flow techniques: net present value and internal rate of return.

Net present value

The net present value (NPV) method discounts future cash flows to their present value (PV) and compares the *present value of future cash flows* to the initial capital investment. The net present value (NPV) is the difference between the present value of future cash flows and the initial investment outflow:

present value (PV) of cash flows = cash flow × discount factor (based on number of years in the future and the cost of capital)

net present value (NPV) = present value of future cash flows – initial capital investment

An investment makes sense financially if the NPV is positive, i.e. that the present value of cash flows exceeds the cost of capital. In this case, the investment is creating shareholder value. If an investment results in a negative NPV, the cost of capital exceeds the present value of cash flows and the investment proposal should be rejected.

The present value of a future cash flow can be derived in four ways:

- using tables (the method used in this chapter);
- using a financial calculator;
- using an Excel spreadsheet (also shown in this chapter); and
- by formula (briefly shown below).

The formula method is $P = F_n (1/(1 + r)^n)$, where:

P is the present value;
F_n is the future cash flow in n years;
r is the cost of capital used as the discount factor; and
n is the number of years.

So for example, £133.10 received in three years using a 10% cost of capital would be calculated as:

$$P = 133.10 \left(1/(1 + .10)^3\right) = 133.10(1/1.331) = 133.10 \times 0.7513 = £100$$

Using the same example, the NPV for Project 1 is shown in Table 14.7. The discount rate can be obtained from the net present value table in the Appendix to this chapter. It can also be obtained using

Table 14.7   NPV for Project 1.

Year	Project 1 cash flows	Discount factor (10%)	Present value of cash flows
1	25,000	.909	22,725
2	25,000	.826	20,650
3	25,000	.751	18,775
4	25,000	.683	17,075
5	25,000	.621	15,525
Present value of cash flows			94,750
Less: Initial investment			100,000
Net present value			–5,250

the @NPV function in an Excel spreadsheet. As the net present value is negative, Project 1 should not be accepted since the present value of future cash flows does not cover the initial investment.

The NPV for Project 2 is shown in Table 14.8. Project 2 can be accepted because it has a positive net present value. However, we need to compare this with Project 3 to see if that alternative yields a higher net present value. The NPV for Project 3 is shown in Table 14.9.

Table 14.8   NPV for Project 2.

Year	Project 2 cash flows	Discount factor (10%)	Present value of cash flows
1	35,000	.909	31,815
2	35,000	.826	28,910
3	35,000	.751	26,285
4	35,000	.683	23,905
5	35,000	.621	21,735
Present value of cash flows			132,650
Less: Initial investment			125,000
Net present value			7,650

Table 14.9   NPV for Project 3.

Year	Project 3 cash flows	Discount factor (10%)	Present value of cash flows
1	60,000	.909	54,540
2	60,000	.826	49,560
3	80,000	.751	60,080
4	30,000	.683	20,490
5	30,000	.621	18,630
Present value of cash flows			203,300
Less: Initial investment			200,000
Net present value			3,300

Despite the faster payback for Project 3, the application of the net present value technique to the timing of the cash flows reveals that the net present value of Project 3 is lower than that for Project 2, and therefore Project 2 – which also showed the highest accounting rate of return – is the recommended investment. However, using the NPV method it is difficult to determine how much better Project 2 (with an NPV of £7,650) is than Project 3 (with an NPV of £3,300) because each has a different initial investment.

One way of ranking projects with different NPVs is cash value added (CVA) or profitability index, which is a ratio of the NPV to the initial capital investment:

$$\text{cash value added} = \frac{\text{NPV}}{\text{Initial capital investment}}$$

In the above example, Project 2 returns a CVA of 6.12% (£7,650/£125,000) while Project 3 returns a CVA of 1.65% (£3,300/£200,000). Companies may have a target CVA such that, for example, to be approved a project must have a CVA of 10% (i.e. the NPV is at least 10% of the initial capital investment). The lower the CVA, the more risk there is of the NPV falling below zero.

The second DCF technique is the internal rate of return.

Internal rate of return

The internal rate of return (IRR) method determines the discount rate that produces a net present value of zero. This involves repeated trial-and-error calculations using the discount tables, applying different discount rates until an NPV of 0 is reached. The discount rate may need to be interpolated between whole percentages in the tables. However, it is much easier to use spreadsheet software like Excel which contains an @IRR function. The IRR for each project, using the spreadsheet function, is:

Project 1	7.9%
Project 2	12.4%
Project 3	10.7%

This is a more informative presentation of the comparison because it presents the cash flows as an effective interest rate. This interest rate is compared to the risk-adjusted cost of capital. The project with the highest internal rate of return would be preferred, provided that the rate exceeds the cost of capital.

Comparison of techniques

In the above example, each technique provides management with an incomplete picture, but taken together, all the methods help to determine the most appropriate decision to invest limited funds. Table 14.10 shows the rankings for each investment using each technique.

Table 14.10   Comparison of techniques.

Project	ARR	Payback	NPV	CVA	IRR
Project 1	10%	4 years	−£5,250		7.9%
Ranking	3	3			
Project 2	16%	3.57 years	$7,650	6.12%	12.4%
Ranking	1	2	1	1	1
Project 3	12%	3 years	£3,300	1.65%	10.7%
Ranking	2	1	2	2	2

Project 1 should not be accepted because it has a negative NPV and is ranked third on ARR and payback measures. Project 2 has the highest ranking on all techniques other than payback. Project 3 has the fastest payback but is otherwise behind Project 2 on all other measures. In this case it would appear that Project 2 is the preferred alternative investment. However, a business would normally set hurdle rates for its ARR, payback, and DCF such that a proposal would need to exceed each hurdle to be accepted. In this case, the board may well send Project 2 back to the managers who submitted it, with a request that forecast cash flows be reviewed to see if they can be improved.

The methods themselves inform management and the board about different aspects of the capital expenditure evaluation. While the accounting rate of return method provides an average after-tax return on the capital investment and a business may select the highest return, commensurate with its ROI and ROCE targets in its financial statements, the method ignores the timing of cash flows. Sometimes where there are high short-term ARRs, managers may prefer those investments even though the longer term impact may be detrimental to the organization. This is because managers may be evaluated and rewarded on their short-term performance (see Chapter 15). On the other hand, projects with a longer-term ARR may be rejected as managers may not gain the benefit of those investment returns, since new managers may well have replaced them. Payback measures the number of years it will take to recover the capital investment and while this takes timing into account, it ignores cash flows after the payback period. Both ARR and payback methods ignore the time value of money.

Discounted cash flow techniques take account of the time value of money and discount future cash flows to their present value using a risk-adjusted weighted average cost of capital. This is generally seen to be a more reliable method of capital expenditure evaluation. Discounted cash flow is similar to the method of calculating shareholder value proposed by Rappaport (1998) which was described in Chapter 2.

However, for investment evaluation, while all projects with a positive net present value are beneficial, a business will usually select the project with the highest net present value, or in other words the highest internal rate of return, sometimes using the initial cash investment (CVA) or the cost of capital (IRR) as a benchmark for the return.

In their 2009 report *Management accounting tools for today and tomorrow*, the Chartered Institute of Management Accountants (CIMA, 2009) found that the payback method was relatively popular, despite it being the least sophisticated appraisal technique. This was so even in the very largest organizations, which typically have larger capital projects and more specialist finance staff. This may reflect the short-term focus of listed companies in producing results under investor pressure, and/or the risk-averse nature of boards of directors who, despite the availability of more sophisticated techniques, like to see quick returns on their investment.

Boards of directors typically set quite high 'hurdle' rates for investing in new assets. These are commonly in terms of payback periods of two to four years or ARR rates of 25–50%. Because of increasing market competition, rapid technological change, and increased demands for short-term shareholder value, the use of discounted cash flow techniques has declined in some businesses. However, for larger investments where returns are expected over many years, discounted cash flow techniques are still important. Business mergers and acquisitions, investments in buildings, major items of plant, mining exploration, and so on commonly use discounted cash flow as methods of capital expenditure evaluation.

Case study 14.1 provides an example of capital expenditure evaluation.

Case study 14.1: Goliath Co. – investment evaluation

Goliath Co. is considering investing in a project involving an initial cash outlay for an asset of €200,000. The asset is depreciated over five years at 20% p.a. Goliath's cost of capital is 10%. The expected cash flows from the project are shown in Table 14.11.

Table 14.11   Expected cash inflows and outflows for Goliath Co.

Year	€ Inflow	€ Outflow
1	75,000	30,000
2	90,000	40,000
3	100,000	45,000
4	100,000	50,000
5	75,000	40,000

The company wishes to consider the accounting rate of return (each year and average), payback, and net present value as methods of evaluating the proposal. The depreciation expense is €40,000 per year. Net cash flows and profits are shown in Table 14.12.

Table 14.12   Cash flow and profit projections for Goliath Co.

Year	Inflow €	Outflow €	Net cash flow €	Depreciation €	Profit €
1	75,000	30,000	45,000	40,000	5,000
2	90,000	40,000	50,000	40,000	10,000
3	100,000	45,000	55,000	40,000	15,000
4	100,000	50,000	50,000	40,000	10,000
5	75,000	40,000	35,000	40,000	–5,000

The accounting rate of returns (ARR) each year for the project are shown in Table 14.13.

Table 14.13   ARRs for Goliath Co.

	1	2	3	4	5
Investment (€)	160,000	120,000	80,000	40,000	0
Profit (€)	5,000	10,000	15,000	10,000	–5,000
ARR	3.125%	8.33%	18.75%	25%	–

The average ARR over the five years is calculated as:

$$\text{Profit } 35,000/5,000 = 7,000$$
$$\text{Investment } 200,000/2,000 = 100,000$$
$$\text{ARR } 7,000/100,000 = 7\%$$

In order to calculate payback, we need cumulative cash flows, which are shown in Table 14.14.

Table 14.14   Cumulative cash flows for Goliath Co.

Year	Cash flow €	Cumulative €
1	45	45
2	50	95
3	55	150
4	50	200

The payback period is at the end of year 4 when €200,000 of cash flows has been recovered. The net present value of the cash flows is shown in Table 14.15.

Table 14.15   Net Present Value calculation for Goliath Co.

Year	Cash flow	Factor	Present value
1	45,000	.9091	40,910
2	50,000	.8264	41,320
3	55,000	.7513	41,321
4	50,000	.6830	34,150
5	35,000	.6209	21,731
Present value of cash flows			179,432
Initial investment			−200,000
Net present value			−20,568

Using the spreadsheet NPV function, the answer is calculated in Table 14.16 (the difference is due to rounding).

Table 14.16   NPV for Goliath Co.

A	B Year 0	C Year 1	D Year 2	E Year 3	F Year 4	G Year 5
Cash flows		45,000	50,000	55,000	50,000	35,000
Present value	179,437					
		=NPV (10%, C36:G36)				
Initial investment	200,000					
NPV	−20,563					

Although the ARR is 7% and the payback is four years, the discounted cash flow shows that the net present value is negative. Therefore the project should be rejected, as the returns are insufficient to recover the company's cost of capital.

Conclusion

In this chapter we have explained the importance of capital expenditure evaluation and its relationship with strategy formulation and implementation. In particular, we have described the main techniques for capital expenditure evaluation: accounting rate of return, payback, and the two discounted cash flow methods: net present value and internal rate of return.

Often, business decisions are made subjectively and then justified after the event by the application of financial techniques. This is particularly so for emergent strategies, described earlier in this chapter. Despite the usefulness of these techniques, the assumption has been that future cash flows can be predicted with some accuracy. This prediction problem is, however, one of the main difficulties in accounting, as we will see in Chapter 16.

References

Ansoff, H. I. (1988). *The New Corporate Strategy*. New York: John Wiley & Sons.

Chartered Institute of Management Accountants (CIMA, 2009). *Management accounting tools for today and tomorrow*. http://www.cimaglobal.com/Documents/Thought_leadership_docs/CIMA%20Tools%20and%20Techniques%2030-11-09%20PDF.pdf.

Kim, W.C. and Mauborgne, R. (2005). *Blue Ocean Strategy*. Boston, MA: Harvard Business School Press.

Maritan, C. A. (2001). Capital investment as investing in organizational capabilities: an empirically grounded process model. *Academy of Management Journal*, 44(3), 513–31.

Mintzberg, H. and Waters, J. A. (1985). Of strategies, deliberate and emergent. *Strategic Management Journal*, 6, 257–72.

Porter, M.E. (1980). *Competitive Strategy: Techniques for Analyzing Industries and Competitors*. New York: Free Press.

Quinn, J. B. (1980). *Strategies for Change: Logical Incrementalism*. Homewood, IL: Irwin.

Rappaport, A. (1998). *Creating Shareholder Value: A Guide for Managers and Investors*. New York: Free Press.

Appendix to Chapter 14: Present value factors

Table 14.17 gives the present value of a single payment received n years in the future discounted at an interest rate of x% per annum. For example, with a discount rate of 6% a single payment of £100 in five years' time has a present value of £74.73 (£100 × 0.7473).

Table 14.17   Present value factors.

Years	1%	2%	3%	4%	5%	6%	7%	8%	9%	10%	11%	12%	13%	14%	15%	16%	17%	18%	19%	20%
1	0.9901	0.9804	0.9709	0.9615	0.9524	0.9434	0.9346	0.9259	0.9174	0.9091	0.9009	0.8929	0.8850	0.8772	0.8696	0.8621	0.8547	0.8475	0.8403	0.8333
2	0.9803	0.9612	0.9426	0.9246	0.9070	0.8900	0.8734	0.8573	0.8417	0.8264	0.8116	0.7972	0.7831	0.7695	0.7561	0.7432	0.7305	0.7182	0.7062	0.6944
3	0.9706	0.9423	0.9151	0.8890	0.8638	0.8396	0.8163	0.7938	0.7722	0.7513	0.7312	0.7118	0.6931	0.6750	0.6575	0.6407	0.6244	0.6086	0.5934	0.5787
4	0.9610	0.9238	0.8885	0.8548	0.8227	0.7921	0.7629	0.7350	0.7084	0.6830	0.6587	0.6355	0.6133	0.5921	0.5718	0.5523	0.5337	0.5158	0.4987	0.4823
5	0.9515	0.9057	0.8626	0.8219	0.7835	0.7473	0.7130	0.6806	0.6499	0.6209	0.5935	0.5674	0.5428	0.5194	0.4972	0.4761	0.4561	0.4371	0.4190	0.4019
6	0.9420	0.8880	0.8375	0.7903	0.7462	0.7050	0.6663	0.6302	0.5963	0.5645	0.5346	0.5066	0.4803	0.4556	0.4323	0.4104	0.3898	0.3704	0.3521	0.3349
7	0.9327	0.8706	0.8131	0.7599	0.7107	0.6651	0.6227	0.5835	0.5470	0.5132	0.4817	0.4523	0.4251	0.3996	0.3759	0.3538	0.3332	0.3139	0.2959	0.2791
8	0.9235	0.8535	0.7894	0.7307	0.6768	0.6274	0.5820	0.5403	0.5019	0.4665	0.4339	0.4039	0.3762	0.3506	0.3269	0.3050	0.2848	0.2660	0.2487	0.2326
9	0.9143	0.8368	0.7664	0.7026	0.6446	0.5919	0.5439	0.5002	0.4604	0.4241	0.3909	0.3606	0.3329	0.3075	0.2843	0.2630	0.2434	0.2255	0.2090	0.1938
10	0.9053	0.8203	0.7441	0.6756	0.6139	0.5584	0.5083	0.4632	0.4224	0.3855	0.3522	0.3220	0.2946	0.2697	0.2472	0.2267	0.2080	0.1911	0.1756	0.1615
11	0.8963	0.8043	0.7224	0.6496	0.5847	0.5268	0.4751	0.4289	0.3875	0.3505	0.3173	0.2875	0.2607	0.2366	0.2149	0.1954	0.1778	0.1619	0.1476	0.1346
12	0.8874	0.7885	0.7014	0.6246	0.5568	0.4970	0.4440	0.3971	0.3555	0.3186	0.2858	0.2567	0.2307	0.2076	0.1869	0.1685	0.1520	0.1372	0.1240	0.1122
13	0.8787	0.7730	0.6810	0.6006	0.5303	0.4688	0.4150	0.3677	0.3262	0.2897	0.2575	0.2292	0.2042	0.1821	0.1625	0.1452	0.1299	0.1163	0.1042	0.0935
14	0.8700	0.7579	0.6611	0.5775	0.5051	0.4423	0.3878	0.3405	0.2992	0.2633	0.2320	0.2046	0.1807	0.1597	0.1413	0.1252	0.1110	0.0985	0.0876	0.0779
15	0.8613	0.7430	0.6419	0.5553	0.4810	0.4173	0.3624	0.3152	0.2745	0.2394	0.2090	0.1827	0.1599	0.1401	0.1229	0.1079	0.0949	0.0835	0.0736	0.0649
16	0.8528	0.7284	0.6232	0.5339	0.4581	0.3936	0.3387	0.2919	0.2519	0.2176	0.1883	0.1631	0.1415	0.1229	0.1069	0.0930	0.0811	0.0708	0.0618	0.0541
17	0.8444	0.7142	0.6050	0.5134	0.4363	0.3714	0.3166	0.2703	0.2311	0.1978	0.1696	0.1456	0.1252	0.1078	0.0929	0.0802	0.0693	0.0600	0.0520	0.0451
18	0.8360	0.7002	0.5874	0.4936	0.4155	0.3503	0.2959	0.2502	0.2120	0.1799	0.1528	0.1300	0.1108	0.0946	0.0808	0.0691	0.0592	0.0508	0.0437	0.0376
19	0.8277	0.6864	0.5703	0.4746	0.3957	0.3305	0.2765	0.2317	0.1945	0.1635	0.1377	0.1161	0.0981	0.0829	0.0703	0.0596	0.0506	0.0431	0.0367	0.0313
20	0.8195	0.6730	0.5537	0.4564	0.3769	0.3118	0.2584	0.2145	0.1784	0.1486	0.1240	0.1037	0.0868	0.0728	0.0611	0.0514	0.0433	0.0365	0.0308	0.0261
21	0.8114	0.6598	0.5375	0.4388	0.3589	0.2942	0.2415	0.1987	0.1637	0.1351	0.1117	0.0926	0.0768	0.0638	0.0531	0.0443	0.0370	0.0309	0.0259	0.0217
22	0.8034	0.6468	0.5219	0.4220	0.3418	0.2775	0.2257	0.1839	0.1502	0.1228	0.1007	0.0826	0.0680	0.0560	0.0462	0.0382	0.0316	0.0262	0.0218	0.0181
23	0.7954	0.6342	0.5067	0.4057	0.3256	0.2618	0.2109	0.1703	0.1378	0.1117	0.0907	0.0738	0.0601	0.0491	0.0402	0.0329	0.0270	0.0222	0.0183	0.0151
24	0.7876	0.6217	0.4919	0.3901	0.3101	0.2470	0.1971	0.1577	0.1264	0.1015	0.0817	0.0659	0.0532	0.0431	0.0349	0.0284	0.0231	0.0188	0.0154	0.0126
25	0.7798	0.6095	0.4776	0.3751	0.2953	0.2330	0.1842	0.1460	0.1160	0.0923	0.0736	0.0588	0.0471	0.0378	0.0304	0.0245	0.0197	0.0160	0.0129	0.0105
26	0.7720	0.5976	0.4637	0.3607	0.2812	0.2198	0.1722	0.1352	0.1064	0.0839	0.0663	0.0525	0.0417	0.0331	0.0264	0.0211	0.0169	0.0135	0.0109	0.0087
27	0.7644	0.5859	0.4502	0.3468	0.2678	0.2074	0.1609	0.1252	0.0976	0.0763	0.0597	0.0469	0.0369	0.0291	0.0230	0.0182	0.0144	0.0115	0.0091	0.0073
28	0.7568	0.5744	0.4371	0.3335	0.2551	0.1956	0.1504	0.1159	0.0895	0.0693	0.0538	0.0419	0.0326	0.0255	0.0200	0.0157	0.0123	0.0097	0.0077	0.0061
29	0.7493	0.5631	0.4243	0.3207	0.2429	0.1846	0.1406	0.1073	0.0822	0.0630	0.0485	0.0374	0.0289	0.0224	0.0174	0.0135	0.0105	0.0082	0.0064	0.0051
30	0.7419	0.5521	0.4120	0.3083	0.2314	0.1741	0.1314	0.0994	0.0754	0.0573	0.0437	0.0334	0.0256	0.0196	0.0151	0.0116	0.0090	0.0070	0.0054	0.0042
35	0.7059	0.5000	0.3554	0.2534	0.1813	0.1301	0.0937	0.0676	0.0490	0.0356	0.0259	0.0189	0.0139	0.0102	0.0075	0.0055	0.0041	0.0030	0.0023	0.0017
40	0.6717	0.4529	0.3066	0.2083	0.1420	0.0972	0.0668	0.0460	0.0318	0.0221	0.0154	0.0107	0.0075	0.0053	0.0037	0.0026	0.0019	0.0013	0.0010	0.0007
45	0.6391	0.4102	0.2644	0.1712	0.1113	0.0727	0.0476	0.0313	0.0207	0.0137	0.0091	0.0061	0.0041	0.0027	0.0019	0.0013	0.0009	0.0006	0.0004	0.0003
50	0.6080	0.3715	0.2281	0.1407	0.0872	0.0543	0.0339	0.0213	0.0134	0.0085	0.0054	0.0035	0.0022	0.0014	0.0009	0.0006	0.0004	0.0003	0.0002	0.0001

Questions

14.1 The Whitton Co. has an opportunity to buy a computer now for €18,000 that will yield annual net cash inflows of €10,000 for the next three years, after which its resale value would be zero. Whitton's cost of capital is 16%.

> Calculate the net present value of the cash flows for the computer using spreadsheet formula.
>
> What is the IRR?

14.2 SmallCo is considering the following project, whose cost of capital is 12% per annum:

Year	0	1	2	3
	£	£	£	£
Cash flows of project	(2,000)	1,000	800	700

Calculate the NPV of the project.

14.3 Goliath Hotel projects the cash flows for three alternative investment projects (in $'000) as:

Project	Year 0	1	2	3	4	5
A	−350	100	200	100	100	140
B	−350	40	100	210	260	160
C	−350	200	150	240	40	0

Depreciation is $70,000 per annum. For each project, calculate: the payback period; accounting rate of return (average); net present value (assuming a cost of capital of 9%); and comment on which (if any) project should be accepted.

14.4 Freddie plc has £5 million to invest this year. Three projects are available and all are divisible, i.e. part of a project may be accepted and the cash flow returns will be pro rata. Details of the projects are:

Project	1	2	3
Cash outlay (£M)	3.0	2.0	1.5
NPV (£M)	1.7	1.1	1.0

What is the ranking of the projects that should be accepted?

14.5   Tropic Investments is considering a project involving an initial cash outlay for an asset of €200,000. The asset is depreciated over five years at 20% p.a. (based on the value of the investment at the beginning of each year). The cash flows from the project are expected to be:

	Inflow	Outflow
	€	€
Year 1	75,000	30,000
Year 2	90,000	40,000
Year 3	100,000	45,000
Year 4	100,000	50,000
Year 5	75,000	40,000

What is the payback period?

What is the accounting rate of return (each year and average)?

Assuming a cost of capital of 10% and ignoring inflation, what is the net present value of the cash flows? (Use the tables rather than a spreadsheet to answer this question.)

Should the project be accepted?

14.6   Creative Tooling wishes to make a capital investment of $750,000 and the management team has produced an analysis (see Table 14.18) for your consideration. Make a recommendation to the board of Creative Tooling as to whether the capital investment should be made, and give reasons to support your answer. Identify the questions that a board of directors may ask the management team in relation to this proposal.

Table 14.18   Capital investment evaluation for Creative Tooling Company.

Capital investment	$750,000					
Cost of capital	12%					
Year	**0**	**1**	**2**	**3**	**4**	**5**
Projected profitability						
Anticipated additional revenue		300,000	350,000	450,000	450,000	400,000
Less anticipated additional costs		60,000	67,500	82,500	75,000	60,000
Less depreciation expense		150,000	150,000	150,000	150,000	150,000
Profit before tax		90,000	132,500	217,500	225,000	190,000
Less income tax expense		66,500	81,375	111,125	96,250	66,500
Profit after tax		23,500	51,125	106,375	128,750	123,500

Year	0	1	2	3	4	5
Projected cash flow						
Profit before tax		90,000	132,500	217,500	225,000	190,000
Add back depreciation		150,000	150,000	150,000	150,000	150,000
Less income tax paid			−66,500	−81,375	−111,125	−96,250
Change in working capital			−60,000	−60,000	−20,000	0
Net cash flow		240,000	156,000	226,125	243,875	243,750
Accounting rate of return						
Asset cost in Balance Sheet		750,000	750,000	750,000	750,000	750,000
Less provision for depreciation		−150,000	−300,000	−450,000	−600,000	−750,000
Net asset value		600,000	450,000	300,000	150,000	0
	Total					
Profit after tax	433,250	23,500	51,125	106,375	128,750	123,500
ARR		3.9%	11.4%	35.5%	85.8%	
Average profits ($433,250/5)	86,650					
Average investment ($750,000/2)	375,000					
Average ARR	23.1%					
Payback						
Net cash flow		240,000	156,000	226,125	243,875	243,750
Cumulative cash flow		240,000	396,000	622,125	866,000	1,109,750
Payback period					3.5 years approx	
Discounted cash flow (NPV at 12%)						
Projected cash flows	−750,000	240,000	156,000	226,125	243,875	243,750
Present value of cash flows	792,897					
Net present value	42,897					
Discounted cash flow (IRR)	14.23%					

CHAPTER 15

Performance Evaluation of Business Units

The shift towards a decentralized, multidivisional business structure and the measurement and management of divisional (i.e. business unit) performance has influenced the development of management accounting. This chapter introduces the structure of business organizations, with emphasis on the divisionalized structure and decentralized profit responsibility. This chapter describes the two main methods by which the performance of divisions and their managers is evaluated: return on investment and residual income. We also consider the issue of controllability and the transfer pricing problem and introduce the theory of transaction cost economics. This chapter suggests that some management accounting techniques may provide an appearance rather than the reality of 'rational' decision making.

Structure of business organizations

Child (1972) defined organization structure as 'the formal allocation of work roles and the administrative mechanisms to control and integrate work activities' (p. 2). Emmanuel, Otley, and Merchant. (1990) described organizational structure as:

> a potent form of control because, by arranging people in a hierarchy with defined patterns of authority and responsibility, a great deal of their behaviour can be influenced or even pre-determined (p. 39).

Galbraith and Nathanson (1976) suggested that the choice of organizational form was the result of choices about five design variables: task; people; structure; reward systems; and information and decision processes. These choices should be consistent with the firm's product–market strategy, i.e. there should be 'fit' or 'congruence' between the variables and the selected organizational structure. Galbraith and Nathanson applied Chandler's (1962) four growth strategies – expansion of volume, geographic dispersion, vertical integration, and product diversification – to see how each affects the form of organizational structure, based on Chandler's thesis that structure follows strategy. Galbraith and Nathanson argued that:

> Variation in strategy should be matched with variation in processes and systems as well as in structure, in order for organizations to implement strategies successfully (p. 10).

Businesses produce products/services through a variety of organizational forms, but predominantly through either a functional structure or a divisionalized structure. The *functional structure* locates decision making at the top of the corporate hierarchy, with functional responsibilities for marketing, operations, human resources, finance, and so on allocated to *departments*, as shown in the typical functional organization chart in Figure 15.1.

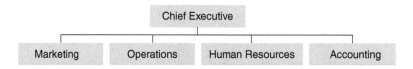

Figure 15.1   Functional organization chart.

In the functional structure, accounting provides a *staff* function to the *line* functions, simplified here as marketing, operations, and human resources. Accounting knowledge tends to be centralized in the accounting department, which collects, produces, reports, and analyses accounting information on behalf of its (internal) customer departments.

The functional structure may be suitable for smaller organizations or those with a narrow geographic spread or a limited product/service range, but it is not generally suitable for larger organizations.

The *divisional structure* is based on a typically small head office with corporate specialists supporting the chief executive, with business units established for major segments of the business. These business units may be based on geographic territories or different products/services, and each division will typically have responsibility for all the functional areas: marketing, operations, human resources, and accounting. The advantage of the divisional structure is that while planning is centrally coordinated, the implementation of plans, decision making, and control is devolved to local management who are closer to customers and have a better understanding of their local operations. The divisions are often referred to as business units to describe their devolved responsibility for a segment of the business. A typical divisional structure showing three divisions (or business units) is shown in Figure 15.2.

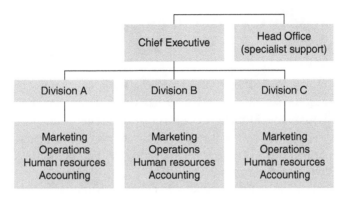

Figure 15.2   Divisional organization chart.

Management within these business units will carry out a significant function in analysing and interpreting financial information as part of their local management responsibilities, typically supported by locally based accounting staff. The role of accounting is quite different in a divisionalized structure as it is more focused on providing advice, information, and support to local management to support local planning, decision making, and control rather than carrying out the monitoring and controlling role that accounting usually undertakes at the corporate head office level. At the local level, accounting will typically be associated with more of the management accounting techniques described in this book than with financial reporting, which will more commonly be a head office role. Accounting therefore influences and is influenced by the organizational structure adopted and the extent of delegated managerial responsibility for business unit performance.

Responsibility centres are business units which, through their managers, are held responsible for achieving certain standards of performance. There are three types of responsibility centres for divisionalized businesses:

- **Cost centres** – where managers are responsible for controlling costs within budget limits. Managers are evaluated on their performance compared to budget in keeping costs within budget constraints.
- **Profit centres** – where managers are responsible for sales performance, achieving gross margins, and controlling expenses, i.e. for the 'bottom-line' profit performance of the business unit. Managers are evaluated on their performance compared to budget in achieving or exceeding their profit target. They have more flexibility than cost centres because they are usually able to exceed their cost budget provided they meet or exceed their profit targets.
- **Investment centres** – where managers have profit responsibility but also influence the amount of capital invested in their business units. Managers are evaluated based on a measure of the return on investment made by the investment centre. These managers have even more flexibility because they are able to influence their return on investment not only by increasing profits but also by increasing or reducing the level of investment in their business units, although such investment will normally still need to be approved at corporate level.

The decentralized organization and divisional performance measurement

While the evaluation of new capital expenditure proposals is a key element in allocating resources across the whole organization (see Chapter 14), a further aspect of strategy implementation is improving and maintaining divisional performance. *Decentralization* implies the devolution of authority to make decisions while *divisionalization* adds to decentralization the concept of delegated profit responsibility (Solomons, 1965). Solomons is recognized for having written the earliest and what still remains the definitive text on divisional performance evaluation.

Divisionalization makes it easier for a company to diversify, while retaining overall strategic direction and control from the corporate head office. Performance improvement is encouraged by assigning individual responsibility for divisional performance to managers, typically linked to executive remuneration (e.g. bonuses, profit sharing, share options). Just as shareholder value is the criterion for overall business success, so divisional performance is the criterion for divisional success. As at the corporate level, divisional performance has moved beyond purely financial measures to incorporate the drivers of financial results, i.e. non-financial performance measures (see Chapter 4).

Solomons (1965) highlighted three purposes for financial reporting at a divisional level:

1. To guide divisional managers in making decisions.
2. To guide top management in making decisions.
3. To enable top management to appraise the performance of divisional management.

The decentralization of businesses has removed the centrality of the head office in larger organizations such that many support functions are now devolved to business units, which may be called subsidiaries (if they are legally distinct entities), divisions, or departments. For simplicity, we will use the term divisionalization in this chapter although the same principle applies to any business unit, whatever it may be called. Divisionalization allows managers to have autonomy over operational aspects of the business, but those managers are then accountable for the performance of their business units (whether they are cost centres, profit centres, or investment centres). While budgets and performance evaluation against budget are the subjects of Chapters 16 and 17, evaluating division-level performance is the subject of this chapter.

There are three methods by which divisional performance can be evaluated:

- absolute profit;
- return on investment;
- residual income.

In each case, we are trying to evaluate the performance of the business unit, and the performance of its management team.

Absolute profit

Under this method, the total profit (usually compared with budget) is the method by which divisional performance is evaluated. Although it is easy to use, being based on standard financial reports, absolute profit is not a good measure because it does not consider the investment in the business or how long-term profits can be affected by short-term decisions such as reducing research, maintenance, and advertising expenditure. These decisions will improve reported profits in the current year, but will usually have a detrimental long-term impact on the division's ability to generate future profits.

Return on investment

The relative success of divisions and managers can be judged by the return on investment (or ROI, which was introduced in Chapter 7). This is the rate of return achieved on the capital employed and was a method developed by the DuPont Powder Company early in the twentieth century. Using ROI, managerial and divisional success is judged according to the rate of return on the investment. As we saw with capital expenditure evaluation in Chapter 14, if a business as a whole wants to achieve a particular ROI, then each investment must contribute to that ROI. Equally, with a divisionalized business, each division must contribute to overall business ROI, hence one way in which divisional ROI can be evaluated is by comparing the divisional ROI with the ROI that is calculated from the company's financial statements.

However, a problem with this approach is whether a high rate of return on a small capital investment is better or worse than a lower return on a larger capital. For example:

	Division A	Division B
Capital invested	€1,000,000	€2,000,000
Operating profit	€200,000	€300,000
Return on investment	20%	15%

In the above example, Division B makes a higher absolute profit but a lower return on the capital invested in the business. While there will always be pressure to improve operating profits, measuring ROI also emphasizes the elimination of under-utilized assets (in Chapter 7 we said that the only reason a business invests in assets is to generate sales and profits).

Solomons (1965) argued that a decision cannot be made about relative performance unless we know the cost of capital, something which we introduced in Chapter 14.

Residual income

A different approach to evaluating performance is residual income, which takes into account the cost of capital. Residual income (or RI) is the profit remaining after deducting the notional risk-adjusted cost of capital from the investment in the division. The RI approach was developed by the General Electric Company and more recently has been compared with Economic Value Added (EVA, see Chapter 2), as both methods deduct a notional cost of capital from the reported profit. Using the same example:

	Division A	Division B
Capital invested	€1,000,000	€2,000,000
Operating profit	€200,000	€300,000
Less cost of capital at 17.5%	€175,000	€350,000
Residual income	€25,000	–€50,000

As the cost of capital is 17.5% in the above example, Division A makes a satisfactory return but Division B does not. Division B is eroding shareholder value while Division A is creating it.

The aim of managers should be to maximize the residual income from the capital investments in their divisions. However, Solomons (1965) emphasized that the RI approach assumes that managers have the power to influence the amount of capital investment. Solomons argued that an RI target is preferred to a maximization objective because it takes into account the differential investments in divisions, i.e. that a larger division will almost certainly produce or should produce a higher residual income in absolute terms. Johnson and Kaplan (1987) believe that the residual income approach:

> overcame one of the dysfunctional aspects of the ROI measure in which managers could increase their reported ROI by rejecting investments that yielded returns in excess of their firm's (or division's) cost of capital, but that were below their current average ROI (p. 165).

This argument can be illustrated with a simple example. Consider a company that in total achieves an ROI of 12% on its assets. However the 'Beta' division achieves 20% ROI (see the Current column in Table 15.1 below) so there are clearly less-well performing divisions in the company. Beta is considering an investment proposal (in the second column of Table 15.1). If the Beta division and its management are evaluated on ROI, the division is likely to reject this proposal as its future performance will appear worse, i.e. its average ROI will fall from 20% to 18.5%. However the new investment will achieve a 14% ROI which is better for the company as a whole so the company is likely to want that proposal to go ahead, as it will earn an additional £15,000 residual income for the company – an additional contribution to shareholder value that will not be achieved if the division rejects the proposal. Measuring performance using residual income is more likely to lead to the Beta division approving the proposal, which is more congruent with the goals of the whole company than is the case using ROI.

One of the problems with both the ROI and RI measures of divisional performance is the calculation of the capital investment in the division: should it be total (i.e. capital employed) or net assets (i.e. equity)? Should it include only non-current assets, or both non-current and current assets? Should

Table 15.1   'Beta' Division's ROI and RI.

	Current	Proposal	Future
Divisional asset investment	£750,000	£250,000	£1,000,000
Operating profit	£150,000	£35,000	£185,000
Return on investment	20.0%	14.0%	18.5%
Cost of capital @ 8%	£60,000	£20,000	£80,000
Residual income	£90,000	£15,000	£105,000

non-current assets be valued at cost or written-down value (i.e. net of depreciation?) Should the book value be at the beginning or end of the period? Solomons (1965) argued that it was the amount of capital put into the business, rather than what could be taken out, that was relevant. The investment value, according to Solomons, should be total assets less *controllable* (see below) liabilities, with non-current assets valued at cost using the value at the beginning of the period. ROI calculations therefore relate *controllable* operating profit as a percentage of *controllable* investment. An RI approach would measure net residual income plus actual interest expense (because the notional cost of capital has already been deducted in calculating RI) against the total investment in the division.

One of the main problems in evaluating divisional performance is the extent to which managers can exercise control over investments and costs charged to their responsibility centres. Hence controllability is an important element in the performance evaluation of business units.

Controllability

The principle of controllability, according to Merchant (1987, p. 316), is that 'individuals should be held accountable only for results they can control' (p. 336). One of the limitations of operating profit as a measure of divisional performance is the inclusion of some costs over which the divisional manager may have no control. The need for the company as a whole to make a profit often results in corporate overheads (see Chapter 13) being allocated to divisions so that these costs can be recovered in the prices charged by the divisions. The problem arises when a division's profit is not sufficient to cover the head office charge. Solomons (1965) argued that so long as corporate expenses are independent of divisional activity, allocating corporate costs is irrelevant because a positive contribution by divisions will cover at least some of those costs (we introduced this concept in relation to segmental profitability in Chapter 10). Note however that controllable costs are not necessarily the same as the avoidable costs we used in calculating segmental profitability in Chapter 10. A cost such as rental for the space occupied by a product line in a division may be uncontrollable by divisional management, but it may be avoidable if the product line is closed. A cost such as depreciation may be controllable by divisional managers in a responsibility centre which can make investment decisions, but that cost may not be avoidable because the asset cannot be disposed of.

Solomons separated the controllable from non-controllable components in the divisional profit report, a simplified example of which is shown in Table 15.2.

Table 15.2   Divisional profit report showing controllability.

Sales		£1,000,000
Less variable cost of goods sold	£200,000	
Other variable expenses	£100,000	£300,000
Contribution margin		£700,000
Less controllable divisional overhead		£250,000
Controllable profit for division		£450,000
Less non-controllable overhead		£175,000
Operating profit for division		£275,000

The controllable profit is the profit after deducting expenses that can be controlled by the divisional manager, but ignoring those expenses that are outside the divisional manager's control. What is controllable or non-controllable will depend on the circumstances of each organization. While the business as a whole may consider the operating profit to be the most important figure for the *business unit*, performance evaluation of the *manager* should only be carried out based on the controllable profit. Solomons (1965) argued that the most suitable figure for appraising divisional managers was the *controllable residual income before taxes*. Using this method, the controllable profit is reduced by the corporate cost of capital. For decisions in relation to a division's performance, the relevant figure is the *net residual income after taxes*.

Case study 15.1 provides an example of divisional performance measurement using ROI and RI techniques.

Case Study 15.1: Majestic Services – divisional performance measurement

Majestic Services has two divisions, both of which have proposed that the company invests $1 million for projects that will generate significant cost savings. Majestic has a cost of capital of 15% and can only invest in one of the projects.

The current performance of each division is as follows:

	Division A	Division B
Current investment	$4 million	$20 million
Profit	$1 million	$2 million

Each division has estimated the additional controllable profit that will be generated from the $1 million investment. A estimates $200,000 and B estimates $130,000.

Each division also has an old asset which they would like to dispose of. A's old asset currently makes an ROI of 19%, while B's old asset makes an ROI of 12%. The business wishes to use ROI and residual income techniques to determine in which of the $1 million projects Majestic should invest, and whether either of the division's identified assets should be disposed of.

Using ROI, the two divisions are compared in Table 15.3.

Table 15.3   ROI on original investment.

	A	B
Current investment	$4 million	$20 million
Current profit	$1 million	$2 million
ROI	25%	10%

While Division B is the larger division and generates a higher profit in absolute terms, Division A achieves a higher return on investment.

Again using ROI, the impact of the additional investment can be seen in Table 15.4.

Table 15.4   ROI on additional investment.

	A	B
Additional investment	$1 million	$1 million
Additional contribution	$200,000	$130,000
ROI on additional investment	20%	13%

Using ROI, Division A may not want its project to be approved as the ROI of 20% is less than the current ROI of 25%. The impact of the new investment would be to reduce the divisional ROI to 24% ($1.2 million/$5 million). However, Division B would want its project to be approved as the ROI of 13% is higher than the current ROI of 10%. The effect would be to increase Division B's ROI slightly to 10.14% ($2.13 million/$21 million). However, the divisional preference for B's investment over A, because of the rewards attached to increasing ROI, are dysfunctional to Majestic. The corporate view of Majestic would be to invest $1 million in Division A's project because the ROI to the business as a whole would be 20% rather than 13%.

The disposal of the old assets can be considered even without knowing their value. If Division A currently obtains a 25% ROI, disposing of the old asset with a return of only 19% will increase its average ROI. Division B would wish to retain its old asset because it generates an ROI of 12% and disposal would reduce its average ROI to below the current 10%. Given a choice of retaining only one old asset, Majestic would prefer to retain Division A's old asset as it has a higher ROI.

The difficulty with ROI as a measure of performance is that it ignores both the difference in size between the two divisions and Majestic's cost of capital. These issues are addressed by using the residual income method.

Using residual income (RI), the divisional performance is compared in Table 15.5. In this case, we can see that Division A is contributing to shareholder value as it generates a positive RI, while Division B is eroding its shareholder value because the profit it generates is less than the cost of capital on the investment.

Table 15.5   RI on original investment.

	A	B
Current investment	$4 million	$20 million
Current profit	$1,000,000	$2,000,000
Cost of capital @ 15%	$600,000	$3,000,000
Residual income (profit–cost of capital)	$400,000	-$1,000,000

Using RI, the impact of the additional investment is shown in Table 15.6. Under the residual income approach, Division A's project would be accepted (positive RI) while Division B's would be rejected (negative RI).

Table 15.6   RI on additional investment.

	A	B
Additional investment	$1 million	$1 million
Additional contribution	$200,000	$130,000
Less cost of capital @ 15%	$150,000	$150,000
Residual income	$50,000	–$20,000

Similarly for the asset disposal, Division A's old asset would be retained (ROI of 19% exceeds cost of capital of 15%), while Division B's old asset would be disposed of (ROI of 12% is less than cost of capital of 15%).

The main problem facing Majestic is that the larger of the two divisions (in terms of both investment and profits) is generating a negative residual income and consequently eroding shareholder value.

Comparison of methods

Each of absolute profit, return on investment, and residual income has its advantages and disadvantages, but like the methods of capital investment evaluation in Chapter 14, the methods should be used together to provide a more holistic picture than any single measure provides on its own. Irrespective of the limitations of absolute profit as a performance measure, the reality is that businesses want more profit in absolute terms. However they also recognize the need not to reduce the return on investment and the importance of ensuring that all investments achieve a satisfactory return as measured by ratio analysis on published financial statements. Where individual business unit ROIs are below expectation, under performing assets can be disposed of, including whole business units which may be sold off or closed. Residual income overcomes some of the dysfunctional consequences whereby ROI measures may distort divisional decisions at the expense of the company as a whole. However, the RI measure may not adequately reflect the scale and size of the investment in one division compared with another.

Whatever method or methods of divisional performance evaluation are chosen, top managers need to bear in mind the importance of achieving shareholder value by ensuring that profits exceed the cost of capital.

A further problem associated with measuring divisional performance is that of transfer pricing.

Transfer pricing

When decentralized business units conduct business with each other, an important question is what price to charge for within-company transactions, as this affects the profitability of each business unit. Transfer pricing may be as simple as one manufacturing business unit selling its finished goods to a sales and marketing business unit whose responsibility is to sell the product at as high a price as possible. However, the situation becomes more complex when multinational companies use transfer pricing as a method of shifting profits to lower tax countries. Transfer prices may be based on:

- *Market price*: where products/services can be sold on the open market, the market price is used, including a normal profit margin. This is the easiest way to ensure that divisional decisions are compatible with corporate profit maximization. However, if there is no external market, particularly for an intermediate product, i.e. one that requires additional processing before it can be sold, this method cannot be used.
- *Full cost or cost-plus*: this method would recover both fixed and variable costs, with or without a profit margin included. This method has the same overhead allocation problem as identified in Chapter 13.
- *Marginal cost*: the transfer price is the incremental (or variable) cost incurred, with or without a profit margin included.
- *Negotiated prices*: this may take into account market conditions, marginal costs, and the need to motivate managers in each division. It tends to be the most practical solution to align the interests of divisions with the whole organization and to share the profits equitably between each division. In using this method, care must be taken to consider differential capital investments between divisions, so that both are treated equitably in terms of ROI or RI criteria.

In an increasingly globalized marketplace, manufacturing, assembly, and selling operations may take place in different countries. In some Japanese companies for example, it is common to leave the profit with the manufacturing division, placing the onus on the marketing division to achieve better market prices. However, transfer prices may often be set with a goal of ensuring that reported profits are earned in countries where lower corporation tax is payable as this maximizes the after-tax earnings (and hence shareholder value) of the multinational corporation as a whole. These arrangements are consequently scrutinized by taxation authorities as well as having ethical implications for companies. In practice, many organizations negotiate transfer prices with taxation authorities and then adopt those prices for transactions between their business units.

However, transfer prices that are suitable for evaluating divisional performance may lead to divisions acting contrary to the corporate interest (Solomons, 1965). Therefore, an important issue in establishing a transfer price is the motivational effect that this may have on managers of both the buying and selling business units, who may prefer to buy and sell on the open market in order to maximize their divisional profits, ROI, or RI, even if that has detrimental results for the business as a whole.

For example, consider a company with two divisions. Division A can produce 10,000 units for a total cost of £100,000, but additional production costs are £5 per unit. Division A sells its output to Division B at £13 per unit in order to show a satisfactory profit. Division B carries out further processing on the product. It can convert 10,000 units for a total cost of £300,000, but additional production costs are £15 per unit. The prices B can charge to customers will depend on the quantity it wants to sell. Market estimates of selling prices at different volumes (net of variable selling costs) are:

Volume	Price
10,000 units	£50 per unit
12,000 units	£46 per unit
15,000 units	£39 per unit

The financial results for each division at each level of activity are shown in Table 15.7.

Table 15.7   Divisional financial results.

Activity level	10,000	12,000	15,000
Division A			
10,000 units	100,000	100,000	100,000
2,000 units @ £5		10,000	
5,000 units @ £5			25,000
Total cost	100,000	110,000	125,000
Transfer price @ £13	130,000	156,000	195,000
Division profit	£30,000	£46,000	£70,000
Division B			
Transfer from Division A	130,000	156,000	195,000
Conversion cost			
10,000 units	300,000	300,000	300,000
2,000 units @ £15		30,000	
5,000 units @ £15			75,000
Total cost	430,000	486,000	570,000
Selling price	@ £50	@ £46	@ £39
Sales revenue	500,000	552,000	585,000
Division profit	£70,000	£66,000	£15,000
Company			
Sales revenue	500,000	552,000	585,000
Division A cost	−100,000	−110,000	−125,000
Division B cost	−300,000	−330,000	−375,000
Company profit	£100,000	£112,000	£85,000

Division A sees an increase in profit as volume increases and will want to increase production volume to 15,000 units. However, Division B sees a steady erosion of divisional profitability as volume increases and will seek to keep production limited to 10,000 units, at which point its maximum profit is £70,000. The company's overall profitability increases between 10,000 and 12,000 units, but then falls when volume increases to 15,000 units. From a whole-company perspective, therefore, volume should be maintained at 12,000 units to maximize profits at £112,000. However, neither division will be satisfied with this result, as both will see it as disadvantaging them in terms of divisional profits, against which divisional managers are evaluated.

For Division A, variable costs over 10,000 units are £5, but its transfer price is £13, so additional units contribute £8 each to divisional profitability. A's average costs reduce as volume increases, as Table 15.8 shows.

Table 15.8   Division A costs.

Activity level	10,000	12,000	15,000
Division A total costs	£100,000	£110,000	£125,000
Average cost per unit	£10.00	£9.17	£8.33

However, for Division B, its variable costs over 10,000 units are £28 (transfer price of £13 plus conversion costs of £15). The reduction in average costs of £2.50 per unit is more than offset by the fall in selling price (net of variable selling costs), as Table 15.9 shows.

Table 15.9   Division B costs.

Activity level	10,000	12,000	15,000
Division B total costs	£430,000	£486,000	£570,000
Average cost per unit	£43.00	£40.50	£38.00
Reduction in average cost per unit		£2.50	£2.50
Reduction in selling price		£4.00	£7.00

Decisions about what the transfer cost should be are therefore important in motivating managers and making divisional decisions that are congruent with the objectives of the business as a whole. Where business units are located in different countries, establishing transfer prices is an important role for management accounting in terms of accurately measuring business unit performance. However, other than the taxation effects (discussed above), transfer prices have no real effect on published financial statements, as all inter-business unit transactions are eliminated when the financial records of each business unit are consolidated into a single set of financial statements.

Transaction cost economics

A useful theoretical framework for understanding divisionalization and the transfer pricing problem is the transactions cost (also called the markets and hierarchies) approach of Oliver Williamson (1975). Williamson is a winner of the Nobel prize for economics, who was concerned with the study of the economics of internal organization. Transaction cost economics seeks to explain why some separate activities that require coordination occur within the organization's hierarchy (i.e. within the multidivisional structure), while others take place through exchanges outside the organization in the wider market (i.e. between arm's-length buyers and sellers). The markets and hierarchies perspective considers the vertical integration of production and decisions about whether organizations should make or buy (we discussed make versus buy considerations in Chapter 11).

Transactions are more than exchanges of goods, services, and money. They incur costs over and above the price for the commodity bought or sold. In Chapter 11 we introduced the total cost of ownership which comprises purchasing costs, the costs of delivery and quality failure, and inventory holding and compliance costs. Understanding the total cost of ownership may reveal that it is more economic to carry out an activity in-house than to accept a market price that appears less costly but which may incur 'transaction' costs that are hidden in overheads. Williamson (1975) argued that the desire to minimize these transaction costs leads to transactions being kept within the organization, i.e. it favours the organizational hierarchy over markets. However, markets are favoured where there are a large number of external suppliers competing for business, as this minimizes the risk of opportunistic behaviour.

The work of business historians such as Chandler (1962) reflects a transaction cost approach in his explanations for the growth of huge corporations such as General Motors (GM) in the first half of the twentieth century, in which hierarchies were developed as alternatives to market transactions. Recent trends, not only in the automotive industry, have reversed this with the strategy being to outsource as much production as possible to the lowest cost producer. In the automotive industry, companies like GM, Ford, and Toyota mainly assemble vehicles, the components for which are manufactured by multiple suppliers.

For managers using accounting information, attention is focused on whether markets or hierarchies are more cost-effective. Transaction cost economics focuses attention on the transaction costs involved in allocating resources within the organization, and determining when the costs associated with one mode of organizing transactions (e.g. markets) would be reduced by shifting those transactions to an alternative arrangement (e.g. the internal structure of an organization). The efficiency of a transaction that takes place within the organization depends on how the behaviour of managers is governed or constrained, how economic activities are subdivided, and how the management accounting system – including the setting of transfer prices – is structured.

Rather than reflecting a concern with utility maximization (the assumption of agency theory – see Chapter 6), the transaction cost framework is more concerned with bounded rationality (see Chapter 4) and gives recognition to power relations in the internal managerial hierarchy that is used to coordinate production.

Conclusion: a critical perspective

In this chapter we have described the divisionalized organization and how divisional performance can be evaluated using return on investment (ROI) and residual income (RI) techniques. The divisional form is a preferred organizational structure because it allows devolved responsibility while linking divisional performance to organizational goals through measures such as ROI and RI. In this chapter we have also discussed the controllability principle and the transfer pricing problem and how these can lead to managers making decisions that benefit their divisions but which may not be optimal for the organization as a whole.

However, a critical stance can be applied to the divisionalized form of organization. Roberts and Scapens (1985) argued that in a divisionalized company there is distance between the division and the head office, such that 'the context within which accounting information is gathered will typically be quite different from the context in which it is interpreted' (p. 452). Like the social construction perspective we introduced in Chapter 5, divisional managers and the corporate head office may see the same financial information in very different ways. This may result in manipulating the appearance of accounting reports. Roberts and Scapens concluded:

> The image of an organization which is given through Accounts will be from a particular point of view, at a particular point in time and will be selective in its focus. Events, actions, etc. which are significant for the organization may be out of focus, or not in the picture at all . . . the image conveyed by the Accounts may misrepresent the actual flow of events and practices that it is intended to record (p. 454).

Managers are often critical that the corporate head office fails to distinguish adequately between controllable and non-controllable overhead. Research by Merchant (1987) showed that the controllability principle was not found in practice and that managers should be evaluated 'using all information that gives insight into their action choices'.

The transaction cost economics approach brings to our attention the theory behind make versus buy decisions and whether different functions are carried out within the organizational hierarchy or through arm's-length markets. Relationships between business units frequently cause friction, particularly in some organizations where the number of business units has been increased to a level that is difficult to manage and where transfer pricing contributes to decisions that may not be in the best interests of the business as a whole.

The political process inherent in transfer pricing between divisions is evidenced in many multinational corporations, where transfer pricing has become more concerned with how to shift profits between countries so as to minimize income taxes and maximize after-tax profits to increase shareholder value. While this is undoubtedly in the interests of individual companies, it usually does need the approval of taxation authorities. However, it raises issues of the ethics of transfer pricing when multinationals minimize their profits and taxation in relatively high-tax countries from which they enjoy many benefits.

References

Chandler, A. D. J. (1962). *Strategy and Structure: Chapters in the History of the American Industrial Enterprise.* Cambridge, MA: Harvard University Press.

Child, J. (1972). Organizational structure, environment and performance: the role of strategic choice. *Sociology*, 6, 122.

Emmanuel, C., Otley, D., and Merchant, K. (1990). *Accounting for Management Control* (2nd edn). London: Chapman & Hall.

Galbraith, J. R. and Nathanson, D. A. (1976). *Strategy Implementation: The Role of Structure and Process.* St Paul, MN: West Publishing Company.

Johnson, H. T. and Kaplan, R. S. (1987). *Relevance Lost: The Rise and Fall of Management Accounting.* Boston, MA: Harvard Business School Press.

Merchant, K. A. (1987). How and why firms disregard the controllability principle. In W. J. Bruns and R. S. Kaplan (Eds), *Accounting and Management: Field Study Perspectives*. Boston, MA: Harvard Business School Press.

Roberts, J. and Scapens, R. (1985). Accounting systems and systems of accountability understanding accounting practices in their organizational contexts. *Accounting, Organizations and Society*, 10(4), 443–56.

Solomons, D. (1965). *Divisional Performance: Measurement and Control*. Homewood, IL: Richard D. Irwin.

Williamson, O. E. (1975). *Markets and Hierarchies: Analysis and Antitrust Implications. A Study in the Economics of Internal Organization*. New York: Free Press.

Questions

15.1   Jakobs Ladder has capital employed of £10 million and currently earns an ROI of 15% per annum. It can make an additional investment of £2 million for a five-year life. The average net profit from this investment would be 14% of the original investment. The division's cost of capital is 12%.

Calculate the residual income before and after the investment.

15.2   China Group has a division with capital employed of €10 million that currently earns an ROI of 15% per annum. It can make an additional investment of €2 million for a five-year life with no scrap value. The average net profit from this investment would be €280,000 per annum after depreciation. The division's cost of capital is 9%.

Calculate the ROI and residual income for the:

* original investment;
* additional investment; and
* total new level of investment.

15.3   Brummy Co. consists of several investment centres. Green Division has a controllable investment of $750,000 and profits are expected to be $150,000 this year. An investment opportunity is offered to Green that will yield a profit of $15,000 from an additional investment of $100,000. Brummy accepts projects if the ROI exceeds the cost of capital, which is 12%.

* Calculate Green's ROI currently, for the additional investment, and after the investment.
* How will Green and Brummy Co. view this investment opportunity?
* Calculate the effect of the new investment opportunity on Green's residual income.

15.4   Anston Industries is the manufacturing division of a large multinational. The divisional general manager is about to purchase new equipment for the manufacture of a new product. He can buy either the Compax or the Newpax equipment, each of which has the same capacity and an expected life of four years. Each type of equipment has different capital costs and expected cash flows, as Table 15.10 shows.

Table 15.10   Capital investment data for two divisions of Anston Industries.

	Compax	Newpax
Initial capital investment	£6,400,000	£5,200,000
Net cash inflows (before tax)		
Year 1	£2,400,000	£2,600,000
Year 2	£2,400,000	£2,200,000
Year 3	£2,400,000	£1,500,000
Year 4	£2,400,000	£1,000,000
Net present value (@ 16% p.a.)	£315,634	£189,615

The equipment will be installed and paid for at the end of the current year (Year 0) and the cash flows accrue at the end of each year. There is no scrap value for either piece of equipment. In calculating divisional returns, divisional assets are valued at net book value at the beginning of each year.

The multinational expects each division to achieve a minimum return before tax of 16%. Anston is just managing to achieve that target. Anything less than a 16% return would make the divisional general manager ineligible for his profit-sharing bonus.

- Prepare accounting rate of return (ARR) and residual income (RI) calculations for the Compax and the Newpax divisions for each year.
- Suggest which equipment is preferred under each method. Compare this with the NPV calculation.

15.5   Magna Products has three divisions, A, B, and C. The current investments in and net profits earned by each division are shown in Table 15.11.

Table 15.11   Investment returns for three divisions of Magna Products.

Division A	
Investment	€1,000,000
Net profit	€75,000
Division B	
Investment	€1,500,000
Net profit	€90,000
Division C	
Investment	€2,000,000
Net profit	€150,000

Each division has put forward to the parent board a capital expenditure proposal for €500,000. Each division expects to produce net profits of €40,000 from that investment. Magna's cost of capital is 7% p.a.

Use ROI and RI calculations to:

- evaluate the current performance of each division; and
- recommend the proposal the board should approve if finance limits the decision to a single proposal.

CHAPTER 16

Budgeting

This chapter is about how organizations carry out budgeting. It begins with an overview of what budgeting is and the budgeting process, and then uses four case studies to illustrate profit budgets for service, retail, and manufacturing businesses, and a cash forecast for retail. The case studies show how sales, cost of sales, and expense predictions are converted using inventory requirements into purchase budgets, and how the cash flow forecast links back to the Statement of Cash Flows that was described in Chapter 6. The chapter concludes with a behavioural perspective on budgeting, and a critique of budgeting practice.

What is budgeting?

Anthony and Govindarajan (2000) described budgets as 'an important tool for effective short-term planning and control' (p. 360). They saw strategic planning (see Chapter 14) as being focused on several years into the future, contrasted with budgeting which focuses on a single year. Strategic planning:

> precedes budgeting and provides the framework within which the annual budget is developed. A budget is, in a sense, a one-year slice of the organization's strategic plan (p. 361).

Anthony and Govindarajan also differentiated the strategic plan from the budget, on the basis that strategy is concerned with product lines while budgets are concerned with responsibility centres.

This is an important distinction, as there is no reason that budgets for products/services cannot be produced, although they tend to stop at the contribution margin level, because of the overhead allocation problem described in Chapter 13. Traditional budgetary reports are produced for responsibility centres and are used for evaluating the performance of business units and their managers, as described in Chapter 15.

A budget is a plan expressed in monetary terms covering a future time period (typically a year broken down into months). Budgets are based on a defined level of activity, either expected sales revenue (if market demand is the limiting factor) or capacity (if that is the limiting factor). While budgets are typically produced annually, rolling budgets add additional months to the end of the period so that there is always a 12-month budget for the business. Alternatively, budgets may be re-forecast part way through a year, e.g. quarterly or six-monthly, to take into account changes since the last budget cycle (hence the common distinction made by organizations between budget and forecast; a forecast usually refers to a revised estimate, or a budgetary update, part-way through the budget period).

Budgeting provides the ability to:

- implement strategy by allocating resources in line with strategic goals;
- coordinate activities and assist in communication between different parts of the organization (whether departments in a functional structure or business units in a divisional structure);
- motivate managers to achieve targets;
- control activities; and
- evaluate managerial performance.

The budgeting process

There are four main methods of budgeting: incremental, priority based, zero based, and activity based. Each is described below.

Incremental budgets take the previous year's budget as a base and add (or subtract) a percentage to give this year's budget. The assumption is that the historical budget allocation reflected organizational priorities and was rooted in some meaningful justification developed in the past.

Priority-based budgets allocate funds in line with strategy. If priorities change in line with the organization's strategic focus, then budget allocations would follow those priorities, irrespective of the historical allocation. A public-sector version of the priority-based budget is *programme budgeting*, which developed from the planning, programming and budgeting system (PPBS) used by the US space programme. Under programme budgeting, budgets are allocated to projects or programmes rather than to responsibility centres. The intention of priority-based and programme budgeting systems is to compare costs more readily with benefits by identifying the resources used to obtain desired outcomes. In the public sector, it is quite common for some budgets to be allocated incrementally, but for new government initiatives to be funded through projects or programmes.

An amalgam of incremental and priority-based budgets is *priority-based incremental budgeting*. Here, the budget-holder is asked what incremental (or decremental) activities or results would follow if budgets increased (or decreased). This method has the advantage of comparing changes in resources with the resulting costs and benefits.

Zero-based budgeting identifies the costs that are necessary to implement agreed strategies and achieve goals, as if the budget-holder were beginning with a new organizational unit, without any prior history. This method has the advantage of regularly reviewing all the activities that are carried out to see if they are still required, but has the disadvantage of the cost and time needed for such reviews. It is also very difficult to develop a 'greenfields' budget while ignoring 'brownfields' resource allocations.

Activity-based budgeting (ABB) is associated with activity-based costing (ABC, see Chapter 13). ABC identifies *activities* that consume resources and uses the concept of *cost drivers* (essentially the causes of costs) to allocate costs to products or services according to how much of the resources of the firm they consume. Activity-based budgeting follows the same process to develop budgets based on the expected activities and cost drivers to meet sales (or capacity) projections.

Whichever method of budgeting is used, there are two approaches that can be applied in setting budgets. Budgets may be top down or bottom up. *Top-down budgets* begin with the sales forecast and, using the volume of sales, predict inventory levels, staffing, and production times within capacity limitations. These are based on bills of materials, labour routings, and standard costs (see Chapter 11). For services, the top-down budget is based largely on capacity utilization and staffing levels needed to meet expected demand. In both cases, senior management establishes spending limits within which departments allocate costs to specific line items (salaries, travel, office expenses, etc.). Senior managers set the revenue targets and spending limits that they believe are necessary to achieve profits that will satisfy shareholders. *Bottom-up budgets* are developed by the managers of each department based on current spending and agreed plans, which are then aggregated to the corporate total.

Top-down budgets can ignore the problems experienced by operational managers and any new ideas they may have for improvement. By contrast, the bottom-up budget may be inadequate in terms of 'bottom-line' profitability or unachievable as a result of either capacity limitations elsewhere in the business or market demand. Unlike managers, boards of directors often have a clear idea of the sales growth and profit requirement that will satisfy stock market expectations. Consequently, most budgets are the result of a combination of top-down and bottom-up processes. By adopting both methods, budget-holders are given the opportunity to bid for resources (in competition with other budget-holders) within the constraints of the shareholder value focus of the business. We discuss the behavioural implications of budget participation later in this chapter.

The budget cycle – the period each year over which budgets are prepared – may last several months, with budget preparation beginning some months before the commencement of each financial year. The typical budget cycle will follow a common sequence:

1. Identify business objectives.
2. Forecast economic and industry conditions, including competition.

3. Develop detailed sales budgets by market sectors, geographical territories, major customers, and product groups.
4. Prepare production budgets (materials, labour, and overhead) for the goods or services needed to satisfy the sales forecast and maintain agreed levels of inventory.
5. Prepare non-production budgets (e.g. selling and administrative expenses).
6. Prepare capital expenditure budgets.
7. Prepare cash forecasts and identify financing requirements.
8. Prepare master budget (profit, financial position, and cash flow).
9. Obtain board approval of profitability and financing (including approval of new borrowings and the debt/equity mix).

Detailed budgeting takes place at the responsibility centre level (see Chapter 15), where good practice involves looking at the opportunities for earning income, the causes of costs, and the business processes in use. Bidding for funds for capital expenditure to fund new initiatives or projects is an important part of budgeting because of the need for growth and continual improvement. The process of budgeting is largely based on making informed judgements about:

- how business-wide strategies will affect the responsibility centre;
- the level of demand placed on the business unit and the expected level of activity to satisfy (internal or external) customers;
- the technology and processes used in the business unit to achieve desired productivity levels, based on past experience and anticipated improvements;
- any new initiatives or projects that are planned and require resources;
- the headcount and historical spending by the business unit.

In preparing a budget it is important to carry out a thorough investigation of current performance, i.e. to get behind the numbers. The complexity of the budget will depend on a number of factors, such as:

- knowledge of past performance;
- understanding of customer demand trends, seasonal factors, competition, etc.;
- whether the business is a price leader or price follower (see Chapter 10);
- understanding the drivers of business costs (see Chapter 13);
- the control that managers are able to exercise over expenses.

How well these factors can be understood and modelled using a spreadsheet will depend on the knowledge, skills, and time available to the business. Typically, budgets either at the corporate or responsibility centre level will contain a number of subjective judgements of likely future events, customer demand, and a number of simplifying assumptions about product/service mix, average prices, cost inflation, etc.

Risk – or uncertainty – is an important element in budgeting practice. Collier and Berry (2002) identified risk as being managed in four different domains: financial, operational, political, and personal. These were the result of the unique circumstances, history, and technology in different organizations that had led to different ideas about risk. These domains of risk revealed how participants in the budgeting process influenced the content of the budget through their unique perspectives. Collier and Berry distinguished the content of budgets from the process of budgeting and contrasted three types of budget. In the risk-modelled process, there was an explicit use of formal probability models to assess the effect of different consequences over a range of different assumptions. In the risk-considered process, informal sensitivity (or what-if) analysis is used to produce (for example) high, medium, and low consequences of different assumptions. The risk-excluded budget manages risk outside the budget process, and the budget relies on a single expectation of performance. Collier and Berry found that little risk modelling was used in practice, and that although risk was considered during the budgeting process, the content of the budget documents largely excluded risk.

Hence most budgets start with current year or past year performance and make adjustment for known changes in strategy, technology, market, or competitive conditions. Sales forecasts begin the process. Budgets for manufacturing are based on standard costs (see Chapter 11) for a defined level of sales demand or production activity. These standard costs should be based on current expectations about supplier prices and productivity levels, etc. In service industries, many costs follow headcount (as we saw in Chapter 12), so it is essential that salary and related costs are accurately estimated, and the impact of recruitment, resignation, and training is taken into account in cost and productivity calculations.

Once the budget is agreed in total, it needs to be allocated over each month. Simply dividing the budget into 12 equal monthly amounts will not be sufficient in any but very small businesses. The process of profiling or time-phasing the budget is commonly based on the number of working days each month and takes into account seasonal fluctuations etc. Profiling is important because the process of budgetary control (see Chapter 17) relies on an accurate estimation of when revenue will be earned and when costs will be incurred.

The profit budget

The sales, cost of sales, and expense budget looks very much like an Income Statement, but with substantially more detail for management than would be provided in the financial statements included in the Annual Report to shareholders. The budgeted profit would be profiled or time-phased over each accounting period (normally 12 monthly budgets) and would be supported by statistical data from which the income, cost of sales, and expense projections were made. The case study of Superior Hotel (Case study 16.1) illustrates the profit budget and how the figures in that budget are derived from the supporting statistical data.

A budget for a retailer will be more complex as it requires an estimation, separate from the sales forecast, of the level of inventory to be held. This results in a purchasing budget. Similarly, a budget for a manufacturing business will involve developing a production budget (materials, labour, and overhead) by cost centre in order to produce the goods or services needed to satisfy the sales forecast and maintain agreed levels of inventory.

The first problem to consider is inventory, which is shown in Case study 16.2.

Case Study 16.1: Superior Hotel – service budget example

Table 16.1 is an example of a budget for a small hotel. It shows some statistics that the Superior Hotel has used for its budget for next year. Both last year's and the current year's figures are shown. For ease of presentation, the budget year has been divided into four quarters and some simplifying assumptions have been made. The hotel capacity is limited to the number of rooms, but in common with the industry, full capacity is rarely achieved, although there are substantial variations both during the week and at peak times. The main income driver is the number of rooms occupied, the price able to be charged (which can vary significantly depending on the number of vacant rooms), and the average spend per head on dining, the bar, and business services.

Table 16.1   Service budget example: Superior Hotel budget statistics.

Superior Hotel	Explanation	Last year	Current year	Qtr 1 Jan–Mar	Qtr 2 Apr–June	Qtr 3 Jul–Sep	Qtr 4 Oct–Dec	Next year
Number of bedrooms		80	80	80	80	80	80	
Days per year (per quarter)		365	365	90	91	92	92	365
Rooms available 365 days/year	No. days × no. rooms	29,200	29,200	7,200	7,280	7,360	7,360	29,200
Average occupancy rate (7-day basis)	Historical	50%	50%	40%	45%	55%	60%	
Average no. rooms occupied	No. rooms × occup. rate	14,600	14,600	2,880	3,276	4,048	4,416	14,620
Average room rate	Historical/planned	$65.00	$70.00	$70.00	$72.00	$75.00	$75.00	
Average spend on dining per room	Historical/planned	$25.00	$25.00	$25.00	$25.00	$25.00	$25.00	
Average spend on bar per room	Historical/planned	$5.00	$5.00	$5.00	$5.00	$5.00	$5.00	
Average spend on business services per room	Historical/planned	$2.00	$2.00	$2.00	$2.00	$2.00	$2.00	

The statistical information, together with estimations of direct costs (food and drink) and expenses, is based on historical experience and expected supplier cost increases. The budget for the year for the Superior Hotel, based on these assumptions, is shown in Table 16.2.

This is of course a simplified presentation and in practice, a great deal more work in analysing past figures would be reflected in underlying spreadsheets.

Table 16.2   Service budget example: Superior Hotel budget.

	Explanation	Last year	Current year	Qtr 1 Jan–Mar	Qtr 2 Apr–June	Qtr 3 Jul–Sep	Qtr 4 Oct–Dec	Next year
INCOME								
Rooms	No. of rooms × average spend	949,000	1,022,000	201,600	235,872	303,600	331,200	1,072,272
Dining	No. of rooms × average spend	365,000	365,000	72,000	81,900	101,200	110,400	365,500
Bar	No. of rooms × average spend	73,000	73,000	14,400	16,380	20,240	22,080	73,100
Business services	No. of rooms × average spend	29,200	29,200	5,760	6,552	8,096	8,832	29,240
Total Income		$1,416,200	$1,489,200	$293,760	$340,704	$433,136	$472,512	$1,540,112
EXPENDITURE								
Direct costs								
Food cost of sales	35% of dining income	127,750	127,750	25,200	28,665	35,420	38,640	127,925
Liquor cost of sales	40% of bar income	29,200	29,200	5,760	6,552	8,096	8,832	29,240
Total cost of sales		156,950	156,950	30,960	35,217	43,516	47,472	157,165
Salaries and wages:								
Hotel staff	increases 3% p.a.	212,000	218,360	56,228	56,228	56,228	56,228	224,911
Dining staff	increases 3% p.a.	75,000	77,250	19,892	19,892	19,892	19,892	79,568
Office staff	increases 4% p.a.	35,000	36,400	9,464	9,464	9,464	9,464	37,856
Management	increases 5% p.a.	50,000	52,500	13,781	13,781	13,781	13,781	55,125
Fuel, light and water	Historical/estimate	12,000	14,000	4,000	4,000	4,000	4,000	16,000
Laundry	Historical/estimate	8,000	9,000	2,500	2,500	2,500	2,500	10,000
Cleaning	Historical/estimate	6,000	7,000	2,000	2,000	2,000	2,000	8,000
Repairs and maintenance	Historical/estimate	12,000	20,000	4,000	4,000	4,000	4,000	16,000
Advertising and promotion	Historical/estimate	10,000	12,000	3,000	3,000	3,000	3,000	12,000
Telephones	Historical/estimate	4,000	5,000	1,500	1,500	1,500	1,500	6,000
Consumables	Historical/estimate	5,000	5,000	1,500	1,500	1,500	1,500	6,000
Other expenses	Historical/estimate	6,000	7,000	2,000	2,000	2,000	2,000	8,000
Total expenditure		$591,950	$620,460	$150,825	$155,082	$163,381	$167,337	$636,624
Profit before interest and taxes		$824,250	$868,740	$142,935	$185,622	$269,755	$305,175	$903,488

Case Study 16.2: Sports Stores Co-operative Ltd – retail budget example

Sports Stores Co-operative (SSC) is a large retail store selling a range of sportswear. Its anticipated sales levels and expenses for each of the next six months are shown in Table 16.3. In this example, sales and expenses are budgeted for each of the six months. Although there are several hundred different items of inventory and the product mix does fluctuate due to seasonal factors, SSC is only able to budget based on an average sales mix and applies an average cost of sales of 40%, reflecting its historical experience.

Table 16.3   Sports stores co-operative sales and expenses estimate.

	Jan	Feb	Mar	Apr	May	Jun	Total
Sales (in £'000)	75	80	85	70	65	90	465
Average cost of sales 40%	30	32	34	28	26	36	186
Gross profit	45	48	51	42	39	54	279
Less expenses:							
Salaries	10	10	10	8	7	10	55
Rent	15	15	15	15	15	15	90
Insurance	1	1	1	1	1	1	6
Depreciation on shop fittings	2	2	2	2	2	2	12
Advertising and promotion	8	8	8	9	9	8	50
Electricity, telephone etc.	5	5	5	5	5	5	30
Total expenses	41	41	41	40	39	41	243
Net profit	4	7	10	2	0	13	36

SSC carries six weeks' inventory, i.e. sufficient inventory to cover six weeks of sales (at cost price). At the end of each month, therefore, the inventory held by SSC will equal all of next month's cost of sales, plus half of the following month's cost of sales. This is shown in Table 16.4.

In Table 16.4, for example, the inventory required at the end of February (£48,000) is the cost of sales for March (£34,000) plus half the cost of sales for April (£14,000). In order to budget for the

Table 16.4   Sports Stores Co-operative inventory calculation.

In £'000	Jan	Feb	Mar	Apr	May	Jun
Inventory required at end of month	49	48	41	44	54	53
Inventory at beginning of month	45	49	48	41	44	54
Increase/-decrease in inventory	4	−1	−7	3	10	−1
Sales during month (at cost)	30	32	34	28	26	36
Total purchases	34	31	27	31	36	35

inventory for May and June, SSC needs to estimate its sales for July and August. As this is the peak selling time, the sales are estimated at £90,000 and £85,000 respectively (not shown in Table 16.4). The cost of sales (based on 40%) is therefore £36,000 for July and £34,000 for August. Using these figures, the inventory required at the end of June (£53,000) is equal to the cost of sales for July (£36,000) and half the cost of sales for August (£17,000).

SSC also needs to know its inventory on 1 January, which is given as £45,000.

Purchases can then be calculated as:

inventory required at end of month – inventory at beginning of month
= increase (or decrease) in inventory
plus the cost of sales for the current month (which need to be replaced)

Table 16.4 shows the calculation of total purchases. However, it can also be shown in the more usual format introduced in previous chapters. This format is shown in Table 16.5.

Table 16.5   Sports Stores Co-operative closing inventory.

	Jan	Feb	Mar	Apr	May	Jun
Opening inventory	45	49	48	41	44	54
Plus purchases	34	31	27	31	36	35
Less cost of sales	–30	–32	–34	–28	–26	–36
Closing inventory	49	48	41	44	54	53

If we move from the example of a retailer to a manufacturer, the budget becomes more complex again as we need to account for the conversion process of raw materials into finished goods. Case study 16.3 is the production budget for a manufacturing business.

Case Study 16.3: Telcon Manufacturing – manufacturing budget example

Telcon is a manufacturer. Its budget is shown in Table 16.6.

Telcon estimates its sales for July and August as 1,400 units per month. Its production budget is based on needing to maintain one month's inventory of finished goods, i.e. the cost of sales for the following month. Its finished goods inventory at the beginning of January is 1,000 units. Table 16.7 shows that the production required of €56,250 is greater than the cost of sales of €53,250 because of the need to produce an additional 400 units at a variable cost of €7.50, i.e. an increase in inventory of €3,000.

However, in order to produce the finished goods, Telcon must also ensure that it has purchased sufficient raw materials. Once again, it wishes to have one month's inventory of raw materials

(2 kg of the materials are required for each unit of finished goods). There are 2,000 units of raw materials at the beginning of January. Table 16.8 shows the materials purchases budget.

Table 16.6   Telcon Manufacturing budget.

In €'000	Jan	Feb	Mar	Apr	May	Jun	Total
Sales units	1,000	1,100	1,200	1,200	1,300	1,300	7,100
Expected selling price	€10	€10	€10	€10	€10	€11	
Revenue	10,000	11,000	12,000	12,000	13,000	14,300	72,300
Cost of sales							
Direct materials @ €4 (2 kg @ €2)	4,000	4,400	4,800	4,800	5,200	5,200	28,400
Direct labour @ €2.50	2,500	2,750	3,000	3,000	3,250	3,250	17,750
Variable overhead @ €1	1,000	1,100	1,200	1,200	1,300	1,300	7,100
Variable costs	7,500	8,250	9,000	9,000	9,750	9,750	53,250
Contribution margin	2,500	2,750	3,000	3,000	3,250	4,550	19,050
Fixed costs (in total)	1,500	1,500	1,500	1,500	1,500	1,500	9,000
Net profit	1,000	1,250	1,500	1,500	1,750	3,050	10,050

Table 16.7   Telcon Manufacturing Production budget.

	Jan	Feb	Mar	Apr	May	Jun	Total
Variable costs per unit	€7.50	€7.50	€7.50	€7.50	€7.50	€7.50	€7.50
Inventory units at end of month	1,100	1,200	1,200	1,300	1,300	1,400	
Inventory units at beginning of month	1,000	1,100	1,200	1,200	1,300	1,300	
Increase in inventory	100	100	0	100	0	100	
Production required							
Units sold	1,000	1,100	1,200	1,200	1,300	1,300	
Increase in inventory	100	100	0	100	0	100	
Total units to be produced	1,100	1,200	1,200	1,300	1,300	1,400	
Production units @ variable cost	8,250	9,000	9,000	9,750	9,750	10,500	56,250
Of which:							
Materials @ €4	4,400	4,800	4,800	5,200	5,200	5,600	30,000
Labour @ €2.50	2,750	3,000	3,000	3,250	3,250	3,500	18,750
Variable overhead @ €1	1,100	1,200	1,200	1,300	1,300	1,400	7,500

Table 16.8 Telcon Manufacturing Materials budget.

	Jan	Feb	Mar	Apr	May	Jun	Total
Total units to be produced	1,100	1,200	1,200	1,300	1,300	1,400	
Total kg of materials (units × 2 kg)	2,200	2,400	2,400	2,600	2,600	2,800	
Inventory units at end of month	2,400	2,400	2,600	2,600	2,800	2,800	
Inventory units at beginning of month	2,000	2,400	2,400	2,600	2,600	2,800	
Increase in inventory	400	0	200	0	200	0	
Materials required							
Kg used in production	2,200	2,400	2,400	2,600	2,600	2,800	
Increase in inventory	400	0	200	0	200	0	
Total kg to be purchased	2,600	2,400	2,600	2,600	2,800	2,800	
Purchase cost @ €2/kg	5,200	4,800	5,200	5,200	5,600	5,600	31,600

The purchases budget of €31,600 is more than the materials usage of €30,000 from the production budget because an additional 800 kg of materials is bought at €2 per kg (i.e. €1,600), due to the need to increase raw materials inventory.

Cash forecasting

Once a profit budget has been constructed, it is important to understand the impact on cash flow. The purpose of the cash forecast is to ensure that sufficient cash is available to meet the level of activity planned by the sales and production budgets and to meet all the other cash inflows and outflows of the business. Cash surpluses and deficiencies need to be identified in advance to ensure effective business financing decisions, e.g. raising short-term finance or investing short-term surplus funds.

There is a substantial difference between profits and cash flow (for a detailed explanation see Chapter 6) because of:

- the timing difference between when income is earned and when it is received (i.e. receivables);
- increases or decreases in inventory for both raw materials and finished goods;
- the timing difference between when expenses are incurred and when they are paid (i.e. payables);
- non-cash expenses (e.g. depreciation);
- capital expenditure;
- income tax;
- dividends;
- new borrowings and repayments; and
- proceeds from new share issues and repurchases of shares.

Case study 16.4 provides a cash forecasting example for a retail business.

Case Study 16.4: Retail News Group – cash forecasting example

Retail News is a store selling newspapers, magazines, books, confectionery, etc. Its profit budget for six months has been prepared and is shown in Table 16.9.

Table 16.9   Retail News Group profit budget.

	Jan	Feb	Mar	Apr	May	Jun	Total
Sales	10,000	12,000	15,000	12,000	11,000	9,000	69,000
Cost of sales (40%)	4,000	4,800	6,000	4,800	4,400	3,600	27,600
Gross profit	6,000	7,200	9,000	7,200	6,600	5,400	41,400
Less expenses							
Salaries and wages	2,000	2,000	2,000	2,200	2,200	2,200	12,600
Selling and distribution expenses (7.5%)	750	900	1,125	900	825	675	5,175
Rent	1,000	1,000	1,000	1,000	1,000	1,000	6,000
Electricity, telephone etc.	500	500	500	500	500	500	3,000
Insurance	500	500	500	500	500	500	3,000
Depreciation	500	500	500	500	500	500	3,000
Total expenses	5,250	5,400	5,625	5,600	5,525	5,375	32,775
Net profit	750	1,800	3,375	1,600	1,075	25	8,625

Retail News makes half of its sales in cash and half on credit to business customers, who typically pay their account in the month following that in which the sale is made. Credit sales in December to customers who will pay during January amount to £3,500. Retail News' sales receipts budget is shown in Table 16.10.

Table 16.10   Retail News Group sales receipts budget.

	Jan	Feb	Mar	Apr	May	Jun	Total
50% of sales received in cash	5,000	6,000	7,500	6,000	5,500	4,500	34,500
50% of sales on credit – 30-day terms	3,500	5,000	6,000	7,500	6,000	5,500	33,500
Total receipts	8,500	11,000	13,500	13,500	11,500	10,000	68,000

Retail News' receivables have increased by £1,000 from £3,500 to £4,500, since 50% of the sales in June (£9,000) will not be received until July.

As in the previous case studies we also need to determine the purchases budget for Retail News, which needs inventory equal to one month's sales (at cost price) at the end of each month. The inventory at the beginning of January is £4,500. The sales and cost of sales estimated for July are £12,000 and £4,800, respectively. The purchases budget is shown in Table 16.11.

Table 16.11   Retail News Group purchase budget.

	Jan	Feb	Mar	Apr	May	Jun	Total
Inventory at end of month	4,800	6,000	4,800	4,400	3,600	4,800	4,800
Inventory at beginning of month	4,500	4,800	6,000	4,800	4,400	3,600	4,500
Increase/-decrease in inventory	300	1,200	−1,200	−400	−800	1,200	300
Sales during month (at cost)	4,000	4,800	6,000	4,800	4,400	3,600	27,600
Total purchases	4,300	6,000	4,800	4,400	3,600	4,800	27,900

Purchases are £27,900 compared with a cost of sales of £27,600, because inventory has increased by £300 (from £4,500 to £4,800). However, purchases are on credit and Retail News has arranged with its suppliers to pay on 60-day terms. Therefore, for example, purchases in January will be paid for in March. Retail News will pay for its November purchases in January (£3,800) and its December purchases in February (£3,500). The creditor payments budget is shown in Table 16.12.

Table 16.12   Retail News Group supplier payments budget.

	Jan	Feb	Mar	Apr	May	Jun	Total
Payment on 60-day terms	3,800	3,500	4,300	6,000	4,800	4,400	26,800

Retail News' payables have increased by £1,100 from £7,300 (£3,800 for November and £3,500 for December) to £8,400 (£3,600 for May and £4,800 for June).

We can now construct the cash forecast for Retail News using the sales receipts budget (Table 16.10) and supplier payments budget (Table 16.12). We also need to identify the timing of cash flows for all expenses. In this case, we determine (using the data from Table 16.9) that salaries and wages, selling and distribution costs, and rent are all paid monthly, as those expenses are incurred. Electricity and telephone are paid quarterly in arrears in March and June. The annual insurance premium of £6,000 is paid in January. Income tax of £5,000 is due in April. As we know, depreciation is an expense that does not involve any cash flow.

However, the business also has a number of other cash payments that do not affect profit. These non-operating payments are:

- capital expenditure of £2,500 committed in March;
- £3,000 of dividends due to be paid in June;
- a loan repayment of £1,000 due in February.

The opening bank balance of Retail News is £2,500. Table 16.13 shows the cash forecast.

Table 16.13   Retail News Group cash forecast.

	Jan	Feb	Mar	Apr	May	Jun	Total
Receipts from sales	8,500	11,000	13,500	13,500	11,500	10,000	68,000
Payments to suppliers	3,800	3,500	4,300	6,000	4,800	4,400	26,800
Salaries and wages	2,000	2,000	2,000	2,200	2,200	2,200	12,600
Selling and distribution expenses	750	900	1,125	900	825	675	5,175
Rent	1,000	1,000	1,000	1,000	1,000	1,000	6,000
Electricity, telephone etc.			1,500			1,500	3,000
Insurance	6000						6,000
Total payments	13,550	7,400	9,925	10,100	8,825	9,775	59,575
Operating cash flow	−5,050	3,600	3,575	3,400	2,675	225	8,425
Income tax paid				5,000			5,000
Capital expenditure			2,500				2,500
Dividends paid						3,000	3,000
Loan repayments		1,000					1,000
Net cash flow	−5,050	2,600	1,075	−1,600	2,675	−2,775	−3,075
Opening bank balance	2,500	−2,550	50	1,125	−475	2,200	
Closing bank balance	−2,550	50	1,125	−475	2,200	−575	

In summary, the bank balance has reduced from an asset of £2,500 to a liability (bank overdraft) of £575 due to a net cash outflow of £3,075. The main issue here is that, in anticipation of the overdrawn position of the bank account in January, April, and June, Retail News needs to make arrangements with its bankers to extend its facility.

One last thing remains, which is for Retail News to produce a cash flow forecast. This is shown in Table 16.14.

Note that Table 16.14 follows the same format as for the Statement of Cash Flows in Chapter 6. The budgeting process will normally produce a forecast Income Statement, Statement of Financial Position, and Statement of Cash Flows for a company as part of the budget process. Ratio analysis (Chapter 7) may even be performed on the forecast financial statements to understand the likely impact of future performance on ratio targets, trends, and benchmark comparisons.

Table 16.14   Retail News Group Statement of Cash Flows (cash forecast).

Cash flows from operating activities		
Operating profit		**£8,625**
Plus non-cash expense		
Depreciation		3,000
		11,625
Less increase in working capital		
Receivables	1,000	
Inventory	300	
Insurance prepayment	3,000	
	4,300	
Less increase in payables	1,100	
Net increase in working capital		−3,200
Cash flow from operations		8,425
Less income tax paid		−5,000
Net cash flow from operations		3,425
Cash flow from investing activities		
Capital expenditure	2,500	
Net cash flow from investing activities		−2,500
Cash flow from financing activities		
Dividend	3,000	
Loan repayment	1,000	
Net cash flow from financing activities		−4,000
Net decrease in cash		£3,075
Opening cash & cash equivalents		2,500
Closing cash & cash equivalents		−£575

A behavioural perspective on budgeting

Although the tools of budgeting and cash forecasting are well developed and made easier by the use of spreadsheet software, the difficulty of budgeting is in predicting the volume of sales for the business, especially the sales mix between different products or services and the timing of income and expenses. This is because there is uncertainty in terms of economic conditions, customer demand, and competitor strategies.

As budget targets are often linked to managerial rewards (promotion, bonuses, share options, etc.) budgets can result in behavioural consequences that are unintended, and often dysfunctional. *Participation* by managers in the budget process has long been recognized as a method of reducing dysfunctional consequences. Participation is only effective if the managers who are accountable for their performance can help develop budget targets and are able to make decisions that can influence the outcomes (see also controllability in Chapter 15).

A top-down budget approach (see earlier in this chapter) does not involve participation while a bottom-up approach does. The more common mixed method may have varying extents of participation depending on whether or not the concerns of managers about targets and controllability are addressed in the final budget outcome. Managers will typically perform better if they feel the budget is 'theirs' rather than budgets having been imposed by a remote head office.

A further behavioural issue is the extent of padding the budget. This is the practice by managers of inflating cost targets and reducing sales targets to make those targets easier to achieve. *Budgetary slack* is the difference between those inflated (or deflated) targets and a realistic estimate of revenues and costs. It is caused by a desire to please a superior manager in what is a competitive managerial hierarchy; because of uncertainty over future events; and because when budget targets are evaluated at higher organizational levels, it is common for those targets to be adjusted. Hence a manager will build in slack knowing that his or her final cost budget will likely be cut while sales targets will be increased. Managers who are rewarded for meeting targets are more likely to incorporate budget slack in their own estimates.

Targets are often set by top managers that are *stretch targets* – targets that are difficult to achieve and stretch managers' abilities. However, if targets are considered unachievable by managers they will not be effective as a motivational tool, but neither will targets that are too easily achieved. Therefore targets need to be achievable with managerial effort but not be so difficult that they are considered by those managers as unrealistic and unachievable. Of course, what is 'realistic' or 'achievable' varies depending on different points of view (we discussed 'socially constructed reality' in Chapter 5).

Samuelson (1986) argued that:

> senior management often articulate one role for the budget but budgetees then perceive that another very different role may be intended (p. 35).

Samuelson contrasted the 'role articulated' by management for budgetary control (as an aid to planning), which may be different from the 'real role', and the 'role intended' by managers (holding people responsible). This dichotomy may be at the heart of tensions in the budget process.

A critical perspective: beyond budgeting?

Budgeting has been criticized in recent years because it can disempower the workforce, discourage information sharing, and slow the response to market developments. The Beyond Budgeting Round Table (BBRT) has identified 10 reasons why budgets cause problems. They:

- are time consuming and expensive;
- provide poor value to users;

- fail to focus on shareholder value;
- are too rigid and prevent fast response;
- protect rather than reduce costs;
- stifle product and strategy innovation;
- focus on sales targets rather than customer satisfaction;
- are divorced from strategy;
- reinforce a dependency culture;
- can lead to unethical behaviour.

BBRT describes 'Beyond Budgeting' as:

> about rethinking how we manage organizations in a post-industrial world where innovative management models represent the only sustainable competitive advantage. It is also about releasing people from the burdens of stifling bureaucracy and suffocating control systems, trusting them with information and giving them time to think, reflect, share, learn and improve (http://bbrt.org/about/what-is-beyond-budgeting).

Hope and Fraser (2003) suggested that budgets should be replaced with a combination of financial and non-financial measures, with performance being judged against world-class benchmarks. Companies that have adopted 'Beyond Budgeting' include American Express, Google, John Lewis Partnership, Southwest Airlines, and Toyota.

Compared with the traditional management model, 'Beyond Budgeting' is a more adaptive way of managing. In place of fixed annual plans and budgets that tie managers to predetermined actions, targets are reviewed regularly through rolling forecasts based on stretch goals linked to performance against world-class benchmarks and prior periods. Instead of a traditional hierarchical and centralized leadership, 'Beyond Budgeting' enables decision making and performance accountability to be devolved to line managers and fosters a culture of decentralized decision making and employee and team empowerment. This, it is argued, leads to increased motivation, higher productivity, and better customer service.

Twelve principles define the 'Beyond Budgeting' management model (see http://www.bbrt.co.uk/beyond-budgeting/bb-principles.html). The first six 'leadership' principles provide a framework for the devolution of responsibility to front-line teams which enables them to respond quickly to emerging events and makes them accountable for continuously improving *relative* performance. (Note that 'relative' performance is in relation to past trends and benchmarks with other organizations. This is not the same as 'absolute' performance improvement that ignores trends and industry conditions.) The second six 'process' principles support a more adaptive set of performance management systems that enable front-line teams to be more responsive to the competitive environment and to customer needs. These twelve principles represent a holistic model although different organizations will place different emphases on each of the principles depending on their circumstances.

The origin of the 'Beyond Budgeting' movement was a case study of Swedish bank Handelsbanken by Jan Wallander. Case study 16.5 provides a summary of Wallender's paper.

Case Study 16.5: Svenska Handelsbanken – is budgeting necessary?

Jan Wallander was an executive director of Handelsbanken. He was appointed to the role when the bank, the largest commercial bank in Sweden, faced a crisis. Handelsbanken's goal was to be the most profitable bank in Sweden and its strategy was to be radically decentralized with nearly all lending authority independent of Head Office. Although at the time Swedish banks did not use budgets, Handelsbanken had started to install a sophisticated budgeting system. Wallander (1999) was very critical of budgeting. He argued:

> You can make forecasts very complicated by putting a lot of variables into them and using sophisticated techniques for evaluating the time series you have observed and used in your work. However, if you see through all this technical paraphernalia you will find that there are a few basic assumptions which determine the outcome of the forecast (p. 408).

The accuracy of the budget therefore depended on how accurate the assumptions were. Wallander argued that there were two reasons to abandon budgeting:

1. If there is economic stability and the business will continue as usual, we use previous experience in order to budget. Wallander argued that we do not need an intricate budgeting system in this case, because people will continue working as they presently are. Even when conditions are not normal, the expectation is that they will return to normal.
2. If events arise that challenge economic stability then budgets will not reflect this, because, Wallander says, 'we have no ability to foresee something of which we have no previous experience' (p. 411).

Wallander concluded that traditional budgeting is 'an outmoded way of controlling and steering a company. It is a cumbersome way of reaching conclusions which are either commonplace or wrong' (p. 419).

Wallander did not reject planning but differentiated the need to plan from the need to prepare budgets. He argued that it is important to have an 'economic model' that establishes the basic relationships in the company, such as the ability to plan production. Wallander used the analogy of making and selling cars: 'If they want to be able to produce X cars a year from now, they have to figure out when they have to place their orders with their subcontractors. In the course of that planning activity they have to make a lot of medium-term forecasts about demand, prices etc. Their natural ambition in this context is to place their orders as late as possible and thus not bind their hands more than necessary and keep their inventories as low as possible. This type of planning is something that is going on all the year round and has nothing to do with the annual budget' (Wallander, 1999, p. 416).

To support this business model, Handelsbanken had an information system that was focused on the information needed to influence actual behaviour. It incorporated both financial and 'Balanced Scorecard' measures at the profit centre level, and performance was benchmarked both externally and internally. Because actual performance could not be compared with budget, the real target was not in absolute monetary terms but a relative one, a return on capital better than what other businesses were achieving, not just in the banking industry but in other industries as well. Handelsbanken thus adopted a true shareholder value model.

The bank rewarded its staff through a profit-sharing scheme, with the profit share dependent on the profitability of the bank relative to the other Swedish banks. Interestingly, the share of the employees in the profits of the bank was only paid to them when they retired, which encouraged them to remain with the bank and continually to improve performance.

Despite its abandonment of budgeting, Handelsbanken remained a very successful bank. Wallander concluded, 'abandoning budgeting, which was an essential part of the changes, had no adverse effect on the performance of the bank compared to other banks, which all installed budgeting systems during the period' (p. 407).

Source: Wallander, J. (1999). Budgeting an unnecessary evil. *Scandinavian Journal of Management*, 15, 405–21.

Østergren and Stensaker (2011) studied how the head office of a large oil and energy company adopted the 'Beyond Budgeting' approach to management control in two business units. Their research found that the means of control that were exercised in the absence of budgets altered the relationship between head office management and division management. Users at division level struggled with the complexity of the 'Beyond Budgeting' approach compared with the better understood budgeting system. One division even implemented its own internal budgets. However, Østergren and Stensaker found that those managers who did come to terms with the 'Beyond Budgeting' approach gained a more holistic understanding of their division's performance than was provided by the financial numbers.

Few companies have abandoned budgeting altogether. This is partly because of the legitimating effect of budgets in the eyes of shareholders and the need for budgets to support applications for finance. In a personal communication between the author and Handelsbanken, I asked whether the bank required budgets from its clients seeking loans. The bank replied: 'Handelsbanken has no formal requirement on receiving a budget when our corporate clients need financing. We naturally want as much information as possible on how the company and its management see the future etc. But no requirement that this is presented in a budget' (email from Bank, September 2014).

There are also behavioural consequences of abandoning budgets as they are seen by many managers as an important element of management control. In their 2009 report *Management accounting tools for today and tomorrow*, the Chartered Institute of Management Accountants (CIMA, 2009) identified the relative popularity of budgeting tools, from financial year forecasts (the most popular overall) to 'Beyond Budgeting' (the least popular). The CIMA report argues that:

> it would need a radical re-invention of budgeting and performance management to persuade users there are alternatives to cash forecasts, and financial year forecasts (both of which are amongst the most used tools) (p. 28).

Conclusion

In this chapter we have seen budgeting as an extension of the strategy formulation and implementation process. We described the budget process and the mechanics of the budgeting cycle. Through a series of four case studies we explored budgeting for a service, retail, and manufacturing organization and how budgets are converted into a cash forecast. The chapter concluded with a behavioural perspective on budgeting, and by drawing on the example of the 'Beyond Budgeting' movement and the case of Handelsbanken we questioned whether budgets are necessary at all. The assumptions behind the production of budgets are important for planning purposes, but crucial when managers are held accountable for achieving budget targets. This is the topic of budgetary control, which is the subject of Chapter 17.

References

Anthony, R. N. and Govindarajan, V. (2000). *Management Control Systems* (10th edn). New York: McGraw-Hill Irwin.

Chartered Institute of Management Accountants (CIMA, 2009). *Management accounting tools for today and tomorrow.* http://www.cimaglobal.com/Documents/Thought_leadership_docs/CIMA%20Tools%20and%20Techniques%2030-11-09%20PDF.pdf.

Collier, P. M. and Berry, A.J. (2002). Risk in the process of budgeting. *Management Accounting Research*, 13, 273–97.

Hope, J. and Fraser, R. (2003). *Beyond Budgeting: How Managers Can Break Free from the Annual Performance Trap.* Boston, MA: Harvard Business School Press.

Østergren, K. and Stensaker, I. (2011). Management Control without Budgets: A Field Study of 'Beyond Budgeting' in Practice. *European Accounting Review*, 20(1), 149–81.

Samuelson, L. A. (1986). Discrepancies between the roles of budgeting. *Accounting, Organizations and Society*, 11(1), 35–45.

Wallander, J. (1999). Budgeting an unnecessary evil. *Scandinavian Journal of Management*, 15, 405–21.

Questions

16.1   April Co. receives payment from customers for credit sales as follows:

30% in the month of sale.
60% in the month following sale.
8% in the second month following the sale.
2% become bad debts and are never collected.

The following sales are expected:

January	£100,000
February	£120,000
March	£110,000

- Calculate how much will be received in March.
- What is the value of receivables at the end of March?

16.2   Creassos Co. was formed in July 2010 with €20,000 of capital. €7,500 of this was used to purchase equipment. The owner's budget is shown in Table 16.15.

Table 16.15   Budget for Creassos Co.

	Sales	Receipts from customers	Purchases	Payments to suppliers	Wages	Other expenses
July	20,000	—	8,000	5,000	3,000	2,000
Aug	30,000	20,000	15,000	10,000	4,000	2,000
Sept	40,000	30,000	20,000	20,000	5,000	3,000

Wages and other expenses are paid in cash. In addition to the above, depreciation is €2,400 per annum. No inventory is held by the company.

- Calculate the profit for each of the three months from July to September and in total.
- Calculate the cash balance at the end of each month.
- Prepare a Statement of Financial Position at the end of September.

16.3   Highjinks Corporation's sales department has estimated revenue of $2,250,000 for East Division. 60% of this will be achieved in the first half year and 40% in the remaining half year. Variable operating costs are typically 30% of revenue and fixed operating costs are expected to be $35,000 per month for the first six months and £40,000 per month thereafter.

The selling expense recharged from the sales department to East Division is $15,000 per month for the first half year, thereafter $12,000. Salaries are $25,000 per month, depreciation is $5,000 per month, and council rates $8,000 per month. Light, heat, and power are expected to cost $3,000 per month for the first half year, falling to $2,000 thereafter.

- Construct a budget for East Division for the year based on the above figures.
- What can you say about the rate of gross profit?

16.4 Griffin Metals Co. has provided the following data.

Anticipated volumes (assume production equals sales each quarter):

Quarter 1	100,000 tonnes
Quarter 2	110,000 tonnes
Quarter 3	105,000 tonnes
Quarter 4	120,000 tonnes

The selling price is expected to be £300 per tonne for the first six months and £310 per tonne thereafter. Variable costs per tonne are predicted as £120 in the first quarter, £125 in the second and third quarters, and £130 in the fourth quarter.

Fixed costs (in £'000 per quarter) have been estimated and are shown in Table 16.16.

Table 16.16   Fixed costs for Griffin Metals Co.

Salaries and wages	£3,000 for the first half year, increasing by 10% for the second half year
Maintenance	£1,500
Council rates	£400
Insurance	£120
Electricity	£1,000
Depreciation	£5,400
Other costs	£2,500 in the first and fourth quarters, £1,800 in the second and third quarters
Interest	£600
Capital expenditure	£6,500 in the first quarter, £2,000 in the second quarter, £1,000 in the third quarter and £9,000 in the fourth quarter
Dividend payment	£10,000 in the third quarter
Debt repayments	£1,000 in the first quarter, £5,000 in the second quarter, £4,000 in the third quarter, and £3,000 in the fourth quarter

Griffin has asked you to produce a profit budget and a cash forecast for the year (in four quarters) using the above data.

16.5 Mega Stores is a chain of 125 retail outlets selling clothing under the strong Mega brand. Its sales have increased from €185 million to €586 million over the last five years. The company's gross profit is currently 83% of sales, giving it a little more than 20% mark-up on the cost of goods and retail store running costs. Corporate overhead is €19 million and the operating profit is €81 million.

Mega Stores' finance director has produced a budget, which has been approved by the board of directors, to increase sales by 35% next year and to improve operating profit margin to 15% of sales. Corporate overheads will be contained at €22 million.

The strategy determined by the marketing director is to continue expanding sales by winning market share from competitors and by increasing the volume of sales to existing customers. It aims to increase use of social marketing to customers, and its television advertising. The company also intends to open new stores to extend its geographic coverage.

Mega Stores also plans to improve its cost-effectiveness by continuing its investments in major regional warehouses and distribution facilities servicing its national network of stores, together with upgrading its information systems to reduce inventory and delivery lead times to its retail network.

You have been asked to produce a report for the senior management team identifying the financial information that is required to support the business strategy. You are also asked to identify any non-financial issues arising from the strategy.

16.6 Placibo Ltd has estimated the sales units and selling prices for its products for each of the next four months. This information is shown in Table 16.17.

Table 16.17   Placibo Ltd.

	June	July	August	September
Forecast sales units	20,000	20,000	22,000	25,000
Selling price per unit	$4.25	$4.50	$4.50	$4.75

Placibo's average cost of sales is 30% of revenue. It incurs overhead costs of $55,000 per month, of which $25,000 per month is depreciation. Placibo receives payment from its customers in the month following the month of sale, and it pays its suppliers in the month following the recognition of the cost of sales in the Income Statement. Overheads are paid in the same month in which they are incurred.

a. Prepare a budgeted Income Statement for each of the three months July–September.
b. Prepare a cash forecast for each of the three months July–September.

Case study question 16.1: Carsons Stores Ltd

Carsons is a retail store that has given the task of preparing its budget for next year to a trainee accountant. The budget is prepared in quarters. Table 16.18 is the profit budget report produced by the trainee.

A cash forecast has also been prepared (see Table 16.19).

Table 16.18   Carsons Stores Ltd.

In £'000	Quarter 1	Quarter 2	Quarter 3	Quarter 4	Year total
Sales	100	110	110	120	440
Cost of sales	40	44	44	48	176
Gross profit	60	66	66	72	264
Expenses:					
Salaries	10	10	10	10	40
Rent	20	20	20	20	80
Depreciation	5	5	5	5	20
Promotional expenses	10	11	11	12	44
Administration expenses	5	5	5	5	20
Total expenses	50	51	51	52	204
Net profit	10	15	15	20	60

Table 16.19   Carsons Stores Ltd.

In £'000	Quarter 1	Quarter 2	Quarter 3	Quarter 4	Year total
Cash inflow from sales	100	110	110	120	440
Purchases		40	44	44	128
Expenses	50	51	51	52	204
Capital expenditure		20			20
Income tax			20		20
Dividends		15	20	25	60
Cash outflow	50	126	135	121	432
Net cash flow	50	−16	−25	−1	8
Cumulative cash flow	50	34	9	8	

What are the questions you would want to ask the trainee accountant in order to satisfy yourself that the budget was realistic and achievable? Can you identify any errors that have been made in the budget or cash forecast? If so, make any corrections that you think are necessary and comment on any problems you have identified.

CHAPTER 17

Budgetary Control

Following on from budgeting in Chapter 16, in this chapter we describe the process of budgetary control that takes place in organizations to manage performance in line with budget targets. We demonstrate variance analysis by using flexible budgets in relation to sales, material, and labour costs and overheads. We separately identify price and efficiency variances for costs that need to be investigated by operational managers as part of the management control process. This chapter also contains a critique of variance analysis in the modern business environment. The chapter concludes with the application of different perspectives to the management accounting techniques covered in Chapters 14 to 17.

What is budgetary control?

Budgetary control is concerned with ensuring that actual financial results are in line with targets. An important part of management control, this *feedback process* (see Chapter 4) is concerned with investigating variations between actual results and budgeted results and taking appropriate corrective action.

Corrective action may include:

- Revising the original budget; and/or
- Changing the behaviour of those responsible for the actual results.

Budgetary control provides a yardstick for comparison and isolates problems by focusing on those variances which provide early warning signals to managers. Budgetary control is typically exercised at the level of each responsibility centre (see Chapter 15). Management reports show, for each line item, the budget income and expenditure, actual income and expenditure, and a variance, usually for both the current accounting period and the year to date.

A typical (but simplified in terms of the number of line items) actual versus budget financial report is shown in Table 17.1.

Table 17.1   Actual v. budget financial report.

	Current Month			Year to date		
	Budget	**Actual**	**Variance**	**Budget**	**Actual**	**Variance**
Sales	€120,000	€110,000	−€10,000	€340,000	€345,000	€5,000
Less: cost of sales						
Materials	€40,000	€45,000	−€5,000	€100,000	€96,000	€4,000
Labour	€21,000	€19,000	€2,000	€30,000	€32,000	−€2,000
Energy	€9,000	€7,000	€2,000	€40,000	€38,000	€2,000
Total cost of sales	€70,000	€71,000	−€1,000	€170,000	€166,000	€4,000
Gross profit	€50,000	€39,000	−€11,000	€170,000	€179,000	€9,000
Selling & admin expenses	€10,000	€2,500	€7,500	€50,000	€55,000	−€5,000
Net profit	€40,000	€36,500	−€3,500	€120,000	€124,000	€4,000

It is important to look at both the current period, which in Table 17.1 shows a profit shortfall compared to budget of €3,500 (budget profit of €40,000 compared with the actual result of €36,500), and the year to date, which shows that the business exceeded profit expectations by €4,000.

It is also important to look at each line item in the budget versus actual comparison, in both the current month and the year to date. In the current month, actual sales were below budget but the cost of sales was over budget, although there were significant savings in selling and administration expenses. However, these differences should not be seen as offsetting each other. Each variance needs to be looked at individually as the causes are likely to be different between, for example, why materials were over spent and why energy was under spent compared with budget.

In the year to date, sales have exceeded budget and cost of sales are less than budget – the result is a big improvement in gross profit compared with budget, but this has been eroded by an overspending on selling and administration compared with budget.

Each month there will be explanations for variances which build to a composite year-to-date explanation. There may be many different causes, even for a single line item. We must be careful to understand what is happening within each line item, and we can only do that by analysing the underlying transactions in the accounting records (see Chapter 3) and by questioning the managers who are accountable for sales, cost of sales, and other expenses. This process is called variance analysis.

Variance analysis

Variance analysis involves comparing actual performance against plan and investigating the causes of the variance. This leads to management taking corrective action to ensure that targets are achieved (although corrective action may also include modifying the targets where they are unrealistic). Variance analysis needs to be carried out for each responsibility centre, product/service (if information is available), and for each line item.

The steps involved in variance analysis are:

1. Ascertain the budget and phasing (see Chapter 16) for each period.
2. Report the actual spending.
3. Determine the variance between budget and actual (and determine whether it is either favourable or adverse).
4. Investigate why the variance occurred.
5. Take corrective action.

There are two types of variance:

- A favourable variance occurs where income exceeds budget and/or expenses are lower than budget (these are positive variance figures in Table 17.1).
- An adverse or unfavourable variance occurs where income is less than budget and/or expenses are greater than budget (these are negative figures in Table 17.1).

Not only adverse variances need to be investigated. Favourable variances provide a learning opportunity so that good practice can be repeated. The questions that need to be asked as part of variance analysis are:

- Is the variance significant?
- Is it early or late in the year?
- Is it likely to be repeated?
- Can it be explained (and understood)?
- Is it controllable?

Only significant variations need to be investigated. However, what is significant can be interpreted differently. Which is more significant, for example, a 5% variation on £10,000 (£500) or a 25% variation on £1,000 (£250)? The significance of the variation may be either an absolute amount or a percentage. Also in terms of significance, a variance later in the year will be more difficult to correct, so variances should be detected so that corrective action can be taken as soon as the variance occurs. Similarly, a one-off variance requires a single corrective action, but a variance that will continue into the future requires more drastic action. A variance that can be understood can be corrected, but if the causes of the variance are not understood or are outside the manager's control, it may be difficult to influence in the future.

The questions senior managers may ask in relation to Table 17.1 include:

- What is the cause of the decline in sales in the current month and is this likely to continue in future months?
- What is the cause of the increase in materials cost in the current month and is this likely to continue in future months?
- What is the cause of the savings in energy costs and is this likely to continue in future months?
- What was the cause of the underspending on selling and administration expenses in the current month, and what are the implications (if any) for future months?

However, a weakness of traditional management reports for budgetary control is that the business may not be comparing like with like. For example, if the business volume is lower than budgeted, then it follows that any variable costs should (in total) be lower than budget. Conversely, if business volume is higher than budgeted, variable costs should (in total) be higher than budget. In many management reports, the distinction between variable and fixed costs (see Chapter 10) is not made and it becomes very difficult to compare the actual costs incurred at one level of activity with budgeted costs at a different level of activity and to make meaningful judgements about managerial performance. Therefore, we need to use a flexible budget.

Flexible budgets and sales variances

If the actual activity level is different to that budgeted, comparing revenue and/or costs at different (actual and budget) levels of activity will produce meaningless figures. Flexible budgets take into account variations in the volume of business activity and provide a better basis for investigating variances than the original budget. A flexible budget is a budget that is *flexed*, that is standard costs per unit (see Chapter 11) are applied to the actual level of business activity. A comparison is then made, and a variance calculated between the actual costs at the actual level of activity and the budgeted (i.e. standard) costs that should apply at the actual level of activity.

Using the same example as in Table 17.1, analysis reveals that budgeted sales were 20,000 units at an average selling price per unit of €6. However actual sales volume was 18,965 units at an average selling price of €5.80. We can use a flexible budget to show a more meaningful variance than simply reporting that sales fell short of budget by €10,000.

	Original Budget	*Flexed Budget*	*Actual*	*Variance*
Sales	€120,000	€113,790	€110,000	−€3,790
	20,000 @ €6	18,965 @ €6	18,965 @ €5.80	

The flexed budget is based on the actual sales volume of 18,965 units at the standard (or budget) selling price of €6. This flexed budget for sales of €113,790 is then compared with the actual sales of €110,000. The difference of €3,790 is an adverse *selling price variance*, caused by 18,965 units being sold at €0.20 below the target price (the small difference in calculation is due to rounding).

In constructing a flexed budget, we don't ignore the original budget because we can separately compare the original with the flexed budget. The difference of €6,210 (€120,000 less €113,790) is an adverse *sales quantity or sales volume variance* because the actual sales volume fell below budget by 1,035 (20,000 – 18,965) at the standard selling price of €6. The two variances – the price variance of €3,790 and the quantity variance of €6,210 – total the original €10,000 variance between budget and actual.

Using flexible budgeting leads to a more meaningful variance analysis because we can identify two separate causes, which may not be controllable by the same managers (we discussed controllability in Chapter 15). For example, market conditions and competition may be an important influence in understanding the volume variance. However, managers may be questioned on why prices fell below standard even though volume also fell.

The same approach can be used to understand cost variances, because explanations need to be sought from different managers in relation to different types of variance:

- material variances: price and quantity of materials used;
- labour variances: wage rate and efficiency/productivity;
- overhead variances.

Flexible budgets and cost variances

Each cost variance for materials, labour, and overhead can be split into two types, a price variance and a usage or efficiency variance. This is because each type of variance may be the responsibility of a different manager. Price variances occur because the cost per unit of resources (labour, material, etc.) is higher or lower than the standard cost. Usage variances occur because the actual quantity of labour or materials used is higher or lower than the standard cost contained in the labour routing or bill of materials (these concepts were covered in Chapter 11). The relationship between price and usage variances is shown in Figure 17.1. In using Figure 17.1, it is important to note that the 'standard quantity' refers to the standard quantity of materials or labour multiplied by the *actual quantity of finished goods*, i.e. it is based on the flexible budget.

Figure 17.1   Price and usage variances.

The variances for material and labour are calculated as follows:

- The usage variance is the difference between the standard and actual quantity, while holding the standard price constant, i.e. it tells us, at the standard or expected price, the excess material, labour, or variable overhead consumed in producing the actual quantity of finished goods.
- The price variance is the difference between the standard price and the actual price, while holding the actual quantity of material or labour used constant, i.e. it tells us, given the actual quantity of resource used, the additional price or rate paid in producing the actual quantity of finished goods.

We can apply Figure 17.1 to the example in Table 17.1 which we can develop with additional information from an analysis of the accounting records and explanations from responsible managers. This analysis reveals that each unit of finished goods sold requires one unit of material at a standard cost of €2. As 18,965 units have been sold, this equates to a flexed budget for material costs of €37,930. Accounting records reveal that 22,959 units of material have been used at an actual cost of €1.96 each.

Table 17.2 shows the calculation of the materials price and usage variances in which the adverse usage variance is shown separately from the favourable price variance for materials (the formulae come from Figure 17.1). Note that we are not comparing actual costs with the original budget for materials of €40,000 because that was based on a different volume of sales of the finished product and such a comparison would not be meaningful.

Table 17.2   Materials price and usage variance.

Materials variance	Standard qty × standard price	Actual qty × standard price	Actual qty × actual price
	18,965 @ €2 €37,930	22,959 @ €2 €45,918	22,959 @ €1.96 €45,000
Usage variance	€7,988 Adverse		
Price variance		€918 Favourable	
Total variance		€,7070 Adverse	

In the same way, we can calculate the usage and rate variances for labour. Each unit of finished goods sold requires about 6 minutes of labour (0.10 of an hour) at a standard labour rate of €10.50. As 18,965 units have been sold, this equates to a flexed budget for labour costs of €19,908 (ignore rounding in the calculation). Accounting records reveal that 1,727 hours of labour have been used at an actual cost of €11 each. Table 17.3 shows the calculation of the labour rate and usage variances.

Table 17.3 shows that a favourable usage variance was due to an efficiency gain which reduced the total labour hours needed in production of the finished products. However, the cost of that labour was

Table 17.3   Labour rate and usage variance.

Labour variance	Standard hours × standard price	Actual hours × standard price	Actual hours × actual price
18,965 × 6 mins = 1896 hours	@ €10.50	1,727 @ €10.50	1,727 @ €11
	€19,908	€18,133	€19,000
Usage variance	€1,775 Favourable		
Rate variance			€867 Adverse
Total variance		€908 favourable	

higher than standard. The reasons for each would need to be investigated. As for materials, we are not comparing actual costs with the original budget for labour of €21,000 because that was based on a different number of sales of the finished product and such a comparison would not be meaningful.

As overheads may be variable or fixed, there can be different reasons for variances in each category. For variable overhead variances, we would need to look at the drivers of overheads (see Chapter 13). In our present example, we can assume that the variance between budget and actual expenditure for selling and administrative expenses is a fixed cost and hence there is no impact of changes in volume on the overhead cost variation (see Chapter 10 for an explanation of fixed and variable costs). There is no need to flex the budget for fixed overheads and in the present example the variance is a favourable €7,500 for the month.

Interpreting variances

There are many possible causes for variances between budget and actual, some of which may be caused by volume changes in the sale of finished products, and others by differences in the quantity of materials or labour hours or the prices for the materials or labour consumed in production.

A (favourable or adverse) materials efficiency variance may be the result of:

* waste or scrap;
* inaccurate bill of materials;
* different quality materials.

Favourable or adverse material price variances may be the result of:

* changes in supplier prices not yet reflected in standard costs;
* purchasing practices that are inconsistent with standard supply arrangements (e.g. as a result of being out of stock of materials).

A (favourable or adverse) labour efficiency variance may be the result of:

- different quality material that requires more or less labour time to work;
- differences in productive efficiency of labour;
- effectiveness of production planning in minimizing downtime.

Labour rate variance may be the result of:

- unplanned overtime payments;
- wage rate changes that have not been included in the standard cost of labour.

As can be seen in these examples, there may be offsetting factors in explaining variances. For example, buying cheaper materials may result in a favourable materials price variation, but the consequences may be that more materials are wasted, leading to an adverse materials usage variance; or that additional labour is required to work with the cheaper materials, leading to an adverse labour efficiency variance.

While the example used above is a manufacturing example, variance analysis is equally applicable to service and retail businesses. In a service business, labour variances will be particularly important but there will be no materials and therefore no materials variance. For example, in professional services, there will be variations between estimated hours that have been quoted to a client and actual hours charged on timesheets to client jobs, as well as labour rate variances where staff with different skills and therefore different charge-out rates (see Chapter 12) from those quoted charge their times to client jobs.

In a retail business, purchases of goods for resale will be a high component of total costs and so material price variance will be important, but labour variances will be irrelevant as there is no production process.

In service, knowledge-based, and financial services industries, overheads often form the largest component of total cost. Nevertheless, investigating the reasons for variations between budget and actual costs, even if those costs are independent of volume, can identify poor budgeting practice, lack of effective cost control, or poor purchasing practices.

Criticism of variance analysis

In his landmark study, Anthony Hopwood (1973) differentiated three styles of evaluation of budget information. The budget-constrained manager is evaluated based on the ability to meet the budget continually on a short-term basis. The profit-conscious manager is evaluated on the basis of the ability to increase the general effectiveness of operations to meet long-term objectives. In the non-accounting style, accounting information plays little part in the evaluation of a manager's performance.

A manager who adopts a budget-constrained style takes budget information at face value and has a short time horizon, considering each month's variances in isolation rather than the trend or the long-term implications. To the budget-constrained manager, an adverse budget variance is an indicator of poor management performance, even though the standards used by the accounting system may be faulty.

By contrast, managers adopting a profit-conscious style realize that accounting information is not a constraint, and that variances are a meaningful guide to action, even though they may be misleading. The profit-conscious manager is more likely to experiment and innovate even though cost may exceed budget in the short term.

Hopwood found that although managers:

> made extensive use of the accounting information, they did so in a rigid manner, either attributing too much validity to the information or being unaware of its intended purposes, with the result that again, despite the thought and consideration which went into the design and operation of the system, its final value was questionable (p. 185).

Hence, as for other management accounting techniques described in this book, the behavioural consequences of budgetary control cannot be ignored.

Standard costing, flexible budgeting, and variance analysis can be criticized as tools of management because these methods emphasize variable costs in a manufacturing environment. While labour costs are typically a low proportion of manufacturing cost, material costs are typically high and variance analysis has a role to play in many organizations that incur high costs for purchased goods (including retailers). However, even in manufacturing the introduction of new management techniques such as just-in-time (JIT) is often not reflected in the design of the management accounting system.

Variance analysis has less emphasis in a JIT environment because price variations are only one component of total cost and a higher cost may be justifiable in exchange for a lower investment in inventory, more flexible deliveries, superior quality, etc. We have already described the total cost of ownership and quality management in Chapter 11 and the implications for cost management. It is important to recognize that reducing variances based on standard costs can be an overly restrictive approach in a continuous improvement environment. This is because an over-focus on variances between budget and actual may result in a tendency to aim at the more obvious cost reductions (cheaper labour and materials) rather than broader issues of quality, reliability, on-time delivery, flexibility, etc. (which will be reflected in the total cost of ownership). An emphasis on variances will also tend to result in employees following standard work instructions rather than being encouraged to adopt an innovative approach to re-engineering business processes.

As we will see in Chapter 18, new approaches to accounting in production environments are concerned with minimizing waste, including wasteful accounting practices. The next chapter will show how backflushing and lean accounting practices can replace detailed time and material recording and obviate variance analysis altogether.

Standard costs and variance analysis are tools that can be used in certain circumstances, but they should not be used blindly without consideration of the wider impact on strategies being implemented by the business. Nevertheless, neither accountants nor non-financial managers should overlook the importance of effectively managing the organization's costs.

Applying different perspectives to management accounting

In Chapters 4 and 5, we considered rational-economic, interpretive, and critical perspectives that help to provide multiple views about the world in which we live. Chapters 14 through 17 have introduced many aspects of how management accounting techniques are used in planning, decision making, and control in relation to investments, business unit evaluation, budgeting, and budgetary control.

Implicit in most of what is contained in these four chapters is an acceptance of the rational-economic paradigm described in Chapter 4. Profit-oriented businesses make investment decisions to maximize profits (Chapter 14), monitor the performance of different business segments (Chapter 15), budget for future profits (Chapter 16), and use variance analysis for control in order to take appropriate corrective action (this chapter). These are rational-economic choices.

However, numbers often reinforce subjective decisions and accounting choices may not be as straightforward as they seem. The interpretive perspective is useful here. For example, different views exist about the choice of investment evaluation method (accounting return, payback, and discounted cash flow in Chapter 14), each of which gives different answers and can result in a different interpretation. There are divergent views about whether divisional performance should be assessed on return on investment or residual income criteria (Chapter 15) and again, different interpretations of performance are possible. Budgeting is itself an estimate of future activity (Chapter 16) involving considerable subjective judgements about the unknowable future, and a wide range of different estimates are possible. Variance analysis itself can be challenged on the basis that in many industries it may no longer be relevant to the way in which modern businesses operate (this chapter).

Equally, we have seen in these chapters that the critical perspective can also apply. Power determines particular choices of approach. The discounted cash flow technique (Chapter 14), for example, can be biased in practice by inflated forecast cash flows that support the proposer's view that an investment should be approved. Evaluation criteria can be altered by boards of directors to raise or lower hurdle rates. The choice of transfer pricing technique (Chapter 15) will depend on the relative power of buying and selling divisions within an organization and top-management influence over the selection of the transfer price. The power of accounting departments over every segment of the business due to accountants' control of the budget process is evident in most companies. The adoption (or non-adoption) of variance analysis (this chapter) is also a significant source of power, especially where accountants can use variances to hold selling, purchasing, and production managers accountable for their decisions and actions.

Conclusion

In this chapter, we have described budgetary control and the use of flexible budgets. We have illustrated sales price and volume variances, and cost variances with the separation of usage (or efficiency) and price (or wage rate) variances for materials and labour. We have concluded the chapter with a critique of variance analysis. Finally, we have seen how different perspectives can be applied to the management accounting techniques covered in Chapters 14–17.

References

Hopwood, A. G. (1973). *An Accounting System and Managerial Behaviour*. London: Saxon House.

Questions

17.1   Conrad Corporation has a budget to produce 2,000 units at a variable cost of $3 per unit, but actual production is 1,800 units with an actual cost of $3.20 per unit.

Calculate the variance based on a flexible budget and determine whether it is favourable or adverse.

17.2   Calculate the material price variance for Cracker Barrel based on the following information:

	Standard	Actual
Quantity purchased (units)	5,000	5,200
Price per unit	€3.10	€3.05

17.3   Gargantua plc has produced budget and actual information in Table 17.4.

Table 17.4   Gargantua budget and actual.

	Budget	**Actual**
Sales units	10,000	11,000
Price per unit	£37.10	£36
Direct materials	5kg @ £2.20	58,000 kg cost £126,075
Labour per unit	2.5 hours @ £7	26,400 hours cost £187,440
Fixed costs	£75,000	£68,000

a.   Prepare a traditional budget versus actual report using the above figures.
b.   Prepare a flexible budget for Gargantua.
c.   Calculate the sales price and volume variances, and the cost efficiency and price variances for materials, labour, and overhead.

17.4   Eggscell Ltd has produced budget and actual information for one of its business units for the previous month. This information is shown in Table 17.5.

Table 17.5   Eggscell Ltd.

	Budget	Actual
Analysis of labour		
Number of hours	10,000	9000
Average rate per hour	$75	$80

a. Show how a traditional budget versus actual variance report would be presented to the manager of this business unit.
b. Use a flexed budget to present an actual versus budget comparison.
c. Explain how the use of a flexed budget provides variance information that is more meaningful to managers.

CHAPTER 18

Strategic Management Accounting

In this final chapter we bring together some of the concepts that have been developed in Part III, and look strategically in three ways. First, we look beyond the narrow accounting period to a long-term view of the organization through its value chain and the product/service life cycle. Second, we look beyond the organizational boundary to see its role in the supply chain from supplier through distributor to end customer. Third, we look at the organization's performance relative to its competitors – the idea of benchmarking. In our view of performance, we also look beyond purely financial numbers to show how non-financial performance measurement and a concern with business processes have extended the ambit of accounting.

In this chapter, we look first at trends in management accounting and then introduce the concept of *strategic* management accounting. We then look at the specific accounting techniques that can be used within the umbrella of strategic management accounting, many developed from the Japanese automobile industry. We conclude this chapter with an overview of lean thinking and how lean accounting has challenged some established management accounting practices.

Trends in management accounting

In their 2009 report *Management accounting tools for today and tomorrow*, the Chartered Institute of Management Accountants (CIMA, 2009) identified a number of trends in the use of the management accounting tools described in this book. In particular the report found that:

- Gross margin after full cost of sales, net profit margin after allocation of overhead, and contribution after variable costs are the most widely used financial measures.

- The balanced scorecard is the most widely used performance measurement system.
- Benchmarking is the dominant management accounting tool for organizations of all sizes.
- There is a high overall level of interest in product/service profitability analysis and customer profitability analysis.

The CIMA report also found that the tools most likely to be introduced by organizations in the following two years were the Balanced Scorecard, customer profitability analysis, and rolling forecasts. The more traditional tools of variance analysis and overhead allocation remain the most popular.

Respondents to the CIMA survey were asked about the main issues currently confronting the management accounting function in their organization. The issues which most concerned them were:

- software issues such as outdated, inflexible, or poorly integrated systems which required manual interventions to create reports;
- the quality of information provided to users in the face of internal customer demands for better, more timely, or bespoke information;
- the lack of suitably qualified finance personnel; and a lack of understanding about the contribution possible from management accountants, including from the accountants themselves (who admitted to inadequate knowledge of tools).

These trends suggest that many of the tools described in this book are commonly used in practice although there remain concerns about the quality of information and support provided by accountants to non-financial managers. The remainder of this chapter looks at more recent management accounting tools that are available to support non-financial managers in strategic decision making.

Strategic management accounting

Bhimani and Bromwich (2010) have shown that products now require far more innovation, flexibility, and differentiation to meet customer expectations and market competition as well as shorter life cycles and continuous quality improvement. Global supply chains and the pursuit of shareholder value have pushed manufacturing out of many Western countries, in part due to the high pre-production investment needed and the high cost of labour. At the same time, the 'number crunching' role of (particularly management) accountants has shifted to a more business advisory role of supporting managers' decision making.

This more strategic role for management accounting and management control is the subject of this chapter, building on Chapters 4 and 5 where we first introduced management control. From a strategic perspective, the definition of management control systems has evolved from a focus on formal, financially quantifiable information and now includes external information relating to markets, customers, and competitors; non-financial information about production processes; predictive infor-mation; and a broad array of decision support mechanisms and informal personal and social controls (Chenhall, 2003).

The term 'strategic management accounting' (SMA) was coined by Simmonds in 1981, who defined it as:

> the provision and analysis of management accounting data about a business and its competitors which is of use in the development and monitoring of the strategy of that business (pp. 278).

Simmonds argued that accounting should be more outward looking and help the firm evaluate its competitive position by collecting and analysing data on costs, prices, sales volumes, market share, and cash flows for its main competitors. Simmonds emphasized the learning curve through early experience with new products that leads to cost reductions and lower prices.

Bromwich (1990) argued that SMA is the management accountant's contribution to corporate strat-egy, and defined SMA as the provision and analysis of financial information on the firm's product mar-kets and competitors' costs and cost structures and the monitoring of the enterprise's strategies and those of its competitors in these markets over a number of periods (p. 28). Lord (1996) argued that firms should match their accounting emphasis with the firm's strategic position.

Tayles *et al.* (2002) argued that SMA has a role to play in providing the tools to assist a company to increase shareholder value, and proposed that greater attention should be given to intangible assets (see Chapter 6) and intellectual capital (see Chapter 7) as measures which could be used for internal and external benchmarking.

The term 'strategic management accounting' is not used widely in practice; nevertheless, the tools that often fall under the umbrella of SMA are available for use by accountants and non-accountants in planning, decision making, and control. These tools and techniques are described in this chapter.

In Chapter 4 we showed how accounting had extended its remit to non-financial performance meas-urement through techniques such as the Balanced Scorecard. Non-financial performance measures pro-vide a more strategic perspective on organizational performance because they provide a broader understanding of trends in performance than financial measures alone and they can be benchmarked between organizations. In Chapter 9, we showed the value of enterprise resource planning (ERP) systems and how a concern with horizontal business processes can be more useful than vertical departmental/business unit structures. ERP systems are being developed in three directions:

* supplier facing (supply chain management);
* customer facing (customer relationship management);
* management facing to support the information and decision-making needs of managers.

Various accounting techniques have been developed to provide more strategic tools for management accounting. Figure 18.1 shows a representation of strategic management accounting in terms of its relationships with suppliers, customers, and competitors over time.

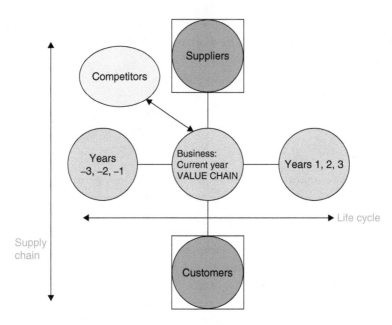

Figure 18.1   Representation of strategic management accounting.

Accounting techniques to support strategic management accounting

Cost management

Cost management is concerned with managing costs. This implies understanding what costs the business incurs and the drivers or causes of those costs. This process involves either reducing costs while maintaining the same levels of productivity, or maintaining costs while increasing levels of productivity through economies of scale or efficiencies in producing goods or services. Because cost management or cost control implies budgetary cuts rather than seeking efficiencies and reducing waste, a more accurate term may be cost improvement. Cost improvement needs to be exercised by all budget holders in order to ensure that limited resources are effectively utilized and budgets are not overspent. This is best achieved by understanding the causes of costs: the cost drivers. Understanding cost drivers and reviewing business processes can be used as tools to help in managing costs such as:

- Projects: why are they being undertaken?
- Employment costs: what tasks are people performing, and why and how are they performing those tasks?
- Material or consumable costs: how much waste is there, and what are the causes of that waste?

- Travel: what causes people to travel to other locations and by what methods? Is video conferencing a better use of time and money?
- Information technology costs: what data is being processed and why? Is the information being provided still used by managers?

The questions that can be asked in relation to most costs are: What is being done? Why is it being done? When is it being done? Where is it being done? How is it being done? The answers to these questions can lead to continuous improvement.

A particular approach, termed cost down in some industries (notably automotive), involves working with suppliers to reduce the cost of purchased materials or components, improve purchasing processes, reduce inventory, and eliminate waste. The Toyota Production System (or TPS) is internationally recognized for its cost down approach.

TPS empowers team members to optimize quality by constantly improving processes and eliminating unnecessary waste in natural, human, and corporate resources. TPS influences every aspect of Toyota's organization and includes a common set of values, knowledge, and procedures. It entrusts employees with well-defined responsibilities in each production step and encourages every team member to strive for overall improvement. TPS comprises: *just-in-time* – having smooth, continuous, optimized workflows rather than investing in inventory; *jidoka* – building in quality rather than post-production inspection for faults; and *kaizen* – improvement as a continuous process (http://www.toyota.com.au/toyota/company/operations/toyota-production-system; and Toyota, undated). Just-in-time, jidoka, and kaizen are described later in this chapter.

Strategic management accounting information such as the total cost of ownership and supplier cost analysis (see Chapter 11) can be used to understand the costs and profits of suppliers and distributors and determine whether excess profits are being earned by some parts of the supply chain. For example, in the automotive industry, the large vehicle assemblers collect vast quantities of information about their suppliers' costs: the cost of labour, the cost of manufacturing equipment and its capacity, and the cost of raw materials. This information supports negotiations between the assembler's purchasing department and its suppliers because the assembler knows the costs the supplier is likely to have or should have if it is efficient after allowing a reasonable profit margin. This is powerful information during the negotiation process and can lead to collaboration to improve efficiencies in the supply chain.

Activity-based management

Chapter 13 introduced activity-based costing as an overhead allocation technique, which was also mentioned in relation to activity-based budgeting in Chapter 16. Activity-based management is a broader concept which focuses on controlling activities that consume resources, i.e. controlling costs at their source. Kaplan and Cooper (1998) defined activity-based management (ABM) as:

> the entire set of actions that can be taken, on a better informed basis, with activity-based cost information. With ABM, the organization accomplishes its outcomes with fewer demands on organizational resources (p. 137).

Kaplan and Cooper differentiated *operational* and *strategic* ABM. The former is concerned with doing things right: increasing efficiency, lowering costs, and enhancing asset utilization. Strategic ABM is about doing the right things, by attempting to alter the demand for activities to increase profitability.

Strategic ABM can be used in relation to product mix and pricing decisions. It works by shifting the mix of activities from unprofitable applications to profitable ones. The demand for activities is a result of decisions about products, services, and customers. Activity-based costing was the first application of activity-based management. It attempted to remove the distortions caused by traditional methods of overhead allocation based on direct labour.

Strategic ABM extends the domain of analysis beyond production costs to marketing, selling, and administrative expenses, reflecting the belief that the demand for resources arises not only from products/ services but from customers, distribution, and delivery channels. Cost information can be used to modify a firm's relationships with its customers, transforming unprofitable customers into profitable ones through negotiations on price, product mix, delivery, and payment arrangements. Strategic ABM can be pushed further back along the value chain to suppliers, designers, and developers where the cost of purchased goods and services can be reduced. ABM can also inform product/service design and development decisions, which can result in a lowering of production costs for new products/services *before* they reach the production stage.

The ABM process involves moving from managing the vertical hierarchical structure to managing horizontal business processes, which we first saw in Chapter 9.

Figure 18.2 shows the CAM-I ABCM model of activity-based cost management. The vertical 'cost assignment view' is about *what products/services cost*. It shows how resources are tracked to cost objects (product/services, processes, customers, etc.) using activity-based costing (ABC) techniques (see Chapter 13). ABC information is used to analyse the sources of profitability (product, customer, distribution channel), improve pricing, and determine whether it is better to make a product in-house or to subcontract it (the make versus buy decision – see Chapter 11). Using ABC techniques, product-related actions can reduce the resources required to produce existing products/services. Pricing and product substitution decisions can shift the mix from difficult-to-produce items to simple-to-produce ones.

The horizontal 'process view' is concerned with *why products/services cost*. The horizontal view takes an activity-based management (ABM) approach and uses a variety of financial and non-financial performance measures to focus on cost reduction, business process re-engineering (see Chapter 9), the cost of quality (Chapter 11), and continuous improvement. By comparing activity-based costs with performance measures such as quality, productivity, cycle time (from order to delivery), etc. it is possible using the horizontal view to make decisions about performance improvement. In the horizontal perspective, redesign, process improvement, focused production facilities, and new technology can enable the same products or services to be produced with fewer resources.

The horizontal view, in reflecting the value chain of an organization and its fundamental business processes, takes a more strategic approach than the financially dominated and typically short-term orientation of the vertical focus on cost objects.

Strategic management accounting also includes other costing approaches. We consider life cycle costing, target costing, and kaizen.

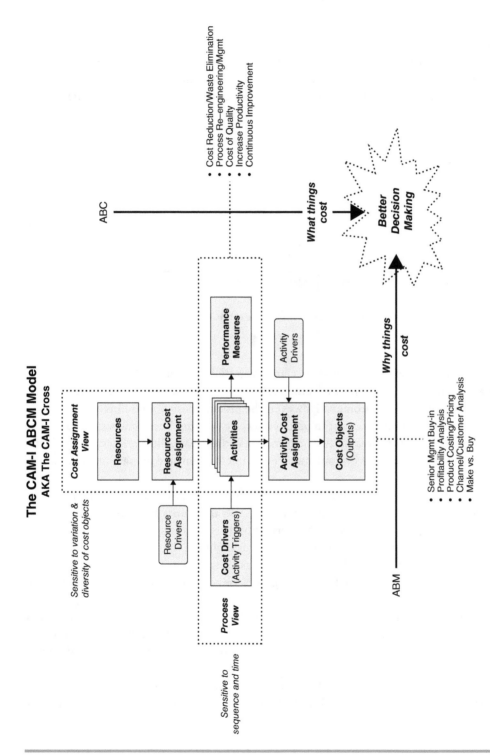

Figure 18.2   CAM-I ABCM model. www.cam-i.org

Life cycle costing

All products and services go through a typical life cycle, from introduction, through growth and maturity to decline. The life cycle of a product is contingent on the product and industry – it may vary from months, as with a high technology product, to many decades, as in the case of mining. The life cycle is represented in Figure 18.3.

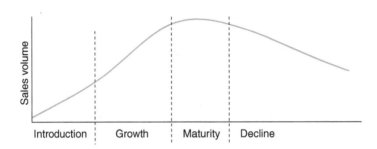

Figure 18.3   Typical product/service life cycle.

Over time, sales volume increases, then plateaus, and eventually declines. Management accounting has traditionally focused on the period after product design and development, when the product/service is in production for sale to customers. However, the product design phase involves substantial costs that may not be taken into account in product/service costing. These costs may have been capitalized (see Chapters 3 and 6) or treated as an expense in earlier years. Similarly, when products/services are discontinued, the costs of discontinuance are rarely identified as part of the product/service cost.

Life cycle costing estimates and accumulates the costs of a product/service over its entire life cycle, from inception to abandonment. This helps to determine whether the profits generated during the production phase cover all the life cycle costs. This information helps managers make decisions about future product/service development and the need for cost control during the development phase. This kind of costing does not appear in financial statements because it ignores the accounting treatment as to whether a cost was capitalized or expensed, and also ignores the accounting period in which payment was made.

The design and development phase can determine up to 80% of costs in many advanced technology industries. This is because decisions about the production process and the technology investment required to support production are made long before the product/services are actually produced. This is shown in Figure 18.4.

Consequently, efforts to reduce costs during the production phase are unlikely to be successful when the costs are committed or locked in as a result of technology and process decisions made during the design phase.

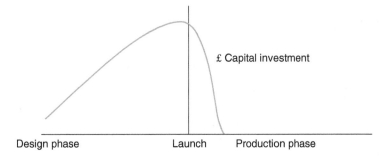

Figure 18.4   Investment decisions.

Target costing

Target costing is concerned with managing whole-of-life costs *during the design phase*. It has four stages:

1. Determining the target price that customers will be prepared to pay for the product/service.
2. Deducting a target profit margin to determine the target cost, which becomes the cost to which the product/service should be engineered.
3. Estimating the actual cost of the product/service based on the current design.
4. Investigating ways of reducing the estimated cost to the target cost.

target price – target profit margin = target cost

The technique was developed in the Japanese automotive industry and is customer oriented. Its aim is to build a product at a cost that can be recovered over the product life cycle through a price that customers will be willing to pay to obtain the benefits (which in turn drive the product cost). Target costing is equally applicable to a service. For example, the design of an internet banking service or an online retail ordering system involves substantial upfront investment, the benefits of which must be recoverable in the selling price over the expected life cycle of the service.

Using a simple example, a new product is expected to achieve a desired volume and market share at a price of £1,000, from which the manufacturer wants a 20% margin, leaving a target cost of £800. Current estimates suggest the cost as £900. An investigation seeks to find which elements of design, manufacture, or purchasing contribute to the costs and how those costs can be reduced, or whether features can be eliminated that cannot be justified in the target price. This is an iterative process, often referred to as *value engineering*, a process of improving the ratio of 'function to cost', in which value can be increased either by improving the function or reducing the cost. Such an investigation is usually a team effort involving designers, purchasing, production/manufacturing, marketing, and accounting staff. The target cost is rarely achieved from the beginning of the manufacturing phase. Japanese companies tend to take a long-term perspective on business (see Chapter 13) and aim to achieve the target cost over the life cycle of the product.

This process is essential if the life cycle costs of the product/service are to be managed and recovered in the (target) selling price. Importantly, this process of estimating costs over the product/service life cycle and establishing a target selling price takes place *before* decisions are finalized about product/service design and the production process to be used.

Kaizen costing

Kaizen is a Japanese term literally meaning 'improvement'. It means the process of making continuous, incremental improvements to the production process. While target costing is applied during the design phase, kaizen costing is applied during the production phase of the life cycle when large innovations may not be possible. Target costing focuses on the product/service. Kaizen focuses on the production process, seeking efficiencies in production, purchasing, and distribution.

Like target costing, kaizen establishes a desired cost-reduction target and relies on teamwork and employee empowerment to improve processes and reduce costs. This is because employees are assumed to have more expertise in the production process than managers. Frequently, cost-reduction targets are set and producers work collaboratively with suppliers who often have cost-reduction targets imposed on them by their customers.

Global competition, the changing demands of the marketplace, and advanced manufacturing technologies have led to the need for more sophisticated approaches to management accounting and how cost information is used for planning, decision making, and control.

Just-in-time

Just-in-time (JIT) aims to improve productivity and eliminate waste by obtaining manufacturing components in the right quantity and quality, at the right time and place to meet the demands of the manufacturing cycle. It requires close cooperation within the supply chain and is generally associated with continuous manufacturing processes with low inventory holdings, a result of eliminating buffer inventories considered waste between the different stages of manufacture. Many of these costs are hidden in a traditional cost accounting system. JIT relies on *kanban*, a Japanese term referring to signals between different points in the production process which provide information on when a raw material or component is required. Rather than relying on comprehensive inventory systems, kanbans can be as simple as visual signals (e.g. the presence or absence of a part in a process) to prompt reordering.

The introduction of JIT by many manufacturing companies is intended to bring components from suppliers to the assembly line as they are required for production, rather than for the manufacturer to hold large quantities of raw materials to meet future production requirements. JIT has resulted in a significant reduction in inventories and so inventory valuation becomes less relevant.

Jidoka

Along with just-in-time and kaizen, jidoka is the third element in the Toyota Production System (see earlier in this chapter). *Jidoka* is sometimes called *autonomation*, meaning automation with human intelligence. In an example made famous by the detailed study of Toyota's methods by Womack, Jones, and Roos (1990), Toyota empowered its production line employees to stop the assembly line when they identified a quality problem. Staff from all the functional areas would work towards solving the *cause* of the problem before restarting the assembly line.

Jidoka highlights the causes of problems because work stops immediately when a problem first occurs. This leads to improvements in the processes that build in quality by eliminating the root causes of defects. While this delayed production output in the short term, the end result was far fewer quality problems in the long run. By contrast, Western manufacturers have traditionally emphasized production line throughput but spent large sums of money on final product inspection and rectification – without solving the causes of quality problems (a good example of analysing the cost of quality into conformance and non-conformance costs is in Chapter 11).

Lean production, lean accounting, and backflush costing

Western organizations became aware of lean production methods in the 1990s, with the publication of *The Machine That Changed the World* (Womack, Jones, and Roos, 1990), a five-year study of the automotive industry which described the Toyota Production System. 'Lean thinking' arose as a result of the shift from mass production to more efficient production techniques that were enabled by modern manufacturing, information, and communications technologies (Womack and Jones, 2003). Lean thinking is a management philosophy that focuses on customer value and results in the use of fewer resources, a reduction of waste, and improved outputs from existing resources. The 'lean' approach focuses on only doing activities that add value and eliminating those that do not.

Lean production focuses on production processes as a continuous flow, rather than on the hierarchical structures in an organization chart. The adoption of flow production (in which products are manufactured in a continuous process) significantly reduces the cycle time from order to delivery. As cycle time decreases, so does the need for work-in-process inventory. The lean production company can begin to produce to meet demand (demand 'pulls' production), rather than build finished goods inventory (production 'pushes' inventory). Automotive assemblers speak of the concept of the 'five-day car' in which a customer's order for a specific vehicle could be assembled and available for delivery within five days of the order being placed. This goal is only achievable with a lean production system. The benefits of lean production are lower costs, reduced waste, higher product quality, and shorter lead times.

While this concept of removing non-value-adding activities is often applied to the actual production of goods, it can also be applied to the work done by accountants. But traditional costing approaches do not recognize the importance of just-in-time, kaizen, and jidoka processes that aim to improve productivity and eliminate waste.

Lean accounting focuses on simplifying processes, reducing waste, and speeding up the accounting function to improve decision making, reduce errors, and add greater value to the organization. It involves using some simpler techniques such as direct costing of items (rather than including overheads – which is a difficult, time-consuming, and often confusing activity, as we saw in Chapter 11), eliminating activities such as standard costing and variance analysis (see Chapter 17), and introducing simplified management reporting to improve decision making.

In Chapter 8, we discussed accounting for inventory in detail. Under traditional costing approaches, each raw material issue transaction is recorded separately. However, under the principle of lean accounting, this is a wasteful bureaucratic process. Backflush costing (or 'backflushing') aims to eliminate detailed transaction processing. Rather than tracking each movement of materials, the output from the production process determines the amount of materials to be transferred from raw materials to finished goods – based on the *expected* (not actual) usage and cost of materials. Importantly, under backflush costing there is no separate accounting for work-in-progress. The timing of the recording of costs is based on a *trigger point*.

In its simplest version, backflush costing transfers the cost of raw materials from suppliers, and conversion costs, to finished goods inventory when production of finished goods is complete (the trigger point). In a modified version of backflush costing, trigger points occur when raw materials are purchased and when finished goods are completed. Variance analysis is impossible under backflush costing as the *standard cost* of labour and materials is used, not the actual cost and quantity.

Instead of these traditional approaches, lean accounting relies on value-stream accounting. Value-stream accounting involves assigning employees and assets to a single value stream, rather than costs being allocated to a department or cost centre, or across multiple business processes. Performance measures (financial and non-financial) are developed for each value stream and overhead costs are directed to specific value streams, resulting in less arbitrary overhead allocations.

Value-stream costing measures how much value is added in each step of the process, by costing the various value streams backwards from the customer to their source. It produces a simple summarized *direct* costing of each value stream, and in many cases its proponents argue that it is not necessary to calculate product or service costs. This is because *value-based pricing* sets the prices of products/services according to the value created for customers. This approach is in contrast to traditional cost-plus pricing methods which can lead to serious errors in pricing because of the assumed (and false) relationship between price and cost. The proponents of value-stream pricing argue that the price of a product is unrelated to the cost of manufacturing and supplying that product. Instead the price of a product or service is entirely determined by the amount of value created by the product in the eyes of the customer.

Case study 18.1 provides an illustration of one company's focus on creating value for its customers, its use of strategic management accounting, and its lean approach to the accounting function.

Case study 18.1: TNA and strategic management accounting

TNA is a multinational packaging equipment supplier providing equipment to the food industry. It is privately owned and hence does not need to satisfy stock market pressures for short-term performance. About 10% of the company's annual sales revenue has been invested in research and development (R&D) through which TNA developed a computer numerically controlled (CNC) packaging machine that was more efficient than its competitors. Although the price of TNA's equipment was 2–3 times more than competitive equipment, it operates 50–100% faster than conventional packers and has a much lower reject rate. Hence, despite its price, TNA's products provide value to their customers that their customers are willing to pay for. TNA's machines have worldwide patents, but despite patent protection, two competitors breached the company's patents and substantial sums were spent to defend TNA's intellectual property. The company has continued to expand geographically and TNA now has offices around the world. The manufacture of the CNC equipment was outsourced to reduce TNA's capital investment and avoid the capacity utilization problem faced by its competitors.

TNA's major operating costs are salaries, premises, travel, advertising, and exhibitions. Most of these costs are driven either by export market development or R&D. In particular, international growth has meant rapidly increasing operating expenses. TNA has had a dual focus on growth and cash flow. However, in developing its business, TNA has not relied on traditional accounting-based financial reports.

TNA did not have profit targets. Short-term profit was not meaningful to the owners as expenditure on R&D, export market development, and patent litigation was incurred a year or more in advance of any income generation. The company instead emphasized sales targets as part of a strategy for market development, along with continual expenditure on R&D. Because there was no attempt to allocate R&D or export marketing costs over products, the direct (subcontracted) manufacturing cost was a relatively small proportion of the selling price. Consequently, product costing did not rely on management accounting data.

As TNA became larger, the owners began to focus more on growth in market share. They developed a sophisticated spreadsheet that contained an industry-level top-down analysis of markets and competitors. It calculated the installed packaging machine base by market segment, adding a factor for market growth and the anticipated replacement of old machines by customers or potential customers. This was then adjusted by the relative performance of competitors' installed machines to produce a theoretical market size at the standard running speed for its own equipment. Using this model, TNA was able to estimate how many machines the company could sell and which of its competitors were likely to lose market share (most had the disadvantage of manufacturing their own equipment and needed to manage an increasingly under-utilized capacity and high fixed cost base). TNA modified its marketing strategy to target the customers of weaker competitors, in order to force those competitors into losses and thereby secure even more market share from their failure. Several of TNA's competitors failed or were purchased by TNA as a result.

TNA's owners developed a network of social contacts from employees and customers to competitors and suppliers by attending industry events such as exhibitions and trade fairs, reading the business press, and entertaining. Over time the owners developed a comprehensive market intelligence that they believed was superior to that of any of their competitors. TNA's spreadsheet model was regularly modified in an iterative fashion after market knowledge was gained through these social events. This knowledge became the driver of TNA's continuous investment in both export market development and R&D.

Market share became a key performance measure. The spreadsheet also led to strategic decisions to expand its product range, first to a stainless steel construction and second to the development of a low-cost machine. Both met emerging market needs and the desire for increased market share. TNA's strategy and its use of the spreadsheet to inform that strategy was an example of the use of strategic management accounting and a lean accounting approach driven by TNA's owner – an engineer.

The full TNA case study is available from Collier, P.M. (2005). Entrepreneurial cognition and the construction of a relevant accounting. *Management Accounting Research*, 16(3), 321–39.

Conclusion

Strategic management accounting provides the opportunity for management accounting and other performance information to be linked with strategy and continuous improvement. In doing so, the scope of management accounting extends beyond the organization and also extends beyond the financial year time horizon. It also moves from a vertical or hierarchical view of organization structure and production of goods and services to an alternate view that sees horizontal business processes as more important. Various techniques are available under the umbrella of strategic management accounting to help managers achieve organizational objectives and compete more cost-effectively. The introduction of lean accounting principles also calls into question some of the taken-for-granted management accounting tools and techniques described in this book, although those techniques remain in common usage.

This book has attempted to integrate the tools and techniques of accounting as though they were rational, while also introducing alternative ways of seeing accounting through interpretive and critical perspectives. It is hoped that this book may also encourage readers to undertake research into accounting, either in an academic environment or in their own business organizations, in order to challenge conventional wisdom and better understand the context in which accounting is practised and the consequences and limitations of the use of accounting information for decision making.

Published financial statements are to a large degree consistent across companies, industries, and nations as a result of IFRS (see Chapter 6), and have the ability to be analysed with common tools. This is a necessity when the *representation* of financial performance is so important for the efficient operation of capital markets. However, the differences in business context and the variety of management accounting techniques that are available, each imbued with their own limitations and assumptions, pose a greater challenge to the solving of organizational problems by managers in product markets.

The power that often accompanies the role of accountants is that they do understand the numbers, both financial and non-financial. The challenge for non-accounting managers is to understand the numbers sufficiently well to be able to contribute to the formulation and implementation of business strategy and communicate with accountants. Those managers who do not understand or who do not want to understand the numbers are likely to be increasingly marginalized in their organizations.

References

Bhimani, A. and Bromwich, M. (2010). *Management Accounting: retrospect and prospect*. London: Elsevier/CIMA Publishing.

Bromwich, M. (1990). The case for strategic management accounting: the role of accounting information for strategy in competitive markets. *Accounting, Organizations and Society*, 15(1/2), 27–46.

Chartered Institute of Management Accountants (CIMA) (2009). Management accounting tools for today and tomorrow. http://www.cimaglobal.com/Documents/Thought_leadership_docs/CIMA%20Tools%20and%20Techniques%20 30-11-09%20PDF.pdf.

Chenhall, R. H. (2003). Management control systems design within its organizational context: findings from contingency-based research and directions for the future. *Accounting, Organizations and Society*, 28, 127–68.

Collier, P. M. (2005). Entrepreneurial cognition and the construction of a relevant accounting, *Management Accounting Research*, 16(3), 321–39.

Kaplan, R. S. and Cooper, R. (1998). *Cost and Effect: Using Integrated Cost Systems to Drive Profitability and Performance*. Boston, MA: Harvard Business School Press.

Lord, B. R. (1996). Strategic management accounting: the emperor's new clothes? *Management Accounting Research*, 7, 347–66.

Simmonds, K. (1981). Strategic management accounting. *Management Accounting*, 59(4), 269.

Tayles, M., Bramley, A., Adshead, N., and Farr, J. (2002). Dealing with the management of intellectual capital: the potential role of strategic management accounting, Accounting, *Auditing and Accountability Journal*, 15(2), 251–67.

Toyota (undated). *Toyota Production System and what it means for your business* http://www.toyota-forklifts.eu/SiteCollectionDocuments/PDF%20files/Toyota%20Production%20System%20Brochure.pdf.

Womack, J. P. and Jones, D. T. (2003). *Lean Thinking: Banish Waste and Create Wealth in Your Corporation*. London: Free Press.

Womack, J. P., Jones, D. T., and Roos, D. (1990). *The Machine that Changed the World*. New York: Rawson Associates.

Further reading

One of the aims of this book has been to encourage readers to access the research-based academic literature of accounting, in particular in relation to the broader social, historical, and contextual influences on accounting; the organizational and behavioural consequences of accounting information; and the assumptions and limitations underlying the tools and techniques used by accountants. For those who wish to read further, whether as part of their preparation for academic research at postgraduate level or as part of their personal pursuit of greater knowledge, some recommended additional reading is listed below.

Books

Alvesson, M. and Willmott, H. (Eds) (1992). *Critical Management Studies*. London: Sage.

Ashton, D., Hopper, T., and Scapens, R.W. (Eds) (1995). *Issues in Management Accounting* (2nd edn). London: Prentice Hall.

Berry, A. J., Broadbent, J., and Otley, D. (Eds) (2005). *Management Control: Theories, Issues and Performance* (2nd edn). London: Palgrave Macmillan.

Bhimani, A. and Bromwich, M. (2010). *Management Accounting: retrospect and prospect*. London: Elsevier/CIMA Publishing.

Chapman, C. S. (Ed.) (2005). *Controlling Strategy: Management, Accounting, and Performance Measurement*. Oxford: Oxford University Press.

Heliar, C. and Bebbington, J. (Eds) (2004). *Taking Ethics to Heart*. Edinburgh: Institute of Chartered Accountants of Scotland.

Hope, J. and Fraser, R. (2003). *Beyond Budgeting: How Managers Can Break Free from the Annual Performance Trap*. Boston, MA: Harvard Business School Press.

Hopwood, A. G. and Miller, P. (1994). *Accounting as Social and Institutional Practice*. Cambridge: Cambridge University Press.

Johnson, H. T. and Kaplan, R. S. (1987). *Relevance Lost: The Rise and Fall of Management Accounting*. Boston, MA: Harvard Business School Press.

Jones, T. C. (1995). *Accounting and the Enterprise: A Social Analysis*. London: Routledge.

Kaplan, R. S. and Cooper, R. (1998). *Cost and Effect: Using Integrated Cost Systems to Drive Profitability and Performance*. Boston, MA: Harvard Business School Press.

Kaplan, R. S. and Norton, D. P. (2001). *The Strategy-Focused Organization: How Balanced Scorecard Companies Thrive in the New Business Environment*. Boston, MA: Harvard Business School Press.

Macintosh, N. and Quattrone, P. (2010). *Management Accounting and Control Systems* (2nd edn). Chichester, UK: John Wiley & Sons.

Munro, R. and Mouritsen, J. (Eds) (1996). *Accountability: Power, Ethos and the Technologies of Managing*. London: Thomson.

Puxty, A. G. (1993). *The Social and Organizational Context of Management Accounting*. London: Academic Press.

Ryan, B., Scapens, R. W., and Theobald, M. (2002). *Research Method and Methodology in Finance and Accounting* (2nd edn). London: Thomson.

Scott, W. R. (1998). *Organizations: Rational, Natural, and Open Systems* (4th edn). London: Prentice Hall.

Articles published in the following journals

- *Accounting, Auditing and Accountability Journal*
- *Accounting, Organizations and Society*
- *British Accounting Review*
- *Critical Perspectives in Accounting*
- *Financial Accountability and Management* (public sector)
- *Journal of Accounting and Organizational Change*
- *Journal of Management Accounting Research* (US)
- *Management Accounting Research* (UK)
- *Qualitative Research in Accounting and Management*.

These articles are generally available online for students through university libraries.

Questions

18.1   Identify the changes to the business environment that have led to a more strategic focus for management control.

18.2   Explain how the role of management accounting has expanded beyond its traditional scope to incorporate a more strategic role.

18.3   Contrast how lean accounting differs from traditional management accounting in relation to product costing.

Supporting Information

Part IV contains the following supplementary material:

- Readings
- Glossary of Accounting Terms
- Solutions to Questions
- Index

Readings

A rationale for this book was to provide a theoretical underpinning to accounting, drawn from accounting research, to assist in interpretation and critical questioning. This underpinning provides a critical perspective on the most common accounting techniques, questioning taken-for-granted assumptions and describing the social and organizational context in which accounting exists. In Part IV, we reproduce two readings from the academic literature. These readings each illustrate very practical issues in management accounting and control.

Readings

1. Cooper and Kaplan (1988). How cost accounting distorts product costs.
2. Dent (1991). Accounting and organizational cultures: a field study of the emergence of a new organizational reality.

The article by Cooper and Kaplan is a classic, explaining clearly how traditional management accounting techniques have distorted management information and the decisions made by managers. The authors criticize the distinction between variable and fixed costs, the limitations of marginal costing, and the arbitrary methods by which overhead costs are allocated to products. The activity-based approach recommended by Cooper and Kaplan treats all costs as variable, although only some vary with volume. This paper was the foundation for the development of activity-based costing which was described in Chapter 13.

Jeremy Dent's case study of EuroRail remains, despite its age, a highly regarded field study of accounting change in which organizations are portrayed as cultures, i.e. systems of knowledge, belief, and values. Prior to Dent's study, the dominant culture in EuroRail was engineering and production, but this culture was displaced by economic and accounting concerns that constructed the railway as a profit-seeking enterprise. Dent traced the introduction of a revised corporate planning system, the amendment of capital expenditure approval procedures, and the revision of budgeting systems, each of which shifted power from railway engineers to business managers. Dent describes how accounting played a role 'in constructing specific knowledges' (p. 727 *in the original source*). This paper provides an important case study of the role of culture and accounting in organizational change, the topic of Chapters 4 and 5.

Reading 1

How Cost Accounting Distorts Product Costs

The traditional cost system that defines variable costs as varying in the short term with production will misclassify these costs as fixed.

by Robin Cooper and Robert S. Kaplan

In order to make sensible decisions concerning the products they market, managers need to know what their products cost. Product design, new product introduction decisions, and the amount of effort expended on trying to market a given product or product line will be influenced by the anticipated cost and profitability of the product. Conversely, if product profitability appears to drop, the question of discontinuance will be raised. Product costs also can play an important role in setting prices, particularly for customized products with low sales volumes and without readily available market prices.

The cumulative effect of decisions on product design, introduction, support, discontinuance, and pricing helps define a firm's strategy. If the product cost information is distorted, the firm can follow an inappropriate and unprofitable strategy. For example, the low-cost producer often achieves competitive advantage by servicing a broad range of customers. This strategy will be successful if the economies of scale exceed the additional costs, the diseconomies of scope, caused by producing and servicing a more diverse product line. If the cost system does not correctly attribute the additional costs to the products that cause them, then the firm might end up competing in segments where the scope-related costs exceed the benefits from larger scale production.

Similarly, a differentiated producer achieves competitive advantage by meeting specialized customers' needs with products whose costs of differentiation are lower than the price premiums charged for special features and services. If the cost system fails to measure differentiation costs properly, then the firm might choose to compete in segments that are actually unprofitable.

Full vs. Variable Cost

Despite the importance of cost information, disagreement still exists about whether product costs should be measured by full or by variable cost. In a full-cost system, fixed production costs are allocated to products so that reported product costs measure total manufacturing costs. In a variable cost system, the fixed costs are not allocated and product costs reflect only the marginal cost of manufacturing.

Academic accountants, supported by economists, have argued strongly that variable costs are the relevant ones for product decisions. They have demonstrated, using increasingly complex models, that setting marginal revenues equal to marginal costs will produce the highest profit. In contrast, accountants in practice continue to report full costs in their cost accounting systems.

The definition of variable cost used by academic accountants assumes that product decisions have a short-time horizon, typically a month or a quarter. Costs are variable only if they vary directly with monthly or quarterly changes in production volume. Such a definition is appropriate if the volume of production of all products can be changed at will and there is no way to change simultaneously the level of fixed costs.

In practice, managers reject this short-term perspective because the decision to offer a product creates a long-term commitment to manufacture, market, and support that product. Given this perspective, short-term variable cost is an inadequate measure of product cost.

While full cost is meant to be a surrogate for long-run manufacturing costs, in nearly all of the companies we visited, management was not convinced that their full-cost systems were adequate for its product-related decisions. In particular, management did not believe their systems accurately reflected the costs of resources consumed to manufacture products. But they were also unwilling to adopt a variable-cost approach.

Of the more than 20 firms we visited and documented, Mayers Tap, Rockford, and Schrader Bellows provided particularly useful insights on how product costs were systematically distorted.[1]

These companies had several significant common characteristics.

They all produced a large number of distinct products in a single facility. The products formed several distinct product lines and were sold through diverse marketing channels. The range in demand volume for products within a product line was high, with sales of high-volume products between 100 and 1,000 times greater than sales of low-volume products. As a consequence, products were manufactured and shipped in highly varied lot sizes. While our findings are based upon these three companies, the same effects were observed at several other sites.

In all three companies, product costs played an important role in the decisions that surrounded the introduction, pricing, and discontinuance of products. Reported product costs also appeared to play a significant role in determining how much effort should be assigned to marketing and selling products.

Typically, the individual responsible for introducing new products also was responsible for setting prices. Cost-plus pricing to achieve a desired level of gross margin predominantly was used for the special products, though substantial modifications to the resulting estimated prices occurred when direct competition existed. Such competition was common for high-volume products but rarely occurred for the low-volume items. Frequently, no obvious market prices existed for low-volume products because they had been designed to meet a particular customer's needs.

Accuracy of Product Costs

Managers in all three firms expressed serious concerns about the accuracy of their product-costing systems.

For example, Rockford attempted to obtain much higher margins for its low-volume products to compensate, on an ad hoc basis, for the gross under-estimates of costs that it believed the cost system produced for these products. But management was not able to justify its decisions on cutoff points to identify low-volume products or the magnitude of the ad hoc margin increases. Further, Rockford's management believed that its faulty cost system explained the ability of small firms to compete effectively against it for high-volume business. These small firms, with no apparent economic or technological advantage, were winning high-volume business with prices that were at or below Rockford's reported costs. And the small firms seemed to be prospering at these prices.

At Schrader Bellows, production managers believed that certain products were not earning their keep because they were so difficult to produce. But the cost system reported that these products were among the most profitable in the line. The managers also were convinced that they could make certain products as efficiently as anybody else. Yet competitors were consistently pricing comparable products considerably lower. Management suspected that the cost system contributed to this problem.

At Mayers Tap, the financial accounting profits were always much lower than those predicted by the cost system, but no one could explain the discrepancy. Also, the senior managers were concerned by their failure to predict which bids they would win or lose. Mayers Tap often won bids that had been overpriced because it did not really want the business, and lost bids it had deliberately underpriced in order to get the business.

Two-Stage Cost Allocation System

The cost systems of all companies we visited had many common characteristics. Most important was the use of a two-stage cost allocation system:

in the first stage, costs were assigned to cost pools (often called cost centers), and in the second stage, costs were allocated from the cost pools to the products.

The companies used many different allocation bases in the first stage to allocate costs from plant overhead accounts to cost centers. Despite the variation in allocation bases in the first stage, however, all companies used direct labor hours in the second stage to allocate overhead from the cost pools to the products. Direct labor hours was used in the second allocation stage even when the production process was highly automated so that burden rates exceeded 1,000%. Figure A.1 illustrates a typical two-stage allocation process.

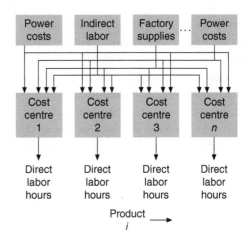

Figure A.1   The two-stage progress.

Of the three companies we examined in detail, only one had a cost accounting system capable of reporting variable product costs. Variable cost was identified at the budgeting stage in one other site, but this information was not subsequently used for product costing. The inability of the cost system to report variable cost was a common feature of many of the systems we observed. Reporting variable product costs was the exception, not the rule.

Firms used only one cost system even though costs were collected and allocated for several purposes, including product costing, operational control, and inventory valuation. The cost systems seemed to be designed primarily to perform the inventory valuation function for financial reporting because they had serious deficiencies for operational control (too delayed and too aggregate) and for product costing (too aggregate).

The Failure of Marginal Costing

The extensive use of fixed-cost allocations in all the companies we investigated contrasts sharply with a 65-year history of academics advocating marginal costing for product decisions. If the marginal-cost concept had been adopted by companies' management, then we would have expected to see product-costing systems that explicitly reported variable-cost information. Instead, we observed cost systems that reported variable as well as full costs in only a small minority of companies.

The traditional academic recommendation for marginal costing may have made sense when variable costs (labor, material, and some overhead) were a relatively high proportion of total manufactured cost and when product diversity was sufficiently small that there was not wide variation in the demands made by different products on the firm's production and marketing resources. But these conditions are no longer typical of many of today's organizations. Increasingly, overhead (most of it considered 'fixed') is becoming a larger share of total manufacturing costs. In addition, the plants we examined are being asked to produce an increasing variety of products that make quite different demands on equipment and support departments. Thus, even if direct or marginal

costing were once a useful recommendation to management, direct costing, even if correctly implemented, is not likely a solution and may perhaps be a major problem for product costing in the contemporary manufacturing environment.

The Failure of Fixed-Cost Allocations

While we consistently observed managers avoiding the use of variable or marginal costs for their product-related decisions, we observed also their discomfort with the full-cost allocations produced by their existing cost systems. We believe that we have identified the two major sources for the discomfort.

The first problem arises from the use of direct labor hours in the second allocation stage to assign costs from cost centers to products. This procedure may have been adequate many decades ago when direct labor was the principal value-adding activity in the material conversion process. But as firms introduce more automated machinery, direct labor is increasingly engaged in setup and supervisory functions (rather than actually performing the work on the product) and no longer represents a reasonable surrogate for resource demands by product.

In many of the plants we visited, labor's main tasks are to load the machines and to act as troubleshooters. Labor frequently works on several different products at the same time so that it becomes impossible to assign labor hours intelligently to products. Some of the companies we visited had responded to this situation by beginning experiments using machine hours instead of labor hours to allocate costs from cost pools to products (for the second stage of the allocation process). Other companies, particularly those adopting just-in-time or continuous-flow production processes, were moving to material dollars as the basis for distributing costs from pools to products. Material dollars provide a less expensive method for cost allocation than machine hours because, as with labor hours, material dollars are collected by the existing cost system, A move to a machine-hour basis would require the collection of new data for many of these companies.

Shifting from labor hours to machine hours or material dollars provides some relief from the problem of using unrealistic bases for attributing costs to products. In fact, some companies have been experimenting with using all three allocation bases simultaneously: labor hours for those costs that vary with the number of labor hours worked (e.g., supervision – if the amount of labor in a product is high, the amount of supervision related to that product also is likely to be high), machine hours for those costs that vary with the number of hours the machine is running (e.g., power – the longer the machine is running the more power that is consumed by that product), and material dollars for those costs that vary with the value of material in the product (e.g., material handling – the higher the value of the material in the product, the greater the material-handling costs associated with those products are likely to be).

Using multiple allocation bases allows a finer attribution of costs to the products responsible for the incurrence of those costs. In particular, it allows for product diversity where the direct labor, machine hours, and material dollars consumed in the manufacture of different products are not directly proportional to each other.

For reported product costs to be correct, however, the allocation bases used must be capable of accounting for all aspects of product diversity. Such an accounting is not always possible even using all three volume-related allocation bases we described. As the number of product items manufactured increases, so does the number of direct labor hours, machine hours, and material dollars consumed. The designer of the cost system, in adopting these bases, assumes that all allocated costs have the same behavior; namely that they increase in direct relationship to the volume of product items manufactured. But there are many costs that vary with the diversity and complexity of products, not by the number of units produced.

The Cost of Complexity

The complexity costs of a full-line producer can be illustrated as follows. Consider two identical plants. One plant produces 1,000,000 units of product A. The second plant produces 100,000 units of product A and 900,000 units of 199 similar products. (The similar products have sales volumes that vary from 100 to 100,000 units.)

The first plant has a simple production environment and requires limited manufacturing-support facilities. Few setups, expediting, and scheduling activities are required.

The other plant presents a much more complex production-management environment. Its 200 products have to be scheduled through the plant, requiring frequent setups, inventory movements, purchases, receipts, and inspections. To handle this complexity, the support departments must be larger and more sophisticated.

The traditional cost accounting system plays an important role in obfuscating the underlying relationship between the range of products produced and the size of the support departments. First, the costs of most support departments are classified as fixed, making it difficult to realize that these costs are systematically varying. Second, the use of volume-related allocation bases makes it difficult to recognize how these support-department costs vary.

Support-department costs must vary with something because they have been among the fastest growing in the overall cost structure of manufactured products. As the example demonstrates, support-department costs vary not with the volume of product items manufactured, rather they vary with the range of items produced (i.e., the complexity of the production process). The traditional definition of variable cost, with its monthly or quarterly perspective, views such costs as fixed because complexity-related costs do not vary significantly in such a short time frame. Across an extended period of time, however, the increasing complexity of the production process places additional demands on support departments, and their costs eventually and inevitably rise.

The output of a support department consists of the activities its personnel perform. These include such activities as setups, inspections, material handling, and scheduling. The output of the departments can be represented by the number of distinct activities that are performed or the number of transactions handled. Because most of the output of these departments consists of human activities, however, output can increase quite significantly before an immediate deterioration in the quality of service is detected. Eventually, the maximum output of the department is reached and additional personnel are requested. The request typically comes some time after the initial increase in diversity and output. Thus, support departments, while varying with the diversity of the demanded output, grow intermittently. The practice of annually budgeting the size of the departments further hides the underlying relationship between the mix and volume of demand and the size of the department. The support departments often are constrained to grow only when budgeted to do so.

Support-department costs are perhaps best described as 'discretionary' because they are budgeted and authorized each year. The questions we must address are: What determines the level of these discretionary fixed costs? Why, if these costs are not affected by the quantity of production, are there eight people in a support department and not one? What generates the work, if not physical quantities of inputs or outputs, that requires large support-department staffs? We believe the answers to these questions on the origins of discretionary overhead costs (i.e., what drives these costs) can be found by analyzing the activities or transactions demanded when producing a full and diverse line of products.

Transaction Costing

Low-volume products create more transactions per unit manufactured than their high-volume counterparts. The per unit share of these costs should, therefore, be higher for the low-volume products. But when volume-related bases are used exclusively to allocate support-department costs, high-volume and low-volume products receive similar transaction-related costs. When only volume-related bases are used for second-stage allocations, high-volume products receive an excessively high fraction of support-department costs and, therefore, subsidize the low-volume products.

As the range between low-volume and high-volume products increases, the degree of cross-subsidization rises. Support departments expand to cope with the additional complexity of more products, leading to increased overhead charges. The reported product cost of all products consequently increases. The high-volume products appear more expensive to produce than previously, even though they are not responsible for the additional costs. The costs triggered by the introduction of new, low-volume products are systematically shifted to high-volume products that may be placing relatively few demands on the plant's support departments.

Many of the transactions that generate work for production-support departments can be proxied by the number of setups. For example, the movement of material in the plant often occurs at the commencement or completion of a production run. Similarly, the majority of the time spent on parts inspection occurs just after a setup or change-over. Thus, while the support departments are engaged in a broad array of activities, a considerable portion of their costs may be attributed to the number of setups.

Not all of the support-department costs are related (or relatable) to the number of setups. The cost of setup personnel relates more to the quantity of setup hours than to the actual number of setups. The number of inspections of incoming material can be directly related to the number of material receipts, as would be the time spent moving the received material into inventory. The number of outgoing shipments can be used to predict the activity level of the finished-goods and shipping departments. The assignment of all these support costs with a transactions-based approach reinforces the effect of the setup-related costs because the low-sales-volume items tend to trigger more small incoming and outgoing shipments.

Schrader Bellows had recently performed a 'strategic cost analysis' that significantly increased the number of bases used to allocate costs to the products; many second-stage allocations used transactions costs to assign support-department costs to products. In particular, the number of setups allocated a sizable percentage of support-department costs to products.

The effect of changing these second-stage allocations from a direct labor to a transaction basis was dramatic. While the support-department costs accounted for about 50% of overhead (or about 25% of total costs), the change in the reported product costs ranged from about minus 10% to plus 1,000%. The significant change in the reported product costs for the low-volume items was due to the substantial cost of the support departments and the low batch size over which the transaction cost was spread.

Table A.1 shows the magnitude of the shift in reported product costs for seven representative products. The existing cost system reported gross margins that varied from 26% to 47%, while the strategic analysis showed gross margins that ranged from –258% to +46%. The trends in the two sets of reported product profitabilities were clear: the existing direct-labor-based system had identified the low-volume products as the most

Table A.1   Comparison of reported product costs at Schrader Bellows.

Product	Sales volume	Existing cost system		Transaction-based system		Percent of change	
		Unit cost[a]	Unit gross margin	Unit cost[a]	Unit gross margin	Unit cost	Unit gross margin
1	43,562	7.85	5.52	7.17	6.19	(8.7)	12.3
2	500	8.74	3.76	15.45	(2.95)	76.8	(178.5)
3	53	12.15	10.89	82.49	(59.45)	578.9	(645.9)
4	2,079	13.63	4.91	24.51	(5.97)	79.8	(221.6)
5	5,670	12.40	7.95	19.99	0.36	61.3	(93.4)
6	11,169	8.04	5.49	7.96	5.57	(1.0)	1.5
7	423	8.47	3.74	6.93	5.28	(18.2)	41.2

[a]The sum of total cost (sales volume × unit cost) for all seven products is different under the two systems because the seven products only represent a small fraction of total production.

profitable, while the strategic cost analysis indicated exactly the reverse.

There are three important messages in the table and in the company's findings in general.

- Traditional systems that assign costs to products using a single volume-related base seriously distort product costs.
- The distortion is systematic. Low-volume products are under-costed, and high-volume products are over-costed.
- Accurate product costs cannot, in general, be achieved by cost systems that rely only on volume-related bases (even multiple bases such as machine hours and material quantities) for second-stage allocations. A different type of allocation base must be used for overhead costs that vary with the number of transactions performed, as opposed to the volume of product produced.

The shift to transaction-related allocation bases is a more fundamental change to the philosophy of cost-systems design than is at first realized. In a traditional cost system that uses volume-related bases, the costing element is always the product. It is the product that consumes direct labor hours, machine hours, or material dollars. Therefore, it is the product that gets costed.

In a transaction-related system, costs are assigned to the units that caused the transaction to be originated. For example, if the transaction is a setup, then the costing element will be the production lot because each production lot requires a single setup. The same is true for purchasing activities, inspections, scheduling, and material movements. The costing element is no longer the product but those elements the transaction affects.

In the transaction-related costing system, the unit cost of a product is determined by dividing the cost of a transaction by the number of units in the costing element. For example, when the costing element is a production lot, the unit cost of a product is determined by dividing the production lot cost by the number of units in the production lot.

This change in the costing element is not trivial. In the Schrader Bellows strategic cost analysis (see table A.1), product seven appears to violate the strong inverse relationship between profits and production-lot size for the other six products. A more detailed analysis of the seven products, however, showed that product seven was assembled with components also used to produce two high-volume products (numbers one and six) and that it was the production-lot size of the components that was the dominant cost driver, not the assembly-lot size, or the shipping-lot size.

In a traditional cost system, the value of commonality of parts is hidden. Low-volume components appear to cost only slightly more than their high-volume counterparts. There is no incentive to design products with common parts. The shift to transaction-related costing identifies the much lower costs that derive from designing products with common (or fewer) parts and the much higher costs generated when large numbers of unique parts are specified for low-volume products. In recognition of this phenomenon, more companies are experimenting with assigning material-related overhead on the basis of the total number of different parts used, and not on the physical or dollar volume of materials used.

Long-Term Variable Cost

The volume-unrelated support-department costs, unlike traditional variable costs, do not vary with short-term changes in activity levels. Traditional variable costs vary in the short run with production fluctuations because they represent cost elements that require no managerial actions to change the level of expenditure.

In contrast, any amount of decrease in overhead costs associated with reducing diversity and complexity in the factory will take many months to realize and will require specific managerial actions. The number of personnel in support departments will have to be reduced, machines may have to be sold off, and some supervisors will become redundant. Actions to accomplish these overhead cost reductions will lag, by months, the complexity-reducing actions in the product line and in the process technology. But this long-term cost response mirrors the way overhead costs were first built up in the factory – as more products with specialized designs were added to the product line, the organization simply muddled through with existing personnel. It was only over time that overworked support departments requested and received additional personnel to handle the increased number of transactions that had been thrust upon them.

The personnel in the support departments are often highly skilled and possess a high degree of firm-specific knowledge. Management is loathe to lay them off when changes in market conditions temporarily reduce the level of production complexity. Consequently, when the workload of these departments drops, surplus capacity exists.

The long-term perspective management had adopted toward its products often made it difficult to use the surplus capacity. When it was used, it was not to make products never to be produced again, but rather to produce inventory of products that were known to disrupt production (typically the very low-volume items) or to produce, under short-term contract, products for other companies. We did not observe or hear about a situation in which this capacity was used to introduce a product that had only a short life expectancy. Some companies justified the acceptance of special orders or incremental business because they 'knew' that the income from this business more than covered their variable or incremental costs. They failed to realize that the long-term consequence from accepting such incremental business was a steady rise in the costs of their support departments.

When Product Costs are not Known

The magnitude of the errors in reported product costs and the nature of their bias make it difficult for full-line producers to enact sensible strategies. The existing cost systems clearly identify the low-volume products as the most profitable and the high-volume ones as the least profitable. Focused competitors, on the other hand, will not suffer from the same handicap. Their cost systems, while equally poorly designed, will report more accurate product costs because they are not distorted as much by lot-size diversity.

With access to more accurate product cost data, a focused competitor can sell the high-volume products at a lower price. The full-line producer is then apparently faced with very low margins on these products and is naturally tempted to deemphasize this business and concentrate on apparently higher-profit, low-volume specialty business. This shift from high-volume to low-volume products, however, does not produce the anticipated higher profitability. The firm, believing in its cost system, chases illusory profits.

The firm has been victimized by diseconomies of scope. In trying to obtain the benefits of economy of scale by expanding its product offerings to better utilize its fixed or capacity resources, the firm does not see the high diseconomies it has introduced by creating a far more complex production environment. The cost accounting system fails to reveal this diseconomy of scope.

A Comprehensive Cost System

One message comes through overwhelmingly in our experiences with the three firms, and with the many others we talked and worked with. Almost all product-related decisions – introduction, pricing, and discontinuance – are long-term. Management accounting thinking (and teaching) during the past half-century has concentrated on information for making short-run incremental decisions based on variable, incremental, or relevant costs. It has missed the most important aspect of product decisions. Invariably, the time period for measuring 'variable,' 'incremental,' or 'relevant' costs has been about a month (the time period corresponding to the cycle of the firm's internal financial reporting system). While academics admonish that notions of fixed and variable are meaningful only with respect to a particular time period, they immediately discard this warning and teach from the perspective of one-month decision horizons.

This short-term focus for product costing has led all the companies we visited to view a large and growing proportion of their total manufacturing costs as 'fixed.' In fact, however, what they call 'fixed' costs have been the most variable and rapidly increasing costs. This paradox has seemingly eluded most accounting practitioners and scholars. Two fundamental changes in our thinking about cost behavior must be introduced.

First, the allocation of costs from the cost pools to the products should be achieved using bases that reflect cost drivers. Because many overhead costs are driven by the complexity of production, not the volume of production, nonvolume-related bases are required. Second, many of these overhead costs are somewhat discretionary. While they vary with changes in the complexity of the production process, these changes are intermittent. A traditional cost system that defines variable costs as varying in the short term with production volume will misclassify these costs as fixed.

The misclassification also arises from an inadequate understanding of the actual cost drivers for most overhead costs. Many overhead costs vary with transactions: transactions to order, schedule, receive, inspect, and pay for shipments; to move, track, and count inventory; to schedule production work; to set up machines; to perform quality assurance; to implement engineering change orders; and to expedite and ship orders. The cost of these transactions is largely independent of the size of the order being handled; the cost does not vary with the amount of inputs or outputs. It does vary, however, with the need for the transaction itself. If the firm introduces more products, if it needs to expedite more orders, or if it needs to inspect more components, then it will need larger overhead departments to perform these additional transactions.

Summary

Product costs are almost all variable costs. Some of the sources of variability relate to physical volume of items produced. These costs will vary with units produced, or in a varied, multiproduct environment, with surrogate measures such as labor hours, machine hours, material dollars and quantities, or elapsed time of production. Other costs, however, particularly those arising from overhead support and marketing departments, vary with the diversity and complexity in the product line. The variability of these costs is best explained by the incidence of transactions to initiate the next stage in the production, logistics, or distribution process.

A comprehensive product cost system, incorporating the long-term variable costs of manufacturing and marketing each product or product line, should provide a much better basis for managerial decisions on pricing, introducing, discontinuing, and reengineering product lines. The cost system may even become strategically important for running the business and creating sustainable competitive advantages for the firm.

The Importance of Field Research

The accompanying article, coauthored with Robin Cooper, is excerpted from *Accounting & Management: Field Study Perspectives* (Boston, Mass., Harvard Business School Press, 1987) William J. Bruns, Jr. and Robert S. Kaplan (eds). The book contains 13 field studies on management accounting innovations presented at a colloquium at the Harvard Business School in June 1986 by leading academic researchers from the U.S. and Western Europe. The colloquium represents the largest single collection of field research studies on management accounting practices in organizations.

The HBS colloquium had two principal objectives. First, the authors were to understand and document the management accounting practices of actual organizations. Some of the organizations would be captured in a process of transition: attempting, and occasionally succeeding to modify their systems to measure, motivate and evaluate operating performance. Other organizations were studied just to understand the system of measurement and control that had evolved in their particular environment.

A second, and even more important, objective of the colloquium was to begin the process by which field research methods in management accounting could be established as a legitimate method of inquiry. Academic researchers in accounting have extensive experience with deductive, model-building, analytic research with the design and analysis of controlled experiments, usually in a laboratory setting; and with the empirical analysis of large data bases. This experience has yielded research guidance and criteria that, while not always explicit, nevertheless are widely shared and permit research to be conducted and evaluated.

At a time when so many organizations are reexamining the adequacy of their management accounting systems it is especially important that university-based researchers spend more time working directly with innovating organizations. We are pleased that *Management Accounting*, through publication of this article, is helping to publicize the existence of the field studies performed to date.

The experiences described in the accompanying article, as well as in the other papers in the colloquium volume, indicate a very different role for management accounting systems in organizations than is currently taught in most of our business schools and accounting departments. We believe that present and future field research and case writing will lead to major changes in management accounting courses. To facilitate the needed changes in curriculum and research, however, requires extensive cooperation between university faculty and practicing management accountants. As noted by observers at the Harvard colloquium:

> There is a tremendous store of knowledge about management accounting practices and ideas out there in real companies. Academicians as a whole are far too ignorant of that knowledge. When academics begin to see the relevance of this data base, perhaps generations of students will become more aware of its richness. Such awareness must precede any real progress on prescribing good management accounting for any given situation.

To observe is also to discover. The authors have observed interesting phenomena. We do not know how prevalent these phenomena are or under what conditions they exist or do not exist. But the studies suggest possible relationships, causes, effects, and even dynamic process in the sense that Yogi Berra must have had in mind when he said, 'Some times you can observe a lot just by watching.'

With the research support and cooperation of the members of the National Association of Accountants, many university professors are looking forward to watching and also describing the changes now under way so that academics can begin to develop theories, teach, and finally prescribe about the new opportunities for management accounting.

Robert S. Kaplan

Endnotes

1. Mayers Tap (disguised name) is described in Harvard Business School, case series 9-185-111. Schrader-Bellows is described in HBS Case Series 9-186-272.

Robin Cooper is an associate professor of business administration at the Harvard Business School and a fellow of the Institute of Chartered Accountants in England and Wales. He writes a column, 'Cost Management Principles and Concepts,' in the *Journal of Cost Management* and has produced research on activity-based costing for the CAM-1 Cost Management System Project. Robert S. Kaplan is the Arthur Lowes Dickinson Professor of Accounting at the Harvard Business School and a professor of industrial administration at Carnegie-Mellon University. Currently, Professor Kaplan serves on the Executive Committee of the CAM-1 Cost Management System Project, the Manufacturing Studies Board of the National Research Council, and the Financial Accounting Standards Advisory Committee.

Reading 2

Reprinted from *Accounting, Organizations and Society*, 16:8, Dent, Jeremy. F, Accounting and organizational cultures: A field study of the emergence of a new organizational reality (1991), with permission from Elsevier.

Accounting and Organizational Cultures: A Field Study of the Emergence of a New Organizational Reality[*]

Jeremy F. Dent
London School of Economics and Political Science

Abstract

Organizations have long been known to have cultural properties. A more recent innovation is the study of organizations as cultures: systems of knowledge, beliefs and values in which action and artifact are vested with expressive qualities. We know little about the way in which accounting is implicated in organizations' cultures. This paper reports a longitudinal field study of organizational change, tracing out the way in which new accounting practices were implicated in an emergent reconstruction of the organization's culture.

The train arrived at Capital City Terminus at 12.10. It was on time despite a delay on the line. Walking up the platform, I saw the train driver leaning out of his cab. He must have driven the train fast to recover the time: the windscreens were spattered with dead insects. He exchanged

This research was generously supported by the Chartered Institute of Management Accountants. Earlier versions of the paper were presented at the AAA Annual Convention, New York, 1986, the EAA Annual Congress, London, 1987, and the EIASM Workshop on Strategy, Accounting & Control, Venice, 1990. Ken Euske, Anthony Hopwood, Keith Hoskins, Kenneth Merchant, Peter Miller and two anonymous reviewers provided helpful comments.

some words with men dressed in smart overalls. Muttering a few words into 'walkie-talkies', they jumped down onto the track to check the engine. Men driving small electric trucks towing streams of trailers with logos on the side collected parcels and mail bags from the guard's van. Others set about replenishing water and food supplies in the train. At the barrier, a man wearing a smile and a dark uniform with red piping on the seams checked my ticket.

Moving on, the concourse was bright and airy, concealed lighting illuminating the white tiled floor. People were milling about. Soft music was playing on the tannoy. Large electronic screens indicated arrival and departure times. There were colourful boutiques displaying ties, handkerchiefs, socks and bags, and cafés where people were drinking coffee and eating croissants. What a change, I thought, from just a short time ago, when the station was dark and grimy, and a grumpy employee had greeted my question about departure times with a crude response.

At the new executive offices across the street I tangled with the revolving glass and stainless steel door. In the foyer, a manicured receptionist called upstairs to say I'd arrived. The security guard, at least I presumed he was a security guard (his appearance was quite like a ticket inspector, but his commanding presence was more like a policeman), showed me to the lift. He deftly pressed the fourth floor button, removing himself before the doors closed. After a few moments the lift doors opened onto what appeared to be open-plan office space, but in fact comprised zones of compartmentalized activity separated by cleverly positioned shoulderheight cabinets and screens. A person came up to me: 'Mr Charles will be here in a minute', he said; 'he's at a retirement do'. The man looked busy; his tie was loose, the top button of his shirt was undone, he must have left his jacket on his chair. He was courteous: 'his

secretary just popped out for a few minutes, but she told me to expect you. Why don't you wait in his office?'

Walking through the office space, I could see over the cabinets. The arrangements were utilitarian. Some people were stabbing at computer keyboards, others were studying documents, others were writing or working out sums on calculators. There were piles of print-out everywhere.

We entered Mr Charles' office through his secretary's room. From the large windows there was a fine view into, and over, the station. I could see trains arriving and leaving. I followed one right into the hills across the city. The office was softly furnished. At one end, there was a large desk, at the other a couple of sofas; opposite the windows there were bookshelves and a cabinet. The lighting was bright but unobtrusive. There wasn't a computer in sight. My guide and I made small talk incidental conversation about the comforts of the new building and the air conditioning. Conscious that his work was pressing and not wishing to detain him, I told him not to worry about me. Eventually he made to leave. 'Ah! Mr General Manager', I heard him say before he had even left the secretary's office. 'Your visitor has arrived'. 'Thanks John', came the reply. Mr Charles, the General Manager, entered the room. 'Good to see you again, Mr Charles', I said to him as we exchanged greetings.

Settling down in one of the sofas he said to me 'I am glad you could come. I think you will find this afternoon's meeting interesting. We're deeply embroiled in cost allocations. Intercity are holding Freight to ransom'. After my query, he continued: 'At night, we push freight up the main line routes. Intercity don't use them at night. You don't want the speed then; after all you can't expect passengers to get off the train at 2 or 3 in the morning. Sleeper trains make their separate way on roundabout routes. Intercity say the wear and tear caused *by freight trains, and they are very heavy, means they need to increase the engineering specification of the track. As it's an Intercity track, they pick up the cost; and they want Freight to pay. They're holding them to ransom. Freight have responded by running their trains slower. This reduces the damage to the track. They don't go very fast anyway, so I mean SLOW. Now Intercity say they can't get back on the track when they want it in the morning. They have threatened not to let Freight use the track unless they pay. It's going to be an interesting meeting. Would you like a drink before we have lunch?'*

Going to the cabinet, he poured two glasses of mineral water . . .

Organizations have long been known to have distinct cultural properties (cf. Weber, 1947; Parsons, 1951). They create and sustain particular work customs. They establish norms for proper and improper behaviour and performance. They propagate stories and myths, and are replete with rituals (Van Maanen & Barley, 1984; Martin *et al.*, 1983). Communities in organizations have particular codes of communication: behaviour, language, dress, presentation, design, architecture, ceremony . . . The operation of work technologies in organizations is not a purely technical-rational affair. Rather it is embedded in a cultural system of ideas (beliefs, knowledges) and sentiments (values), in which actions and artifacts are vested with symbolic qualities of meaning. The appreciation of organizational dynamics requires a sensitivity to local frames of significance and interpretation.

Accounting practices are a common feature of most work organizations. Planning and budgeting activities, systems of hierarchical accountability, performance appraisal procedures, budgetary controls and remuneration arrangements, all rely to a greater or lesser extent on accounting practices. Inevitably, therefore, accounting is likely to be implicated in organizations' cultural systems. But

how, and in what way? Drawing on the insights of Meyer & Rowan (1977), Pfeffer & Salancik (1978), DiMaggio & Powell (1983), Scott (1987), Zucker (1988) and others, one theme in the literature appeals to accounting's potential significance in the context of wider societal values and beliefs. Put crudely, organizations depend on a flow of resources for survival; society has beliefs in the efficacy of 'rational' management practices; organizations which adopt such practices are more likely to be rewarded. Thus, recent empirically grounded studies (Berry *et al.*, 1985; Ansari & Euske, 1987; Covaleski & Dirsmith, 1988) have cast accounting as a culturally expressive symbol of rationality, particularly oriented towards powerful external constituencies, moderating environmental control. In this view, following especially Meyer & Rowan's (1977) discussion, accounting is often seen to be neutral in its effects within the organization. It is kept at arm's length, symbolically construed as necessary but irrelevant, and, as it were, not taken seriously. It is purposefully uncoupled from organizations' core technological activities.

All knowledges and practices can be reflexive, however. Accounting can reflect back on those institutions which adopt it. Hopwood (1987), Hines (1988), Miller & O'Leary (1987) and others have argued for its constitutive role in the construction of organizational life. Finely crafted notions of costliness, efficiency, profitability, earnings-per-share and so forth, actively construct particular definitions of reality which privilege the financial and economic sphere. Rather than being kept at arm's length, uncoupled from organizations' core technological activities, these can permeate into organizational settings, leading to the creation of particular agendas (in the sense of objectives and priorities and the means for their achievement), stylized definitions of success and failure, the characterization of heroic performance and the mobilization of particular dynamics of change. This suggests the possibility of a more intimate involvement of accounting in organizational cultures.

In fact, evidence in the field suggests that accounting practices are not uniformly implicated in organizational activities (Goold & Campbell, 1987; Miles & Snow, 1978). In some organizations, accounting is centrally involved in work rituals: financial achievement is celebrated; budgets are massaged, pored over, and matter. In others, accounting is incidental, perhaps existing as a practice, but with no particular significance. Similarly, entrepreneurial risk taking is sometimes valued for its own sake. Dynamic, decisive, action-oriented men and women who innovate are heroes, almost irrespective of the financial consequences. In other organizations, risk taking is valued only if successful in financial terms. Arguably, the multi-faceted interplay of accounting with organizations' cultural and technical systems is under-researched. More empirically grounded research is needed to ascertain the way in which accounting is drawn upon by actors within organizations in the creation and maintenance of cultures.

Responding, with others, to appeals for field studies (e.g. Bruns & Kaplan, 1987) and for the study of accounting in its organizational and social context (e.g. Hopwood, 1978, 1983; Dent, 1986), this paper reports a longitudinal study undertaken in one organization to research this issue. The organization is a railway company. The study focuses on its senior management élite: a group of approximately 120 people including head office executives, senior line management and people in senior staff positions (i.e. finance and engineering). Prior to the study, the dominant culture within this management group was well established, and centred on engineering and production concerns. Accounting was incidental in this culture: it was necessary in the technical-rational sense of ensuring that revenues were accounted for and suppliers were paid, but it was not incorporated into the culture among the senior management élite in any significant way. Rituals, symbols and language celebrated the primacy of the engineering and production orientation. During the course of the study, a new culture emerged. The previously dominant orientation was displaced by a new preoccupation with economic and accounting concerns. New accounts were crafted. Gradually, through action and interaction, they were coupled to organizational activities to reconstitute interpretations of organizational endeavour. Accounting actively shaped the dominant meanings given to organizational life, ultimately obtaining a remarkable significance in the senior management culture. A new set of symbols, rituals and language emerged to celebrate an economic rationale for organized activity. This paper carefully traces the events and interactions through which accounting was endowed with significance.

The paper is written from a cultural perspective, but in a very real sense the study is also concerned with power and influence in the organization. A new culture can be a major source of power, particularly if it gains ascendancy to become dominant, for it effectively alters the legitimacy of accepted criteria for action.

The next section of the paper outlines the cultural approach adopted in the subsequent analysis. The following section explains the method employed in the study. Two sections then document the study itself. Thereafter, some implications for accounting and culture are drawn out. Finally, there is a concluding comment.

Culture

In recent years, a prolific literature has emerged to offer a wide array of perceptual, symbolic and processual characterizations of organization (e.g. Hedberg *et al.*,1976; Jonsson & Lundin, 1977; Hedberg & Jonsson, 1978; Pondy, 1978; Weick, 1979; Ranson *et al.*,1980; Argyris & Schon, 1981; Pfeffer, 1981; Starbuck, 1982; Pondy *et al.*, 1983; Brunsson, 1985; Greenwood & Hinings, 1988). As a result, we are now used to conceptualizing organizations as bodies of thought, variously described as myths, causal schema, theories-of-action, interpretive schemes, ideologies, paradigms and so forth. The concept of culture, drawn from anthropology and ethnography, has entered the organizational literature as a framework for extending this ideational understanding of organizations[1] (Pettigrew, 1979; Smircich, 1983a; Allaire & Firsirotu, 1984; Van Maanen & Barley, 1984; Meek, 1988).

Culture is an elusive concept.[2] Here, drawing on Geertz' (1973, 1983) interpretive anthropology, it is defined to be the broad constellation of interpretive structures through which action and events are rendered meaningful in a community. Balinese cockfights, a sheep raid in Morocco, funeral rites in Java – or nearer home, the graduation ceremony, the distinguished lecture series, the publication of papers in prestigious journals – all have singular meanings in their respective communities (as does all social action). Culture is the 'ordered clusters of significance' (Geertz, 1973, p. 363), the shared 'webs of significance' (p. 5) through which people appreciate the meaningfulness of their experience, and are guided to action. Culture, as an ideational system, is produced and reproduced through action and interaction. But it is not just lodged in people's minds. Culture is public, the product of minds, between minds. Culturally significant events give public expression to the ideational system.

The appreciation of organizations as cultures brings the interpretive, experiential aspects of their activities to the foreground of analysis, emphasizing their expressive qualities[3] (Van Maanen, 1979, 1988; Feldman, 1986). Looking at the railway, for example, the train is not seen as cold technology; the concourse is not just glass and marble; 'Mr General Manager' is not an anybody; cost allocations are not mere calculations: everything is expressive. Local knowledge, beliefs and values vest them with symbolic qualities of meaning. The train may be vested with a sacred quality (or not, as the case may be) quite beyond its technical properties; beliefs about the skills required to operate a railway and appropriate forms of organizing may endow the General Manager with special status and privilege (or not). Cultural analysis attempts to uncover these meanings and to trace the underlying thematic relationships. The objective is interpretation and 'thick description': the production of rich contextually laden accounts conveying the symbolic content of social action.

Meaning systems may differ within organizations, of course. The train, the framing of the routing problem as a cost allocation issue and so on are likely to be interpreted differently by different groups. Within the overarching concept of an organization as a culture, it is sensible to recognize the possibility and likelihood of distinct subcultures existing among managerial teams, occupational groups, members of different social classes and so on; many of which may transcend organizational boundaries (Van Maanen & Barley, 1984). As a limiting case, these subcultures may be isomorphic; more commonly, they may only partially overlap.[4] Also, some may be dominant-cultures and others counter-cultures (Martin & Siehl, 1983), perhaps partially uncoupled from each other (Berry *et al.*,1985), or co-existing in an 'uneasy symbiosis' (Martin & Siehl, 1983), or in contest with each other for dominance (Gregory, 1983; Riley, 1983; Pettigrew, 1985; Feldman, 1986). Moreover, cultures in organizations are not independent of their social context. They are interpenetrated by wider systems of thought, interacting with other organizations and social institutions, both importing and exporting values, beliefs and knowledge.

Accounting is likely to be differentially implicated in these subcultures in organizations. Accounting systems, and information systems more generally, inevitably offer highly stylized views of the world. Any representation is partial, an interpretation through a particular framing of reality, rendering some aspects of events important and others unimportant; counter-interpretations are possible (Hedberg & Jonsson, 1978). Accounting systems embody particular assumptions about organization, rationality, authority, time and so forth. These may be more or less consonant with local subcultures in organizations (cf. Markus & Pfeffer, 1983). For example, to senior managers in some organizations accounting may symbolize efficiency, calculative rationality, order and so forth: 'the name of the game is profit'. This may motivate the development of sophisticated accounting systems measuring economic performance this way and that. To others (nearer the ground?), accounting may symbolize confusion or irrelevance: 'no one understands the business'; 'when all else fails they resort to the numbers' (see Jones & Lakin, 1978, chapter 11, for a graphic example). Similarly, meanings may differ across occupational groups. Commercial managers may appreciate accounting rather differently to engineers, for example.

It is useful to think of societal cultures as emergent, unfolding through time[5] (Geertz, 1973; Douglas, 1966), and similarly with organizational cultures (Pettigrew, 1985; Feldman, 1986). That is not to say that given cultures do not survive for long periods, or that changes may be proactively managed: organizational cultures probably have inertial tendencies (cf. Miller & Friesen, 1984), perhaps sometimes not even incorporating changes

in wider patterns of social thought[6] (cf. Burns & Stalker's, 1961, pathological responses in mechanistic firms). Rather, the implication is that culture is not programmed or static. The processes of cultural change in organizations are poorly understood, however. Perhaps cultural change is a political process: subcultures competing with one another for legitimacy and dominance (Pettigrew, 1985). Perhaps cultural change is akin to the diffusion of organizational forms, whole fields of organizations rapidly adopting knowledge innovations in leading firms (cf. Fligstein, 1990). Perhaps in a Kuhnian sense, cultural change is precipitated by crisis: the adoption of new cultural knowledge only being possible when faith is undermined, for example by the failure of strategies for subsistence. Maybe new cultures are autonomously crafted in organizations (cf. 'groping' towards 'solutions-in-principle' and their subsequent elaboration: Mintzberg, 1978; Jonsson & Lundin, 1977); or perhaps they are already there, 'lying around' in counter-cultures, waiting to be discovered by others (cf. Cohen et al., 1972); alternatively, cultures may be imported from the environment through new actors (cf. Starbuck & Hedberg, 1977).

Clearly, there are multiple modes and possibilities for cultural change. However, the point of importance for this paper is the conceptualization of cultural change as the uncoupling of organizational action from one culture and its recoupling to another (cf. Greenwood & Hinings, 1988; Hedberg, 1981). It is a process of fundamental reinterpretation of organizational activities. Things cease to be what they were and become what they were not: a new reality, if you will. In the railway, for example, the sacred train could turn into cold steel, or the priest-like general manager could become an anybody. Moreover, this process of uncoupling and recoupling is unlikely to be sudden, but emergent: the gradual disintegration of one coupling and the crystallization of another. This crystallization may be around an idea not fully understood, a kind of ill-articulated new knowledge, perhaps imported from the environment. In the railway, this idea was a new accounting.

Research Method

Arm's length analysis is clearly inappropriate for cultural analysis of the kind described here. Instead, it calls for closer engagement in the research setting and 'interpretive' methodology (Geertz, 1973; Burrell & Morgan, 1979; Denzin, 1983). Necessarily, this precludes the imposition of exteriorized accounts, and radical critique. In part, the goal is 'to grasp the native's point of view, his relation to life, to realise his vision of his world' (Malinowski, 1922, p. 25); in part it is to reflect on the processes through which that vision comes to be and is sustained.[7]

This kind of research is necessarily qualitative. Data consist of descriptions and accounts provided by participants in the research site, together with the *researcher's observations* on activities and interactions and the context in which they take place. Data must be collected over an extended period of time so that processes can be recorded. The researcher, in general, does not seek to test a prior hypothesis. Rather, he or she seeks to theorize through the data in an inductive manner. Analysis of the data is itself an emergent process.

The researcher seeks gradually to develop an empathy with the data, to understand what they tell of participants' realities and the process through which they unfold. The researcher must constantly construct alternative interpretations ('readings': Levi Strauss, quoted in Turner, 1983) until he or she is satisfied that the representation is a faithful account. Interpretations must be grounded in context and consistent with the chronological ordering of events and interactions. Finally, research results must be presented in such a way that the reader can independently judge their credibility, as far as is possible.[8]

The study reported here was conducted over a period of two years, with follow up visits one year and two years later. It involved ongoing iterations between data collection and analysis. Access to the organization was gained through various channels and contacts. The researcher was given freedom to interview anyone he wished. At no point in the data collection process did the researcher express opinions, save where it was necessary to prompt interviewees. Data were collected from staff within the organization in several ways. The first source was a series of unstructured interviews. Approximately 30 managers were interviewed, sometimes twice or more times at the researcher's request. These included head office executives and their advisors or assistants, senior line management and people in senior staff positions (finance and engineering). Interviews averaged one and a half hours in length, and were spread over the period of the research. They were tape-recorded and transcribed. Secondly, access was granted to various internal meetings. Debates were observed and dialogue noted. Activities in these meetings were subsequently written up in abbreviated form. Thirdly, data were collected through casual conversations and by simply 'being around'.

As the project progressed, the data were repeatedly analysed. At first, it seemed that there was a real probability of drowning in the data. Transcripts and notes were accumulating rapidly, and the material appeared to be incoherent. This is apparently a common feature of the initial stages of cultural research (Smircich, 1983b). But different ways of making sense of it all were explored and gradually a pattern began to emerge. At each stage emerging appreciations were checked against the next round of data in an attempt to confirm the researcher's understanding of the situation. This continued until such time as the subsequent data became predictable.

It may be useful to indicate the precise way in which the data were found to give a coherent picture. Ultimately, the analysis hinged on three dimensions: role (function), and level of hierarchy of the subject, and time. Firstly, the data were categorized according to content and underlying values. Opinions, sentiments, interpretations, confusions and so forth in each interview transcript were noted. This was done without reference to the identity of the person who had been interviewed. The data collected at any one time seemed to fall naturally into distinct constellations or clusters (in the sense that groups of people expressed similar views). Attaching identity to the data, it transpired that these constellations corresponded broadly to interviewees' roles and positions in the hierarchy. Among those performing similar roles (functions) at a similar level in the hierarchy, there was a marked similarity of perspective. Perspectives differed, however, across roles and at different levels of the hierarchy. These data were set up on a two-dimensional space with role on one axis and hierarchy on the other.

This exercise was repeated on data collected at different times, and found to give similar results, in the sense that the data again fell into role-hierarchy clusters. The specific content of the data differed over time, however. So, the two-dimensional spaces were set out in chronological order. In effect, a third dimension was added to the space, representing elapsed time. Studying the content of the data as one moved through time, it transpired that the opinions, sentiments and interpretations of each group were in fact evolving in a systematic way. In this three-dimensional space was a story of unfolding meanings in the organization.

This was indicative of the existence of different cultures in the organization, and some systematic underlying trajectory in the emergence of those cultures. In fact, during the data collection process, it became clear that new interviewees' views were predictable, given a knowledge of (a) the role (function) of the participant, (b) his or her position in the hierarchy, and (c) the time of the interview.

At this point, the data were analysed from a different perspective. Specifically, the level of analysis shifted from content to process. The data were re-examined to see if the process through which the new meanings were emerging was observable. Some key turning points were obvious in the data. There was a series of events and interactions through which the emergence of the new meaning structure could be traced. These are documented in following sections. Finally, the findings of the research project were noted and informally discussed with various participants.[9]

The Organization: An Overview

The research was undertaken in a major railway company. The company is referred to here as ER[10] ('Euro Rail'). It is, and has been for some while, in public sector ownership. It is large by any standards, employing approximately 160,000 people. It has a distinguished history.

History and traditions

ER has its origins in the great private-sector railway companies set up in the middle decades of the last century. These each built and operated a main line out of the capital city, i.e. radial routes and associated branch lines.[11] The companies are legendary. They raised capital to fund their projects on an unprecedented scale. Their railways were built by world-famous engineers who pioneered emerging industrial technology, designing magnificent steam locomotives and tracks and bridges which the world admired. The railways were, and are, a visible celebration of Victorian accomplishment.

These companies enjoyed a monopoly in the nation's transport well into this century. They had good relationships with successive governments. They paid consistent dividends and their shares were blue-chip stocks. This monopoly position and government patronage, coupled with a remarkable continuity in the underlying nature of their operations, rendered them highly bureaucratic: rules and procedures were well defined, there were clear chains of command and formalized systems for managing operations.[12] Their managements were conservative, cultivating a belief in the uniqueness of railway management and the wisdom of practices built up over many decades.

Importantly, though, while established as commercial concerns and earning their founders a handsome return,[13] these companies also embraced a spirit of public service, for the railway network provided a transport infrastructure much needed for the pursuit of trade and manufacturing, and for social mobility. This notion of public service was significant in the managements' interpretations of the railways: they took the rough with the smooth. They were run by 'railway men': engineers and operators who took pride in the professional management of the railway and its public service.

The railway companies were nationalized in the late 1940s. In many respects, this was of limited significance. The nationalized railway consolidated the old management structure: it was organized by region, each representing one of the radial routes out of the capital city; and each still managed by a General Manager (the same title as before). An Executive Committee was established to oversee policy decisions and to interface with government. This committee comprised the regional General Managers together with the Chief Executive of ER and various engineering chiefs.[14] Management practices of the former railways survived intact. Furthermore, nationalization reinforced the public service orientation, for this was the era of the Welfare State. Public-sector ownership established the railway as a social service. Its prime purpose was to provide a transport infrastructure. Profitability was secondary.

This interpretation of the railway remained dominant among senior managers for thirty years or more. Post-nationalization governments, faced with deficits and huge investment sums required for modernization, frequently sought to contain the costs of maintaining this infrastructure. Following a fundamental review in the 1960s many branch lines were closed. Later, during the 1970s, the government imposed investment ceilings and set out expectations for the maximum level of its support. But, although now tempered with a concern for thrift and the avoidance of waste, old traditions endured. Financial deficits continued. ER remained a bureaucratic organization with a heritage of railway engineering and public service. The railways were still run for practical purposes by regional General Managers, each one of these standing in a direct line of descent from a founding pioneer. They occupied the same grand offices. There were portraits of previous incumbents on their walls. They were, very consciously, carrying on a tradition of professional railway management.

This was the reality of the dominant 'railway culture'. The railway was a public service. The purpose of the railway was to run trains. In so doing profitability was secondary. The accepted professional concerns were to do with railway engineering and the logistical problems of operating trains. And although the 'golden age' of steam had passed, new electrical and electronic technologies still offered scope for railway people to further their engineering heritage.[15]

The emergence of the economic perspective

In a profound sense, nationalization thirty years before had created a relationship of dependence for the railways, a dependence on government for sustenance. In the early 1980s the implications of this became clear. Government policy became stringent. Social aims ceased to be a legitimate criterion for support. Government sought to impose harsh economic disciplines in all areas of public and private endeavour. Declaring a determination to 'take on' the public services in particular, it orchestrated a campaign challenging the competence of public-sector management. For the railway, government 'expectations' were translated into more specific financial 'objectives'. These were progressively tightened. Investment funds were withheld. Reporting escalating losses, ER found itself in a malign, resource constrained environment.

We need, for a moment, to backtrack. Apparently, in the late 1970s, the Chief Executive of the railway had set up a strategy think-tank to improve long-term planning.[16] Embryonic ideas developed there, and subsequently nurtured by a small group of executives, were now rolled out for more general consideration. Senior managers, by this time fully appreciative of the real hostility of government and the precarious position of the railway, fastened onto the ideas as a solution to the current problems. The organization, through the Executive Committee, created new management positions. For the first time, 'Business Managers' were appointed. For analytical purposes (only), railway operations were broken down into market sectors: for example, long distance passenger traffic, short distance passenger traffic, freight, parcels and postal traffic. Business Managers were assigned responsibility for developing strategies to enhance financial performance in each sector in effect to manage the 'bottom line(s)'.

These people were appointed outside the main line-management hierarchy of the railway. They were long-range planning people in staff positions at the Head Office, with no formal control or authority over railway operations. In fact, their initial responsibilities were thought to be confined to the identification of market-related initiatives. The Business Managers reported to the Chief Executive and joined the Executive Committee. But the regional management hierarchies remained intact. Regional General Managers, carrying on the old traditions, continued to run the railway.

The appointment of Business Managers was to have far reaching consequences, however, for it introduced a new 'business' culture, a counterculture. They brought a different interpretation of reality. For them the railway was a business, its purpose was to make profit. Engineering and logistical operations were essentially a means for extracting revenues from customers. Professional management was about making the railway profitable.

Business Managers were appointed without staff or support at the margins of the organization. But during the course of the study, they gained influence at the expense of the regional General Managers. They persuaded many around them of their idea of a business railway. Gradually, people converted to the 'business culture'. Others left the organization. The nature of dialogue and debate changed. Appeals to the old traditions of railway excellence and public service were repudiated. New kinds of policy decisions emerged, motivated by the business logic. Operational activities out in the regions began to be informed by the new rationale.

Now, the old world view, the preoccupation with engineering and logistics, the belief in the railway as a social service, the railway culture, has been substantially displaced by the business perspective, the belief that railways should be instrumental in making profit and managed to that end. The counter-culture has emerged to become the dominant-culture among the senior management. Traditions established over longer than a century were quickly overthrown.

Tracing the Dynamics of Change

The story is one of evolving interpretations, meanings and perceived possibilities. No one in the organization foresaw the outcome at the start, not even the Business Managers. At first, their 'business culture' was vague and indistinct, a kind of abstract generality. But as events unfolded, it became more specific. Possibilities for coupling their business reality to organizational action were perceived. Gradually, as people elaborated the new logic for organized activity, momentum was created. Capturing the emergent nature of these developments, one senior manager described the experience as 'a voyage of discovery and development'.

This section traces the dynamics of change. Firstly, it considers the context surrounding the appointment of Business Managers. Then it outlines the crafting of new accounting systems. Subsequently, it traces the process through which the new accounting was coupled to organizational activities and endowed with meaning. Finally, it gives an account of the regional General Managers' perspective in these events. The section is interspersed with representative comments from managers in the organization.

People and context

The context of the Business Managers' appointments in ER is important in appreciating the trajectory of events. The railway was under acute threat. The competence of public-sector management was openly under challenge. The railway was charged with being 'old fashioned'. Governmental pressures for profitability were onerous, and sanctions were being applied. These threats were clearly appreciated by senior management. The railway has always prided itself on being modern in its technological activities. The charge of being 'old-fashioned' in its management practice was deeply challenging. Moreover, there was some recognition that the old traditions were not, in themselves, proving sufficient to manage the threats away, and needed to be supplemented in some way. The skills the Business Managers brought, marketing, long-term planning, 'bottom line' management, had an image of modernity, enabling the railway to throw off the charge of being 'old-fashioned', and were thought to be a useful supplementation of the railway traditions. Moreover, they were thought to be unintrusive, a 'grafting-on' to the old traditions. The Business Managers had no operational authority. They were 'back office' planning people. Their roles were defined through a remote accounting construct, the 'bottom line', outside the prevailing mainstream understanding of railway activities. In bringing new knowledge to bear to cope with environmental pressures, they were not expected to disrupt the railway or existing patterns of authority. Senior managers commented:

> Everything has its time. You've got to realize the environment of the (transport) industry. We're now in the most competitive environment the railway has ever faced. And there were clear objectives emerging from the Government. These things made people think differently . . . It's all in the market place in the end, and how to exploit the market place. The traditional railway wasn't sensitive to the market place (Senior Executive).

> We were weak in marketing and business issues generally. The government targets were stiff. We needed those skills (General Manager).

Equally important are the personalities and backgrounds of the Business Managers. While they had all at some time worked in or with the railway, practically all had also worked outside. Thus, while they understood the railway culture and could talk railway talk, they also appreciated what they saw as wider business practice: 'managing for profit'. Furthermore, these men became evangelists, hungry people with a mission. They developed a zeal to convert the railway from a social service to a business enterprise.

In addition, the nature of their appointments was rather unusual (at least for a mechanistic organization). There were no briefs or manuals. Ultimate intentions were not articulated. Business Managers were just told to see what they could do.

> We introduced it in an evolutionary way. We said: 'Let's appoint Business Managers and then let it evolve. Be patient and let it evolve' (Senior Executive).

> When the Chief Executive introduced the Business Managers he didn't have any idea how to take the concept forward. I think he deliberately chose people who would win the day, and left them to get on with it. It was up to each of us to build our influence. The regional General Managers had great centres of power: buildings and armies of people. They were the Gods on high, the last remnants of the Railway Companies. He wanted to stand back from it all, and see what would happen (Business Manager).

They had, at best, a vague job description, one which they could legitimately expand.

Subsequent events were not independent of changes in the social and political climate during the decade. It was one dominated by economic liberalism: deregulation in many spheres of activity, privatization of state owned enterprises, and a sea change in attitudes towards the public services and the Welfare State. These substantive effects were to come later, but there was already a clear 'idealization' by government of private sector management practices, and a belief that they could be introduced in the public sector. (Industrialists were rationalizing 'old fashioned' work routines in the Civil Service, for example.) There was also a stated political agenda to subject the public services to 'market disciplines' wherever possible.

Evolutionary change and organizational acclimatization

The railway has long traditions and consensually accepted preoccupations. At first, the Business Managers could only see limited opportunities for coupling their concept to day-to-day activities. But as events unfolded, tentative new possibilities were perceived. Stage-by-stage, as if in episodes, their abstract notion of the business railway became more concrete.

The railway is a very formal organization. People in it describe the management process in bureaucratic analogies, talking of 'chains-of-command' and 'good old soldiers falling into line'. In meetings, people are often referred to through their official titles. There is much deference to authority. The Business Managers recognized the significance of this formal management style in their quest to convert the railway. In fact they worked through it. As their ideas evolved, in each episode they sought first to persuade the Chief Executive and his advisors. These people were likely to be the most sympathetic to their economic rhetoric, for they interfaced with government and felt the external pressures most immediately. Carefully negotiating in principle a course of action, often after much private and closed debate, then, sure of their support, the Business Managers set out to convert a wider group.

Each episode involved a fairly small incremental step. None, in isolation, was especially threatening or difficult to accommodate in the old railway culture. Indeed, at first, even those who ultimately stood to lose influence and status appreciated the blending of the business perspective into the railway culture. As the organization became acclimatized to each change, however, as each episode had a chance to 'soak', so new possibilities were perceived. Repeatedly, new episodes were enacted.

Commenting on the way in which they operated, a Business Manager reflected:

> In the early days, there was nothing in writing, except that we had a responsibility for improving the bottom line. There were no organization charts. This made life difficult. It was all about relationships. We had to persuade everyone around us . . . As we did so, our ideas evolved. We became increasingly aware of the potential of the Businesses.

Senior Executives recalled:

> Our ideas were constrained because we were . . . well I was going to say traditional railwaymen. We were coloured by the views of the complexity of running a railway. No one foresaw the present state as a possibility. Our minds were opened.

> It takes time to change an organization like the railways and to change attitudes. There's 150 years' history. You don't overturn that lightly. Nor would you want to, or the railways would cease to operate . . . The Business Managers recognized that. First, they convinced a small group, then gradually widened that group until everyone was aboard . . .

> They operated in stages . . . Incremental changes were easier to sell. It was easier to build commitment and minimize opposition from those who stood to lose . . . They took each stage to the limit.

Creating an alternative account

For the Business Managers the purpose of the railway was to make a profit. The significance of customers was revenues; the significance of operations, that is, trains, infrastructure and staff, was cost. Upon their appointment, however, there was no account of the railway's activities in each market sector consistent with their reality. While profit or loss was measured for the organization as a whole, and was used in dealings with government, no such measures existed for component parts of the railway.[17]

In fact, during the 1970s, primarily for analytical purposes (rather than for responsibility accounting), the railway had moved towards a system of contribution accounting, matching directly traceable costs to revenues for various market segments.[18] Common costs were not allocated to the segments. The railway is a remarkably integrated activity, with common staff, infrastructure and, to some extent, train-related activities, so these unallocated costs were very substantial. Senior accounting executives had long argued, both privately and publicly, that allocation was neither possible nor meaningful. Fundamental to the Business Managers' appointments, however, was not just a profit-contribution responsibility, but a 'bottom line' responsibility, and this called for the allocation of common costs. In a definite way, this 'bottom line' responsibility had a normative symbolism – private sector managers were concerned with the 'bottom line'. But there was a more practical logic: this was to ensure that one or other of the Business Managers would be responsible for all costs, and motivated, as events unfolded, to ask questions about the necessity and consequences of incurring cost. A Senior Executive commented:

> You appoint a Business Manager and say: 'We believe this is freight'. The first thing he says is:

'What's mine? What are the boundaries of my business?' Then he pursues questions such as: 'How are costs being allocated to me? I want to know more about it. Let me analyse and fillet all the cost you are suggesting is mine' . . . Then he asks: 'How do these costs relate to my revenues'.

An individual within the accounting department was appointed to develop profit or loss measures by business sector. This person was in rather an invidious position. Given senior finance officials' former public repudiation of the possibility of developing these measures, he had to tread carefully. He later recalled:

At first I was not convinced that it was either sensible or feasible. There's a whole history of avoiding cost allocations in the railway. But if the Business Managers were to take responsibility, they needed different Management Accounting. I was persuaded of this new way to run the railway. I wanted Finance to play a fundamental part in supporting it.

When I was appointed I spent several months bouncing ideas off walls – walls not people – because finance people didn't believe you could or should develop the information they needed.

He became involved in intensive discussions with the Business Managers, and with representatives of the Chief Executive's office. Different ways of apportioning costs were discussed, and a firm of accountants consulted. The guiding principle was 'cost exhaustion' – all costs incurred by the railway had somehow to be attributed to one or more of the businesses.

The precise details of the method of arriving at the profit or loss for each business are unimportant here. It suffices to say that it was founded on principles reflecting the primacy of use of resources, and that the development of computer systems to operationalize the principle in full took some while. The significant point is that these measures were introduced, manually at first, and that they were fundamental to the emergence of the new culture.

Business Managers were appointed without any operational authority. Their positions were an abstract economic construct. They were made meaningful through the new accounting constructs. Moreover, the accounting measures provided a means through which they could later couple debate on operational and physical concerns to an economic calculus. Reflecting on the penetration of the new account of organizational activities, one Business Manager observed:

It's my impression that the engineers, and after all we are an engineering company, had no real understanding of what they were doing in terms of the 'bottom line' . . . Now the engineers know what a 'bottom line' specification really is and they can respond to it.

One regional General Manager commented:

I always behaved with the 'bottom line' in mind. But the Business Managers took it further. They challenge to a much greater extent. Making the railway profitable is the real meaning of the Business.

And another:

I didn't realize the extent to which budgets would be challenged, and challenged so vehemently.

Coupling railway activities to the new account

At the head of the railway is the office of Chief Executive. Attached to this are various staff functions – Finance, Engineering Directorates and so forth. Reporting to the Chief Executive in a line-management relationship are the General Managers of the regions. Underneath these are the railway operations. Overlaid on this management structure are formal planning and decision-making systems of various kinds.

The Business Managers were appointed in staff positions outside the formal line-management structure of the railway organization. They wished to explore their reality with others. But, there was, at first, no formal context for them to interact with others. Neither did they have the formal status they perceived necessary to influence others. In a sequence of moves, they sought, first, to institutionalize their status, and then to secure bases for participating in an increasing range of dialogue and debate.

Securing status. First they lobbied the Chief Executive and his advisors for a change in reporting relationships. If he was serious about the idea of marketing and business planning in the railway, they argued, then they had to have comparable status to the regional General Managers. After some considerable debate, a new management structure was introduced. The Chief Executive appointed two Joint Managing Directors, one taking a responsibility for the regions – the operations side of the railway, the regional General Managers; the other taking a responsibility for planning and marketing – in effect, the Business Managers. In a symbolic sense, although not at first in practice, this gave the Business Managers parity with the regional General Managers. It also stood for the Chief Executive's acknowledgement of the legitimacy of the 'business' reality, the reality of the railways being managed for profit. Commenting on the significance of this, one Business Manager observed:

> The General Managers used to report directly to the Chief Executive. The joint Managing Directors gave us parity.

Creating contexts for interaction. Later, in subsequent episodes, they lobbied for successive changes in the formal planning and decision-making systems. Changes, they argued at each juncture, were necessary to provide a balance to the overbearing influence of the regional General Managers and engineers. Over the period of the study, three changes were forthcoming. Each change secured opened up possibilities for perceiving the potential of the next. Firstly, the corporate planning system was revised. This dealt with longer-term matters. Formerly, regional General Managers prepared plans and presented them to the Executive Committee for ratification. The change gave Business Managers a formal input into the preparation of plans. In fact, the planning process became 'business-led', with these managers setting financial and other objectives for the regions, the regions being required to identify actions to achieve those objectives. Next, capital expenditure approval procedures were amended. Formerly, regional General Managers and engineering chiefs had significant autonomy in the approval of capital expenditures. The new system required expenditure proposals to be underwritten by one or more Business Managers, and effectively gave them a right to veto if they thought the proposals were uneconomic. Finally, budgeting systems were revised. Budgets emanating from each region were analysed by market sector. Business Managers became involved in their review.

The significance of these changes is that, in the context of ER's formal management style, formal systems and procedures imply rights to participate in and influence decisions and actions. The Business Managers' participation in the operation of these systems gave them a context to interact with others and question the rationale underlying railway decisions. In meetings, they could be seen translating operational and engineering concerns into the new profit calculus, feeding their financial vocabulary back into the stream of discourse.

Appealing to the 'ideal' of the profit-conscious customer-oriented private sector manager, they challenged and sometimes ridiculed beliefs.

Thus, participation in the planning procedures enabled them to reinterpret longer-run engineering and operational initiatives in business terms: what does it mean for the customer? Will it improve journey times and punctuality? What implications does it raise in terms of costs and revenues? Their sponsorship of capital investments enabled them to ask: will it improve train reliability, eliminating the need for back up resources? Can the businesses afford it? What are the investment options? The redesign of the budgeting system gave them opportunities to challenge the cost effectiveness and profit implications of operational issues like train routing, train scheduling and the programming of maintenance.

Moving from the remote concerns of long-term planning, through capital investments, to immediate issues of train scheduling and maintenance programming, they recast management debate into a language of the 'bottom line'. Others began to take up their vocabulary. Railway matters gradually came to be discussed as financial matters. Furthermore, planning and budgeting activities began to assume a new significance. Formerly, they were introverted acts of cost containment. Now they came to symbolize the search for profit-maximizing opportunities.

Commenting on the importance of these changes in formal systems, a Business Manager observed:

> We had responsibility for improving the profitability of the railway. But it wasn't clear who was in control – I think there was some diffidence in spelling that out with the utmost clarity. We lobbied to get control of the planning process. Clarity has emerged, now that we have taken responsibility for planning and budgeting. That's become our power base.

Over time, these changes cumulatively extended the opportunity for Business Managers to interact with engineers and operators far beyond their original remit. Through this interaction, their ideas became more specific. But they were still located in the Head Office. Accordingly, in a later episode, they set about extending their influence into the regional organizations. They appealed to the Chief Executive for the appointment of individuals to represent their interests within the regions. These Regional Business Managers, once appointed, carried the economic perspective deep into the regional organizations, carving underneath the regional General Managers and giving Business Managers a direct line of influence to operational activities. One commented:

> People in the regions are used to doing things without asking. They find themselves subject to our scrutiny. I can take things up in a big way, if necessary, and howl for their blood.

And commenting on their influence, an operations manager in the regions observed:

> Five years ago it would have been revolutionary to challenge what an engineer wanted to spend money on. Now it happens frequently.

Consolidating the emerging reality through symbolic events. Through interaction in meetings and elsewhere, many in the organization began to understand the Business Managers' emerging reality. Most also found it appealing. The continual attacks on the competence of public sector managers had worn morale down. To be business-like was 'good', it gave them pride, and made the railway modern. Increasingly people came to share the normative symbolism of the 'bottom line'. But to a large extent this was uncoupled from their concrete day-to-day activities. Meaningful symbols relating to everyday tasks, events and recollections through which people could connect the business reality to their ongoing decisions and actions, were absent.

As the situation unfolded, this changed, however. In parallel with the formal changes, a sequence of important events was enacted. The Business Managers staged 'contests' with the regional General Managers, forcing collisions between the railway culture and the business culture. As before, they worked through the bureaucratic structure of the railway. Focusing, in each episode, on a specific issue demonstrative of their concerns, they sought first to persuade the Chief Executive and his advisors. Once sure of this group's support they set out to convert a wider group. Finally, they forced the issue for resolution. Again, each issue resolved opened up the possibility of the next. Three events stand out. They are reported in sequence.

The first concerned the disposition of locomotives and rolling stock. Over a period of time, one regional General Manager had been successful in acquiring resources to invest in high speed trains for passenger transport. These he zealously guarded against suggestions from other regional General Managers that they should be more widely dispersed on the railway network. The relevant Business Manager's analysis suggested that this situation was uneconomic. Profit could be improved by relocating some of these train sets to other regions. This Business Manager lobbied the Chief Executive and his advisors to have the location decision determined by economic criteria. This was supported and the trains were moved. Commenting on this event, the relevant Business Manager observed:

> Regional prejudices had stopped the movement of high speed trains to the areas where they could earn the most money. The General Managers were barons. You just didn't go into

> their territory. It was a sort of unwritten law. I got those trains moved early on, it was one of the first things I did.

A second event concerned capital investments. In this case, a major track was being upgraded to take faster trains. According to engineering precedent, it was usual to renew signalling equipment at the same time. The Business Manager's analysis indicated that this was neither necessary nor economic. Again, the Chief Executive was lobbied. The signalling was not renewed. As the Business Manager observed:

> The main line was being electrified at significant expense. When wires are being strung over the track, it is customary to renew signalling equipment at the same time.

> We can't afford it. Anyway, the existing signalling will last another 15 years. All we needed to do was immunize the signals for electrification. The General Manager and his engineers were horrified. 'This isn't the way to run a railway', they said. 'It's a cash flow decision'.

A third decision concerned the scheduling of trains. Note that this is getting down to operational and logistical detail, by any standards the province of professional railway operators. Traditionally, train schedules had been set to maximize operational convenience. For the sake of passenger convenience, a Business Manager wanted to alter the schedule on a route. This intervention was bitterly resented by the regional General Managers. Even in this case, the Business Manager's judgement was supported by the Chief Executive.

> Traditionally, timetables have been set for operational convenience. I was dissatisfied and wanted to change the frequency of trains on the route.

The General Manager was determined not to have it. I took it to the Chief Executive. I said to the General Manager half an hour before the meeting: 'I've got to win, and will win, the writing's on the wall whether you like or not. I like you, why are you putting your head in a noose? Why don't you back off?'. But he didn't (Business Manager).

All these events came to have a significance way beyond the decisions themselves. Each stood for a whole class of decisions, signifying the primacy of the business reality in relation to those kinds of decisions. The high speed train issue redefined all decisions concerning the location of locomotives and rolling stock as economic decisions. The signalling decision redefined all investment decisions as economic decisions. The scheduling decision established the economic nature of detailed operational issues.

These events coupled the business culture to concrete railway activities. They were widely celebrated in the organization, both in public documents and in internal discussions, and are recalled in explanations of the emergence of the business rationale for railway management. Cumulatively, they embrace almost all aspects of the railway. People used them to attribute a new meaning to their everyday activities.

Not all decisions went in the Business Managers' favour, though. Secure in their conversion of the majority of the senior management élite, the Business Managers sought to explore their new reality with those within the organization. As already noted, representatives were appointed in regional offices: Regional Business Managers. At first, these individuals reported formally to the regional General Managers, and were on their payroll. The Business Managers wanted to pay their salaries from their own budgets to avoid them having divided loyalties. Regional General Managers found this unacceptable.

Apparently the Business Managers acted too soon; they lost. But the momentum they had already established was too great and they came back to win support some weeks later. A Business Manager explained:

There was a famous breakfast meeting where I soundly lost. The organization was not ready. But of course, one rises again. Later, we were on firmer ground. I raised the matter again, and I won the votes of everyone.

In the regions, a similar process of change seems to be being enacted. These individuals appear to be following a similar strategy, gaining contexts for interaction, persuading others of their views, and staging contests. The 'bottom line' for each business is now decomposed into subsidiary 'bottom line' accounts. In regional meetings, these managers reinterpret dialogue and debate through the subsidiary accounts. A sequence of new symbolic events is being enacted in each region. Commenting on his experiences, one Regional Business Manager observed:

At first we had to stand out there in front battling on our own. But now it's like a tide coming in. Nobody can actually fight the tide. I'm coming in on a surfboard really.

The picture then, is one of sequencing, momentum and cumulation. The Business Managers started on their mission with a vague concept of a business railway. They secured increasing contexts for interaction. Their ideas gradually became more concrete and they persuaded others around them. In an episodic manner, moving from the general to the particular, they secured changes to reporting relationships and systems. Each episode was punctuated by a key event. These events became symbols of the business culture, endowing railway activities with a new meaning, and provided a basis for continual and cumulative reinterpretations of railway operations.

Of course, there was tension. These decisions challenged the status of the regional General Managers and others who still subscribed to old beliefs. There was resentment and hostility. But the Business Managers let each step 'soak' so the organization could acclimatize, before embarking on the next episode, and a majority of the senior management gradually converted to the 'business culture'. Appealing to another metaphor, a Senior Executive commented:

> We've lit a bonfire and it's burning like mad.

The Regional General Managers' perspective

Regional General Managers were steeped in tradition. They were the descendants of the railway pioneers, the bastions of the railway culture. The business culture struck at their values and beliefs. When asked why and how they had let these things happen, they responded:

> It wasn't obvious at the time. The Business Managers were planners. We didn't expect the railway operations to change (General Manager).

One quoted from a memo he had written to his staff immediately after the Executive Committee meeting which had approved the principle of the Business Managers' appointment:

> The respective roles of Headquarters and the Regions will not change . . . Policies, as now will evolve from discussions. The Regions will participate . . .

In fact, from the General Managers' perspective, the story is one of initial seduction, followed by surprise and ambivalence, defection and resignation. They were aware of external pressures for financial performance. Some thought it was a whim, and would pass. But most perceived a need for a business perspective, and supported the creation of the Business Managers' positions in the Executive Committee. When the Business Managers were appointed, most welcomed their influence. At an early stage, one General Manager commented:

> This is good for us. I'm quite pleased at the way the culture is changing. You talk around now and nobody is in any doubt that the railway is business-led.

And another, commenting on the decision to relocate the high speed trains:

> Why do we have fancy train sets? It's not for General Managers to play trains. It's to make the businesses more profitable.[19]

One joined the Senior Executives, representing the Business Managers. According to his critics, he is reputed to have seen 'which way the wind was blowing', but he himself described it thus:

> Initially I was opposed. But I saw the logic of the changes. I was converted.

Thus, most found the abstract normative symbolism of the 'bottom line' appealing. They thought it 'good' to be more business-like. They aspired to 'private sector practice'. Few perceived the underlying momentum of events or their potential significance. Acting out the new rationale, they thought they need have no fear for the railway traditions. In fact, sitting in their grand offices with portraits and plaques around their walls and other symbols of former grandeur, it was inconceivable to them that the railway traditions could be undermined by anything.

As the significance of the economic reality emerged through subsequent events, however, the situation became less congenial for them. It threatened their pride as professional railway operators. Commenting on the resignalling decision noted earlier, a General Manager said:

> We'll have to do it all again in 15 years' time. It's not a sensible long-term decision.

Furthermore, the appointment of Regional Business Managers within their own organizations undermined their authority.

At this point, they protested vigorously. This prompted a report from the centre discussing the relationship between Businesses and the Regions. The report placated them with the soothing idea of Business Managers and regional General Managers as equals in a team-based organization. Nevertheless, the business perspective continued to impinge on operational matters.

Many General Managers became unhappy. They thought the emerging decisions unprofessional, and feared for the quality of the railway. By this time, however, their appeals fell on deaf ears. Most others among the senior management élite had converted to the business culture. The General Managers were characterized as reactionary, protective and old-fashioned.

Towards the end of the study, most of them left the organization or took 'early retirement'. One stayed in office a while longer. Shortly before his retirement he had this to say:

> With the benefit of hindsight, I think the Chief Executive was right in allowing it through . . . But it's gone too far . . .
>
> While I've been in office, through good engineering management, I've just about managed to get rid of all the speed restrictions on the main line. Business Managers are taking a maintenance

holiday [i.e. neglecting maintenance]. In five years someone will be faced with exactly the situation I inherited.

Former regional General Managers have been replaced with sympathetic men. They repudiate the old traditions. They are proud to subscribe to the business culture. A newly appointed General Manager had this to say:

> I personally feel that this new approach is right. I support the businesses. I see it as my job to influence my current staff to accept the business managers.

Far from being equals in a team, the regional General Managers are seen to be subservient to Business Managers. 'Business managers set policy and standards; regions implement'. Career patterns have changed. To become a regional General Manager was the ultimate aspiration for a railwayman; by the end of the field research it was to become a Business Manager. There was open discussion of removing the regional General Managers from the Railway Executive.

Accounting and Culture

Initially, there was a dominant 'railway' culture. The Business Managers brought a counter 'business' culture. This cascaded across the senior management élite to become dominant. The Business Managers had an abstract idea of a business railway. New accounts were crafted representing the railway as a series of businesses. The Business Managers gained contexts to interact with others. In these contexts, they recast dialogue and debate from a railway language of operations and engineering to their business language of markets and profit. Gradually the idea of a business railway became more specific. Moving from remote concerns to immediate issues, they persuaded others of their interpretations. There were contests over the definition of specific activities. The outcomes became symbols through which people attributed new meaning to railway operations. Momentum built up behind the business culture. People converted, others left. For senior managers, the abstract idea became a tangible, energizing reality, a source of pride. Now the railway culture is repudiated.

A broad range of theories can be brought to bear to interpret the pattern of these events. Fundamental to this account is the notion of culture as a system of ideas: beliefs, knowledges and values in which action and artifacts are vested with expressive qualities (Geertz, 1973, 1983); and the idea that organizations have distinctive cultures (Pettigrew, 1979). This is exemplified in the contrasting 'railway' and 'business' cultures described. Associated with this is the conceptualization of organizational change as a process of uncoupling and recoupling (cf. Greenwood & Hinings, 1988): exemplified in the railway by the uncoupling of activities from the railway culture and their recoupling to the business culture.[20] We can also see a theory of inertia in operation, change being precipitated by crisis (cf. Starbuck & Hedberg, 1977; Jonsson & Lundin, 1977; Mintzberg, 1978; Miller & Friesen, 1984). The railway culture was remarkably resilient over many previous decades, despite several attacks; real threats only being perceived when the severity of the current onslaught on the public services became apparent. There are also traces of the 'garbage can' (Cohen et al., 1972; March & Olsen, 1976): the Business Management idea was developed independently of the crisis, only subsequently coupled to the threats facing the organization.

Continuing, change was emergent (March & Olsen, 1976; Pettigrew, 1985). This was not a controlled process, relying on plans and rational analy-ses engineered by those standing outside, untainted as it were; the whole management group was bound up in the creation of the business culture. The process unfolded through tentative initiatives, buffeted by the timing of events, the ambition and (relative) political skills of the 'champions' (Kanter, 1983) and other actors involved, and their failures and successes. Nor were the vagaries of chance unimportant[21] (Pettigrew, 1985). Moreover, we see changes in systems (planning, capital investment, budgeting) interpenetrating the emergence and elaboration of the business culture.

It also is possible to appeal to the insights of institutional theory (Meyer & Rowan, 1977; DiMaggio & Powell, 1983; Scott, 1987; Zucker, 1988). Government, the railway's key environmental constituency, was intolerant of (what it saw as) managerial incompetence. The Business Management initiative could be interpreted as a symbol of the railway becoming more modern and business-like: the 'bottom line' idea standing for the railway adopting private sector practices. Such solutions may have real and unintended internal consequences, however. One was the Business Managers amassing power and influence at the expense of the General Managers. Although a theoretically impoverished theory in this context, there is some link here with the strategic contingencies' perspective of intraorganizational power (Hickson et al.,1971; Hinings et al.,1974). Subsequent to the appointment of the Business Managers, the railway managed to persuade government to make funds available, on a one-off basis, for a major electrification project (giving rise to the signalling controversy discussed earlier). Apparently, approval was forthcoming as a result of the 'rigorous business case' orchestrated by the relevant Business Manager.

The purpose here is not to discuss these theories further, however. It is to develop a cultural appreciation of accounting. The study shows that accounting was implicated differently in the two cultures described. At this point, it is appropriate to explicate its linkages to underlying knowledge, values and beliefs.

A cultural system incorporates, among other things, knowledge about environments, and strategies for extracting subsistence from them. This knowledge is quite different in the two cultures. In the railway culture it revolved around the public service idea, later coupled to notions of thrift. Essentially, the knowledge was this: if the organization provided the nation with a transport infrastructure (without undue waste), then sustenance would be forthcoming from government. This knowledge is not unique to the railway culture. The expectation that low-cost, generally available services will be rewarded by the state is common to many public service organizations in Europe, for example the health and education services. Given this knowledge, accounting was incidental in the railway culture: it was necessary to ensure that revenues were accounted for and suppliers paid, and perhaps to contain waste, but that was the limit of its significance in the structures of meaning. The purpose of the railway was to run trains; operating the railway would be rewarded by government. In this knowledge, the train, therefore, was endowed with a special significance.

The business culture, revolving around the 'bottom line', incorporates a quite different knowledge. Rather obviously, in view of events in ER, the bottom line constructs the notion of the railway as a profit-seeking enterprise. This is not just a matter of 'cost efficiency', however, although that is important. More importantly, in ER it constructs the idea of looking to product markets, rather than to government, for sustenance. There is nothing somehow uniquely 'public service' about the railway network in this construction. Rail transport is a product (or service), to be bought and sold like any other; in fact it is a series of prod-

ucts: intercity travel, freight, suburban commuting, etc. Revenues from these products, rather than government support, must cover costs; and, critically, revenues are earned in the market place. Survival depends on extracting resources from these markets, perhaps in competition with other firms. Hence the new-found concern for competition with other means of transport (road, air, buses), expressed by railway managers early in the account above, a concern which in the railway culture would have been probably inconsequential.[22] Given this knowledge, accounting activities become hugely significant. The search for profit opportunities, and the elimination of non-profit-making activities, is a quest for survival. It is now the customer, not the train, which has special importance.

No culture is completely coherent, of course. Each has ambiguities and contradictions. In ER, residues of the past create tensions. One is the partial incompatibility of the business culture with the restrictions placed on it by state ownership. ER is not allowed to borrow in financial markets to fund investment, for example, and as government funds are tight, this means investments necessary for competitive purposes cannot always be made. It also has statutory obligations to keep certain branch lines open, even if they are unprofitable. Here it still looks to government for support (although a government conceptualized as a customer). Nevertheless, the underlying knowledge systems are quite different, and constitute different realities.

This shift in knowledge which accounting helps to construct, the shift from looking to the state for subsistence to looking to markets, is fundamental, and it interpenetrates the operation and management of ER's core technology with pervasive effects. For a start, it changes the appropriate form of organization. In the old knowledge, the prime task was the operation of trains. The meaningful management structure was one which facilitated operations. The physical facilities of the railway are geographically laid out along the radial routes of the old prenationalization companies. Thus the appropriate management organization was around these routes, i.e. the regional management structures. The regional General Managers and engineers, because of their acknowledged expertise in operating trains, were afforded substantial status and influence.

Now, in the new knowledge, this is 'mere' production, subservient to markets. The prime task is serving markets. The meaningful form of management organization is one which reflects and confronts markets. Since the long distance intercity travel market is not confined to one main line, for example, or the freight market confined to one region, the regional and business forms of organization do not map perfectly onto one another. Hence the reorientation of management structures and systems around the Business Managers, and their subsequent elaboration through the Business Manager's subordinates located in the regions. Of course, there is still an operational task to be performed: trains, tracks, maintenance and so forth. But in this new knowledge it is Business Managers, with supposed expertise in markets and extracting resources from them, who attract status and influence.

The changing knowledge also redefines the appropriate form of action. In the old knowledge, that of the celebration of the train, there were norms that made things intrinsically necessary. 'Of course' professional railwaymen renewed signalling equipment when they electrified the track, for example; it was inconceivable not to do so. The train needs to be taken care of and nurtured. The interest in thrift, the avoidance of waste, also meant the elimination of activities not strictly necessary for the operation of trains: training staff to smile at customers, for example. In the new knowledge, activities are neither intrinsically necessary, nor intrinsically wasteful. Rather they are judged for their consequences in the market. Through the 'bottom line', activities become desirable to the extent that they add more 'value' than they cost. This is not simply cost minimization: the avoidance of unnecessary gold-plating. The 'bottom line engineering specification', mentioned earlier, means designing for the market, as it were: adding comfort, reliability, speed, customer service where its returns outweigh its cost. Attractive concourse design is not wasteful extravagance, it is reinterpreted as a 'good' thing which brings in custom.

Action is also judged against a different concept of time. In the old knowledge, time was practically infinite. The railways were built to last for decades, for centuries. The nation would always need a transport infrastructure. Professional standards were oriented towards doing a long-lasting thorough job. Government would reward the railway for maintaining the viability of the network into the future. In the new knowledge, the concept of time is much shorter. Survival is a day-to-day affair. Markets are ephemeral. Don't spend money now on activities that you can put off until the future. Take 'maintenance holidays' where you can: deterioration of the infrastructure can be remedied later.

The point being made here is that accounting can play a significant role in constructing specific knowledges. Accounting systems embody particular assumptions about rationality, organization, authority, time and so forth. If these permeate into underlying values, knowledges and beliefs they can have very real consequences. Above we see accounting coming into the organization to construct a new theory of subsistence, which in turn implies particular modes of organizing, patterns of influence and authority, criteria for action and a new concept of time.

The cultural knowledge described here was not discovered completely formed. Nor was it coupled to the railway's management structures (or to action) in an instant. Rather the meaning of the bottom line gradually crystallized around the initial accounts, and the coupling had to be actively crafted. The business culture unfolded in episodes: bursts of exhausting creativity, each building on what had previously been accomplished, and punctuated by a concluding event; followed by a pause for consolidation, recovery and imagination before the next. Successive episodes moved from the abstract realm to the particular; from long-term issues to immediate issues. In each, senior management struggled to reconceptualize a class of activities; then it was uncoupled, or perhaps one should say wrenched, from the railway culture and recoupled to the business culture. Again and again these episodes continued, until cumulatively practically all classes of railway activity were redefined. Later, in the regions, a similar process of episodic uncoupling and recoupling was enacted. In the process, linkages to the railway culture were only bit-by-bit ruptured.

The general point arising is that organizations have different classes of activity. Cultural change is not simply uncoupling and recoupling, or even reconceptualization. Each class of activity may need to be separately uncoupled and recoupled. During the process, different classes of activity may be informed by different rationales and knowledge. In ER, this led to a strange schizophrenia in the organization (and difficulties in making sense of the data), in which some activities were railway-culture issues, and some business-culture issues. It also led to strange disjunctures between the interpretive schemes brought to bear in the head office and in the regions. Only towards the end of the research did this schizophrenia begin to be resolved.

This process, however, needs to be enveloped in an awareness of the conditions for its possibility, conditions for the emergence of the particular culture described. In some ways, perhaps, the business culture in ER may be seen to be inevitable. Today, the belief in markets (as an optimal form of organization) seems to be firmly entrenched in Anglo-American political cultures, and in those of some continental-European states. Governmental pressures, inevitably, in this view, led to investment in financial calculation and the construction of the railway as a business enterprise. Support for this 'theory of inevitability' might be sought by retrospective application of the present political determination to privatize ER, or at least some of its businesses.

As Fligstein (1990) notes, in a rather different critique, such an interpretation relies on understandings of the present to construct appreciations of the past: interpreting the past through the present, rather than the present through the past. ER had a remarkably strong heritage which survived previous attacks. In the early 1980s, its privatization was not just undiscussed, it was inconceivable. Arguably, the business culture in ER, the reconstruction of the railway through the 'bottom line(s)' as a series of businesses, actually created preconditions for the discussion of privatization, not vice versa.

For sure, the early 1980s witnessed the beginnings of the sea change in attitudes towards the public services that swept across the political culture later in the decade. Through influential right-wing think-tanks the idea of subjecting public services to an entrepreneurial principle was then emerging, later to be manifested in the 'rolling back' of the public sector through the privatization of many public utilities and attempts to introduce market mechanisms in others. Associated with this was the emerging idea of the 'dependence' culture, and its repudiation; to be replaced by an 'enterprise' culture. Individuals, and organizations, were expected to take a responsibility for their own destiny.

However, the initiative for business management in ER, conceived in the late 1970s, preceded these political developments, and appears to have been a substantially autonomous development in a separate arena: as one of the initiators in the senior management group explained, it was 'the product of thinking railwaymen'. Explicating this claim would require careful analysis of historical materials beyond the scope of this paper. But such evidence as is available supports the view that the initiative was developed largely independently of political ideas, its private sector leanings probably owing more to the advice of a few business consultants than to any political agenda. Certainly it was not government-inspired; indeed government was initially sceptical, only later endorsing the ideas (and applying them to its own ends).

That said, the initiative was congruent with the ideas emerging outside, and its subsequent elaboration into the business culture undoubtedly owes much to their development. Even here, though, due importance must be attached to the specific circumstances within the organization. Public sector management was under challenge, morale was low. Many in the senior management group were receptive to the new ideas. Business Management was seen as a home-grown solution to governmental attack. It expressed some kind of empowerment, a potential freedom from the yoke of government restriction, and an opportunity for managers to show their entrepreneurial capabilities.

Concluding Comment

The purpose of this paper is to articulate a cultural analysis of accounting in organizations. The appreciation of organizations as cultures provides a rich insight into organizational life, drawing out the expressive qualities of action and artifact. Cultural knowledge in organizations vests organizational activities with symbolic meanings; so also it vests accounting with symbolic meaning. A cultural analysis of accounting seeks to uncover these particular meanings, and to locate them in underlying local knowledges, values and beliefs.

The paper has sought to apply this cultural perspective in an empirical setting. Through a field study of organizational change, it showed how accounting can be vested with different meanings in local cultures. And it showed how accounting can enter into organizational settings to constitute cultural knowledge in particular ways, creating particular rationalities for organizational action; and in turn how this can lead to new patterns of organization, of authority and influence, new concepts of time and legitimate action. The study also traced the emergent, episodic process through which cultural knowledge was constituted in this organization, and coupled to organizational activities.

The study certainly fleshes out the constitutive potential of accounting proposed by Hopwood (1987), Hines (1988) and others. However, the specific findings of the field study – the reorientation of a strategy for subsistence from government to markets, and its subsequent elaboration; and the process through which this realization was accomplished – are not offered as a general proposition on the cultural significance of accounting. Accounting systems are implicated in organizational cultures in different, possibly unique ways. The cultural knowledge constructed in this organization is but one possibility; there are many others. In this, as in other fields, 'the road to the grand abstractions of science winds through a thicket of singular facts' (Geertz, 1973, p. 145).

Rather, the purpose of the field study is to explicate a mode of theorizing linkages between accounting and culture. The mode of theorizing is interpretive, getting underneath surface descriptions to understand the significance of accounting in local settings; and it is reflective, in the sense that the theorist reflects on that significance in the context of the underlying ideational system. Applying this mode of analysis in different settings would contribute hugely to our emergent appreciation of the way in which accounting is used in organizations, usefully supplementing the more quantitative approaches to research pursued by contingency theorists, for example. It may be particularly valuable also in the development of comparative theories of the use of accounting in different social contexts. We know, for example, that accounting systems within organizations in different countries are often not that dissimilar to Anglo-American designs; it seems, however, that they may be used quite differently. The mode of theorizing advanced here would enable us to address this issue in a productive way.

Finally, while the paper has deliberately refrained from casting judgements on the developments described in the organization studied, it is probably worth acknowledging that there is widespread criticism of 'bottom line' orientations such as those described here, particularly for their construction of time. Far from creating an underlying competitiveness in organizations, the preoccupation with the 'bottom line' is seen to discourage technological innovation and investments in operational capability (e.g. Hayes & Abernathy, 1980; Johnson & Kaplan, 1987). ER, it seems, has adopted this vocabulary just as those organizations that have it are being exhorted to move towards longer-term, more strategic appreciations of time. In the railway, assets have long lives and the lead-time on capital investment is also long. To some extent the maintenance of the infrastructure is inevitably compromised by its new culture. Quite possibly with innovations in transport, the railway network will be an irrelevance in 50 years' time; on the other hand, it may not be. The green lobby, in particular, might argue that it is sensible to keep options open in a way that at present may not be possible.

Postscript

The process of change in ER continues. The regional management structure is today being dissolved. The operational side of the railway is currently being reorganized and assimilated into the businesses. The crafted accounts representing the railway as a series of businesses have now permeated through management structures and systems to operations on the ground. The railway quite literally has become its businesses. There are no longer any regional General Managers, no vestiges of the railway culture . . . or are there? High up on a building above one of the main-line termini, out of sight except to observant motorists on a nearby flyover, there is a residue of the past: a large illuminated logo, the logo of a pre-nationalization railway.

Bibliography

Aldrich, H. E., *Organizations & Environments* (Englewood Cliffs, NJ: Prentice Hall, 1979).

Allaire, Y. & Firsirotu, M. E., Theories of Organizational Culture, *Organizational Studies* (1984) pp. 51–64.

Ansari, S. & Euske, K. J., Rational, Rationalizing and Reifying Uses of Accounting Data in Organizations, *Accounting, Organizations and Society* (1987) pp. 549–570.

Argyris, C. & Schon, D. A., *Organizational Learning* (Reading, MA: Addison-Wesley, 1981).

Barley, S. R., Meyer, G. W. & Gash, D. C., Cultures of Culture: Academics, Practitioners and the Pragmatics of Normative Control, *Administrative Science Quarterly* (March 1988) pp. 24–60.

Berry, A., Capps, T., Cooper, D., Fergusson, P., Hopper, T. & Lowe, A., Management Control in an Area of the National Coal Board, *Accounting, Organizations and Society* (1985) pp. 3–28.

Blau, P. M., *The Dynamics of Bureaucracy: A Study of Interpersonal Relationships in Two Government Agencies* (Chicago, IL: University of Chicago Press, 1955).

Bruns, W. & Kaplan, R. S. (eds), *Accounting and Management: A Field Study Perspective* (Cambridge, MA: Harvard Business School Press, 1987).

Brunsson, N., *The Irrational Organization* (New York: Wiley, 1985).

Bryer, R. A., Accounting for the Railway Mania of 1845 A Great Railway Swindle?, *Accounting, Organizations and Society* (1991) pp. 439–486.

Burns, T. & Stalker, G. M., *The Management of Innovation* (London: Tavistock Press, 1961).

Buroway, M., *Manufacturing Consent* (Chicago, IL: University of Chicago Press, 1979).

Burrell, G. & Morgan, G., *Sociological Paradigms and Organizational Analysis* (London: Heineman, 1979).

Chandler, A. D., *The Railroads* (New York: Harcourt, Brace & World, 1965).

Clifford, J. & Marcus, G. E. (eds), *Writing Culture* (Berkeley, CA: University of California Press, 1986).

Cohen, M. D., March, J. G. & Olsen, J. P., A Garbage Can Model of Organizational Choice, *Administrative Science Quarterly* (March 1972) pp. 1–25.

Covaleski, M. & Dirsmith, M., The Use of Budgetary Symbols in the Political Arena: An Historically Informed Field Study, *Accounting, Organizations and Society* (1988) pp. 1–24.

Crapanzano, V., Hermes Dilemma: The Masking of Subversion in Ethnographic Description, in Clifford, J. & Marcus, G. E. (eds), *Writing Culture* (Berkeley, CA: University of California Press, 1986) pp. 51–76.

Crozier, M., *The Bureaucratic Phenomenon* (London: Tavistock, 1964).

Dalton, M., *Men Who Manage* (New York: Wiley, 1959).

Deal, T. E. & Kennedy, A. A., *Corporate Culture: The Rites and Rituals of Corporate Life* (Reading, MA: Addison-Wesley, 1982).

Dent, J. F., Organizational Research in Accounting: Perspectives, Issues and a Commentary, in Hopwood, A. G. & Bromwich, M., *Research and Current Issues in Management Accounting* (London: Pitman, 1986).

Denzin, N. K., *Interpretive Interactionism*, in Morgan, G. (ed), *Beyond Method* (Beverly Hills, CA: Sage, 1983) pp. 129–146.

DiMaggio, P. J. & Powell, W. W., The Iron Cage Revisited: Institutional Isomorphism and Collective Rationality in Organizational Fields, *American Sociological Review* (April 1983) pp. 147–160.

Douglas, M., *Purity and Danger: An Analysis of Concepts of Pollution and Taboo* (London: Routledge & KeganPaul, 1966).

Evans Pritchard, E. E., *Witchcraft, Oracles and Magic among the Azande* (Oxford: Oxford University Press, 1937).

Evans Pritchard, E. E., *The Nuer* (Oxford: Oxford University Press, 1940).

Feldman, S. P., Management in Context: An Essay on the Relevance of Culture to the Understanding of Organizational Change, *Journal of Management Studies* (November 1986) pp. 587–607.

Fligstein, N., *The Transformation of Corporate Control* (Cambridge, MA: Harvard University Press, 1990).

Geertz, C., *The Interpretation of Cultures* (New York: Basic Books, 1973).

Geertz, C., *Local Knowledge* (New York: Basic Books, 1983).

Geertz, C., *Works and Lives: The Anthropologist as Author* (Cambridge: Polity Press, 1988).

Goffman, E., *The Presentation of Self in Everyday Life* (New York: Doubleday, 1959).

Goodenough, W. H., *Culture, Language and Society* (Reading, MA: Addison-Wesley, 1971).

Goold, M. & Campbell, A., *Strategies and Styles* (Oxford: Blackwell, 1987).

Gouldner, A. W., *Patterns of Industrial Bureaucracy* (New York: Free Press, 1954).

Gourvish, T. R., *British Railways 1948–73: A Business History* (Cambridge University Press, 1986).

Gourvish, T. R., British Rail's 'Business Led' Organization, 1977–90: Government–Industry Relations in Britain's Public Sector, *Business History Review* (1990) pp. 109–149.

Greenwood, R. & Hinings, C. R., Organization Design Types, Tracks and the Dynamics of Strategic Change, *Organization Studies* (1988) pp. 293–316.

Gregory, K. L., Native-View Paradigms: Multiple Cultures & Culture Conflicts in Organizations, *Administrative Science Quarterly* (September 1983) pp. 359–377.

Harris, M., *Cultural Materialism: the Struggle for a Science of Culture* (New York: Random House, 1979).

Hayes, R. & Abernathy, S. J., Managing Our Way to Economic Decline, *Harvard Business Review* (July–August 1980) pp. 67–77.

Hedberg, B. L. T., How Organizations Learn and Unlearn, in Nystrom, P. C. & Starbuck, W. H. (eds), *Handbook of Organization Design: Volume 1* (Oxford: Oxford University Press, 1981).

Hedberg, G. & Jonsson, S., Designing Semi-confusing Information Systems for Organizations in Changing

Environments, *Accounting, Organizations and Society* (1978) pp. 47–65.

Hedberg, B., Nystrom, P. C. & Starbuck, W. H., Camping on See Saws: Prescriptions for a Self-Designing Organization, *Administrative Science Quarterly* (March 1976) pp. 41–65.

Hickson, D. J., Hinings, C. R., Lee, C. A., Schneck, R. E. & Pennings, J. M., A Strategic Contingencies' Theory of Intra Organizational Power, *Administrative Science Quarterly* (June 1971) pp. 216–229.

Hines, R., Financial Accounting: In Communicating Reality, We Construct Reality, *Accounting, Organizations and Society* (1988) pp. 251–261.

Hinings, C. R., Hickson, D. J., Pennings, J. M. & Schneck, R. E., Structural Conditions of Intra Organizational Power, *Administrative Science Quarterly* (March 1974) pp. 22–44.

Hopwood, A. G., Towards an Organizational Perspective for the Study of Accounting and Information Systems, *Accounting, Organizations and Society* (1978) pp. 3–13.

Hopwood, A. G., On Trying to Study Accounting in the Contexts in which it Operates, *Accounting, Organizations and Society* (1983) pp. 287–305.

Hopwood, A. G., The Archaeology of Accounting Systems, *Accounting, Organizations and Society* (1987) pp. 207–234.

Hughes, E. C., *Men and their Work* (Glencoe, IL: Free Press, 1958).

Johnson, H. T. & Kaplan, R. S., *Relevance Lost: The Rise and Fall of Management Accounting* (Cambridge, MA: Harvard, 1987).

Jones, P. R. & Lakin, C., *The Carpet Makers* (Maidenhead: McGraw-Hill, 1978).

Jonsson, S. & Lundin, R. A., Myths and Wishful Thinking as Management Tools, in Nystrom, P. C. & Starbuck, W. H. (eds), *Prescriptive Models of Organization*, pp. 157–170 (Amsterdam: North-Holland, 1977).

Kanter, R., *The Change Masters: Corporate Entrepreneurs at Work* (New York: Simon & Schuster, 1983).

Kilmann, R. H., Saxton, M. J. & Serpa, R. (eds), *Gaining Control of the Corporate Culture* (San Francisco: Jossey Bass, 1985).

Lawrence, P. R. & Lorsch, J. W., *Organization and Environment: Managing Differentiation and Integration* (IL: Irwin, [1967] 1969).

Levi Strauss, C., *Structural Anthropology* (New York: Basic Books, 1963).

Levi Strauss, C., *The Savage Mind* (Chicago, IL: University of Chicago Press, [1962] 1966).

Malinowski, B., *Argonauts of the Western Pacific* (London: Routledge & Kegan Paul, 1922).

March, J. G. & Olsen, J. P., *Ambiguity and Choice in Organizations* (Oslo: Universitetforlaget, 1976).

Marcus, G. E. & Cushman, R., Ethnographies as Texts, *Annual Review of Anthropology* (1982) pp. 25–69.

Marcus, G. E. & Fischer, M. M. J., *Anthropology as Cultural Critique* (Chicago, IL: University of Chicago Press, 1986).

Markus, M. L. & Pfeffer, J., Power and the Design and Implementation of Accounting and Control Systems, *Accounting, Organizations and Society* (1983) pp. 205–218.

Martin, J., Fieldman, M. S., Hatch, M. J. & Sitkin, S. M., The Uniqueness Paradox in Organizational Stories, *Administrative Science Quarterly* (September 1983) pp. 438–453.

Martin, J. & Siehl, C., Organizational Culture and Counterculture: An Uneasy Symbiosis. *Organizational Dynamics* (Autumn 1983) pp. 52–64.

Meek, V. L., Organizational Culture: Origins and Weaknesses, *Organization Studios* (1988) pp. 453–473.

Meyer, J. W. & Rowan, B., Institutionalized Organizations: Formal Structure as Myth and Ceremony, *American Journal of Sociology* (1977) pp. 340–363.

Miles, R. E. & Snow, C. C., *Organizational Strategy, Structures and Process* (New York: McGraw-Hill, 1978).

Miller, D. & Friesen, P. H., *Organizations: A Quantum View* (Englewood Cliffs, NJ: Prentice Hall, 1984).

Miller, P. & O'Leary, T., The Construction of the Governable Person, *Accounting, Organizations and Society* (1987) pp. 235–265.

Mintzberg, H., Patterns in Strategy Formulation, *Management Science* (May 1978) pp. 934–948.

Ouchi, W., *Theory Z: How American Business Can Meet the Japanese Challenge* (Reading, MA: Addison-Wesley, 1981).

Parsons, T., *The Social System* (New York: Free Press, 1951).

Peters, T. J. & Waterman, R. A., *In Search of Excellence: Lessons from America's Best Run Companies* (New York: Harper & Row, 1982).

Pettigrew, A., On Studying Organizational Cultures, *Administrative Science Quarterly* (December 1979) pp. 570–581.

Pettigrew, A., *The Awakening Giant, Continuity and Change in ICI* (Oxford: Blackwell, 1985).

Pfeffer, J., Management as Symbolic Action: The Creation and Maintenance of Organizational Paradigms, in Cummings, I. L. & Staw, B. M. (eds), *Research in Organizational Behavior*, pp. 1–52 (Greenwich, CT: JAI Press, 1981).

Pfeffer, J. & Salancik, G. R., *The External Control of Organizations* (New York: Harper & Row, 1978).

Pondy, L. R., Leadership is a Language Game, in McCall, M. W. & Lombardo, M. M. (eds), *Leadership: Where Else Can We Go?* (Durham, NC: Duke University Press, 1978).

Pondy, L. R., Frost, P. J., Morgan, G. & Dandridge, T. C. (eds), *Organizational Symbolism* (Greenwich, CT: JAI Press, 1983).

Radcliffe-Brown, A. R., *Structure and Function in Primitive Society* (Oxford: Oxford University Press, 1952).

Ranson, S., Hinings, R. & Greenwood, R., The Structuring of Organizational Structures, *Administrative Science Quarterly* (March 1980) pp. 1–17.

Riley, P., A Structurationist Account of Political Culture, *Administrative Science Quarterly* (September 1983) pp. 414–437.

Roethlisberger, F. J. & Dickson, W. J., *Management and the Worker* (Cambridge, MA: Harvard University Press, 1939).

Roy, D., Efficiency and 'the Fix': Informal Intergroup Relations in a Piecework Machine Shop, *American Journal of Sociology* (November 1954) pp. 255–266.

Roy, D., Banana Time: Job Satisfaction and Informal Interactions, *Human Organization* (Winter 1960) pp. 158–168.

Scott, W. R., The Adolescence of Institutional Theory, *Administrative Science Quarterly* (December 1987) pp. 493–511.

Selznick, P., *TVA and the Grass Roots* (Berkeley, CA: University of California Press, 1949).

Smircich, L., Concepts of Culture and Organizational Analysis, *Administrative Science Quarterly* (September 1983a) pp. 339–358.

Smircich, L., Studying Organizations as Cultures, in Morgan, G. (ed.), *Beyond Method*, pp. 160–172 (Beverley Hills, CA: Sage, 1983b).

Starbuck, W. H., Congealing Oil: Inventing Ideologies to Justify Acting Ideologies Out, *Journal of Management Studies* (January 1982) pp. 3–27.

Starbuck, W. H. & Hedberg, B., Saving an Organization from a Stagnating Environment, in Thorelli, H. B. (ed.), *Strategy + Structure = Performance*, pp. 249–258 (Bloomington, IN: Indiana University Press, 1977).

Turner, S., Studying Organization Through Levi Strauss' Structuralism, in Morgan, G. (ed.), *Beyond Method*, pp. 189–201 (Beverley Hills, CA: Sage, 1983)

Van Maanen, J., The Fact of Fiction in Organizational Ethnography, *Administrative Science Quarterly* (December 1979) pp. 539–550.

Van Maanen, J., *Tales of the Field* (Chicago, IL: University of Chicago Press, 1988).

Van Maanen, J. & Barley, S. R., Occupational Communities: Culture and Control in Organizations, in Cummings, L. L. & Staw, B. M. (eds), *Research in Organizational Behavior*, pp. 287–365 (Greenwich, CT: JAI Press, 1984).

Weber, M., *The Theory of Social and Economic Organization* (New York: Collier-Macmillan, 1947).

Weick, K. E., *The Social Psychology of Organizing*, 2nd edn (Reading, MA: Addison-Wesley, 1979).

Whyte, W. F., *Human Relations in the Restaurant Industry* (New York: McGraw-Hill, 1948).

Whyte, W. F., *Street Corner Society* (Chicago, IL: University of Chicago Press, [1943] 1955).

Wuthnow, R., Hunter, J. D., Bergesen, A. & Kurzweil, E., *Cultural Analysis* (London: Routledge & KeganPaul, 1984).

Wuthnow, R. & Witten, M., New Directions in the Study of Culture, *Annual Review of Sociology* (1988) pp. 49–67.

Zucker, L. G. (ed.), *Institutional Patterns and Organizations* (Cambridge, MA: Ballinger, 1988).

Endnotes

1. Cultural ideas are not new to organizational research. They surface in many classic descriptive studies of organizational behaviour (e.g. Roethlisberger & Dickson, 1939; Whyte, 1948, [1943] 1955; Selznick, 1949; Gouldner, 1954; Blau, 1955; Roy, 1954, 1960; Goffman, 1959; Hughes, 1958; Dalton, 1959; Buroway, 1979). Only in the late 1970s, however, did organizational culture emerge as an explicit theme.

2. In cultural anthropology, culture is used in different ways. The broad idea of culture as a 'total way

of life' of a community, developed by classical anthropologists (e.g. Radcliffe-Brown, 1952; Malinowski, 1922; Evans Pritchard, 1937, 1940), is continued by Harris (1979), among others. More commonly, culture is used to denote a system of ideas, a position associated in different ways with Goodenough (1971), Levi Strauss (1963, [1962] 1966) and Geertz (1973, 1983). Allaire & Firsirotu (1984) trace implications of these different perspectives on culture for organizational research. Wuthnow & Witten (1988) discuss the use of culture in contemporary sociology, see also Wuthnow et al. (1984).

3. With Meek (1988), Feldman (1986) and others, I wish to distance myself from the current vogue of 'pop-culture' literature on the management of meaning, which is ill-informed in the anthropological tradition: e.g. Ouchi (1981), Peters & Waterman (1982), Deal & Kennedy (1982), Kilmann et al. (1985). No one has a monopoly of meanings (Smircich, 1983b). See Barley et al. (1988) for an interesting discussion of the contaminating effects of this literature.

4. Geertz' (1973, pp. 407–408) analogy is relevant here: 'Systems need not be exhaustively connected . . . They may be densely interconnected or poorly . . . the problem of cultural analysis is as much a matter of determining independencies as interconnections, gulfs as well as bridges. The appropriate image . . . of cultural organisation, is . . . the octopus, whose tentacles are in large part separately integrated, neurally quite poorly connected with one another and with what in an octopus passes for a brain, and yet who nonetheless manages to get around and to preserve himself, for a while anyway, as a viable if somewhat ungainly entity'. He goes on: 'Culture moves like an octopus too – not all at once in a smoothly coordinated synergy of parts, a massive coaction of the whole, but by disjointed movements of this part, then that, and now the other which somehow cumulate to directional change'.

5. Douglas (1966, p. 5) states: '. . . we think of ourselves as passively receiving our native language, and discount responsibility for shifts it undergoes in our life time. The anthropologist falls into the same trap if he thinks of a culture he is studying as a long established pattern of values'.

6. There is a link here to the cultural adaptation literature (Harris, 1979), but it is not developed in this paper; cf. Lawrence & Lorsch ([1967] 1969), Aldrich (1979).

7. For Geertz (1983, p. 58): 'The trick is not to get yourself into some inner correspondence of spirit with your informants . . . The trick is to figure out what they think they are up to'. While one may attempt to move towards an 'experience near' understanding in the field, however, the presentation of an ethnography inevitably will recast these understandings through the 'experience far' theoretical categories of the reader. Crapanzano (1986) argues that this claim to 'native view' interpretations is illusory: 'There is only the constructed understanding of the constructed native's constructed point of view' (p. 74). See also Marcus & Fischer (1986) for contemporary critique.

8. The anthropological literature is brimming with reflexive discussion of ethnographic writing styles. See Geertz (1988), Marcus & Cushman (1982), Clifford & Marcus (1986), also Van Maanen (1988).

9. There were several fascinating aspects of this last stage in the field. One was that many managers had simply forgotten what had happened, or at least had retrospectively reconstructed it. In particular, some seemed to forget how tentative their initiatives had been, the anguish and stress of trying to imagine a new future, the tense moments at the heights of political intrigue and the sheer uncertainty of the outcomes. They read the past through the present. Geertz' (1973, p. 19) notion, drawn from Ricoeur, of the ethnographer '. . . tracing the curve of social discourse; fixing it in inspectable form . . . He turns it from a passing event which exists only in its own moment of occurrence, into an account, which . . . can be reconsulted', is particularly pertinent here. Secondly, my intervention at this stage actually constructed a past (and hence a present) for participants; in other words, the theory developed here on the constitutive potential of accounting may be a general theory of accounts.

10. The company's name has been disguised.

11. This is an oversimplification, for in fact there were then a multitude of local regional railway companies in addition. It was only in the 1920s that government inspired mergers led to their consolidation around the major routes.

12. This was not unique to ER. See Chandler (1965), Crozier (1964) and Gourvish (1986).

13. In this connection, Bryer's (1991) account of the differential returns to investors in Britain's railways is interesting.

14. Committee structures were continually revised and amended during the post-nationalization period. My terminology anticipates the structure in place in the early 1980s, at the start of this research. Broadly speaking, this structure is not unrepresentative of early patterns, for the representation of interests in railway management committees was constant throughout this period. The railway companies were also diversified into related businesses, however, e.g. engineering, shipping, harbours, property and hotels, which were also represented in the management structure. These other businesses are not discussed here. They only accounted for about 25% of headcount and turnover, and the railway operations remained the dominant managerial concern. For the record, they were gradually privatized during and after the period of this research.

15. A notorious example of this was the development of an advanced passenger train in the late 1970s. Powered by a gas turbine, it employed a revolutionary suspension technology, the whole train tilting as it went round corners. In trials, the prototypes proved unreliable, and made passengers sick. The project was shelved in the subsequent 'business regime' of the 1980s. A prototype was sent to a railway museum.

16. I am indebted to independent archival research for this information. In the railway folklore these events are shrouded in the mystery of (recent) time. This pattern of events is not unique: see Gourvish (1990) for comparable accounts.

17. Under existing systems, costs were accounted for by region, corresponding to the physical location of the operational activities concerned. The regions were thus essentially cost centres. Revenue responsibility was more diffuse, for passengers and freight were frequently transported across two or more regions. In fact it was not as simple as this, but in practical terms, the railway network alone was a huge profit centre.

18. These did not precisely correspond to the present market sectors, but provided a basis on which to build the subsequent measures.

19. This General Manager claimed that he had repeatedly requested some of these train sets himself.

20. This characterization, of course, emphasizes change; and there is also a sense in which there is continuity. The railway still runs trains, it still provides a transport infrastructure (of sorts), and it is still a very mechanistic bureaucracy. Nevertheless, managers in the organization currently emphasize change, and there is a sense in which linkages with the past have been ruptured, for the railway, as I will explain, is interpreted quite differently.

21. In ER, subsequent to the events described, there was an unfortunate accident in which one crowded commuter train collided into the back of another. A formal inquiry found that basic supervision of electrical rewiring in a signalling scheme had been neglected, attributing blame, in part, to ER's pursuit of profit. It is interesting to speculate how outcomes might have differed had this accident happened two years before.

22. A Business Manager's comment on market research is also interesting in this respect: 'The single most important question we ask is: "Are you more likely or less likely to travel on the railway as a result of your most recent journey?"' This question would have been substantially irrelevant in the railway culture.

Glossary of Accounting Terms

Absorption costing	A method of costing in which all fixed and variable production costs are charged to products or services using an allocation base. See also *Allocation base*.
Account	An explanation or report in financial terms about the transactions of an organization.
Accountability	The process of satisfying stakeholders in the organization that managers have acted in the best interests of the stakeholders, a result of the stewardship function of managers, which takes place through accounting.
Accounting	A collection of systems and processes used to record, report, and interpret business transactions.
Accounting equation	The representation of the double-entry system of accounting such that assets are equal to liabilities plus equity.
Accounting period	The period of time for which financial statements are produced. See also *Financial year*.
Accounting rate of return (ARR)	A method of investment appraisal that measures the profit generated as a percentage of the investment. See also *Return on investment*.
Accounting standards	See *International Financial Reporting Standards (IFRS)*.
Accounting system	A set of accounts that summarize the transactions of a business that have been recorded on source documents.
Accounts	'Buckets' within the ledger, part of the accounting system. Each account contains similar transactions (line items) that are used for the production of financial statements. 'Accounts' is also commonly used as an abbreviation for financial statements.
Accrual	An expense for profit purposes even though no payment has been made.
Accruals accounting	A method of accounting in which profit is calculated as the difference between income *when it is earned* and expenses *when they are incurred*. See also *Matching principle*.

Activity-based budgeting	A method of budgeting that develops budgets based on expected activities and cost drivers. See also *Activity-based costing*.
Activity-based costing	A method of costing that uses cost pools to accumulate the cost of significant business activities and then assigns the costs from the cost pools to products or services based on cost drivers (the causes of activity).
Allocation base	A measure of activity or volume such as labour hours, machine hours, or volume of production used to apportion overheads to products and services.
Amortization	See *Depreciation*, but usually in relation to intangible assets such as goodwill, or to leased assets.
Annual Report	The report required by the Stock Exchange for all listed companies, containing the company's financial statements, chairman's, statutory, and audit reports.
Assets	Things that the business owns. IASB definition: a resource controlled by an entity as a result of past events and from which future economic benefits are expected to flow to the entity. An entity acquires assets to produce goods or services capable of satisfying customer needs. Physical form is not essential.
Audit	A periodic examination of the accounting records of a company carried out by an independent auditor to ensure that those records have been properly maintained and that the financial statements which are drawn up from those records comply with legislation and accounting standards, and give a true and fair view.
Avoidable costs	Costs that are identifiable with and able to be influenced by decisions made at the business unit (e.g. division) level.
Backflush costing	A method of costing that aims to eliminate detailed transaction processing. Rather than tracking each movement of materials, the output from the production process determines (based on the *expected* usage and cost of materials) the amount of materials to be transferred from raw materials to finished goods. See also *Lean accounting*.
Balance Sheet	See *Statement of Financial Position*.
Balanced Scorecard	A system of non-financial performance measurement that links innovation, customer, and process measures with financial performance and strategy.
Bank	Money in a bank cheque account, the difference between receipts and payments.
Bank overdraft	Money owed to the bank in a cheque account where payments exceed receipts.
Bill of materials	A listing of all the materials and quantities that comprise a completed product.

Breakeven point	The point at which total costs equal total revenue, i.e. where there is neither a profit nor a loss.
Budget	A plan expressed in monetary terms covering a future period of time and based on a defined level of activity.
Budget cycle	The annual period over which budgets are prepared.
Budgetary control	The process of ensuring that actual financial results are in line with targets. See also *Variance analysis*.
Capacity	The maximum volume of products or services that can be produced given limitations of space, people, equipment, or financial resources.
Capacity utilization	The proportion of capacity that is able to be utilized to fulfil customer demand for products or services.
Capital	The shareholders' investment in the business; the difference between the assets and liabilities of a business. See also *Equity*.
Capital employed	The total of debt and equity, i.e. the total funds in the business, however financed.
Capital investment or capital expenditure (often abbreviated as 'cap ex')	Spending money now in the hope of getting it back later through future cash flows. See also *Capitalize*.
Capitalize	To make a payment that might otherwise be an expense (in the Income Statement) or an asset (in the Statement of Financial Position).
Capital market	The market in which investors buy and sell shares of companies or debt, normally associated with a Stock Exchange.
Cash accounting	A method of accounting in which profit (or surplus) is calculated as the difference between income *when it is received* and expenses *when they are paid*.
Cash cost	The amount of cash expended for something.
Cash flow	Cash flow is the change in cash and cash equivalents during an accounting period. It arises from one of three activities – operations, investing, or financing. Cash flow from operations is calculated by adjusting profit by non-cash expenses (such as depreciation) and for changes in working capital, and deducting income tax payments. Cash flow from investing is the net effect of purchasing new capital assets and the proceeds of sale of capital assets disposed of. Cash flow from financing is the net effect of borrowings and repayments, share issues and buy-backs, interest and dividends paid. Cash flow specifically ignores accruals and prepayments which are used in calculating profit.
Cash Flow Statement	See *Statement of Cash Flows*.
Cash value added (CVA)	A method of investment appraisal that calculates the ratio of the net present value of an investment to the initial capital investment.

Contribution	The difference between the selling price and variable costs, which can be expressed either per unit or in total.
Contribution margin	The contribution (see above) expressed as a percentage of the selling price.
Controllable profit	The profit made by a division after deducting only those expenses that can be controlled by the divisional manager and ignoring those expenses that are outside the divisional manager's control.
Conversion costs	The production labour and production overhead associated with continuous manufacture. In a process costing system, conversion costs are added to the cost of raw materials and divided by production volume in order to calculate the cost of manufacture of finished goods produced under continuous manufacture.
Corporate Governance	A set of principles for corporate governance.
Cost	A resource sacrificed or forgone to achieve a specific objective, usually defined in monetary terms.
Cost behaviour	The idea that fixed costs and variable costs react differently to changes in the volume of products/services produced.
Cost centre	A division or unit of an organization that is responsible for controlling costs.
Cost control	The process of either reducing costs while maintaining the same level of productivity or maintaining costs while increasing productivity.
Cost driver	The most significant cause of the cost of an activity, a measure of the demand for an activity by each product/service enabling the cost of activities to be assigned from cost pools to products/services. See also *Activity-based costing*.
Cost object	Anything for which a measurement of cost is required – inputs, processes, outputs, or business units.
Cost of capital	The costs incurred by an organization to fund all its investments, comprising the risk-adjusted cost of equity and debt weighted by the mix of equity and debt.
Cost of goods sold	See *Cost of sales*.
Cost of quality	The difference between the actual costs of production, selling, and service and the costs that would be incurred if there were no failures during production or usage of products or services.
Cost of sales	The manufacture or purchase price of goods sold in a period or the cost of providing a service.
Cost-plus pricing	A method of pricing in which a mark-up is added to the total product/service cost.

Cost pool	The costs of (cross-functional) business processes, irrespective of the organizational structure of the business. See also *Activity-based costing*.
Cost–volume–profit analysis (CVP)	A method for understanding the relationship between revenue, cost, and sales volume.
Credit	Buying or selling goods or services now with the intention of payment following at some time in the future (as opposed to buying or selling goods or services for cash).
Creditors	See *Payables*.
Current assets	Amounts receivable by the business within a period of 12 months, including bank, receivables, inventory, and prepayments.
Current liabilities	Amounts due and payable by the business within a period of 12 months, e.g. bank overdraft, payables, and accruals.
Debt	Borrowings from financiers.
Debtors	See *Receivables*.
Depreciation	An expense that spreads the cost of an asset over its useful life.
Direct costs	Costs that are readily traceable to particular products or services.
Discounted cash flow (DCF)	A method of investment appraisal that discounts future cash flows to present value using a discount rate, which is the risk-adjusted weighted average cost of capital.
Dividend	The payment of part of after-tax profits to shareholders as their share of the profits of the business for an accounting period.
Double entry	The system of recording business transactions in two accounts in an accounting system.
Earnings before interest and tax (EBIT)	The operating profit before deducting interest and taxes.
Earnings before interest, tax, depreciation, and amortization (EBITA)	The operating profit before deducting interest, taxes, depreciation, and amortization.
Economic Value Added	Operating profit, adjusted to remove distortions (EVATM) caused by certain accounting rules, less a charge to cover the cost of capital invested in the business.
Equity	Funds raised from shareholders. The residual interest in the assets of the entity after deducting all its liabilities. See also *Shareholders' funds*. See also *Capital*.
Equivalent units	A measure of the volume of production under continuous manufacture used in a process costing system. Equivalent units combine the number of completed units of production with the proportion of partially completed units expressed as completed units (e.g. 1,000 units 50% complete are calculated as the equivalent of 500 completed units).

Expenses	The costs incurred in buying, making, or producing goods and services.
Feedback	The retrospective process of measuring performance, comparing it with plan, and taking corrective action.
Feedforward	The process of determining prospectively whether strategies are likely to achieve the target results that are consistent with organizational goals.
Financial accounting	The production of financial statements, primarily for those interested parties who are external to the business.
Financial statements	A Statement of Financial Position, Income Statement, Statement of Comprehensive Income, Statement of Changes in Equity, and Statement of Cash Flows together with explanatory Notes.
Financial year	The accounting period adopted by a business for the production of its financial statements.
Finished goods	Inventory that is ready for sale, either having been purchased as such or the result of a conversion from raw materials through a manufacturing process.
Fixed assets	See *Non-current assets*.
Fixed costs	Costs that do not change with increases or decreases in the volume of goods or services produced, within the relevant range.
Flexible budget	A method of budgetary control that flexes, i.e. adjusts the original budget, by applying standard prices and costs per unit to the actual production volume.
Forecast	A revised budget estimate or update, part-way through a budget period.
Framework for the Preparation and Presentation of Financial Statements	Part of International Financial Reporting Standards (IFRS) that sets out the concepts underlying the preparation and presentation of financial statements for external users, including the objectives of financial statements; the qualitative characteristics that determine decision usefulness; and the definition, recognition, and measurement of the elements from which financial statements are constructed.
Free cash flow	A measure of financial performance defined as operating cash flow after deducting capital expenditure. Free cash flow = operating profit before tax + depreciation & amortization +/– change in working capital – capital expenditure.
Gains	A form of income not in the ordinary course of business, such as income from the disposal of non-current assets or revaluations of investments.
Gearing	A measure of the extent of long-term debt in comparison with shareholders' funds.

Goodwill	Goodwill arises where a company buys a business and pays more than the fair value of the tangible assets. Goodwill is an intangible asset and represents the value of brands, customer lists, location, reputation, etc. It is reflected in the expectation of future profits.
Governance	See *Corporate governance*.
Gross margin	Gross profit, expressed as a percentage of sales.
Gross profit	The difference between the price at which goods or services are sold and the cost of sales.
Income	The revenue generated from the sale of goods or services.
Income Statement	A financial statement measuring the profit or loss of a business income less expenses for an accounting period. Previously known as a Profit and Loss Account and now part of a Statement of Comprehensive Income.
Incremental budget	A budget that takes the previous year as a base and adds (or deducts) a percentage to arrive at the budget for the current year.
Indirect costs	Costs that are necessary to produce a product/service but are not readily traceable to particular products or services. See also *Overhead*.
Intangible assets	Non-physical assets, e.g. customer goodwill or intellectual property (patents and trademarks).
Integrated reporting	A concise communication about how an organization's strategy, governance, performance, and prospects lead to the creation of value over the short, medium, and long term.
Interest	The cost of money, received on investments or paid on borrowings.
Internal rate of return (IRR)	A discounted cash flow technique used for (IRR) investment appraisal that calculates the effective cost of capital that produces a net present value of zero from a series of future cash flows and an initial capital investment.
International Financial Reporting Standards (IFRS)	Standards that set out recognition, measurement, presentation, and disclosure requirements dealing with transactions and events that are important in general purpose financial statements.
Inventory	Goods bought or manufactured for resale but as yet unsold, comprising raw materials, work-in-progress, and finished goods.
Investment centre	A division or unit of an organization that is responsible for achieving an adequate return on the capital invested in the division or unit.
Job costing	A method of accounting that accumulates the costs of a product/service that is produced either customized to meet a customer's specification or in a batch of identical products/services.
Just-in-time (JIT)	A method of purchasing that aims to improve productivity and eliminate waste by obtaining manufacturing components in the right quantity, at the right time and place to meet the demands of the manufacturing cycle with minimal inventory.

Kaizen	A method of costing that involves making continual, incremental improvements to the production process during the manufacturing phase of the product/service life cycle, typically involving setting targets for cost reduction.
Labour oncost	The non-salary or wage costs that follow from the payment of salaries or wages, e.g. National Insurance (in the UK) and pension contributions.
Lean accounting	A method of accounting and costing that relies on value stream accounting rather than traditional management accounting tools like standard costing, activity-based costing, variance reporting, cost-plus pricing, transaction reporting systems, and financial statements that are often confusing to non-financial managers. See *Value stream accounting*.
Lean production	A method of production that focuses on production processes as a continuous flow (in which products are manufactured in a continuous process), rather than on the hierarchical structures. This significantly reduces the cycle time from order to delivery, which reduces the need for work-in-process inventory.
Leasing	A method of finance for equipment used by business organizations, in which a business needing equipment (the lessee) 'rents' that equipment from a financial institution (the lessor) which in turn pays the supplier for the equipment. The lessee pays a fixed monthly sum over a number of years to the lessor in payment of the debt.
Ledger	A collection of all the different accounts of the business that summarize the transactions of the business.
Liabilities	Debts that the business owns. IFRS definition: a present obligation of the entity arising from past events, the settlement of which is expected to result in an outflow from the entity of resources embodying economic benefits.
Life cycle costing	An approach to costing that estimates and accumulates the costs of a product/service over its entire life cycle, i.e. from inception to abandonment.
Limiting factor	The production resource that, as a result of scarce resources, limits the production of goods or services.
Line item	Generic types of assets, liabilities, income, or expense that are common to all businesses and used as the basis of financial reporting, e.g. rent, salaries, advertising.
Liquidity	A measure of the ability of a business to pay its debts as they fall due. See also *Working capital*.
Losses	A form of expense not arising from the ordinary course of business, such as those resulting from disasters such as fire and flood and following the disposal of non-current assets.

Management accounting	The production of financial and non-financial information used in planning for the future; making decisions about products/services, prices, and what costs to incur; and ensuring that plans are implemented and achieved.
Margin	The margin that profit represents as a percentage of selling price.
Margin of safety	A measure of the difference between the anticipated and breakeven levels of activity.
Marginal cost	The cost of producing one extra unit.
Mark-up	The amount added to a lower figure to reach a higher figure, expressed as a percentage of the lower figure, e.g. cost is marked up by a percentage to cover the desired profit to determine a selling price.
Matching principle	The accruals basis of accounting under which income earned is matched with expenses incurred in earning that income during an accounting period.
Net assets	On the Statement of Financial Position, the difference between total assets and total liabilities.
Net present value (NPV)	A discounted cash flow technique used for investment appraisal that calculates the present value of future cash flows and deducts the initial capital investment.
Net profit	See *Operating profit*.
Non-current assets	Things that the business owns and are part of the business infrastructure. Non-current assets may be tangible or intangible.
Non-current liabilities	Amounts owing which do not have to be repaid within the next 12 months.
Non-production overhead	A general term referring to period costs, such as selling, administration, and financial expenses.
Operating and Financial Review (OFR)	Part of the Annual Report. A report by directors to shareholders which discusses and analyses the business's performance and the factors underlying its results and financial position, in order to assist users to assess for themselves the future potential of the business.
Operating margin	Operating profit, expressed as a percentage of sales.
Operating profit	The profit made by the business for an accounting period, equal to gross profit less selling, finance, administration, etc. expenses, but before deducting interest or taxation.
Opportunity cost	The opportunity forgone by making a choice among alternatives, which involves the inability to undertake the alternative not selected. The opportunity cost may be financial or non-financial.
Optimum selling price	The price at which profit is maximized, which takes into account the cost behaviour of fixed and variable costs and the relationship between price and demand for a product/service.

Overhead	Expenditure on labour, materials, or services that cannot be economically identified with a specific saleable cost unit. Any cost other than a direct cost of production (i.e. traceable to a specific product/service) – overhead may refer to an indirect production cost and/or to a non-production expense.
Overhead allocation	The process of spreading production overhead equitably over the volume of production of goods or services.
Payables	Purchases of goods or services from suppliers on credit to whom the debt is not yet paid.
Payback	A method of investment appraisal that calculates the number of years taken for the cash flows from an investment to cover the initial capital outlay.
Period costs	The costs that relate to a period of time, not to a product/service.
Planning, programming, and budgeting system (PPBS)	A method of budgeting in which budgets are allocated to projects or programmes rather than to responsibility centres.
Prepayment	A payment made in advance of when it is treated as an expense for profit purposes.
Pricing	The act of setting a selling price which customers may be prepared to pay for the desired volume of a product or service that a business wishes to sell. The price should reflect both the actions of competitors and the benefits a customer receives or perceives. The price should exceed the cost to the business of producing those benefits.
Prime cost	The total of all direct costs.
Priority-based budget	A budget that allocates funds in line with strategies.
Process costing	A method of costing for continuous manufacture in which costs for an accounting period are compared with production for the same period to determine a cost per unit produced.
Product cost	The cost of goods or services produced.
Product market	A business's investment in technology, people, and materials in order to make, buy, and sell products or services to customers.
Product/service mix	See *Sales mix*.
Production overhead	A general term referring to indirect costs of production.
Profiling	A method of budgeting that takes into account seasonal fluctuations and estimates of when revenues will be earned and costs will be incurred over each month in the budget period.
Profit	The difference between income and expenses.
Profit and Loss account	See *Income Statement*.
Profit before interest and taxes (PBIT)	See *Earnings before interest and tax (EBIT)*.

Profit centre	A division or unit of an organization that is responsible for achieving profit targets.
Profitability index	See *Cash value added*.
Provision	Estimates of possible future liabilities that may arise, but where there is uncertainty as to timing or the amount of money.
Ratio analysis	A method of analysing financial reports to interpret trends and make comparisons by using ratios. A ratio is two numbers, with one generally expressed as a percentage of the other.
Raw materials	Unprocessed goods bought for manufacture, part of inventory.
Receivables	Sales to customers who have bought goods or services on credit but who have not yet paid their debt.
Relevant cost	The cost that is relevant to a particular decision – future, incremental cash flows.
Relevant range	The upper and lower levels of activity within which the business expects to be operating within the short-term planning horizon (the budget period).
Residual income (RI)	The profit remaining after deducting from profit a notional cost of capital on the investment in a business or division of a business.
Responsibility centre	A division or unit of an organization for which a manager is held responsible – may be a cost centre, profit centre, or investment centre.
Retained profits	The amount of profit after deducting interest, taxation, and dividends that is retained by the business and is an addition to equity.
Return on capital employed (ROCE)	The operating profit before interest and tax as a percentage of the total shareholders' funds plus the long-term debt of the business.
Return on investment (ROI)	The net profit after tax as a percentage of the shareholders' investment in the business.
Revenue	A form of income that arises in the ordinary course of business. Typically income earned from the sale of goods and services, including fees, interest, dividends, royalties, and rent.
Rolling budgets	A method of budgeting in which as each month passes, an additional budget month is added such that there is always a 12-month budget.
Routing	A list of all the labour or machining processes and times required to convert raw materials into finished goods or to deliver a service.
Sales mix	The mix of products/services offered by the business, each of which may be aimed at different customers, with each product/service having different prices and costs.
Semi-fixed costs	Costs that are constant within a defined level of activity but that can increase or decrease when activity reaches upper and lower levels.
Semi-variable costs	Costs that have both fixed and variable components.

Sensitivity analysis	An approach to understanding how changes in one variable are affected by changes in the other variables, e.g. in cost–volume–profit analysis between selling price, costs, and profit.
Set-up	The time required to make ready a machine or process for production, e.g. changing equipment settings. Also known as make-ready.
Shareholder value	Increasing the value of the business to its shareholders, achieved through a combination of dividend and capital growth in the value of the shares.
Shareholder value-based management	The process of increasing shareholder value through new or redesigned products/services, cost management, performance management systems, and improved decision making.
Shareholders' funds	The capital invested in a business by the shareholders, including retained profits. See also *Equity*.
Source document	The document that records a transaction and forms the basis for recording in a business's accounting system.
Standard costs	A budget cost for materials and labour used for decision making, usually expressed as a per unit cost that is applied to standard quantities from a bill of materials and to standard times from a routing.
Statement of Cash Flows	A financial report that shows the movement in cash for a business during an accounting period.
Statement of Comprehensive Income	The profit (or loss) of a business for a financial period (after income tax is deducted) together with other comprehensive income such as movements in the price or valuation of something resulting in a change in measurement
Statement of Financial Position	A financial statement showing the financial position of a business – its assets, liabilities, and equity – at the end of an accounting period.
Stock	See *Inventory*.
Strategic management accounting	The provision and analysis of management accounting data about a business and its competitors, which is of use in the development and monitoring of strategy.
Sunk costs	Costs that have been incurred in the past.
Supplier performance index	The ratio of the total overhead costs to the supplier's invoiced price.
Tangible assets	Physical assets that can be seen and touched, e.g. buildings, machinery, vehicles, computers.
Target costing	A method of costing that is concerned with managing whole-of-life costs of a product/service during the product design phase – the difference between target price (to achieve market share) and the target profit margin.

Target rate of return pricing	A method of pricing that estimates the desired return on investment to be achieved from the company's total capital investment and includes that return in the price of a product/service.
Throughput contribution	Sales revenue less the cost of materials.
Total cost of ownership	The total cost of the supply arrangement with a supplier, including purchasing costs, delivery failure, quality failure, inventory holding, and compliance costs.
Transaction	The financial description of a business event.
Transfer price	The price at which goods or services are bought and sold within divisions of the same organization, as opposed to an arm's-length price at which sales may be made to an external customer.
True and fair view	A judgement made by directors and auditors about the content and presentation of financial statements.
Turnover	The business income or sales of goods and services.
Unavoidable costs	A cost that cannot be influenced at the business unit level but is controllable at the corporate level.
Value added tax (VAT)	A form of indirect taxation (in the UK), levied on the sale of most goods and services.
Value-based management	A variety of approaches that emphasize increasing shareholder value as the primary goal of every business.
Value-stream accounting	Assigning employees and assets to a single value stream, rather than costs being allocated to a department or cost centre, or across multiple business processes. A value stream is everything done to create value for customers and that can reasonably be associated with a product or product group. Performance measures are developed for each value stream and overhead costs are directed to specific value streams, resulting in less arbitrary overhead allocations. Value streams are the unit of financial reporting under lean accounting.
Value-stream costing	The measurement of how much value is added in each step of the production process, by costing the various value streams backwards from the customer to their source.
Variable cost	A cost that increases or decreases in proportion with increases or decreases in the volume of production of goods or services.
Variable costing	A method of costing in which only variable production costs are treated as product costs and in which all fixed (production and non-production) costs are treated as period costs.
Variance analysis	A method of budgetary control that compares actual performance against plan, investigates the causes of the variance, and takes corrective action to ensure that targets are achieved.
Weighted average cost of capital	See *Cost of capital*.

Work-in-progress	Goods or services that have commenced the production process but are incomplete and unable to be sold.
Working capital	Current assets less current liabilities. Money that revolves in the business as part of the process of buying, making, and selling goods and services, particularly in relation to receivables, payables, inventory, and bank.
Zero-based budgeting	A method of budgeting that ignores historical budgetary allocations and identifies the costs that are necessary to implement agreed strategies.

Solutions to Questions

One of the problems that most students of accounting face is being able to tackle calculation problems. The 'fear of numbers' is quite common with postgraduate students and practising managers. Students often look back to find a similar 'model question' and then try to repeat the calculation, simply replacing the numbers. This is not good practice as it does not help the student to think about the concepts involved. Each problem is different, and this mirrors day-to-day business decisions. Solving these problems is about applying the underlying concepts.

The questions in each chapter require the reader to perform calculations. In attempting to solve these problems, you need to think about:

- what the business problem is;
- the information that is provided to solve the problem;
- the most appropriate technique to apply to the problem; and
- how to apply the technique to solve the problem.

If you are not able (as is most likely with some questions) to answer a question or answer it incorrectly on your first attempt, study the answer and if necessary go back to the relevant section in the text book. Then, at a later time, go back to the same question and try to answer it again, but this time without looking at the solution. This is the best examination preparation technique.

Solutions for Chapter 1

1.1

Accounting is a collection of systems and processes used to record, report, and interpret business transactions. An account is an explanation or report in financial terms about those transactions. Accountability arises from the stewardship function under which managers have to provide an account to other stakeholders in the business.

1.2

(i) The main activities of financial accountants involve collecting financial transaction data in the company's accounting system; classifying those transactions in terms of their effect on income, expenses, assets, liabilities, and equity; and producing regular financial reports (e.g. Income Statement, Statement of Financial Position) for publication to interested parties (e.g. shareholders, banks, financiers).

(ii) The main activities of management accountants include participation in planning, primarily through budgets; generating, analysing, presenting, and interpreting information to support decision making; and monitoring and controlling performance. Management accountants will use financial accounting data but will produce it more frequently and in greater detail for the internal users.

1.3

The critical view of accounting comes essentially from Marxist historians. It reveals how accounting and accountants have been intertwined with the growth of capitalism, particularly since the Industrial Revolution and the rise in mass production in the early twentieth century. The critical view highlights the exploitation of labour with low wages and British colonialism (subsequently replaced by the American industrial powerhouse), which took advantage of cheap labour in developing countries. Cheap capital and rising prices led to high profits and while this fed investment, there was no consideration of the human, social, and environmental costs and no questioning as to why the allocation of the surplus of production (i.e. profits) all went to the suppliers of capital.

Solutions for Chapter 2

2.1

Value-based management uses a variety of techniques to measure increases in shareholder value, which is assumed to be the primary goal of all business organizations. Shareholder value refers to the economic value of an investment by discounting future cash flows to their present value using the cost of capital for the business. To achieve shareholder value, a business must generate profits in its markets for goods and services (product markets) that exceed the cost of capital (the weighted average cost of equity and borrowings) in the capital market.

2.2

The responsibilities of the board include setting the company's strategic goals, providing leadership to senior management, monitoring business performance, and reporting to shareholders. The last two of these explicitly relate to accounting, and the first two implicitly do so. In the UK the Combined Code, in Australia the Corporations Act, and in the USA the Sarbanes–Oxley Act include important responsibilities of the board in relation to financial statements and performance management. The role of a board is to provide leadership of the company within a framework of prudent and effective controls which enable risk to be assessed and managed. These controls include many accounting controls such as budgets and capital expenditure evaluations. The financial reports of a company are the responsibility of the board, which must ensure that the company keeps proper accounting records that disclose with reasonable accuracy the financial position of the company at any time and that the financial reports comply with the relevant legislation. The board is also responsible for safeguarding the company's assets and for taking reasonable steps to prevent and detect fraud.

2.3

The shareholder value approach privileges the rights of shareholders, with the primary goal of companies being to increase shareholder wealth through dividends out of profits, and capital growth in share prices over time.

The stakeholder approach is based on the responsibility of companies to a broader range of stakeholders (those who influence, or are influenced by, the company) including shareholders, employees, customers, suppliers, government, and society as a whole. Stakeholder theory argues that organizations carry a broader responsibility than returns to shareholders and should consider the social and environmental as well as the economic aspects of their activities.

Solutions for Chapter 3

3.1

Answer c.

3.2

Answer d. Note there also is an associated entry for the cost of sales: increase cost of sales and reduce inventory.

3.3

Answer b.

Profit	Sales	100,000
	Cost of sales	−35,000
	Salaries	−15,000
	Rent	−4,000
	Advertising	−8,000
		£38,000
Cash	Equity	£25,000
	Sales	100,000
	Salaries	−15,000
	Rent	−4,000
	Advertising	−8,000
	Inventory	−40,000
		£58,000
Equity	Initial	£25,000
	Plus profit	38,000
		£63,000

Assets

$$Cash\ 58{,}000 + Equipment\ 20{,}000 + Inventory\ 5{,}000 = 83{,}000$$

Liabilities

$$Creditors\,(Equipment)\ 20{,}000 + Equity\ 63{,}000 = 83{,}000$$

3.4

Answer b.

$$Capital = Assets - Liabilities = 240{,}000 - 125{,}000 = 115{,}000$$

3.5

Answer c.

3.6

Transaction	Profit = Income – Expenses	Cash flow	Assets (excluding cash)	Liabilities/Equity
Issues shares to public		Increases		Increases (equity)
Borrows money over 5 years		Increases		Increases (long-term debt)
Pays cash for equipment		Decreases	Increases (non-current asset)	
Buys inventory on credit			Increases (current asset: inventory)	Increases (current liability: payables)
Sells goods on credit	Increases (selling price less cost price)		1. Increases (current asset: receivables at selling price) 2. Decreases (current asset: inventory at cost price)	
Pays cash for salaries, rent, etc.	Decreases (expenses)	Decreases		
Pays cash to suppliers		Decreases		Decreases (current liability: payables)
Receives cash from customers		Increases	Decreases (current asset: receivables)	

3.7

a. Profit is £35,000 (income £135,000 less expenses of advertising £15,000, rent £10,000, and salaries £75,000).
b. Equity at end of year is £106,000 (£71,000 plus profit for year of £35,000).

The Statement of Financial Position would show assets of £117,000 (non-current assets £100,000, bank £5,000, and receivables £12,000) less liabilities (payables £11,000) therefore net assets of £106,000 (equal to equity).

Solutions for Chapter 4

4.1

The key ingredients of a cybernetic management control system are:

- An objective or target to be achieved;
- A predictive model that helps to explain how the business will be conducted to achieve its targets, by a clear understanding of cause–effect or action–outcome relationships;
- A method of measuring actual performance;
- A means of comparing actual to target performance;
- The ability to take corrective actions to reduce the deviation between actual and target performance.

4.2

The Balanced Scorecard is a way of monitoring organizational performance through non-financial as well as financial measures, separating those measures that are leading indicators (generally non-financial) from the typically lagging financial measures, and recognizing the need to achieve both short-term and long-term performance. Hence, organizations are able to take earlier action to correct deviations from target based on the leading indicators.

The measures are 'balanced' between the four perspectives based on organizational strategy and competitive position. The perspectives and the measures follow an assumed cause–effect relationship. This benefits the organization by having to articulate cause–effect relationships in their business model.

The four Balanced Scorecard perspectives are financial, customer, internal business process, and learning and growth. These are inter-related such that learning and growth leads to continuous improvement in business processes, which in turn leads to more satisfied customers and in turn to improved financial performance. Assuming these cause–effect relationships are valid, the four perspectives provide a more holistic view of organizational performance and enable managers to shift resource allocations and priorities to the perspective where they may be needed most to achieve strategy and performance targets.

4.3

The economic-rational perspective in relation to management control systems and accounting is a way of viewing the world that privileges the pursuit of shareholder value through setting goals and strategies to achieve those goals. The rational approach follows a particular reasoning, with alternatives being evaluated and decisions made as a result of economic preferences, typically profit maximization and the pursuit of shareholder value.

In this perspective, organizations are collectivities of people bound by a common purpose to achieve common goals, with organizations being highly formalized with clear rules governing behaviour and the roles of individual members, based typically on the division of labour and specialization of tasks leading to efficiency and reduced costs.

The notion of contract is at the centre of this perspective which determines how management control and accounting systems are used in the organization, principally to provide information, and to measure and monitor performance in pursuit of organizational goals.

Solutions for Chapter 5

5.1

Research in management control usually takes one of two forms.

The normative view – or what *should* happen – is an economically rational approach that is based on the assumption that there is 'one best way' to do things. In this view, management control and accounting are rational tools that accurately monitor and report organizational performance, aid decision making, and contribute to the goal of improving shareholder value.

The interpretive/critical view – or what *does* happen – explains how management control and accounting develop and come to be used in specific organizational settings. This view rejects the assumption that people always make economically rational decisions but holds rather that they have limited information and limited abilities to understand and interpret that information. This view also holds that people are influenced not only by formal structures and systems but by the norms and values of their social groups – e.g. professional or organizational cultures – and by relations of power in the organization.

5.2

Socially constructed reality is a way of viewing the world from an interpretive perspective. Reality in the interpretive paradigm is subjective rather than objective. The interpretive approach rejects the assumption that everything is fact-based, measurable, and observable, but holds rather that it is based on interpretations and points of view, involving experience, emotion, and judgement.

Individuals perceive things and events differently as a result of their education, past experiences, values, etc. and then act towards those things or events on the basis of the meaning they have for the individual.

However, meaning is given to things and events, not just as a result of individual perceptions, but influenced by the social groups to which the individual belongs: e.g. family, ethnic or religious group, occupation or profession, etc. These groups tend to both construct and share the meanings of things, and so these meanings are said to be socially constructed, internalized, and shared within the group. In this way, members of the social group make sense of reality in a similar way.

5.3

Discourse is an informed conversation through which arguments and counter-arguments are considered. It is central to critical theory, which is concerned with opening up the discourse beyond the economic-rational application of management control and accounting to question its underlying assumptions and its often dysfunctional consequences.

Control and accounting are important to consider in such a discourse because both purport to present objective 'facts' which are dominated by an economic-rational logic. As Miller and O'Leary (1987) state in 'Accounting and the construction of the governable person', *Accounting, Organizations and Society*, 12(3), 235–65 at 239, accounting 'serves to construct a particular field of visibility'.

Critical theory does not necessarily imply a Marxist view of the world and a rejection of capitalism, but it does imply a questioning and critical approach to the role of management control and accounting with an aim to change (where appropriate) practices which may be historically or politically derived but which are no longer justifiable. This questioning is an integral part of discourse.

The proponents of critical theory emphasize the need to develop choice through meaningful debate rather than through established power structures that reinforce the status quo. It is only through the application of this kind of critical debate that organizations have begun to consider their social and environmental responsibilities and adopted more ethical practices, introducing more social and environmental factors into their reports to shareholders. However, much of that change has arguably been forced on organizations by government, the media, and public interest groups.

Solutions for Chapter 6

6.1

Kazam Services' accounting records are shown in Table S6.1.

Table S6.1

	Non-current assets	Receivables	Bank	Payables	Long-term loan	Equity	Income	Expenses
Opening balance	+500,000	+125,000	−35,000	+90,000	+300,000	+200,000		
Takes out loan for new building	+150,000				+150,000			
Money from Receivables		−45,000	+45,000					
Reduction of Payables			−30,000	−30,000				
Invoice for services performed		+70,000					+70,000	
Pay salaries			−15,000					+15,000
Pay office expenses			−5,000					+5,000
Depreciation	−20,000							+20,000
	630,000	150,000	−40,000	60,000	450,000	200,000	70,000	40,000
Profit transferred						+30,000 230,000	30,000	

Notes:
+ indicates the account increases.
− indicates the account decreases.
The bank account is a liability (withdrawals exceed deposits) and is shown here as a minus to distinguish it from an asset.

Kazam Services
Income Statement

Income	70,000
Less expenses	40,000
Operating profit	30,000

Statement of Financial Position
Assets:

Non-current assets	650,000	
Less depreciation	20,000	630,000

Current assets

Receivables	150,000
Total assets	780,000

Liabilities:
Non-current liabilities

Long-term loan	450,000

Current liabilities

Bank overdraft	40,000
Payables	60,000
	100,000

Total liabilities	550,000
Net assets	230,000
Equity	
Share capital	200,000
Retained earnings	30,000
Total Equity	230,000

6.2

See Table S6.2.

Table S6.2

Current assets	125,000
Payables	−75,000
Working capital	50,000
Non-current assets	250,000
Current assets	125,000
Capital employed	375,000
Long-term debt	−125,000
Shareholders' capital (equity)	175,000

6.3

Answer e: although the operating profit has increased (from €137,000 to €139,000), the operating margin has decreased (from 11.6% to 11.1%) as a result of a reduction in the gross margin (from 39% to 37%) and higher expenses (from €323,000 to €324,000), despite sales growth (of 6.4%). See Table S6.3.

Table S6.3

	2015	2014
Sales	1,250,000	1,175,000
Sales growth	6.4%	
Cost of sales	787,000	715,000
Gross profit	463,000	460,000
Gross margin	37%	39%
Selling and admin expenses	324,000	323,000
Operating profit	139,000	137,000
Operating margin	11.1%	11.6%

6.4

a. Prepayment

The annual payment is 24 × $400 = $9,600 (this is $800/month). The prepayment at 31 March is 9/12 (Apr–Dec) @ $800 = $7,200.

Profit is reduced by $2,400 (expense: 3 months @ $800).

Asset in the Statement of Financial Position is increased by $7,200 (prepayment is an asset: 9 months @ $800).

Cash flow is reduced by $9,600 (payment 31 December).

NB: the effect of the prepayment of $7,200 is to carry forward the expense to the next financial year.

b. Accrual

The simple solution is to divide $6,000 by 12 months and charge $500/month to profit. However, this ignores seasonal fluctuations and cash flow differences from quarter to quarter.

The quarterly bills have been paid during the year, but the last quarterly bill was in November. Therefore the business is missing one month's expense (i.e. December). To determine the amount we need to calculate the seasonal charges:

$6,000 × 70% = $4,200 for September–February/6 = $700/month

$6,000 × 30% = $1,800 for March–August/6 = $300/month

Accrue for one month (December) = $700

Profit reduced by $700 (expense). This is the profit adjustment. In total, expenses are $6,000 for the year.

Statement of Financial Position reduced by $700 (accrual is a current liability).

Cash flow has no impact (no money yet paid).

NB: the effect of the accrual is to reduce by $700 the expense impact of the expected bill for three months of $2,100, which will be received in February. This leaves $1,400 as the expense ($700 for each of January and February).

c. Depreciation

Depreciation is 20% of $12,000 = $2,400 p.a. or $200/month. As depreciation is charged from the next month, it needs to be provided for the period July–March. For that period, depreciation is $200 x 9 = $1,800.

Profit reduced by $1,800 (depreciation expense).

Statement of Financial Position increased by $12,000 (new asset) and reduced by $1,800 (depreciation), leaving a net value of $10,200.

Cash flow reduced by $12,000 (payment for new system).

NB: the Statement of Financial Position value of the asset will be reduced by $2,400 p.a. until the asset is written down to a nil value, or sold or disposed of.

6.5

Plant & Equipment	£7,000,000
Receivables	£1,500,000

Inventory	£2,300,000
	£10,800,000
Payables	£500,000
Net assets	£10,300,000
Purchase price	£12,000,000
Goodwill	£1,700,000
Amortization over 10 years:	
£170,000 per annum	£170,000
Net goodwill in Statement of Financial Position at end of first year	£1,530,000

6.6

Depreciation and interest

Payments made to the lessor are apportioned between the interest cost which is treated as an expense in the Income Statement and a reduction of the liability in the Statement of Financial Position. The asset is depreciated in the Income Statement and reduces the Statement of Financial Position asset value as though it was owned.

6.7

As a loss (not expense, see below).

6.8

As a gain (not revenue, see below).

Note re 6.7 and 6.8:

Revenue arises in the ordinary course of business (e.g. sales, fees, interest, dividends, royalties, and rent). Gains represent other items such as income from the disposal of non-current assets or revaluations of investments.

Expenses arise in the ordinary course of business (e.g. salaries, advertising). Losses represent other items such as those resulting from disasters such as fire and flood and following the disposal of non-current assets or losses following from changes in foreign exchange rates.

6.9

Gross sales are $5,875,000. Sales tax is 17.5%, therefore net sales are $5,875,000/1.175 giving net sales in the Income Statement of $5,000,000.

6.10

Income statement

Depreciation	30,000
Advertising	5,000
Loss	−35,000

Statement of Cash Flows

Loss	−35,000
Depreciation added back	30,000
Cash flow from operations	−5,000
Asset purchase	−150,000
Cash flow from investing	−150,000
Borrowing	200,000
Cash flow from financing	200,000
Change in cash	45,000

Statement of Financial Position

Non current assets	120,000
Current asset: Bank	45,000
Total assets	165,000
Non-current liability	−200,000
Net assets	−35,000
Equity (Loss)	−35,000

Workings: this question can be answered by using the double entry format introduced in Chapter 3 and illustrated in Tables 6.7 and 6.8 of Chapter 6.

	Asset	Loan	Bank	Depreciation	Advertising
Loan		200,000	200,000		
Asset purchase	150,000		−150,000		
20% depreciation	−30,000			30,000	
Advertising			5,000		−5,000
	120,000	200,000	45,000	30,000	5,000

Solutions for Chapter 7

7.1

	2014	2013
Return on (shareholders') investment (ROI)		
$\dfrac{\text{net profit after tax}}{\text{shareholders' funds}}$	$\dfrac{13.8}{131.5} = 10.5\%$	$\dfrac{16.3}{126.6} = 12.9\%$

Return on capital employed (ROCE)

$$\frac{\text{profit before interest and tax}}{\text{shareholders' funds} + \text{long-term debt}}$$

$$\frac{27.2}{131.5+96.7} = 11.9\%$$
$$= 228.2$$

$$\frac{29.5}{126.6+146.1} = 10.8\%$$
$$= 272.7$$

Operating profit/sales

$$\frac{\text{profit before interest and tax}}{\text{sales}}$$

$$\frac{27.2}{141.1} = 19.3\%$$

$$\frac{29.5}{138.4} = 21.3\%$$

Sales growth

$$\frac{\text{sales year 2} - \text{sales year 1}}{\text{sales year 1}}$$

$$\frac{141.1-138.4}{138.4} = 2.7$$
$$= +1.95\%$$

Expense growth

$$\frac{\text{expenses year 2} - \text{expenses year 1}}{\text{expenses year 1}}$$

$$\frac{113.9-108.9}{108.9} = 5$$
$$= +4.6\%$$

Gearing ratio

$$\frac{\text{long-term debt}}{\text{shareholders' funds} + \text{long-term debt}}$$

$$\frac{96.7}{131.5+96.7} = 42.3\%$$
$$= 228.2$$

$$\frac{146.1}{126.6+146.1} = 53.5\%$$
$$= 272.7$$

Asset turnover

$$\frac{\text{sales}}{\text{total assets}}$$

$$\frac{141.1}{266.7+28.3} = 47.8\%$$
$$= 295$$

$$\frac{138.4}{265.3+35} = 46.1\%$$
$$= 300.3$$

ROI has reduced but ROCE has increased. This is because shareholders' funds have increased but total assets have declined relative to the small change in profits. There has been a very small sales growth (less than 2%, but remember the effect of inflation) but expenses have increased by 4.6%. Consequently, operating profit has fallen, as has profit as a percentage of sales. The fall in profits and the increase in shareholders' funds and capital employed have resulted in the decline in ROI. Gearing has also fallen as a result of a large reduction in long-term debt. Asset turnover has improved marginally. The reduced total assets and lower gearing has resulted in a higher ROCE. Although two years is too short a period to draw any meaningful trends, we can say that Drayton needs to increase its sales and/or contain its expenses.

7.2

Conclusions include:

- Profit has declined on each of the measures.
- Liquidity: working capital has deteriorated and customers are taking longer to pay their accounts.

- Gearing: long-term debt has increased in proportion to shareholders' funds and there is less profit to pay a higher amount of interest.
- Assets are being used less efficiently to generate sales.

Overall, Jupiter's performance on all four criteria has been worse in the current year.

7.3

Receivables/average daily sales

$$\frac{200,000}{1,200,000/250} = \frac{200,000}{4,800} = 41.7 \text{ days' sales outstanding}$$

Inventory turnover
Cost of sales/inventory

$$\frac{450,000}{200,000} = 2.25 \text{ times p.a.}$$

or every 100 days (250/2.5).
Payables/average daily purchases

$$\frac{100,000}{450,000/250} = \frac{100,000}{1,800} = 55.5 \text{ days' purchases outstanding}$$

7.4

Sales (in £m)	2014	2013	2012	2011	2010
	155	144	132	130	120

Sales growth	$\frac{155-144}{144}$	$\frac{144-132}{132}$	$\frac{132-130}{130}$	$\frac{130-120}{120}$	
	7.6%	9.1%	1.5%	8.3%	

7.5

Overheads are €65 million. Sales are €155 million. The overhead/sales ratio is 65/155 or 41.9%.

Solution to case study question 7.1: Paramount Services plc

It is important to remember that ratio analysis is really only useful to identify trends and comparisons. Trends require more than two years' data, while comparisons require either budget data or industry/competitor results that can be used as a performance benchmark.

Nevertheless, although the two years' data is limited, some conclusions can be drawn from the ratios. Sales growth is high (17.2%) but overhead growth is greater (26.9%), suggesting the need to control expenses. Consequently, profit growth (9.4%) has not been maintained at the same level as sales growth. Interest cost has increased due to higher long-term borrowings and consequently the interest cover has fallen, a slightly more risky situation for lenders.

All profitability measures (PBIT/Sales, ROCE, and ROI) have fallen, as a result of the above-mentioned reasons. However, dividend payout has increased in total (and consequently per share for a constant number of shares) while the yield has increased, predominantly a result of the fall in the share price. For the same reason (a reduced share price) the price/earnings ratio has fallen.

Asset efficiency is constant at 1.2, although Paramount does appear to have a very high level of investment in non-current assets in relation to its income from services. Days' sales outstanding have increased significantly from 60 days to 76 days, a reflection of a credit control problem. Although payables have also increased, the working capital ratio has increased and is adequate at 1.7. Gearing has increased, but the level of long-term debt is quite low in comparison to the investment in non-current assets, an indication that a substantial part of the capital and reserves has been invested in non-current assets, possibly real estate.

Perhaps the major area of concern is whether the large non-current asset investment can be justified in terms of the business services that the company carries out.

Solution to case study question 7.2: General Machinery Ltd

After a decline, the company's profitability (ROI, ROCE, operating margin) has improved recently. However, the gross margin has dropped for five consecutive years, suggesting that selling prices are not being increased to pass on purchase (or production) cost increases. This deteriorating gross margin is a significant risk for the company as profits have only been increased by the large reduction in overhead as a percentage of sales in 2014. If gross margins continue to erode and if overheads as a percentage of sales cannot be continually cut, profits may be at serious risk. The company needs to continue to increase sales growth, fix its gross margins, and continue to manage overheads.

One of the impacts on the depressed margins may be the company's inability to negotiate cost of sales reductions with suppliers due to the late payment of suppliers. Days' purchases outstanding (DPO) are 78, representing over 2.5 months. This is likely to give the company a poor credit rating and may impact its ability to maintain continuity of supply. Although the DPO has reduced over the five years, it is still taking too long to pay suppliers.

Working capital has been at extremely high levels but has fallen to close to 2:1, an improvement, but with an acid test greater than 1, it is probably still too high. This is demonstrated by the relatively high days' sales outstanding (60- against 30-day terms), which even though it has improved is still too high. Inventory represents the biggest concern to working capital as at 3.3 it represents an average stockholding of 110 days (365/3.3). The company needs to manage its ordering to a just-in-time basis. Reduction of outstanding receivables and inventory would assist the company to pay its suppliers more quickly and potentially achieve savings in cost of sales, thereby improving the gross margin.

The Statement of Cash Flows shows that most cash has been used in 2014, hence working capital is strained by a lack of cash and slow receivables collections and inventory turnover. The Statement of Cash Flows reveals that net cash from operating activities, after deducting dividend payments, is very low. The major cash flow impacts are capital expenditure of €300,000 over the last three years and borrowings of €150,000. The balance of €150,000 has been funded from operating activities and has been the cause of the reduction in the closing bank balance to €20,000. This in turn has affected the working capital ratio (cash at bank is the only other item in working capital not measured by the three efficiency ratios for receivables, inventory, and payables).

Asset turnover has steadily increased, a trend which needs to continue. It is likely that there is a time lag between the high capital expenditure in the most recent year so it might be expected that sales (and asset turnover) should increase in subsequent years.

The company has spent money on capital expenditure that has worsened its ability to pay suppliers more quickly. An alternative would have been to use the available cash to pay suppliers more quickly and to borrow the balance of €150,000. The question 'should the company have borrowed more?' is interesting because on the surface it needs to do so to replenish the bank balance. This is because it is less risky for non-current assets to be financed by non-current liabilities. However, further borrowings would be disguising poor credit control and inventory practices. It would be better for the company to fix its inventory problems and collect its debts on time, pay its overdue creditors, and then look to see how much additional borrowing was required.

Gearing at 42% has increased slightly over five years but is at acceptable levels (anything in the range 40–60% being very common). However, interest cover has fallen significantly and is less than 2:1, with banks and financiers likely to consider this as risky in terms of the company's long-term ability to make interest payments. Hence any further borrowing would need to be offset by increases in profit to improve the interest cover.

Shareholder ratios are somewhat erratic with a lack of consistency in dividend per share likely to make some investors nervous. Dividend payout remains at about the 50% level, consistent with common practice, although it is noticeable that depressed profits seem to have led to a reduction in the dividend per share in 2012 and 2013, made worse by the dividend payment being a higher proportion of after-tax profits. The dividend yield is very low compared to risk-free government securities or bank interest rates. The P/E ratio of 16 (years) is an improvement and probably reflects market optimism about the company's future sustainable cash flows as a result of recent capital expenditure.

So there are three major issues the company needs to address: (i) Fix the declining gross margin to maintain profitability; (ii) Fix the inventory and receivables problem to improve cash flow; (iii) Reduce its payables by paying its suppliers on time and try to use faster payments to negotiate lower cost of sales with suppliers. Profitability needs to be increased and if gross margins cannot be increased, there will be further pressure to reduce overheads, perhaps to unrealistic levels. Whether or not the company needs to borrow further will only be clear after the effects of these improvements are seen.

Solutions for Chapter 8

8.1

Answer c.

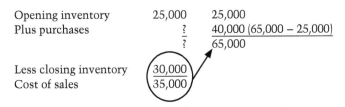

Opening inventory	25,000	25,000
Plus purchases	?	40,000 (65,000 – 25,000)
	?	65,000
Less closing inventory	30,000	
Cost of sales	35,000	

8.2

Answer b.

8.3

Answer c.

The lower of cost or net realizable value is the discounted selling price of £1,350 less transport cost of £100 = £1,250. The even lower scrap value of £1,100 – £100 = £1,000 is irrelevant as the higher net realizable value is £1,250.

8.4

a. Weighted average:

6,000 @ $2	$12,000
3,000 @ $2.20	6,600
2,000 @ $2.30	4,600
11,000	$23,200
$23,200/11,000 = $2.11	
Cost of sales 8,000 @ $2.11	$16,873
Inventory 3,000 @ $2.11	$6,327
	$23,200

b. FIFO:

Purchased	Cost of sales	Inventory
6,000 @ $2	6,000 @ $2 = $12,000	0
3,000 @ $2.20	2,000 @ $2.20 = $4,400	1,000 @ $2.20 = $2,200
2,000 @ $2.30	0	2,000 @ $2.30 = $4,600
Total	8,000 = $16,400	3,000 = $6,800
	$23,200	

8.5

	Units
Opening WIP	20,000
Units commenced	60,000
	80,000
Closing WIP	15,000
Completed	65,000

Cost per unit:

	Opening WIP £	Cost for month £	Total £	Completed units	WIP Equivalent units	Total equivalent units	Cost per equivalent unit £
Material	62,000	192,000	254,000	65,000	15,000	80,000	£3.175
Conversion	25,000	85,150	110,150	65,000	4,500*	69,500	£1.585
					*15,000 @ 30%		
Total	£87,000	£277,150	£364,150				£4.76

Work-in-progress:
Materials 15,000 @ £3.175   £47,625
Conversion 4,500 @ £1.585   £7,132
                                             £54,757

Finished goods:
65,000 units @ £4.76   £309,400
Total costs   £364,157 (difference due to rounding)

8.6

	Raw materials	Job A101 Qty: 40	Job B202 Qty: 60
Materials purchased:			
400 sqm timber @ £14.50 =	£5,800		
80 l glue @ £6 =	480		
Materials issued:			
200 sqm timber @ £14.50			
150 @ £14.50	(5,075)	2,900	2,175
20 l glue @ £6	(240)	120	120
Labour			
200 hours @ £30		6,000	
100 hours @ £30			3,000

Overhead		
200 DLH @ £25	5,000	
100 DLH @ £25		2,500
Total job cost	£14,020	£7,795
	Completed	**WIP**
	£14,020/40 =	Inventory
	£350.50 each	
Raw materials inventory	£965	
Transferred to finished goods	£14,020	
Less 30 sold @ cost of £350.50	10,515	
Finished goods inventory	**£3,505**	
Sales	£15,000	
Cost of sales	10,515	
Gross profit	**£4,485**	

8.7

Costs incurred to date	€850,000
Estimated costs to complete	€2,650,000
	€3,500,000
Estimated profit	500,000
Contract price	€4,000,000

Percentage completed is €850,000/€3,500,000 = 24.3%

24.3% of estimated profit of €500,000 = €121,500 (ignore any rounding differences).

8.8

Manufacturing statement

	$	$
Material:		
Raw material at beginning of period	100,000	
Purchases of raw materials	250,000	
Raw material available for use	350,000	
Less raw material at end of period	150,000	
Raw material usage in production		200,000
Labour		450,000
Manufacturing overhead:		
Factory rental	75,000	
Depreciation of plant & equipment	50,000	
Light & power	25,000	
Salaries & wages of factory labour	100,000	250,000
Total manufacturing costs		900,000
Add work-in-progress at beginning of period		300,000
		1,200,000

Less work-in-progress at end of period		400,000
Cost of goods manufactured		800,000

Cost of goods sold statement

Finished goods at beginning of period	150,000
Cost of goods manufactured	800,000
Goods available for sale	950,000
Less finished goods at end of period	250,000
Cost of goods sold	700,000

Income statement

Sales	900,000
Less cost of goods sold	700,000
Gross profit	200,000
Less selling and administrative expenses	75,000
Net profit	125,000

The inventory valuation in the Balance Sheet totals $800,000 and comprises:

Inventory raw materials	150,000
Inventory work-in-progress	400,000
Inventory finished goods	250,000

Solutions for Chapter 9

9.1

Transaction processing systems are accounting based, containing details of all business transactions recorded for accounting purposes. They have little value to management for planning or decision making other than through simple summarization and exception reports but do provide a valuable audit trail of transactions.

Management information systems extend to incorporate non-financial as well as financial data. They are typified by more sophisticated reporting using graphs and colour coding of performance relative to targets. However these systems do not integrate the different aspects of business operations.

Enterprise resource planning systems take a more holistic perspective, integrating information across multiple organizational functions such as sales, production, purchasing, distribution, and accounting.

9.2

The hierarchical or vertical perspective is that contained within the organization chart, with financial information accumulated by functional department or business unit, where specialists carry out defined tasks. This reporting is used to produce financial information about the performance of those organizational units. However, this perspective provides no holistic picture about business activities that cross department or business unit boundaries.

The horizontal or business process perspective records financial information for collections of business activities associated with business processes that cross over multiple departments or business units in the hierarchical perspective. The focus is not on the organizational unit that carries out tasks but on the process of doing something (e.g. processing a customer order, or purchasing goods and services) irrespective of the department in which the activities take place.

Organizations will get most value from information about both perspectives. The vertical perspective provides information for internal financial reporting, comparing actual with budget performance and holding managers accountable for the performance of their departments or business units. The horizontal perspective provides information about business processes that help to focus on the costs of those processes relative to pricing, and also helps to improve those processes, e.g. by reducing duplication and streamlining.

9.3

Information systems design is important because there is a significant risk in any new system that it does not meet user needs, is late, or costs more than was estimated. This is even the case with established systems through providers such as SAP and Oracle as these systems often require customization.

Systems development should take place under the control of a steering committee with responsibility for delivering the system to quality, time, and cost requirements. Development comprises feasibility, design, testing, and implementation. The key elements of project management for information systems include: specification of requirements and obtaining top management support; defining the role and responsibilities of the steering committee and project manager; allocating sufficient resources in both staff and money; quality control and progress monitoring; and user participation and involvement.

Information system controls are essential to ensure the security of data and the reliability of information once an information system is in use. The main types of information system controls are over security and access; application controls to prevent, detect, and correct errors; network controls to prevent hacking and viruses; and those covering contingencies such as backup and disaster recovery.

Solutions for Chapter 10

10.1

See Table S10.1.

Table S10.1

Sales		1,100,000
Less cost of sales		
Opening inventory	150,000	
Purchases	650,000	
	800,000	
– Closing inventory	200,000	
Cost of sales		600,000
Gross profit		500,000
– Expenses		275,000
Operating profit		225,000

10.2

See Table S10.2.

Table S10.2

Units	Fixed Costs	Variable costs @ €7	Total costs	Average cost
100,000	645,000	700,000	1,345,000	€13.45
150,000	645,000	1,050,000	1,695,000	€11.30
200,000	645,000	1,400,000	2,045,000	€10.22

10.3

Volume	Variable cost	Fixed cost	Total cost	Actual cost	Marginal cost
150,000	1,050,000	300,000	1,350,000		7.00
140,000	980,000	300,000	1,280,000	9.14	

The actual cost per unit is $9.14 – this is the actual average production cost per unit. The marginal cost per unit is $7.00 – this is the variable cost per unit.

10.4

Volume	Variable cost	Fixed cost	Total cost	Average cost/unit
10,000	70,000	100,000	170,000	£17
20,000	140,000	100,000	240,000	£12

The average cost reduces by £5 from £17 to £12. This is because the fixed costs of £100,000 are spread over 20,000 documents (£5 per document) rather than 10,000 documents (£10 per document).

The marginal cost is £7, i.e. the variable cost. It does not change per unit irrespective of volume within the relevant range.

The costs per unit at each activity level are:

	10,000	20,000
Variable costs	£7	£7
Fixed costs	£10	£5
Average cost	£17	£12

10.5

Current position:

	Eastern	Western	Total
	€	€	€
Sales	550,000	500,000	1,050,000
Variable costs	275,000	200,000	475,000
Divisional fixed costs	180,000	150,000	330,000
Contribution to corporate costs	95,000	150,000	245,000
Allocated corporate costs	170,000	135,000	305,000
Operating profit	(75,000)	15,000	(60,000)

After closure of Eastern division:

	Eastern	Western	Total
	€	€	€
Sales	–	500,000	500,000
Variable costs	–	200,000	200,000
Divisional fixed costs	–	150,000	150,000
Allocated corporate costs	–	305,000	305,000
Operating profit	–	(155,000)	(155,000)

The Eastern division should not be closed. It currently contributes €95,000 towards corporate costs. If the division were closed, the corporate costs would remain unchanged and the current loss of €60,000 would increase to €155,000.

10.6

	Last year		Current year
Sales price	80		
Variable cost	55		
Contribution margin	25	+20% (£5)	30
Units	5,000		5,000
Contribution	125,000		150,000
Fixed costs	25,000	−10% (£2,500)	22,500
Operating profit	100,000		127,500

Contribution margin is £25 (£80−£55) + 20% = increase of £535,000 units =   +£25,000
Fixed costs £25,000 Reduction of 10% =   +£2,500
Increase in profit is   £27,500

10.7

Variable costs are $750,000/300,000$ batons = $2.50/baton.
As the selling price is $5/baton, the normal contribution/baton = $2.50 ($5–$2.50).

If 240,000 batons are sold at the normal price:

Contribution = 240,000 @ $2.50	$600,000
−Fixed costs	450,000
Operating profit	$150,000

If 60,000 batons are sold at a 40% discount:
Sales = 60% of $5 = $3/baton, and contribution is 50p ($3−variable costs $2.50)

Contribution = 60,000 @ 50p/baton	$30,000
Total operating profit	$180,000

10.8

Profit = selling price per unit × no. units (VC/unit × no. units + fixed costs) therefore, £40,000 = SP × 320,000 ((£8 × 20,000) + £100,000)

$$\text{Selling price} = \frac{£40,000 + £160,000 + £100,000}{20,000 \text{ units}}$$
$$= £300,000/20,000 \text{ units} = £15$$

10.9

Breakeven is:

$$\frac{(10,000 \times 35) + 450,000 + 0}{10,000} = \frac{800,000}{10,000} = 80$$

Or:

Profit = price × no. units (fixed costs + variable costs × no. units)
0 = 10,000P − (450,000 + 35 × 10,000)
0 = 10,000P − (450,000 + 350,000)
0 = 10,000P − 800,000
800,000 = 10,000P
P = 800,000/10,000 = 80
Proof
10,000 × (80 − 35) = 10,000 × 45 = 450,000 − 450,000 = 0

10.10

Contribution per unit is 75 − 30 = 45
Fixed costs are 1,000 × 12 = 12,000

$$\text{Breakeven} = \frac{12,000 + 10,000}{45} = 489 \text{ p.a.}$$

10.11

$$\frac{200,000 \times 12\%}{18,000 \text{ units}} = \frac{£24,000}{18,000} = £1.33 \text{ per unit}$$

10.12

Selling price	20
Variable costs	13
Contribution margin	7

$$\text{Breakeven} = \frac{7,000 + 5,000}{7} = \frac{12,000}{7} = 1,714$$

10.13

See Table S10.13.

Table S10.13

Price	Variable costs	Contribution p.u.	Quantity	Total contribution
26	15	11	1,075	11,825
27	15	12	1,000	12,000
28	15	13	925	12,025
29	15	14	850	11,900
30	15	15	775	11,625

The maximum contribution is at a selling price of £28. Note that this is not necessarily the highest sales revenue. The highest contribution will also be the highest profit because the same amount of fixed costs is deducted from each level of activity (within the relevant range).

10.14

Labour costs	25.00
Variable costs	4.00
Fixed costs $250,000/20,000	12.50
Target return (750,000 × 25%)/20,000	9.38
Price	50.88

10.15

See Table S10.15.

Table S10.15

Number of rooms sold	Price per room per night	Revenue £	Variable costs @ £25	Contribution £
120	90	10,800	3,000	£7,800
100	105	10,500	2,500	£8,000
80	135	10,800	2,000	£8,800
60	155	9,300	1,500	£7,800
50	175	8,750	1,250	£7,500

Contribution maximized at £135 (80 rooms). This is an occupancy rate of 67% (80/120).

Solutions for Chapter 11

11.1

Variable costs are £2 per unit (£10,000/5,000), for December 10,000 @ £2 = £20,000.

Fixed costs do not change with activity, for December £30,000.
As total costs are £75,000, semi-variable costs for December are £25,000 (£75,000 − £20,000 − £30,000).

11.2

	Product R	Product S
Selling price	12	20
Materials	4	11
Throughput contribution	€8	€9
Machine hours	4	3
Return per machine hour	€2	€3
Ranking	2	1

Product S generates more throughput contribution per machine hour (the limiting factor). Labour hours are irrelevant.

11.3

	Hours	Cost $
	15,000	345,000
	7,000	185,000
Increase	8,000	160,000

The increase in hours sold of 8,000 has generated a higher cost of $160,000. This cost must be a variable cost as, by definition, fixed costs do not vary with the volume of activity. Therefore variable costs are $160,000/8,000 or $20 per hour.

At the 15,000 level of activity: 15,000 @ $20 = $300,000. Therefore fixed costs are $45,000 ($345,000 − $300,000).

At the 7,000 level of activity: 7,000 @ $20 = $140,000. Therefore fixed costs are $45,000 ($185,000 − $140,000).

However, this only applies in the relevant range, as outside the relevant range the cost structure of fixed and variable costs may alter.

11.4

Materials	40 @ 2.50		100
Labour	7 @ £12	84	
	4 @ £7	28	112
	11		212
Variable overhead	11 @ £5 =		55
Variable production cost			267
Fixed production overhead			
£1,000,000/12,500			80
Total production cost			347

11.5

Production will be 8,000 units special order plus 12,000 units regular sales to give a maximum production capacity of 20,000 units.

Variable costs are €49 per unit (€588,000/12,000 units).
Fixed costs are €345,000 (€245, 000 + €100,000).

Sales 12,000 units at €100	€1,200,000
Sales 8,000 @ €95	760,000
Total	€1,960,000
Variable costs 20,000 @ €49	980,000
Contribution margin	980,000
Fixed costs	345,000
Operating profit	€635,000

11.6

As the material is in regular use and has to be replaced, it is irrelevant that some is already in stock as the relevant cost − the future, incremental cash flow (in this case the replacement cost) − is 150 kg @ $12.50, a total of $1,875. The scrap value is not relevant.

11.7

	Macro	Mezzo	Micro
Contribution per unit	£6	£9	£14
Machine hours	2	2	2
Contribution per hour	£3	£4.50	£7
Ranking	3	2	1

Therefore the ranking should be to maximize production of Micro, followed by Mezzo, and finally Macro.

11.8

	Cost to produce in-house €	Outsourcing cost €
Raw materials	15,000	
Production labour	10,000	
Fixed manufacturing costs	7,000	3,000
Outsourcing cost	0	27,000
Total costs	32,000	30,000
Production units	4,000	4,000
Cost per Widget	€8	€7.50

On a purely financial basis Europa should outsource production, although there may be many non-financial reasons that compensate for the cost saving.

11.9

See Table S11.9.

Table S11.9

Sales		$850,000
Less cost of production		
Materials	450,000	
Labour	175,000	
Variable manufacturing expense	30,000	
Cost of production	655,000	
Opening inventory	120,000	
	775,000	
– Closing inventory	95,000	
Cost of sales		680,000
Contribution margin		170,000
– Fixed non-manufacturing expenses		65,000
– Selling and administrative expenses		40,000
Operating profit		$65,000

Solutions for Chapter 12

12.1

	£
Salary	40,000
National Insurance 11%	4,400
Pension 6%	2,400
Total employment cost	46,800
Working weeks per person	
52 – 4 – 2 = 46	
Cost per week 46,800/46	£1,017
Chargeable hours per week	25
Hourly rate (£1,017/25)	£40.68 or £41 to the nearest hour

12.2

	Volume	Cost
	1,200,000	€850,000
	1,000,000	€750,000
Increase	200,000	€100,000

Variable costs = €100,000/200,000 = €0.50
1,200,000 @ .50 = €600,000. Therefore fixed costs are €250,000 (€850,000 – €600,000).

12.3

Raw materials and variable costs are relevant costs as they are only incurred if manufacture takes place. Production labour is avoidable, i.e. it will only be incurred if Cardinal makes the part. As 60% of the fixed costs will continue regardless of the decision, only 40% of the fixed costs are relevant for the decision. Therefore, relevant costs of in-house manufacture are:

Raw materials	$4
Production labour	16
Variable costs	8
Fixed costs (40% of $10)	4
Total $32 × 20,000 units = $640,000	$32

Relevant costs of outsourcing to Oriole are:

Purchase cost $36 × 20,000 units = $720,000

Consequently, based on relevant costs, it is cheaper to manufacture the part in-house.

Note: the fixed manufacturing overhead of $10 per unit is an arithmetic calculation of total fixed costs divided by the number of units produced. This does *not* mean that the cost is a variable cost, just because it is expressed as a cost per unit.

12.4

The manufactured cost is £235 (120 + 60 + 30 + 25). The relevant costs are raw materials £120 and variable overhead £30, a total of £150. Production labour and fixed costs are not relevant. Production labour cannot be avoided as the business has spare capacity and wishes to retain its skilled employees. As the cost of purchasing the component is £140, on a relevant cost basis Cirrus should buy the component rather than make it.

12.5

Partners' cost	€200,000
Total hours 800 =	€250 per hour
Juniors' cost	€450,000
Total hours 5,000 =	€90 per hour

See Table S12.5.

Table S12.5

	Accounting	Audit	Tax	Total
Partner hours	150	250	400	800
@ €250	37,500	62,500	100,000	200,000
Junior hours	1,200	2,800	1,000	5,000
@ €90	108,000	252,000	90,000	450,000
Total	€145,500	€314,500	€190,000	€650,000

Audit services cost €314,500.

12.6

The comparison of costs under each alternative is shown in Table S12.6a.

Table S12.6a

	Manufacture 100	Purchase 100
Production labour 100 @ $200	20,000	20,000
Raw material 100 @ $600	60,000	
Variable overhead 100 @ $100	10,000	
Fixed overheads 100 @ $300	30,000	30,000
Supplier price 100 @ $1,000	0	100,000
Total	$120,000	$150,000

Production labour and fixed overheads are irrelevant in making a choice between alternatives. Raw materials and variable overheads will not be incurred if the components are purchased, and are therefore relevant costs. Relevant costs are as in Table S12.6b.

Table S12.6b

	Manufacture 100	Purchase 100
Raw material	60,000	
Variable overhead	10,000	
Supplier price		100,000
Total	$70,000	$100,000

If employees were on a temporary contract, labour cost would be avoidable and therefore the comparison of costs would be as in Table S12.6c.

Table S12.6c

	Manufacture 100	Purchase 100
Production labour 100 @ $200	20,000	
Raw material 100 @ $600	60,000	
Variable overhead 100 @ $100	10,000	
Fixed overheads 100 @ $300	30,000	30,000
Supplier price 100 @ $1,000		100,000
Total	$120,000	$130,000

Fixed overheads are irrelevant in making a choice between alternatives. Production labour, raw materials, and variable overheads will not be incurred if the components are purchased, and are therefore relevant costs.

Relevant costs are as in Table S12.6d.

Table S12.6d

	Manufacture 100	Purchase 100
Production labour	20,000	
Raw material	60,000	
Variable overhead	10,000	
Supplier price		100,000
Total	$90,000	$100,000

Costs based on stock valuation are not relevant since they are sunk costs, as we are concerned with future incremental cash flows only.

12.7

An alternative format for these figures is shown in Table S12.7.

Table S12.7

	Franklin Industries	Engineering Partners	Zeta	Other customers	Total (average)
Sales	1,000,000	1,500,000	2,000,000	1,500,000	6,000,000
Cost of materials	250,000	600,000	750,000	750,000	2,350,000
Contribution	750,000	900,000	1,250,000	750,000	3,650,000
% contribution	75%	60%	62.5%	50%	(60.8%)
Cost of labour	300,000	200,000	300,000	75,000	875,000
Gross profit	450,000	700,000	950,000	675,000	2,775,000
% Gross profit	45%	46.7%	47.5%	45%	(46.25%)
No. of hours (labour/£100)	3,000	2,000	3,000	750	8,750
Contribution per labour hour	£250	£450	£417	£1,000	(£417)

This format shows that at 75% the contribution margin as a percentage of sales (i.e. after deducting material) is in fact highest for Franklin. However, calculating the contribution per labour hour (we can divide the cost of labour for each customer by the cost per labour hour of £100 to give the number of hours required) verifies the lower contribution by Franklin per unit of the limiting factor, i.e. labour capacity. This is reflected in the rate of gross profit being the lowest of the three main customers.

The issues that arise from these figures are:

1. Labour is in effect a fixed cost given the circumstances of the business and its allocation to different products is questionable, other than in terms of determining the most profitable utilization of the limited capacity.
2. Can the high labour cost for Franklin be reduced by automation given that Franklin contributes almost 17% of total sales (£1,000,000/£6,000,000) with the highest contribution margin of 75%?
3. While Engineering Partners and Zeta are the most profitable customers in the accountant's report, the revised format shows the highest contribution per labour hour from the 'other' customer segment. Zeta, which, on the accountant's figures, appears more profitable than Engineering Partners, is using the revised format, less profitable per labour hour.
4. Do the corporate overheads, presently allocated arbitrarily in proportion to sales volume (overheads are 30% of sales), accurately reflect the different cost structure of each segment of the business in terms of space utilization (rent), capital investment in production processes (depreciation), non-production salaries, selling, and administration expenses? A more meaningful allocation of costs may lead to a different decision as to the profitability of different business segments.

12.8

Total costs	Cost to make	Cost to buy
Materials	$1.25	
Labour	$0.70	
Variable overheads	$0.20	
Total variable cost	$2.15	
Cost for 100,000 eggs	$215,000	
Cost to buy from int'l company @ $2.50 per egg		$250,000
Transport cost 100,000 @ $0.25		$25,000
Fixed costs	$150,000	$100,000
Total cost for each alternative	$365,000	$375,000

Relevant costs	Cost to make	Cost to buy
Variable production/purchase cost for 100,000 eggs	$215,000	$250,000
Plus transport		$25,000
Fixed costs	$50,000	
Relevant costs	$265,000	$275,000

Both approaches show that it is more cost-effective by $10,000 to make in-house rather than to buy from the international company. The maximum price that could be paid by Seaford which would result in the same cost as currently incurred to produce in-house is $2.40 ($265,000–$25,000 = $240,000/100,000).

Solution to case study question 12.1: Call Centre Services plc

The staffing level in the call centre provides a capacity of 60,000 calls (10 staff @ 6,000), but 70,000 calls have been taken. The telemarketing division has subsidized the operations of the call centre. In the short term, all costs in CCS are fixed costs. The standard cost of a call is €250,000/60,000 calls = €4.17. The standard cost for 70,000 calls is €291,900. It could therefore be argued that a more accurate presentation of the divisional performance is as in Table S12csa.

Table S12csa   Call Centre Services.

	Call centre	Telemarketing	Total
Number of calls	70,000	25,000	
Revenue	350,000	250,000	600,000
@ standard cost (€4.17)	291,900	148,100	440,000
Operating profit	€58,100	€101,900	€160,000

Note: telemarketing expenses have been calculated as total expenses (€440,000) less standard cost for 70,000 calls in the call centre (€291,900).

This shows quite a different picture. However, the telemarketing manager is likely to point out that his staff are paid considerably more than call centre staff (€22,000 compared to €15,000) and that the standard cost is based on a salary of €15,000.

The appropriate staffing for the call centre to handle 70,000 calls is 12 staff (70,000/6,000 = 11.7). Given the recruitment freeze, two of the telemarketing staff costs should be transferred to the call centre. Rental costs are adjusted accordingly. It is arguable as to whether the lease costs should be allocated 50/50, but in the absence of more information this is left unchanged. The revised profitability is shown in Table S12csb.

Table S12csb   Call Centre Services.

	Call centre	Telemarketing	Total
Number of calls	70,000	25,000	
Fee per call	€5	€10	
Revenue	€350,000	€250,000	€600,000
Less expenses			
Staff costs			
10 @ €15,000 p.a.	150,000		
2 @ €22,000 p.a.	44,000		
3 @ €22,000 p.a.		66,000	260,000
Lease costs on telecoms and IT equipment (shared 50/50)	20,000	20,000	40,000
Rent (shared in proportion to staffing: 4/5, 2/5)	96,000	24,000	120,000
Telephone call charges		20,000	20,000
Total expenses	310,000	130,000	440,000
Operating profit	€40,000	€120,000	€160,000

Whether based on standard costs or a reallocation of expenses between the divisions, the originally reported profit of €100,000 to the call centre and €60,000 to telemarketing is distorted. As the standard cost and reallocation calculations demonstrate, the call centre is making a much smaller profit and telemarketing a much larger profit than originally reported.

Solutions for Chapter 13

13.1

See Table S13.1.

Table S13.1

Division	1	2	3	Total
Overheads	50%	30%	20%	
	250,000	150,000	100,000	500,000
Hours	4,000	2,000	3,000	9,000
Hourly rate	$62.50	$75	$33.33	$55.55

13.2

	Machining	Assembly	Finishing	Total
Overhead costs	€120,000	€80,000	€30,000	€230,000
Labour hours	20,000	10,000	10,000	40,000
Hourly rate	€6	€8	€3	€5.75
Costing:				
Material			€300	
Labour			€150	
Overhead	10 @ €6	60		
	7 @ €8	56		
	3 @ €3	9	125	
Total			€575	

13.3

	Dept A	Dept B	Dept C	Total
Overheads	£150,000	£200,000	£125,000	£475,000
Direct labour hours	5,000	10,000	5,000	20,000
Overhead per hour	£30	£20	£25	£23.75
Hours for GH1	10	12	5	27
Overhead per product	£300	£240	£125	£641.25

Using plant-wide rate:

Direct materials	£150
Direct labour	£75
Overhead	£641
Total	£866

Using cost centre rate:

Direct materials		£150
Direct labour		£75
Overhead	(£300 + £240 + £125)	£665
Total		£890

13.4

Cost pool	Estimated cost	Expected activity Product A	Product B	Total	Rate $/activity
Activity 1	$20,000	100	400	500	40.00
Activity 2	$37,000	800	200	1,000	37.00
Activity 3	$91,200	800	3,000	3,800	24.00

Product A:

		Total	per unit (/8,000)
Activity 1:	$40.00 × 100	$4,000	$0.50
Activity 2:	$37.00 × 800	$29,600	$3.70
Activity 3:	$24.00 × 800	$19,200	$2.40
			$6.60

Product B:

		Total	per unit (/6,000)
Activity 1:	$40.00 × 400	$16,000	$2.67
Activity 2:	$37.00 × 200	$7,400	$1.23
Activity 3:	$24.00 × 3,000	$72,000	$12.00
			$15.90

13.5

a. Set-up costs €66,000

Production runs $12 + 5 + 8 = 25$
Cost per set-up €66,000/25 = €2,640
Product A has 12 runs @ €2,640 = €31,680
And 4,000 units are produced
Cost per set-up per unit is €31,680/4,000 = €7.92

b. Materials handling costs €45,000

Stores orders $12 + 6 + 4 = 22$
Cost per store order €45,000/22 = €2,045
Product B has 6 stores orders @ €2,045 = €12,270
And 3,000 units are produced
Cost per stores order per unit is €12,270/3,000 = €4.09

13.6

Purchasing cost	£120,000
No. purchase orders	240
Cost per purchase order	£500
L uses 80 @ £500	£40,000
For 20,000 units =	£2 per unit
M uses 160 @ £500	£80,000
For 20,000 units =	£4 per unit

If £120,000 of costs were recovered over the number of units produced (20,000 + 20,000 = 40,000), the purchasing cost per unit would be £3 (£120,000/40,000 units) for both L and M.

13.7

	Purchasing	Quality control	Dispatch
Total cost	$60,000	$40,000	$30,000
Driver	12,000	4,000	2,000
Cost/driver	$5	$10	$15
Hekla uses	5	8	2
Overhead	$25	$80	$30
Total overhead $25 + 80 + 30 =	$135		
Direct materials	$100		
Direct labour	$75		
Total cost	$310		

13.8

a.

Cost pool	Estimated cost	Expected activity			Cost/activity
		X	Y	Total	
Activity 1	€12,000	300	500	800	12,000/800 = €15
Activity 2	€15,000	100	400	500	15,000/500 = €30
Activity 3	€32,000	400	1,200	1,600	32,000/1,600 = €20

X		Y	
300 @ €15 = 4,500		500 @ €15 = 7,500	
100 @ €30 = 3,000		400 @ €30 = 12,000	
400 @ €20 = 8,000		1,200 @ €20 = 24,000	
Total €15,500		Total €43,500	
Units 3,000		2,000	
Overhead cost per unit €5.17		Overhead cost per unit €21.75	

b.

	X	Y	Total
Units	3,000	2,000	
Machine hours	5	5	
Total machine hours	15,000	10,000	25,000
Hourly rate €59,000/25,000 = €2.36 per hour			
Overhead cost	5 @ €2.36	5 @ €2.36	
Overhead cost per unit	€11.80	€11.80	

13.9

Traditional absorption costing
Machining overheads:

Widgets	50,000 × 2 @ £1.20	120,000
Gadgets	40,000 × 5 @ £1.20	240,000
Helios	30,000 × 4 @ £1.20	144,000

Assembly overheads:

Widgets	50,000 × 7 @ £0.825	288,750
Gadgets	40,000 × 3 @ £0.825	99,000
Helios	30,000 × 2 @ £0.825	49,500

See Table S13.9a.

Table S13.9a

	Widgets	Gadgets	Helios
Sales volume	50,000	40,000	30,000
Selling price	45	95	73
Direct labour and materials	32	84	65
Contribution per unit	13	11	8
Total contribution	650,000	440,000	240,000
Less machining overheads	120,000	240,000	144,000
Less assembly overheads	288,750	99,000	49,500
Profit	£241,250	£101,000	£46,500

Total profit £388,750.

Activity-based costing
See Tables S13.9b and S13.9c.

Table S13.9b

	Machining	Assembly	Set-ups	Order processing	Purchasing
Cost pool	£357,000	£318,000	£26,000	£156,000	£84,000
Cost drivers	420,000	530,000	520	32,000	11,200
Rate	£0.85	£0.60	£50	£4.875	£7.50
	per machine hour	per direct labour hour	per set-up	per customer order	per supplier order

Table S13.9c

	Widgets	Gadgets	Helios
Sales volume	50,000	40,000	30,000
Total contribution	£650,000	£440,000	£240,000
Machining @ £0.85	85,000	170,000	102,000
Assembly @ £0.60	210,000	72,000	36,000
Set-up @ £50	6,000	10,000	10,000
Order processing @ £4.875	39,000	39,000	78,000
Purchasing @ £7.50	22,500	30,000	31,500
Profit/(loss)	£287,500	£119,000	£ (17,500)

Total £389,000.

The total overhead and therefore the total profit is the same under both methods of overhead allocation (the difference is due to rounding). Each method has simply allocated the total overheads in different ways. The activity-based approach charges overheads to products based on the activities that are carried out in producing each product. This demonstrates, for example, that the Helios is actually making a loss as its high overheads compared with its low volume are not being recovered in the selling price. Under traditional absorption costing, the Helios is being subsidized by the other two products.

13.10

See Table S13.10a.

Table S13.10a

	A	B	C	Total
No. units	150,000	200,000	350,000	
Selling price	$50	$35	$25	
Variable costs	$20	$17	$14	
Contribution per unit	$30	$18	$11	
Sales revenue	7,500,000	7,000,000	8,750,000	23,250,000
Variable costs	3,000,000	3,400,000	4,900,000	11,300,000
Contribution (total)	4,500,000	3,600,000	3,850,000	11,950,000
Fixed expenses				6,900,000
Operating profit				$5,050,000

Preferred services

Based on volume of production (Production Dept preference?):

C, B, A

Based on sales revenue (Sales Dept preference?):

C, A, B

Based on contribution per unit of volume:

A, B, C

Based on total contribution (Accounting Dept preference?):

A, C, B

Strategy should be to shift sales mix as far as possible to Product A (highest contribution per unit).

Absorption of overhead

See Table S13.10b.

Table S13.10b

	A	B	C	Total
Absorption costs based on sales value	7,500,000	7,000,000	8,750,000	23,250,000
	32.2%	30.1%	37.7%	
Variable costs	3,000,000	3,400,000	4,900,000	11,300,000
Fixed expenses	2,221,800	2,076,900	2,601,300	6,900,000
Total costs	$5,221,800	$5,476,900	$7,501,300	$18,200,000
Cost per unit of volume	$34.81	$27.38	$21.43	
Absorption costs based on volume	150,000	200,000	350,000	700,000
	21.4%	28.6%	50%	
Variable costs	3,000,000	3,400,000	4,900,000	11,300,000
Fixed expenses	1,476,600	1,973,400	3,450,000	6,900,000
Total costs	$4,476,600	$5,373,400	$8,350,000	$18,200,000
Cost per unit of volume	$29.84	$26.87	$23.86	
Absorption costs based on equal allocation				
Variable costs	3,000,000	3,400,000	4,900,000	11,300,000
Fixed expenses	2,300,000	2,300,000	2,300,000	6,900,000
Total costs	5,300,000	5,700,000	7,200,000	18,200,000
Cost per unit of volume	$35.33	$28.50	$20.57	

    While there is not much difference between using sales value and equal allocations for overhead, the volume method leads to lower costs for Products A and B and higher costs for Product C. The important point here is that different methods of overhead allocation (of the same value of overhead) can lead to different costs for products and services.

Breakeven

See Table S13.10c.

Table S13.10c

	A	B	C	Total
No. units	150,000	200,000	350,000	700,000
Sales revenue	7,500,000	7,000,000	8,750,000	23,250,000
Variable costs	3,000,000	3,400,000	4,900,000	11,300,000
Contribution (total)	4,500,000	3,600,000	3,850,000	11,950,000
Average contribution per unit of volume				$17.07

Fixed costs	$6,900,000	404,218 units of volume
Contribution per unit	$17.07	

Maintaining the same sales mix, the breakeven sales units of each product are:

86,619 of A
115,490 of B
202,109 of C

Solutions for Chapter 14

14.1

Formula for present value = NPV (16%, C3:E3). The cash flows are entered in columns C (Year 1) to E (Year 3). See Table S14.1.

Table S14.1

Col A	Col B Year 0	Col C Year 1	Col D Year 2	Col E Year 3
Cash flows		10,000	10,000	10,000
Present value	22,459			
Initial investment	−18,000			
NPV	€4,459			

To calculate IRR using the spreadsheet function, a negative figure (the initial cash investment) must be part of the range of values.
Formula for IRR = IRR(B3:E3).

	Year 0	Year 1	Year 2	Year 3
Cash flows	−18,000	10,000	10,000	10,000
IRR	31%			

14.2

See Table S14.2.

Table S14.2

	Year 0	Year 1	Year 2	Year 3
Cash flows		1,000	800	700
Present value	2,029			
Initial investment	−2,000			
NPV	£29			

14.3

Payback

Project A	2.5 years	$(100 + 200 + 1/2 \times 50)$
Project B	3 years	$(40 + 100 + 210)$
Project C	2 years	$(200 + 150)$

Accounting rate of return

	Total cash flow	Depreciation	Profit	Average profit	ARR
Project A	640	350	290	58	33.1%
Project B	770	350	420	84	48%
Project C	630	350	280	56	32%

Average investment $350,000/2=\$175,000$

$$\text{ARR is } \frac{\text{average profit (profit/5 years)}}{\text{Average investment}}$$

NPV

See Table S14.3.

Table S14.3

	Year 0	Year 1	Year 2	Year 3	Year 4	Year 5
Project A						
Cash flows		100	200	100	100	140
Present value	499					
Initial investment	−350					
NPV	$149					
Project B						
Cash flows		40	100	210	260	160
Present value	571					
Initial investment	−350					
NPV	$221					
Project C						
Cash flows		200	150	240	40	0
Present value	523					
Initial investment	−350					
NPV	$173					
IRR						
Project A	24%					
Project B	26%					
Project C	33%					

The ranking is different depending on the technique:

On a payback basis, the ranking of projects (with preference to the quickest payback) is C, then A, then B.

The accounting rate of return method favours B, then A, then C.

The NPV method ranks B followed by C then A.

The IRR suggests that Project C has the highest return (as the cash flows are returned more quickly).

No absolute preference is clear, although Project A is slightly less attractive. As the accounting profits are likely to be important in terms of satisfying shareholders, this may be the optimum solution.

14.4

Project	1	2	3
NPV	1.7	1.1	1.0
Outlay	3.0	2.0	1.5
PI	.57	.55	.67
	57%	55%	67%
Ranking	2	3	1
Select	All	Part	All
Ranking 1:	Project 3 requires	£1.5 million	
Ranking 2:	Project 1 requires	£3 million	
Ranking 3:	Project 2	£0.5 million available	
		(25% of project)	
Total investment		£5 million	

14.5

Payback period

End of year 4, i.e. €200,000.

ARR

Year	1	2	3	4	5
Investment	200	160	120	80	40
Cash flows	45	50	55	50	35
– Depreciation 20%	40	40	40	40	40
Profit	5	10	15	10	−5
ARR	2.5%	6.25%	12.5%	12.5%	−12.5%

Over the 5 years:

Profit €35,000/5,000 = €7,000

Investment €200,000/2 = €100,000

ARR 7,000/100,000 = 7%

NPV

	Inflow	Outflow	Net	Factor	PV
Year 1	75,000	30,000	45,000	.9091	40,910
Year 2	90,000	40,000	50,000	.8264	41,320
Year 3	100,000	45,000	55,000	.7513	41,321
Year 4	100,000	50,000	50,000	.6830	34,150
Year 5	75,000	40,000	35,000	.6209	21,731
PV of cash flows					179,432
Cash outflow					−200,000
NPV					−20,568

Although the project has a payback of four years and an ARR of 7%, it should not be accepted as the NPV is negative, i.e. the cash flows do not cover the cost of capital.

14.6

The average accounting rate of return is 23.1%, although the annual ARR ranges from 3.9% in year 1 to 85.8% as a result of the reducing asset value after depreciation. The 5-year average is quite a high ARR.

The payback of about 3.5 years suggests some risk, in that market or technology changes could impact on the company's ability to generate the forecast profits and cash flow. A shorter payback period would usually be preferred.

The NPV is positive, and the amount of $42,897 represents a cash value added of 5.7% of the initial investment. The IRR is 2.23% above the cost of capital. While these DCF techniques do support a positive return, the return is relatively small and even a small reduction or delay in forecast profits and cash flows would likely result in a longer payback period and could lead to a negative NPV.

Despite the high ARR, the payback and DCF techniques suggest that while this is potentially a positive investment for shareholders, it is a marginal one at best, given the risks associated with the profit and cash flow projections.

The very high ARR should be challenged by the board. The questions that should be asked of the management team include: What are the assumptions behind the additional sales revenue that has been forecast and the relatively low additional costs? Are these figures realistic? Do they take into account the impact of competition? Does the asset have a life of five years, and if so, how much risk is associated with the profit and cash flow projections in years 3–5?

In addition, the board would be advised to set hurdle rates for each of the ARR, payback period, and IRR. The board should also validate the 12% cost of capital as being correct and reflecting the risks involved.

On balance, therefore, until such time as the management team is able to answer these questions satisfactorily, and in the absence of any known hurdle rates, it is recommended that the proposal be rejected given the low return based on DCF measures, and the fairly long payback period, despite the high ARR.

Note for students: while your actual answer may vary from the above (it is not incorrect to support the project), it is important that reasons are given to support the recommendation. In giving reasons, you must be critical of the figures presented, and not accept them at face value.

Solutions for Chapter 15

15.1

	Original	Additional	New
Investment	£10,000,000	£2,000,000	£12,000,000
ROI	15%	14%	14.8%
Profit	£1,500,000	£280,000	£1,780,000
Cost of capital 12%	1,200,000	240,000	1,440,000
RI	£300,000	£40,000	£340,000

15.2

	Original	Additional	New
Investment	€10,000,000	€2,000,000	€12,000,000
ROI	15%	14% (280/2000)	14.8% (1,780/12,000)
Profit	€1,500,000	€280,000	€1,780,000
Cost of capital 9%	900,000	180,000	1,080,000
RI	€600,000	€100,000	€700,000

15.3

	Current	Additional	After
Controllable investment	$750,000	$100,000	$850,000
Profit	$150,000	$15,000	$165,000
ROI	20%	15%	19.4%

Green may not want to accept the investment as it decreases the divisional ROI, but for Brummy Co. the project is better than the cost of capital (15% compared to 12%) and will increase shareholder value.

	Current	Additional	After
Controllable investment	750,000	100,000	850,000
Profit	150,000	15,000	165,000
Cost of capital 12%	90,000	12,000	102,000
RI	$60,000	$3,000	$63,000

Using residual income, both Green and Brummy Co. see an increase and will support the investment.

15.4

Compax

Figures in £m	1	2	3	4	Total
Cash flow	2.4	2.4	2.4	2.4	9.6
Depreciation	1.6	1.6	1.6	1.6	
Profit	.8	.8	.8	.8	3.2
Asset value -					
Opening value	6.4	4.8	3.2	1.6	
Closing value	4.8	3.2	1.6	0	
Cost of capital – 16% of opening asset value	1.02	.77	.51	.26	
RI	-.22	.03	.29	.54	0.64
ARR	12.5%	16.67%	25%	50%	

Average ARR

Average profit 3.2/4 = 0.8
Average investment = 6.4/2 = 3.2
Average ARR = 0.8/3.2 = 25%

Newpax

Figures in £m	1	2	3	4	Total
Cash flow	2.6	2.2	1.5	1.0	7.3
Depreciation	1.3	1.3	1.3	1.3	
Profit	1.3	.9	.2	-.3	2.1
Asset value -					
Opening value	5.2	3.9	2.6	1.3	
Closing value	3.9	2.6	1.3	0	
Cost of capital – 16% of opening asset value	.83	.62	.42	.21	
RI	.47	.28	-.22	-.51	.02
ARR	25%	23%	7.7%	23%	

Average ARR

Average profit 2.1/4 = 0.525

Average investment = 5.2/2 = 2.6
Average ARR = 0.525/2.6 = 20.2%

The NPV calculations show that Compax has a higher NPV at £315,634, giving a cash value added of 4.9% (315,634/6,400,000). Newpax has an NPV of £189,615 and a cash value added of 3.6% (189,615/5,200,000).

Overall, Compax has a higher ROI (the ARR calculation above is the same as the ROI), a higher RI and a higher cash value added based on the NPV. This is the preferred investment. However, it is important to realize that the returns for Compax are in the third and fourth years. Newpax looks more appealing in the first two years, when both its ARR/ROI and RI are higher. This may make Newpax more attractive from a divisional perspective or if Anston has a short-term focus.

15.5

See Table S15.5.

Table S15.5

	Division A €	Division B €	Division C €
Original investment	1,000,000	1,500,000	2,000,000
Original net profit	75,000	90,000	150,000
Original ARR	7.5%	6.0%	7.5%
Cost of capital 7%	70,000	105,000	140,000
Original RI	€5,000	−€15,000	€10,000
Additional investment	500,000	500,000	500,000
Additional profit	40,000	40,000	40,000
Additional ARR	8.0%	8.0%	8.0%
Cost of capital at 7%	35,000	35,000	35,000
Additional RI	€5,000	€5,000	€5,000
New investment	1,500,000	2,000,000	2,500,000
New profit	115,000	130,000	190,000
New ARR	7.7%	6.5%	7.6%
New cost of capital	105,000	140,000	175,000
New RI	€10,000	−€10,000	€15,000

Before the new investment, Divisions A and C have the highest ROI and Division C has the highest residual income. The additional investment achieves the same ROI and RI for each division. After the new investment, Division A has the highest ROI and Division C the highest RI. Division B has a negative RI before and after the new investment because the current ROI of 6% is less than the cost of capital of 7%. The additional investment improves that position, but Division B still erodes shareholder value.

Solutions for Chapter 16

16.1

Cash received (in £'000)		Jan	Feb	Mar	later	Never
Sales made in Jan	100	30	60	8		2.0
Sales made in Feb	120		36	72	9.6	2.4
Sales made in Mar	110			33	74.8	2.2
	330	30	96	113	84.4	6.6

Cash received in March £113,000
Receivables at end of March 84.4 + 6.6 = £91,000

16.2

Profit

See Table S16.2a.

Table S16.2a

	July	August	September	Total
Sales	20,000	30,000	40,000	90,000
Purchases	8,000	15,000	20,000	43,000
Gross profit	12,000	15,000	20,000	47,000
Wages	3,000	4,000	5,000	12,000
Other expenses	2,000	2,000	3,000	7,000
Depreciation	200	200	200	600
Operating profit	€6,800	€8,800	€11,800	€27,400

Note: Depreciation is €2,400 p.a. or €200 per month.

Cash

See Table S16.2b.

Table S16.2b

	July	August	September	Total
Receipts		20,000	30,000	50,000
Payments to creditors	–5,000	–10,000	–20,000	–35,000
Wages	–3,000	–4,000	–5,000	–12,000
Other expenses	–2,000	–2,000	–3,000	–7,000
Net cash flow	–10,000	4,000	2,000	–4,000
Opening balance	12,500	2,500	6,500	12,500
Closing bank balance	€2,500	€6,500	€8,500	€8,500

Note. Depreciation does not involve any cash flow. The opening bank balance is the capital of €20,000 less the equipment purchased of €7,500.

Statement of Financial Position

Non current assets	7,500	
Less depreciation	600	6,900
Current assets:		
Receivables	40,000	
Bank	8,500	
	48,500	
Total assets	55,400	
Liabilities:		
Payables	8,000	
Net assets	47,400	
Equity:		
Share capital	20,000	
Retained earnings	27,400	
	€47,400	

Note. Receivables €90,000 – 50,000 = €40,000

Payables €43,000 – 35,000 = – €8,000

16.3

See Table S16.3.

Table S16.3

Budget (in $'000)	Apr	May	Jun	Jul	Aug	Sep	Oct	Nov	Dec	Jan	Feb	Mar	Total
Revenue	225	225	225	225	225	225	150	150	150	150	150	150	2,250
Variable operating costs	68	68	68	68	68	68	45	45	45	45	45	45	675
Fixed operating costs	35	35	35	35	35	35	40	40	40	40	40	40	450
Total operating costs	103	103	103	103	103	103	85	85	85	85	85	85	1,125
Gross profit	123	123	123	123	123	123	65	65	65	65	65	65	1,125
Overheads:													
Sales charge	15	15	15	15	15	15	12	12	12	12	12	12	162
Salaries	25	25	25	25	25	25	25	25	25	25	25	25	300
Depreciation	5	5	5	5	5	5	5	5	5	5	5	5	60
Council rates	8	8	8	8	8	8	8	8	8	8	8	8	96
Heat, light and power	3	3	3	3	3	3	2	2	2	2	2	2	30
Total overheads	56	56	56	56	56	56	52	52	52	52	52	52	648
Operating profit	$67	$67	$67	$67	$67	$67	$13	$13	$13	$13	$13	$13	$477

The gross profit is 55% in the first half year and 43% in the second half year, because an increased fixed cost is spread over a lower volume of sales.

16.4

See Table S16.4.

Table S16.4

Budget data	Qtr 1	Qtr 2	Qtr 3	Qtr 4	Total
Volume (tonne)	100,000	110,000	105,000	120,000	
Selling price (per tonne)	300	300	310	310	
Variable costs (per tonne)	120	125	125	130	
Budget in £'000					
Sales and production	30,000	33,000	32,550	37,200	132,750
Variable costs (raw materials)	12,000	13,750	13,125	15,600	54,475
Contribution	18,000	19,250	19,425	21,600	78,275
Fixed costs:					
Salaries and wages	3,000	3,000	3,300	3,300	12,600
Maintenance	1,500	1,500	1,500	1,500	6,000
Council rates	400	400	400	400	1,600
Insurance	120	120	120	120	480
Electricity	1,000	1,000	1,000	1,000	4,000

Table S16.4 Continued

Budget data	Qtr 1	Qtr 2	Qtr 3	Qtr 4	Total
Depreciation	5,400	5,400	5,400	5,400	21,600
Other costs	2,500	1,800	1,800	2,500	8,600
Total fixed costs	13,920	13,220	13,520	14,220	54,880
Operating profit	4,080	6,030	5,905	7,380	23,395
Interest expense	600	600	600	600	2,400
Profit after interest	3,480	5,430	5,305	6,780	20,995
Cash forecast					
Profit after interest	3,480	5,430	5,305	6,780	20,995
Add back depreciation	5,400	5,400	5,400	5,400	21,600
	8,880	10,830	10,705	12,180	42,595
Less capital expenditure	6,500	2,000	1,000	9,000	18,500
Less dividend			10,000		10,000
Less debt repayments	1,000	5,000	4,000	3,000	13,000
Net cash flow	1,380	3,830	–4,295	180	1,095
Cumulative cash flow	1,380	5,210	915	1,095	

16.5

The known information is:

	Current year € mill	Next year € mill
Sales	586	+ 35% = 791
Cost of sales	486	
Gross profit	17% 100	
Overheads	–19	–22
Operating profit	13.8% 81	15% 119

Therefore, gross profit can be calculated as 141 or 17.8% of sales.

Sales	586	+ 35% = 791
Cost of sales	486	(791 – 41) = 650
Gross profit	17% 100	17.8% (119 + 22) = 141
Overheads	–19	–22
Operating profit	13.8% 81	15% 119

The company plans to increase sales substantially and improve margins through better purchasing and/or higher prices, and will incur significant costs in store openings, warehousing, and IT systems while maintaining only a 15% increase in corporate overheads.

A detailed budget projection would need to support these broad figures. The budget should identify, as a minimum:

- The sales mix by whatever categories are relevant (products, geographic sales, type of customer, etc.).
- The margins on different categories of sales.
- The cost of materials, retail store salaries, and property costs that are deducted to arrive at gross profit.
- The warehousing and distribution costs.
- Central overhead costs.

In terms of marketing, there are three distinct market strategies in existence:

- Increasing sales to existing customers through social marketing.
- Winning market share through television advertising.
- Increasing sales in new geographic areas through opening new stores.

The information needed to support these strategies is the expected contribution from each strategy, drawing from past experience. Questions to be asked include:

- How effective is social marketing likely to be, given that this is a relatively new domain?
- What is the cost of TV advertising and what additional sales and margins does it contribute?
- What is the cost of new store openings and what is the impact on capital expenditure (and therefore on cash flow) and the effect on running costs (especially salaries and property costs, including non-cash depreciation)?

The cost-effectiveness of operations may improve by investing in warehousing and distribution facilities and IT systems, but the cost/benefit of this needs to be demonstrated. Questions include:

- What is the current level of inventory and delivery lead time and how much is this expected to improve through new warehousing and IT systems?
- How does this saving compare with the additional capital expenditure?
- What is the impact of additional capital expenditure on operating costs?

This information needs to be modelled to determine whether the strategies will in fact lead to the desired profit target. The impact on capital expenditure, cash flow, and financing also has to be determined.

Non-financial issues include whether the existing staff in stores, distribution, and head office will be able to cope with the extra volume of business that is expected while retaining at least current standards of customer satisfaction, delivery lead time, and product quality.

16.6

Table S16.6a shows the Income Statement for Placibo Ltd.

Table S16.6a   Income Statement.

	June	July	August	September	3 mth total
Forecast sales units	20,000	20,000	22,000	25,000	
Selling price per unit	$4.25	$4.50	$4.50	$4.75	
Forecast revenue	$85,000	$90,000	$99,000	$118,750	$307,750
Cost of sales 30%	$25,500	$27,000	$29,700	$35,625	$92,325
Gross profit	$59,500	$63,000	$69,300	$83,125	
Overheads	$30,000	$30,000	$30,000	$30,000	
Depreciation	$25,000	$25,000	$25,000	$25,000	
Operating profit	$4,500	$8,000	$14,300	$28,125	

Table S16.6b shows a cash forecast for Placibo Ltd.

Table S16.6b   Cash forecast.

	June	July	August	September	3 mth total
Receipts - 30-day terms		$85,000	$90,000	$99,000	$274,000
Payables - 30-day terms		–$25,500	–$27,000	–$29,700	$82,200
Overheads - current month	–$30,000	–$30,000	–$30,000	–$30,000	
Operating cash flow		$29,500	$33,000	$39,300	

Table S16.6b provides a sufficient answer, but it can also be shown in the format of a Statement of Cash Flows, as shown in Table S16.6c.

Table S16.6c   Cash forecast (detailed version).

	June	July	August	September	3 mth total
Operating profit		$8,000	$14,300	$28,125	
Add Depreciation		$25,000	$25,000	$25,000	
		$33,000	$39,300	$53,125	
Change in working capital					
Increase in receivables		–$5,000	–$9,000	–$19,750	$33,750
Decrease in payables		$1,500	$2,700	$5,925	$10,125
Operating cash flow		$29,500	$33,000	$39,300	

Note in Table S16.6c that the increase in receivables is calculated by subtracting the receipts from sales from the forecast revenue in the Income Statement. The decrease in payables is calculated by subtracting the payments to suppliers from the cost of sales.

Solution to case study question 16.1: Carsons Stores Ltd

The first set of questions to be asked is how the level of sales was arrived at. In particular, have the sales been analysed by department/product? Have managers been consulted to see if the budget sales figures are achievable? Is the seasonal increase over the four quarters consistent with past trends, consumer spending patterns, and market share? Does it reflect changing prices and competitive trends?

The second set of questions is in relation to the rate of gross profit $(264/440 = 60\%)$. In particular, is this broken down by product or supplier? Is the cost of sales consistent with previous trading? Does it reflect current negotiations with suppliers? Does it reflect changing prices?

The third set of questions is in relation to expenses. Is the salary budget consistent with the headcount and approved salary levels for each grade of staff? Has an allowance for across-the-board (i.e. inflation-adjusted) salaries been built in? Have all the oncosts been included? Is the rental figure consistent with the property lease? How has depreciation been calculated (e.g. what is the asset value and expected life)? Promotional expenses appear to be 10% of sales – is this consistent with past experience and/or with marketing strategy? Are administration expenses consistent with past experience and any changes that have been introduced in the administration department?

The fourth set of questions is in relation to the cash flow. Are all sales for cash (because there is no assumption about delayed receipts for sales on credit)? Cost of sales appear to be on 30-day terms, but there is no payment showing for Quarter 1 – the payments for purchases made in Quarter 4 of the previous year have not been included. It also appears from the pattern of payments for purchases that there is no increase or decrease in inventory – is this correct given the trend of increasing sales over the year? All expenses have been treated as cash expenses, i.e. no allowance has been made for payment to suppliers for credit purchases – is this correct? The inclusion of depreciation expense in the cash flow is incorrect. Have the assumptions as to the timing and amount of capital expenditure, income tax, and dividends been checked with the appropriate departments?

An adjusted cash forecast, taking into account the missing purchases figure (assume £40,000) and removing depreciation as a cash outflow, is shown in Table S16cs.

Table S16cs   Carsons Stores.

In £'000	Quarter 1	Quarter 2	Quarter 3	Quarter 4	Year total
Cash receipts from sales	100	110	110	120	440
Purchases	40	40	44	44	168
Expenses	45	46	46	47	184
Capital expenditure		20			20
Income tax			20		20
Dividends		15	20	25	60
Cash outflow	85	121	130	116	452
Net cash flow	15	−11	−20	4	−12
Cumulative cash flow	15	4	−16	−12	

The previous cash flow of £8,000 has been increased by the non-cash depreciation expense of £20,000 and reduced by the omission of the estimated Quarter 1 purchases of £40,000. This results in a negative cash flow of £12,000. Importantly, this raises the question as to whether Carsons has an adequate overdraft facility to cover the negative cash flows in the third and fourth quarters. Due to the errors, this was not disclosed by the trainee accountant's cash forecast.

Note: there are many possible answers to this case study. The indicative answer provided above is intended to demonstrate the wide-ranging questions that need to be asked in relation to any budget projections and the assumptions behind budget figures.

Solutions for Chapter 17

17.1

	Budget	Flex	Actual
Units	2,000	1,800	1,800
@	$3	$3	$3.20
Cost	$6,000	$5,400	$5,760
Variance			$360 adverse

17.2

(Standard price – actual price) × quantity purchased
(€3.10 – €3.05) × 5200 = €260 favourable

17.3

a. See Table S17.3a.

Table S17.3a

	Budget	Actual
Sales units	10,000	11,000
Price per unit	£37.10	£36
Sales revenue	£371,000	£396,000
Direct materials	10,000 × 5kg @ £2.20	58,000
	£110,000	£126,075
Labour per unit	25,000 hours @ £7	26,400 hrs @ £7.10
	£175,000	£187,440
Total direct costs	285,000	313,515

Table S17.3a   Continued

	Budget	Actual
Contribution margin	86,000	82,485
Fixed costs	75,000	68,000
Profit	£11,000	£14,485

Note: an additional column could be included showing the variance between budget and actual.

b. See Table S17.3b.

Table S17.3b

	Budget	Flexible budget	Actual
Sales units	10,000	11,000	11,000
Price per unit	£37.10	£37.10	£36
Sales revenue	371,000	408,100	396,000
Direct materials	110,000	11,000 × 5kg @ £2.20 = £121,000	126,075
Labour	175,000	11,000 × 2.5 = 27,500 @ £7 = 192,500	187,440
Total direct costs	285,000	313,500	313,515
Contribution margin	86,000	94,600	82,485
Fixed costs	75,000	75,000	68,000
Profit	11,000	19,600	14,485

Note: an additional column could be included showing the variance between the flexed budget and actual.

c. See Table S17.3c.

Table S17.3c

Sales variances

	Original budget	Flexed budget	Actual	Variance
Sales	10,000 @ £37.10 = £371,000	11,000 @ £37.10 = £408,100	11,000 @ £36 = £396,000	
Selling price variance				11,000 @ £1.10 = £12,100 Adverse
Sales quantity variance		1,000 @ £37.10 = £37,100 Favourable		

Total sales variance £25,000 Favourable (£37,100 F − £12,100 A)

Table S17.3c   Continued

Cost variances

	Standard Quantity × Standard Price	Actual Quantity × Standard Price	Actual Quantity × Actual Price
Materials	11,000 × 5kg @ £2.20 = £121,000	58,000 @ £2.20 = £127,600	58,000 @ £2.17 = £126,075
Variance	Quantity £6,600 A		Price £1,525 F
		Total materials variance £5,075 A	
Labour	11,000 × 2.5 = 27,500 hrs @ £7 = £192,500	26,400 @ £7 = £184,800	26,400 @ £7.10 = £187,440
Variance	Quantity £7,700 F		Price £2,640 A
		Total labour variance £5,060 F	
Fixed costs	75,000	75,000	68,000
Variance			**Total fixed cost variance 7,000 F**

17.4

a. See Table S17.4a.

Table S17.4a

	Budget	Actual	Budget – Actual Variance
Analysis of labour			
Number of hours	10,000	9,000	
Average rate per hour	$75	$80	
Value of labour	$750,000	$720,000	$30,000

b. See Table S17.4b.

Table S17.4b

	Budget	Flex budget	Actual	Flex – Actual Variance
Analysis of labour				
Number of hours	10,000	9,000	9,000	
Average rate per hour	$75	$75	$80	
Value of labour	$750,000	$675,000	$720,000	–$45,000

c. In the traditional budget report, the variance cannot be interpreted properly because we are comparing the value of labour when the number of hours in the budget and actual data is not the same. The variance using the flexed budget equates the actual number of hours and compares the cost difference based on the same number of units. In this second example we can see that the variance is more sensible at $45,000, being 9,000 hours @ $5 ($80 – $75). This overspending on the average rate per hour cannot be determined from the traditional budget report.

Solutions for Chapter 18

18.1

As competition has increased and customers increasingly demand higher quality, choice, and lower costs, products now require far more innovation, flexibility, and differentiation to meet customer expectations and market competition. With technological change, products now have shorter life cycles and global competition demands continuous quality and cost improvement. Global supply chains need faster and better information to coordinate business activities, while high labour costs have led to more outsourcing, especially internationally, which has exacerbated the problem of management control.

18.2

A more strategic focus means that organizations should match their management control and accounting emphasis with the organizational strategy. In this strategic role, the scope of management accounting extends beyond the organization and beyond the financial year time horizon. It also moves from a vertical view of the organization structure to a view that sees horizontal business processes as being more important. Consequently, the role of management control has expanded from an inwards-looking focus on financial and non-financial information from an organization's own accounting and performance measurement systems to encompass information relating to markets, customers, and competitors; non-financial information about production processes; predictive information; and a broad array of decision support mechanisms and informal controls.

In its more strategic role, management accounting is more outward looking and helps the organization by collecting and analysing data on costs, prices, sales volumes, market share, and cash flows for its main competitors, which becomes the benchmark against which the organization's own performance is compared.

The crucial role for management accountants is to contribute to corporate strategy through the provision and analysis of financial information on the firm's product markets and competitors' costs and cost structures and the monitoring of organizational strategies compared with those of its competitors.

Accountants should be providing the tools to assist a company to increase shareholder value and moving from a 'number crunching' role to a more business advisory role of supporting managerial decision making.

18.3

Traditional management accounting establishes standard costs, records the issue of materials and labour times to production, and allocates overheads to products. It then carries out variance analysis to determine usage and price variances for materials and labour.

However, traditional management accounting does not recognize the importance of just-in-time, kaizen, and jidoka processes that aim to improve productivity and eliminate waste.

The introduction of lean accounting principles calls into question some taken-for-granted management accounting tools and techniques, simplifying management accounting routines in order to reduce waste and speed up the accounting function to improve decision making and reduce errors.

Lean accounting involves simpler techniques such as direct costing of items (without allocating overheads), and using backflush costing to replace detailed transaction recording of material issues and labour hours. It eliminates overhead allocation, standard costing, and variance analysis and introduces simplified management reporting to improve management decision making.

Index

4 Ps marketing strategy 199
5 forces (Porter) 197–8

ABC analysis 138–9
absolute profit 321, 326
absorption costing 274–8, 282–5
academic research 70–2, 401–2
accountability 3–5
accountant, fundamental principles 88–9
accounting
   critical perspective 14–15
   definitions 3–5
   financial vs management 12–14
   functions 7
   history 5–6
   lean 381–3
   limitations 11, 152–6
   overview 3–17
   principles 42–5
   recent developments 10–12
   role 7–10
Accounting Council 98
accounting entity 43
accounting equation 39
accounting in action 76
accounting period 43
accounting rate of return (ARR) 301–3,
   307, 308
   see also return on investment
Accounting Standards Board (ASB) 98, 130
Accounting Standards Committee (ASC) 98
accounting system 34
account types 34
accruals accounting 109–11
   see also matching principle
accuracy, product costing 392–3

acid test ratio 135, 139–40, 151
activity-based budgeting (ABB) 337
activity-based costing (ABC) 273, 278–85
   cost pools 278–81
   time-driven 281–2, 283–4
activity-based management (ABM) 11, 375–7
activity/efficiency ratio 136–7, 144, 151
adverse selection 120–1
advocacy threats 89
agency theory 73–5, 120–1
   contract 65
   rational-economic perspective 161
allocation base 274, 282
allocation systems
   cost accounting 393–5, 397–8
   two-stage systems 393–4, 397
   unavoidable costs 212
   see also overhead allocation
alternative perspectives
   budgetary control 368
   cybernetics 69, 75
   financial statements 156–7, 161–2
   institutional theory 75
   management accounting 51–67, 368
   natural perspectives 73
   non-rational perspectives 69–93
   radical perspectives 78–9
   social constructionism 75–7
   see also critical perspectives; interpretive
     perspectives; rational-economic
     perspectives
Amazon 187
amortization 112
annual impairment test 114
Annual Reports 129–30
Ansoff, H.L. 297

Anthony, R. 51–2, 55, 58, 335
Apple 44
application controls 193
arbitrary cost allocation 282
Armstrong, M. 251
ARR *see* accounting rate of return
Arthur Andersen 26, 86, 88, 162
ASB (Accounting Standards Board) 98, 130
ASC (Accounting Standards Committee) 98
assets
    Balance Sheets 107–9
    financial statements 102, 107–9
    IASs 113
    leases 115–16
    transaction recording 34, 38–42
asset turnover ratio 136–7, 143
attention-directing accounting function 7
audits 27
automatic teller machines (ATMs) 217
autonomation 380
avoidable costs 212, 213, 232

backflush costing 381–2
BACS (Bank Automated Clearing System) 217
bad debts 138
Balanced Scorecard 58, 59–61, 65, 240, 373
Balance Sheets 8, 12, 97, 98, 100, 148
    Annual Reports 130
    Carrington Printers 153–5
    depreciation 111–12
    differences from other financial statements 118–19
    financial position 107–9
    historic cost 44
    history 6
    leases 115, 116
    ratio analysis 141–3, 148
    transaction recording 38, 39
batch manufacture 175
batch-related costing activities 284
behavioural aspects 73–5, 199–200, 287–9
benchmarking 132, 143, 153
Berry, A.J. 52, 226, 339
Beyond Budgeting Round Table 350–1
big data 188
bill of materials 225, 269
bottlenecks 231–2
'bottom line' management 159, 414, 416, 417, 419, 421, 424–9
bottom-up budgets 337
bounded rationality 64
BP *Deepwater Horizons* accident 242

BPR (business process re-engineering) 192
breakeven, CVP analysis 202–7
    with multiple products 204–6
breakeven point 202, 203–4, 206, 207
budgetary control 359–70
    flexible budgeting 362–5
    variance analysis 361–8
budget-constrained managers 366–7
budget cycle 337–8
budgeting 335–58
    behavioural perspectives 349–50
    budgeting cycle 337–8
    cash forecasting 345–9
    control 359–70
    critical perspective 350–3
    definition 335–6
    EuroRail 418
    examples 340–5
    organizational culture 406, 418
    overhead rates 274–8
    processes 336–9
    Sports Stores Co-operative Ltd 342–3
    Superior Hotel 340–1
    Svenska Handelsbanken 352–3
    Telcon Manufacturing 343–5
Burchell, S. 288
business aspects
    culture 413, 414, 423–4, 425, 427
    events 33–5
    units 317–34
Business Excellence model 11
business organizations, structure of 317–19
business processes 190–2
business process re-engineering (BPR) 192
business-to-business activities (B2B) 187
business-to-consumer sales (B2C) 187
business-wide budgeted overhead rates 274–8

calculations, profit 34
Call Centre Services plc 265
CAM-I ABCM model 376, 377
capacity utilization 229–31, 242–3
capital
    Balance Sheets 107–9
    calculating capital 34
    decision-making 297–315
    employed 20
    expenditure (cap ex) 40, 420
    intellectual capital 157
    maintenance 103
    markets 19–21
    transaction recording 34, 39

working capital 40, 135, 139–40
  see also investment
capitalism 14–15
capitalizing assets 111
capitalizing expenses 40
Carrington Printers 153–6
case studies
  Arthur Andersen 86
  budgeting 339–45, 346–9, 352–3, 357–8
  Call Centre Services plc 265
  Carrington Printers 44, 153–6
  Carsons Stores Ltd 357–8
  Database Management Company 257–60
  decentralized organizations 324–6
  easyJet 81–4
  Enron 85
  EuroRail 389, 403–34
  General Machinery Ltd 168–9
  Goliath Co. 309–11
  Helo Europe 176–7
  human resource decisions 257–61, 265
  investment appraisal 309–11
  job costing 176–7
  Kazoo 178
  long-term contract costing 179–80
  Macro Builders 179–80
  Majestic Services 324–6
  marketing 214–16
  Marquet Company 217
  operating decisions 242–6
  Paramount Services plc 166–8
  performance evaluation 324–6
  Planet Engineering 245–6
  pricing for capacity utilization 242–3
  process costing 177, 178–9
  Quality Printing Company 242–3
  Retail Stores plc 214–16
  Royal Bank of Scotland 87
  segmental profitability 214–16
  Sports Stores Co-operative Ltd 342–3
  Superior Hotel 339–41
  Supertech 218–19
  Svenska Handelsbanken 352–3
  Tektronix Portables 290
  Telcon Manufacturing 343–5
  TNA 382–3
  Trojan Sales 260–1
  Vehicle Parts Co. 243–5
  Voxic Co. 177
  W H Smith PLC 146–52
  WorldCom 86

  see also examples
cash
  cash accounting 109
  cash cost 46
  double entry accounting 35
  equivalents 117
  forecasting 345–9
cash flow, budgeting 345
Cash Flow Statements 8, 12, 97, 98, 100, 116–18, 145–6
  Annual Reports 130
  case study 146–52
  decision-making 297–315
  differences from other financial statements 118–19
  discounted cash flow 304–7
  investment appraisal 299–301
  net present value 304–7
  ratio analysis 149
  strategic investment 299–301, 304–7
cash value added (CVA) 306–7, 308
chairman's report, Annual Reports 129–30
Chandler, A.D.J. 6, 318
change
  accounting roles 272–3
  cultural change 409, 424, 427
  EuroRail 414–23
Chartered Institute of Management Accountants 13
Child, J. 317
classification, costs 267–71
closed systems 73, 74
Code of Ethics for Professional Accountants 88–9
Collier, P.M. 226, 339
companies *see* organizations
Companies Act (2006) 25, 98, 103, 130–1
comparability, financial statements 101–2
compliance costs 237
comprehensive cost systems 400
computerization 12
conflict
  power issues 78
  radical perspectives 78
conformance costs 240–1
conservative accounting 45
  see also traditional accounting critiques
consistent accounting 45
constraints theory 231–2
Construction Contracts (IAS11) 113, 179
contingency theory
  control 193
  decision-making 285–6
  open systems 75

continuous improvement 239, 240, 367, 375
continuous manufacture 175
contract 65, 120
contribution accounting 416
contribution margin 200
control 7, 51–67
   budgeting 359–70
   contract 120
   cybernetic control 55–6, 64, 69, 75
   definitions 51–2
   information systems 192–3
   internal control 28–9
   organizational culture 77–8
   planning 52, 54–8
   power 80–4
   systems design 285
   technocratic 77
controllability
   decentralized organizations 323–4
   profit 323–4
conversion costs 175
Cooper, D.J. 288
Cooper, R. 278, 288, 290, 375–6, 389, 390–402
corporate finance 7
corporate governance 25–8
Corporate Report 158
corporate social responsibility 158–61
corrective action, variances 361
cost *see* costs
cost accounting 8–9, 389, 390–402
   allocation systems 393–5, 397–8
   complexity problems 395–6
   comprehensive systems 400
   diseconomies of scope 399
   fixed-cost allocations 394–5
   marginal costing 394
   product cost accuracy 392–3
   transaction costing 396–8, 400
   two-stage allocation systems 393–4, 397
cost centres
   budgeted overhead rate 274, 276–7
   decentralized organizations 319
   performance evaluation 319
cost down 375
cost formulae, inventory 173
cost improvement 374
costing
   ABC 278–85, 337
   absorption costing 274–8, 282–5
   kaizen costing 380
   lifecycle costing 378–9
   long-term product costing 400
   spare capacity 228–9
   standard costing 225–6
   target costing 379–80
cost of goods sold 36
cost of sales 36
cost-plus pricing 208–9, 327
costs
   allocation basis 274, 282
   avoidable costs 212, 213, 232
   batch-related activities 284
   cash cost 46
   cause-and-effect basis 285
   classification 267–71
   control 374
   conversion 171–2, 175
   cost behaviour 199–200
   cost objects 45–6
   cost of capital 21
   definition 45
   drivers 278–80, 374, 400
   easyJet 81–4
   equipment replacement 233–4
   EuroRail 416–17
   external failure 240, 241
   facility-sustaining activities 284
   flow 172–3
   goods sold 172
   internal failure 240, 241
   inventory 171–3
   labour 252–60
   management 374–5
   marginal cost 200, 327, 394
   measurement 241
   operating decisions 232–7
   period costs 267–9
   pools 278–80, 284
   prevention 240, 241
   prime costs 270
   product costs 267–9, 284, 390–402
   purchase 171–2
   quality issues 239–41
   relationships 271
   sales 268–9
   supplier cost analysis 237–9
   support departments 395–9
   terms and concepts 45–7
   total cost of ownership 237–9
   transaction costs 120, 329–30, 396–8, 400
   unavoidable costs 212, 213, 232
   unit costs 284, 398
   variances 363–5
   weighted average cost of capital 21
   see also expenses; fixed costs; overheads;
      variable costs

cost–volume–profit (CVP) analysis 201–8
  breakeven 202–7
  limitations 207–8
  margin of safety 204
  operating leverage 206–7
creative accounting 84–90
credit 36
creditors 36, 107, 139
  see also liabilities
critical perspectives 14–15, 69–93
  budgetary control 368
  budgeting 350–3
  critical theory 79
  easyJet 84
  financial statements 162
  performance evaluation 330–1
  shareholder value 29–30
  see also alternative perspectives
culture 407–10
  see also organizational culture
current assets 107
current cost 102
current liabilities 107–8
customer order processing 190–2
customer profitability analysis 216–19
customer relationship management 198, 373
custom manufacture 175
CVA (cash value added) 306–7, 308
CVP *see* cost–volume–profit (CVP) analysis
cybernetics
  alternative perspectives 69, 75
  control 55–6, 64, 69, 75

Database Management Company 257–60
data collection methods 186–8
data warehouse 189
days' payables outstanding 151
days' purchases outstanding (DPO) 139–40
days' sales outstanding (DSO) 138,
    139–40, 151
DCF (discounted cash flow) 304–7, 308
debt 20–1, 34, 36, 111, 135–6
debtors 6, 36, 107, 138
decentralized organizations 320–9
  absolute profit 321, 326
  case study 324–6
  controllability 323–4
  cost centres 319
  investment centres 319
  performance evaluation 320–3
  profit centres 319
  residual income 321–3, 326
  ROI 321

decision-making 7, 69–93
  accounting definitions 4
  capital investment 297–315
  EuroRail 420–1
  human resources 251–65
  investment appraisal 298–301
  marketing 197–222
  operations 223–49
  shareholder value 22
  strategic investment 297–315
decision support systems (DSS) 189
delivery failure costs 237
Dent, J.F. 289, 389, 403–34
depreciation 111–12
design, control systems 285
differential pricing 208
direct costs 269–71
direct labour 229, 252
direct labour cost per unit of production 229, 253
direct labour costs 269–70
direct labour hours 393–5
direct materials 269
directors
  corporate governance 25, 27, 28
  responsibilities 27
discounted cash flow (DCF) 304–7, 308
discount rates 304–7, 311
discourse, critical theory 79
diseconomies of scope 399
distortion, cost accounting 390–402
distribution requirements planning (DRP) 189
dividend payout ratio 140, 152
dividend per share 140, 152
dividends 21, 106–7, 140–1, 152
dividend yield 141, 152
divisional business structures 318–19
  performance measurement 320–3
  see also business aspects
DMAIC 240
double entry accounting 35–8
doubtful debts 111
drivers
  cost 278–80, 374, 400
  shareholder value 22–3
DuPont 6, 321

earnings before interest and taxes (EBIT) 105, 143
earnings before interest, taxes, depreciation, and
    amortization (EBITDA) 112
earnings management 43, 85
earnings per share 152
earnings per share ratio 141, 145
easyJet 81–4

EBIT 105, 143
EBITDA 112
Economic Value Added™ (EVA) 23
efficiency
    activity/efficiency ratio 136–7, 144, 151
    labour variances 366
EFTPOS (electronic funds transfer at point
    of sale) 217
eighty/twenty rule 138
elastic demand 209
electronic data interchange (EDI) 187
electronic funds transfer at point of sale
    (EFTPOS) 187
electronic point-of-sale (EPOS) 186–7
elements, financial statements 102–3
emergent properties, systems 394
Emmanuel, C. 317
Employee Benefits (IAS19) 113
Enron 11, 25, 26, 85, 88, 99, 162
enterprise resource planning (ERP) 12, 189, 190, 192,
    193, 373
entity principle 43
environmental cost management 241–2
environmental issues 158–61
equipment replacement 233–4, 243–5
equity, definition 20, 108
equivalent units 175
ethics 84, 88–90, 160, 162
    see also moral issues
EuroRail (ER) study 289, 403–34
    accounting and culture 423–8
    change dynamics 414–23
    organization overview 411–14
    research method 410–11
EVA (Economic Value Added Economic Value
    Added™) 23
evaluation
    budgetary information 366
    investment 298–301, 309–11
    performance 317–34
examples
    budgeting 340–5
    fixed/variable costs 199–200
    manufacturing 343–5
    see also case studies
executive information systems (EIS) 189
expenditure, EuroRail 420
expenses
    capitalizing expenses 40
    disclosure 104
    period costs 268
    transaction recording 34
expert systems 189–90

eXtensible Business Reporting Language
    (XBRL) 161
external failure costs 240, 241

facility-sustaining activity costs 284
failure costs 218, 240, 241
familiarity threats 89
FASB (Financial Accounting Standards Board) 99
feedback control 54–5, 56, 64, 65
    budgetary control 359
feedforward control 54–5, 56, 64, 65
finance leases 115–16
financial accounting 7–8, 24
    vs management accounting 12–14
    recent developments 10–12
Financial Accounting Standards Board (FASB) 99
financial information 38–42
financial management 18, 21
financial position 107–9
Financial Reporting Council (FRC) 27, 98, 99
Financial Reporting Standard for Smaller Entities
    (FRSSE) 99
Financial Reporting Standards (FRSs) 98, 99, 124–5
financial reports
    accruals accounting 109–11
    agency theory 120–1
    Annual Reports 129–30
    capital maintenance 103
    Cash Flow Statements 116–18
    comparability 101–2
    critical perspective 121–2, 156–7, 162
    depreciation 111–12
    directors' responsibilities 27
    elements 102–3
    financial position 107–9
    Framework 97, 100–3
    IFRSs 98–100
    interpretation 129–69
    liabilities 102, 107–9
    limitations of 152–6
    objectives 101
    qualitative characteristics 101–2
    ratio analysis 132–7
    role 7–8
    theoretical perspective 120–1
    see also Balance Sheets; Income Statements
financial statements 7, 9, 44, 97, 100–3, 181, 198, 274
    constructing 97–127
    context 131
    differences between 118–19
    interpretation of 129–69
finished goods 172, 225
first-in-first-out (FIFO) 173, 174, 179

Fisher, J. 285
Fitzgerald, L. 227–8
fixed assets 107
fixed costs 199
   allocations 394–5
   budgetary control 362
   comprehensive cost systems 400
   example 199–200
flexible budgeting 362–5
flowcharting 190
Ford, Henry 6
Ford Motor Co. 330
forecasting 336, 345–9
Framework for the Preparation and Presentation of Financial Statements (*Framework*) 97, 100–3
free cash flows 22, 299
full cost 209, 327, 391–2
functional organization structure 318
future cost 46

GAAP (Generally Accepted Accounting Principles) 10, 99
gains, disclosure 104
Galbraith, J.R. 318
'garbage-can' decision-making approach 73
gearing ratios 135–6, 140, 144, 151
General Electric Co. 321
Generally Accepted Accounting Principles (GAAP) 10, 99
General Machinery Ltd 168–9
General Managers, EuroRail 418–23
General Motors 6, 330
global financial crisis (GFC) 11, 21–2, 25
global harmonization 98
Global Reporting Initiative (GRI) 159–60
goal congruence 120
going concern basis, financial reporting 44
Goliath Co. case study 309–11
goodwill 114–15
Gosselin, M. 281
Govindarajan, V. 335
graphical user interface (GUI) 189
GRI (Global Reporting Initiative) 159–60
gross margin 105, 134, 147–9, 397
gross profit 104–5

harmonization
   financial reporting 286
   global 98
historic cost 44, 46–7, 102, 103
Hobsbawm, E. 14
Hopper, T. 70, 72, 75
Hopwood, A.G. 366–7

hotel budget example 340–1
human resources 251–65

IASB (International Accounting Standards Board) 98
IASC (International Accounting Standards Committee) 98
IASs *see* International Accounting Standards
IFRSs *see* International Financial Reporting Standards
impairment assessments 113
Impairment of Assets (IAS36) 113
impairment testing 114
income
   income tax 106, 108, 347
   profitability 104
   transaction recording 34
Income Statements 12, 97–8, 100, 104–7
   Annual Reports 130
   depreciation 111
   differences from other financial statements 118–19
   leases 116
   ratio analysis 141–2
   transaction recording 38
   see also financial reports
incremental budgets 336, 337
indirect costs 252–4, 269–71
indirect labour 252
indirect labour costs 270
individual theories 76
Industrial Revolution 6, 8, 9, 14
inelastic demand 209–10
inflation 152
information accounting
   agency theory 120–1
   financial information 38–42
   ratio analysis 143–5
information asymmetry 121
information management (IM) 186
information systems 185–94
   big data 188
   business processes 190–2
   designs and controls 192–3
   development 193
   types 188–90
information technology (IT) 12, 186
institutional investors 158
institutional theory
   alternative perspectives 75
   EuroRail 424
   financial statements 158
   organizations 158
intangible assets 107, 113
Intangible Assets (IAS38) 113
integrated reporting 160–1

intellectual capital 157
interest
  cash flow 117
  EBIT 105, 143
  EBITDA 112
  equity 106, 108
  gearing ratios 135–6, 144
  leases 115–16
  operating profit 105
  PBIT 105, 143
  winning sales 218–19
interest cover ratio 135
internal control 28–9, 192–3
internal failure costs 240, 241
internal rate of return (IRR) 307–8
international accounting comparisons 286–7
International Accounting Standards (IASs) 112–13
  see also International Financial Reporting
    Standards
International Accounting Standards Board (IASB) 98
International Accounting Standards Committee
    (IASC) 98
International Financial Reporting Standards (IFRSs)
    10, 97, 98–100, 121, 123–4, 286
  Framework 100–3
  IAS1 Presentation of Financial Statements 108, 112
  IAS2, Inventory 113, 171, 273, 284
  IAS11, Construction Contracts 113, 179
  IAS16, Property, Plant & Equipment 113
  IAS17, Leases 113
  IAS19, Employee Benefits 113
  IAS21, Foreign Exchange 113
  IAS36, Impairment of Assets 113
  IAS37, Provisions, Contingent Liabilities and
    Contingent Assets 113
  IAS38, Intangible Assets 113
  IAS39, Financial Instruments 113
  IFRS2, Share Based Payment 112–13
International Integrated Reporting Council
    (IIRC) 160
International Standards Organization (ISO)
  ISO 9000: 239, 240, 241
  ISO 14000: 241
interpretation, financial statements 129–69
interpretive perspectives 69–93
  budgetary control 368
  easyJet 83–4
  EuroRail study 427
  financial statements 161–2
  management accounting 71
  social constructionism 75–7
  see also alternative perspectives
intimidation threats 89

inventory 36, 105, 111, 341, 342–3
Inventory (IAS2) 113, 171, 273, 284
inventory accounting 171–84
inventory holding costs 237
inventory management 138–9
inventory turnover (turn) 138, 151
investment
  appraisal 298–301, 309–11
  capital investment 40, 298–301
  centres 319
  evaluation 298–301, 309–11
  see also strategic investment
investment centres 319
IRR (internal rate of return) 307–8
ISO see International Standards Organization
isomorphism 158
Italian city-states 5–6
iTunes 187

Japan 287
jidoka 375, 380–1
JIT (just-in-time) systems 139, 226, 367, 375, 380
job costing 175, 225
  case study 176–7
Johnson, H.T. 9–10, 58–9, 272–3, 322
just-in-time (JIT) systems 139, 226, 367, 375, 380

kaizen costing 375, 380
Kaplan, R.S. 9–10, 58–61, 65, 71, 272–3, 278, 322, 375–6,
    289, 390–402
keiretsu principle 287
key performance indicators (KPIs) 131
  see also Operating and Financial Review
King Committee on Corporate Governance, South
    Africa 29
knowledge
  cultural knowledge 428
  EuroRail 425–7
  systems 425–7
KPIs (key performance indicators) 131

labour
  costs 252–60
  definition 252
  labour oncost 252
  labour process 78
  variances 364–5, 366
last-in, first-out (LIFO) 173
Latin terms 6
lean accounting 12, 381–3
lean production 381
leases 113, 115–16
ledgers 37–8, 42

legislation
    Companies Act (2006) 25, 98, 103, 130–1
    Sarbanes–Oxley Act (2002) 26
legitimacy, institutional theory 158
liabilities
    Balance Sheets 107–9
    creditors 34, 107, 139
    financial statements 102, 107–9
    IAS37 113
    leases 115–16
    transaction recording 34, 38–42
lifecycle costing 378–9
limitations
    accounting 11, 152–6
    Carrington Printers 153–6
    limiting factors 229–30, 336
    ratio analysis 152–6
    scarce resources 229
limited liability 19
limiting factors 229–30, 336
line items 42, 46
liquidation, Carrington Printers 155
liquidity 117, 126, 131, 135, 144, 151
Listing Rules, Stock Exchange 27–8, 103
logical incrementalism 298
longitudinal study, ER 403–34
long-term contract costing 179–80
long-term product costing 400
long-term variable cost 398–9
loss 89, 90, 91, 104, 106, 213

machine hours 394–5
maintenance
    capital 103
    EuroRail 429
Majestic Services 324–6
make-ready time 227
make-versus-buy decisions 232–3
management
    activity-based management 11, 375–7
    control systems 51–4
    EuroRail 417–23
    financial management 18, 21
    operations 225–7
    payables 137, 139
    performance 53, 58, 60–1, 63–4
    quality management 11
    receivables 137–8
    strategic accounting 12
    value-based management 11, 21–3
    working capital 137, 138–9
    see also control
management accounting 7, 8–10, 24
    alternative perspectives 51–67, 368
    behavioural implications 287–9
    changes 272–3
    financial accounting vs 12–14
    internal control 28–9
    Japan 287
    rational-economic perspective 51–67
    recent developments 10–12
    research 70–2, 401–2
    statements 180–1
    theoretical aspects 64–5, 70–2
    trends 371–2
management control systems see control
management information systems (MIS) 189
managerialism 72
manufacturing
    costing inventory 175–80
    examples 343–5
    finished goods 225
    JIT systems 226
    operating decisions 225–7
    types 225
    variance analysis 366, 367
manufacturing resource planning (MRP2)
        systems 189
margin, definition 209
marginal cost 200, 327, 394
margin of safety 204
marketing decisions 197–222
    case studies 214–16, 218–19
    marketing strategy 197–9
    pricing 208–12
    segmental profitability 212–16
markets
    capital 19–21
    EuroRail 425, 426
    penetration 198, 208
    products 19–21, 425
    segments 208, 383
    skimming 198, 208
    transfer pricing 327
market-to-book ratio (MBR) 44
market value added (MVA) 22
mark-up, definition 209
Marquet Company 217
Marxism 14, 78, 79
matching principle 41, 43, 97, 104, 105, 109–11, 172
    see also accruals accounting
material dollars 394–5
material requirements planning (MRP) 189
materials 225, 235–7, 364, 365, 366
Mayers Tap 392, 393
MBR (market-to-book ratio) 44

meanings 76, 408–10
measurement
  costs 241
  financial elements 102–3
  monetary measurement 44
  performance 11, 58–64, 82–3
Medici family 6
Microsoft 44
mix
  product 198, 229–31
  sales 198
  services 229
monetary measurement 44
moral issues
  accounting consequences 15
  creative accounting 84
  ethics and accounting 84, 88–90
  moral hazard 120–1
  non-financial performance measurement 58–64
MVA (market value added) 22

Nathanson, D.A. 318
nationalization, railways 412, 413
natural perspectives 73, 74
negotiated prices 327
net assets 108
net present value (NPV) 304–8
  see also present value
net profit 104, 105, 201
net realizable value 175
net residual income after taxes 324
network controls 193
Nobes, C. 286
non-conformance costs 240–1
non-current assets 107
non-current liabilities 108
non-cybernetic control 75
non-financial performance
  accounting limitations 11
  control systems 58–64
  non-rational perspectives 73
non-production overheads 270
non-rational perspectives 69–93
normative view, research 71
Norton, D.P. 59–61, 65
notes, Annual Reports 130
NPV see net present value

OFR (Operating and Financial Review) 130–1
open systems 73, 74, 75
Operating and Financial Review (OFR) 130–1
operating decisions 223–49
  case studies 242–6

managing operations 225–8
  manufacturing 225–7
  operations function 223–5
  relevant costs 232–7
  services 227–8
operating leases 115, 116
operating leverage 206–7
operating margin 105, 134
operating profit 104, 105
opportunity cost 46, 232, 255
optimum selling price 209–10
organizational culture 77–8, 403–34
  accounting aspects 77–8, 423–8
  business culture 413, 414, 423–4, 425, 427
  concept of culture 407–10
  cultural change 409, 424, 427
  EuroRail study 389, 403–34
  isomorphism 158
  knowledge 425–7
  meanings 408–10
  'railway' culture 412, 422, 423–8
  reality 403–34
organizational structure 317–19
organizations
  company regulation 130
  corporate governance 25–8
  institutional theory 158
Otley, D. 52, 53, 54, 56, 57, 58, 69, 72, 90, 285–6
outsourcing, labour costs 256–7
overhead allocation
  ABC 278–81
  alternative methods 273–82
  case studies 290
  decisions 267–96
  problem 271–2
  variable costing 273, 283
overheads
  definition 269
  overheads/sales ratio 134
  over- or under-recovery 282
  ratio analysis 149–51
  variance analysis 365, 366

Pacioli, Luca 6
paradigm, definition 64
Paramount Services plc 166–8
Pareto principle 138
Parker, R.H. 286
payables, management 137, 139
payback
  CVA 306–7
  IRR 307
  NPV 304–7

strategic investment 304
technique comparisons 307–8
PBIT (profit before interest and taxes) 105, 143
penetration, markets 198, 208
P/E ratio (price/earnings ratio) 141, 145, 152
performance
  absolute profit 321, 326
  business units 317–34
  case study 324–6
  control system standards 55
  cost centres 319
  critical perspective 330–1
  decentralized organizations 320–3
  evaluation 317–34
  investment centres 319
  management 53, 58, 60–1, 63–4
  measurement 11, 58–64, 82–3
  profit centres 319
  ratio analysis 153
  residual income 321–3, 324, 325–6
  ROI 321, 324–6
  transaction costs 329–30
  transfer pricing 327–9
Performance Management for Turbulent
    Environments (PM⁴TE) model 63–4
Performance Prism 62–3
period costs 267–9
physical capital maintenance 103
Planet Engineering 245–6
planning 7
  control 52, 54–8
  EuroRail 413, 414, 418
  horizon 301
  strategic planning 336
planning, programming and budgeting system
    (PPBS) 336
political economy 78
population ecology theory 75
Porter's five forces 197–8
Porter's value chain 224–5
power
  control 80–4
  critical perspective 78
  organizational culture 406
  radical perspective 78
PPBS (planning, programming and budgeting
    system) 336
predictive models 56–7
prepayments 110
present value (PV) 103, 304–7, 311–12
prevention costs 240, 241
price/earnings (P/E) ratio 141, 145, 152
price elasticity of demand 209–10

price-maker 208
price-taker 208
price variances 362–5
pricing
  alternative approaches 208–12
  capacity utilization 242–3
  cost-plus pricing 208–9
  differential pricing 208
  marketing decisions 208–12
  optimum selling price 209–10
  products 392
  special decisions 210–12
  target rate of return 209
  transfer pricing 327–9
prime costs 270
principles, accounting 42–5
priority-based budgets 336–7
privatization, EuroRail 427
problem-solving 7
process costing
  case studies 177, 178–9
  systems 175, 225, 226
process mapping 190–2
production
  overheads 270
  resources 228–9
production run 175
products
  capacity utilization 229–31
  costs 267–9, 270–1, 390–402
  markets 19–21
  overheads 270
  parts in common 398
  product/service mix 198, 229
  sustaining activities 284
  variety 394
  volume 395–9
product/service mix 198, 229
profiling 339
profit
  absolute 321, 326
  budget 339–45
  calculations 34
  capital maintenance 103
  cash forecasting 345
  centres 319
  controllability 323–4
  CVP analysis 201–8
  EuroRail 416–17, 418, 419
  market segments 212–16
  net profit 104, 105, 201
  profitability index 306–7
  profit-conscious managers 366–7

profit (*continued*)
  profit–volume graph 204
  ratio analysis 133–5, 143–4, 147–51
  strategic accounting 23
  transaction recording 38, 40
profitability 133–5, 143–4, 147–51
Profit and Loss Account 97, 106
  see also financial statements; Income Statements
profit before interest and taxes (PBIT) 105, 143
Property, Plant & Equipment (IAS16) 113
provisions 108, 110–11
*Provisions, Contingent Liabilities and Contingent
    Assets* (IAS37) 113
public service, EuroRail 412, 415, 425, 427
purchasing
  ABC 279
  cash forecasting 345–9
  costs 237
  double entry 36
  materials 235–6
  retail budgets 343, 345
Purple Book *see* Listing Rules, Stock Exchange
PV (present value) 103, 304–7, 311–12

qualitative aspects
  financial statements 101–2
  research 410
quality failure costs 237
quality issues
  costs 239–41
  management 11
  Six Sigma approach 11, 239–40
  TQM 239–40, 367
  see also standards
Quality Printing Company 242–3
quantity, sales variance 363
quick ratio 135
Quinn, J.B. 298

radical perspectives 78–9
  see also alternative perspectives
railway company 403–34
  see also EuroRail (ER) study
'railway' culture 412, 422, 423–8
rates, labour variance 366
ratio analysis 132–7
  activity/efficiency ratio 136–7, 144, 151
  gearing 135–6, 140, 144, 151
  information interpreting 143–5
  inventory management 138–9
  limitations 152–6
  liquidity 135, 144, 151
  profit 133–5, 143–4, 147–51

receivables 138
  relationship between financial ratios 141–3
  shareholder return 140–1, 144–5, 152
  W H Smith PLC 146–52
  working capital 137
rational-economic perspectives
  budgetary control 368
  easyJet 83
  financial statements 161
  management accounting 51–67
  see also alternative perspectives
rationality 64–5
  closed systems 73
  contract 65
  organizational culture 406
rational perspective 63, 73, 75
ratios, working capital 138–9
raw materials 172, 225
readings 389
  cost accounting 390–402
  organizational culture 403–34
reality 403–34
realizable value 103
receivables 36, 137–8
recognition, definition 102
recording transactions 33–49
re-engineering, business processes 192
regulatory aspects
  Companies Act (2006) 25, 98, 103, 130–1
  Framework 97, 100–3
  GAAP 99
  IFRSs/IASs 98–100, 286
  King Committee 29
  OFR 130–1
  Sarbanes–Oxley Act (2002) 26
  TUPE 254
  UK Corporate Governance Code 25–6, 28
relevance, financial statements 101
Relevance Lost (Johnson and Kaplan) 9–10
relevant cost of labour 255–7
reliability, financial statements 101
replacement, equipment 233–4, 243–5
Reporting Standards *see* International Financial
    Reporting Standards
reports *see* financial reports
research
  academic research 70–2, 401–2
  EuroRail study 403–34
  field studies 401–2
  financial reports 115
  qualitative research 410
residual income (RI) 321–3, 324, 325–6, 330
resource dependence theory 75

resources, production 228–9
responsibilities, directors 27
responsibility centres 46, 319
retail budget example 342–3
retail method 175
Retail News Group 346–9
Retail Stores plc 214–16
return on capital employed (ROCE) 21, 134, 143,
    144, 151
return on investment (ROI) 6, 21, 326, 330
    decentralized organizations 321, 326
    performance evaluation 321, 322–3, 326
    profit 133, 134, 144, 151
    see also accounting rate of return
revenue 104
reviews, OFR 130–1
risk 28–9, 339
ROCE (return on capital employed) 21, 134, 143,
    144, 151
Rockford 392–3
ROI *see* return on investment
rolling budgets 336
routing 205, 225
Royal Bank of Scotland 87
rules systems 53

Sainsbury 131
sales
    breakeven 202–7
    costs 268
    days' sales outstanding 138
    growth 134–5
    mix 198
    overheads/sales ratio 134
    ratio analysis 134–5
    selling price 209–10
    SuperTech 218–19
    tax 114
    variances 362–3
Samuelson, L.A. 350
Sarbanes–Oxley Act (2002) 26
satisficing behaviour 64
scheduling incident, EuroRail 420–1
Schrader Bellows 392, 393, 397–8
scientific management 73
scorekeeping accounting function 7
securitisation 22
security controls 193
segmental profitability 212–16
segments, markets 208, 383
self-interest threats 89
self-review threats 89
selling price 209–10

SEM (strategic enterprise management) 189
semi-fixed costs 200
semi-variable costs 181, 200
sensitivity analysis 202
services
    budget example 340–1
    managing operations 227–8
    mix 229
    overheads 270
    product/service mix 198, 229
    public service 412, 415, 425, 427
setups 227, 397, 398
Share Based Payment (IFRS2) 112–13
share buyback 145
shareholders
    audits 27
    return ratios 133–4, 140–1, 144–5, 152
    shareholder value 19–31, 73, 145,
        161–2
shareholder value added (SVA) 22–3
sharing rule 120
short-term financial performance 58
short-term product costing 400
short-term variable cost 392
signals renewal incident, ER 420, 421, 424
significance, variance analysis 361
Simmonds, K. 373
Six Sigma approach 11, 239–40
Skandia Navigator 157
skimming, marketing 198, 208
SMA *see* strategic management accounting
smoothing 84–5
social constructionism 75–7
socialization 68, 77
socio-technical systems theory 75
Solomons, D. 320, 321, 322, 323, 324, 327
source documents 34
spare capacity 228–9
special pricing decisions 210–12
Sports Stores Co-operative Ltd 342–3
stakeholders 29, 97, 158–9
stakeholder theory 75
standard costing 225–6
standards
    control systems performance 55
    global harmonization 98
    IASB 112–13
    IFRSs 98–100, 112–13
Statement of Cash Flows *see* Cash Flow
        Statements
Statement of Changes in Equity 8, 100
    Annual Reports 130
    ratio analysis 148

Statement of Comprehensive Income 8, 97–8, 100, 104–7
  Annual Reports 130
Statement of Financial Position *see* Balance Sheets
Statements of Standard Accounting Practice (SSAPs) 99
Stern Stewart & Co. 23
stocks 36, 138–9
  see also inventory accounting
strategic accounting 23–4
strategic cost analysis 397–8
strategic enterprise management (SEM) 189
strategic investment 297–315
  cash flow 299–301, 304–7
  comparison of techniques 307–8
  decision-making 297–315
  investment appraisal 298–301
  payback 304
  present value 304–7, 311–12
  strategy formulation 297–8
strategic management accounting (SMA) 371–86
  accounting techniques 374–81
strategic planning 29–30, 336
strategy mapping 61–2
sunk costs 47, 232
Superior Hotel 339–41
SuperTech 218–19
supplier cost analysis 237–9
supplier performance index 239
supply chain management 237–9, 375
support departments 395–9
sustainability 159–60
Sustainability Reporting Guidelines, GRI 159
sustaining activities, products 284
SVA (shareholder value added) 22–3
Svenska Handelsbanken 352–3

tableaux de bord measurement system 59
takeover movement 21
tangible assets 107
target costing 379–80
target rate of return pricing 209
taxation 108, 114, 347
technology 218–19
Tektronix Portables 290
Telcon Manufacturing 343–5
Tesco 131
theoretical issues
  management accounting 64–5, 70–2
  theorizing modes 429
  see also individual theories
Theory of Constraints (ToC) 231–2
threats 89

throughput contribution, definition 231
time-driven activity-based costing (TDABC) 281–2, 283–4
time-phasing, budgeting 339
time-recording system 269
time value of money 282, 304
TNA case study 382–3
ToC (Theory of Constraints) 231–2
top-down budgets 337
total cost of ownership 237–9, 367, 375
total employment cost 252–4
total quality management (TQM) 11, 239–40, 367
total shareholder return (TSR) 22
Toyota 330, 375, 380, 381
TQM (total quality management) 11, 239–40, 367
traditional accounting critiques 389–434
  cost accounting 390–402
  organizational culture 403–34
transaction cost economics 65
transaction costs 120, 329–30, 396–8, 400
transaction recording 33–49
Transfer of Undertakings Protection of Employment (TUPE) 254
transfer pricing 327–9
trigger point 382
triple bottom line 159
Trojan Sales 260–1
true and fair view 27, 103–4
TSR (total shareholder return) 22
TUPE (Transfer of Undertakings Protection of Employment) 254
turnover 138
two-stage cost allocation system 393–4, 397

unavoidable costs 212, 213, 232
understandability, financial statements 101
unit contribution 202
unit costs 284, 398
United Kingdom (UK), *Corporate Governance Code* 25–6, 28
United States (US)
  GAAP 99
  Sarbanes–Oxley Act (2002) 26
  units
  business 317–34
  equivalent 175
usage variances 363, 364–5

value
  chains 224–5, 376
  organizational cultures 77–8
  shareholders 19–31, 145, 161–2

Value Added Tax (VAT) 114
value-based management (VBM) 11, 21–3
value-based pricing 382
value engineering 379
value gap 21
value stream 382
value-stream accounting 382
value-stream costing 382
variable costs 199
    budgetary control 362
    cost accounting 391–2, 396, 398–9
    example 199–200
    overhead allocation 273, 283
variable overhead variances 365
variance analysis 361–8
    budgetary control 361–8
    cost variances 363–5
    criticisms 366–7
    flexible budget 362–5
    interpreting variances 365–6
    sales variance 362–3
VAT (Value Added Tax) 114

VBM (value-based management) 11, 21–3
Vehicle Parts Co. 243–5
volume
    CVP analysis 201–8
    products 395–9

Wallander, Jan 351–2
weighted average cost of capital 21
weighted average method 173–4, 178–9
W H Smith PLC 146–52
Williamson, O. 329, 330
working capital 40, 135
    management 137, 138–9
working capital ratio 135, 139–40, 151
work-in-progress 172, 177, 225
WorldCom 11, 25, 26, 43, 45, 85, 86, 88, 99, 162

XBRL 161

Yellow Book see Listing Rules, Stock Exchange

zero-based budgets 337

Printed in the USA
CPSIA information can be obtained
at www.ICGtesting.com
LVHW081523181023
761402LV00005B/107